America

Since 1945
Fourth Edition

America

Since 1945
Fourth Edition

Edited by

Robert D. Marcus

and

David Burner

St. Martin's Press

New York

Acknowledgments

PART ONE 1945–1960

"Russia and the Cold War" by Averell Harriman. From *America and Russia in a Changing World* by Averell Harriman. Copyright © 1970, 1971 by W. Averell Harriman. Reprinted by permission of Doubleday & Company Inc.

"The Cold War: A Revisionist View" by Barton J. Bernstein. From "American Foreign Policy and the Origins of the Cold War" in *Politics and Policies of the Truman Administration* by Barton J. Bernstein (ed.). Copyright © 1970 by Quadrangle Books. Reprinted by permission of Franklin Watts, Inc.

"Harry Truman and the Fair Deal" by Alonzo L. Hamby. Abridged from "The Vital Center, the Fair Deal, and the Quest for a Liberal Political Economy" by Alonzo L. Hamby, *American Historical Review*, LXXVII (June 1972), 653–678. Copyright © 1972, 1976 by Alonzo L. Hamby. Reprinted by permission of the author.

"McCarthyism as Mass Politics" by Michael Paul Rogin. Reprinted from *The Intellectuals and McCarthy* by Michael Paul Rogin, by permission of The M.I.T. Press, Cambridge, Mass. Copyright © 1967 by the Massachusetts Institute of Technology. Footnotes omitted.

"Eisenhower: What Manner of Man?" by Fred I. Greenstein. From *The Hidden-Hand Presidency* by Fred I. Greenstein. © 1982 by Basic Books, Inc. Publishers. Reprinted by permission of the Publisher.

"Nixon Agonistes: The Checkers Speech" by Garry Wills. From *Nixon Agonistes* by Garry Wills. Copyright © 1969, 1970 by Garry Wills. Reprinted by permission of Houghton Mifflin Company.

"The Texture of Poverty" by Michael Harrington. Reprinted with permission of Macmillan Publishing Co., Inc., from *The Other America* by Michael Harrington. Copyright © Michael Harrington 1962, 1969.

"The Feminine Mystique" by Betty Friedan. Reprinted from *The Feminine Mystique* by Betty Friedan by permission of W. W. Norton & Company, Inc. Copyright © 1983, 1974, 1973, 1963 by Betty Friedan.

PART TWO 1960–1973

"An Imperial President in Foreign Policy?" by David Burner. From *The Torch Is Passed: The Kennedy Brothers and American Liberalism*. Copyright © 1984 David Burner and Thomas R. West. Reprinted with permission of Atheneum publishers.

"Freedom Riders" by Howell Raines. Reprinted by permission of G. P. Putnam's Sons from *My Soul Is Rested: Movement Days in the Deep South Remembered*, by Howell Raines. Copyright © 1977 by Howell Raines.

"Letter from Birmingham Jail" by Martin Luther King, Jr. from *Why We Can't Wait* by Martin Luther King, Jr. Reprinted by permission of Harper & Row, Publishers, Inc.

Acknowledgments and copyrights continue at the back of the book on page 408, which constitutes an extension of the copyright page.

Preface

In two successive presidential elections—1976 and 1980—the American people chose political outsiders offering a fresh vision. Whether these results represent a new and realistic approach to the remainder of the twentieth century or a nostalgia for a seemingly simpler past remains a question.

Keeping in mind this search for perspective, we have selected for the fourth edition of *America Since 1945* articles that consider and link together the most significant political and social events of the past four decades. For example, on foreign affairs we have included the views of Averell Harriman and Barton Bernstein on the cold war, Henry F. May and Michael Herr on American involvement in Vietnam, and Walter LaFeber on American policy in Central America. On domestic issues we have included not only classic political articles, such as Garry Wills's reevaluation of Richard Nixon's famous "Checkers" speech and Jonathan Schell on Watergate, but also pieces that deal with some of the social transformations of the period, including selections from Betty Friedan's *The Feminine Mystique,* Michael Harrington's *The Other America,* Ruth Schwartz Cowan's *More Work for Mother,* and a piece on popular culture: Greil Marcus's analysis of the Elvis Presley phenomenon. Throughout we have attempted to offer an interesting combination of primary and secondary materials; thus we have included excerpts from such primary sources as the speeches and writings of John F. Kennedy, Lyndon B. Johnson, Martin Luther King, Jr., and Malcolm X, the memoirs of Richard Nixon and Henry Kissinger, and personal accounts of the civil rights movement assembled by Howell Raines.

There are twelve new selections in this edition. In addition to the readings by May, LaFeber, Cowan, Marcus, Raines, and King, other new essays include a study of McCarthyism, fresh evaluations of Eisenhower and Kennedy, an analysis of the American economy by Allen Matusow, and studies of Jimmy Carter's and Ronald Reagan's approaches to the presidency. We have also updated the Suggested Further Readings section.

Robert D. Marcus
David Burner

Contents

Preface   v

Part One   1945–1960   1

Russia and the Cold War, *from* America and Russia in a
    Changing World, *Averell Harriman*   3

The Cold War: A Revisionist View, *from* American Foreign
    Policy and the Cold War, *Barton J. Bernstein*   14

Harry Truman and the Fair Deal, *from* The Vital Center,
    The Fair Deal, and Liberalism, *Alonzo L. Hamby*   39

McCarthyism as Mass Politics, *from* The Intellectuals and
    McCarthy, *Michael Paul Rogin*   51

Eisenhower: What Manner of Man? *from* The Hidden-Hand
    Presidency, *Fred I. Greenstein*   70

Nixon Agonistes: The Checkers Speech, *from* Nixon Agonistes,
    Garry Wills   93

The Texture of Poverty, *from* The Other America,
    Michael Harrington   108

The Feminine Mystique, *from* The Feminine Mystique,
    Betty Friedan   123

Part Two   1960–1973   139

The John F. Kennedy Inaugural Address   141

An Imperial President in Foreign Policy? *from* The Torch Is
    Passed: The Kennedy Brothers and American Liberalism,
    David Burner   145

Freedom Riders, *from* My Soul Is Rested: Movement Days in
    the Deep South Remembered, *Howell Raines*   169

Letter from Birmingham Jail, *from* Why We Can't Wait,
    Martin Luther King, Jr.   185

On Revolution, *from* Malcolm X Speaks, *Malcolm X*   199

The Port Huron Statement,
    Students for a Democratic Society   203

The Great Society, *Lyndon B. Johnson*   221

Keynesian Economics in the 1960s, *from* The Unraveling of
    America: A History of Liberalism in the 1960s,
    Allen Matusow   225

Vietnam: The Bed of Procrustes, *from* Lessons of the Past:
The Use and Misuse of History in American Foreign
Policy, *Ernest May*   240

Report from Vietnam, *from* Dispatches, *Michael Herr*   262

Cambodia and Kent State: Two Memoirs, *from* RN: The
Memoirs of Richard Nixon *and* White House Years,
Richard Nixon and *Henry Kissinger*   273

Part Three   1974–Present   295

Watergate, *from* Time of Illusion, *Jonathan Schell*   297

The Environmental Decline, *from* The Closing Circle,
Barry Commoner   314

More Work for Mother, *from* More Work for Mother,
Ruth Schwartz Cowan   322

The Elvis Presley Phenomenon *from* Mystery Train,
Greil Marcus   339

A Crisis of Confidence, *from* It Seemed Like Something
Happened, *Peter Carroll*   350

Nicaragua: The System Overthrown, *from* Inevitable
Revolutions: The United States in Central America,
Walter LaFeber   371

Ronald Reagan: Cold War Certainties, *from* Ronald Reagan:
The Politics of Symbolism, *Robert Dallek*   388

Suggested Further Readings   405

PART ONE

1945-1960

In 1945 World War II ended and the atomic age began. It was a year of high drama: the final defeat of the Axis powers, the establishment of the United Nations, and the beginning of what some people hoped would be a great "American century" in which, under the guidance of the United States, the world would know a long era of peace and progress. Although Americans eagerly awaited demobilization and the sweet harvest of victory, they were uneasy. The great leader Franklin D. Roosevelt was dead and was replaced by a modest ex-haberdasher from Missouri. Europe was devastated; victory over Japan introduced the world to the horror of nuclear weapons; and in America the end of

1

the war raised the question of whether the economy, which had been depressed for a decade before the war, would lapse into the same dismal state from which war production had roused it.

Many hopes and even more fears were realized in the next few years. The United Nations survived, the United States remained the greatest world power, and the domestic economy showed little inclination to slip back into severe depression. But the image of an "American century" rapidly gave way to the reality of cold war. Reforms and programs begun under Roosevelt were continued, and bipartisan forces also vigorously pursued an ideological conflict with the Soviet Union. Amid confusion and ill-feeling the nation rearmed to fight an inconclusive war in Korea, created an economy dependent on military spending, and moved irregularly toward a social order which, in the 1950's, seemed more stable than in fact it was. In reaction to a threatening world, Americans in 1952 closed ranks behind a popular and decidedly unmilitaristic general whom they hoped—correctly as it turned out—would put the sour era of postwar adjustment behind them.

The age of Eisenhower—that era of allged serenity and order that has long been an object of nostalgia—was shorter than we remember. In 1953 Eisenhower became president, the Korean War ended, and Joseph Stalin died. However, Senator Joseph McCarthy was still a power for potential disruption and the economy was in a slump in the immediate aftermath of Korea. Serenity, in short, was hardly a reality. By the end of the Eisenhower years anxiety had been stirred by Soviet achievements in space, spacecrafts, colonial revolutions, and the growing civil-rights movement—foretastes of major issues of the 1960's.

The Eisenhower years offered a respite from war but did not bring long-term social stability. In the interchangeable suburbs, Americans were adopting new life-styles that included new attitudes toward money and family behavior. An economy increasingly based on consumer credit undermined old habits of savings and thrift. This great social flux was obscured by the public's affirmation of traditional values and by political stalemate. But it was manifested in the push for black equality; in the awakening of a vocal movement on the political right; and in the growing unrest among the youth of the country.

Before this decade's end, a fresh spirit of criticism abounded. The Supreme Court had spoken in a historic school segregation case, and blacks had already discovered the techniques that could force change. In 1955 in Montgomery, Alabama, Martin Luther King had demonstrated their methods to an uneasy nation. John Kennedy emerged as a practical hero of liberals and an enemy of the Right. An era of muckraking, which began late in the decade with the writings of C. Wright Mills, John Kenneth Galbraith, Michael Harrington, and others, revealed areas of national shame and failure. The nation would soon come to noisy confrontation over the changes the 1950's had quietly wrought.

Russia and the Cold War

AVERELL HARRIMAN

From 1926 when he bargained with Leon Trotsky in Moscow over a manganese concession until 1968 when he conferred in Paris with the North Vietnamese, Averell Harriman has probably been our most experienced and influential representative to the Communist world. His reminiscences are important not only for the insights he has acquired about Communist governments over the years, but for what they reveal about developing American foreign policy.

Harriman never conceived of American-Soviet relations as a struggle to the death between hostile forces, one destined to conquer, the other to die. He had contempt for the crusading cold-warrior mentality in international affairs and strongly criticized Eisenhower's Secretary of State, John Foster Dulles, for taking "the position that Communism was evil and that countries were either for us or against us in our struggle with it."

Harriman's opinions are quite typical of American policy makers in the immediate postwar era. He himself called it "a fairly glorious period, perhaps the most creative period in American foreign policy." The idealism he expresses—as in his account of the Marshall Plan—is undoubtedly genuine. Although some critics such as Barton J. Bernstein (in the next selection) have suggested that those liberal ideals actually defined the world in a way that made the Cold War inevitable, Harriman contends that Stalin's intransigence led to an unavoidable collapse of the wartime alliance.

There has grown a myth about Yalta that somehow or other Roosevelt and Churchill sold out Eastern Europe to Stalin. That wasn't true at all. I can't imagine why Stalin went to such extreme lengths in breaking the Yalta agreements if it had been true that they were so much to his advantage. It was agreed that the people in these countries were to decide on their own governments through free elections. But Stalin didn't permit it.

One wonders why he broke his agreement on Poland so soon. It's rather hard to guess. Personally, I think one of the reasons was that Bierut, the leading member of the Lublin Polish government—the Communist government—was in Moscow on Stalin's return from Yalta. He may have told Stalin that if he carried out his plan for free elections, Bierut and his comrades couldn't deliver Poland. Stalin had the idea that the Red Army would be accepted as a liberating army. In fact, he told me so. In this regard, perhaps the Communist partisans had reported too optimistically to Moscow. At any rate I think the Kremlin leaders were awfully hurt when they found that the Red Army was looked upon by the Poles, the Romanians, and others as a new invading force.

In addition, there appeared to be two schools of thought in the Kremlin hierarchy—the Politburo itself. One is apt to think of the Communist government as one single brain; it isn't. It is made up of men with sometimes differing views; this was true even under Stalin. I was conscious of the fact that members of Politburo even during the war had different views on different subjects. Let me quickly say that there was free discussion in the Politburo on *new* subjects only. On anything Stalin had decided, that was it. That couldn't be questioned. I think it is fair to say that in these discussions about new matters, Stalin listened, smoked his pipe, and walked up and down the room. Then, when he had heard enough, he said, "This is what we are going to do." If anyone left the room with a shrug of his shoulders, he might find himself on the way to Siberia the next afternoon. That may be somewhat of an exaggeration, but I think it's pretty nearly right.

In any event, I feel sure that there was a difference of opinion as to whether it would be wise for the Soviet Union in the immediate postwar period to soft-pedal Communist expansion for a time and continue to collaborate with the Western Allies to get the value of loans and trade, technical assistance, and other cooperation for the terrific job of reconstruction they faced; or whether they should push ahead and use the extraordinary opportunities in the dislocations in Europe and elsewhere to extend Communist control. Stalin once told me, "Communism breeds in the cesspools of capitalists." In this sense, Europe looked as if it were going to be in a mire.

I was so concerned about this that in early 1945, I sent messages about the need to help Western Europe, urging that the recovery of Europe would require much more than most people thought. I said that UNRRA would not be enough, food would not be enough. We would have to supply working capital and raw materials to get trade going again. Imports would be needed for raw materials for industrial production as well as for reconstruction. Without that, there would be vast unemployment and misery, in which the Communists might well take over.

I believe that Stalin hoped to get to the Atlantic, and that was perhaps the reason why he didn't carry out the Yalta agreements. The prospects for Communist takeover simply looked too good.

He said a number of things on different occasions, some of them contradictory, and it is hard to know what he had in mind. After Teheran he sent President Roosevelt a telegram in which, among other things, he said, "Now it is assured that our people will act together, jointly and in friendship, both at the present time and after the completion of the war." This is only one of the many expressions of that kind which gave some indication that he had in mind postwar cooperation. But that didn't happen. Roosevelt died, and I know that before he died he realized that his hopes had not been fully achieved; he knew Stalin had already broken some of the Yalta agreements. I know that from the telegrams I received from him to deliver to Stalin and also from some of the people who talked to him just before his death.[1] . . .

While I was home, I did spend several weeks in San Francisco during the United Nations Conference. At the request of Ed Stettinius, the Secretary of State, I had three off-the-record talks with editors, columnists, and reporters to give them some background on our growing problems with the Soviet government. I told them we would have real difficulties with the Soviet Union in the postwar period. This came as a great shock to many of them. At one meeting, I explained that our objectives and the Kremlin objectives were irreconcilable; they wanted to communize the world, and we wanted a free world. But I added that we would have to find ways to compose our differences if we were to live in peace on this small planet. Two men were so shocked that they got up and left. Some of the press at that time criticized me for being so unkind to what were then known as "our gallant allies," and some even suggested that I should be recalled as Ambassador. It was one of the few times in my experience that members of the press have broken the confidence of an off-the-record talk.

People ask when and why I became convinced we would have difficulties with the Soviets. This judgment developed over a period of time. . . .

A talk I had with Stalin at Potsdam in July 1945 is illuminating. The first time I saw him at the conference I went up to him and said that it must be very gratifying for him to be in Berlin, after all the struggle and the tragedy. He hesitated a moment and then replied, "Czar Alexander got to Paris." It didn't need much of a clairvoyant to guess what was in his mind.

I don't think there is any doubt that, with the strong Communist Parties both in Italy and in France, he would have extended his domination to the Atlantic, if we had not acted to frustrate it. In all probability, the Communist leaders in those countries had reported to Moscow that they could take over, and I think they would have succeeded if we had not helped Western Europe to recover. Some of Western Europe would have had Communist governments under the control of Moscow. One doesn't know what the rest of Europe would have been like, but perhaps some countries would have been something less independent than Finland and allowed to be cautiously neutral at the grace of Moscow.

But that isn't what happened. I know that some young people

1. Mrs. Hoffman wrote me a letter some years later describing her conversation with Roosevelt on March 24, 1945, his last day in Washington:

The President was in his wheel chair as we left the room, and both Mrs. Roosevelt and I walked at his side. He was given a message which I learned later was a cable from you which had been decoded. He read it and became quite angry. He banged his fists on the arms of his wheel chair and said, "Averell is right; we can't do business with Stalin. He has broken every one of the promises he made at Yalta." He was very upset and continued in the same vein on the subject.

These were his exact words. I remembered them and verified them with Mrs. Roosevelt not too long before her death.

think that everything that has been done before them wasn't just right, but we did have a fairly glorious period, perhaps the most creative period in American foreign policy, immediately after the war. It was due to the leadership of President Truman and the effective cooperation of Senator Vandenberg, the Republican Senator from Michigan, who was then Chairman of the Foreign Relations Committee. The undertakings included aid to Greece, which was under Communist attack, and Turkey, which was threatened at that time; the Marshall Plan, which was an extraordinarily ambitious and successful venture in cooperation; and that led to NATO. These things developed one from the other. Public opinion in the West was deeply disturbed by the Czech coup of March 1948 and then the Berlin blockade three months later. . . .

I was involved in the Marshall Plan, in charge of operations in Europe for more than two years. This was a European effort, with United States help. By the way, I should recall that General Marshall's offer of aid was made to all of Europe, including Russia and Eastern Europe. In fact, Molotov came to the meeting of Foreign Ministers of the European countries called in Paris in July 1947 to consider Marshall's offer with a staff of sixty, including senior economists. However, he demanded that each country act independently. He wanted the European nations to reply to the United States along these lines, "Tell us how much money you will give us, and we will divide it on the basis of those who suffered most will get the most. Then each country will look after its own recovery." But Marshall's proposal was that the European countries should cooperate together in a mutual recovery program. Bevin and Bidault, the British and French Foreign Ministers, stood firm for the cooperative concept, and Molotov left in a huff. The Czechs and the Poles had wanted to join the Marshall Plan, but the Kremlin ordered them not to do so.

At that time the Soviets organized the Cominform and declared war on the Marshall Plan, calling it an "American imperialist plot to subjugate Western Europe." Needless to say, that was just exactly the reverse of what we wanted. We wanted a strong, united and independent Europe. Everything that we did was to minimize our role and maximize the cooperative effort of the Europeans. "Self-help and mutual aid" was the slogan. It was amazingly successful—a spirit of cooperation and unity developed within Europe which had never before existed. They abandoned some of the restrictive business and labor practices of the intra-war years and accepted the necessity of an expanding economy as the basis for a rising standard of living. . . .

Now, Western Europe is more vital and dynamic than ever. When De Gaulle was in control, France was, perhaps, a little too nationalistic. But today the Europeans are again moving toward greater integration and closer cooperation. This was part of the objective of the Congress, and certainly of President Truman in initiating the Marshall Plan. . . .

The Berlin blockade in June of 1948 was a startling event and led to the pressure for NATO. You have to remember that never in history has a nation destroyed its armed strength as rapidly as we did after the

Second World War. The demand for bringing the boys home was irresistible. No one was to blame; it was the deep desire of the American people. We thought we had won the war and everyone in the world would want peace. We had the strongest military force in being at the end of the war, but after the Japanese surrendered, it was dissipated. The Russians didn't do that. They strengthened their forces. They developed new weapons. We in Moscow reported to Washington in late 1945 evidence which indicated that Soviet research expenditure was being doubled, that production of certain new weapons and military equipment was continuing at wartime levels, and that combat training for the Red Army was being emphasized.

Although for a time we had a monopoly in nuclear weapons, Stalin ordered the highest priority be given to developing nuclear capability. Much to the surprise of most people at the time, the Soviets exploded their first nuclear device in September 1949.

The Berlin blockade was countered not by direct force. There has been a lot of argument about that at the time and since. People can argue whether Truman's decision was right or wrong—whether to try to drive our forces through and threaten a nuclear attack, or whether to supply Berlin by airlift. In any event, the least provocative of these responses—the airlift—was chosen, and with full British cooperation it was successful. The Soviets lifted the blockade a year later.

We have had difficulty over Berlin ever since, some times more dangerous than others. Of course, one can criticize the arrangements which made Berlin the capital of occupied Germany. Frankly, Ben Cohen and I favored at the time a capital in a new location, where the three zones came together, just north of Magdeburg. I was influenced in part by the appalling way in which the Soviets had stripped Berlin of most everything they could take out, between V-E Day and the Potsdam meeting. The factories, particularly, were emptied of all machinery and machine tools. But these arrangements had been made by the European Advisory Commission in London. They had been accepted by the three Allies and would have been pretty hard to change at Potsdam.

Sometimes I have thought our presence in Berlin was of great value. Other times I have wondered if it was worthwhile. These are things that historians can argue about. But we are there in West Berlin, and the division of Germany continues along the line of the Soviet occupational zone.

Some think that General Eisenhower should have taken Berlin, but if he had done that, our Third Army wouldn't have been in Austria, and Austria, which is a free and independent country, probably would have been occupied largely by the Red Army and might have been turned into a satellite.

These are all questions which one can weigh. It is hard to say what might have been done. If one objective had been gained, something else would have been lost. I think by and large with the Soviet recalcitrance it would have made very little difference.

Some people have even argued that if General Eisenhower had

liberated Prague somehow or other Czechoslovakia would be free today. That's nonsense! The Czech government under President Benes was set up under an agreement in Moscow, negotiated by Benes with Czech party leaders, including the Communists. This government returned to Czechoslovakia from the East, as the Red Army, joined with four or five Czech divisions, advanced. Under the agreement Benes had to take Communists into the government.

I had several talks with Benes when he came to Moscow from London in March 1945 before returning to Czechoslovakia. He told me that he was not too well satisfied with the composition of the new government, but he added, "It might have been worse." Benes was confident he could control the situation in Czechoslovakia as he believed the people would support him. He told me that Stalin had assured him that the Soviets would not interfere in Czech internal affairs.

Unfortunately, Benes was ill in March 1948 when the coup took place. Of course, the Red Army had long since retired. It had withdrawn from Czechoslovakia more than two years earlier. Our troops had also withdrawn long before, so nothing we did in 1945 would have affected the outcome. Whether or not it would have been different if Benes had been well and vigorous, and whether he could have held his own, I don't know. But the Communist coup was successful without the participation of the Red Army, but undoubtedly with Moscow's collusion.

I had long talks with Jan Masaryk in San Francisco in May 1945. He was Benes' Foreign Minister. He told me I must understand that in the United Nations he would have to vote with Molotov. The Soviets were insisting that the Czech government support them in foreign policy. In return, he thought they would have a free hand at home. Unfortunately, it did not work out that way, and Masaryk himself came to a violent end in March 1948.

The Truman period was an exciting period. President Truman was a man of great determination. He was very humble at the start. He said he had not been elected; Roosevelt had been elected, and it was his responsibility to carry out Roosevelt's policies. He did the best he could. Very early he showed that he recognized the unique problems facing the United States in the world, and he had the extraordinary courage to undertake new policies and programs. And I think they were extraordinarily successful.

President Truman proposed in January 1949 the Point Four Program, announcing that since science and technology had developed to such a point that the old enemies of mankind—hunger, misery, poverty, and disease—could be overcome, it was the obligation of the United States and other more technologically advanced nations to help. That concept has moved ahead. There have been some outstanding successes in some ways and in some countries—some disappointments in others. Unfortunately, our development assistance is in rather a low state today —one of the casualties of Vietnam.

There have been lasting constructive results from the Truman period. Germany has revived and has become a strong ally; Japan has revived and is becoming a strong partner. Western Europe is more productive and united than ever. Other countries have made progress as well and are on their way to sustained economic development, for example in Asia, Korea, and Taiwan, and in Latin America, Mexico, Venezuela, and Colombia. There have been disappointments, of course. The developing countries as a whole have not been able to advance as rapidly as had been hoped, and the gap between them and the industrial nations has widened.

China was an enigma. Roosevelt first of all wanted to get the Soviet Union into the war against Japan. There was never any doubt in my mind that Stalin would attack Japan when it suited him. We could not have kept him out. The question was whether that would be soon enough to do us good. Our Chiefs of Staff estimated that it would take eighteen months after the fall of Germany to defeat the Japanese and would require an amphibious landing on the plains of Tokyo. American casualties were estimated to run up near a million with perhaps a couple of hundred thousand killed. This was a grim prospect to President Roosevelt. Yet, if the Russians attacked the Japanese Kwangtung Army in Manchuria, the Japanese strength to defend the home islands would be reduced. President Roosevelt had a deep sense of responsibility to protect American lives, and it was hoped that possibly, with Russia in the war and with American use of Soviet airfields in Siberia, we could bring Japan to surrender without invasion. Therefore, Soviet intervention seemed of vital importance.

It didn't turn out to be important because, unexpectedly, the nuclear bomb became operative and events moved so rapidly. At Yalta, when plans about Soviet entry into the war against Japan were agreed to, the nuclear bomb had not yet been completed, and nobody knew whether it would work. Even five months later at Potsdam, after the first test explosion took place, one of the most distinguished Navy officers bet an apple that it would not go off as a bomb. Of course, after things happen they seem so easy and so obvious that people say, "Why didn't you think of this at the time?"

Apart from Soviet entry into the war, Roosevelt also wanted to get Stalin to accept Chiang Kai-shek's Nationalist government as the government of China. And that, too, was part of the agreements reached at Yalta about the Far East. This was formalized in a treaty negotiated by T. V. Soong, Premier of the Nationalist government, with Stalin six months later. During these negotiations in Moscow I saw T. V. Soong almost every day. He was finally well satisfied, and in fact the world applauded the agreement. . . .

There were certain concessions to the Russians related to the railroads and ports in Manchuria for a thirty-year period, but the important point for Chiang was that the Soviets accepted Chinese sovereignty over the area. Some of us had been concerned when the Russians got into Manchuria they would establish a "Manchurian People's Republic" just as they had the Mongolian People's Republic. The fact that the Soviets accepted Chinese sovereignty was the thing that impressed Chiang.

Curiously, Stalin did not have much respect for Mao Tse-tung. During the war he spoke about him several times, and at one time he called him a "margarine Communist." That created a great deal of puzzlement in Washington. Some didn't know what it means. It would be entirely clear to any dairy farmer what he meant—a fake, not a real product. I gained the impression from several of my talks with Stalin that he was not keen to support Mao Tse-tung in China and that, perhaps, he wanted to see a new group more amenable to Moscow, take over the Chinese Communist Party before he gave his full support.

After the war, in January 1946, he told me that he had "poor contacts with the Communists." He said that the Soviet government's "three representatives in Yenan had been recalled" and that the Soviet influence with the Chinese Communists was not great. I think there is other evidence to that effect. For example, the Red Army not only stripped Manchuria of its industrial machinery for use in the Soviet Union but also blew up facilities such as blast furnaces. However, the Mao Communists were stronger than Stalin thought, and Chiang was weaker. As events developed, Chiang's forces collapsed in 1949, and he was driven out of mainland China.

Some people have said, "We lost China." It just happens that we never owned China. Whatever we had done in China over the years had had only a limited impact. And although it is unfortunate that a government friendly to us did not survive, we could not have involved ourselves in a major war at that time in China. President Truman, in spite of all the initiatives we had taken in other parts of the world, was wise enough to exercise restraint and not become involved in a civil war in mainland China.

So not all the postwar developments were favorable. Some of them did not go as well as we had hoped they might. . . .

President Kennedy handled the Cuban missile crisis with consummate skill and induced Khrushchev to take the offensive missiles out of Cuba. He was able to go on to an agreement with him on a limited test ban. The signing and ratification of the Limited Nuclear Test Ban Treaty marked a high water point in our relations with the Soviet Union. There were of course unsolved critical problems, particularly in regard to Germany and Southeast Asia. But the change in less than a year from the Cuban missile crisis to the test ban was so striking that I believe President Kennedy began to think seriously of a visit to the Soviet Union early in his second term should he be re-elected. But President Kennedy was assassinated three months later.

Within a year new personalities were to take over in Moscow. Khrushchev was removed from office, Brezhnev took his place as Secretary of the Party and Kosygin as Chairman of the Council of Ministers. . . .

QUESTIONS AND ANSWERS

Q—Do you believe that there is anything America could have done to assist Chiang, particularly in the latter period when we did withdraw our support?

A—I don't think so. I went to Chunking to talk with Chiang Kai-shek in January 1946. General Marshall was there at the time. Chiang had grave doubts about coming to an agreement for a coalition with the Communists, and he may have been justified in his fears. I asked him why he did not strengthen his government at once by bringing in the Democratic League, which included the leading Chinese intellectuals. They had recently participated in a Consultative Conference which had attempted to reconcile the contending parties. I also asked him why he didn't get rid of some of his warlords and some of the obviously corrupt people around him. He replied that they were the only ones he could count on for support if he brought the Communists into the government.

Perhaps the outcome might have been better if we had had quite a different approach. Looking at things from Moscow, my idea at the time was that we might better accept temporarily a divided China. If we could have prevented Chiang from sending his best troops into Manchuria where they were chewed up, he would have been far better off. It was hopeless for him to expect to take over the rule of Manchuria when he was having difficulty in controlling even the area where his forces were concentrated—southern China.

I also had grave doubts about the attempts to form a coalition government with the Communists. It seemed to me at the time that Chiang was too weak and the Communists too strong for him to have had much of a chance of survival.

In any event, General Marshall was sent out to attempt to mediate between the Nationalists and the Communists, and he did everything he could under his instructions. Despite General Marshall's patience and skill, the reluctance and suspicion of both sides and the inherent weakness of the Kuomintang made successful mediation impossible. . . .

Q—Mr. Ambassador, would you comment on the motivation of Soviet foreign policy? Do you think the motivation is primarily that of power politics and national power concerns, or of Communist ideology, or are they both equally determining factors?

A—It is a combination of both. Stalin had both. He was a Russian imperialist with ambitions similar to the Czars. He was also utterly determined to promote world Communist revolution with the oracle in Moscow. Since Stalin's death the world situation has changed, but the Kremlin still has both motivations. . . .

Q—If you could relive history, what changes would you make in the United States foreign policy during the wartime conferences and what effect that might have had on the future?

A—Well, I don't think much would have been different. You can argue about a lot of different things. People blame Eisenhower for not going to Berlin, but there had been a decision made in which the occupational zones of Germany were set. It was considered important that we should not meet and clash with the Russians, that we should decide in advance the zones each would occupy to avoid that possibility. The agreed zones were considered to be very favorable by our chiefs of staff at the time they were decided upon. They thought the Russians would be much further into Germany than they got and that we would not have gotten as far as we did. It didn't work out that way. I am not critical of them for this, as no one could have foreseen the military events.

Now if we had tried to do what Churchill proposed after V-E Day—stand on the Elbe until there was a political settlement about Eastern Europe—I don't think it would have done any good, and we would then have been held responsible for the cold war. Furthermore, our military plans required a redeployment of our forces in Europe to the Pacific. Churchill wanted to force a political settlement about the areas occupied by the Red Army before we withdrew from the Elbe. But even if we had gotten an agreement and free elections had been held, the governments elected would, in all probability, not have lasted. There was, in fact, a free election in Hungary in 1945 in which the Smallholders party (the small peasants' party) got over 50 per cent of the votes and the Communists only about 18 per cent. The government established after this election lasted only a short time, and the Communists—supported by the Red Army—took over and squeezed out the others.

There was no way we could have prevented any of these events in Eastern Europe without going to war with the Russians. There were a few military people who considered that. This wasn't De Gaulle, but a few French and American officers talked about going in and cleaning them up while we had such superiority in air power. It is perfectly absurd to think the American people would have stood for it, even if the President wanted to do it, which he didn't.

I think it was very important that Roosevelt and Churchill made the effort to come to an agreement with Stalin. One achievement was the establishment of the United Nations. With all the disappointments, it has been effective in many activities during the twenty-five years of its life, although handicapped by the differences that exist between the great powers. The fact that Stalin broke the agreements about Eastern Europe exposed his perfidy and aggressive designs. This aroused the suspicion of the West and eventually led to steps for mutual defense.

There is a group of historians who are now attempting to rewrite the history of that time. Arthur M. Schlesinger, Jr., has pointed out that such attempts to rewrite history have happened frequently in the past. These revisionists are creating myths about what happened and what our objectives were. Some of them take facts out of context and try to build up a case for imagined objectives. Some conveniently overlook Stalin's failure to cooperate, his violation of specific agreements and aggressive actions. Of course, I am not talking about those thoughtful analysts who, with the advantage of hindsight, point out more clearly the significance of events and perhaps mistakes than was possible at the time.

The military alternatives were perhaps more obvious than the political. At the time some people wanted us to go to Vienna, up the Ljubljana Gap, and get there before the Russians, instead of landing in the south of France as we did. Yet as things have turned out, Austria is free today anyway.

Churchill was always very much worried about attempting to cross the Channel. It turned out successfully. It would have been disastrous for the British if it hadn't. Churchill wanted to go at Hitler from the south—"the soft underbelly," as he called it. He didn't want to take the risk of crossing the Channel. Stalin, after having berated and even insulted us for two years for not establishing a second front in Europe by crossing the Channel, said to me after we had successfully landed, "The history of war has never witnessed such a grandiose operation." He added neither Napoleon nor Hitler had dared attempt it. Later, after he had received detailed reports, he spoke to me again about crossing the Channel, as "an unheard of achievement in the history of warfare." The number of men and the vast amount of equipment which had been thrown into France impressed him greatly. He added "the world had never seen an individual operation of such magnitude— an unbelievable accomplishment." He was unconcerned by the fact that he had previously minimized its difficulties and had accused us of cowardice in not having undertaken it before.

Undoubtedly mistakes were made, and undoubtedly many things might have been improved. Your question is an interesting one, and I have thought a lot about it. But the facts are that, although militarily unprepared, we fought a war successfully on two fronts. With our allies in Europe, we completely defeated Hitler, and almost alone we defeated Japan in the Pacific. That was an extraordinary achievement— and particularly as it was done in less than four years. As far as our relations with the Soviet Union since the end of the war are concerned, I doubt whether any different wartime military or political decisions would have had much effect.

The Cold War:
A Revisionist View

BARTON J. BERNSTEIN

*"There is no nation which has
attitudes so pure that they cannot
be bettered by self-examination."*
—John Foster Dulles (1946)

*"We are forced to act in the world
as it is, and not in the world as
we wish it were, or as we would
like it to become."*
—Henry L. Stimson (1947)

*Barton J. Bernstein is one of the "revisionists" whom Averell Harriman
criticizes for "creating myths about what happened [in the Cold War]
and what our objectives were." The revisionist position, expressed repeatedly during the 1960's, holds that Stalin was basically cautious
rather than aggressive in his actions immediately after World War II;
that the United States government, aiming to preserve American access
to a world trading empire, overlooked legitimate Soviet security needs;
and that, possessing preponderant power in the world, America refused
to cooperate with the Soviet Union, forcing the Kremlin into a hostile
posture in Eastern Europe to protect itself from future military threats.*

*Only a small proportion of American diplomatic historians has
totally accepted this analysis of American foreign policy, but the revisionist argument has influenced virtually every student in the field.
The central point of revisionist thinking, that the postwar power of
the United States gave it wider options than the Soviet Union ever had,
seems hard to question. Some theorists also maintain that American
and Soviet social and economic policies would eventually have con-
verged, and that such abrasive conflict between the two ideologies need
not have occurred at all. Yet we know so little of what Stalin was
thinking, and he gave so many contradictory signals that almost any
interpretation is possible. The experience of Vietnam, the breakdown
of monolithic power blocs, both East and West, and the emergence of
"détente" have all provided continuing stimulus for Cold War re-
visionism.*

Despite some dissents, most American scholars have reached a general consensus on the origins of the Cold War. As confirmed international-ists who believe that Russia constituted a threat to America and its European allies after World War II, they have endorsed their nation's acceptance of its obligations as a world power in the forties and its desire to establish a world order of peace and prosperity. Convinced that only American efforts prevented the Soviet Union from expanding past Eastern Europe, they have generally praised the containment policies of the Truman Doctrine, the Marshall Plan, and NATO as evidence of America's acceptance of world responsibility. While chiding or condemning those on the right who opposed international involve-ment (or had even urged preventive war), they have also been deeply critical of those on the left who have believed that the Cold War could have been avoided, or that the United States shared substantial responsi-bility for the Cold War.

Whether they are devotees of the new realism or open admirers of moralism and legalism in foreign policy, most scholars have agreed that the United States moved slowly and reluctantly, in response to Soviet provocation, away from President Franklin D. Roosevelt's conciliatory policy. The Truman administration, perhaps even belatedly, they suggest, abandoned its efforts to maintain the Grand Alliance and acknowledged that Russia menaced world peace. American leaders, ac-cording to this familiar interpretation, slowly cast off the shackles of innocence and moved to courageous and necessary policies.

Despite the widespread acceptance of this interpretation, there has long been substantial evidence (and more recently a body of scholar-ship) which suggests that American policy was neither so innocent nor so nonideological; that American leaders sought to promote their conceptions of national interest and their values even at the conscious risk of provoking Russia's fears about her security. In 1945 these lead-ers apparently believed that American power would be adequate for the task of reshaping much of the world according to America's needs and standards.

By overextending policy and power and refusing to accept Soviet interests, American policy-makers contributed to the Cold War. There was little understanding of any need to restrain American political efforts and desires. Though it cannot be proved that the United States could have achieved a *modus vivendi* with the Soviet Union in these years, there is evidence that Russian policies were reasonably cautious and conservative, and that there was at least a basis for accommodation.

The author wishes to express his gratitude for generous counsel to Gar Alpero-vitz, H. Stuart Hughes, Gabriel Kolko, Walter LaFeber, Lloyd Gardner, Allen J. Matusow, Thomas G. Paterson, Athan Theoharis, and Samuel Williamson. Research was conducted with the assistance of grants from the Rabinowitz Foundation, the American Philosophical Society, the Harry S. Truman Library Institute, the Charles Warren Center of Harvard University, and the Institute of American History at Stanford University. Portions of this paper were presented at the Warren Center in November 1967, at the John F. Kennedy Institute at Harvard in 1967–1968, and at the annual meeting of the Southern Historical Association in November 1968.

But this possibility slowly slipped away as President Harry S. Truman reversed Roosevelt's tactics of accommodation. As American demands for democratic governments in Eastern Europe became more vigorous, as the new administration delayed in providing economic assistance to Russia and in seeking international control of atomic energy, policy-makers met with increasing Soviet suspicion and antagonism. Concluding that Soviet-American cooperation was impossible, they came to believe that the Soviet state could be halted only by force or the threat of force.

The emerging revisionist interpretation, then, does not view American actions simply as the necessary response to Soviet challenges, but instead tries to understand American ideology and interests, mutual suspicions and misunderstandings, and to investigate the failures to seek and achieve accommodation.

I

During the war Allied relations were often marred by suspicions and doubts rooted in the hostility of earlier years. It was only a profound "accident"—the German attack upon the Soviet Union in 1941 —that thrust that leading anti-Bolshevik, Winston Churchill, and Marshal Josef Stalin into a common camp. This wartime alliance, its members realized, was not based upon trust but upon necessity; there was no deep sense of shared values or obvious similarity of interests, only opposition to a common enemy. "A coalition," as Herbert Feis has remarked, "is heir to the suppressed desires and maimed feelings of each of its members." Wartime needs and postwar aims often strained the uneasy alliance. In the early years when Russia was bearing the major burden of the Nazi onslaught, her allies postponed for two years a promised second front which would have diverted German armies. In December 1941, when Stalin requested recognition of 1941 Russian borders as they had been before the German attack (including the recently annexed Baltic states), the British were willing to agree, but Roosevelt rebuffed the proposals and aroused Soviet fears that her security needs would not be recognized and that her allies might later resume their anti-Bolshevik policies. So distrustful were the Allies that both camps feared the making of a separate peace with Germany, and Stalin's suspicions erupted into bitter accusations in March 1945, when he discovered (and Roosevelt denied) that British and American agents were participating in secret negotiations with the Germans. In anger Stalin decided not to send Vyacheslav Molotov, the Foreign Minister, to San Francisco for the April meeting on the founding of the United Nations Organization.

So suspicious were the Americans and British that they would not inform the Soviet Union that they were working on an atomic bomb. Some American leaders even hoped to use it in postwar negotiations with the Russians. In wartime, American opposition to communism had not disappeared, and many of Roosevelt's advisers were fearful of

Soviet intentions in Eastern Europe. In turn, Soviet leaders, recalling the prewar hostility of the Western democracies, feared a renewed attempt to establish a *cordon sanitaire* and resolved to establish a security zone in Eastern Europe.

Though Roosevelt's own strategy often seems ambiguous, his general tactics are clear: they were devised to avoid conflict. He operated often as a mediator between the British and Russians, and delayed many decisions that might have disrupted the wartime alliance. He may have been resting his hopes with the United Nations or on the exercise of America's postwar strength, or he may simply have been placing his faith in the future. Whatever future tactics he might have been planning, he concluded that America's welfare rested upon international peace, expanded trade, and open markets:

. . . it is our hope, not only in the interest of our own prosperity, but in the interest of the prosperity of the world, that trade and commerce and access to materials and markets may be freer after this war than ever before in the history of the world. . . . Only through a dynamic and soundly expanding world economy can the living standards of individual nations be advanced to levels which will permit a full realization of our hopes for the future.

His efforts on behalf of the postwar world generally reflected this understanding.

During the war Roosevelt wavered uneasily between emphasizing the postwar role of the great powers and minimizing their role and seeking to extend the principles of the Atlantic Charter. Though he often spoke of the need for an open postwar world, and he was reluctant to accept spheres of influence (beyond the Western hemisphere, where American influence was pre-eminent), his policies gradually acknowledged the pre-eminence of the great powers and yielded slowly to their demands. By late 1943 Roosevelt confided to Archbishop Francis Spellman (according to Spellman's notes) that "the world will be divided into spheres of influence: China gets the Far East; the U.S. the Pacific; Britain and Russia, Europe and Africa." The United States, he thought, would have little postwar influence on the continent, and Russia would probably "predominate in Europe," making Austria, Hungary, and Croatia "a sort of Russian protectorate." He acknowledged "that the European countries will have to undergo tremendous changes in order to adapt to Russia; but he hopes that in ten or twenty years the European influence would bring the Russians to become less barbarous."

In 1944 Roosevelt recognized the establishment of zones of influence in Europe. The Italian armistice of the year before had set the pattern for other wartime agreements on the control of affairs of liberated and defeated European nations. When Stalin requested the creation of a three-power Allied commission to deal with the problems of "countries falling away from Germany," Roosevelt and Churchill first rebuffed the Russian leader and then agreed to a joint commission for Italy which would be limited to information gathering. By excluding Russia from sharing in decision-making in Italy, the United States and Great Britain, later concluded William McNeill, "prepared the way for their own exclusion from any but a marginal share in the affairs of Eastern Europe."

When Roosevelt refused to participate in an Anglo-American invasion of southeastern Europe (which seemed to be the only way of restricting Russian influence in that area), Churchill sought other ways of dealing with Russian power and of protecting British interests in Greece. In May 1944 he proposed to Stalin that they recognize Greece as a British "zone of influence" and Rumania as a Russian zone; but Stalin insisted upon seeking Roosevelt's approval and refused the offer upon learning that the United States would not warmly endorse the terms. When the Soviets liberated Rumania in September they secured temporarily the advantages that Churchill had offered. They simply followed the British-American example in Italy, retained all effective power, and announced they were "acting in the interests of all the United Nations." From the Soviet Union, W. Averell Harriman, the American ambassador, cabled, "The Russians believe, I think, that we lived up to a tacit understanding that Rumania was an area of predominant Soviet interest in which we should not interfere. . . . The terms of the armistice give the Soviet command unlimited control of Rumania's economic life" and effective control over political organization.

With Russian armies sweeping through the Balkans and soon in a position to impose similar terms on Hungary and Bulgaria, Churchill renewed his efforts. "Winston," wrote an associate, "never talks of Hitler these days; he is always harping on the dangers of Communism. He dreams of the Red Army spreading like a cancer from one country to another. It has become an obsession, and he seems to think of little else." In October Churchill journeyed to Moscow to reach an agreement with Stalin. "Let us settle our affairs in the Balkans," Churchill told him. "Your armies are in Rumania and Bulgaria. We have interests, missions and agents there. Don't let us get at cross-purposes in small ways." Great Britain received "90 per cent influence" in Greece, and Russia "90 per cent influence" in Rumania, "80 per cent" in Bulgaria and Hungary, and "50 per cent" in Yugoslavia.

In the cases of Hungary and Bulgaria the terms were soon sanctioned by armistice agreements (approved by the United States) which left effective power with the Soviets. "The Russians took it for granted," Cordell Hull, then Secretary of State, wrote later, "that . . . Britain and the United States had assigned them a certain portion of the Balkans, including Rumania and Bulgaria, as their sphere of influence." In December Stalin even confirmed the agreement at a considerable price: he permitted British troops to put down a rebellion in Greece. "Stalin," wrote Churchill later, "adhered strictly and faithfully to our agreement . . . and during all the long weeks of fighting the communists in the streets of Athens, not one word of reproach came from *Pravda* or *Izvestia*."

At Yalta in February 1945 Roosevelt did not seem to challenge

Soviet dominance in east-central Europe, which had been established by the Churchill-Stalin agreement and confirmed by the armistices and by British action in Greece. What Roosevelt did seek and gain at Yalta was a weak "Declaration on Liberated Europe"—that the powers would consult "where in their judgment conditions require" assistance to maintain peace or to establish democratic governments. By requiring unanimity the declaration allowed any one power to veto any proposal that seemed to threaten that power's interests. In effect, then, the declaration, despite its statements about democratic governments, did not alter the situation in Eastern Europe. The operative phrases simply affirmed the principle that the three powers had already established: they could consult together when all agreed, and they could act together when all agreed. At Yalta the broadly phrased statement provoked little discussion—only a few pages in the official proceedings. Presumably the Russians did not consider it a repudiation of spheres of influence, only as rhetoric that Roosevelt wanted for home consumption. Despite later official American suggestions, the Yalta agreement was not a product of Roosevelt's misunderstanding of the Soviet meaning of "democracy" and "free elections." Rather, it ratified earlier agreements, and the State Department probably understood this.

While accepting the inevitable and acknowledging Russian influence in these areas, Roosevelt had not been tractable on the major issue confronting the three powers: the treatment of postwar Germany. All three leaders realized that the decisions on Germany would shape the future relations of Europe. A dismembered or permanently weakened Germany would leave Russia without challenge on the continent and would ease her fears of future invasion. As Anthony Eden, the British Foreign Minister explained, "Russia was determined on one thing above all others, that Germany would not again disturb the peace of Europe. . . . Stalin was determined to smash Germany so that it would never again be able to make war." A strong Germany, on the other hand, could be a partial counterweight to Russia and help restore the European balance of power on which Britain had traditionally depended for protection. Otherwise, as Henry Morgenthau once explained in summarizing Churchill's fears, there would be nothing between "the white snows of Russia and the white cliffs of Dover."

The Allied policy on Germany had been in flux for almost two years. At Teheran in 1943 the Allies had agreed in principle (despite Churchill's reluctance) that Germany should be dismembered, and in 1944 Roosevelt and a reluctant Churchill, much to the distress of Foreign Minister Anthony Eden, had agreed on a loosely phrased version of the Morgenthau Plan for the dismemberment and pastoralization of Germany. Not only would the plan have eliminated German military-industrial potential and thereby allayed Russian fears, but by stripping Germany it would also have provided the resources for Russian economic reconstruction. Churchill, despite his fear of Russia and his desire for Germany as a counterweight on the continent, had temporarily agreed to the plan because it seemed to be a prerequisite for increased American economic aid and promised to eliminate German industry as a postwar rival for the trade that the debt-ridden British economy would need. Many in the State and War Departments charged that the plan was economic madness, that it would leave not only Germany but also much of war-torn Western Europe (which would need postwar German production) without the means for economic reconstruction. (Secretary of the Treasury Morgenthau concluded after discussion with many officials that they wanted a strong Germany as a "bulwark against Bolshevism.") Yielding to the pleas of the War and State Departments, Roosevelt decided upon a plan for a stronger postwar Germany, and Churchill, under pressure from advisers, also backed away from his earlier endorsement of the Morgenthau Plan and again acted upon his fears of an unopposed Russia on the continent. At Yalta, he resisted any agreement on the dismemberment of Germany. Stalin, faced with Anglo-American solidarity on this issue, acceded. The final communiqué patched over this fundamental dispute by announcing that the three powers had pledged to "take such steps including the complete disarmament, demilitarization, and dismemberment of Germany as they deem requisite for future peace and security." The strategy of postponement had triumphed. Unable to reach a substantive agreement, the Big Three agreed to submit these problems (and the related, vital issues of reparations and boundaries) to three-power commissions.

Though Yalta has come to represent the triumph of the strategy of postponement, at the time it symbolized Allied accord. Stalin accepted a limitation of the veto power on certain quasi-judicial issues in the U.N. Security Council; Roosevelt conceded to Russia the return of the Kurile Islands, which stretched between Japan and Siberia, and special rights in Dairen and Port Arthur in Manchuria; Stalin promised to enter the Pacific war within three months of the end of the European conflict. "Stalin," as William McNeill explained, "had conceded something to the British in Yugoslavia; and Churchill had yielded a good deal in Poland."

II

Roosevelt's successor was less sympathetic to Russian aspirations and more responsive to those of Roosevelt's advisers, like Admiral William Leahy, Chief of Staff to the Commander in Chief; Harriman; James Forrestal, Secretary of the Navy; and James F. Byrnes, Truman's choice for Secretary of State, who had urged that he resist Soviet efforts in Eastern Europe. As an earlier self-proclaimed foe of Russian communism, Truman mistrusted Russia. ("If we see that Germany is winning the war," advised Senator Truman after the German attack upon Russia in 1941, "we ought to help Russia, and if Russia is winning we ought to help Germany and in that way kill as many as possible.") Upon entering the White House, he did not seek to follow Roosevelt's tactics of adjustment and accommodation. Only eleven days in the presidency and virtually on the eve of the United Nations conference,

Truman moved to a showdown with Russia on the issue of Poland.

Poland became the testing ground for American foreign policy, as Truman later said, "a symbol of the future development of our international relations." At Yalta the three powers had agreed that the Soviet-sponsored Lublin Committee (the temporary Polish government) should be "recognized on a broader democratic basis with the inclusion of democratic leaders from Poland itself and from Poland abroad." The general terms were broad: there was no specific formula for the distribution of power in the reorganized government, and the procedures required consultation and presumably unanimity from the representatives of the three powers. The agreement, remarked Admiral Leahy, was "so elastic that the Russians can stretch it all the way from Yalta to Washington without ever technically breaking it." ("I know, Bill—I know it. But it's the best I can do for Poland at this time," Roosevelt replied.)

For almost two months after Yalta the great powers haggled over Poland. The Lublin Committee objected to the Polish candidates proposed by the United States and Great Britain for consultation because these Poles had criticized the Yalta accord and refused to accept the Soviet annexation of Polish territory (moving the eastern boundary to the Curzon Line). In early April Stalin had offered a compromise— that about 80 per cent of the cabinet posts in the new government should be held by members of the Lublin Committee, and that he would urge the committee to accept the leading Western candidates if they would endorse the Yalta agreement (including the Curzon Line). By proposing a specific distribution of power, Stalin cut to the core of the issue that had disrupted negotiations for nearly three months, and sought to guarantee the victory he probably expected in Poland. Roosevelt died before replying, and it is not clear whether he would have accepted this 4 to 1 representation; but he had acknowledged that he was prepared to place "somewhat more emphasis on the Lublin Poles."

Now Truman was asked to acknowledge Soviet concern about countries on her borders and to assure her influence in many of these countries by granting her friendly (and probably non-democratic) governments, and even by letting her squelch anti-communist democrats in countries like Poland. To the President and his advisers the issue was (as Truman later expressed Harriman's argument) "the extension of Soviet control over neighboring states by independent action; we were faced with a barbarian invasion of Europe." The fear was not that the Soviets were about to threaten all of Europe but that they had designs on Eastern Europe, and that these designs conflicted with traditional American values of self-determination, democracy, and open markets.

Rushing back to Washington after Roosevelt's death, Harriman found most of FDR's advisers (now Truman's) sympathetic to a tougher approach. At a special White House meeting Harriman outlined what he thought were the Soviet Union's two policies—cooperation with the United States and Great Britain, and the creation of a unilateral security ring through domination of its border states. These policies, he contended, did not seem contradictory to Russian leaders, for "certain elements around Stalin" misinterpreted America's generosity and desire to cooperate as an indication of softness and concluded "that the Soviet Government could do anything that it wished without having any trouble with the United States." Before Roosevelt's death, Harriman had cabled: "It may be difficult . . . to believe, but it still may be true that Stalin and Molotov considered at Yalta that by our willingness to accept a general wording of the declaration on Poland and liberated Europe, by our recognition of the need of the Red Army for security behind its lines, and of the predominant interest of Russia in Poland as a friendly neighbor and as a corridor to Germany, we understood and were ready to accept Soviet policies already known to us."

Harriman wanted the American government to select a few test cases and make the Russians realize they could not continue their present policies. Such tactics, he advised, would place Russian-American relations on a more realistic basis and compel the Soviet Union to adhere to the American interpretation of the issues in dispute. Because the Soviet government "needed our [economic assistance] . . . in their reconstruction," and because Stalin did not wish to break with the United States, Harriman thought Truman "could stand on important issues without running serious risks." As early as January 1944 Harriman had emphasized that "the Soviet Government places the utmost importance on our cooperation" in providing economic assistance, and he had concluded: "it is a factor which should be integrated into the fabric of our overall relations." In early April Harriman had proposed that unless the United States were prepared "to live in a world dominated largely by Soviet influence, we must use our economic power to assist those countries that are naturally friendly to our concepts." In turn, he had recommended "tying our economic assistance directly into our political problems with the Soviet Union.

General George Marshall, the Army Chief of Staff, and Secretary of War Henry Stimson, however, recommended caution. Stimson observed "that the Russians perhaps were being more realistic than we were in regard to their own security," and he feared "that we would find ourselves breaking our relations with Russia on the most important and difficult question which we and Russia have gotten between us." Leahy, though supporting a firm policy, admitted that the Yalta agreement "was susceptible to two interpretations." Secretary of State Edward Stettinius read aloud the Yalta decision and concluded "that this was susceptible of only one interpretation."

Having heard his advisers' arguments, Truman resolved to force the Polish question: to impose his interpretation of the Yalta agreement even if it destroyed the United Nations. He later explained that this was the test of Russian cooperation. If Stalin would not abide by his agreements, the U.N. was doomed, and, anyway, there would not be enough enthusiasm among the American electorate to let the United States join the world body. "Our agreements with the Soviet Union so far . . . [have] been a one-way street." That could not continue, Truman told his advisers. "If the Russians did not wish to join us, they could go to hell." ("FDR's appeasement of Russia is over," joyously wrote Senator Arthur Vandenberg, the Republican leader on foreign policy.) Continuing in this spirit at a private conference with Molotov, the new President warned that economic aid would depend upon Russian behavior in fulfilling the Yalta agreement. Brushing aside the diplomat's contention that the Anglo-American interpretation of the Yalta agreement was wrong, the President accused the Russians of breaking agreements and scolded the Russian Foreign Minister. When Molotov replied, "I have never been talked to like that in my life," Truman warned him, "Carry out your agreement and you won't get talked to like that."

At the United Nations conference in San Francisco, when Anthony Eden, the British Foreign Minister, saw a copy of Truman's "blunt message" about Poland to Stalin, "he could scarcely believe his eyes . . . and cheered loudly," reported Vandenberg. But the policy of firmness was not immediately successful. American-Russian relations were further strained by the disputes at the meeting to create the U.N.—over the veto, the admission of fascist Argentina, and the persistent question of Poland. Despite Soviet objections and Roosevelt's promise at Yalta to exclude Argentina from the U.N., the United States supported the Latin American state's candidacy for membership. In committee Molotov, whom Stalin had sent to establish good will with the new President, tried to block the admission of Argentina until the Lublin Poles were also admitted, but his proposed bargain was overwhelmingly defeated. Later in the plenary session, when only three nations voted with Russia, the Soviets found additional evidence for their fears of an American bloc directed against their interests. The Truman administration's action also gave the Soviets more reason to doubt America's explanations that her interests in Poland were inspired simply by a desire to guarantee representative, democratic governments. Moreover, because of the American bloc and Soviet fears that the U.N. (like the League of Nations) might be used against her, Molotov was at first unwilling to accede to the demands of the United States and the smaller nations who wished to exclude procedural questions before the Security Council from the great power veto.

The Soviets were further embittered when the United States abruptly curtailed lend-lease six days after V-E Day. Though Truman later explained this termination as simply a "mistake," as policy-making by subordinates, his recollection was incomplete and wrong. Leo Crowley, the director of lend-lease, and Joseph Grew, the Under Secretary of State, the two subordinates most closely involved, had repeatedly warned the President of the likely impact of such action on relations with Russia, and the evidence suggests that the government, as Harriman had counseled, was seeking to use economic power to achieve diplomatic means. Termination of lend-lease, Truman later wrote, "should have been done on a gradual basis which would not have made it appear as if somebody had been deliberately snubbed." Yet, despite this later judgment, Truman had four days after signing the order in which to modify it before it was to be implemented and announced, and the lend-lease administrator (in the words of Grew) had made "sure that the President understands the situation." The administrator knew "that we would be having difficulty with the Russians and did not want them to be running all over town for help." After discussing the decision with Truman, Grew, presumably acting with the President's approval, had even contrived to guarantee that curtailment would be a dramatic shock. When the Soviet chargé d'affaires had telephoned Grew the day before the secret order was to become effective, the Under Secretary had falsely denied that lend-lease to Russia was being halted. Harriman, according to Grew's report to the Secretary of State, "said that we would be getting 'a good tough slashback' from the Russians but that we would have to face it."

Presumably to patch the alliance, Truman dispatched to Moscow Harry Hopkin's, Roosevelt's former adviser and a staunch advocate of Soviet-American friendship. Hopkins denied that Truman's action was an American effort to demonstrate economic power and coerce Russia ("pressure on the Russians to soften them up," as Stalin charged). Instead he emphasized that "Poland had become a symbol of our ability to work out our problems with the Soviet Union." Stalin acknowledged "the right of the United States as a world power to participate in the Polish question," but he stressed the importance of Poland to Soviet security. Within twenty-five years the "Germans had twice invaded Russia via Poland," he emphasized. "All the Soviet Union wanted was that Poland should not be in a position to open the gates to Germany," and that required a government friendly to Russia. There was "no intention," he promised, "to interfere in Poland's internal affairs" or to Sovietize Poland.

Through the Hopkins mission, Truman and Stalin reached a compromise: 70 per cent of the new Polish government (fourteen of twenty ministers) should be drawn from the Lublin Committee. At the time there was reason to believe that such heavy communist influence would not lead to Soviet control. Stalin had reaffirmed the pledge of free elections in Poland, and Stanislaw Mikolajczyk, former Prime Minister of the exile government in London and Deputy Prime Minister in the new coalition government, was optimistic. He hoped (in Harriman's words) that "a reasonable degree of freedom and independence can be preserved now and that in time after conditions in Europe can become more stable and [as] Russian turns her attention to her internal development, controls will be relaxed and Poland will be able to gain for herself her independence of life as a nation even though he freely accepts that Poland's security and foreign policy must follow the lead of Moscow."

Truman compromised and soon recognized the new Polish government, but he did not lose his hopes of rolling back the Soviets from their spheres of influence in Eastern Europe. Basing most of his case on the Yalta "Declaration on Liberated Europe" (for which he relied on State Department interpretations), Truman hoped to force Russia to permit representative governments in its zones, and expected that free elections would diminish, perhaps even remove, Soviet authority. Refusing to extend diplomatic recognition to Rumania and Bulgaria, he emphasized that these governments were "neither representative of nor responsive to the will of the people."

"The opportunities for the democratic elements in Rumania and Bulgaria are not less than, say, in Italy, with which the Governments of of the United States and the Soviet Union have already resumed diplomatic relations," replied Stalin, who was willing to exaggerate to emphasize his case. The Russians were demanding a *quid pro quo,* and they would not yield. At Potsdam, in late July, when Truman demanded "immediate reorganization" of the governments of Hungary and Bulgaria to "include representatives of all significant democratic elements" and three-power assistance in "holding . . . free and unfettered elections," Stalin pointed to Greece, again to remind Truman of the earlier agreements. The Russians were "not meddling in Greek affairs," he noted, adding that the Bulgarian and Rumanian governments were fulfilling the armistice agreements while in Greece "terrorism rages . . . against democratic elements." (One member of the American delegation later claimed that Stalin at one point made his position clear, stating that "any freely elected government [in Eastern Europe] would be anti-Soviet and that we cannot permit.") In effect, Stalin demanded that the United States abide by his construction of earlier agreements, and that Truman acknowledge what Roosevelt had accepted as the terms of the sphere-of-influence agreements—that democratic forms and anti-communist democrats of Eastern Europe be abandoned to the larger cause of Russian-American concord.

Though the Allies at Potsdam were not able to settle the dispute over influence in Eastern Europe, they did reach a limited agreement on other European issues. In a "package" deal the Soviets accepted Italy in the U.N. after a peace treaty could be arranged; the United States and Great Britain agreed to set the temporary western border of Poland at the Oder-Neisse line; and the Soviets settled for far less in reparations than they had expected. The decisions on Germany were the important settlements, and the provision on reparations, when linked with American avoidance of offering Russia economic aid, left Russia without the assistance she needed for the pressing task of economic reconstruction.

Russia had long been seeking substantial economic aid, and the American failure to offer it seemed to be part of a general strategy. Earlier Harriman had advised "that the development of friendly relations [with Russia] would depend upon a generous credit," and recommended "that the question of the credit should be tied into our overall diplomatic relations with the Soviet Union and at the appropriate time the Russians should be given to understand that our willingness to cooperate wholeheartedly with them in their vast reconstruction problem will depend upon their behavior in international matters." In January 1945 Roosevelt had decided not to discuss at Yalta the $6 billion credit to the Soviet Union, explaining privately, "I think it's very important that we hold this back and don't give them any promises until we get what we want." (Secretary Morgenthau, in vigorous disagreement, believed that both the President and Secretary of State Stettinius were wrong, and "that if they wanted to get the Russians to do something they should . . . do it nice. . . . Don't drive such a hard bargain that when you come through it does not taste good.") In future months American officials continued to delay, presumably using the prospect of a loan for political leverage. Shortly before Postdam, the administration had secured congressional approval for a $1 billion loan fund which could have been used to assist Russia, but the issue of "credits to the Soviet Union" apparently was never even discussed.

Shunting aside the loan, the United States also retreated from Roosevelt's implied agreement at Yalta that reparations would be about $20 billion (half of which the Soviets would receive); Truman's new Secretary of State, James F. Byrnes, pointed out that the figures were simply the "basis" for discussion. (He was technically correct, but obviously Roosevelt had intended it as a general promise and Stalin had so understood it. Had it not been so intended, why had Churchill refused to endorse this section of the Yalta agreement?) Because Byrnes was unwilling to yield, the final agreement on reparations was similar to the terms that would have prevailed if there had been no agreement: the Soviet Union would fill her claims largely by removals from her own zone. That was the substance of the Potsdam agreement. The Russians also surrendered any hopes of participating in control of the heavily industrialized Ruhr, and confirmed the earlier retreat from the policy of dismemberment of Germany. They settled for an agreement that they could trade food and raw materials from their zone for 15 per cent of such industrial capital equipment from the Western Zones "as is unnecessary for the German peace economy," and that the allies would transfer from the Western Zones "10 percent of such industrial capital equipment as is unnecessary for the German peace economy"—but the agreement left undefined what was necessary for the economy.

Potsdam, like Yalta, left many of the great questions unresolved. "One fact that stands out more clearly than others is that nothing is ever settled," wrote Lord Alanbrooke, Chief of the British Staff, in his diary. As he observed, neither the United States nor Russia had yielded significantly. Russia had refused to move from the areas that her armies occupied, and the United States had been vigorous in her efforts, but without offering economic assistance to gain concessions. Though the atomic bomb may not have greatly influenced Truman's actions in the months before Potsdam, the bomb certainly influenced his behavior at Potsdam. When he arrived he still wanted (and expected) Russian intervention in the Japanese war. During the conference he learned about the successful test at Alamogordo. With Russian intervention no longer necessary, Truman's position hardened noticeably. As sole possessor of the bomb, he had good reason to expect easier future dealings with Stalin. For months Stimson had been counseling that the bomb would be the "master card," and Truman, acting on Stimson's advice, even delayed the Potsdam Conference until a time when he would know about the bomb. On the eve of the conference the President had confided to an adviser, "If it explodes, as I think it will, I'll certainly have a hammer on those boys [the Russians]."

III

At Potsdam President Truman was "delighted" when Stimson brought him the news about the bomb on July 16. Upon learning more about the results of the test, Truman (according to Stimson) said "it gave him an entirely new feeling of confidence and he thanked me for having come to the conference and being present to help him in this way." The President's enthusiasm and new sense of power were soon apparent in his meetings with the other heads of state, for as Churchill notes (in Stimson's words), "Truman was evidently much fortified by something that had happened and . . . he stood up to the Russians in a most emphatic and decisive manner." After reading the full report on the Alamogordo explosion, Churchill said. "Now I know what happened to Truman yesterday. I couldn't understand it. When he got to the meeting after having read this report he was a changed man. He told the Russians just where they got off and generally bossed the whole meeting."

"From that moment [when we learned of the successful test] our outlook on the future was transformed," Churchill explained later. Forced earlier to concede parts of Eastern Europe to the Russians because Britain did not have the power to resist Soviet wishes and the United States had seemed to lack the desire, Churchill immediately savored the new possibilities. The Prime Minister (Lord Alanbrooke wrote in his diary about Churchill's enthusiasm) "was completely carried away . . . we now had something in our hands which would redress the balance with the Russians. The secret of this explosive and the power to use it would completely alter the diplomatic equilibrium. . . . Now we had a new value which redressed our position (pushing out his chin and scowling); now we could say, 'If you insist on doing this or that well . . . And then where were the Russians!' "

Stimson and Byrnes had long understood that the bomb could influence future relations with Russia, and, after the successful test, they knew that Russian entry was no longer necessary to end the Japanese war. Upon Truman's direction, Stimson conferred at Potsdam with General Marshall and reported to the President that Marshall no longer saw a need for Russian intervention. "It is quite clear," cabled Churchill from Potsdam, "that the United States do not at the present time desire Russian participation in the war against Japan."

"The new explosive alone was sufficient to settle matters," Churchill reported. The bomb had displaced the Russians in the calculations of American policy-makers. The combat use of the bomb, then, was not viewed as the only way to end the Far Eastern war promptly. In July there was ample evidence that there were other possible strategies—a noncombat demonstration, a warning, a blockade. Yet, before authorizing the use of the bomb at Hiroshima, Truman did not try *any* of the possible strategies, including the three most likely: guaranteeing the

position of the Japanese Emperor (and hence making surrender conditional), seeking a Russian declaration of war (or announcement of intent), or waiting for Russian entry into the war.

As an invasion of the Japanese mainland was not scheduled until
about November 1, and as Truman knew that the Japanese were sending out "peace feelers" and that the main obstacle to peace seemed to
be the requirement of unconditional surrender (which threatened the
position of the Emperor), he could wisely have revised the terms of surrender. At first Under Secretary of State Grew and then Stimson had
urged Truman earlier to revise the terms in this way, and he had been
sympathetic. But at Potsdam Stimson found that Truman and Byrnes
had rejected his advice. As a result the proclamation issued from Potsdam by the United States, Great Britain. and China retained the demand for unconditional surrender when a guarantee of the Emperor's
government might have removed the chief impediment to peace.

Nor was Truman willing to seek a Russian declaration of war (or
even an announcement of intent). Even though American advisers had
long believed that the *threat* of Russian entry might be sufficient to
compel Japanese capitulation, Truman did not invite Stalin to sign the
proclamation, which would have constituted a statement of Russian
intent. There is even substantial evidence that Truman sought to delay
Russian entry into the war.

Pledging to maintain the position of the Emperor, seeking a Russian declaration of war (or announcement of intent), awaiting Russian
entry—each of these options, as well as others, had been proposed in the
months before Hiroshima and Nagasaki. Each was available to Truman.
Why did he not try one or more? No *definite* answer is possible. But it
is clear that Truman was either incapable or unwilling to reexamine his
earlier assumption (or decision) of using the bomb. Under the tutelage
of Byrnes and Stimson, Truman had come to assume by July that the
bomb should be used, and perhaps he was incapable of reconsidering
this strategy because he found no compelling reason not to use the
bomb. Or he may have consciously rejected the options because he
wanted to use the bomb. Perhaps he was vindictive and wished to retaliate for Pearl Harbor and other atrocities. (In justifying the use of
the bomb against the Japanese, he wrote a few days after Nagasaki,
"The only language they seem to understand is the one we have been
using to bombard them. When you have to deal with a beast you have
to treat him as a beast.") Or, most likely, Truman agreed with Byrnes
that using the bomb would advance other American policies: it would
end the war before the Russians could gain a hold in Manchuria, it
would permit the United States to exclude Russia from the occupation
government of Japan, and it would make the Soviets more manageable
in Eastern Europe. It would enable the United States to shape the
peace according to its own standards.

At minimum, then, the use of the bomb reveals the moral insensitivity of the President—whether he used it because the moral implications did not compel a reexamination of assumptions, or because he
sought retribution, or because he sought to keep Russia out of Man-

churia and the occupation government of Japan, and to make her more manageable in Eastern Europe. In 1945 American foreign policy was not innocent, nor was it unconcerned about Russian power, nor did it assume that the United States lacked the power to impose its will on the Russian state, nor was it characterized by high moral purpose or consistent dedication to humanitarian principles.

IV

Both Secretary of War Stimson and Secretary of State Byrnes had foreseen the importance of the bomb to American foreign policy. To Stimson it had long promised to be the "master card" for diplomacy. After Hiroshima and Nagasaki Byrnes was eager to use the bomb as at least an "implied threat" in negotiations with Russia. and Truman seems to have agreed to a vigorous course in trying to roll back Russian influence in Eastern Europe.

Truman seemed to be rejecting Stimson's recommendations that international control of atomic energy be traded for important Russian concessions—"namely the settlement of the Polish, Rumanian, Yugoslavian, and Manchurian problems." In his report on the Potsdam Conference the day after the second bomb, the President asserted that Rumania, Bulgaria, and Hungary "are not to be the spheres of influence of any one power" and at the same time proclaimed that the United States would be the "trustees" of the atomic bomb.

Following Truman's veiled threat, Byrnes continued his efforts to roll back the Soviet Union's influence. Assisted by a similar protest by the British, who clearly recognized the power of the bomb, he gained postponement of the Bulgarian election, charging that the government was not "adequately representative of important elements . . . of democratic opinion" and that its arrangements for elections "did not insure freedom from the fear of force or intimidation." In Hungary, Russia also acceded to similar Anglo-American demands and postponed the scheduled elections. It is not unreasonable to conclude that the bomb had made the Russians more tractable. "The significance of Hiroshima was not lost on the Russians," Alexander Werth, British correspondent in the Soviet Union, later reported. "It was clearly realized that this was a New Fact in the world's power politics, that the bomb constituted a threat to Russia. . . . Everybody . . . believed that although the two [atomic] bombs had killed or maimed [the] . . . Japanese, their real purpose was, first and foremost, to intimidate Russia."

Perhaps encouraged by his successes in Bulgaria and Hungary, Byrnes "wished to have the implied threat of the bomb in his pocket during the [September] conference" of foreign ministers in London. Stimson confided to his diary that Byrnes "was very much against any attempt to cooperate with Russia. His mind is full of his problems with the coming meeting . . . and he looks to having the presence of the bomb in his pocket . . . as a great weapon to get through the thing he has. He also told me of a number of acts of perfidy . . . of Stalin which they had encountered at Potsdam and felt in the light of those that we would not rely upon anything in the way of promises from them."

The London conference ended in deadlock, disbanding without even a joint communiqué. Despite American possession of the bomb, Molotov would not yield to American demands to reorganize the governments of Bulgaria and Rumania. In turn, he demanded for Russia a role in the occupation government of Japan, but Byrnes rebuffed the proposal. Unprepared for this issue, Byrnes was also unwilling or unable to understand Soviet anxieties about the security of their frontiers, and he pressed most vigorously for the reorganization of the Rumanian government. He would not acknowledge and perhaps could not understand the dilemma of his policy: that he was supporting free elections in areas (particularly in Rumania) where the resulting governments would probably be hostile to the Soviet Union, and yet he was arguing that democracy in Eastern Europe was compatible with Soviet demands for security. Unable to accept that Byrnes might be naive, Molotov questioned the Secretary's sincerity and charged that he wanted governments unfriendly to the Soviet Union. From this, Byrnes could only conclude later, "It seemed that the Soviet Union was determined to dominate Europe."

While the United States in the cases of these Eastern European nations chose to support traditional democratic principles and neither to acknowledge its earlier agreements on spheres of influence nor to respect Russian fears, Byrnes would not admit the similarity between Russian behavior in Rumania and British action in Greece. As part of the terms of his agreement with Churchill, Stalin had allowed the British to suppress a revolutionary force in Greece, and as a result the Greek government could not be accurately interpreted as broadly representative nor as a product of democratic procedures. Yet, as Molotov emphasized, the United States had not opposed British action in Greece or questioned the legitimacy of that government, nor was the United States making a reversal of British imperialism in Greece a condition for the large loan that Britain needed.

Some American observers, however, were aware of this double standard. In the northern Pacific and in Japan, America was to have the deciding voice, but in Eastern Europe, emphasized Walter Lippmann, "we invoke the principle that this is one world in which decisions must not be taken unilaterally." Most Americans did not see this paradox, and Byrnes probably expressed crystallizing national sentiment that autumn when he concluded that the dispute with Russia was a test of whether "we really believed in what we said about one world and our desire to build collective security, or whether we were willing to accept the Soviet preference for the simpler task of dividing the world into two spheres of influence."

Despite Byrnes's views, and although he could not secure a reorganization of the Rumanian government, communist influence was weakened in other parts of Eastern Europe. In Budapest free elections were held and the Communist party was routed; and early in November, just two days after the United States recognized Hungary, the Communists lost in the national elections there. In Bulgaria elections took place in "complete order and without disturbance," and despite American protests, a Communist-dominated single ticket (representing most of the political parties) triumphed.

While the Soviet Union would not generally permit in Eastern Europe conditions that conformed to Western ideals, Stalin was pursuing a cautious policy and seeking accommodation with the West. He was willing to allow capitalism but was suspicious of American efforts at economic penetration which could lead to political dominance. Though by the autumn of 1945 the governments in Russia's general area of influence were subservient in foreign policy, they varied in form and in degree of independence—democracy in Czechoslovakia (the only country in this area with a democratic tradition), free elections and the overthrow of the Communist party in Hungary, a Communist-formed coalition government in Bulgaria, a broadly based but Communist-dominated government in Poland, and a Soviet-imposed government in Rumania (the most anti-Russian of these nations). In all of these countries Communists controlled the ministries of interior (the police) and were able to suppress anti-Soviet groups, including anti-communist democrats.

Those who have attributed to Russia a policy of inexorable expansion have often neglected this immediate postwar period, or they have interpreted it simply as a necessary preliminary (a cunning strategy to allay American suspicions until the American Army demobilized and left the continent) to the consolidation and extension of power in east-central Europe, From this perspective, however, much of Stalin's behavior becomes strangely contradictory and potentially self-defeating. If he had planned to create puppets rather than an area of "friendly governments," why (as Isaac Deutscher asks) did Stalin "so stubbornly refuse to make any concessions to the Poles over their eastern frontiers?" Certainly, also, his demand for reparations from Hungary, Rumania, and Bulgaria would have been unnecessary if he had planned to take over these countries. (America's insistence upon using a loan to Russia to achieve political goals, and the nearly twenty-month delay after Russia first submitted a specific proposal for assistance, led Harriman to suggest in November that the loan policy "may have contributed to their [Russian] avaricious policies in the countries occupied or liberated by the Red Army.")

Russian sources are closed, so it is not possible to prove that Soviet intentions were conservative; nor for the same reason is it possible for those who adhere to the thesis of inexorable Soviet expansion to prove their theory. But the available evidence better supports the thesis that these years should be viewed not as a cunning preliminary to the harshness of 1947 and afterward, but as an attempt to establish a *modus vivendi* with the West and to protect "socialism in one country." This interpretation explains more adequately why the Russians delayed nearly three years before ending dissent and hardening policies in the countries behind their own military lines. It would also explain why the Communist parties in France and Italy were cooperating with the coalition governments until these parties were forced out of the coalitions in 1947. The American government had long hoped for the exclusion of these Communist parties, and in Italy, at least, American intimations of greater economic aid to a government without Communists was an effective lever. At the same time Stalin was seeking to prevent the revolution in Greece.

If the Russian policy was conservative and sought accommodation (as now seems likely), then its failure must be explained by looking beyond Russian actions. Historians must reexamine this period and reconsider American policies. Were they directed toward compromise? Can they be judged as having sought adjustment? Or did they demand acquiescence to the American world view, thus thwarting real negotiations?

There is considerable evidence that American actions clearly changed after Roosevelt's death. Slowly abandoning the tactics of accommodation, they became even more vigorous after Hiroshima. The insistence upon rolling back Soviet influence in Eastern Europe, the reluctance to grant a loan for Russian reconstruction, the inability to reach an agreement on Germany, the maintenance of the nuclear monopoly—all of these could have contributed to the sense of Russian insecurity. The point, then, is that in 1945 and 1946 there may still have been possibilities for negotiations and settlements, for accommodations and adjustments, if the United States had been willing to recognize Soviet fears, to accept Soviet power in her areas of influence, and to ease anxieties.

V

In October 1945 President Truman delivered what Washington officials called his "getting tough with the Russians" speech. Proclaiming that American policy was "based firmly on fundamental principles of righteousness and justice," he promised that the United States "shall not give our approval to any compromise with evil." In a veiled assault on Soviet actions in Eastern Europe, he declared, "We shall refuse to recognize any government imposed on any nation by the force of any foreign power." Tacitly opposing the bilateral trading practices of Russia, he asserted as a principle of American foreign policy the doctrine of the "open door"—all nations "should have access on equal terms to the trade and the raw materials of the world." At the same time, however, Truman disregarded the fact of American power in Latin America and emphasized that the Monroe Doctrine (in expanded form) remained a cherished part of American policy there: ". . . the sovereign states of the Western Hemisphere, without interference from outside the Western Hemisphere, must work together as good neighbors in the solution of their common economic problems."

"Soviet current policy," concluded a secret report by the Deputy Director of Naval Intelligence a few months later, "is to establish a Soviet Monroe Doctrine for the area under her shadow, primarily and urgently for security, secondarily to facilitate the eventual emergence of the USSR as a power which could not be menaced by any other world combination of powers." The report did not expect the Soviets ". . . to take any action during the next five years which might develop into hostilities with Anglo-Americans," but anticipated attempts to build up intelligence and potential sabotage networks, "encouragement of Communist parties in all countries potentially to weaken antagonists, and in colonial areas to pave the way for 'anti-imperialist' disorders and revolutions as a means of sapping the strength of . . . chief remaining European rivals, Britain and France." "Present Soviet maneuvers to control North Iran," the report explained, were conceived to "push . . . from their own oil . . . and closer to the enemy's oil." There was no need to fear military expansion beyond this security zone, suggested the report, for the Soviet Union was economically exhausted, its population undernourished and dislocated, its industry and transportation "in an advanced state of deterioration." Despite suggestions that Soviet policy was rather cautious, Truman was reaching a more militant conclusion. "Unless Russia is faced with an iron fist and strong language," asserted Truman to his Secretary of State in January, "another war is in the making. Only one language do they understand—'how many divisions have you' . . . I'm tired of babying the Soviets."

During the winter months Byrnes, Senator Vandenberg, and John Foster Dulles, a Republican adviser on foreign policy, publicly attacked Russian policies. Vandenberg warned "our Russian ally" that the United States could not ignore "a unilateral gnawing away at the status quo." After these attacks, Churchill, accompanied by the President, delivered at Fulton, Missouri, a speech that announced the opening of the Cold War. "From Stettin in the Baltic to Trieste in the Adriatic, an iron curtain has descended across the Continent," declared the former British war leader. Condemning the establishment of "police governments" in Eastern Europe and warning of "Communist fifth columns or   . . . parties elsewhere," Churchill, with Truman's approval, called for an Anglo-American alliance to create "conditions of freedom and democracy as rapidly as possible in all [these] countries." The Soviet Union, he contended, did not want war, only "the fruits of war and the indefinite expansion of their power and doctrines." Such dangers could not be removed "by closing our eyes to them . . . nor will they be removed by a policy of appeasement." While he said that it was "not our duty *at this time* . . . to interfere forcibly in the internal affairs" of Eastern European countries, Churchill implied that intervention was advisable when Anglo-American forces were strengthened. His message was clear: ". . . the old doctrine of the balance of power is unsound. We cannot afford . . . to work on narrow margins, offering temptations to a trial of strength."

This was, as James Warburg later wrote, the early "idea of the containment doctrine . . . [and] the first public expression of the idea of a 'policy of liberation,'" which Dulles would later promulgate. Truman's presence on the platform at Fulton implied that Churchill's statement had official American endorsement, and though the President lamely denied afterward that he had known about the contents of the speech, he had actually discussed it with Churchill for two hours. Despite official denials and brief, widespread popular opposition to Churchill's message (according to public opinion polls), American policy was becoming clearly militant. It was not responding to a threat of immediate military danger; it was operating from the position of overwhelming power, and in the self-proclaimed conviction of right-eousness.

Undoubtedly Truman also agreed with the former Prime Minister when Churchill said at Fulton:

It would . . . be wrong and imprudent to intrust the secret knowledge of experience of the atomic bomb, which the United States, Great Britain and Canada now share, to the world organization. . . . No one in any country has slept less well in their beds because this knowledge and the method and raw material to apply it are at present . . . in American hands. I do not believe that we should all have slept so soundly had the positions been reversed and some Communist or neo-Fascist state monopolized, for the time being, these dread agencies. . . . Ultimately, when the essential brotherhood of man is truly embodied and expressed in a world organization, these powers may be confided to it.

Here, in classic form, was a theme that would dominate the American dialogue on the Cold War—the assertion of the purity of Anglo-American intentions and the assumption that the opposing power was malevolent and had no justifiable interests, no justifiable fears, and should place its trust in a Pax Americana (or a Pax Anglo-Americana). Under Anglo-American power the world could be transformed, order maintained, and Anglo-American principles extended. Stalin character-ized Churchill's message as, "Something in the nature of an ultimatum: 'Accept our rule voluntarily, and then all will be well: otherwise war is inevitable.' "

VI

Churchill's assurances notwithstanding, Russia had reason to fear the atomic bomb, particularly after Byrnes's efforts to use it as an "implied threat." For Byrnes the nuclear monopoly seemed to promise the possibility of creating on American terms a lasting structure of peace. Since this monopoly would last at least seven years, according to his estimates, America could achieve its objectives and presumably avoid an arms race. (A few days after Hiroshima, Byrnes instructed J. Robert Oppenheimer, the nuclear physicist, that "for the time being . . . international agreement was not practical and that he and the rest of the gang should pursue their work [on the hydrogen weapon] full force.")

Byrnes's strategy was briefly and unsuccessfully challenged by an-other member of the administration, Henry Stimson. Earlier Stimson had hoped that America's possession of the bomb could lead to the offer of a partnership with the Russians in return for a *quid pro quo*—

"the settlement of the Polish, Rumanian, Yugoslavian, and Manchurian problems," and the liberalization of the Soviet regime. Russia would have to roll back her curtain of secrecy and move toward an open society, reasoned Stimson, for "no permanently safe international relations can be established between two such fundamentally different national systems." The bomb, he believed, could not be shared until Russia liberalized her regime, and he hoped that the need for international controls would pry back the lid of secrecy. But his conversations with Harriman at Potsdam had made Stimson pessimistic about Russia's easing her restrictions, and after the bombing of Japan, as he watched Byrnes's strategy unfolding, he moved more strongly toward international cooperation. On September 5 the Secretary of War met with the President, explaining "that both my plan and Byrnes's plan contained chances which I outlined and I said that I thought that in my method there was less danger than in his and also we would be on the right path towards establishment of an international world, while on his plan we would be on the wrong path in that respect and would be tending to revert to power politics."

Rejecting his earlier idea of using possession of the bomb "as a direct lever" to produce "a change in Russian attitudes toward individual liberty," Stimson urged the President to invite the Soviet Union to share the secret "upon a basis of cooperation and trust."

It is true [he wrote to the President] if we approach them now, as I would propose, we may be gambling on their good faith and risk their getting into production of bombs sooner than they would otherwise. To put the matter concisely, I consider the problem of our satisfactory relations with Russia as not merely connected with but virtually dominated by the problem of the atomic bomb. Except for the problem of the control of that bomb, those relations, while vitally important, might not be immediately pressing. The establishment of relations of mutual confidence between her and us could afford to await the slow process of time. But with the discovery of the bomb, they become immediately emergent. *Those relations may be irretrievably embittered by the way in which we approach the solution of the bomb with Russia. For if we fail to approach them now and merely continue to negotiate with them, having this weapon rather ostentatiously on our hip, their suspicions and their distrust of our purposes and motives will increase.*

"The chief lesson I have learned in a long life," concluded Stimson, "is the only way you can make a man trustworthy is to trust him; and the surest way you can make a man untrustworthy is to distrust him and show your distrust." A week after learning that Byrnes planned to use the bomb as an "implied threat," Stimson warned Truman that a direct and forthright approach should be made before using *"express or implied threats* in our peace negotiations."

While Byrnes was at the unsuccessful London conference in mid-September, Stimson was lining up support for his new approach. The President seemed to approve of Stimson's memorandum. Truman "thought that we must take Russia into our confidence," wrote Stimson in his diary. Dean Acheson, the Under Secretary of State, also seemed "strongly on our side in the treatment of Russia," Stimson recorded. Robert P. Patterson, Stimson's Under Secretary who was scheduled to replace the Secretary upon his retirement later in the month, was convinced (in Stimson's words): "The safest way is not to try to keep the secret. It evidently cannot be kept . . . and that being so it is better to recognize it promptly and try to get on [better] terms with the Russians."

At a special cabinet meeting on September 21, Stimson outlined his proposal: "(1) that we should approach Russia at once with an opportunity to share on proper *quid pro quo* the bomb and (2) that this approach to Russia should be to her directly and not through the . . . [United Nations] or a similar conference of a number of states." He received support from Patterson, Robert Hannegan, the Postmaster General, Henry Wallace, the Secretary of Commerce, and Acheson, who was representing the State Department in Byrnes's absence. Explaining that he could not "conceive of a world in which we were hoarders of military secrets from our Allies, particularly this great Ally," Acheson (reported Forrestal) "saw no alternative except to give the full information to the Russians . . . for a *quid pro quo*."

Forrestal, Fred Vinson, the Secretary of the Treasury, Tom Clark, the Attorney General, and Clinton Anderson, the Secretary of Agriculture, opposed sharing the secret. Vinson compared it to the decision at the end of World War I to sink ships, and Anderson emphasized that the President must retain the confidence of the nation in his ability to "handle Russia." He warned that giving up information on atomic energy and the bomb would dangerously weaken that confidence. Forrestal, apparently the most vigorous opponent, objected to any attempt to "buy [Russian] understanding and sympathy. We tried that once with Hitler." Concluding that "trust had to be more than a one-way street," he recommended that the United States exercise "a trusteeship over the . . . bomb on behalf of the United Nations."

Twelve days later, on October 3, Truman publicly announced his decision: the United States would seek international control of atomic energy but would not share the secret of the bomb. Byrnes, who had just returned from the London conference, resisted even this plan: he opposed the sharing of any information with the Russians. Since he believed that his diplomacy had been frustrated by Russian secrecy and suspicions, he did not see how inspection could operate. Convinced that the United States should delay until it had achieved a "decent" peace, he urged the President to stall. He realized that the United States was relying more heavily on the bomb and sharply cutting back conventional forces, and he was unwilling to risk yielding nuclear mastery.

For more than two months the American government delayed even approaching the Russians. "The insistence by the inventors of mankind's most horrible weapon on withholding the secret from their ally has produced a most evident reaction in Moscow," reported the *New York Times*. It also led to Molotov's uneasy public boasting in November that Russia too would develop the bomb. ("We will have atomic energy and many other things too.") Finally, four months after Hiroshima, at the Moscow Conference of Foreign Ministers in late December, Byrnes invited Russia to join in recommending that the United Nations establish a commission on atomic energy.

During the next five months, while the Cold War intensified, the Truman administration organized to formulate a policy. In March it released a preliminary study (the Acheson-Lilienthal report) which sought to minimize the problems of inspection by recommending the establishment of an international Atomic Development Authority (ADA), which would control all significant nuclear activities. The ADA would be established in stages, and at each stage the United States would provide the necessary information, with the specific information on the bomb withheld until the final stage.

Probably this plan would have been unacceptable to the Russians. It would have left the secret of the bomb as an American trust for at least a few years, and it would have meant Russia's relinquishing possible control of a source of great economic potential to an international authority dominated by Western powers. In its emphasis, however, the report also conflicted with the desires of many American officials. It stressed generosity and negotiations when most were emphasizing fear and suspicion. It saw no need for punishment. A violation by any nation, under the proposed arrangements, would have been obvious and would have been a warning to other nations, and all would have returned at that point to big-power politics. The plan emphasized the necessity of international control and was willing to countenance small risks for world security when most emphasized the primacy of American security. ("We should not under any circumstances throw away our gun until we are sure that the rest of the world can't arm against us," asserted Truman.)

The final American plan was formulated and presented by Bernard Baruch, whom Truman had appointed as American representative to the U.N. Atomic Energy Commission. It emphasized "sanctions" and "condign punishments," and called for the elimination of the Security Council veto on matters of atomic energy. The issue of the veto was unnecessary; if any nation violated the treaty after the sharing of atomic energy, what action could be vetoed? In turn, until the nations reached the last stages of the plan, a violation, whatever the situation in the U.N., would lead to the withdrawal of other nations from the plan. Also, rather than following Stimson's advice and first approaching the Soviets privately on control of atomic energy, Baruch insisted upon negotiations in the public forum where positions could easily harden. Lacking the flexibility of the earlier plan but relying upon similar stages, the Baruch plan guaranteed the United States a nuclear monopoly for some years. Thus it left the United States with the option of using the bomb for leverage or even blackmail. While Byrnes and Truman may no longer have wanted to use the bomb as an "implied threat," its value was clear to the Joint Chiefs of Staff who had so counseled Baruch. The atomic bomb, "because of its decisive power is now an essential part of our military strength," explained General Carl

Spaatz, the Air Force Chief of Staff. "Our monopoly of the bomb, even though it is transitory, may well prove to be a critical factor in our efforts to achieve [peace]." Separately the military chiefs had outlined the strategy which the Baruch plan followed: "We should exploit [the nuclear monopoly] to assist in the early establishment of a satisfying peace. . . . It will be desirable for international agreements concerning the atomic bomb to follow the European peace treaties and definitely to precede the time when other countries would have atomic bombs."

Though the Western world generally viewed the plan as magnanimous and interpreted Russia's objections as further evidence of her refusal to negotiate sincerely, the Soviet criticisms were actually quite reasonable. The Baruch plan in its early stages *did* endanger Soviet security. Russia would have had to allow investigations of natural resources and mapping of the interior—thus surrendering a principal military advantage. The Baruch plan, charged Molotov, "proceeds from the desire to secure for the United States the monopolistic possession of the bomb." (Vandenberg had reportedly told Molotov privately, "We have the atomic bomb and we are not going to give it up. We are not going to compromise or trade with you. We are not going to give up our immortal souls.") American leaders, as the Soviets understood, were demanding absolute security for their own nation and refusing to trust Russia at the same time that they were demanding that the Soviets trust the United States and risk the possibility of having the American nuclear monopoly frozen.

The Russian plan, on the other hand, was clearly unacceptable to American leaders. It called for nuclear disarmament and the sharing of secrets first while delaying the establishment of controls. In effect it asked the United States to surrender its nuclear advantage and promised that the nations could thereafter wrestle with the problems of controls. For the Truman administration the Russian plan was further evidence of Soviet insincerity. American leaders could not understand objections to the suspension of the veto, nor, perhaps, why the Soviets feared a plan that could guarantee the American monopoly. Yet Baruch had been explicitly counseled earlier on the advantages of the monopoly, Byrnes had tried to exploit the monopoly, and presumably Truman had understood it. Perhaps because these men so thoroughly believed that their intentions were honorable, that their aim was to establish a just and lasting peace, and that the United States would never use the bomb first, they could not grant the validity of Soviet objections.

Harry Truman and the Fair Deal

ALONZO L. HAMBY

President Harry S Truman enunciated a program called the Fair Deal that was to be an extension of Franklin Roosevelt's New Deal. The rhetoric of Truman's speeches, especially his inaugural address of 1949, promised much, and Hamby argues that the Fair Deal definitely extended FDR's work. But Truman was by nature a moderate, a border-state politician whose very essence was compromise, and he operated in a period of rapprochement between government and business. Some centers of Democratic strength, notably the urban machines, seem to stand still rather than to grow in social awareness. Did local leaders urge the Truman administration to "go slow" because welfare laws jeopardized their organizations? One historian even asks whether "the Democratic coalition had ceased to be a 'have-not' coalition and had become interested chiefly in maintaining earlier gains." To question the possibilities of policies in the New Deal and Fair Deal is to ask about the possibilities of government today.

"Every segment of our population and every individual has a right to expect from our Government a fair deal," declared Harry S Truman in early 1949. In 1945 and 1946 the Truman administration had almost crumbled under the stresses of postwar reconversion; in 1947 and 1948 it had fought a frustrating, if politically rewarding, battle with the Republican Eightieth Congress. Buoyed by his remarkable victory of 1948 and given Democratic majorities in both houses of Congress, Truman hoped to achieve an impressive record of domestic reform. The president systematized his past proposals, added some new ones, and gave his program a name that would both connect his administration with the legacy of the New Deal and give it a distinct identity. The Fair Deal, while based solidly upon the New Deal tradition, differed from its predecessor in significant aspects of mood and detail. It reflected not only Truman's own aspirations but also a style of liberalism that had begun to move beyond the New Deal during World War II and had come to maturity during the early years of the cold war—"the vital center."

. . .

The legislative goals Truman announced for his administration, while not devised to meet the needs of an abstract theory, were well in tune with the vital-center approach: anti-inflation measures, a more progressive tax structure, repeal of the Taft-Hartley Act, a higher minimum wage, a farm program based on the concepts of abundant production and parity income, resource development and public power programs, expansion of social security, national medical insurance, fed-

39

eral aid to education, extensive housing legislation, and civil rights bills. The president's most controversial request was for authority to increase plant facilities in such basic industries as steel, preferably through federal financing of private enterprise but through outright government construction if necessary. Roundly condemned by right-wing opponents as "socialistic" and soon dropped by the administration, the proposal was actually intended to meet the demands of a prosperous, growing capitalist economy and emerged from the Fair Deal's search for the proper degree of government intervention to preserve the established American economic structure. "Between the reactionaries of the extreme left with their talk about revolution and class warfare, and the reactionaries of the extreme right with their hysterical cries of bankruptcy and despair, lies the way of progress," Truman declared in November 1949.

The Fair Deal was a conscious effort to continue the purpose of the New Deal but not necessarily its methods. Not forced to meet the emergencies of economic depression, given a solid point of departure by their predecessors, and led by a president more prone than FDR to demand programmatic coherence, the Fair Dealers made a systematic effort to discover techniques that would be at once more equitable and more practical in alleviating the problems of unequal wealth and opportunity. Thinking in terms of abundance rather than scarcity, they attempted to adapt the New Deal tradition to postwar prosperity. Seeking to go beyond the New Deal while preserving its objectives, the Truman administration advocated a more sweeping and better-ordered reform agenda. Yet in the quest for political means, Truman and the vital-center liberals could only fall back upon one of the oldest dreams of American reform—the Jacksonian-Populist vision of a union of producing classes, an invincible farmer-labor coalition. While superficially plausible, the Fair Deal's political strategy proved too weak to handle the burden thrust upon it.

The Fair Deal seemed to oscillate between militancy and moderation. New Dealers had frequently gloried in accusations of "liberalism" or "radicalism"; Fair Dealers tended to shrink from such labels. The New Dealers had often lusted for political combat; the Fair Dealers were generally more low keyed. Election campaigns demanded an aggressiveness that would arouse the Democratic presidential party, but the continued strength of the conservative coalition in Congress dictated accommodation in the post-election efforts to secure passage of legislative proposals. Such tactics reflected Truman's personal political experience and instincts, but they also developed naturally out of the climate of postwar America. The crisis of economic depression had produced one style of political rhetoric; the problems of prosperity and inflation brought forth another.

The Fair Deal mirrored Truman's policy preferences and approach to politics; it was no more the president's personal creation, however, than the New Deal had been Roosevelt's. Just as FDR's advisers had formulated much of the New Deal, a group of liberals developed much of the content and tactics of the Fair Deal. For the most part these were the men who had formed a liberal caucus within the administration in early 1947 shortly after the Republican triumph in the congressional elections of 1946, had worked to sway the president toward the left in his policy recommendations and campaign tactics, and had played a significant, if not an all-embracing, role in Truman's victory in 1948. Truman's special counsel, Clark M. Clifford, was perhaps the most prominent member of the group, but Clifford, although a shrewd political analyst, a persuasive advocate, and an extremely valuable administrative chief of staff, was neither the caucus's organizer nor a creative liberal thinker. Others gave the Fair Deal its substance as a program descending from the New Deal yet distinct from it.

. . .

The administration took the next step in April with the introduction in Congress of a new farm program, which had been drawn up under Brannan's direction. The Brannan Plan was difficult and complex in detail, but essentially it was an effort to maintain farm income at the record high level of the war and immediate postwar periods while letting market prices fall to a natural supply-demand level. Brannan thus proposed to continue the New Deal policy of subsidizing the farmers, but he broke dramatically with the New Deal technique of restricting production and marketing in order to achieve artificially high prices.

Many agrarian progressives, including Henry A. Wallace himself, had long been troubled by the price-support mechanisms and had sought methods of unleashing the productive capacity of the farms. Brannan seemed to show the way. He proposed the maintenance of farm income through direct payments to farmers rather than through crop restriction. In order to encourage and protect the family farm, moreover, he recommended supporting a maximum of about $26,100 worth of production per farm. To the consumer he promised milk at fifteen cents a quart, to the dairy farmer a sustained high income. To the Democratic party he offered an apparently ingenious device that would unite the interests of farmers and workers.

Liberals generally were enthusiastic over both the principles and the politics of the Brannan proposals. "The new plan lets growers grow and eaters eat, and that is good," commented Samuel Grafton. "If Brannan is right, the political miracle of 1948 will become a habit as farmers, labor and consumers find common political goals," wrote agricultural columnist Angus MacDonald. James Patton called the Brannan Plan "a milestone in the history of American agriculture," and the *Nation* asserted that the average consumer should devote all his spare time to support of the program.

The plan immediately ran into the opposition of the conservatives who dominated Congress. Republicans feared that the political coalition Brannan was trying to build would entrench the Democrats in power. Large producers, most effectively represented by the powerful Farm Bureau Federation, regarded the plan as discriminatory, and many Democrats with ties to the Farm Bureau refused to support it, among them Senate majority leader Scott Lucas and Clinton Anderson, now the freshman senator from New Mexico. By June it was obvious to most political analysts that the Brannan Plan had no chance of passage in

1949. The administration and most liberals nevertheless remained optimistic. The issue seemed good, the alignment of interests logical and compelling: enough political education and campaigning could revive the scheme and revolutionize American politics.

Both the CIO and the Farmers Union undertook campaigns to spread the message of farmer-labor unity. An article in the *National Union Farmer* typified the effort:

Workers today are in a tough spot. just like farmers. Production has been steadily declining, and that means fewer jobs and lower wages. And that means smaller markets for farm products. This worries everybody but Big Business, but these advocates of scarcity still rule the roost. Monopoly wants less production, less employment, lower wages, fewer family farmers, less collective bargaining, lower farm prices and less competition except for jobs. . . . There is little basic difference between the labor fight against the Taft-Hartley law, and our fight against attempts to tax cooperatives out of existence. . . . Labor's strong objections to 40¢ an hour as a minimum is no different than our equally strong objections to 60% of parity.

Brannan campaigned extensively for his program. "Farm income equals jobs for millions of American workers," he told a labor gathering in a typical effort. "Together, let workers and farmers unite in achieving a full employment, full production economy." The administration sponsored regional farmer-labor conferences around the country. The one attracting the most attention was held in June at Des Moines, Iowa, and featured prominent labor leaders, important Democratic congressmen, and Vice-President Alben Barkley. Other such grass-roots meetings were organized as far east as upstate New York, and the Democratic National Committee prepared a pamphlet on the Brannan Plan for mass distribution. On Labor Day the president devoted two major appearances, one in Pittsburgh and the other in Des Moines, to the Brannan Plan and to farmer-labor unity. "Those who are trying to set these two great groups against each other just have axes of their own to grind," he warned his Pittsburgh audience. "Price supports must . . . give consumers the benefit of our abundant farm production," he told his Des Moines listeners.

Many liberals and Democratic politicians remained convinced that they had an overwhelming political strategy. "In 1950 and '52, the Brannan Plan will be the great issue in the doubtful states," wrote journalist A. G. Mezerik. "After that, Congress will enact a new farm bill—one which is based on low prices for consumers and a high standard of living for family farmers." In early 1950 the Brannan Plan seemed to be gaining popular support. Liberals inside and outside the administration continued to hope for vindication at the polls in November. They could not, of course, foresee the Korean War and the ways in which it would change the shape of American politics.

Even without the Korean War, however, even without the disruptive impact of McCarthyism, it is doubtful that the Brannan Plan would have worked the miracles expected of it. The liberals inside and outside the administration who had created or worked for it assumed that urban and rural groups could be united simply on grounds of mutual self-interest. They failed to understand that these groups were not deeply concerned with *mutual* self-interest; both sides had practiced with some success methods that had taken care of their own self-interest. The rhetoric about urban-rural interdependence was extremely superficial, talked but not deeply felt. Most farm and labor leaders, even those progressive in their outlook, hardly had a basis for communication. The ADA conference of February 1949 included some of the best-informed figures from the unions and the farms. Yet one of the labor leaders had to ask for an explanation "in simple language" of the concept of parity. One of the farm leaders then admitted that he had no idea what the dues check-off was or how it worked. The farm leaders also frankly commented that their constitutents were strongly against such things as a minimum wage applied to farm workers, the extension of social security to cover farm labor and farmers in general, and especially the re-establishment of any sort of price controls. The situation at Des Moines seems to have been much the same. Even some of the Farmers Union officials at the conference were annoyed by the presence of the labor people. "Some farmers wondered if they wern't being sucked in to help the forces of labor fight the Taft-Hartley Act," reported journalist Lauren Soth. Such ideas, of course, were not entirely fanciful. Most of the observers at Des Moines sensed the artificiality of the whole affair, but they continued to hope that further contacts would consummate the union of city and country.

The farm leaders harbored a provincial suspicion of labor, while the reverse was true in the cities. "While labor has given general support to the Brannan plan, I have had the suggestion made, almost ironically, that labor might be given a guaranteed income if such were to be granted to farmers," remarked Jim Loeb in November 1949. Many liberals felt that, as proposed by the administration, the Brannan Plan was too generous. The Chicago *Sun-Times* and the *Nation* agreed that the principles and machinery of the Brannan system were excellent, but both dissented from Brannan's proposal to support farm income at record heights. "The country as a whole should not undertake to support farm income at a higher level than is fair and just," warned the *Sun-Times,* adding that it would always be easier to raise supports than to lower them. Chester Bowles went a step further when he proposed that the whole matter of agricultural subsidies should be tied to urban employment with no supports at all during periods of full employment. Such ideas were hardly the current of a new urban-rural coalition.

Many urban liberals found the plan itself difficult to grasp and could not work up much enthusiasm about it. "Most of us do not understand it completely," admitted Jim Loeb a month and a half after its introduction. A group of ADA leaders had a cordial meeting with Brannan in June 1949 and pledged their support. Actually, however, the ADA did little to promote the program. In the spring of 1950 a Philadelphia liberal wrote to the organization asking for information on the issue, but Violet Gunther, the legislative director, replied that the ADA had published nothing other than an endorsement in the platform, nor could she think of any group other than the Farmers Union that might have something available. The *Nation* and the *New Republic* gave only occasional mention to the plan. Most liberals could heartily endorse and even get excited about Brannan's political objectives, but understanding and identifying with the scheme itself was quite a different matter.

For a time in early 1950 declining farm prices seemed to generate a surge of support for the Brannan Plan. At the beginning of June, Albert Loveland, the undersecretary of agriculture, won the Iowa Democratic senatorial primary on a pro-Brannan platform and thereby encouraged the administration to believe that the Midwest was moving in its direction. Just a few weeks later, however, the Korean War began, creating situations and pressures that doomed most of the Fair Deal.

Even if the Brannan Plan had become law, it is far from certain that it would have created the dream farmer-liberal coalition. Most leading agricultural economists, including those of a progressive outlook, were convinced that the proposal would be unworkable and prohibitively expensive. Some liberal economists condemned its failure to give the rural poor at least as much aid as the middle-class family farm. Even assuming that the economists were wrong, there is no guarantee that a smoothly functioning Brannan program could have performed the neat trick of uniting the very different cultures of urban liberalism and rural insurgency; such a feat probably would have required more than mutual economic benefits. The down-to-earth, church-social ethos of the Farmers Union would not automatically homogenize with the sophisticated, intellectual progressivism of the city liberals or the wage-and-hour, union-shop, reformism of labor.

During 1949 and early 1950 the Truman administration managed a record of substantial legislative accomplishment, but it consisted almost entirely of additions to such New Deal programs as the minimum wage, social security, and public power. The Housing Act of 1949, with its provisions for large-scale public housing, appeared to be a breakthrough, but weak administration, local opposition, and inadequate financing subsequently vitiated hopes that it would help the poor. Acting on his executive authority, Truman took an important step by forcing the army to agree to a policy of desegregation. The heart of the Fair Deal, however—repeal of the Taft-Hartley Act, civil rights legislation, aid to education, national medical insurance, and the Brannan Plan—failed in Congress. Given the power of the well-entrenched conservative coalition and a wide-spread mood of public apathy about big new reforms, Truman could only enlarge upon the record of his predecessor.

Democratic strategists hoped for a mandate in the congressional elections of 1950. In the spring Truman made a successful whistle-stop tour of the West and Midwest, rousing party enthusiasm and apparently demonstrating a solid personal popularity. Loveland's victory provided further encouragement, and in California the aggressive Fair

Dealer Helen Gahagan Douglas won the Democratic nomination for the Senate by a thumping margin. Two incumbent Fair Deal supporters— Frank Graham of North Carolina and Claude Pepper of Florida—lost their senatorial primaries, but, as Southerners who had run afoul of the race issue, they did not seem to be indictors of national trends. Nevertheless, the hope of cutting into the strength of the conservative opposition ran counter to the historical pattern of mid-term elections. The beginning of the Korean War at the end of June destroyed any chances of success.

The most immediate impact of Korea was to refuel an anti-Communist extremism that might otherwise have sputtered out. Senator Joseph R. McCarthy had begun his rise to prominence in February 1950, but he had failed to prove any of his multiple allegations and seemed definitively discredited by the investigations of a special Senate committee headed by Millard Tydings. McCarthy, it is true, was a talented demagogue who should have been taken more seriously by the liberals and the Truman administration in early 1950, but it seems probable that his appeal would have waned more quickly if the cold war with communism had not suddenly become hot. As it was, many of his Senate colleagues rushed to emulate him. In September 1950 Congress passed the McCarran Internal Security Act; only a handful of congressional liberals dared dissent from the overwhelming vote in favor. Truman's subsequent veto was intelligent and courageous, but was issued more for the history books than with any real hope of success. In the subsequent campaign, liberal Democrats, whether they had voted for the McCarran Act or not, found themselves facing charges of softness toward communism.

The war hurt the administration in other ways. It touched off a brief but serious inflation, which caused widespread consumer irritation. By stimulating demand for agricultural products it brought most farm prices up to parity levels and thereby undercut whatever attractiveness the Brannan Plan had developed in rural areas. Finally it removed the Democratic party's most effective spokesman—the president —from active participation in the campaign. Forced to play the role of war leader, Truman allowed himself only one major partisan speech, delivered in St. Louis on the eve of the balloting.

The Fair Deal might have been a winning issue in a nation oriented toward domestic concerns and recovering from an economic recession; it had much less appeal in a country obsessed with Communist aggression and experiencing an inflationary war boom. The reaction against the administration was especially strong in the Midwest. Indiana's Democratic aspirant for the Senate asked Oscar Ewing to stay out of the state. In Iowa, Loveland desperately attempted to reverse his identification with the Brannan Plan. In Missouri the managers of senatorial candidate Thomas C. Hennings, Jr. privately asked White House aides to make Truman's St. Louis speech a foreign policy address that would skip lightly over Fair Deal issues. A few days before the election the columnist Stewart Alsop returned from a Midwestern trip convinced that the region had never been more conservative. Nevertheless, Truman's political advisers, and probably Truman himself, felt that the Fair Deal still had appeal. Given the basic strength of the economy and the victories in Korea that followed the Inchon landing, the White House believed that the Democrats could easily rebut generalized charges of fumbling or softness toward communism. In mid-October the Democratic National Committee and many local leaders were so confident of success that their main concern was simply to get out the vote.

The November results, however, showed a Democratic loss of twenty-eight seats in the House of Representatives and five seats in the Senate. Truman seized every opportunity to remind all who would listen that the numbers were small by traditional mid-term standards. Liberal political analysts, including Kenneth Hechler, a White House staffer, and Gus Tyler of the International Ladies Garment Workers Union, subjected the returns to close scrutiny and all but pronounced a Democratic victory. All the same, most of the Democrats who went under had been staunch Fair Dealers. Republican candidates, including John Marshall Butler in Maryland, Richard M. Nixon in California, Everett McKinley Dirksen in Illinois, and Robert A. Taft in Ohio, scored some of the most spectacular GOP victories by blending right-wing conservatism with McCarthyism. The Midwestern losses were especially disappointing. Hechler argued that the corn-belt vote primarily reflected urban defections and that the Democrats had done comparatively well among farmers. Perhaps so, but for all practical purposes the results put an end to the Brannan strategy of constructing a farmer-labor coalition. Truman was probably more accurate than Hechler when, with characteristic overstatement, he privately expressed his disappointment: "The main trouble with the farmers is that they hate labor so badly that they will not vote for their own interests."

Thereafer, with the Chinese intervention transforming the Korean War into a more serious conflict and with the dismissal of General Douglas MacArthur in April 1951, Truman faced a tough attack from a Republican opposition determined to capitalize upon the frustrations of Korea. Finding it necessary to place party unity above all else, he quietly shelved most of his domestic legislative program and sought to bring the conservative wing of his party behind his military and defense policies. He secretly asked Richard B. Russell of Georgia, the kingpin of the Southern conservatives, to assume the Democratic leadership in the Senate. Russell, content with the substance of power, declined and gave his nod to Ernest W. McFarland of Arizona, an amiable tool of the Southern bloc; Truman made no effort to prevent McFarland's selection as Senate majority leader. The president's State of the Union message was devoted almost entirely to foreign policy and defense mobilization and mentioned social welfare programs only as an afterthought. Subsequently Truman told a press conference that while he supported the Fair Deal as much as ever, "first things come first, and our defense programs must have top priority."

Truman's success in achieving a minimum degree of party unity became apparent in the weeks of investigation and accusation that followed General MacArthur's return to America. Russell, playing the role of parliamentarian-statesman to the hilt and cashing in on his great prestige with senators of both parties, chaired the Senate committee that looked into the MacArthur incident, and he saw to it that the administration was able to deliver a thorough rebuttal to the general. The Northern liberal, Brien McMahon of Connecticut, relentlessly grilled hostile witnesses. The Western representative of oil and gas interests, Robert S. Kerr of Oklahoma, lashed out at MacArthur himself with a vehemence and effectiveness that no other Democrat could match. The tandem efforts of Russell, McMahon, and Kerr demonstrated the new party solidarity, but in terms of the Fair Deal the price was high.

In July 1951 the Federal Power Commission renounced the authority to regulate "independent" (non-pipeline-owning) natural gas producers. The ruling amounted to an adminstrative enactment of a bill, sponsored by Kerr, which Truman had vetoed a year earlier; Truman's close friend and most recent appointee to the Federal Power Commission, Mon Wallgren, cast the deciding vote. Although he talked like a militant liberal in a private conversation with ADA leaders, the president stalled throughout 1951 on repeated demands for the establishment of a Korean War Fair Employment Practices Committee. In December the administration established an ineffective Committee on Government Contract Compliance. Other domestic programs were soft-pedaled to near-invisibility.

Yet even the Korean War was not entirely inimical to reform. Its exigencies forced the army to transform its policy of integration into practice. Korea also provided a test for one of the basic underpinnings of the Fair Deal—Leon Keyserling's philosophy of economic expansion. Truman did not in the end fully embrace Keyserling's policies, but in the main he followed the guidance of his chief economic adviser. The Korean War years demonstrated the extent to which Keyserling's economics diverged from conventional New Deal–World War II Keynesianism and revealed both the strengths and weaknesses of his approach.

From the outbreak of the fighting, most liberals favored either immediate strong economic controls akin to those that had held down inflation in World War II or at least the establishment of stand-by machinery that could impose them rapidly. Truman disliked such measures on the basis of both principle and politics. He and his diplomatic advisers also wanted to signal the Soviet Union that the United States regarded the North Korean attack as a limited challange meriting a limited response. Keyserling's expansionary economics provided an attractive alternative to the liberal clamor for controls. Convinced that extensive controls would put the economy in a strait jacket and retard the expansion necessary to meet both consumer and defense needs and assuming a North Korean defeat in a few months, the administration decided to accept a short-term, war-scare inflation (probably unavoidable in any case) and concentrate on economic growth, which would be underwritten in large measure by tax incentives for business. An expanding economy would be the best long-term answer to inflation:

growth policies could fit a small war into the economy, avoid the social and political strains accompanying wartime controls, and reduce inflationary pressures to a level at which fiscal and monetary policies could contain them. Liberals outside the administration watched with alarm as prices went up, but Truman and Keyserling continued to gamble on a quick end to the war and the development of an economy capable of producing both guns and butter.

Their plan might have worked fairly well had the United States not overreached itself militarily in Korea. The Chinese intervention of November 1950 wrecked hopes of a quick recovery, set off another round of scare buying, and intensified war demands upon the economy. The administration quickly threw up a price-wage control structure, but by the end of February 1951, eight months after the beginning of the Korean conflict, the consumer price index had risen eight per cent (an annual rate of twelve per cent). Keyserling agreed that the new situation necessitated controls, but he accepted them with reluctance and sought to keep them as simple as possible, even at the risk of benefiting profiteers. "We'll never be able to out-control the Russians," he told a Senate committee, "but we can out-produce them." Speaking to an ADA economic conference, he asserted that many liberals, in their opposition to tax breaks for large business and in their demands for stronger controls, were confusing the Korean War with World War II and "engaging merely in hackneyed slogans out of the past."

Most liberals disagreed with Keyserling's emphases. As production was his first imperative, an end to the wage-price spiral was theirs. "Unless we are willing seriously to endanger the basis of existence of the American middle class, we must stop prices from rising," wrote Hans Landsberg in the *Reporter*. The liberals assumed that economic expansion was possible within a framework of rigid, tightly administered controls. Chester Bowles observed that the controlled economy of World War II had turned out a twofold increase in industrial production. John Kenneth Galbraith rejected the idea that Keyserling's expansionary policies could outrun the inflationary pressures they themselves created. The bulk of liberals regarded the administration approach as dangerous, the product of political expediency rather than sound economic analysis.

Neither Keyserling nor the more conventional liberals won a complete victory. Truman, who understood all too well the political dangers of a prolonged inflation, made substantial concessions to the controllers, led by Michael V. DiSalle, head of the Office of Price Stabilization. In the interest of fairness Truman approved a more complex system of price controls than Keyserling thought desirable, giving DiSalle considerable leeway to roll back some prices while approving advances in other areas. By March 1951 inflation was under control; during the final ten months of the year the cost-of-living index increased by less than two and one-half per cent. The waves of scare buying that followed the North Korean attack and the Chinese intervention had subsided. Higher taxes and restraints on credit were beginning to affect consumer buying. The Federal Reserve System, despite opposition from

the administration, initiated a stringent monetary policy. Tax breaks
for businesses expanding plant facilities presaged increased productive
capacity. All these factors, along with the government stabilization
program, discouraged an inflationary psychology.

At the time, however, it appeared to most economic observers that
the lull was only temporary. Many of the administration's liberal critics
refused even to admit the existence of a lull and called for tougher
controls as if prices were still skyrocketing. More moderate analysts
feared that the impact of large government defense orders would set
off another inflationary spiral in the fall. Influenced by such expectations, Truman ostentatiously mounted an anti-inflation crusade, demanding that Congress not only extend his control authority, due to
expire on June 30, but actually strengthen it. In fact the Defense Production Act of 1951 weakened the president's powers considerably.
Truman signed it reluctantly, comparing it to "a bulldozer, crashing
aimlessly through existing pricing formulas, leaving havoc in its wake."
A subsequent tax bill failed to meet administration revenue requests
and increased the danger of serious inflation.

Yet price stability persisted through 1952, in large measure because
defense production, hampered by multiple shortages and bottlenecks,
lagged far behind its timetable. In late 1951 these problems and the
fear of renewed inflation led Truman to decide in favor of a "stretch-
out" of defense production schedules; in doing so he overrode Keyserling's urgings for an all-out effort to break the bottlenecks and concentrate relentlessly upon expansion. Given the serious problems in
defense industry, the stretch-out decision may have seemed necessary to
Truman, but it also carried the dividend of economic stability.

The president had steered a course between the orthodox liberal
obsession with inflation and Keyserling's easy disregard of its perils;
perhaps as a result the economy failed to expand at the rate Keyserling
had hoped. On balance, however, Truman's approach to the political
economy of the Korean War was closer to Keyserling's, and the conflict
produced a dramatic economic growth. Before the war the peak gross
national product had been $285 billion in 1948; by the end of 1952 the
GNP (measured in constant dollar values) had reached a rate of $350
billion. The production index of durable manufactured goods had
averaged 237 in 1950; by the last quarter of 1952 it had reached 313.
The expansion, even if less than Keyserling had wanted, was breathtaking. Moreover, aside from the probably unavoidable inflation that
accompanied the early months of the war, this remarkable growth had
occurred in a climate of economic stability. Using a somewhat more
orthodox approach than Keyserling preferred, the administration had
achieved one of the central goals of the Fair Deal.

In its efforts to carry on with the reforming impulse of the New
Deal the Truman administration faced nearly insuperable obstacles.
A loosely knit but nonetheless effective conservative coalition had controlled Congress since 1939, successfully defying Franklin Roosevelt
long before it had to deal with Truman. Postwar prosperity muted
economic liberalism and encouraged a mood of apathy toward new

reform breakthroughs, although Truman's victory in 1948 indicated that most of the elements of the old Roosevelt coalition were determined to preserve the gains of the New Deal. The cold war probably made it more difficult to focus public attention upon reform and dealt severe blows to civil liberties. It did, however, give impetus to the movement for Negro equality.

The Fair Deal attempted to adapt liberalism to the new conditions. Under the intellectual leadership of Leon Keyserling it formulated policies that sought to transcend the conflicts of the New Deal era by encouraging an economic growth that could provide abundance for all Americans. With Charles Brannan pointing the way, the Truman administration tried to translate abundance into a political coalition that could provide the votes for its social welfare policies. The political strategy, ambitious but unrealistic, collapsed under the weight of the Korean War. Keyserling's economics, on the other hand, received a lift from Korea; in a period of adversity the Fair Deal was able to achieve at least one of its objectives.

McCarthyism as Mass Politics

MICHAEL PAUL ROGIN

Wisconsin Senator Joseph R. McCarthy was a dominant force in American politics for nearly five years in the early 1950's, affecting the decisions of presidents and Congress as well as shattering lives of those he accused of communism. The political success of McCarthy's anti-Communist crusade, his charges of Communist infiltration of the government, and the fear he inspired in rival politicians raised questions about American political values that a generation of theorists struggled to understand. Sociologists, psychologists, historians, and political scientists who had labored to explain the rise of totalitarianism in Germany and the Soviet Union feared that McCarthy's brutal tactics, his disregard for the truth, and the apparent hysteria of his followers represented an analogous threat to American political values. These social theories that explained McCarthyism—described by Rogin as "cultural pluralism"—strongly influenced the understanding of American politics throughout the 1950's and even the 1960's.

The Intellectuals and McCarthy, in which Rogin analyzes both the explanations of McCarthy's rise to power and the hard evidence of who did and did not support him, is one of the most thorough criticisms of a generation's social thought. The social thinkers of the 1950's, Rogin claims, distrusted mass movements, which they saw as irrational projections of social fears. However, people who felt that their importance in society was shrinking tended to view the political world as a vast conspiracy, and they uncritically followed demagogic leaders like McCarthy because they were impatient with the orderly processes of government, such as the constitutional guarantees protecting speech and privacy. Instead they supported a leader who promised to enact instantly the "will of the people" with little regard for the traditions of "civility" that customarily guided American political life.

Rogin demonstrates the inadequacy of this early explanation of Joseph McCarthy's rise. Relying heavily on a statistical analysis of McCarthy's support both in public opinion polls and in the ballot boxes, Rogin promotes a rethinking of this critical episode in American life and offers an alternative interpretation.

From 1950 through 1954, Joseph McCarthy disrupted the normal routine of American politics. But McCarthyism can best be understood as a product of that normal routine. McCarthy capitalized on popular concern over foreign policy, communism, and the Korean War, but the animus of McCarthyism had little to do with any less political or more developed *popular* anxieties. Instead it reflected the specific traumas of conservative Republican activists—internal Communist subversion, the New Deal, centralized government, left-wing intellectuals, and the corrupting influences of a cosmopolitan society. The resentments of these Republicans and the Senator's own talents were the driving forces behind the McCarthy movement.

Equally important, McCarthy gained the protection of politicians and other authorities uninvolved in or opposed to the politics motivating his ardent supporters. Leaders of the GOP saw in McCarthy a way back to national power after twenty years in the political wilderness. Aside from desiring political power, moderate Republicans feared that an attack on McCarthy would split their party. Eisenhower sought for long months to compromise with the Senator, as one would with any other politician. Senators, jealous of their prerogative, were loath to interfere with a fellow senator. Newspapers, looking for good copy, publicized McCarthy's activities. When the political institutions that had fostered McCarthy turned against him, and when, with the end of the Korean War his political issue became less salient, McCarthy was reduced to insignificance.

Politics alone does not explain McCarthyism; but the relevant sociopsychology is that which underpins normal American politics, not that of radicals and outsiders. Psychological insights are not relevant alone to the peculiar politics of the American Right. Equally important, the ease with which McCarthy harnessed himself to the everyday workings of mainstream politics illuminates the weaknesses of America's respectable politicians.

Attention to sociology and psychology must be concentrated within the political stratum, not among the populace as a whole. It is tempting to explain the hysteria with which McCarthy infected the country by the hysterical preoccupations of masses of people. But the masses did not levy an attack on their political leaders; the attack was made by a section of the political elite against another and was nurtured by the very elites under attack. The populace contributed to McCarthy's power primarily because it was worried about communism, Korea, and the cold war.

The analysis of McCarthyism presented here focuses on political issues, political activists, and the political structure. As an alternative to this interpretation of McCarthyism, the pluralists have suggested an analysis that goes further beneath the surface of American politics. To be sure, unlike La Follette and Hitler, McCarthy mobilized no cohesive, organized popular following. Nevertheless, for the pluralists the concept of mass politics captures both the flavor of McCarthy's appeals and the essence of his threat to American institutions.

In the first place, they argue, McCarthyism drew sustenance from the American "populist" tradition. "Populists," suspicious of leadership, seek to register the unadulterated popular will at every level of government. . . .

The alleged mass character of McCarthyism flows, in the second place, from the character of the popular resentments he exploited. He is said to have mobilized feelings of uneasiness over a sophisticated, cosmopolitan, urban, industrial society. He focused these vague discontents, the argument continues, on such specific symbols as intellectuals, striped-pants diplomats, homosexuals, and effete eastern aristocrasts. McCarthyite status politics was thus radical in its rejection of industrial society as well as in its suspicion of responsible political leadership. . . .

THE CONTEXT

[But] the entry of the Senator from Wisconsin onto the political stage did not split apart a previously united Republican Party. The split in the GOP between the East and the western Middle West goes back decades before McCarthyism. In Populist and progressive days, the West North Central states were the center of liberal opposition to an eastern-dominated Republican Party. During the New Deal and World War II, the two wings of the Republican Party switched places. On "traditional economic issues" as well as on foreign policy, midwest Republicans had been more conservative than their eastern counterparts for a decade before McCarthyism. The midwest wing of the party had been more isolationist for perhaps half a century.

It was this wing that mobilized itself behind McCarthy. It supported him on the censure resolution in the Senate, and Republican businessmen in the Middle West were more sympathetic to McCarthyism than those in the East. McCarthy did not split apart an elite, the parts of which had been equally conservative before him. He rather capitalized on an existing liberal-conservative split within the existing Republican elite.

Former centers of agrarian radicalism, like the plains states, sent right-wing Republicans who supported McCarthy to the Senate. But McCarthy was not the agent who disrupted the traditional agrarian radical base. Before these states supported McCarthy, they had already undergone an evolution from agrarian radicalism to extreme conservatism. (Of the states analyzed here, South Dakota was typical of the trans-Mississippi West and North Dakota the exception.)

The decline of agrarian radicalism increased conservative power in the trans-Mississippi West, but there have been important continuities in the conservative outlook. An ambiguity about the state of the country continues to plague these conservatives; in some ways they are satisfied and in others they are not. The right wing of the Republican Party reveals an uneasiness about cosmopolitan values and styles of life, about large cities and big bureaucracies. In this sense it seeks to change American institutions, not to conserve them. At the same time, it profoundly wishes to preserve the status quo in its own areas—not simply in terms of rural virtues but in terms of the local prestige and economic power of the elites that have since the decline of agrarian radicalism controlled the Republican Parties of the rural and small-town Middle West. This ambiguity—complacency at home and fear of the outside world—is nothing new for midwest conservatism. Half a century ago, it motivated midwestern conservative opposition to agrarian radical movements, which were perceived as alien imports from the bureaucratized and hostile outside world. McCarthy sprang from this conservative background. . . .

The activists around McCarthy were traditional conservatives, rejoicing in McCarthy's attack on the party of Roosevelt. Like the businessmen in the *Fortune* study, they would have deserted the Senator had he developed a demagogic "liberal" economic program.

Democratic control of national politics added to Republican discontent. By 1952, the GOP had been out of power for twenty consecutive years. And Republicans were not accustomed to opposition; between 1856 and 1932 they failed to control the presidency for a total of only twenty years.

The international situation brought the frustrations of midwest conservatism to a head and at the same time seemed to offer a political issue and a way out. The new long-term importance of foreign policy reinforced an already powerfully moralistic political approach. Much as some progressives at the turn of the century had reacted with defensive moralism to the waves of immigrants, so conservatives now reacted to the Communist threat. There had not yet been time to become accustomed to the new situation.

Traditionally, the Middle West has been isolationist for both ethnic and geographic reasons. Many of the region's political leaders thought Roosevelt had forced the country into a war against Germany; now Truman seemed afraid to fight a much worse enemy. Communism represented to them the epitome of an alien world—atheism, immorality, destruction of the family, and socialism. But far from defeating this enemy or withdrawing from the outside world that it contaminated, the Democratic Party dealt in an ambiguous atmosphere of international involvement, limited war, and compromise with evil.

Communism in the abstract was threatening enough. The danger became concretized and symbolized by two traumatic events. The first of these was the "loss of China." The right wing insisted with a stridency born of inner doubt that only a failure to apply traditional American values and tactics could have caused this defeat. The loss of China was a loss of American potency; it could only cease to be frightening if those responsible were identified.

Following hard upon the loss of China came the Korean War. Wars in America often produce superpatriotism, and this in turn claims victims. Those suspected of opposing wars have often been the victims of 100 percent Americanism. But during the Korean War the superpatriots perceived the very prosecutors of the war as the ambivalent ones. This again was something new and reinforced right-wing Republican fears that the centers of power in the society were working against them. If Woodrow Wilson had not approved of all the excesses of the superpatriots during and following World War I, he at least approved of the war. In the Korean War, the powers that be seemed unenthusiastic; one had to seek support for superpatriotism elsewhere. This was fertile ground for McCarthy.

If China preoccupied conservative elites, the Korean War attracted the attention of the population as a whole. Here real fighting brought to a head amorphous cold war anxieties and intensified concern over communism. McCarthy's prominence coincides with the years of the Korean War. He made his famous Wheeling speech in February 1950, and as its impact appeared to be ending the Korean War began in June. Three years later a truce was signed, and a year after that the Senate censured McCarthy.

Less than 1 percent of a national sample interviewed in the early 1950's volunteered communism as something they worried about. Many more, however—34 percent—checked it off a checklist of things they had recently talked about. In addition, almost all families knew someone fighting in Korea. The poll data did not suggest a mass political uprising over the question of communism, but no more did it suggest the issue's political irrelevance. . . .

This analysis failed to comprehend that McCarthyism was the product less of attitude syndromes at the mass level than of the character of political leaders whom the people supported. Parsons failed to see that fear of communism was generally most salient among those who already voted conservative. He overlooked the fact that McCarthy and anticommunism were far more salient to the conservative elite—from precinct workers to national politicians—than to the mass of voters. If the attitude structure at the popular level was not coherent, those whom the people supported did have a coherent set of attitudes. McCarthyism fed into an existing conservative tradition at the elite level, very conservative on both domestic and foreign questions. (Similarly, Parsons found evidence for the "mass" character of McCarthyism in its strength in former agrarian radical territory because he missed the intervention of conservative elites in the political evolution of those states.) This underestimation of the role of political elites in structuring McCarthyism recurs in pluralist analysis, and we will return to it.

Those who did not stress foreign policy in explaining McCarthyism had additional difficulties. They rightly saw that their analysis had to explain why some people supported McCarthy and others did not; presumably everyone was anti-Communist. Therefore they examined the American social structure to find groups particularly prone to status political appeals of the type McCarthy employed. In this view, McCarthy's concern with communism and foreign policy was only the immediate condition which enabled status seeking and populist groups to act out their frustrations. For example, Lipset wrote, "On the national scene, McCarthy's attacks are probably more important in terms of their appeal to status frustrations than to resentful isolationism." . . .

The alleged mass character of McCarthyism flows, in the second place, from the character of the popular resentments he exploited. He is said to have mobilized feelings of uneasiness over a sophisticated, cosmopolitan, urban, industrial society. He focused these vague discontents, the argument continues, on such specific symbols as intellectuals, striped-pants diplomats, homosexuals, and effete eastern aristocrats. McCarthyite status politics was thus radical in its rejection of industrial society as well as in its suspicion of responsible political leadership. . . .

THE IDEOLOGY

When they first became prominent in the middle 1950's, pluralist interpretations of McCarthyism relied very little on empirical evidence. They focused instead on McCarthy's ideological appeals, where the evidence for McCarthy's anticosmopolitan "populism" was strongest. But even McCarthy's ideology was rooted in traditional conservative rhetoric. . . .

To his most devoted followers McCarthy was fighting more than the Communists; in this the pluralists are certainly right. Speaking in eulogy of the Senator from Wisconsin, Congressman Smith of Kansas said, "In a world which has lost its understanding of the concepts of right and wrong, truth and error, good and evil, and seeks only to adjust itself to what is expedient, a man like Senator McCarthy is a living contradiction of such Machiavellianism." This sentiment was reiterated in newspaper obituaries. A study of McCarthyism in a Wisconsin county found the same emotion among McCarthy supporters at the grass roots.

That McCarthy should be so widely viewed as a moral figure is no paradox to the pluralists. It is just in his cultivation of a political concern with good and evil that they find his relation to agrarian radicalism. But McCarthy attacked the traditional devils of the conservatives. Just as traditional conservatives had feared the intrusion of alien bureaucrats, alien social legislation, and alien agrarian radicals into their stable world, so McCarthy attacked communism. Godless radicals, intellectuals, and bureaucrats were targets of American conservatism many decades before McCarthyism. If he was more extreme than many conservatives, he was extreme within that tradition.

Moreover, one cannot counterpose McCarthy's moralism to a healthier American pragmatism. For one thing, by McCarthy's use of the document-filled briefcase and the elaborated and detailed untruth, he was able to play upon the devotion of Americans to concrete detail. He promised always to "name names"; he always knew of a specific number of Communists; he had lists, affidavits, reports, right in his hand. McCarthy's "fact-fetishism" played upon our attention to the "real world." Had McCarthy not capitalized on the American weakness in the face of the practical and concrete, he would have been far less effective.

Nor was McCarthy's appeal an alternative to the corrupt but safer image of the ordinary politician. In many ways, such as his insistent friendliness with men he had just pilloried, McCarthy was a caricature of the ordinary politician. He was deliberately crude and liked to be thought of as a "guts fighter," a tough guy. There was something quite prurient in his atmosphere. As a punishing figure, he could immerse himself in the evil around him—loving both the immersion and the punishing in good sadistic fashion. Perhaps his supporters, turning their guilt at their own illicit desires into anger at the corruption of the outside world, could permit themselves to experience McCarthy's lasciviousness vicariously, since he was wreaking vengeance against their external enemies. In any case, dichotomies between a politics of purity and one tolerant of human corruption hardly do justice to the seaminess of McCarthy's appeal.

McCarthy's rhetoric was hardly principled; what principles there were had traditional conservative antecedents. Yet did not McCarthy attack traditional conservative institutions and defend the virtues of the plain people? How is this part of a traditional conservative approach?

In his Wheeling speech McCarthy attacked

the traitorous actions of those men who have been treated so well by this Nation . . . who have had all the benefits that the wealthiest nation on earth has to offer—the finest homes, the finest college educations, and the finest jobs in Government we can give. . . . The bright young men [in the State Department] who are born with silver spoons in their mouths are the ones who have been most traitorous. . . . [Acheson is a] pompous diplomat in striped pants with a phony British accent.

Demonstrating his disdain for established institutions, McCarthy appealed for classified information from State Department employees. When Senator McClellan charged, "Then you are advocating government by individual conscience as against government by law," McCarthy replied, "The issue is whether the people are entitled to the facts."

A gigantic rally called in honor of McCarthy sang "Nobody Loves Joe But the People," suggesting that if political leaders and institutions could not be relied on, the people could. Other alleged examples of McCarthy's "populism," such as his calling for telegrams against Eisenhower, are examples less of "populism" than of traditional American political practice. Nevertheless, the antielitist flavor of McCarthy's rhetoric is clear.

This fact alone, however, does not remove McCarthy from the conservative tradition. Since the decline of the Federalists, American conservatives have used "populist" rhetoric; in American politics this rhetoric is essential. "Populist" rhetoric does not necessarily reflect a reality of popular enthusiasm and power; often it disguises the power resting in the hands of local and national elites. "Populism" is often an ideological formula used to gain legitimacy, not a factual description of reality.

Moreover, nothing in McCarthy's rhetoric would have frightened several conservative elite groups away. In so far as McCarthy's appeal transcended anticommunism, its roots were in groups disturbed about cosmopolitanism and about the prestige given to the educated and the established families and businesses of the East. Success in their own bailiwick did not insulate the political and economic elites of the Middle West from these concerns any more than prosperity per se insulated the population at large. The nouveaux riches, however wealthy, could still be upset about those born with silver spoons in their mouths. The midwest political elite, however long established, was still upset about striped-pants diplomacy, intellectuals in the State Department, Harvard intellectuals, and British "pinkos." These were McCarthy's targets, and in the Middle West attacks on such targets did not frighten the elite. Furthermore, McCarthy and other mid-western conservatives never went beyond rhetorical attacks on eastern corporate patricians. They never proposed to injure the vital interests of eastern businessmen, who were, like their midwestern business counterparts, members of the moneyed classes.

Nevertheless, there was in McCarthy's rhetoric a heightened sense of betrayal by the rich and well-born. In part this reflected the growing anxiety of midwestern conservatism in the face of the New Deal and the "liberalism" of Wall Street. Equally important, McCarthy himself was personally very different from other midwestern conservatives. Far from being a man of dangerous principles, McCarthy was a thorough-going nihilist. Other conservatives—Goldwater is the prime example—believe in something; he believed in nothing. Whatever the psychological roots of McCarthy's political approach, its sociological roots lay in his one-man struggle for power and prestige, handicapped by a background of relative poverty most unusual in a successful American politician.

McCarthy's personal and social makeup fitted him for the role of destroyer. Perhaps his destructiveness found a sympathy denied his more righteous conservative colleagues. Certainly his outrageous gall catapulted him to a position of power he could exploit.

But McCarthyism is alleged to be more than the exploits of a single man; it is said to reveal the stresses and strains of the American social structure. Analysis of the Senator and of the ideology he employed tells us little about his reception. Did McCarthy's rhetoric in fact embolden the masses to an attack on modern industrial society? Did his "populist" rhetoric in fact attract ex-radicals, or even ex-Democrats? Did the danger from McCarthyism in fact flow from popular passions?

THE POPULAR FOLLOWING

In January 1954, a majority of the American population approved of Senator McCarthy. For the next eleven months, one third of the total population consistently supported him; eliminate those with no opinion, and the figure rises to 40 percent. This man, terribly dangerous in the eyes of sophisticated observers of American politics, had obtained the backing of millions of American people.

McCarthy's popularity in the polls reenforced a growing belief among intellectuals that the mass of people could not be relied on to defend civil liberties and democratic rights. The Stouffer study of popular attitudes toward communism and civil liberties, published the year following the censure of McCarthy, seemed to demonstrate the willingness of the mass of people to deny civil liberties to socialists and atheists, much less Communists. Community leaders, on the other hand, were much more tolerant of divergent and unpopular points of view. Leaving issues of democratic rights up to the people was apparently a dangerous business; better if they could be decided among political leaders without resort to popular passions. McCarthy had apparently achieved his successes by taking questions of communism and civil liberties out of the hands of the political elite.

In a simplified form, this theory of McCarthy's power ran into trouble. There is evidence to suggest that mass attitudes are not so different in other countries, such as Britain, without producing anything like McCarthyism. Therefore Lipset has suggested that one must look beyond popular attitudes to the political structure that mobilizes and channels those attitudes. This is an important argument, which could have led the pluralists to question the association between popular attitudes and McCarthy's power. But the pluralists contented themselves with pointing to two elements in the American political structure that *fostered* the translation of popular attitudes into political programs. First, it is alleged that McCarthy supporters lacked group ties to the institutions of modern industrial society. Second, Americans are said to lack deference for political leaders; they are not willing to permit a sufficient amount of elite autonomy. With this "populist" outlook, they will be more willing to trust their own (anti-civil libertarian) views than the views of their elected representatives.

Pluralist explanations focused on the "mass" character of McCarthy's appeal, challenging political leaders and cutting across party lines. But perhaps the single most important characteristic of supporters of McCarthy in the national opinion polls was their party affiliation; Democrats opposed McCarthy, and Republicans supported him. In April 1954, Democrats outnumbered Republicans more than two to one among those having an unfavorable opinion of McCarthy; 16 percent more Republicans than Democrats had a favorable opinion of the Senator. Totaling support for McCarthy in a series of Gallup Polls in the early 1950's reveals that 36 percent of the Democrats favored McCarthy while 44 percent opposed him. The comparable Republican figures were 61 percent for and 25 percent against. Democrats were 8 percentage points more against McCarthy than for him, Republicans 36 points more for him than against him. The total percentage point spread by party was 44 points. In these polls, as in the data reported by Polsby, no other single division of the population (by religion, class, education, and so forth) even approached the party split.

Similarly, in October 1954 respondents were asked whether they would be more or less likely to vote for a candidate endorsed by McCarthy. The strong Republicans split evenly, the strong Democrats were five to one against the senator, and the weak and independent Democrats divided four to one against McCarthy. By that date, only hard-core Republicans were actively sympathetic to the Wisconsin senator; even the weak and independent Republicans strongly opposed him.

As Lipset suggests, there is evidence that pro-McCarthy sentiment influenced party preference as well as vice versa. Nevertheless, the great disproportion in support for McCarthy along the lines of previous party commitment was not predicted by the pluralist approach. Pluralism stressed McCarthy's roots in the social structure but not his roots in the existing political structure.

Support for McCarthy was also reasonably close to attitudes on political and economic questions of the day. On a whole range of foreign policy issues, McCarthy adherents had right-wing preferences. Perhaps more surprising, "McCarthy also drew disproportionately from economic conservatives. Measures of such attitudes as position on liberalism in general, laws to prevent strikes, a federal health program, and support of private development of national resources all indicate that the conservative position on these issues was associated with greater support for McCarthy."

On the other hand, Trow found in Bennington that those with a hostile attitude toward big business as well as big labor were most likely to support McCarthy. This suggested McCarthy's roots in a small business, nineteenth-century mentality. But in a national sample such a relationship did not hold. The antibusiness, pro-labor group was more anti-McCarthy than any other group, and the "nineteenth-century liberals" were no more pro-McCarthy than those who were anti-labor and pro-big business or those favoring both big business and big labor. This evidence further locates McCarthy's roots in existing political cleavages.

Clearly McCarthy drew support from the traditional constituency and traditional attitudes of the Republican right wing. However, he also received considerable backing in the polls from traditional Democratic ethnic and social groups. The relevant survey data comes from a variety of different sources, and although the pattern of support for the Senator is consistent, the degree of cleavage varies. Without holding the influence of party constant, religion and occupation best distinguish opponents of McCarthy from supporters. Professional people were more anti-McCarthy than any other occupational group. On five or six reported polls they were the most anti-McCarthy group, and on four of these polls they were far more anti-McCarthy than any other group. Wealthy businessmen were also apparently anti-McCarthy although there is less evidence about them. Unskilled workers and small businessmen were the most consistently pro-McCarthy groups. However, union membership significantly increased the opposition to McCarthy among laborers. Apparently the liberal impact of the union leadership reached significant numbers of workers who would otherwise have been neutral or ignorant about McCarthy.

Farmers also tended to be pro-McCarthy, but their degree of support varied sharply from poll to poll. Perhaps this provides further evidence of farmer political volatility. In one combined group of polls, farmers were clearly the most pro-McCarthy group; in other polls they were no more for McCarthy than were unskilled workers and small businessmen.

The occupational impact on support for McCarthy is clear. In several polls, occupational differences at the extremes equaled or exceeded the party differences. The size of both party and occupational differences is particularly striking since these usually worked against each other. Professionals tended to belong to the pro-McCarthy party, workers to the anti-McCarthy party.

Like occupation, the impact of religion also cut across party loyalties, with the exception of the heavily anti-McCarthy, pro-Democratic Jews. Lipset does not report religious data except within the political parties. Other studies demonstrate that in spite of Catholic and Protestant party affiliations, Catholics were significantly more pro-McCarthy than Protestants. In these polls, the religious differences were greater than the occupational differences, but they were not greater than the occupational differences reported by Lipset, whose occupational measures were more discriminating.

Within the parties the influence of religion was even more apparent. The percentage point spread in attitudes toward McCarthy between strong Democratic Protestants and Catholics was 33. The difference between strong Republican Catholics and Protestants was 21. On the other hand, for strong party identifiers party seems to have been even more important than religion. Strong Democratic Protestants differed in their attitudes from strong Republican Protestants even more than they did from strong Democratic Catholics. And Republican Catholics were closer to Republican Protestants than to Democratic Catholics. Since workers tend to be Catholics, religion and class reinforced each other. Either factor might have declined in importance if the other had been held constant.

Ethnic data also cut across party lines to some extent. Irish and Italian Catholics, traditionally Democratic, were highly pro-McCarthy. However, the influence of party may explain the greater support McCarthy received from German than Polish Catholics, as the latter are strongly Democratic. Among Protestants, differences by ethnic background were small and inconsistent, although Germans were clearly more pro-McCarthy than British.

Finally, level of education was of great significance in explaining support for McCarthy. Without holding party constant, differences are apparent, but they are less significant than occupational influences. However, when party is held constant the effect of education upon support for McCarthy is truly pronounced. The percentage point spread between graduate-school Democrats and grade-school Republicans was 65, the largest spread in all the poll data. However, college-educated Republicans were no more anti-McCarthy than grammar-school Democrats.

The polls provide us with considerable evidence about support for McCarthy, and reveal a broadly consistent pattern. When the influence of party is eliminated and often even when it is not, the lower socioeconomic groups, the more poorly educated, and the Catholics tended to support McCarthy, the big business and professional classes, the better educated, and the Protestants to oppose him. . . .

The McCarthy years were also the Eisenhower years. Far from demonstrating their discontent with respectable political leadership, the mass of Americans responded to the political anxieties of the cold and Korean wars and whatever social and personal anxieties may also have been relevant by electing Eisenhower. Eisenhower's personal and political appeal depended on the belief that he could be trusted to take care of things without disrupting the society. Eisenhower politics was the politics of deference to responsible leadership, of apolitical moderation. Support for Eisenhower indicates more about the mood of the populace in the America of the 1950's than does support for McCarthy. And McCarthy became prominent in the vacuum of popular apathy and moderation, not on a wave of radical mass mobilization.

What are we to conclude, then, about McCarthy's "mass" appeal? McCarthy's popular following apparently came from two distinct sources. There was first the traditional right wing of the midwestern Republican Party. Here was a group to whom McCarthy was a hero. He seemed to embody all their hopes and frustrations. These were the militants in the McCarthy movement. They worked hardest for him and were preoccupied with his general targets. To them, communism was not the whole story; their enemies were also the symbols of welfare capitalism and cosmopolitanism. These militants were mobilized by McCarthy's "mass" appeal. Yet this appeal had its greatest impact upon activists and elites, not upon the rank-and-file voters. And while Mc-Carthy mobilized the Republican right wing, he did not change its traditional alliances. This was not a "new" American Right, but rather an old one with new enthusiasm and new power.

McCarthy's second source of popular support were those citizens mobilized because of communism and the Korean War. Concern over these issues throughout the society increased Republican strength, although this increase in popular support accrued not so much to Mc-Carthy as to Eisenhower. McCarthy's strength here was not so much due to "mass," "populist," or "status" concerns as it was to the issues of communism, Korea, and the cold war. At the electoral level, there was little evidence that those allegedly more vulnerable to "mass" appeals were mobilized by McCarthy to change their traditional voting patterns.

McCarthy had real support at the grass roots, but this was hardly a "movement in which popular passions wreaked their aggression against the structure of the polity." In a period in which the populace gave overwhelming support to Eisenhower, it can hardly be accused of failing to show deference to responsible political leadership. In so arguing, I by no means wish to minimize the danger of McCarthyism. But the pluralists, writing in a context of fear of the masses, have misunderstood both the source and the nature of that danger. They see a rebellious populace threatening the fabric of society. In fact, McCarthy did immense damage to the lives and careers of countless individuals. He exercised an inordinate influence over policy making. But popular enthusiasm for his assault on political institutions simply cannot explain the power he wielded. In so far as McCarthy challenged political decisions, political individuals, and the political fabric, he was sustained not by a revolt of the masses so much as by the actions and inactions of various elites.

THE ELITES

Conservative Republican activists provided McCarthy with the core of his enthusiastic support. In addition, groups ranging from Catholic Democratic workers to conservative southern senators contributed to McCarthy's power—the workers by verbal approval in the polls, the senators by their actions and silences in Washington. Having examined the contribution of the masses to McCarthyism, we turn now to the elites.

The pluralists argue that McCarthy was not simply attacking Communists, but also had as his targets the eastern, educated, financial, political, and intellectual elite. There is merit in this view; nevertheless, McCarthy enjoyed the support of some wealthy and influential political elites, and even some of those he attacked played a role in augmenting his power. The existence of a powerful Republican right wing, the new appeal of the issues of communism and foreign policy, and McCarthy's own tactical brilliance raised McCarthyism to a place of national prominence. But there was more to McCarthy's success than this. The response of a variety of political elites—by no means simply allies of the Wisconsin senator—enabled him to harness himself to the everyday workings of American politics. Those already part of this machinery often did not approve of McCarthy. Some, like moderate Republicans in their battle with the Democrats, congressmen in their battle with the executive, newspapers in their search for news, thought they could use him. Others, like southern Democrats, saw no need to treat McCarthy differently than they treated other senators. Still others, moderate Republicans in their desire for party unity, liberal Democrats in their desire for reelection, were afraid of him. Political and psychological reasons made a variety of political elites anxious to avoid a confrontation with McCarthy. Until it became clear to them that McCarthyism was more than politics as usual, they failed effectively to challenge it.

We have already pointed to the importance of the political structure in influencing McCarthy's mass support. Regardless of attitudes toward civil liberties and even toward McCarthy in the abstract, traditional political allegiances kept the workers in the Democratic Party in the 1950's and business and professional men in the GOP. McCarthy's "mass" appeal did not register directly in politics because many who supported him cared more about the Democratic Party, the New Deal, their trade unions, or their wives and families than they cared about McCarthy. They therefore did not break their traditional political habits.

Just as the political structure limited the sustenance McCarthy could derive from the grass roots, so it influenced the behavior of political elites. We look now at conservative Republicans and GOP moderates, at the Senate and the southern Democrats, at the press and at the liberals.

Most of those who mobilized behind McCarthy at the national level were conservative politicians and publicists, businessmen, and retired military leaders discontented with the New Deal, with bureaucracy, and with military policy. Of nineteen businessmen in the leadership of the Ten Million Americans mobilizing for McCarthy, only one had inherited wealth. These men had been part of the Republican right wing before McCarthy; they were joined by an occasional ex-agrarian radical like Burton Wheeler. Numbers of former Marxist intellectuals such as Louis Bundenz, James Burnham, and John Chamberlain became McCarthy publicists, but they lacked political influence or popular support. The political conservatism of the elite supporters of McCarthy ran the gamut of domestic and international policy.

We have already discussed the historical reasons for McCarthy's conservative support. The evolution of politics in the Middle West and the nation had had two political consequences for conservatives. They were in heretofore unprecedented positions of political power at the state level and political weakness at the national level. Their desperation is suggested by Taft's famous advice to McCarthy, "If one case doesn't work, then bring up another." This political elite sustained McCarthy. It helped dramatize his issues and fight his fights. Conservative Republican activists provided money and enthusiasm for the Senator's cause. In Wisconsin, for example, McCarthy did not mobilize the mass of voters. But he did mobilize the local elites of the Republican Party. The near-hysterical enthusiasm with which they identified with the Senator gave the movement its emotional intensity. The regular Wisconsin Republican organization—in an action almost unprecedented in American politics—put up a candidate to oppose Wisconsin's other incumbent Republican senator because he had not voted against McCarthy's censure.

How to explain the mentality of these McCarthy supporters? Lipset, analyzing American politics as a conflict between values of achievement and egalitarian populism, argues that political excesses such as McCarthyism derive from America's egalitarian strain. Thus it is argued that Britain was spared a McCarthyite episode because the populace had deference for its established leaders. But a more important difference between Britain and the United States on this score is the character of conservative politics of the two countries. The British example suggests by comparison what American conservatives were willing to do. Certainly these conservatives were unrestrained by aristocratic traditions, but to ascribe this to populist values rather than to the capitalist-achievement ethic is perverse. In a Protestant, competitive society, an individual can blame only himself for failure, and the fear of failure appears at all levels of the social structure. The attendant insecurities and frustrations will often produce conspiracy theories, scapegoat hunting, and terrible resentments. McCarthy was supported by the activists of a party that emphasizes free enterprise, achievement, and individual responsibility. The politics of these people seems more sensibly explained by their preoccupations with achievement and failure than by their populistic concerns.

McCarthy, however, was not simply another conservative Republican. Mundt, Wherry, and a host of other right-wing Republicans had sought to dramatize the communism issue, but only McCarthy succeeded. And McCarthy succeeded while the others did not in part because of his thoroughgoing contempt for the rules of political controversy. This contempt stemmed partly from his career pattern. McCarthy came from relatively low social origins, and was elected to the Senate without either the inherited status position of some senators or the record of political or professional accomplishment of others. In the period from 1947 to 1956, this was true of only 4 percent of America's senators. Moreover, McCarthy did not conform to Senate folkways; thus he voted with small minorities against large majorities more than most of his colleagues. Clearly, McCarthy had less commitment to established norms than other conservative Republicans; in fact, his career pattern and behavior in the Senate resembled Langer's.

It is important to stress McCarthy's uniqueness, but the pluralists stress it for the wrong reasons. McCarthy's significance as an individual did not derive from new alliances he personally mobilized to assault the social fabric. It lay rather in the fact that he personally, not the masses or even elites behind him, did tremendous damage and wielded great power. And this personal power in large part derived from his willingness not to play by the rules—he was, after all, an extremist. But without the issue of communism and without the enthusiasm he evoked from right-wing Republicans who did conform to Senate folkways and orthodox career patterns, he would have been merely what Langer was —a maverick without influence.

Moderate Republicans were clearly less enthusiastic about McCarthy than the conservative wing of the party, yet without their support as well McCarthy would have been far less powerful. Eastern and moderate Republicans and their allies desired political power, and were also genuinely concerned about the Communist question. For a long time, they acquiesced in McCarthy's power. Viereck writes that McCarthy's targets were not the Communists, but those who had always stood for the rule of law and moderation, like Senator Watkins. By the time Watkins headed the committee which recommended McCarthy's censure, he was an anti-McCarthy pillar of strength. Earlier, however, he had been one of many Republican signers of a statement attacking the Truman administration and the Gillette committee investigation of McCarthy. The official Republican leadership did not sign this pro-McCarthy statement, but Watkins and other future McCarthy critics did.

There are other examples of support for McCarthy by moderate Republicans. Senator Carlson, an Eisenhower Republican, hammered hard at the Communist issue during the early 1950's. He called McCarthy's 1952 primary victory a "great victory." Later that year, Eisenhower deleted a favorable reference to General Marshall from a Wisconsin campaign speech under McCarthy's pressure. After his victory, the President decided that the use of his office to attack McCarthy would split the Republican Party and aid the Democrats. A timid chief executive, Eisenhower also wanted to avoid making enemies, particularly in Congress. Orders went out telling members of the administration not to criticize McCarthy—and those like Stassen who did were publicly humiliated. In appointing a McCarthy man as Personnel Officer, Eisenhower gave the Senator an effective veto over appointments to the State Department. He made every effort to avoid a fight with him over the army. "Among the opponents of McCarthy in the administration (and he also had friends)," reports one chronicler, "the view was that McCarthy should be handled behind closed doors." If McCarthy benefited from airing his charges to the public, he benefited also from moderate unwillingness to combat him openly. By 1954 moderate Republicans were appeasing McCarthy because they feared splitting the party more than because they hoped they could use him. But in both cases McCarthy was able to capitalize on existing political alliances. He had succeeded in harnessing respectable elites and respectable institutions, to which the populace paid deference.

McCarthy's popularity itself in large part depended on his moderate Republican support. Before the 1952 elections gave the GOP control of the Senate, most Americans had not heard of McCarthy and only 15 percent had a favorable opinion of him. By the middle of 1953, McCarthy had sent Cohn and Schine to Europe, had control of a Senate committee, and had been legitimized by the Republican Party; 35 percent of the population approved of him. Having achieved the instruments of Senate power and publicity, McCarthy could keep his name before the public day after day.

In this achievement, he was aided not only by the moderate Republicans but also by the Senate and by the press. Seniority gave McCarthy his committee chairmanship, and Senate traditions permitted him virtually unchecked power. Individual senators were unwilling to interfere with committee prerogatives or with the power of McCarthy as chairman, since their own personal influence depended in large part upon their own committee positions. Many senators also feared that interferences with McCarthy's activities as an individual senator could later rebound to their disadvantage; they feared creating unpleasant precedents. The famed individualism encouraged by the Senate thus worked to McCarthy's advantage.

Moreover, McCarthy capitalized on congressional-executive rivalry. Always a factor in American politics, this institutional conflict was at its height in the McCarthy period. The growing power of the executive, attributable to the New Deal and to the importance of foreign policy, produced congressional concern over the decline in congressional prerogatives and prestige. Relations were further strained by the presence in Washington of New Deal administrators, so different in outlook from the more particularistic, locally oriented congressmen. McCarthy tried to make himself the champion of congressional power and at least succeeded in exploiting the executive-congressional rift.

The Senate in the McCarthy period was dominated by conservative Republicans and southern Democrats. About the former enough has already been said. The southern Democrats, embodying the institutional traditions of the Senate, were unwilling to jeopardize the prerogatives of an individual senator or of the Senate as a whole. As McClellan of Arkansas remarked, "I do not want to do unto one of my colleagues what I would not want him to do unto me under the same circumstances." Southern senators were not pro-McCarthy. But they were perhaps not unhappy to see their northern liberal colleagues and the Fair Deal administration embarrassed. (Reprisals from the populist masses hardly worried these safe-seat senators, particularly since southerners opposed this Catholic Republican in the polls.)

Without the newspaper treatment he received, McCarthy's impact would have been far milder. Large numbers of newspapers, particularly outside the major metropolitan centers, actively supported him.

The respectable press opposed the Wisconsin senator, which suggests to the pluralists McCarthy's absence of elite backing. But McCarthy benefited from their treatment of him in the news columns. Desiring to dramatize the news, the wire services featured McCarthy's activities without regard to their importance. Stories and headlines gave the impression that charges were facts. Even *The New York Times* fostered the myth that McCarthy's investigations had some connection with demonstrated espionage. The coverage of the other anti-McCarthy press was no better. McCarthy's popularity in the polls reached its all-time high during the well-publicized Fort Monmouth investigations.

Eventually *The Times* realized that McCarthy had taken them in. Columnist Peter Kihss concluded a series of articles setting the record straight (lacking the prominence of the earlier stories) with the observation,

For the newspapers Fort Monmouth has been a lesson that will not be quickly forgotten, but the reading public should understand that it is difficult if not impossible to ignore charges by Senator McCarthy just because they are usually proved exaggerated or false. The remedy lies with the reader.

Thus newsmen like politicians sought to lay the blame for McCarthy's prominence on the public and argue that their own hands were tied. Newsmen like Kihss often justify their activities by saying that they print the news and the news is what happens. To understand the role of the press in the McCarthy period one must realize that a figure who gains notoriety sells more papers, and that to ignore such a figure is to risk losing sales to competing publishers.

Finally, many prominent liberals failed actively to oppose McCarthy. Here McCarthy could feed upon feelings of guilt and insecurity pervading the nation's capital. Democratic politicians and government bureaucrats had to adjust to replacing the Popular Front, the New Deal, and the wartime Soviet alliance with the new cold war attitudes. This change weakened the will of the elites to resist McCarthy, since they felt vaguely guilty of his accusations. In addition, liberal politicians were simply afraid of McCarthy's power to retaliate at the polls. They saw Millard Tydings oppose McCarthy and go down to defeat in 1950, William Benton attack him and lose his Senate seat in 1952. The evidence suggests that although McCarthy may have contributed to Tydings' defeat he had no impact on Benton's. Certainly his power at the polls was greatly exaggerated.

Nevertheless, Lippmann and others argued at the time that liberals had lost the confidence of the country over the issues of communism and foreign policy which sustained McCarthy and that only the moderates and conservatives could stop him. If this argument is true, it cuts both ways. For if the moderate Republicans and southern Democrats had this power, why did they not exercise it earlier? McCarthy's influence and his popularity reached their heights during the Eisenhower administration. If moderates and conservatives can take credit for McCarthy's defeat, they must share a large portion of the blame for his successes.

The failure of American elites to confront McCarthy immeasurably enhanced his power. This unwillingness cannot be explained as a response to mass pressures. But if these existed in the minds of observers of McCarthyism, surely they were also in the minds of the political actors themselves. If the populist attitudes of the masses did not enhance McCarthy's power, what of leadership fear of popular pressure? Shils, for example, argues that a "populist" system of authority weakens the will of elites in America. Political leaders lack confidence in themselves, it is alleged, because the value system promotes suspicion of independent leadership. The environment of the legislator makes him too willing to accede to real or imagined popular whims. In this view, the people may not seek to wreak their passions against the body politic, but the politicians, victims of populist rhetoric, will accede to demands which seem to speak for popular passions. Where the politician can look to other sources of authority besides the people—institutions, established procedures, groups, values—he can be more autonomous.

About the desire for elite autonomy more will be said subsequently. We can agree now, however, that one would have preferred elites whose will to resist McCarthy had been firmer. But to blame this weakness on a populist system of authority, holding out pluralist values as alternatives, is too simple a view. An urge to give in to real or imagined popular passions is not a democratic virtue. But the question is not the attitudes of the people in the abstract or the attitudes of the leaders about the people in the abstract. The question is what one wants protection against. Groups often use "populist" rhetoric to insulate themselves from popular control. They may speak of the grass roots to protect their bailiwicks against outside, popularly supported political leaders. A wider political constituency, often sustained by "populist" rhetoric and appeals to principle, can strengthen political leadership against group pressure. It can help political elites confront such figures as McCarthy. The relation between populism and pluralism is more complex than is suggested by the image of practical and procedure-conscious organizations opposed to ideological and authoritarian masses. The "masses" did not produce McCarthyism in America, and groups and their leaders alone did not save us from him.

Consider first the specific reasons for elite tractability, called forth by the nature of McCarthy's issue. Other movements—agrarian radical ones for example—have played on a populist system of authority without achieving anything like the inroads and the power of McCarthy. Racist Governor George Wallace captured the support of masses of northern, urban whites during the 1964 presidential primaries without hindering the passage of a pending civil rights bill. But McCarthy's situation was uniquely favorable. On the one hand, he benefited from the nondivisiveness of his issue: many groups, elites, and institutions were for "Wall Street," the railroads, or "the interests," but no one was for communism. But at the same time, McCarthy could capitalize on divisions and insecurities within the elite structure. Wallace was up against a northern elite consensus on civil rights (created, paradoxically enough, by mass Negro pressure). But McCarthy fed upon Republican suspicion of Democrats, Democratic anxieties about their past policies, and a mood of temporization and passivity in Washington.

Second, here as elsewhere the symbiosis between "populism" and pragmatism cannot go unnoticed. One might blame elite weakness on the instrumentalism and pragmatism of political leaders, which made them less willing to stand up for principle and more willing to give in to the line of least resistance. It was easier to remain silent than to oppose McCarthy, so many remained silent. Individuals did not want to risk their personal gains by opposing the Wisconsin senator. Perhaps the business orientation and narrow self-concern in the society make politicians unwilling to stand up for the commonweal. The principled politics feared by the pluralists might have been an asset here.

Third, institutional restraint and traditional allegiances may be alternatives to populist values, but they augmented McCarthy's power. The Senator capitalized on the routine politics of the political stratum —Senate traditions, executive-legislative rivalry, Republican party loyalty, anxiety to keep disputes out of the limelight. The general unwillingness of American politicians to assume responsibility for controversial actions became increasingly bizarre during the years of McCarthy's hegemony. This monumental insistence that politics continue as usual is surely a classic example of the banality of evil.

One would have hoped for a greater presidential appreciation of the dignity of the executive branch. One would have welcomed greater respect for the rule of law and for individual rights. Yet when Eisenhower finally fought for executive dignity and the rule of law, he had to resort to the instruments of publicity and open confrontation. Only with the publicity of the Army-McCarthy hearings did American politicians gain the confidence and integrity openly to oppose and then to ignore McCarthy.

Temporization and surrender having failed, the Eisenhower administration finally challenged McCarthy directly. Big businessmen who had heretofore supported the Senator began to back away, as he attacked their administration and an institution (the army) with which they identified. After the censure, the Senate "club" would have even less than usual to do with him. The respectable press, allegedly forced to publicize McCarthy's charges because they were news, stopped giving him coverage. Meanwhile, the Korean War had ended, and the tensions of the cold war eased. Observers agree that McCarthy's influence then reached a low point from which it never recovered. All McCarthy had left was the support of those in the populace basically hostile to American society. Undaunted, perhaps even encouraged by his attacks on the institutions in American life from which they were alienated, these anomic "masses" continued to support the Wisconsin Senator. They had no more influence on his power than they had ever had. When McCarthy became a real antagonist of the institutions which conservatives respected—the Republican Party, the Senate, and the Army—he lost influence both among moderately conservative political leaders and among the population at large. As McCarthy became "radical," he lost his hold on American politics.

Eisenhower: What Manner of Man?

FRED I. GREENSTEIN

It has become a cliché to say that the presidency of the United States is the world's toughest job. Dwight Eisenhower was the last American president to complete two terms in office and make the job look easy. Among the most beloved of American presidents, he seemed, in Rexford Tugwell's words, "the least partisan president" since George Washington. In public pose at least, he stood where the people apparently wanted him: firmly above the political battle. This, in turn, rendered the battle beneath, the world of such men as Vice President Richard Nixon and Senate Majority Leader Lyndon Johnson, that much less interesting. Depression and war had meant a generation of political excitement and conflict. After 1952, however, Americans enjoyed respite from turbulance, sat back, and left things to Ike.

Eisenhower almost singlehandedly created the façade of the placid 50's: a period, critics quipped, of "the bland leading the bland." But after a quarter century of assassinations, impeachments, resignations, and failed administrations, Eisenhower's two terms in office, with no war, no economic collapse, no runaway inflation, and only mild scandals, seemed an accomplishment. Though Ike made it look easy, shaping the presidency into a symbol of stability was both difficult and significant. How Eisenhower accomplished this difficult balancing act of providing stability and legitimacy while exercising political influence with a "hidden hand" is the subject of Fred I. Greenstein's analysis of Eisenhower's leadership style.

Eisenhower's vice-president, Richard Nixon, was not the only one to remark on his complexity, many others acquainted with the nonpublic man, made similar observations. What most of them appear to have recognized was the obvious intricacy of the political psychology of a leader who in many respects displayed antithetical qualities in public and in private. The testimonies of three such observers—a journalist, a congressman, and a presidential advisor—point to an array of Eisenhower's personal qualities, each differing in its public and private manifestations, that shaped his leadership style.

Journalist Theodore White reports that in the course of covering Eisenhower at NATO in 1951 and observing him closely he was forced to reverse the impression he had formed on the basis of Eisenhower's public persona. "I made the mistake," White confessed, "so many observers did of considering Ike a simple man, a good straightforward soldier."

Yet Ike's mind was not flaccid, and gradually, reporting him as he performed, I found his mind was tough, his manner deceptive, that the rosy private smile could give way, in private, to furious outbursts of temper; that the tangled rambling rhetoric of his off-the-record remarks could, when he wished, be disciplined by his own pencil into clean hard prose.

Congressman Stuyvesant Wainwright, an Eisenhower Republican, discovered a world of difference between the impression left by the *New York Times,* which "always made him out to be a mediocre, fumbling, ignorant boob," and the informed, issue-involved president with whom he had periodic conferences. Moreover, his bond as an Eisenhower loyalist was strengthened by his awareness of the president's depth of knowledge about public affairs:

When I went in there to talk with him, I used to come away on cloud nine, I was so impressed. And not just by the man. I was impressed because he knew exactly what he was talking about. I'd read about how he had been out in the morning taking putting practice, but when we went there he knew his business. He would ask us about paragraph three of section 4B. And I used to say, "Mr. President, someone must have briefed you pretty well five minutes ago," and he would say, "No, I looked it over last night." He knew what was in the bill, and he knew what to ask. It was just the opposite from what the papers said!

It was Henry Kissinger, however, whose perception of Eisenhower changed most dramatically. He first met the former president during the last months of his life. Though physically enfeebled, Eisenhower nevertheless still exhibited a vividly forceful personality and great political sophistication and interest. Kissinger met Eisenhower in Walter Reed Hospital shortly after Nixon's election and again, with Nixon, soon after his inauguration, only seven weeks before Eisenhower's death. On the first visit Kissinger's purpose was to seek advice on how to coordinate national foreign policy-making machinery. Eisenhower's practice had been to coordinate agencies responsible for making foreign policy in the Executive Office of the President, but Kennedy had abolished this procedure and Johnson had experimented with a State Department-led interdepartmental group that promptly became the object of rivalry among agencies competing for foreign policy-making primacy. Kissinger recalls that Eisenhower

was emaciated by his illness and largely immobilized by a heart pacemaker. I had never met him before, and held about him the conventional academic opinion that he was a genial but inarticulate war hero who had been a rather ineffective President. Two of my books and several articles deplored the vacuum of leadership of his Administration—a view I have since changed. Successive heart attacks had left little doubt that he had not long to live. Despite this, his forcefulness was surprising. His syntax, which seemed so awkward in print, became much more graphic when enlivened by his cold, deep blue, extraordinarily penetrating eyes and when given emphasis by his still commanding voice.

Eisenhower promptly displayed his sensitivity to the realities of Washington politics, warning Kissinger that bureaucratic competition would doom the Johnson-initiated arrangements. The Defense Department would not "accept State Department domination of the national security process. It would either attempt end-runs or counterattack by leaking."

Kissinger's second meeting with Eisenhower was on February 2, 1969. He and Nixon told Eisenhower of a State Department proposal that the United States take a direct part in international negotiations designed to force Israeli concessions in the interest of achieving détente in the Middle East. They discussed this and other national security issues with Eisenhower, who "seemed even more emaciated" than the last time Kissinger had seen him.

He spent much of the time warning Nixon against leaks of NSC proceedings. Nixon told him about our Middle East discussion. Eisenhower argued against major American involvement in the negotiations. Probably reflecting the agony he went through over Suez in 1956, he thought the best course was to let the parties work it out themselves. If we became active we would be forced in the end to become an arbiter and then offer the parties our own guarantee of whatever final arrangement emerged. This would keep us embroiled in Middle East difficulties forever. The next day, I had not been in my office many minutes before an irate Eisenhower was on the phone. He had just read a *New York Times* story reporting that the NSC meeting had determined that the United States would not pursue a more active policy in the Middle East. With a vigor that belied my memory of his frailty—and a graphic vocabulary at variance with his sunny smile—he berated me for letting down the President by not restricting the number of participants.

These accounts reveal apparent contradictions in Eisenhower's personal qualities that I will illustrate and analyze. My illustrations of the man, however, also often illuminate his leadership style. Both White's and Kissinger's accounts capture a particularly striking dichotomy between the public man whose "tangled, rambling rhetoric" made him seem on first impression to be a vague thinker, and the private one who expressed himself with clear incisiveness, reflecting a keen analytic mind. Eisenhower channeled both the public vagueness and the private precision into his style of leadership.

Wainwright and Kissinger detected a second apparent contradiction in Eisenhower's political psychology: he professed and appeared to be nonpolitical but clearly understood and sought seriously to influence politics and policy.

Wainwright's implication that leaving meetings with Eisenhower "on cloud nine" strengthened his attachment to him points to a third aspect of the man: his extraordinary capacity to win the support of other political leaders. This "trait" paralleled the truly distinctive capacity Eisenhower had for winning support from the American public. Both in winning and sustaining this support Eisenhower *seemed* totally artless, in White's phrase "a simple man." However, underlying his capacity to win support was a dimension he did not make public, that of self-conscious artfulness. An Eisenhower whose strong temper and emotions contrasted with the beaming visage on the campaign buttons emerges in White's and Kissinger's remarks. This raises yet another consideration—that of—the nature of his feelings and energies and the ways he expressed and channeled them in his leadership. Finally, there is the matter of his specifically political feelings—his beliefs and convictions. Only an awareness of them makes possible an understanding of certain of his political actions, which, notably in domestic policy, differed from his publicly stated policy positions.

PUBLIC VAGUENESS AND PRIVATE PRECISION

Since Eisenhower's press conference transcripts were the single most influential source of his reputation for vague expressions and muddled thinking, it is well to keep in mind Kissinger's observation that, even when Eisenhower's sentences did not parse, his meaning was hammered home by the force and vividness of his personality. Compare the transcript of an Eisenhower press conference with a recording of it. In the recording, the muddled syntax recedes and his voice emphatically and persuasively conveys his message. The films of Eisenhower, which became regular fare for the television viewers—who by the mid-1950s included virtually the entire electorate—are even more effective. His mobile, expressive face and dignified but comfortable comportment, emerge as the expression of a manifestly warm human being who speaks earnestly of his and the nation's ideals. He comes across as solid and full of common sense—a reassuring figure who lived up to his own premise that, as the visible symbol of the nation, the president should exhibit a "respectable image of American life before the world."

By no stretch of the imagination, however, could the bulk of his press conference discourse be said to reveal sharply honed reasoning. Even when he dealt with some of the complexities of an issue, he usually did so through broad simplifications and in a colloquial manner. And asserting that he was not informed about them, he often refused to discuss complexities. He conveyed the impression of a leader who took it for granted that much of the detailed content of contemporary issues was "non-presidential," frequently referring questioners to cabinet secretaries for answers to issues that he said were in their domain, not his, or had not yet been sufficiently studied by subordinates to come to his attention.

The intellectual thinness and syntactical flaws in press conference texts, Eisenhower would later write, resulted from caution. With press conferences open to quotation and broadcast, "an inadvertent misstatement in public would be a calamity." But, he continued, realizing that "it is far better to stumble or speak guardedly than to move ahead smoothly and risk imperilling the country," by consistently focusing on ideas rather than on phrasing, he "was able to avoid causing the nation a serious setback through anything I said in many hours, over eight years of intensive questioning." Then, in the understated mode he used when he chose to draw attention to one of his strengths, he went on to add, "I soon learned that ungrammatical sentences in the transcripts caused many to believe I was incapable of using good English: indeed, several people who have my private papers, many in my handwriting, have expressed outright astonishment that in my writings syntax and grammatical structure were at least adequate."

They were, as he well knew, more than adequate. The Eisenhower Library files contain many letters and memoranda he composed, some marked "private and confidential," others classified for security purposes, reflecting the clean, hard writing, and, by extension, thinking, to which White refers. They include dispassionate, closely reasoned assessments of contemporary issues and personalities that belie the amiable, informal, and often vague usages of his press conference discourse. Startlingly, for a man who seemed, to as acute an observer as Richard Rovere, to have an "unschematic" mind, many of his confidential writings display geometric precision in stating the basic conditions shaping a problem, deducing their implications, and weighing the costs and benefits of alternative possible responses. Eisenhower's reasoning ability and method are best revealed in one of his confidential analyses of a particularly complex, controversial issue, a six-page single-spaced letter to his one-time chief of staff, then NATO Commander Alfred Gruenther, on the "offshore islands" dispute. . . .

THE "NONPOLITICIAN" AS A POLITICAL MAN

The letter to Gruenther reveals more than Eisenhower's rhetorical and cognitive style; it indicates that he had a capacity for practical political thought. He assessed the political motivations of others, anticipating their likely responses to alternative courses of action, and had an explicit decision-making criterion—a decision must be in the long-term public interest *and* must be acceptable domestically so that congressional support can be assured. In short, the Eisenhower who was widely thought of as nonpolitical, who himself insisted that he was not a politician, and who in private used the words "politics" and "politician" pejoratively employed reasoning processes that bespoke political skill and sensitivity.

Eisenhower's inclination and capacity to analyze the behavior of others in terms of their political motives became apparent immediately after his rise to public visibility. During his 1942 dealings with the Vichy France commander in North Africa, Admiral Jean Darlan, Eisenhower explained to Marshall what it was about the behavior of Darlan and the other Vichy leaders that led him to work with the admiral and to shape his own action in ways that would best maintain Darlan's cooperation. Acknowledging that he had "some appreciation of all the political problems created by the necessity we have met of dealing with Darlan," he noted that nevertheless "the source of all practical help here has been Darlan."

All the others . . . await his lead and will do nothing definitive unless he speaks. So far he has refused us nothing. If he is playing a crooked game with us locally it is so deep that he can afford to give away initial advantages of every kind, even those upon which our existence depends in our present attenuated condition.

Given this, Eisenhower felt it essential to "preserve the attitude that we are dealing with a friend rather than an enemy."

I feel it is a mistake to demand cooperation and a friendly attitude on the one hand and on the other to act here like we have a conquering Army which enforces its will by threat and views with intense suspicion every proposal of these people. This explanation is submitted to you personally so you may understand why in certain details that appear to us relatively unimportant we attempt to be magnanimous and ostentatiously trustful.

The reference to Darlan's "game" fits perfectly with an account of Eisenhower's analytic bent by a long-time aid, General Andrew J. Goodpaster, who was present at many of Eisenhower's strategy conferences at NATO and in the White House. Pointing out that Eisenhower's apprenticeship during a 1922–24 tour of duty as executive officer in Panama with the legendary military intellectual, General Fox Conner, and his work at the Command and General Staff College had instilled in him "the orderly process of reasoning and analysis that is represented in the commander's estimate of the situation," Goodpaster observed that this called for thinking of collective activities in terms of the options open to the various parties. Goodpaster perceived a parallel between Eisenhower's political (as well as military) reasoning and game theory, the formal, mathematical, decision-making mode developed in the 1940s and 1950s and extensively used in cold war nuclear deterrence calculations. "Anything that's based on the theory of games, or a doctrine or technique that conforms to that," Goodpaster commented, "fits well into . . . the way that General Eisenhower's mind works."

He's a great poker player, and extremely good bridge player. He plays bridge very much in poker style and he's a tremendous man for analyzing the other fellow's mind, what options are open to the other fellow, and what line he can best take to capitalize or exploit the possibilities, having figured the options open to the other man. Under Fox Conner . . . he became keenly interested in the command process, not just the mechanics of it so much as the analysis of what was in the commander's mind—what was in Lee's mind, for example, at Gettysburg.

In analyzing "the other fellow's mind" Eisenhower used the reasoning process he described to Gruenther: stripping a problem "down to its simplest possible form." He did not dwell on the sources or subtleties of personalities. Rather, he parsimoniously identified principal traits, focusing on those that bore directly on public performance. As he stressed in conversations with Goodpaster, he formed in his mind explicit sketches of what he called the "personal equations" of his counterparts.

An example is Eisenhower's effort to unravel President Lyndon B. Johnson's motives for announcing after the Tet offensive in Vietnam that he would cease bombing the North "in the hope that this would lead to a satisfactory peace" and that he would not accept renomination. "This abrupt change in policy, without any *quid pro quo* from Hanoi, will," Eisenhower reflected, "of course, further bewilder the United States." As far as he could see, Johnson's shift lacked a cogent rationale.

It appears to be not only contrary to the President's announced determination in the matter, but a partial capitulation, at least, to the "peace at any price" people in our country. . . . The final and most puzzling feature of his talk was his declaration that he would not seek and would not accept the nomination of his Party for the Presidency of the United States. . . . To me it seems obvious that the President is at war with himself and while trying vigorously to defend the actions and decisions he has made in the past, and urging the nation to pursue those purposes regardless of cost, he wants to be excused from the burden of office to which he was elected. He made no mention of the leader from his own Party who should now, in his stead, carry forward the effort. Indeed, I was left with the conclusion that the President had not truely analyzed the implications of his speech. . . .

I am besieged by papers and others to "make a statement." I am . . . refusing to say anything until I can convince myself of the true motivation of this performance.

Johnson's "equation," Eisenhower felt, revolved around extreme readiness to be opportunistic about policies. He also was aware that Johnson as a congressional leader had been a pragmatic analyst of political consequences. Since even an opportunistic motive for the announcement was difficult for Eisenhower to infer, he was suspending judgment.

Eisenhower's diagnosis of Johnson, with whom he had worked closely in the party, was exceedingly negative. . . .

Eisenhower, however, would have considered it politically unwise to make public his distaste for Johnson. He managed, in fact, to maintain the affection of that thin-skinned man. . . .

Eisenhower's impulse to avoid personal disagreements with other political figures was established in his long years in Washington. A vignette from his first term as Chief of Staff is especially telling, because it establishes a link between his personal feelings about politics and his leadership style.

Eisenhower prevented what might have been an ugly dispute between the War Department and the vociferous Mississippi Congressman John Rankin, who usually confined his efforts to assailing blacks, Jews, and Reds. Early in 1945, Rankin had called for an investigation of one of Eisenhower's chief wartime officers, General Mark Clark, who had commanded a World War II engagement in which the casualties were great, the Rapido River crossing. Rankin was echoing the demand by backers of the National Guard division that participated in the action that the army take "the necessary steps to correct a military system that will permit an inefficient and inexperienced officer, such as General Mark Clark, in a high command to destroy the young manhood of the country."

In response, Eisenhower dealt first with Clark and then with Congress. Urging Clark to ignore Rankin, he predicted that a reply would "initiate unnecessarily a public quarrel" which would have

many unfortunate effects, among these being a tendency to drag forward as a volunteer witness every single individual who may through venom, spite, or mere love of personal publicity, see a chance of doing a bit of damage. You must remember that on our side we have only facts and honest conclusions to combat arguments based largely on sentiment and emotional appeal.

Fearing the unruly emotions that would be unloosed in a public exchange, he arranged that a formal report be forwarded to Congress. The high casualty river crossing, the army reported, was a diversion drawing German troops from the Anzio landing site. The congressional military affairs leaders quietly accepted the army's explanation.

The issue threatened to emerge again later in the year when Clark's promotion to permanent major general went to the Senate, but his promotion went through without public outcry. Eisenhower explained his rationale to Clark: it was that nonconfrontation, lubricated by informal negotiations on the Hill is the best way to get results in such a situation. "I wanted," he stressed, "very much to avoid a name-calling campaign." This was why he had urged Clark to ignore Rankin. But Eisenhower had not remained passive. He noted,

I did talk personally to several members of the committee and they knew I was prepared to go down and do my stuff if it became necessary. What I was going to do was dwell upon Grant's second charge at Cold Harbor and Pickett's charge at Gettysburg, directed by Lee. I'd figured that the proper treatment of these two incidents would do more than to argue about the specific tactical situation existing on the Rapido.

The testimony that never occurred not only illuminates Eisenhower's conflict-avoiding approach to potentially ugly rows, it also shows how he could manipulate situations to his own ends while still maintaining the personal image of a neutral spokesman for the national interest. His plan after all had been to defuse an attempt to examine a specific wartime episode by changing the topic. He proposed not to discuss the Rapido battle at all except by analogy to nineteenth-century events. It is unlikely that the lawmakers would have cared to debate with a popularly acclaimed, recently victorious supreme commander about technical problems of assault tactics and the fine points of Civil War military engagements. Moreover, his ploy probably would have succeeded, even if he were not a national hero, because he had the personal confidence and support of the bulk of Congress, who like other leaders he met face to face, found him admirable and compellingly attractive.

ARTLESSNESS AND ART IN WINNING THE
SUPPORT OF OTHER LEADERS

Every World War II buff knows that a crucial part of Eisenhower's contribution to the Axis defeat was holding together the strong-minded, diverse leaders of the Western alliance. When asked to explain how Eisenhower managed this, his associates often sought recourse in such ambiguities as "the mystery of leadership." The biographer of Eisenhower's war years, Stephen Ambrose, gets closer to the heart of the matter in his own response to a question posed to Secretary of War Henry Stimson by a group of American senators visiting Eisenhower's North African headquarters: "Cunningham commands the naval forces, Tedder commands the air forces, and Alexander commands the ground forces. What in hell does Eisenhower command?" Ambrose retorts, "He commanded Cunningham, Alexander, and Tedder. Eisenhower brought this about not through any structural change, but by holding weekly meetings with the three British officers, by having frequent casual conversations with them individually, by acting as referee to settle their inter-service disputes, and above all by the force of his personality."

Clearly this personal force in face-to-face leadership was palpable to those who worked with him even though they had difficulty finding precise words to express the experience of working with Eisenhower. One cabinet aide, for example, characterizes Eisenhower's presence in meetings as "electric." Harvard law and political science professor Robert Bowie, an observer whose accounts of events usually subordinate personal feelings to analytic interpretation, recounts his first meeting with Eisenhower (in 1945, during Eisenhower's brief stint as military governor of Germany) not in terms of its content, but of the emotions induced in him and others by Eisenhower's manner. "What struck me," Bowie recalls, "was the vibrant personality, the very magnetic appeal which he had, even in dealing with people that he hadn't met or known before." Although he had just defeated them, he even "created an immediate sense of friendliness with the Germans and avoided any memory or recollection of prior relationships which could have made it awkward."

Whatever the elements in Eisenhower's "electricity," they had been longstanding, even if they were dormant during his many desk-bound years as a staff officer. Eisenhower's secretary, Mrs. Whitman, discovered a letter dated 1918, when Eisenhower led an army training unit. The author, a junior officer under his command, though describing times and circumstances far removed from presidential demands, picturesquely captures Eisenhower's ease in whipping up subordinates' enthusiasm, his appealing mixture of humor and seriousness, and the other outgoing, personable qualities that encouraged spontaneous identification with him.

Our new captain, Eisenhower by name, is, I believe one of the most efficient and best Army officers in the country. He is a . . . corker and has put more into us in three days than we got in all the previous time we were here. He is a giant for build and at West Point was a noted football and physical culture fiend. He knows his job, is enthusiastic, can tell us what he wants us to do and is pretty human, though wickedly harsh and abrupt. . . . He gets the fellows' imaginations worked up and hollers and yells and makes us shout and stamp until we go tearing into the air as if we mean business. . . . Every now and then Eisenhower would jump on us and say we were having too good a time, call us to attention and put us through the manual for five minutes, but you could see that he enjoyed it all too.

Later accounts describe similar, quite tangible sources of Eisenhower's effectiveness in face-to-face leadership conferences. One source, his capacity for earnest, forceful exhortations was especially effective with associates, such as his cabinet members who had joined the administration because of their admiration for him.* His cabinet included a number of strong personalities who ranged in viewpoint from deep conservatism to middle-of-the-road Republicanism, but who nevertheless all accepted him as an appropriate spokesman for the national interest.

Speech writer Emmet Hughes provides an action portrait of how Eisenhower would rally the cabinet members during their regular meetings. His "ears never seemed to leave the discourse around him." Eisenhower's "interjections" in the discussions "were sudden, sometimes sharp or even explosive."

Again and again the President would seize on some particular matter of legislation or administration as spark for a warm homily on his personal views—the world need for free trade, or the practical necessity (and "cheapness") of programs of mutual security, or the need to temper austere "businesslike" administration with signs of concern for "the little fellow," or the "unthinkable" dimensions of nuclear war. For almost all the persons present these fervent sermons carried an authority almost scriptural.

Eisenhower's comments impressed his colleagues not simply because they were made with intensity, but also because they reflected his extensive personal knowledge of governmental affairs. The cabinet members, Hughes sensed, were especially impressed by his personal acquaintance with other world leaders—for example, "the warmth of his friendship for Harold Macmillan or his tolerance of the idiosyncrasies of Charles de Gaulle." Especially to those members of the cabinet with limited experience in national and international affairs, "such a range of acquaintanceship with things and with people seemed no less than dazzling."

Robert Bowie did not confine his explanation of Eisenhower's effectiveness to "vibrancy." Eisenhower also impressed him in settings such as National Security Council meetings because he displayed two precisely definable qualities. One, which many other observers remark on, was his ability to make decisions, "to face the issues . . . and resolve them." The other was his ability to cut through complex discussions and make persuasive, though unpretentious sounding, judgments.

* No one asked to serve in his cabinet "declined an invitation from the great World War II leader—a statistic unique in the modern presidency."

Often the discussion would be marked by impressive analysis by various individuals who, as intellectuals, struck you as sometimes more articulate than he. But at the end, I felt that he frequently came out with a commonsense appraisal . . . which was wiser than the input which he'd received from the separate advisors. Somehow, almost in an intuitive way, in a way which quite clearly wasn't a one, two, three lawyer's type of analysis, nevertheless he came out with a net judgment which often struck me as wiser or more sensible than the specific positions taken by any individual.*

Eisenhower's ability to win support in group settings may have seemed artless, but it actually represented a conscious application of what he realized were proven tactics for effective leadership, although his use of such tactics no doubt became second nature to him, requiring little conscious forethought. One of the closest observers of Eisenhower's practices over an extended period of demanding leadership, his World War II Chief of Staff, Walter Bedell Smith, explained that Eisenhower consulted subordinates as much to win them over as to canvass their views:

His personality is such that it impresses itself immediately upon senior subordinates as completely frank, completely honest, very human and very considerate. . . . He has great patience, and he disdains no advice regardless of source. One of his most successful methods in dealing with individuals is to assume that he himself is lacking in detailed knowledge and liable to make an error and is seeking advice. This is by no means a pose, because he actually values the recommendations and suggestions he receives, although his own better information and sounder judgment might cause them to be disregarded.

Subordinates so consulted, Smith observed, tended to be highly loyal and to accept Eisenhower's policies readily, presumably because they were flattered to be taken seriously and to feel that whatever line of action Eisenhower embarked upon had been informed by consultation with them.

C. D. Jackson, the Time Inc. executive who in 1953 and early 1954 worked closely with Eisenhower as a national security consultant and speech writer, also noted Eisenhower's habitual close attentiveness to others, by observing that "the only time his features seem to sag is when he is bored." But it was clear to Jackson that Eisenhower took pains to master this appearance. Even the sag in his features, Jackson commented, "is only momentary, because his almost fantastically patient courtesy comes into play almost instantly in order to give the bore the impression that he is being listened to with interest."

Appointments Secretary Robert Gray also noted that Eisenhower's skill and ease in dealing with visitors to his office was built on experience and technique. Eisenhower's meetings with visitors were "never stiff," Gray reported, though he "could manage a near complete sched-

* We have seen that Eisenhower's letter to Gruenther did in fact follow a "one, two, three" reasoning mode. This explicitly deductive reasoning style is especially evident in Eisenhower's written communications. In discussions, he presented his main points and his conclusion, giving his rationale in a comfortably conversational, less formal way.

ule of important appointments at quarter-hour intervals, clear his mind in the seconds it took me to escort out his old visitor and bring in the new, and be locked on the fresh subject in full concentration by the time I withdrew." If the visitor became tongued-tied in Eisenhower's presence, "the President could carry the conversation single-handedly," finding common ground through small talk until "the visitor had settled back on his chair prepared to discuss the . . . business that had brought him."

The artfulness that Eisenhower applied to what he called "leadership in conference" is revealed in his ability to advise others on how to win over groups and individuals. Evidence of what Goodpaster described as Eisenhower's keen "interest in the command process" appears in a lengthy 1948 memorandum to Defense Secretary James Forrestal discussing how the secretary should go about seeking to harmonize the centrifugal demands of the members of the Joint Chiefs of Staff. The methods suggested were those that Eisenhower was often to employ in meetings when he was president. Whenever a member shows "a tendency to become a special pleader," he wrote, "the subject should be skillfully changed and a constant effort made to achieve unanimity of conclusion, first upon broad generalities and these gradually brought closer to concrete application to particular problems."

In a wartime letter to his son, Eisenhower commented, "The one quality that can be developed by studious reflection and practice is the leadership of men." Eisenhower undoubtedly overestimated the transferability of his leadership qualities. Nevertheless as a leader of other leaders he did more than effortlessly exude charm and warmth. He worked at the job.

ARTLESSNESS AND ART IN WINNING PUBLIC SUPPORT

Eisenhower's equal success in rallying and sustaining public support also was not arrived at without effort, though it was based on a personal public attractiveness to people with which few leaders are endowed. Films of Eisenhower's public appearances reveal an animated, enthusiastic man inspiring in the public a reciprocal enthusiasm. This is evident in the wartime newsreels showing a smiling, confident, unpretentious general, easily making his way through formations of troops; in the ticker-tape parades celebrating his return to the United States in 1945; and finally in films showing the motorcades with Eisenhower, both as a candidate and president, standing in open cars, beaming, waving, and signaling the familiar V for victory as he entered the cheering communities where he was making appearances.

The sober Bradley and staid Marshall never could have elicited a comparable response. And the other World War II general to win national popularity, MacArthur, seemed to reinforce his long association with political conservatives by his austere martial air. Numerous public opinion polls at that time reveal that, although both MacArthur and Eisenhower received strong support as "most-admired American," MacArthur's support was parochial, concentrated largely among conservative Republicans, while Eisenhower's crossed partisan and ideological lines.

Striking evidence that Eisenhower took the buoyant displays that won over first troops and later electorates as still another part of his responsibility—an appearance to be cultivated if necessary—can be found in an introductory chapter he did not use in *Crusade in Europe,* but which is preserved in draft form in the Eisenhower Library. The published book deals predominantly with events, not emotions and perceptions. The omitted introduction addresses itself to suppressing and countering feelings of despondency when faced by setbacks, stalemates, or stasis.

Eisenhower recalls the tense weeks he spent in the dank tunnels of Gibraltar immediately before the North African invasion in 1942 when

following upon many months of work and planning, conducted sometimes at almost hysterical intensity, a great Allied amphibious force had sailed from its ports to attack North Africa and my staff and I were condemned to days of almost complete passivity . . . as we awaited the outcome. During those anxious hours I first realized, I think, how inexorably and inescapably strain and tension wear away at the leader's endurance, his judgment and his confidence. The pressure becomes more acute because of the duty of a staff constantly to present to the commander the worst side of an eventuality . . . and the commander inherits an additional load in preserving optimism in himself and in his command. Without confidence, enthusiasm and optmism in the command, victory is scarcely obtainable.

Realizing that "optimism and pessimism are infectious and they spread more rapidly from the head downward than in any other direction," Eisenhower "clearly saw the dual advantages to be obtained from a commander's cheerful demeanor and constant outward optimism." One was that "the habit . . . tends to minimize potentialities within the individual himself" to become demoralized. The other was that it

has a most extraordinary effect upon all with whom he comes in contact. With this clear realization, I firmly determined that my mannerisms and speech in public would always reflect the cheerful certainty of victory—that any pessimism and discouragement I might ever feel would be reserved for my pillow. To translate this conviction into tangible results . . . I adopted a policy of circulating through the whole force to the full limit imposed by physical considerations . . . I did my best to meet everyone from general to private with a smile, a pat on the back and a definite interest in his problems.

Eisenhower realized that a leader must inspire confidence and support, no matter how he feels. Describing his 1952 campaign in *Mandate for Change,* Eisenhower speaks of "the candidate's stepping blithely out to face the crowd, doing his best to conceal with a big grin the ache in his bones and the exhaustion in his mind." Yet he insisted on appearing in motorcades, which was a grueling physical ordeal. And he urged politicians to follow his own practice of projecting a sense of warm enthusiasm. As one aide remembers, "I moved around with him a great deal and I've heard him tell professional politicians: 'Now here's what you do. Get out there. Don't look so serious. Smile. When the people are waving at you wave your arms and move your lips, so you look like you're talking to them. It doesn't matter what you say. Let them see you're reacting to them.' "

The smiling, confident exterior often concealed more than "pessimism and discouragement." It concealed the hard-driving side of this complex man as well as a fiery temper that he kept in check out of a deep commitment to subordinate personal feelings to the duties of leadership. The Democratic jibe that Eisenhower's was an era in which the bland led the bland is contradicted by a multitude of firsthand observations.

THE EASYGOING LEADER AS DYNAMO, THE SMILE AND THE TEMPER

In wartime letters reflecting on the demands of his job, Eisenhower observed that an "inexhaustible fund of nervous energy" is needed to carry out the responsibilities of a higher commander. Ambrose discloses that as supreme commander Eisenhower normally slept only five hours a day. He never napped, he rarely missed work because of illness, and he regularly worked seven-day weeks, taking holidays only when ordered by Marshall to do so. And he chain-smoked—a four-pack-a-day habit.

This intense work and the smoking habit neither began nor ended with his World War II duty. As he later reminisced, "My immoderate use of tobacco was matched by immoderate working hours whenever a big job was to be done. I was, when working, driven by the need to go at top speed, day after day, starting early and continuing past midnight." In March 1949, while on leave from Columbia University to help weld the new Defense Department, he was seized with severe gastrointestinal disorder (one he first experienced in the Philippines and which later was diagnosed as ileitis and was successfully treated by surgery in 1956). When told that he would have to cut back on smoking, he was as forceful as he had been in the relentless workaholic routines his smoking accompanied. In an act of will that can be best understood by an ex-tobacco addict, he simply stopped cold turkey.

As a national figure in constant demand for public appearances, a regularly consulted statesman, *and* a university president, Eisenhower was less successful in finding respite from a relentlessly full schedule of activities than in abandoning cigarettes. His physicians and his own sense of his health reached parallel conclusions. His blood pressure and susceptibility to digestive-tract disorder were high. His sense of well-being was low. The prescription—imperfectly adhered to but nevertheless helpful—was for him to block out time every several weeks for genuine rest, if possible physically removing himself from town.

By the time he entered the presidency at age 62, Eisenhower had already attacked his life's work with an intensity that would have broken the constitution of a man who did not have a fundamentally sound and resilient physical and emotional makeup. Physically he was helped by the hard manual work and exposure to the outdoors made possible by his rural upbringing, by the early years of his military career when he was not constantly deskbound, and by the stamina he had built up as an athlete. Emotionally, he had a capacity to turn from worries to congenial, typically gregarious entertainment; although, except for his hobbies of painting and cooking, his preferred distractions were less relaxations than shifts from intense work to intense play. Golfing companions describe the stubborn determination he would pour into replaying an unsatisfactory shot. And what he liked about bridge was the opportunity it gave him to focus sharply on the solution to a logical problem and at the same time master the psychology of effective cooperation with his partner and competition with his opponents.

In his White House years, he continued the regimens he and his friend and longtime personal physician, Dr. Howard Snyder, had established to put periodic dampers on his restless energy. The much publicized golfing trips, the working vacations, and even the Wild West stories he read at bedtime, which many critics suggested were the outward signs of a passive president with a flaccid mind, paradoxically were prescriptions for winding down a man whose drive and intensity needed to be kept in check. This was even more the case after his three major illnesses, all typical of the "immoderate" worker—a heart attack in 1955, an ileitis episode in 1956, and a slight stroke in 1957. Despite the remonstrances of some critics and political advisors to abjure golf or at least conceal his participation in it, Eisenhower let the relaxations become part of the image, perhaps recognizing that a golfing Ike was a more reassuring symbol than a harried chief executive presiding over circumstances so unsettled that the fairways were off limits. And the Gallup Poll, in support, found that the majority of the public had no objection to the time he spent on golf courses.

The eyewitness accounts of his behavior at meetings uniformly point to an energetic, restless temperament. Though he subjected himself to the passive context of regular long meetings and more tightly packed, longer work schedules than he chose to publicize, his physical comportment in meetings revealed his force and drive. His concentration was intense: his excess energy spilled over as he would doodle, finger his glasses, swivel in his chair, and look at other speakers with piercing bright blue eyes that innumerable observers sensed as windows to an inner dynamism.

National Security Advisor Dillon Anderson was one of many people who described the way Eisenhower would get up and pace the floor in an informal meeting as his enthusiasm mounted. "He was a man of a lot of native animal energy, which came out when a subject stirred him up, and he used to get up and walk the floor." Anderson, a dignified Texas banker who chaired Eisenhower's National Security Council staff briefly in 1955 and 1956, found himself nonplussed to be looking up at a striding president. "When he would get up, I would get up, and he would say, 'God damn it, sit down' and I would sit back down. Finally I got to where I could be comfortable sitting down in a room where the President of the United States was not seated." Visiting Eisenhower in 1960, his last year in office, Anderson noted the same energy and restless stride. His several illnesses and the approach of his seventieth birthday had not made him placid.

In earlier years Eisenhower's dynamism was even more visible. When William Robinson initiated negotiations with Eisenhower after the war about writing a memoir, Eisenhower seemed "to get on fire" as Robinson talked about how an account of Eisenhower's wartime leadership would make a fundamental contribution to maintaining postwar allied unity. Robinson reported to his boss,

He would, every few minutes, arise from the chair in which he was sitting and stride up and down the office, talking about his limitations at one moment and in the next outlining the manner in which he would like to be of service, the things he would like to say, the guidance he would like to give historians in setting forth the facts of his mission in Europe. He was completely free, unguarded to the point even of indiscretion. There was no pose, no pretence, no attempt to establish anything for the record, no attempt to build an impression of any kind. He was natural, alive, alert, spirited, and gave the impression of having an intense amount of unloosened energy, both intellectual and physical. . . . His high spirit and his great emotional potentiality might conceivably develop a highly unbalanced entity in a person of lesser intellectual capacity.

White House appointment lists carefully document everyone with whom the president met and state whether these meetings were on or off the record. They cover his official weekday working hours—usually from 8 A.M. to 5 or 5:30 P.M.—and often record Saturday and Sunday work, as well as evening activities, including entertainment of state guests and "stag dinners" for prominent citizens. They show a steady level of activity (excluding periods when he was ill or on a real rather than working vacation) through the end of his second term.

The official lists fail to record his informal workday. Most days he had business breakfasts at 7:30, often with confidants such as his brother Milton or Lucius Clay. By then he had read several newspapers, even examining items tucked away on the business pages. Both his press secretary and the men who briefed him on intelligence reports recognized that, although Eisenhower often chided his associates for wasting time reading the newspapers, he frequently tripped them up by mentioning information they had not noticed in the morning's news.

Even before rising his mind often was at work. Eisenhower told his boyhood friend "Swede" Hazlett that he had never wholly been able to overcome the annoyance of a wartime habit of waking very early in the morning, but he felt that the abbreviated sleep was a healthy sign.

Ever since the hectic days of the North African campaign, I find that when I have weighty matters on my mind I wake up extremely early, apparently because a rested mind is anxious to begin grappling with knotty questions. Incidentally, I never worry about what I did the day before. Likewise, I spend no time fretting about what enemies or critics have said about me. I have never indulged in useless regrets. Always I find, when I have come awake sufficiently to figure out what may be then engaging my attention, that I am pondering the same question that is still unanswered.

So I think it is fair to say that it is not worry about the past, but a desire to attack the future, that gets me into this annoying habit.

At the end of the workdays when he had no evening obligations, Eisenhower often continued to conduct presidential business informally over drinks in the residential quarters of the White House. Sometimes his cocktail time was purely social, but frequently he used it for such purposes as culling information or mending fences. It was in this setting that he and one or two of his legislative liaison aides would meet with Democratic House and Senate leaders, Sam Rayburn and Lyndon Johnson, so that neither his partisans nor those of the Democratic leaders could complain that party purity was being undermined by bipartisan conniving.

Eisenhower preferred to avoid evening work, but he frequently edited speeches, read government reports, and did other homework. He chose not to publicize these nocturnal activities, just as he chose not to make available a complete listing of his daily meetings for the appointment calendars published in the newspaper each day. Publicity of his nighttime work (like complete lists of all his appointments) would have been discordant with the impression he conveyed of being a president who so successfully maintained national and international order that he did not have to work intensively around-the-clock.

In fact, however, like other presidents, he had associates who were empowered to "re-open the day" after he retired for the evening. "One evening in 1958, around midnight," Eisenhower's legislative liaison chief Bryce Harlow remembers,

Speaker Sam Rayburn telephoned me about an urgent requirement on an important bill then in intense controversy in the House of Representatives. He needed a Presidential decision at once, but Eisenhower had retired for the night. I told him to stand by, went to the President's rooms, had him awakened, explained the problem, got his decision, and reported back to the Speaker, well within 20 minutes.

Anyone in regular, informal contact with Eisenhower knew that his energy was not always manifested in a dulcet mood. Accounts of his proclivity to flare up in red-faced anger go back to his preteen years in Abilene. Without attempting to psychoanalyze the diverse sources of what Harlow called his "Bessemer furnace" personality we can note that he himself suggested a role model, referring to the awesome temper of his patriarchal Pennsylvania Dutch father, David Eisenhower. He also claimed he learned to control his temper from his gentle, pacifistic mother, but one aide commented, "I thought to myself what a poor job she had done." Childhood models notwithstanding, the very energy he poured into problem solving needed outlet when nevertheless things went wrong—often his anger was not directed at a person but at an impersonal obstacle.

Eisenhower erupting was by all accounts impressive. As he remarked in an early 1960's CBS interview,

I told my staff . . . once in a while you people have just got to be my safety-valve. So I'll get you in here and I will let go, but this is for you and your knowledge, and your knowledge only. Now I've seen these people going out, and I've gotten a little bit extreme, a little white, but pretty soon one of them comes in and laughs and says, "Well, you were in good form this morning, Mr. President," or "General," or whatever it was at the time.

Former staff members who witnessed it agreed that although his temper was formidable it was also short-lived—summer thunderstorms followed by balmy good humor.

Eisenhower's capacity to fly into towering rages was not unique among modern presidents. Both Lyndon Johnson and Richard Nixon were known for their tempers. Unlike Johnson, Eisenhower did not smolder and bear long-term grudges. If he believed someone to have grave character defects and there were no reasons of state for dealing with him, Eisenhower would simply cut off his association with that person. Also unlike Johnson, he did not bully subordinates.

Eisenhower's awareness and attempts to control his temper distinguished him from Richard Nixon. For Eisenhower, there was no denial of angry impulses. Nixon appears sometimes to have repressed anger, driving it from consciousness, only to have it surface in outbursts that conveyed the impression of meanness of spirit. Eisenhower's practice was suppression, not repression, and suppression for practical reasons. Public loss of temper was inconsistent, he felt, with a leader's duties. "I learned a long time ago," he told his CBS interviewer, "that . . . anybody that aspired to a position of leadership of any kind . . . must learn to control his temper."

In the internecine conflicts within the World War II alliance, Eisenhower showed this ability to control his temper in the face of extreme provocation in order to realize his policy aims. The most striking example is his forbearance in dealing with the caustic, self-centered Field Marshall Bernard Montgomery, who, though Eisenhower's subordinate, refused ever to visit his headquarters. He repeatedly criticized Eisenhower's performance as a general, urging that he himself be named to replace him. Because of Montgomery's great popularity in Britain, it was impossible either to relieve him of his position or publicly chastise him. Eisenhower curbed expression of animus toward Montgomery by analyzing that bantam cock, thus mentally putting him in his place rather than allowing conflict with Montgomery to surface. As he told Marshall, while he did not voluntarily choose Montgomery as a subordinate, "I have his personal equation and have no lack of confidence in my ability to handle him." Drawing on his reading of Montgomery's character, Eisenhower reasoned with the Field Marshall when necessary, gave him his way when he felt it appropriate, but had no hesitation about overruling him.

Although Eisenhower viewed his bad temper as a special curse, his awareness of it and his capacity to control it enabled him to turn it to practical use on occasion. Vernon A. ("Dick") Walters, Eisenhower's translator in NATO negotiations, recounts a time when Eisenhower deliberately indulged himself in a blowup in order to terminate a disagreement he felt was not worth negotiating through to a conclusion.

We stopped in Italy to see Defense Minister Pacciardi. He had insisted that the Greek and Turkish forces be under an Italian commander. Both, however, had told Eisenhower that this was out of the question. During the discussion Eisenhower suddenly appeared to misunderstand something that Pacciardi had just said and I had translated. Pacciardi, after a few feeble attempts to explain that he had been misunderstood, gave in and accepted a U.S. commander for the Greek and Turkish sector of NATO. I was greatly crestfallen as it appeared to Pacciardi that I had mistranslated what he had said and that this had provoked Eisenhower's anger. . . . The matter of the command settled, we returned to Naples airport and took off for Paris. I was sitting in the forward cabin feeling quite glum when General Eisenhower came forward, tapped me on the shoulder and said, "Dick, if I sometimes appear to misunderstand what you say, it is just that I need a hook on which to hang my anger." He added with a grin, "It worked, too."

Eisenhower's quick reference in the CBS interview to temper and the need for a successful leader to control it does, however, show that he knew his own "equation" and factored it into his leadership. One reason why he controlled his temper so successfully was that he had an even more powerful conviction that leaders are charged with responsibilities and must suppress personal impulse if duty so dictated.

Eisenhower's capacity for controlling outward manifestations of his feelings also undoubtedly stemmed from his conviction that a leader's *duty* is to keep his impulses in check and act rationally. Barber is correct in emphasizing the centrality of feeling of duty to Eisenhower's political psychology. These feelings, captured in the old fashioned-sounding abstract nouns of the West Point motto—"duty, honor, country"—resonated with the verities of his rural turn-of-the-century background and surely were strengthened by his immersion as a child in a pietist tradition revolving around the principle that the individual is ultimately responsible to a Supreme Being and to values higher than self-interest.

Eisenhower reminisced in *At Ease* that his early military career had included a frustrating sequence of unchallenging assignments. What kept him going was his resolution "to perform every duty given me . . . to the best of my ability . . . no matter what [its] . . . nature." This sense of duty eventually extended to becoming President of the United States. His diary entries for 1950 leave little doubt that he was profoundly ambivalent about adding the burden of a presidency (it seemed certain that he *could* be nominated and elected) to an already full career. He reflected irritably on how to respond to the constant demands of politicians and business friends, among others, that he become a candidate. His efforts to think aloud on paper revolved around the issue of where his duty lay. Even if he did not want to run, he asked himself, was he morally obliged to do so if it were the only way of achieving the public policies to which he was committed?

Perhaps the most influential single man in forcing him to a decision, his old friend Lucius Clay mercilessly pressed him on this ground. Reflecting in 1954 on how he could best retire at the end of his first term, Eisenhower returned to his diary. Clay had been pressing him anew, striking at what Eisenhower knew to be his most vulnerable point: "All that a person has to say to me is 'the good of the country'," he wrote, "and . . . I probably yield far too easily to generalizations instead of demanding proof."

Ironically, Eisenhower's heart attack, which incapacitated him for much of the fall of 1955, may have insured that he would feel duty bound to run again. He evidently had been disposed—with Milton's aid—to groom a candidate or field of candidates to replace him, but his illness prevented him from doing so in time. When he finally had medical approval to complete his first term and run again, it was clear there was no other Republican candidate in the wings who would both satisfy Eisenhower's aims and be assured of election.

BELIEFS—AS HELD AND AS EXPRESSED

Political convictions—more precisely a core of convictions concerning war and peace, international community, and broad domestic policy principles—were intensely important to Eisenhower. For most people political beliefs are peripheral personality structures, a combination of habitual assumptions and short-lived responses to immediate circumstances and events. To an issue oriented political leader like Eisenhower, however, beliefs are usually stable and can have a profound impact on feeling and action. Clear beliefs and policy positions founded on them are powerful instruments for leadership, since the leader who possesses them is better able to set priorities, communicate a public stance, and delegate specifics to associates by giving them clear guidelines for making detailed decisions.

Eisenhower's most deeply felt concern—the preoccupation that led him to take on the presidency at an age when he was giving thought to reducing his involvement in public service—was with the state of world order. Foreign and international politics clearly were his prime focus, though he recognized their integral link to domestic politics and policy.

The phrase "collective security" best describes his major short-run policy aim—that of welding a sturdy cold war coalition of Western and other non-Communist nations. This coalition, he was convinced, could not merely be military. It needed a solid political, economic, and ideological framework. He believed that if such a coalition could be achieved, there would be a greater likelihood of attaining the most fundamental long-run need of mankind, international harmony. Given time and Western steadfastness, "world communism" might lose its monolithic expansionistic qualities, and a strong, resourceful West could then take the lead in dissipating the cold war. And détente, he was convinced, would have to occur eventually to prevent the ultimate catastrophe—global nuclear war.

Eisenhower recurrently sought to bring home to Republican conservatives the awful significance of nuclear weaponry. Senior Republican Senator Styles Bridges of New Hampshire, for example, in 1957 rumbled publicly that the administration's foreign policy proposals were not true to cold war orthodoxy. The recording machine that from time to time was used to monitor conversations in the Oval Office captured an extended, impassioned Eisenhower exercise in setting Bridges straight. In response to Bridges's concern about "this atomic treaty"— reference to the administration's disarmament proposals—Eisenhower stressed, "this is part of a great program we have to pursue if we are going to save us from some catastrophe."

Eisenhower: Even assuming that we could emerge from a global war today as the acknowledged victor, there would be a destruction in the country [such] that there would be no possibility of our exercising a representative free government for, I would say, two decades at the minimum. . . . Did you ever see one of those net evaluation studies given to me every year?

Bridges: No.

Eisenhower: I will give you just one figure. . . . On a single attack . . . [one in which] we had enough warning for some preparation with our people and weapons . . . we figure something like 25 million killed, 60 million had to go to hospitals, and there were not enough hospitals. When you begin to think of things like that you know there must not be war.

As he put it to one correspondent in a 1958 letter, nuclear weapons had changed the character of war more in the twenty-one years since 1945 than any change between the beginning of the sixteenth century and Hiroshima. The usual notion of war was now obsolete; the new weaponry of extermination would leave no winner. There remained no alternative to finding means of East-West accommodation.

Eisenhower viewed his attempts as president to assure collective security in the West and bargain from strength to begin building a peaceful East-West relationship as a direct extension of his activities in the postwar years that culminated in his NATO leadership. And he thought of his efforts as a coalition builder after 1945 as a continuation of his allied leadership in the war. In his postwar prepresidential years Eisenhower harnessed his long-standing but never publicly expressed or sharply defined conservatism on domestic policy to his views on collective security. Although he felt that the American defense establishment was underfunded and precipitously demobilized in the immediate postwar years, he also was acutely sensitive to the possibility that high taxes and governmental expenditures—whether for military or domestic purposes—would weaken economic productivity through excessive federal regulation and reduction of incentives to invest. And he was preoccupied with the potential costs of an inflation that might be spurred by government spending, including "unproductive" spending on arms.*

* He appears to have done much of this thinking about the need to balance adequate spending for collective security and the requirements of a sound economy when

Eisenhower was conservative enough to view the nomination of the man widely held to personify standpat Republicanism—Robert A. Taft —with equanimity in terms of domestic policy. The problem, however, was that Taft seemed prepared to lead the Republican party to abandon the Atlantic Alliance and other internationalist policies that Eisen- however deemed essential for national survival.

Just before leaving to command NATO in January 1951, Eisen- hower met with Taft privately in the Pentagon. Eisenhower brought to this meeting a prepared statement in which Taft was to commit him- self broadly to internationalist foreign policy principles and Eisenhower would renounce a candidacy. But when he and Taft could not agree, Eisenhower destroyed the statement and left himself in a position to accept the Republican nomination on the grounds that keeping open the option of seeking nomination was his only weapon against choice by the Republicans in 1952 of an isolationist candidate. As he put it in a 1967 interview:

I wasn't going to remove the threat of possibly becoming a candidate, although I had no idea of ever doing it, I assure you. But I just didn't want to let these people nail me down, neutralize me completely, and then still go their own happy way, one I thought was wrong.

Once Eisenhower was president and Taft was Senate Republican leader, it became clear that Eisenhower's private domestic political convictions were *more* conservative than Taft's, even though through- out the convention and campaign Eisenhower was judged further to the left on the political spectrum than either Taft or the bulk of senior Republicans.* . . .

THE EISENHOWER DICHOTOMIES

Eisenhower the man shaped the distinctive Eisenhower leadership style. His personal makeup was permeated by contrasts. Each element in his makeup has the same duality between what the public saw in him and the private man. As a thinker, the public saw a folksy, common- sense replica of the man on the street. The confidential records show

---

he was chief of staff under Defense Secretary Forrestal. In his diary as early as January 1949 he notes his agreement with Forrestal on the central national security premise that "we must hold our position of strength without bankrupting ourselves." This prepresidential reflection prepared the way for his presidential "New Look" defense policy, which relied on high retaliatory power in order to restrain national security costs.

* In fact, during the six months before Taft's death when the two worked together, Eisenhower resisted such Taft proposals as an aid to education bill, which he ex- plained several years after Taft's death to Ohio Congressman Clarence Brown, was "far more 'liberal and radical' than anything to which I could ever agree." Shortly after Taft died, Eisenhower wrote in his diary, "In some things, I found him ex- traordinarily 'leftish.' This applied specifically to his attitude toward old-age pen- sions. He told me he believed every individual in the United States, upon reaching the age of 65, should automatically go on a minimum pension basis, paid by the Fed- eral government."

a man with extraordinary capacities for detached, orderly examination of problems and personalities. In public he seemed to be removed from the political arena. But the inner Eisenhower reasoned about political contingencies with greater rigor and readiness than many political professionals and drew on a long-standing acquaintance with the labyrinths of national and international governance. His ability to win friends and influence people—both face to face and in the mass—seemed to result simply from the magnetism of his sunny personality. But he worked at his apparent artlessness, consciously choosing strategies that made people want to support him. And on occasion the sunny personality masked anger or despondency, since he viewed it as a duty of the responsible leader to exude optimism.

As president, he conveyed a warm, reassuring presence and presided over a peaceful and reasonably prosperous decade while seeming not to work at it. In fact, he pushed and disciplined himself relentlessly. Finally, his political convictions were more intense than those of many who spend their entire careers in party or elective office. But he curbed his strongly felt conservatism to profess the extent of domestic liberalism that seemed necessary to win his party middle-of-the-road support. And he moderated the harsh side of his cold war world view by taking the lead in making peace initiatives.

This was a man with a striking propensity to establish "space" between his private and public self. While this propensity also characterizes hypocrites, Eisenhower, in no letter, conversation, or diary entry reveals the mark of a hypocrite, if that term is taken to connote contradictory public and private behavior informed by cynicism. Responding to a war correspondent's description of Eisenhower's use of profanity, one letter writer suggested that a supreme commander's language ought to reflect his dependence on divine guidance. Eisenhower expostulated: "Why, dammit, I *am* a religious man!" His private political comments show a similar impatiently intense idealism, as he chafed at politicians and business and labor leaders whom he viewed as too shortsighted to act in the national interest.

Compartmentalizing public and private elements of his personal makeup required considerable effort, self-discipline, and a conception of his duties in which eschewing expression of impolitic impulses was taken for granted as an obligation of responsible leadership. Many of the Eisenhower dichotomies reflect a reassuringly benign-seeming public self and a private one with a well-developed capacity for tough-minded political realism. A personality capable of maintaining this division is perfectly suited for adapting to the contradictory public expectations that the president serve both as uncontroversial chief of state and potentially divisive prime minister. Such a person is also well suited to carry out the organizational procedures necessary to rationalize the official routines of public leadership while maintaining a capacity to develop flexible unofficial means for adapting organizational leadership to the complexities and idiosyncracies of the people he is leading.

Nixon Agonistes: The Checkers Speech

GARRY WILLS

Nixon-watching, like Johnson-watching and Kennedy-watching, has become a minor national pastime. Men who get to be President usually are highly complex people, and political success at any level often requires a certain amount of evasion, what Richard Nixon himself has called being "devious . . . in the best sense." However understandable evasiveness may be, it is ironic that a large amount of the unflattering reputation for deviousness that has accompanied Nixon throughout his political career comes from his famous "Checkers" speech of 1952— a talk given in defense against charges that the candidate had spent campaign funds on personal needs. ("Checkers" was the Nixons' cocker spaniel, an irrelevant animal Nixon dragged into the speech along with his wife's "cloth" coat.) As Garry Wills shows, this was in many ways the most open moment of Nixon's career, an occasion when he was forced to tear aside the veil of privacy which has been his primary way of handling the ferocious demands of public life. Unlike Lyndon Johnson, Richard Nixon is not comfortable before the crowds.

The Checkers speech ushered in the age of television politics. Estes Kefauver, investigating criminals in 1950, had made himself a household name in a series of nationally televised hearings, but he had not tailored the medium to his ends. Nixon was the first politician to realize the immense possibilities of television and to exploit every subtle popular response the new medium could evoke. Intellectuals have always held the Checkers speech in bad odor, seeing in it a disgusting exhibition of bathos and an unvarnished attempt to manipulate public emotions. But Wills details the tensions and political infighting which surged around the vice-presidential candidate during the week preceding the speech. He argues persuasively that the Checkers speech was both Nixon's only chance to save his career and also a direct confrontation with the presidential candidate, Dwight D. Eisenhower.

One other thing I probably should tell you, because if I don't they'll probably be saying this about me too, we did get something—a gift—after the election. A man down in Texas heard Pat on the radio mention the fact that our two youngsters would like to have a dog. And, believe it or not, the day before we left on this campaign trip we got a message from Union Station in Baltimore saying that they had a package for us. We went down to get it. You know what it was? It was a little cocker spaniel dog in a crate that he sent all the way from Texas. Black and white spotted. And our little girl— Tricia, the six-year-old—named it Checkers. And you know the kids love that dog and I just want to say this right now, that regardless of what they say about it, we're going to keep it.—The Checkers Speech

Riding in the staff bus during Nixon's 1968 campaign, I talked with one of his speech writers about the convention in Miami. Nixon's wooing of Strom Thurmond had been much criticized. But Nixon's man now said the acceptance speech eclipsed everything that went before: "That was so clearly the major event of the convention—a brilliant job. To talk about that convention is, simply, to talk about that speech. What did *you* think of it?" I answered that it reminded me of the Checkers speech. The comment seemed to horrify my interlocutor; and Professor Martin Anderson, traveling with Nixon as an adviser on urban matters, turned around in the seat before us to object: "People forget that the Checkers speech was a political master stroke, an act of political genius!" But I had not forgotten: that was, I assured him, my point.

Professor Anderson's defensiveness was understandable. Nixon has often been sneered at, over the years, for his television speech in the campaign of 1952. The very term "Checkers speech," reducing the whole broadcast to its saccharine doggy-passage, is a judgment in itself. But that broadcast saved Nixon's career, and made history. By the beginning of the 1968 campaign, sixteen years later, it was a journalistic commonplace that Nixon did not appear to advantage on television. His wan first TV encounter with John Kennedy had dimmed the public's earlier impression. But Nixon only risked that debate with Kennedy because he had such a record of success on the TV screen: in the history of that medium, his 1952 speech was probably a greater milestone than the presidential debate that came eight years later. Nixon first demonstrated the political uses and impact of television. In one half hour Nixon converted himself from a liability, breathing his last, to one of the few people who could add to Eisenhower's preternatural appeal— who could gild the lily. For the first time, people saw a living political drama on their TV sets—a man fighting for his whole career and future —and they judged him under that strain. It was an even greater achievement than it seemed. He had only a short time to prepare for it. The show, forced on him, was meant as a form of political euthanasia. He came into the studio still reeling from distractions and new demoralizing blows.

Nixon, naturally, puts the Checkers speech, along with the whole "fund crisis," among the six crises he survived with credit. It belongs there. He probably displayed more sheer nerve in that crisis than in any of the others. As a freshman in Congress, he did not stand to lose so much by the Hiss investigation. He had, moreover, an unsuspected hoard of evidence in that encounter; and he was backed by dedicated men like Father Cronin, while backing another dedicated man, Whittaker Chambers. In the crises he deals with after 1952, he was a Vice-President, in some way speaking for the nation, buoyed by its resources, defending it as much as himself; never totally without dignity. But at the time when he went onto the TV screen in 1952, he was hunted and alone. Nine years later he would write of that ordeal, "This speech was to be the most important of my life. I felt now that it was my battle alone. I had been deserted by so many I had thought were friends but who panicked in battle when the first shot was fired." It was, without exaggeration, "the most searing personal crisis of my life." It was also the experience that took the glitter out of politics for Mrs. Nixon. . . .

The first news story broke on Thursday, September 18. There had been warnings in the Nixon camp all the four preceding days. A newsman in Washington asked Nixon about the fund on Sunday. Monday, three other reporters checked facts with Dana Smith, the administrator of the fund. By Wednesday, Jim Bassett, Nixon's press secretary, heard something was brewing from his old reporter friends. The candidate had just begun his first major tour—a whistlestop north through California; when the train stopped for water around midnight, a worried staff man waited with more rumors. Thursday, it broke: the New York *Post* had a story with the headline, SECRET RICH MEN'S TRUST FUND KEEPS NIXON IN STYLE FAR BEYOND HIS SALARY. The story did not justify that sensational summary, and neither did subsequent investigation. The fund was public, independently audited, earmarked for campaign expenses, and collected in small donations over two years by known Nixon campaign backers. It was neither illegal nor unethical. And the press soon discovered that the Democratic nominee, Adlai Stevenson, had similar funds, only larger in their amount and looser in their administration. Why, then, was so much made of Nixon's fund, and so little of Stevenson's?

Nixon's official explanation, at the time, was his standard charge: the commies were behind it all. By Friday morning, the day after the charge was published, there were hecklers at his train stops to shout "Tell us about the sixteen thousand!" At a town called Marysville, he did tell them. His own version of that speech, included in his book, is more moderate than some others; but even his excerpts seem gamy enough: "You folks know the work that I did investigating Communists in the United States. Ever since I have done that work the Communists and the left-wingers have been fighting me with every possible smear. When I received the nomination for the Vice Presidency I was warned that if I continued to attack the Communists in this government they would continue to smear me. And believe me, you can expect that they will continue to do so. They started it yesterday. They have tried to say that I had taken $16,000 for my personal use." The *they* is conveniently vague throughout. They—i.e., the New York *Post* and other papers—published the charge. Go far enough back up the paragraph, through intervening "theys," and you find that the antecedent is, more immediately, "the Communists in this Government," and, in the first place, "Communists and [broad sweep here] left-wingers." The explanation is beautifully lucid and inclusive (if a little unspecific about the machinery that makes the nation's press perform the communists' bidding): since the publicizing or nonpublicizing of fund scandals is at the disposal of communists, who were (naturally) supporting Adlai Stevenson, the Stevenson fund got (naturally) no publicity like that accorded to Nixon.

Behind this funny explanation, there are scattered but clear indications, in his book, of the true story, a sad one. At one point Nixon asks why his own statement of the "basic facts" about the fund received so little attention from the press. His answer ignores the conspiratorial explanation given eight pages earlier, and supplies four reasons, two of them technical (denials never get as big a play as accusations in the press, news travels east to west and he was in California), and two more substantive: reporters are mainly Democrats (though Nixon admits that publishers are mainly Republicans, which makes for some balance), and "the big-name, influential Washington reporters cover the presidential candidates while the less-known reporters are assigned to the vice presidential candidates." The last reason, the real one, looks like another point of newspaper mechanics—the mere logistics of press assignment; until we ask why that should matter. The answer, in Nixon's own words, is that his own press release "got lost in the welter of news and speculation over whether General Eisenhower would or would not choose to find a new running mate." *That* was the news on Eisenhower's train—because Ike's advisers were known to be searching for a way to dump Nixon, and Ike was a man who at this stage followed his advisers almost blindly. In short, the Nixon fund was a big story because Eisenhower, by his silence and hints and uneasiness, made it one. For no other reason.

It was natural for Eisenhower to acquiesce in a staff decision to drop Nixon. That staff had presented him with Nixon in the first place. (Ike's knowledge of his running mate was very slim—he thought, for instance, he was forty-two rather than thirty-nine.) The General had, in fact, learned of Nixon's choice at exactly the same time Nixon did. When Herb Brownell asked Ike what he thought of Nixon, the presidential nominee expressed surprise that the decision was his to make. He said he would leave the matter to Brownell, provided the latter consulted "the collective judgment of the leaders of the party" (the top man, in military politics, protects himself by putting a subordinate in charge of the operation, under staff scrutiny). So Brownell called a meeting of the party's leaders, and went through the form of considering Taft and others. But then Dewey got up, to speak for the winning camp. Nixon he said, and Nixon it was. That decision made, Brownell went to the phone, dialed Nixon, and had him listen in while, on another phone, he told Eisenhower that the choice had been made.

As the fund story broke, Nixon wondered where Ike stood. Thursday went by, and Friday. No word from the General—to the public, or to Nixon. But the Establishment was at work: the very thing that had made Nixon good "for balance" made him unpalatable in himself, seen through Establishment eyes. He was there to draw in the yokels. If there was any doubt about his ability to do that, no one would feel compunction at his loss: Ike was too valuable a property to be risked with anyone who might hurt him. This was the attitude on Eisenhower's train, and it spread to Nixon's as newsmen jumped over from the main tour to watch the death throes in the smaller one. The machinery of execution made itself visible Saturday morning, when the New York *Herald Tribune*—the voice of the Eastern Establishment—asked for Nixon's resignation from the ticket. It was, Nixon realized, an order. The same voice that had summoned him was now dismissing him. A waiting game had been played for three days to see if he would go without having to be ordered, and Nixon had not gone. The Saturday editorial (written Friday), following so close on the *Post*'s revelation, appearing before Nixon had conferred with Eisenhower, was the first of several "hints" that he was not wanted. Despite his studied deference toward Eisenhower, Nixon makes it clear he was not dense: "The publishers and other top officials of the *Tribune* had very close relations with Eisenhower and" (for which read, *I mean*) "with some of his most influential supporters. I assumed that the *Tribune* would not have taken this position editorially unless it also represented the thinking of the people around Eisenhower. And, as I thought more about it, it occurred to me" (the little light bulb above a cartoon character's head—Nixon must play this role straight) "that this might well be read as" (*obviously had to be*) "the view of Eisenhower himself, for I had not heard from him since the trouble began two days before."

At ten o'clock Friday night a reporter told him the next day's *Herald Tribune* would ask him to resign. Nixon, who had not heard this, was stunned. He summoned his closest advisers, Chotiner and Bill Rogers (who would, after more of Nixon's crises, at last be his Secretary of State). These two had received the editorial an hour and a half earlier, but they were not going to tell him about it till morning—afraid he would lose sleep if he saw it (a judgment events confirmed). He asked for the editorial and read: "The proper course of Senator Nixon in the circumstances is to make a formal offer of withdrawal from the ticket." So that was it. Nixon is quite candid here: "I knew now the fat was in the fire. That sounded like the official word from Eisenhower himself." He spent four hours discussing his options with Chotiner and Rogers. Then, at two in the morning, he told his wife, and went through the whole discussion again with her.

The next day, Saturday, three days after the story broke, with newsmen plaguing him for his decision, he had to brace himself for defiance of the Establishment. It was an all-day job. He asked Chotiner and Rogers to get the ultimatum spelled out, if they could, from Ike's inner circle—Chotiner tried to reach Dewey, Rogers called Fred Seaton. They got no direct answer. But the indirect command was growing more insistent; sharper and sharper "hints" were thrown to the public (and, by this roundabout path, to Nixon). Sherman Adams had summoned a man all the way from Hawaii to join the Eisenhower train, and the man was all too obviously a second-string Nixon: Bill Knowland, tough anticommunist and Californian. Eisenhower had finally spoken too, off the record. The newsmen on his train had taken a poll that came out forty-to-two for dumping Nixon; news of this was passed along to Ike's press secretary (Dewey's press man in the last campaign, Jim Hagerty), along with the newsmen's opinion that Ike might be stalling to arrange a whitewash job for Nixon. Ike did not like such talk; it questioned not only Nixon's honesty, but his. He invited the newsmen into his compartment for a talk off the record—but the main part of it was soon made public. "I don't care if you fellows are forty-to-two against me, but I'm taking my time on this. Nothing's decided, contrary to your idea that this is all a setup for a whitewash of Nixon. Nixon has got to be clean as a hound's tooth." Again, Nixon got the point: "Our little group was somewhat[!] dismayed by reports of Eisenhower's attitude.

I must admit it made me feel like the little boy caught with jam on his face."

By Saturday night, then, the issue was clear: knuckle under, or defy the closest thing modern America has had to a political saint. Nixon, here as in all his crises, claims the decision was made on purely selfless grounds: he was thinking of Ike's own welfare—switching men in mid-campaign might make the General unpopular. (This is like worrying that the Milky Way might go out.) Not that Nixon is insincere in his claim. Politicians are very deft at persuading themselves that the world's best interests just happen to coincide with the advancement of their own careers. He says he put the question to his four advisers (Chotiner, Rogers, Bassett, and Congressman Pat Hillings) this way: "Forget about me. If my staying on the ticket would lead to Eisenhower's defeat, I would never forgive myself. If my getting off the ticket is necessary to assure his victory, it would be worth it, as far as any personal embarrassment to me is concerned. Looking at it this way—should I take the initiative and resign from the ticket at this time?"

But Nixon does not feel obliged to present his friends as men crippled by nobility. Chotiner, for instance, plays straight man here, saying all the "natural" things Nixon is too lofty for: "How stupid can they be? If these damned amateurs around Eisenhower just had the sense they were born with they would recognize that this is a purely political attack . . . This whole story has been blown up out of all proportion because of the delay and indecision of the amateurs around Eisenhower." Not even good old Murray, though, blunt fellow as he is, can be described in this book as attacking the Big Man himself—just the little men around him. When Nixon's friends start criticizing Eisenhower, the veil of anonymity must be lowered over them: "But now, some were beginning to blame Eisenhower, for not making a decision one way or the other." Nixon himself would never dream of questioning his leader: "What had happened during the past week had not shaken my faith in Eisenhower. If, as some of my associates thought, he appeared to be indecisive, I put the blame not on him but on his lack of experience in political warfare and on the fact that he was relying on several equally inexperienced associates. I could see his dilemma."

The decision to be made at this session was simple: obey the order relayed by the *Herald Tribune,* or risk disobedience. But, after a full day of campaigning through Oregon, he sat up with his inner circle, in Portland, debating the matter till three in the morning. Then, left alone, he went over the whole thing in his mind for two more hours. By five o'clock Sunday morning, he had set himself on a course he meant never to abandon: he would not resign. Sunday brought blow on blow meant to shake that resolution. First, there was a long telegram from Harold Stassen, still trying to clear some path for himself. He recommended, for Nixon's own good ("it will strengthen you and aid your career"), that a resignation be sent right off to Ike. Then, that afternoon, Dewey called to give Nixon the decision of "all the fellows here in New York." Dewey had a plan for breaking the stalemate caused by Nixon's refusal to resign and Eisenhower's refusal to back him: Nixon must plead his cause before the people. If the response was big enough, he could stay. And when Dewey said big enough, he meant the impossible—near-unanimity. Nixon reports the ultimatum this way: "You will probably get over a million replies, and that will give you three or four days to think it over. At the end of that time, if it is sixty percent for you and forty percent against you, say you are getting out, as that is not enough of a majority. If it is ninety to ten, stay on." It is no wonder Nixon—or, rather, "some of the members of my staff"—felt wary of this offer: "They feared a concerted campaign might be put under way to stack the replies against me." The whole plan was stacked against him. It started with the presumption that Nixon was through, and with feigned generosity gave him a chance to climb back onto the ticket. If Nixon took the offer and (as was expected) lost, then he must abide by the consequences. It was a brilliant way of forcing resignation on a man who was determined not to resign.

Nixon said he would consider it. Chotiner got in touch with Party Chairman Arthur Summerfield, to find out how the broadcast would be handled. Summerfield said they had offers from some TV sponsors to give Nixon one of their spots. Chotiner naturally protested: Nixon could hardly go on the air to defend himself against the charge of being a messenger boy for California businessmen, and explain this on time given him by some large corporation! He told Summerfield the National Committee would have to buy the time, if they expected any show at all. (Money had already been set aside for two half-hour appearances by the vice-presidential candidate. But now Summerfield was in the unfortunate position of not knowing who would be the candidate: if he gave one of the periods to Nixon, and Nixon failed, that left only one spot for his successor. At $75,000 a throw, these were not shows to be granted easily.)

Nixon had to deliver a scheduled speech that night (Sunday) at the Portland Temple Club. He was still considering the TV broadcast when he came back to his hotel. He knew this contest was not what it appeared—Nixon against the press, or the Democrats, or the people. It was Nixon against Ike—a contest that, as Stevenson would learn twice over, no one can expect to win. Candidates simply do not get 90 percent victories in America—and Nixon was being told to produce that figure or get lost. He was asked to do it in circumstances that told against him. Eisenhower had been presented by his managers as the voice of a purgative honesty meant to remedy corruption. The very fact that this arbiter of morals was silent, that Nixon was sent out to argue on his own, was an implied judgment on him. He would be guilty until proved innocent, and he could not call on the one character witness who, in this set of circumstances, mattered.

Meanwhile, the Eisenhower camp had received no answer to its "offer." Now was the time to turn the screw. No escape was to be left him. The phone rang in Portland. Ike. For the first and last time during the crisis. Giving the ultimatum all his personal weight: "I think you ought to go on a nationwide television program and tell them everything there is to tell, everything you can remember since the day you

entered public life. Tell them about any money you have ever received."
The public self-revelation for which Nixon would be blamed in later
years was being forced on him, against all his own inclinations, personal
and political. By temperament and conditioning, Nixon is reserved,
with Quaker insistence on the right of privacy. Nixon's mother, a
woman of tremendous self-control, later said of the Checkers speech:
"At the point when he gave that itemized account of his personal expenditures, I didn't think I could take it."

Nixon asked Eisenhower if he meant to endorse him. The response
was put in a particularly galling way: "If I issue a statement now backing you up, in effect people will accuse me of condoning wrongdoing."
Ike knew, and Nixon knew he knew, that the results of a vast survey of
Nixon's affairs would be available in a matter of hours. This study had
been going on for three days; Sherman Adams, at the outset of the
scandal, called Paul Hoffman, one of the architects of Eisenhower's
candidacy, and ordered a thorough inquest into Nixon's finances. Hoffman went to the best. He put Price Waterhouse to work checking
Nixon's accounts, and the law firm of Gibson, Dunn and Crutcher went
over all legal aspects of the matter. Fifty lawyers and accountants worked
on a round-the-clock basis. The results of this scrutiny were being com-
piled Sunday night. No wrongdoing would be found. The objective
moral evidence would soon be in Eisenhower's hands. But he refused
to make his own judgment based on this evidence. He wanted the people, who could not know as much as he did, to decide whether Nixon
was honest, and he would follow them. The people, meanwhile, were
waiting to hear Ike's decision so they could follow *him*. Nixon was
caught between two juries, each of which was waiting for the other to
reach a verdict before it would move.

He tried to strike a bargain: if Eisenhower was satisfied with the
TV broadcast, would he *at that point* make a decision to endorse
Nixon? (If he did not, then a victory scored on the TV screen would
be subject to attrition, as lingering or renewed doubts worked on a
situation inexplicably unresolved.) But Ike was not making bargains:
he said he would need three or four days (the same period Dewey had
mentioned) for the popular reaction to be accurately gauged—during
which time, Nixon would presumably be stalled in Los Angeles waiting
for the response, his campaign tour all too noticeably suspended. Nixon
finally blew: "There comes a time when you have to piss or get off the
pot!" But Seraphim piss not, neither Cherubim. The great Cherub sat
blithely there, enthroned on his high pot. Nixon sculpts and prettifies
the unyielding refusal: "One of Eisenhower's most notable characteristics is that he is not a man to be rushed on important decisions."

There was nothing he could do now but go ahead with the show.
And if so, the sooner the better. Chotiner was back on the phone getting
clearance for the $75,000. Sherman Adams and Arthur Summerfield
finally yielded that point around midnight. The press corps had been
alerted, an hour before, that there would be an announcement. It was
one o'clock in the morning when Nixon came down; newsmen thought
this must be it—his resignation. He deliberately built up suspense by

saying he was breaking off—tense pause—his campaign tour. To make a statement over television. Two days from now. Tuesday night. He let them think it might still be his resignation he would announce. The more interest he could generate in the next two days, the bigger his audience on Tuesday night.

That was Monday morning. He got little sleep before he boarded a plane for Los Angeles that afternoon; during the flight, he drafted the first of a series of outlines for his talk. In Los Angeles, he got the reports from Price Waterhouse and Gibson, Dunn in time to put their findings in presentable summary. After midnight, he called his old English and history teachers at Whittier College, with a request that they find some suitable Lincoln quotes for the speech. They phoned two quotes to him by ten o'clock that morning—one witty and one maudlin (he used the latter). Nixon walked the streets with Bill Rogers, discussing approaches he might take. He was keyed up, and thought he just might bring it off.

And then the last blow fell. Tuesday, after a mere four hours of sleep, he kept at his outline resolution, as is his way. He did not go to El Capitan Theater to check the TV set or props or lighting; he wanted every minute for his preparation—it was a pattern familiar to those who have watched Nixon key himself up for a crisis by mood-setting spiritual exercises. And then, with less than an hour before he must leave for the studio, the cruel blow came, shattering his schedule, his carefully programmed psychological countdown. It was Dewey on the phone again, with a last demand: "There has been a meeting of all of Eisenhower's top advisers. They have asked me to tell you that it is their opinion that at the conclusion of the broadcast tonight you should submit your resignation to Eisenhower." The Establishment was taking no chances that its scheme might misfire. Nixon asked if that was the word from the General's own mouth. Dewey answered that the men he spoke of would not have commissioned him to make such a call at such an hour unless they were speaking for the master. (But, as usual, Ike was protected: afterward he could write, "Just before the broadcast Governor Dewey telephoned him from New York reporting the conviction of some of my supporters there"—two can play at that "some of the staff" game—"that he should resign, which the young Senator later said he had feared represented my views." Poor Senator, so fearful, so young, so avuncularly cared for in this retrospective benediction. Those who have called Nixon a master of duplicity should contrast his account of the fund crisis with the smoothed-over version in Eisenhower's book, which does not even mention the "hound's tooth" remark.)

Nixon stalled on the line to Dewey, stalled and wriggled. He said it was too late to change his prepared speech. Dewey said he could, of course, deliver his personal defense and accounting; all he had to do was tack on, at the end, a formal resignation offered to Ike. Nixon said he had to leave for the studio. Dewey: "Can I say you have accepted?" Nixon: "You will have to watch the show to see—and tell them I know something about politics too!"

Nixon had a half hour to tell his staff of this new lightning bolt, get their reaction, shower, shave, dress for the show, making meanwhile his own decision—and trying to collect his wits and memory over the notes for his talk. It had been five days full of pressure, sleeplessness, betrayal, ultimatums—climaxed with the most unsettling demand of all, made when he was at a poise of tension and could be knocked off balance so easily. A whole series of crises. Thursday: answer the charges? Friday: dodge newsmen, or face them; rely on the formal answer or return to the defense again and again; stall or throw oneself upon Ike's mercy? Saturday: heed the *Trib* and resign? Sunday: do the TV show? Monday: what to say on the show? And now, at the last minute, Tuesday: defy Dewey (and, through him, Ike)? Already the strain had shown in Nixon. Sunday in Portland, when Hillings brought a wire from Nixon's mother with the Quaker understated promise of prayers WE ARE THINK-ING OF YOU, Nixon broke down and cried. "I thought I had better leave the room," Hillings said, "and give him time to compose himself." Chotiner, busy calling party people to get money for the show, remembered "I was more worried about Dick's state of mind than about the Party. He was edgy and irritable."

Even the inner circle could not tell for sure whether Nixon would stand up to the pressure, or give in while he spoke. After reporting Dewey's call, he was silent, his mind working desperately at the problem. During the twenty-five-minute ride to the studio, he went over his notes (on debater-type cards). He had withdrawn to his last ditch, to make an entirely lone stand there. The one thing he demanded in studio arrangements was that even Chotiner and Rogers be kept out. Only his wife would be present, within camera range, visible to Nixon. It is as if he were dramatizing, to himself more than others, the isolation he stood in at this dying moment of defiance.

One of the criticisms made of Nixon's television speech is that the hoarse voice and hurt face, hovering on the edge of tears, were either histrionic or (if unfeigned) disproportionate and "tasteless." But no one who knows the full story can suspect Nixon of acting, or blame him for the tension he felt and conveyed—it would be like blaming a recently flayed man for "indecent exposure." Nixon was deserted, in more ways than he could tell. And he was fighting back with more nerve than anybody knew. Besides concentrating fiercely on his appeal to the audience, which had to succeed if anything else were to follow, he was reaching out across their heads to touch swords in a secret duel with Ike.

And Eisenhower understood. Stewart Alsop, in his useful little book *Nixon and Rockefeller,* quotes from an interview with one who watched Eisenhower's reactions throughout the TV show. The General had to give a speech in Cleveland as soon as Nixon went off the air; the audience for that talk was watching a large screen in the auditorium, while Eisenhower and thirty of his people clustered by the TV set in a backstage office. Even this entourage, predominantly opposed to Nixon, was touched as the show progressed; some wept openly. But Eisenhower was calm, tapping a yellow pad with his pencil, ready to jot down comments on the speech. He took no notes while the talk was in progress, though the tapping stopped twice. Nixon, forced to act like a criminal who must clear himself, deftly made his actions look like those of a man with nothing to fear. And he issued a challenge: the *other* candidates must have something to fear, unless they followed his example. He devoted much of his half hour to this challenge, dictating terms to his accusers. (It is this part of the speech—moving onto the offensive—that so pleased Chotiner.)

Now I'm going to suggest some courses of conduct.

First of all, you have read in the papers about other funds. Now, Mr. Stevenson, apparently, had a couple—one of them in which a group of business people paid and helped to supplement the salaries of state employees. Here is where the money went directly into their pockets.

I think what Mr. Stevenson should do is come before the American people, as I have, and give the names of the people who have contributed to that fund, and give the names of the people who put this money into their pockets at the same time they were receiving money from their state government, and see what favors, if any, they gave out for that.

I don't condemn Mr. Stevenson for what he did. But, until the facts are in there, a doubt will be raised.

As far as Mr. Sparkman is concerned, I would suggest the same thing. He's had his wife on the payroll. I don't condemn him for that. But I think he should come before the American people and indicate what outside sources of income he has had.

I would suggest that under the circumstances both Mr. Sparkman and Mr. Stevenson should come before the American people, as I have, and make a complete statement as to their financial history. If they don't it will be an admission that they have something to hide. And I think you will agree with me.

Because, remember, a man who's to be President and a man who's to be Vice President must have the confidence of all the people. That's why I'm doing what I'm doing, and that's what I suggest that Mr. Stevenson and Mr. Sparkman, since they are under attack, should be doing.

Eisenhower stopped tapping with his pencil—jabbed it, instead, down into the yellow pad—when Nixon said any candidate who did not reveal his finances must have something to hide. Of course, Nixon did not mention Eisenhower, and his phrase about other candidates joining him "since they are under attack" left a loophole for the General. But the overall force of the passage could not be missed. All candidates, he was arguing, should act as he had. That meant *Eisenhower,* too—as Ike realized, and events were to prove. After this all the candidates did make their statements.

There were reasons why it was inconvenient for Eisenhower to make his books public—e.g., the special tax decision on earnings of his *Crusade in Europe.* Besides, as Alsop delicately puts it, "the military rarely get into the habit of making charitable contributions . . ." More important, Nixon was turning the tables on Ike. Eisenhower had brought him to this revelation. Nixon would force the same hard medicine down his mentor's throat.

Yet an even defter stroke followed. Dewey had been vague on how the speech should be judged. He told Nixon to have telegrams addressed to Los Angeles, and measure the talk's impact by their content. This arrangement, besides tying Nixon down for several days, still left the matter with Eisenhower. The real decision would be made by the General, assessing news reaction. Nixon would be left to play games with his switchboard and his mail, unable to vindicate himself if Eisenhower decided the show had not cleared him.

But when it came time for Nixon to mention the sending of telegrams, he said: "I am submitting to *the Republican National Committee* tonight, through this television broadcast, the decision *it is theirs to make* . . . Wire and write *the Republican National Committee* whether you think I should stay or whether I should get off; and whatever *their decision* is, I will abide by it." (Italics added.) The General stabbed again, pencil into pad, a sword struck down as he fenced that image on the screen, and lost. Nixon has always been a party man; his strength lay there. Karl Mundt and Robert Humphreys, manning the Washington headquarters of the National Committee while Chairman Arthur Summerfield traveled with Ike, had routinely issued statements backing Nixon from the very first day of his troubles. Now, by a cool disarming maneuver, Nixon was taking the matter away from the Eastern Establishment and putting it in the hands of men sympathetic to the regulars, to grassroots workers—people who respond in a partisan way to partisan attacks upon one of their own, people most vulnerable to the planned schmaltz and hominess of the Checkers reference, people with small debts of their own and Republican cloth coats. If the decision was theirs to make, then—the real point of the broadcast as Nixon had reshaped it—*it was not Ike's.* It is no wonder that, while others in Cleveland wept, the man who had directed OVERLORD, the largest military operation in the world's history, the *General,* made an angry stab. He knew enough about maneuver to see he was outflanked. Alsop's informant said: "Before that, I'd always liked and admired Ike, of course, but I'd often wondered how smart he really was. After that, I knew Ike got what Dick was getting at right away."

The importance of that decision, redirecting the appeal to the National Committee, explains Nixon's breakdown when he saw he had gone off the air. Under the pressure of the performance, undertaken without rehearsal, using sketchy notes, he had done something rare for him—missed the countdown toward sign-off by a minute or two: "Time had run out. I was cut off just as I intended to say where the National Committee was located and where the telegrams and letters should be sent." He had based everything on this point; he needed every wire that would reach Washington. What if the telegrams were diffused ineffectually about the country, sent to him, to Ike, to TV channels and local campaign offices? He needed a crushing weight of response all directed to one point, and now (he thought) he would not get it. (The wires in fact did go everywhere, but in such breathtaking numbers that all doubt was swept before them.) He threw his cards to the floor in a spasm, told Pat he had failed; when Chotiner came into the studio, elated by the skilled performance, Nixon just shook his head and claimed, "I was an utter flop." Outside the theater, as his car pulled away, an Irish setter friskily rocked alongside barking: Nixon turned,

Bill Rogers would remember, and twisted out a bitter, "At least I won the dog vote tonight." The end, he thought, of the Checkers speech. He was touching bottom. That night he would finally, after all his earlier resistance, resign.

But it took more kicks and blows to bring him to it. During the first hours after his broadcast, others were jubilant and support poured in; but no call came from the General (a wire had been sent off, but was stuck in the traffic-jam of them at Nixon's hotel switchboard—no one called from the Cleveland camp to give Nixon its message). The first notice he had of the telegram came over the news wires—and it brought word of still another ultimatum. Eisenhower did not often lose wars of attrition. They were his kind of battle.

The crowd waiting for Ike in Cleveland was hoarse with shouts and praise for the TV show they had witnessed. Eisenhower's own first comment was to Chairman Summerfield, about the $75,000: "Well, Arthur, you got your money's worth." Hagerty came back from the auditorium and told Eisenhower he could not deliver his prepared talk on inflation with this crowd. He would have to speak to the Nixon issue. The General knew. He had already chosen his strategy. He fashioned its main lines on the yellow pad, and tried it on his advisers. First, a sop to the crowd: "I like courage . . . Tonight I saw an example of courage . . . I have never seen anyone come through in such a fashion as Senator Nixon did tonight . . . When I get in a fight, I would rather have a courageous and honest man by my side than a whole boxcar full of pussyfooters."

All the praise was a cover, though. Eisenhower was a master of the basics—supply, firepower, and retention of position. After praising Nixon for courage, Ike added that he had not made his mind up on the main subject—whether Nixon would remain on the ticket: "It is obvious that I have to have something more than one single presentation, necessarily limited to thirty minutes, the time allowed Senator Nixon." But if Eisenhower, who had chosen him as his running mate, who had access to the research of the lawyers and accountants, to the advice of top politicians in the party, could not make up his mind after watching the TV show, then how could anyone in the public do so? There is only one explanation for this performance: Ike was determined not to let Nixon take the decision out of his hands. "I am not going to be swayed by my idea of what will get most votes . . . I am going to say: Do I myself believe this man is the kind of man America would like to have for its Vice President?" That is, at one minute he will not be swayed by what the people want and would vote for, and the next minute he is accepting the sacred pledge of finding out what the public wants and will vote for!

Then Eisenhower read them his telegram to Nixon, which shows the real thrust of his remarks: "While technically no decision rests with me, you and I know the realities of the situation require a pronouncement which the public considers decisive." (Or: Get your National Committee support, and see how far it carries you without me.) "My personal decision is going to be based on personal conclusions." (Or: I won't judge you by reaction to your talk—which is what he had promised he *would* do.) "I would most appreciate it if you can fly to see me at once." (Or: Here, Rover.) "Tomorrow evening I will be at Wheeling, W. Va." (Or: Tomorrow *you* will be at Wheeling, W. Va.) Not only was Eisenhower reasserting the personal jurisdiction Nixon had challenged; he wanted a public dramatization of the lines of authority. Having cleared himself with the public, Nixon must appear before a superior tribunal, summoned there to make his defense again, in greater detail, while judgment was pointedly suspended.

Nixon could not submit; yet, once the demand was made public, he could not go further in public defiance, either. He gave in. Rose Woods took down his dictated telegram of resignation.

But he would get in one last blow of his own. The wire was not directed toward Eisenhower, as Dewey had insisted it should be. He addressed it to the National Committee! As Rose Woods went out of the room to send the message, Chotiner followed her and tore off the top sheet of her pad. Rose said she could not have sent it anyway. Nixon is, by his own admission, subject to sharp lapses and lowering of his guard in the emotional depletion that follows on conflict. In four of his book's six crises he finds an example of that pattern: and the example for the fund crisis is his telegram to the National Committee. His loss of grip began the minute the show went off the air and he threw his cards to the floor. " 'What more can he possibly want from me?' I asked . . . I didn't believe I could take any more of the suspense and tension of the past week." Chotiner went to work on him, however, and persuaded him that he could avoid both of the unpalatable things being forced on him—resignation, or compliance with Eisenhower's summons. If he just resumed his interrupted campaign-schedule (next step, Missoula, Montana), the General would have to back down. The wave of public response was already seismic. Nixon reports Chotiner's counsel this way: "Chotiner, particularly, insisted that I not allow myself to be put in the position of going to Eisenhower like a little boy to be taken to the woodshed, properly punished, and then restored to a place of dignity." At this point, there was a call from Ike's camp. Arthur Summerfield, pleased that things had turned out well, was asking for Chotiner—who soon dashed his spirits. Murray said Nixon had just dictated his resignation; he admitted, when Summerfield gasped, that the telegram was torn up—"but I'm not so sure how long it's going to stay torn." Summerfield said things could be smoothed over when Dick reached Wheeling. But Dick was not going to Wheeling: "We're flying to Missoula tonight." Summerfield wanted to know how to head off this disaster—so Chotiner set terms: Nixon will not come unless he is sure of a welcoming endorsement, without further inquisition. This was, of course, a demand that Eisenhower back down on the stated purpose of the summons, which was to go into greater detail than thirty minutes would allow.

Eisenhower, realistic about cutting his losses, saw when this news reached him that the idea of further investigation could not be sustained. He let Summerfield give Nixon's camp the proper assurances.

But Nixon would still be answering a humiliating public call. Just before the plane took off for Missoula, Bert Andrews, who had worked with Nixon all through the Hiss affair, called from the Eisenhower press room in Cleveland: Ike would have no choice now but to receive Nixon warmly; Nixon would have to lose a little face in order to avoid flouting the General's summons. Nixon agreed, and let his staff arrange a flight to Wheeling after the stop at Missoula. Ike was at the airport, to throw his arm around him and call him "my boy"—looking gracious, kind, generous, as if supporting an embattled man rather than picking up strength from a victorious one. The only thing that could resolve the crisis—Ike's blue-eyed smile of benediction—had been bestowed.

But they did not forget the night when they touched swords. There would never be any trust between them. And Nixon had begun a tutelage that would gall him and breed resentment through years of friction and slights.

The Texture of Poverty

MICHAEL HARRINGTON

The poor, Michael Harrington urges us, "need an American Dickens to record the smell and texture and quality of their lives." Yet his own brilliant mixture of reporting and social analysis served the essential purpose of encouraging a compassionate view of the poor, which meant first forcing people to see them. The book remains curiously stirring— what we might expect from a novel, but not from a book which constantly quotes the findings of empirical social science.

The Other America, from which this excerpt by Harrington is taken, was one of several muckraking social-science works that forced a new perspective on poverty in modern America. John Kenneth Galbraith in The Affluent Society *had pointed to the persistence of poverty amid affluence and questioned whether economic growth alone would eradicate it. Robert Lampman and Gabriel Kolko demonstrated that the New Deal had not significantly changed the distribution of wealth. All these writers cleave the path for a new liberal program that, ironically, undermined the claims of older liberals that the New Deal had reformed the economy in the interest of poorer Americans.*

Harrington's book continues to be the most vital of the many polemics that muckraked American society in the late fifties and the sixties. It was an important book because it helped launch a war on poverty which, for all its shortcomings, has made a real difference. For one thing the poor are no longer so invisible or politically powerless. They make themselves known despite official efforts to eliminate the word "poverty" from the national vocabulary. This is not to say that they may never become "invisible" again: The job that Harrington did in the early sixties (like Dickens' a century before) will need constant redoing.

I

There are perennial reasons that make the other America an invisible land.

Poverty is often off the beaten track. It always has been. The ordinary tourist never left the main highway, and today he rides interstate turnpikes. He does not go into the valleys of Pennsylvania where the towns look like movie sets of Wales in the thirties. He does not see the company houses in rows, the rutted roads (the poor always have bad roads whether they live in the city, in towns, or on farms), and everything is black and dirty. And even if he were to pass through such a place by accident, the tourist would not meet the unemployed men in the bar or the women coming home from a runaway sweatshop.

Then, too, beauty and myths are perennial masks of poverty. The traveler comes to the Appalachians in the lovely season. He sees the hills, the streams, the foliage—but not the poor. Or perhaps he looks at a run-down mountain house and, remembering Rousseau rather than seeing with his eyes, decides that "those people" are truly fortunate to be living the way they are and that they are lucky to be exempt from the strains and tensions of the middle class. The only problem is that "those people," the quaint inhabitants of those hills, are undereducated, underprivileged, lack medical care, and are in the process of being forced from the land into a life in the cities, where they are misfits.

These are normal and obvious causes of the invisibility of the poor. They operated a generation ago; they will be functioning a generation hence. It is more important to understand that the very development of American society is creating a new kind of blindness about poverty. The poor are increasingly slipping out of the very experience and consciousness of the nation.

If the middle class never did like ugliness and poverty, it was at least aware of them. "Across the tracks" was not a very long way to go. There were forays into the slums at Christmas time; there were charitable organizations that brought contact with the poor. Occasionally, almost everyone passed through the Negro ghetto or the blocks of tenements, if only to get downtown to work or to entertainment.

Now the American city has been transformed. The poor still inhabit the miserable housing in the central area, but they are increasingly isolated from contact with, or sight of, anybody else. Middle-class women coming in from Suburbia on a rare trip may catch the merest glimpse of the other America on the way to an evening at the theater, but their children are segregated in suburban schools. The business or professional man may drive along the fringes of slums in a car or bus, but it is not an important experience to him. The failures, the unskilled, the disabled, the aged, and the minorities are right there, across the tracks, where they have always been. But hardly anyone else is.

In short, the very development of the American city has removed poverty from the living, emotional experience of millions upon millions of middle-class Americans. Living out in the suburbs it is easy to assume that ours is, indeed, an affluent society.

This new segregation of poverty is compounded by a well-meaning ignorance. A good many concerned and sympathetic Americans are aware that there is much discussion of urban renewal. Suddenly, driving through the city, they notice that a familiar slum has been torn down and that there are towering, modern buildings where once there had been tenements or hovels. There is a warm feeling of satisfaction, of pride in the way things are working out: the poor, it is obvious, are being taken care of.

The irony in this . . . is that the truth is nearly the exact opposite to the impression. The total impact of the various housing programs in postwar America has been to squeeze more and more people into existing slums. More often than not, the modern apartment in a towering building rents at $40 a room or more. For, during the past decade and a half, there has been more subsidization of middle- and upper-income housing than there has been of housing for the poor.

Clothes make the poor invisible too: America has the best-dressed poverty the world has ever known. For a variety of reasons, the benefits of mass production have been spread much more evenly in this area than in many others. It is much easier in the United States to be decently dressed than it is to be decently housed, fed, or doctored. Even people with terribly depressed incomes can look prosperous.

This is an extremely important factor in defining our emotional and existential ignorance of poverty. In Detroit the existence of social classes became much more difficult to discern the day the companies put lockers in the plants. From that moment on, one did not see men in work clothes on the way to the factory, but citizens in slacks and white shirts. This process has been magnified with the poor throughout the country. There are tens of thousands of Americans in the big cities who are wearing shoes, perhaps even a stylishly cut suit or dress, and yet are hungry. It is not a matter of planning, though it almost seems as if the affluent society had given out costumes to the poor so that they would not offend the rest of society with the sight of rags.

Then, many of the poor are the wrong age to be seen. A good number of them (over 8,000,000) are sixty-five years of age or better; an even larger number are under eighteen. The aged members of the other America are often sick, and they cannot move. Another group of them live out their lives in loneliness and frustration: they sit in rented rooms, or else they stay close to a house in a neighborhood that has completely changed from the old days. Indeed, one of the worst aspects of poverty among the aged is that these people are out of sight and out of mind, and alone.

The young are somewhat more visible, yet they too stay close to their neighborhoods. Sometimes they advertise their poverty through a lurid tabloid story about a gang killing. But generally they do not disturb the quiet streets of the middle class.

And finally, the poor are politically invisible. It is one of the cruelest ironies of social life in advanced countries that the dispossessed at the bottom of society are unable to speak for themselves. The people of the other America do not, by far and large, belong to unions, to fraternal organizations, or to political parties. They are without lobbies of their own; they put forward no legislative program. As a group, they are atomized. They have no face; they have no voice. . . .

II

Out of the thirties came the welfare state. Its creation had been stimulated by mass impoverishment and misery, yet it helped the poor least of all. Laws like unemployment compensation, the Wagner Act, the various farm programs, all these were designed for the middle third in the cities, for the organized workers, and for the upper third in the country, for the big market farmers. If a man works in an extremely low-paying job, he may not even be covered by social security or other welfare programs. If he receives unemployment compensation, the payment is scaled down according to his low earnings.

One of the major laws that was designed to cover everyone, rich and poor, was social security. But even here the other Americans suffered discrimination. Over the years social security payments have not even provided a subsistence level of life. The middle third have been able to supplement the Federal pension through private plans negotiated by unions, through joining medical insurance schemes like Blue Cross, and so on. The poor have not been able to do so. They lead a bitter life, and then have to pay for that fact in old age.

Indeed, the paradox that the welfare state benefits those least who need help most is but a single instance of a persistent irony in the other America. Even when the money finally trickles down, even when a school is built in a poor neighborhood, for instance, the poor are still deprived. Their entire environment, their life, their values, do not prepare them to take advantage of the new opportunity. The parents are anxious for the children to go to work; the pupils are pent up, waiting for the moment when their education has complied with the law.

Today's poor, in short, missed the political and social gains of the thirties. They are, as Galbraith rightly points out, the first minority poor in history, the first poor not to be seen, the first poor whom the politicians could leave alone.

The first step toward the new poverty was taken when millions of people proved immune to progress. When that happened, the failure was not individual and personal, but a social product. But once the historic accident takes place, it begins to become a personal fate.

The new poor of the other America saw the rest of society move ahead. They went on living in depressed areas, and often they tended to become depressed human beings. In some of the West Virginia towns, for instance, an entire community will become shabby and defeated. The young and the adventurous go to the city, leaving behind those who cannot move and those who lack the will to do so. The entire area becomes permeated with failure, and that is one more reason the big corporations shy away.

Indeed, one of the most important things about the new poverty is that it cannot be defined in simple, statistical terms. Throughout this book a crucial term is used: aspiration. If a group has internal vitality, a will—if it has aspiration—it may live in dilapidated housing, it may eat an inadequate diet, and it may suffer poverty, but it is not impoverished. So it was in those ethnic slums of the immigrants that played such a dramatic role in the unfolding of the American dream. The people found themselves in slums, but they were not slum dwellers.

But the new poverty is constructed so as to destroy aspiration; it is a system designed to be impervious to hope. The other America does not contain the adventurous seeking a new life and land. It is populated by the failures, by those driven from the land and bewildered by the city, by old people suddenly confronted with the torments of loneliness and poverty, and by minorities facing a wall of prejudice.

In the past, when poverty was general in the unskilled and semiskilled work force, the poor were all mixed together. The bright and the dull, those who were going to escape into the great society and those who were to stay behind, all of them lived on the same street. When the middle third rose, this community was destroyed. And the entire invisible land of the other Americans became a ghetto, a modern poor farm for the rejects of society and of the economy.

It is a blow to reform and the political hopes of the poor that the middle class no longer understands that poverty exists. But, perhaps more important, the poor are losing their links with the great world. If statistics and sociology can measure a feeling as delicate as loneliness (and some of the attempts to do so will be cited later on), the other America is becoming increasingly populated by those who do not belong to anybody or anything. They are no longer participants in an ethnic culture from the old country; they are less and less religious; they do not belong to unions or clubs. They are not seen, and because of that they themselves cannot see. Their horizon has become more and more restricted; they see one another, and that means they see little reason to hope.

Galbraith was one of the first writers to begin to describe the newness of contemporary poverty, and that is to his credit. Yet because even he underestimates the problem, it is important to put his definition into perspective.

For Galbraith, there are two main components of the new poverty: case poverty and insular poverty. Case poverty is the plight of those who suffer from some physical or mental disability that is personal and individual and excludes them from the general advance. Insular poverty exists in areas like the Appalachians or the West Virginia coal fields, where an entire section of the country becomes economically obsolete.

Physical and mental disabilities are, to be sure, an important part of poverty in America. The poor are sick in body and in spirit. But this is not an isolated fact about them, an individual "case," a stroke of bad luck. Disease, alcoholism, low IQ's, these express a whole way of life. They are, in the main, the effects of an environment, not the biographies of unlucky individuals. Because of this, the new poverty is something that cannot be dealt with by first aid. If there is to be a lasting assault on the shame of the other America, it must seek to root out of this society an entire environment, and not just the relief of individuals.

But perhaps the idea of "insular" poverty is even more dangerous. To speak of "islands" of the poor (or, in the more popular term, of "pockets of poverty") is to imply that one is confronted by a serious, but relatively minor, problem. This is hardly a description of a misery that extends to 40,000,000 or 50,000,000 people in the United States. They have remained impoverished in spite of increasing productivity and the creation of a welfare state. That fact alone should suggest the dimensions of a serious and basic situation.

And yet, even given these disagreements with Galbraith, his achievement is considerable. He was one of the first to understand that there are enough poor people in the United States to constitute a subculture of misery, but not enough of them to challenge the conscience and the imagination of the nation.

Finally, one might summarize the newness of contemporary poverty by saying: These are the people who are immune to progress. But then the facts are even more cruel. The other Americans are the victims of the very inventions and machines that have provided a higher living standard for the rest of the society. They are upside-down in the economy, and for them greater productivity often means worse jobs; agricultural advance becomes hunger.

In the optimistic theory, technology is an undisguised blessing. A general increase in productivity, the argument goes, generates a higher standard of living for the whole people. And indeed, this has been true for the middle and upper thirds of American society, the people who made such striking gains in the last two decades. It tends to overstate the automatic character of the process, to omit the role of human struggle. (The CIO was organized by men in conflict, not by economic trends.) Yet it states a certain truth—for those who are lucky enough to participate in it.

But the poor, if they were given to theory, might argue the exact opposite. They might say: Progress is misery.

As the society became more technological, more skilled, those who learn to work the machines, who get the expanding education, move up. Those who miss out at the very start find themselves at a new disadvantage. A generation ago in American life, the majority of the working people did not have high-school educations. But at that time industry was organized on a lower level of skill and competence. And there was a sort of continuum in the shop: the youth who left school at sixteen could begin as a laborer, and gradually pick up skill as he went along.

Today the situation is quite different. The good jobs require much more academic preparation, much more skill from the very outset. Those who lack a high-school education tend to be condemned to the economic underworld—to low-paying service industries, to backward factories, to sweeping and janitorial duties. If the fathers and mothers of the contemporary poor were penalized a generation ago for their lack of schooling, their children will suffer all the more. The very rise in productivity that created more money and better working conditions for the rest of the society can be a menace to the poor.

But then this technological revolution might have an even more disastrous consequence: it could increase the ranks of the poor as well as intensify the disabilities of poverty. At this point it is too early to make any final judgment, yet there are obvious danger signals. There are millions of Americans who live just the other side of poverty. When a recession comes, they are pushed onto the relief rolls. (Welfare payments in New York respond almost immediately to any economic decline.) If automation continues to inflict more and more penalties on the unskilled and the semiskilled, it could have the impact of permanently increasing the population of the other America.

Even more explosive is the possibility that people who participated in the gains of the thirties and the forties will be pulled back down into poverty. Today the mass-production industries where unionization made such a difference are contracting. Jobs are being destroyed. In the process, workers who had achieved a certain level of wages, who had won working conditions in the shop, are suddenly confronted with impoverishment. This is particularly true for anyone over forty years of age and for members of minority groups. Once their job is abolished, their chances of ever getting similar work are very slim.

It is too early to say whether or not this phenomenon is temporary, or whether it represents a massive retrogression that will swell the numbers of the poor. To a large extent, the answer to this question will be determined by the political response of the United States in the sixties. If serious and massive action is not undertaken, it may be necessary for statisticians to add some old-fashioned, pre-welfare-state poverty to the misery of the other America.

Poverty in the 1960's is invisible and it is new, and both these factors make it more tenacious. It is more isolated and politically powerless than ever before. It is laced with ironies, not the least of which is that many of the poor view progress upside-down, as a menace and a threat to their lives. And if the nation does not measure up to the challenge of automation, poverty in the 1960's might be on the increase.

There are mighty historical and economic forces that keep the poor down; and there are human beings who help out in this grim business, many of them unwittingly. There are sociological and political reasons why poverty is not seen; and there are misconceptions and prejudices that literally blind the eyes. The latter must be understood if anyone is to make the necessary act of intellect and will so that the poor can be noticed.

Here is the most familiar version of social blindness: "The poor are that way because they are afraid of work. And anyway they all have big cars. If they were like me (or my father or my grandfather), they could pay their own way. But they prefer to live on the dole and cheat the taxpayers."

This theory, usually thought of as a virtuous and moral statement, is one of the means of making it impossible for the poor ever to pay their way. There are, one must assume, citizens of the other America who choose impoverishment out of fear of work (though, writing it down, I really do not believe it). But the real explanation of why the poor are where they are is that they made the mistake of being born to the wrong parents, in the wrong section of the country, in the wrong industry, or in the wrong racial or ethnic group. Once that mistake has been made, they could have been paragons of will and morality, but most of them would never even have had a chance to get out of the other America.

There are two important ways of saying this: The poor are caught in a vicious circle; or, The poor live in a culture of poverty.

In a sense, one might define the contemporary poor in the United States as those who, for reasons beyond their control, cannot help themselves. All the most decisive factors making for opportunity and advance are against them. They are born going downward, and most of them stay down. They are victims whose lives are endlessly blown round and round the other America.

Here is one of the most familiar forms of the vicious circle of poverty. The poor get sick more than anyone else in the society. That is because they live in slums, jammed together under unhygienic conditions; they have inadequate diets, and cannot get decent medical care. When they become sick, they are sick longer than any other group in the society. Because they are sick more often and longer than anyone else, they lose wages and work, and find it difficult to hold a steady job. And because of this, they cannot pay for good housing, for a nutritious diet, for doctors. At any given point in the circle, particularly when there is a major illness, their prospect is to move to an even lower level and to begin the cycle, round and round, toward even more suffering.

This is only one example of the vicious circle. Each group in the other America has its own particular version of the experience, and these will be detailed throughout this book. But the pattern, whatever its variations, is basic to the other America.

The individual cannot usually break out of this vicious circle. Neither can the group, for it lacks the social energy and political strength to turn its misery into a cause. Only the larger society, with its help and resources, can really make it possible for these people to help themselves. Yet those who could make the difference too often refuse to act because of their ignorant, smug moralisms. They view the effects of poverty—above all, the warping of the will and spirit that is a consequence of being poor—as choices. Understanding the vicious circle is an important step in breaking down this prejudice.

There is an even richer way of describing this same, general idea: Poverty in the United States is a culture, an institution, a way of life.

There is a famous anecdote about Ernest Hemingway and F. Scott Fitzgerald. Fitzgerald is reported to have remarked to Hemingway, "The rich are different." And Hemingway replied, "Yes, they have money." Fitzgerald had much the better of the exchange. He understood that being rich was not a simple fact, like a large bank account, but a way of looking at reality, a series of attitudes, a special type of life. If this is true of the rich, it is ten times truer of the poor. Everything about them, from the condition of their teeth to the way in which they love, is suffused and permeated by the fact of their poverty. And this is sometimes a hard idea for a Hemingway-like middle-class America to comprehend.

The family structure of the poor, for instance, is different from that of the rest of the society. There are more homes without a father, there are less marriage, more early pregnancy and if Kinsey's statistical findings can be used, markedly different attitudes toward sex. As a result of this, to take but one consequence of the fact, hundreds of thousands, and perhaps millions, of children in the other America never know stability and "normal" affection.

Or perhaps the policeman is an even better example. For the middle class, the police protect property, give directions, and help old ladies. For the urban poor, the police are those who arrest you. In almost any slum there is a vast conspiracy against the forces of law and order. If someone approaches asking for a person, no one there will have heard of him, even if he lives next door. The outsider is "cop," bill collector, investigator (and, in the Negro ghetto, most dramatically, he is "the Man").

While writing this book, I was arrested for participation in a civil-rights demonstration. A brief experience of a night in a cell made an abstraction personal and immediate: the city jail is one of the basic in-stitutions of the other America. Almost everyone whom I encountered in the "tank" was poor: skid-row whites, Negroes, Puerto Ricans. Their poverty was an incitement to arrest in the first place. (A policeman will be much more careful with a well-dressed, obviously educated man who might have political connections than he will with someone who is poor.) They did not have money for bail or for lawyers. And, perhaps most important, they waited their arraignment with stolidity, in a mood of passive acceptance. They expected the worst, and they probably got it.

There is, in short, a language of the poor, a psychology of the poor, a world view of the poor. To be impoverished is to be an internal alien, to grow up in a culture that is radically different from the one that dominates the society. The poor can be described statistically; they can be analyzed as a group. But they need a novelist as well as a sociologist if we are to see them. They need an American Dickens to record the smell and texture and quality of their lives. The cycles and trends, the massive forces, must be seen as affecting persons who talk and think differently.

I am not that novelist. Yet in this book I have attempted to de-scribe the faces behind the statistics, to tell a little of the "thickness" of personal life in the other America. Of necessity, I have begun with large groups: the dispossessed workers, the minorities, the farm poor, and the aged. Then, there are three cases of less massive types of poverty, including the only single humorous component in the other America. And finally, there are the slums, and the psychology of the poor.

Throughout, I work on an assumption that cannot be proved by Government figures or even documented by impressions of the other America. It is an ethical proposition, and it can be simply stated: In a nation with a technology that could provide every citizen with a decent life, it is an outrage and a scandal that there should be such social misery. Only if one begins with this assumption is it possible to pierce through the invisibility of 40,000,000 to 50,000,000 human beings and to see the other America. We must perceive passionately, if this blind-ness is to be lifted from us. . . .

III

There are few people in the United States who accept Rousseau's image of the "noble savage," of primitive, untutored man as being more natural than, and superior to, his civilized descendants. Such an idea could hardly survive in a society that has made technological progress one of its most central values. There are occasional daydreams about "getting away from it all," of going to an idyllic countryside, but these are usually passing fancies.

Yet, there is a really important remnant of Rousseau's myth. It is the conviction that, as far as emotional disturbance and mental disease go, the poor are noble savages and the rich are the prime victims of tension and conflict.

There are the literature of the harried executive, the tales of suburban neurosis, the theme of the danger of wealth and leisure. It is not so much that anyone says that the poor are healthy in spirit because they are deprived of material things. Rather, the poor are just forgotten, as usual. The novels and the popular sociology are written by the middle class about the middle class, and there is more than a little strain of self-pity. The result is an image in which personal maladjustment flourishes at the top of the society, the price the well-off pay for their power. As you go down the income scale, this theory implies, life becomes more tedious and humdrum, if less upset. (However, it should be noted that the white-collar strata have the chronicler of their quiet desperation in Paddy Chayevsky.)

The truth is almost exactly opposite to the myth. The poor are subject to more mental illness than anyone else in the society, and their disturbances tend to be more serious than those of any other class. This conclusion has emerged from a series of studies made over the past few decades. There is still considerable controversy and disagreement with regard to the reasons behind this situation. But the fact itself would seem to be beyond dispute.

Indeed, if there is any point in American society where one can see poverty as a culture, as a way of life, it is here. There is, in a sense, a personality of poverty, a type of human being produced by the grinding, wearing life of the slums. The other Americans feel differently than the rest of the nation. They tend to be hopeless and passive, yet prone to bursts of violence; they are lonely and isolated, often rigid and hostile. To be poor is not simply to be deprived of the material things of this world. It is to enter a fatal, futile universe, an America within America with a twisted spirit.

Perhaps the most classic (but still controversial) study of this subject is the book *Social Class and Mental Illness* by August B. Hollingshead and F. C. Redlich. Published in 1958, it summarizes a careful research project in New Haven, Connecticut. It is an academic, scholarly work, yet its statistics are the description of an abyss.

Hollingshead and Redlich divided New Haven into five social classes. At the top (Class I) were the rich, usually aristocrats of family as well as of money. Next came the executives and professionals more newly arrived to prestige and power. Then, the middle class, and beneath them, the workers with decent paying jobs. Class V, the bottom class, was made up of the poor. About half of its members were semi-skilled, about half unskilled. The men had less than six years of education, the women less than eight.

As it turned out, this five-level breakdown was more revealing than the usual three-class image of American society (upper, middle, and lower). For it showed a sharp break between Class V at the bottom and Class IV just above it. In a dramatic psychological sense, the skilled unionized worker lived much, much closer to the middle class than he did to the world of the poor. Between Class IV and Class V, Hollingshead and Redlich found a chasm. This represents the gulf between working America, which may be up against it from time to time but which has a certain sense of security and dignity, and the other America of the poor.

Perhaps the most shocking and decisive statistic that Hollingshead and Redlich found was the one that tabulated the rate of treated psychiatric illness per 100,000 people in New Haven. These are their results:

Classes I and II	556 per 100,000
Class III	538
Class IV	642
Class V	1,659

From the top of society down to the organized workers, there are differences, but relatively small ones. But suddenly, when one crosses the line from Class IV to Class V, there is a huge leap, with the poor showing a rate of treated psychiatric illness of almost three times the magnitude of any other class.

But the mental suffering of the poor in these figures is not simply expressed in gross numbers. It is a matter of quality as well. In Classes I and II, 65 percent of the treated psychiatric illness is for neurotic problems, and only 35 percent for the much graver disturbances of psychoses. But at the bottom, in Class V, 90 percent of the treated illness is for psychosis, and only 10 percent for neurosis. In short, not only the rate but also the intensity of mental illness is much greater for the poor.

One of the standard professional criticisms of Hollingshead and Redlich is that their figures are for treated illness (those who actually got to a doctor or clinic) and do not indicate the "true prevalence" of mental illness in the population. Whatever merits this argument has in relation to other parts of the study, it points up that these particular figures are an understatement of the problem. The higher up the class scale one is, the more likely that there will be recognition of mental illness as a problem and that help will be sought. At the bottom of society, referral to psychiatric treatment usually comes from the courts. Thus, if anything, there is even more mental illness among the poor than the figures of Hollingshead and Redlich indicate.

The one place where this criticism might have some validity is with regard to the intensity of emotional disturbance. Only 10 percent of the poor who received treatment are neurotics, yet the poor neurotic is the least likely person in the society to show up for treatment. He can function, if only in an impaired and maimed way. If there were something done about this situation, it is quite possible that one would find more neurosis in the other America at the same time as one discovered more mental illness generally.

However, it is not necessary to juggle with statistics and explanations in order to corroborate the main drift of the New Haven figures. During the fifties the Cornell University Department of Psychiatry undertook an ambitious study of "Midtown," a residential area in New York City. The research dealt with a population of 170,000 from every social class, 99 percent of them white. (By leaving out the Negroes, there probably was a tendency to underestimate the problem of poverty generally, and the particular disabilities of a discriminated minority in particular.) The goal of the study was to discover "true prevalence," and there was interviewing in depth.

The Cornell scholars developed a measure of "mental health risk." They used a model of three classes, and consequently their figures are not so dramatic as those tabulated in New Haven. Yet they bear out the essential point: the lowest class had a mental health risk almost 40 percent greater than the highest class. Once again the world of poverty was given definition as a spiritual and emotional reality.

The huge brute fact of emotional illness in the other America is fairly well substantiated. The reasons behind the fact are the subject of considerable controversy. There is no neat and simple summary that can be given at the present time, yet some of the analyses are provocative for an understanding of the culture of poverty even if they must be taken tentatively.

One of the most interesting speculations came from the Cornell study of "Midtown" in New York City. The researchers developed a series of "stress factors" that might be related to an individual's mental health risk. In childhood, these were poor mental health on the part of the parents, poor physical health for the parents, economic deprivation, broken homes, a negative attitude on the part of the child toward his parents, a quarrelsome home, and sharp disagreements with parents during adolescence. In adult life, the stress factors were poor health, work worries, money worries, a lack of neighbors and friends, marital worries, and parental worries.

The Cornell team then tested to see if there was any relationship between these factors and mental health. They discovered a marked correlation. The person who had been subjected to thirteen of these stress factors was three times more likely to be mentally disturbed than the person who had felt none of them. Indeed, the researchers were led to conclude that the sheer number of stress factors was more important than the quality of stresses. Those who had experienced any three factors were of a higher mental risk than those who had experienced two.

If the Cornell conclusions are validated in further research, they will constitute an important revision of some widely held ideas about mental health. The Freudian theory has emphasized the earliest years and the decisive trauma in the development of mental illness (for example, the death of a parent). This new theory would suggest a more cumulative conception of mental illness: as stress piles upon stress over a period of time, there is a greater tendency toward disturbance. It would be an important supplement to the Freudian ideas.

But if this theory is right, there is a fairly obvious reason for the emotional torment of the other America. The stress factors listed by the Cornell study are the very stuff of the life of the poor: physical illness, broken homes, worries about work and money, and all the rest. The slum, with its vibrant, dense life hammers away at the individual. And because of the sheer, grinding, dirty experience of being poor, the personality, the spirit, is impaired. It is as if human beings dilapidate along with the tenements in which they live.

However, some scholars have attempted to soften the grimness of this picture with a theory about "drift." The poor, they argue, have a high percentage of disturbed people, not because of the conditions of life in the urban and rural slums, but because this is the group that gets all the outcasts of society from the rest of the classes. If this thesis were true, then one would expect to find failures from the higher classes as a significant group in the culture of the poor.

Hollingshead and Redlich tested this theory in New Haven and did not find any confirmation for it. The mentally impaired poor had been, for the most part, born poor. Their sickness was a product of poverty, instead of their poverty being a product of sickness. Similarly, in the Midtown study, no evidence was turned up to indicate that the disturbed poor were the rejects from other classes. There are some exceptions to this rule: alcoholics, as noted before, often tend to fall from a high position into the bitterest poverty. Still, current research points to a direct relationship between the experience of poverty and emotional disturbance.

And yet, an ironic point turned up in the Midtown research. It was discovered that a certain kind of neurosis was useful to a minority of poor people. The obsessive-compulsive neurotic often got ahead; his very sickness was a means of advancement out of the other America and into the great world. And yet, this might only prepare for a later crisis. On the lower and middle rungs of business society, hard work, attention to detail, and the like are enough to guarantee individual progress. But if such a person moves across the line, and is placed in a position where he must make decisions, there is the very real possibility of breakdown.

IV

Someone in trouble, someone in sorrow, a fight between neighbors, a coffin carried from a house, were things that coloured their lives and shook down fiery blossoms where they walked.—Sean O'Casey

The feelings, the emotions, the attitudes of the poor are different. But different from what? In this question there is an important problem of dealing with the chaotic in the world of poverty.

The definition makers, the social scientists, and the moralists come from the middle class. Their values do not include "a fight between neighbors" as a "fiery blossom." Yet that is the fact in the other America. (O'Casey was talking about Ireland; he might as well have been describing any slum in the United States.) Before going on and exploring the emotional torment of the poor, it would be well to understand this point.

Take the gangs. They are violent, and by middle-class standards they are antisocial and disturbed. But within a slum, violence and disturbance are often norms, everyday facts of life. From the inside of the other America, joining a "bopping" gang may well not seem like deviant behavior. It could be a necessity for dealing with a hostile world. (Once, in a slum school in St. Louis, a teacher stopped a fight between two little girls. "Nice girls don't fight," she told them. "Yeah," one of them replied, "you should have seen my old lady at the tavern last night.")

Indeed, one of the most depressing pieces of research I have ever read touches on this point. H. Warren Dunham carefully studied forty catatonic schizophrenics in Chicago in the early forties. He found that none of them had belonged to gangs or had engaged in the kind of activity the middle class regards as abnormal. They had, as a matter of fact, tried to live up to the standards of the larger society, rather than conforming to the values of the slum. "The catatonic young man can be described as a good boy and one who has all the desirable traits which all the social agencies would like to inculcate in the young men of the community."

The middle class does not understand the narrowness of its judgments. And worse, it acts upon them as if they were universal and accepted by everyone. In New Haven, Hollingshead and Redlich found two girls with an almost identical problem. Both of them were extremely promiscuous, so much so that they eventually had a run-in with the police. When the girl from Class I was arrested, she was provided with bail at once, newspaper stories were quashed, and she was taken care of through private psychotherapy. The girl from Class V was sentenced to reform school. She was paroled in two years, but was soon arrested again and sent to the state reformatory.

James Baldwin made a brilliant and perceptive application of this point to the problem of the Negro in a speech I heard not long ago. The white, he said, cannot imagine what it is like to be Negro: the danger, the lack of horizon, the necessity of always being on guard and watching. For that matter, Baldwin went on, the Negro problem is really the white problem. It is not the Negro who sets dark skin and kinky hair aside as something fearful, but the white. And the resolution of the racial agony in America requires a deep introspection on the part of the whites. They must discover themselves even more than the Negro.

This is true of all the juvenile delinquents, all the disturbed people, in the other America. One can put it baldly: their sickness is often a means of relating to a diseased environment. Until this is understood, the emotionally disturbed poor person will probably go on hurting himself until he becomes a police case. When he is finally given treatment, it will be at public expense, and it will be inferior to that given the rich. (In New Haven, according to Hollingshead and Redlich, the poor are five times more likely to get organic therapy—including shock treatment—rather than protracted, individual professional care.)

For that matter, some of the researchers in the field believe that sheer ignorance is one of the main causes of the high rate of disturbance among the poor. In the slum, conduct that would shock a middle-class neighborhood and lead to treatment is often considered normal. Even if someone is constantly and violently drunk, or beats his wife brutally, people will say of such a person, "Well, he's a little odd." Higher up on the class scale an individual with such a problem would probably realize that something was wrong (or his family would). He will have the knowledge and the money to get help.

One of the researchers in the field who puts great stress on the "basic universals" of the Freudian pattern (mother figure, father figure, siblings) looks upon this factor of ignorance as crucial. He is Dr. Lawrence Kubie. For Dr. Kubie, the fundamental determinants of mental health and illness are the same in every social class. But culture and income and education account for whether the individual will handle his problem; whether he understands himself as sick; whether he seeks help, and so on. This theory leaves the basic assumptions of traditional psychoanalysis intact, but, like any attempt to deal with the poor, it recognizes that something is different.

For the rich, then, and perhaps even for the better-paid worker, breakdowns, neurosis, and psychosis appear as illness and are increasingly treated as such. But the poor do not simply suffer these disturbances; they suffer them blindly. To them it does not appear that they are mentally sick; to them it appears that they are trapped in a fate.

The Feminine Mystique

BETTY FRIEDAN

Women have always been a majority treated like a minority: discriminated against in politics, in schools, and on the job, condescended to in nearly every social relationship, scoffed at for almost every aspiration. It is true that certain benefits have accompanied this second-class citizenship. Millions of women enjoyed the advantage of being discounted as a force in society, took the pleasures of prosperity and apparently paid few of the tangible costs in meaningless work or early death. But women as a group have suffered from a remarkably consistent discrimination, and throughout the industrialized countries they have fought back, winning a place for themselves in the economic, cultural, and political worlds.

But something went wrong in the United States in the twentieth century; while women in other countries increasingly found satisfying careers outside the home, American women seemed to be retreating. More of them worked, but at less demanding or rewarding jobs. And they had more children than their peers in other countries. Safely ensconced in the growing suburbs after World War II, apparently uninterested in politics or a career, they seemed calm and safe—the envy, one assumed, of the world. But they had one problem. "The Problem," Betty Friedan called it, "that has no name": more and more of them were miserable. The bored housewife syndrome became a national parlor game, broadcast through the mass media, discussed in countless living rooms and doubtless in as many bedrooms. Betty Friedan brought the problem into the open in her influential The Feminine Mystique *(1963), a book that heralded a new assertiveness on the part of American women such as had not been seen since the women's suffrage movement.*

In part, this new militancy reflects the general climate of political activism in the 1960's; in part it grows from new opportunities open to women. But clearly much of it is a direct and understandable response to the peculiar circumstances of the postwar era, whose attitude toward woman's role Betty Friedan has captured in vigorous polemic.

In the early 1960's *McCall's* has been the fastest growing of the women's magazines. Its contents are a fairly accurate representation of the image of the American woman presented, and in part created, by the large-circulation magazines. Here are the complete editorial contents of a typical issue of *McCall's* (July, 1960):

1. A lead article on "increasing baldness in women," caused by too much brushing and dyeing.
2. A long poem in primer-size type about a child, called "A Boy Is A Boy."

3. A short story about how a teenager who doesn't go to college gets a man away from a bright college girl.

4. A short story about the minute sensations of a baby throwing his bottle out of the crib.

5. The first of a two-part intimate "up-to-date" account by the Duke of Windsor on "How the Duchess and I now live and spend our time. The influence of clothes on me and vice versa."

6. A short story about a nineteen-year-old girl sent to a charm school to learn how to bat her eyelashes and lose at tennis. ("You're nineteen, and by normal American standards, I now am entitled to have you taken off my hands, legally and financially, by some beardless youth who will spirit you away to a one-and-a-half-room apartment in the Village while he learns the chicanery of selling bonds. And no beardless youth is going to do that as long as you volley to his back-hand.")

7. The story of a honeymoon couple commuting between separate bedrooms after an argument over gambling at Las Vegas.

8. An article on "how to overcome an inferiority complex."

9. A story called "Wedding Day."

10. The story of a teenager's mother who learns how to dance rock-and-roll.

11. Six pages of glamorous pictures of models in maternity clothes.

12. Four glamorous pages on "reduce the way the models do."

13. An article on airline delays.

14. Patterns for home sewing.

15. Patterns with which to make "Folding Screens—Bewitching Magic."

16. An article called "An Encyclopedic Approach to Finding a Second Husband."

17. A "barbecue bonanza," dedicated "to the Great American Mister who stands, chef's cap on head, fork in hand, on terrace or back porch, in patio or backyard anywhere in the land, watching his roast turning on the spit. And to his wife without whom (sometimes) the barbecue could never be the smashing summer success it undoubtedly is . . ."

There were also the regular front-of-the-book "service" columns on new drug and medicine developments, child-care facts, columns by Clare Luce and by Eleanor Roosevelt, and "Pots and Pans," a column of readers' letters.

The image of woman that emerges from this big, pretty magazine is young and frivolous, almost childlike; fluffy and feminine; passive; gaily content in a world of bedroom and kitchen, sex, babies, and home. The magazine surely does not leave out sex; the only passion, the only pursuit, the only goal a woman is permitted is the pursuit of a man. It is crammed full of food, clothing, cosmetics, furniture, and the physical bodies of young women, but where is the world of thought and ideas, the life of the mind and spirit? In the magazine image, women do no work except housework and work to keep their bodies beautiful and to get and keep a man.

This was the image of the American woman in the year Castro led a revolution in Cuba and men were trained to travel into outer space; the year that the African continent brought forth new nations, and a plane whose speed is greater than the speed of sound broke up a Summit Conference; the year artists picketed a great museum in protest against the hegemony of abstract art; physicists explored the concept of anti-matter; astronomers, because of new radio telescopes, had to alter their concepts of the expanding universe; biologists made a breakthrough in the fundamental chemistry of life; and Negro youth in Southern schools forced the United States, for the first time since the Civil War, to face a moment of democratic truth. But this magazine, published for over 5,000,000 American women, almost all of whom have been through high school and nearly half to college, contained almost no mention of the world beyond the home. In the second half of the twentieth century in America, woman's world was confined to her own body and beauty, the charming of man, the bearing of babies, and the physical care and serving of husband, children, and home. And this was no anomaly of a single issue of a single women's magazine.

I sat one night at a meeting of magazine writers, mostly men, who work for all kinds of magazines, including women's magazines. The main speaker was a leader of the desegregation battle. Before he spoke, another man outlined the needs of the large women's magazine he edited:

Our readers are housewives, full time. They're not interested in the broad public issues of the day. They are not interested in national or international affairs. They are only interested in the family and the home. They aren't interested in politics, unless it's related to an immediate need in the home, like the price of coffee. Humor? Has to be gentle, they don't get satire. Travel? We have almost completely dropped it. Education? That's a problem. Their own education level is going up. They've generally all had a high-school education and many, college. They're tremendously interested in education for their children—fourth-grade arithmetic. You just can't write about ideas or broad issues of the day for women. That's why we're publishing 90 per cent service now and 10 per cent general interest.

Another editor agreed, adding plaintively: "Can't you give us something else besides 'there's death in your medicine cabinet'? Can't any of you dream up a new crisis for women? We're always interested in sex, of course."

At this point, the writers and editors spent an hour listening to Thurgood Marshall on the inside story of the desegregation battle, and its possible effect on the presidential election. "Too bad I can't run that story," one editor said. "But you just can't link it to woman's world."

As I listened to them, a German phrase echoed in my mind— "*Kinder, Kuche, Kirche,*" the slogan by which the Nazis decreed that women must once again be confined to their biological role. But this was not Nazi Germany. This was America. The whole world lies open to American women. Why, then, does the image deny the world? Why does it limit women to "one position, one role, one occupation"? Not long ago, women dreamed and fought for equality, their own place in the world. What happened to their dreams; when did women decide to give up the world and go back home?

A geologist brings up a core of mud from the bottom of the ocean and sees layers of sediment as sharp as a razor blade deposited over the years—clues to changes in the geological evolution of the earth so vast that they would go unnoticed during the lifespan of a single man. I sat for many days in the New York Public Library, going back through bound volumes of American women's magazines for the last twenty years. I found a change in the image of the American woman, and in the boundaries of the woman's world, as sharp and puzzling as the changes revealed in cores of ocean sediment.

In 1939, the heroines of women's magazine stories were not always young, but in a certain sense they were younger than their fictional counterparts today. They were young in the same way that the American hero has always been young: they were New Women, creating with a gay determined spirit a new identity for women—a life of their own. There was an aura about them of becoming, of moving into a future that was going to be different from the past. The majority of heroines in the four major women's magazines (then *Ladies' Home Journal, McCall's, Good Housekeeping, Woman's Home Companion*) were career women—happily, proudly, adventurously, attractively career women —who loved and were loved by men. And the spirit, courage, independence, determination—the strength of character they showed in their work as nurses, teachers, artists, actresses, copywriters, saleswomen— were part of their charm. There was a definite aura that their individuality was something to be admired, not unattractive to men, that men were drawn to them as much for their spirit and character as for their looks.

These were the mass women's magazines—in their heyday. The stories were conventional: girl-meets-boy or girl-gets-boy. But very often this was not the major theme of the story. These heroines were usually marching toward some goal or vision of their own, struggling with some problem of work or the world, when they found their man. And this New Woman, less fluffily feminine, so independent and determined to find a new life of her own, was the heroine of a different kind of love story. She was less aggressive in pursuit of a man. Her passionate involvement with the world, her own sense of herself as an individual, her self-reliance, gave a different flavor to her relationship with the man. The heroine and hero of one of these stories meet and fall in love at an ad agency where they both work. "I don't want to put you in a garden behind a wall," the hero says. "I want you to walk with me hand in hand, and together we could accomplish whatever we wanted to" ("A Dream to Share," *Redbook,* January, 1939).

These New Women were almost never housewives; in fact, the stories usually ended before they had children. They were young because the future was open. But they seemed, in another sense, much older, more mature than the childlike, kittenish young housewife heroines today. One, for example, is a nurse ("Mother-in-Law," *Ladies' Home Journal,* June, 1939). "She was, he thought, very lovely. She hadn't an ounce of picture book prettiness, but there was strength in her hands, pride in her carriage and nobility in the lift of her chin, in her blue eyes. She had been on her own ever since she left training, nine years ago. She had earned her way, she need consider nothing but her heart."

One heroine runs away from home when her mother insists she must make her debut instead of going on an expedition as a geologist. Her passionate determination to live her own life does not keep this New Woman from loving a man, but it makes her rebel from her parents; just as the young hero often must leave home to grow up. "You've got more courage than any girl I ever saw. You have what it takes," says the boy who helps her get away ("Have a Good Time, Dear," *Ladies' Home Journal,* May 1939).

Often, there was a conflict between some commitment to her work and the man. But the moral, in 1939, was that if she kept her commitment to herself, she did not lose the man, if he was the right man. A young widow ("Between the Dark and the Daylight," *Ladies' Home Journal,* February, 1939) sits in her office, debating whether to stay and correct the important mistake she has made on the job, or keep her date with a man. She thinks back on her marriage, her baby, her husband's death . . . "the time afterward which held the struggle for clear judgment, not being afraid of new and better jobs, of having confidence in one's decisions." How can the boss expect her to give up her date! But she stays on the job. "They'd put their life's blood into this campaign. She couldn't let him down." She finds her man, too—the boss!

These stories may not have been great literature. But the identity of their heroines seemed to say something about the housewives who, then as now, read the women's magazines. These magazines were not written for career women. The New Woman heroines were the ideal of yesterday's housewives; they reflected the dreams, mirrored the yearning for identity and the sense of possibility that existed for women then. And if women could not have these dreams for themselves, they wanted their daughters to have them. They wanted their daughters to be more than housewives, to go out in the world that had been denied them.

It is like remembering a long-forgotten dream, to recapture the memory of what a career meant to women before "career woman" became a dirty word in America. Jobs meant money, of course, at the end of the depression. But the readers of these magazines were not the women who got the jobs; career meant more than job. It seemed to mean doing something, being somebody yourself, not just existing in and through others.

I found the last clear note of the passionate search for individual identity that a career seems to have symbolized in the pre-1950 decades in a story called "Sarah and the Seaplane," (*Ladies' Home Journal,* February, 1949). Sarah, who for nineteen years has played the part of docile daughter, is secretly learning to fly. She misses her flying lesson to accompany her mother on a round of social calls. An elderly doctor houseguest says: "My dear Sarah, every day, all the time, you are committing suicide. It's a greater crime than not pleasing others, not doing justice to yourself." Sensing some secret, he asks if she is in love. "She found it difficult to answer. In love? In love with the good-natured, the beautiful Henry [the flying teacher]? In love with the flashing water and the lift of wings at the instant of freedom, and the vision of the smiling, limitless world? 'Yes,' she answered, 'I think I am.' "

The next morning, Sarah solos. Henry "stepped away, slamming the cabin door shut, and swung the ship about for her. She was alone. There was a heady moment when everything she had learned left her, when she had to adjust herself to be alone, entirely alone in the familiar cabin. Then she drew a deep breath and suddenly a wonderful sense of competence made her sit erect and smiling. She was alone! She was answerable to herself alone, and she was sufficient.

" 'I can do it!' she told herself aloud. . . . The wind blew back from the floats in glittering streaks, and then effortlessly the ship lifted itself free and soared." Even her mother can't stop her now from getting her flying license. She is not "afraid of discovering my own way of life." In bed that night she smiles sleepily, remembering how Henry had said, "You're my girl."

"Henry's girl! She smiled. No, she was not Henry's girl. She was Sarah. And that was sufficient. And with such a late start it would be some time before she got to know herself. Half in a dream now, she wondered if at the end of that time she would need someone else and who it would be."

And then suddenly the image blurs. The New Woman, soaring free, hesitates in midflight, shivers in all that blue sunlight and rushes back to the cozy walls of home. In the same year that Sarah soloed, the *Ladies' Home Journal* printed the prototype of the innumerable paeans to "Ocupation: Housewife" that started to appear in the women's magazines, paeans that resounded throughout the fifties. They usually begin with a woman complaining that when she has to write "housewife" on the census blank, she gets an inferiority complex. ("When I write it I realize that here I am, a middle-aged woman, with a university education, and I've never made anything out of my life. I'm just a housewife.") Then the author of the paean, who somehow never is a housewife (in this case, Dorothy Thompson, newspaper woman, foreign correspondent, famous columnist, in *Ladies' Home Journal,* March, 1949), roars with laughter. The trouble with you, she scolds, is you don't realize you are expert in a dozen careers, simultaneously. "You might write: business manager, cook, nurse, chauffeur, dressmaker, interior decorator, accountant, caterer, teacher, private secretary—or just put down philanthropist. . . . All your life you have been giving away your energies, your skills, your talents, your services, for love." But still, the housewife complains, I'm nearly fifty and I've never done what I hoped to do in my youth—music—I've wasted my college education.

Ho-ho, laughs Miss Thompson, aren't your children musical because of you, and all those struggling years while your husband was finishing his great work, didn't you keep a charming home on $3,000 a year, and make all your children's clothes and your own, and paper the living room yourself, and watch the markets like a hawk for bargains? And in time off, didn't you type and proofread your husband's manuscripts, plan festivals to make up the church deficit, play piano duets with the children to make practicing more fun, read their books in high-school to follow their study? "But all this vicarious living—through others," the housewife sighs. "As vicarious as Napoleon Bonaparte," Miss Thompson scoffs, "or a Queen. I simply refuse to share your self-pity. You are one of the most successful women I know."

As for not earning any money, the argument goes, let the housewife compute the cost of her services. Women can save more money by their managerial talents inside the home than they can bring into it by outside work. As for woman's spirit being broken by the boredom of household tasks, maybe the genius of some women has been thwarted, but "a world full of feminine genius, but poor in children, would come rapidly to an end. . . . Great men have great mothers."

And the American housewife is reminded that Catholic countries in the Middle Ages "elevated the gentle and inconspicuous Mary into the Queen of Heaven, and built their loveliest cathedrals to 'Notre Dame—Our Lady.' . . . The homemaker, the nurturer, the creator of children's environment is the constant recreator of culture, civilization, and virtue. Assuming that she is doing well that great managerial task and creative activity, let her write her occupation proudly: 'housewife.' "

In 1949, the *Ladies' Home Journal* also ran Margaret Mead's *Male and Female*. All the magazines were echoing Farnham and Lundberg's *Modern Woman: The Lost Sex,* which came out in 1942, with its warning that careers and higher education were leading to the "masculinization of women with enormously dangerous consequences to the home, the children dependent on it and to the ability of the woman, as well as her husband, to obtain sexual gratification."

And so the feminine mystique began to spread through the land, grafted onto old prejudices and comfortable conventions which so easily give the past a stranglehold on the future. Behind the new mystique were concepts and theories deceptive in their sophistication and their assumption of accepted truth. These theories were supposedly so complex that they were inaccessible to all but a few initiates, and therefore irrefutable. It will be necessary to break through this wall of mystery and look more closely at these complex concepts, these accepted truths, to understand fully what has happened to American women.

The feminine mystique says that the highest value and the only commitment for women is the fulfillment of their own femininity. It says that the great mistake of Western culture, through most of its history, has been the undervaluation of this femininity. It says this femininity is so mysterious and intuitive and close to the creation and origin of life that man-made science may never be able to understand it. But however special and different, it is in no way inferior to the nature of man; it may even in certain respects be superior. The mistake, says the mystique, the root of women's troubles in the past is that women envied men, women tried to be like men, instead of accepting their own nature, which can find fulfillment only in sexual passivity, male domination, and nurturing maternal love.

But the new image this mystique gives to American women is the old image: "Occupation: housewife." The new mystique makes the housewife-mothers, who never had a chance to be anything else, the model for all women; it presupposes that history has reached a final and glorious end in the here and now, as far as women are concerned. Beneath the sophisticated trappings, it simply makes certain concrete, finite, domestic aspects of feminine existence—as it was lived by women whose lives were confined, by necessity, to cooking, cleaning, washing, bearing children—into a religion, a pattern by which all women must now live or deny their femininity.

Fulfillment as a woman had only one definition for American women after 1949—the housewife-mother. As swiftly as in a dream, the image of the American woman as a changing, growing individual in a changing world was shattered. Her solo flight to find her own identity was forgotten in the rush for the security of togetherness. Her limitless world shrunk to the cozy walls of home.

The transformation, reflected in the pages of the women's magazines, was sharply visible in 1949 and progressive through the fifties. "Femininity Begins at Home," "It's a Man's World Maybe," "Have Babies While You're Young," "How to Snare a Male," "Should I Stop Work When We Marry?" "Are You Training Your Daughter to be a Wife?" "Careers at Home," "Do Women Have to Talk So Much?" "Why GI's Prefer Those German Girls," "What Women Can Learn from Mother Eve," "Really a Man's World, Politics," "How to Hold On to a Happy Marriage," "Don't Be Afraid to Marry Young," "The Doctor Talks about Breast-Feeding," "Our Baby Was Born at Home," "Cooking to Me is Poetry," "The Business of Running a Home."

By the end of 1949, only one out of three heroines in the women's magazines was a career woman—and she was shown in the act of renouncing her career and discovering that what she really wanted to be was a housewife. In 1958, and again in 1959, I went through issue after issue of the three major women's magazines (the fourth, *Woman's Home Companion,* had died) without finding a single heroine who had a career, a commitment to any work, art, profession, or mission in the world, other than "Occupation: housewife." Only one in a hundred heroines had a job; even the young unmarried heroines no longer worked except at snaring a husband.

These new happy housewife heroines seem strangely younger than the spirited career girls of the thirties and forties. They seem to get younger all the time—in looks, and a childlike kind of dependence. They have no vision of the future, except to have a baby. The only active growing figure in their world is the child. The housewife heroines are forever young, because their own image *ends* in childbirth. Like Peter Pan, they must remain young, while their children grow up with the world. They must keep on having babies, because the feminine mystique says there is no other way for a woman to be a heroine. Here is a typical specimen from a story called "The Sandwich Maker" (*Ladies' Home Journal,* April, 1959). She took home economics in college, learned how to cook, never held a job, and still plays the child bride, though she now has three children of her own. Her problem is money. "Oh, nothing boring, like taxes or reciprocal trade agreements, or foreign aid programs. I leave all that economic jazz to my constitutionally elected representative in Washington, heaven help him."

The problem is her $42.10 allowance. She hates having to ask her husband for money every time she needs a pair of shoes, but he won't trust her with a charge account. "Oh, how I yearned for a little money of my own! Not much, really. A few hundred a year would have done it. Just enough to meet a friend for lunch occasionally, to indulge in extravagantly colored stockings, a few small items, without having to appeal to Charley. But, alas, Charley was right. I had never earned a dollar in my life, and had no idea how money was made. So all I did for a long time was brood, as I continued with my cooking, cleaning, cooking, washing, ironing, cooking."

At last the solution comes—she will take orders for sandwiches from other men at her husband's plant. She earns $52.50 a week, except that she forgets to count costs, and she doesn't remember what a gross is so she has to hide 8,640 sandwich bags behind the furnace. Charley says she's making the sandwiches too fancy. She explains: "If it's only ham on rye, then I'm just a sandwich maker, and I'm not interested. But the extras, the special touches—well, they make it sort of creative." So she chops, wraps, peels, seals, spreads bread, starting at dawn and never finished, for $9.00 net, until she is disgusted by the smell of food, and finally staggers downstairs after a sleepless night to slice a salami for the eight gaping lunch boxes. "It was too much. Charley came down just then, and after one quick look at me, ran for a glass of water." She realizes that she is going to have another baby.

"Charley's first coherent words were 'I'll cancel your lunch orders. You're a mother. That's your job. You don't have to earn money, too.' It was all so beautifully simple! 'Yes, boss,' I murmured obediently, frankly relieved." That night he brings her home a checkbook; he will trust her with a joint account. So she decides just to keep quiet about the 8,640 sandwich bags. Anyhow, she'll have used them up, making sandwiches for four children to take to school, by the time the youngest is ready for college.

The road from Sarah and the seaplane to the sandwich maker was traveled in only ten years. In those ten years, the image of American woman seems to have suffered a schizophrenic split. And the split in the image goes much further than the savage obliteration of career from women's dreams.

In an earlier time, the image of woman was also split in two—the good, pure woman on the pedestal, and the whore of the desires of the flesh. The split in the new image opens a different fissure—the feminine woman, whose goodness includes the desires of the flesh, and the career woman whose evil includes every desire of the separate self. The new feminine morality story is the exorcising of the forbidden career dream, the heroine's victory over Mephistopheles: the devil, first in the form of a career woman, who threatens to take away the heroine's husband or child, and finally, the devil inside the heroine herself, the dream of independence, the discontent of spirit, and even the feeling of a separate identity that must be exorcised to win or keep the love of husband and child.

In a story in *Redbook* ("A Man Who Acted Like a Husband," November, 1957) the child-bride heroine, "a little freckle-faced brunette" whose nickname is "Junior," is visited by her old college roommate. The roommate Kay is "a man's girl, really, with a good head for business . . . she wore her polished mahogany hair in a high chignon, speared with two chopstick affairs." Kay is not only divorced, but she has also left her child with his grandmother while she works in television. This career-woman-devil tempts Junior with the lure of a job to keep her from breast-feeding her baby. She even restrains the young mother from going to her baby when he cries at 2 A.M. But she gets her comeuppance when George, the husband, discovers the crying baby uncovered, in a freezing wind from an open window, with blood running down its cheek. Kay, reformed and repentant, plays hookey from her job to go get her own child and start life anew. And Junior, gloating at the 2 A.M. feeding—"I'm glad, glad, glad I'm just a housewife" starts to dream about the baby, growing up to be a housewife, too.

With the career woman out of the way, the housewife with interests in the community becomes the devil to be exorcised. Even PTA takes on a suspect connotation, not to mention interest in some international cause (see "Almost a Love Affair," *McCall's*, November, 1955). The housewife who simply has a mind of her own is the next to go. The heroine of "I Didn't Want to Tell You" (*McCall's*, January, 1958) is shown balancing the checkbook by herself and arguing with her husband about a small domestic detail. It develops that she is losing her husband to a "helpless little widow" whose main appeal is that she can't "think straight" about an insurance policy or mortgage. The betrayed wife says: "She must have sex appeal and what weapon has a wife against that?" But her best friend tells her: "You're making this too simple. You're forgetting how helpless Tania can be, and how grateful to the man who helps her . . ."

"I couldn't be a clinging vine if I tried," the wife says. "I had a better than average job after I left college and I was always a pretty independent person. I'm not a helpless little woman and I can't pretend to be." But she learns, that night. She hears a noise that might be a burglar; even though she knows it's only a mouse, she calls helplessly to her husband, and wins him back. As he comforts her pretended panic, she murmurs that, of course, he was right in their argument that morning. "She lay still in the soft bed, smiling sweet, secret satisfaction, scarcely touched with guilt."

The end of the road, in an almost literal sense, is the disappearance of the heroine altogether, as a separate self and the subject of her own story. The end of the road is togetherness, where the woman has no independent self to hide even in guilt; she exists only for and through her husband and children.

Coined by the publishers of *McCall's* in 1954, the concept "togetherness" was seized upon avidly as a movement of spiritual significance by advertisers, ministers, newspaper editors. For a time, it was elevated into virtually a national purpose. But very quickly there was sharp social criticism, and bitter jokes about "togetherness" as a substitute for larger human goals—for men. Women were taken to task for making their husbands do housework, instead of letting them pioneer in the nation and the world. Why, it was asked, should men with the capacities of statesmen, anthropologists, physicists, poets, have to wash dishes and diaper babies on weekday evenings or Saturday mornings when they might use those extra hours to fulfill larger commitments to their society?

Significantly, critics resented only that men were being asked to share "woman's world." Few questioned the boundaries of this world for women. No one seemed to remember that women were once thought to have the capacity and vision of statesmen, poets, and physicists. Few saw the big lie of togetherness for women.

Consider the Easter 1954 issue of *McCall's* which announced the new era of togetherness, sounding the requiem for the days when women fought for and won political equality, and the women's magazines "helped you to carve out large areas of living formerly forbidden to your sex." The new way of life in which "men and women in ever-increasing numbers are marrying at an earlier age, having children at an earlier age, rearing larger families and gaining their deepest satisfaction" from their own homes, is one which "men, women and children are achieving together . . . not as women alone, or men alone, isolated from one another, but as a family, sharing a common experience."

The picture essay detailing that way of life is called "a man's place is in the home." It describes, as the new image and ideal, a New Jersey couple with three children in a gray-shingle split-level house. Ed and Carol have "centered their lives almost completely around their children and their home." They are shown shopping at the supermarket, carpentering, dressing the children, making breakfast together. "Then Ed joins the members of his car pool and heads for the office."

Ed, the husband, chooses the color scheme for the house and makes the major decorating decisions. The chores Ed likes are listed: putter around the house, make things, paint, select furniture, rugs and draperies, dry dishes, read to the children and put them to bed, work in the garden, feed and dress and bathe the children, attend PTA meetings, cook, buy clothes for his wife, buy groceries.

Ed doesn't like these chores: dusting, vacuuming, finishing jobs he's started, hanging draperies, washing pots and pans and dishes, picking up after the children, shoveling snow or mowing the lawn, changing diapers, taking the baby-sitter home, doing the laundry, ironing. Ed, of course, does not do these chores.

For the sake of every member of the family, the family needs a head. This means Father, not Mother. . . . Children of both sexes need to learn, recognize and respect the abilities and functions of each sex. . . . He is not just a substitute mother, even though he's ready and willing to do his share of bathing, feeding, comforting, playing. He is a link with the outside world he works in. If in that world he is interested, courageous, tolerant, constructive, he will pass on these values to his children.

There were many agonized editorial sessions, in those days at *McCall's*. "Suddenly, everybody was looking for this spiritual significance in togetherness, expecting us to make some mysterious religious movement out of the life everyone had been leading for the last five years—crawling into the home, turning their backs on the world—but we never could find a way of showing it that wasn't a monstrosity of dullness," a former *McCall's* editor reminisces. "It always boiled down to, goody, goody, goody, Daddy is out there in the garden barbecuing. We put men in the fashion pictures and the food pictures, and even the perfume pictures. But we were stifled by it editorially.

"We had articles by psychiatrists that we couldn't use because they would have blown it wide open: all those couples propping their whole weight on their kids but what else could you do with togetherness but child care? We were pathetically grateful to find anything else where we could show father photographed with mother. Sometimes, we used to wonder what would happen to women, with men taking over the decorating, child care, cooking, all the things that used to be hers alone. But we couldn't show women getting out of the home and having a career. The irony is, what we meant to do was to stop editing for women as women, and edit for the men and women together. We wanted to edit for people, not women."

But forbidden to join man in the world, can women be people? Forbidden independence, they finally are swallowed in an image of such passive dependence that they want men to make the decisions, even in the home. The frantic illusion that togetherness can impart a spiritual content to the dullness of domestic routine, the need for a religious movement to make up for the lack of identity, betrays the measure of women's loss and the emptiness of the image. Could making men share the housework compensate women for their loss of the world? Could vacuuming the living-room floor together give the housewife some mysterious new purpose in life?

In 1956, at the peak of togetherness, the bored editors of *McCall's* ran a little article called "The Mother Who Ran Away." To their amazement, it brought the highest readership of any article they had ever run. "It was our moment of truth," said a former editor. "We suddenly realized that all those women at home with their three and a half children were miserably unhappy."

But by then the new image of American woman, "Occupation:

housewife," had hardened into a mystique, unquestioned and permitting no questions, shaping the very reality is distorted.

By the time I started writing for women's magazines, in the fifties, it was simply taken for granted by editors, and accepted as an immutable fact of life by writers, that women were not interested in politics, life outside the United States, national issues, art, science, ideas, adventure, education, or even their own communities, except where they could be sold through their emotions as wives and mothers.

Politics, for women, became Mamie's clothes and the Nixons' home life. Out of conscience, a sense of duty, the *Ladies' Home Journal* might run a series like "Political Pilgrim's Progress," showing women trying to improve their children's schools and playgrounds. But even approaching politics through mother love did not really interest women, it was thought in the trade. Everyone knew those readership percentages. An editor of *Redbook* ingeniously tried to bring the bomb down to the feminine level by showing the emotions of a wife whose husband sailed into a contaminated area.

"Women can't take an idea, an issue, pure," men who edited the mass women's magazines agreed. "It had to be translated in terms they can understand as women." This was so well understood by those who wrote for women's magazines that a natural childbirth expert submitted an article to a leading woman's magazine called "How to Have a Baby in a Atom Bomb Shelter." "The article was not well written," an editor told me, "or we might have bought it." According to the mystique, women, in their mysterious femininity, might be interested in the concrete biological details of having a baby in a bomb shelter, but never in the abstract idea of the bomb's power to destroy the human race.

Such a belief, of course, becomes a self-fulfilling prophecy. In 1960, a perceptive social psychologist showed me some sad statistics which seemed to prove unmistakably that American women under thirty-five are not interested in politics. "They may have the vote, but they don't dream about running for office," he told me. "If you write a political piece, they won't read it. You have to translate it into issues they can understand—romance, pregnancy, nursing, home furnishings, clothes. Run an article on the economy, or the race question, civil rights, and you'd think that women had never heard of them."

Maybe they hadn't heard of them. Ideas are not like instincts of the blood that spring into the mind intact. They are communicated by education, by the printed word. The new young housewives, who leave high school or college to marry, do not read books, the psychological surveys say. They only read magazines. Magazines today assume women are not interested in ideas. But going back to the bound volumes in the library, I found in the thirties and forties that the mass-circulation magazines like *Ladies' Home Journal* carried hundreds of articles about the world outside the home. "The first inside story of American diplomatic relations preceding declared war"; "Can the U.S. Have Peace After This War?" by Walter Lippmann; "Stalin at Midnight," by Harold Stassen; "General Stilwell Reports on China"; articles about the last days of Czechoslovakia by Vincent Sheean; the persecution of Jews in Germany; the New Deal; Carl Sandburg's account of Lincoln's assassination; Faulkner's stories of Mississippi, and Margaret Sanger's battle for birth control.

In the 1950's they printed virtually no articles except those that serviced women as housewives, or described women as housewives, or permitted a purely feminine identification like the Duchess of Windsor or Princess Margaret. "If we get an article about a woman who does anything adventurous, out of the way, something by herself, you know, we figure she must be terribly aggressive, neurotic," a *Ladies' Home Journal* editor told me. Margaret Sanger would never get in today.

In 1960, I saw statistics that showed that women under thirty-five could not identify with a spirited heroine of a story who worked in an ad agency and persuaded the boy to stay and fight for his principles in the big city instead of running home to the security of a family business. Nor could these new young housewives identify with a young minister, acting on his belief in defiance of convention. But they had no trouble at all identifying with a young man paralyzed at eighteen. ("I regained consciousness to discover that I could not move or even speak. I could wiggle only one finger of one hand." With help from faith and a psychiatrist, "I am now finding reasons to live as fully as possible.")

Does it say something about the new housewife readers that, as any editor can testify, they can identify completely with the victims of blindness, deafness, physical maiming, cerebral palsy, paralysis, cancer, or approaching death? Such articles about people who cannot see or speak or move have been an enduring staple of the women's magazines in the era of "Occupation: housewife." They are told with infinitely realistic detail over and over again, replacing the articles about the nation, the world, ideas, issues, art and science; replacing the stories about adventurous spirited women. And whether the victim is man, woman or child, whether the living death is incurable cancer or creeping paralysis, the housewife reader can identify. . . .

A baked potato is not as big as the world, and vacuuming the living room floor—with or without makeup—is not work that takes enough thought or energy to challenge any woman's full capacity. Women are human beings, not stuffed dolls, not animals. Down through the ages man has known that he was set apart from other animals by his mind's power to have an idea, a vision, and shape the future to it. He shares a need for food and sex with other animals, but when he loves, he loves as a man, and when he discovers and creates and shapes a future different from his past, he is a man, a human being.

This is the real mystery: why did so many American women, with the ability and education to discover and create, go back home again, to look for "something more" in housework and rearing children? For, paradoxically, in the same fifteen years in which the spirited New Woman was replaced by the Happy Housewife, the boundaries of the human world have widened, the pace of world change has quickened, and the very nature of human reality has become increasingly free from biological and material necessity. Does the mystique keep American woman from growing with the world? Does it force her to deny reality, as a woman in a mental hospital must deny reality to believe she is a queen? Does it doom women to be displaced persons, if not virtual schizophrenics, in our complex, changing world?

It is more than a strange paradox that as all professions are finally open to women in America, "career woman" has become a dirty word; that as higher education becomes available to any woman with the capacity for it, education for women has become so suspect that more and more drop out of high school and college to marry and have babies; that as so many roles in modern society become theirs for the taking, women so insistently confine themselves to one role. Why, with the removal of all the legal, political, economic, and educational barriers that once kept woman from being man's equal, a person in her own right, an individual free to develop her own potential, should she accept this new image which insists she is not a person but a "woman," by definition barred from the freedom of human existence and a voice in human destiny?

The feminine mystique is so powerful that women grow up no longer knowing that they have the desires and capacities the mystique forbids. But such a mystique does not fasten itself on a whole nation in a few short years, reversing the trends of a century, without cause. What gives the mystique its power? Why did women go home again?

PART TWO

1960-1973

When John F. Kennedy was inaugurated in 1961, the second youngest man ever elected president replaced what at the time was the oldest man ever to serve in the office. The generation that came of age in the era of World War I was giving way to a new breed shaped by World War II, men like Richard Nixon, Robert McNamara, William Westmoreland, and Barry Goldwater. Kennedy's administration stirred the nation far beyond what any of his policies would have suggested. This generation did not always have fresh perspectives, but it did have a new style.

The new generation paced a hard path: assassinations, domestic disorders, and occasional disastrous foreign adventures obscured its record before its policies had a chance to bear fruit. Many of Kennedy's ideas resulted in legislation only after his death, when Lyndon Johnson pushed his Great Society program through Congress. The 1960's were years of extraordinary self-consciousness. The awareness of self was so encompassing—my people, my generation, my "thing"—that the nation became almost ungovernable in traditional ways. Everyone had to be met directly (the process of "confrontation"), had to be self-directed (black power, women's liberation, student power), yet had to fit into a more crowded and interdependent nation (computerized data banks, tax records, the desire for law and order).

Americans—to their credit—have never been an easy people to govern. This old, near anarchic virtue asserted itself more strongly than ever in the 1960's. The decade ended with accomplishments that would have astonished people of a generation before: the end of legal and de facto racial segregation, widespread government-financed medical and educational services, the longest economic boom in our history, and the landing of men on the moon. Yet it also finished amidst potential chaos, with the legitimacy of nearly every major institution—political parties, churches, universities, corporations, the government itself—deeply eroded.

The year 1968 was the climax of this period, a turning point that did not turn. The young generation seemed to fall into more disarray, the men who depended for inspiration largely on the New Deal vanished from the national political scene, and an administration that described itself as conservative came to power. The new Nixon bureaucrats were another group of hard young men—now growing old—who had come out of World War II. Leading the nation into a new era, they lacked the sharp assertiveness of the previous decade during which John F. Kennedy had announced in his inaugural address the coming into power of a "new generation." Rather, the nation was now ruled by a man long familiar to the electorate, as an anti-Communist crusader in Congress in the 1940's and as Eisenhower's vice president in the 1950's. When Nixon became president in 1969, the war in Vietnam, already the longest in the history of the United States, still dragged on. As Eisenhower had done in the 1950's, Nixon eventually settled a war he had not started, thereby calming a nation too long distracted by political agitation caused by an unpopular foreign war.

The history of the 1950's and 1960's was not repeated. America's involvement in the Vietnam War ended during Nixon's second administration. For the most part, demonstrations ceased after several young people had been shot to death on college campuses. But instead of an expected tranquility following the resolution of the war, a new period of political excitement and constitutional crisis developed. Even before the end of the war in Vietnam, the economy, buffeted by major shifts in world economic relations, entered periods of severe recession. People fretted over the irresponsibility of multinational corporations and economic blackmail by the oil producing nations. The nation entered a crisis of confidence and legitimacy that marked the entire decade of the 1970's.

The John F. Kennedy
Inaugural Address

John F. Kennedy set proud goals for his administration in 1961, promising that "a new generation of Americans" would march forth to do battle with "the common enemies of man: tyranny, poverty, disease and war itself." But the Kennedy administration was to be a brief one —two years and ten months from the "trumpet summons" of the inauguration to the muffled drums and caissons marching slowly up Pennsylvania Avenue in November 1963. This foreshortened story of beginnings and promises, then, is a hard one to interpret. Were the hopes real? Was the vitality an illusion? Was there substance behind the glittering style? Was the New Frontier a beckoning horizon or an armed border, a fresh direction or only a new rhetoric? The answers remain "blowing in the wind"—a phrase directly from the Kennedy era.

Kennedy's inaugural address set the tone for his administration as few such addresses have ever done. The elevation, the magnetic tone of dedication and of hope comes across in the way of words chiseled in granite. Thousands, perhaps millions, of Americans have read these words first spoken on that bitterly cold day in Washington. Yet a close reading of this famous speech reveals subtle counterthemes that suggest possible answers to the questions that were subsequently raised after John F. Kennedy's death: about his place in American history, his administration's continuity, or discontinuity, with his predecessors' policies, and the substance lodged beneath the glittering language. Ask yourself what the various publics listening to this speech would have understood by it. What would a civil rights worker have derived from it? A conservative congressman? A Pentagon policy planner? The Soviet foreign ministry? John F. Kennedy was never easy to evaluate, and his untimely death left a legacy of controversy and unanswered questions surrounding him that history may never resolve.

We observe today not a victory of party but a celebration of freedom— symbolizing an end as well as a beginning—signifying renewal as well as change. For I have sworn before you and Almighty God the same solemn oath our forebears prescribed nearly a century and three quarters ago.

The world is very different now. For man holds in his mortal hands the power to abolish all forms of human poverty and all forms of human life. And yet the same revolutionary beliefs for which our forebears fought are still at issue around the globe—the belief that the rights of man come not from the generosity of the state but from the hand of God.

We dare not forget today that we are the heirs of that first revolution. Let the word go forth from this time and place, to friend and foe alike, that the torch has been passed to a new generation of Americans—born in this century, tempered by war, disciplined by a hard and bitter peace, proud of our ancient heritage—and unwilling to witness or permit the slow undoing of those human rights to which this nation has always been committed, and to which we are committed today at home and around the world.

Let every nation know, whether it wishes us well or ill, that we shall pay any price, bear any burden, meet any hardship, support any friend, oppose any foe to assure the survival and the success of liberty.

This much we pledge—and more.

To those old allies whose cultural and spiritual origins we share, we pledge the loyalty of faithful friends. United, there is little we cannot do in a host of cooperative ventures. Divided, there is little we can do—for we dare not meet a powerful challenge at odds and split asunder.

To those new states whom we welcome to the ranks of the free, we pledge our word that one form of colonial control shall not have passed away merely to be replaced by a far more iron tyranny. We shall not always expect to find them supporting our view. But we shall always hope to find them strongly supporting their own freedom—and to remember that, in the past, those who foolishly sought power by riding the back of the tiger ended up inside.

To those peoples in the huts and villages of half the globe struggling to break the bonds of mass misery, we pledge our best efforts to help them help themselves, for whatever period is required—not because the communists may be doing it, not because we seek their votes, but because it is right. If a free society cannot help the many who are poor, it cannot save the few who are rich.

To our sister republics south of our border, we offer a special pledge —to convert our good words into good deeds—in a new alliance for progress—to assist free men and free governments in casting off the chains of poverty. But this peaceful revolution of hope cannot become the prey of hostile powers. Let all our neighbors know that we shall join with them to oppose aggression or subversion anywhere in the Americas. And let every other power know that this Hemisphere intends to remain the master of its own house.

To that world assembly of sovereign states, the United Nations, our last best hope in an age where the instruments of war have far outpaced the instruments of peace, we renew our pledge of support—to prevent it from becoming merely a forum for invective—to strengthen its shield of the new and the weak—and to enlarge the area in which its writ may run.

Finally, to those nations who would make themselves our adversary, we offer not a pledge but a request: that both sides begin anew the quest for peace, before the dark powers of destruction unleashed by science engulf all humanity in planned or accidental self-destruction.

We dare not tempt them with weakness. For only when our arms are sufficient beyond doubt can we be certain beyond doubt that they will never be employed.

But neither can two great and powerful groups of nations take comfort from our present course—both sides overburdened by the cost of modern weapons, both rightly alarmed by the steady spread of the deadly atom, yet both racing to alter that uncertain balance of terror that stays the hand of mankind's final war.

So let us begin anew—remembering on both sides that civility is not a sign of weakness, and sincerity is always subject to proof. Let us never negotiate out of fear. But let us never fear to negotiate.

Let both sides explore what problems unite us instead of belaboring those problems which divide us.

Let both sides, for the first time, formulate serious and precise proposals for the inspection and control of arms—and bring the absolute power to destroy other nations under the absolute control of all nations.

Let both sides seek to invoke the wonders of science instead of its terrors. Together let us explore the stars, conquer the deserts, eradicate disease, tap the ocean depths and encourage the arts and commerce.

Let both sides unite to heed in all corners of the earth the command of Isaiah—to "undo the heavy burdens . . . [and] let the oppressed go free."

And if a beach-head of cooperation may push back the jungle of suspicion, let both sides join in creating a new endeavor, not a new balance of power, but a new world of law, where the strong are just and the weak secure and the peace preserved.

All this will not be finished in the first one hundred days. Nor will it be finished in the first one thousand days, nor in the life of this Administration, nor even perhaps in our lifetime on this planet. But let us begin.

In your hands, my fellow citizens, more than mine, will rest the final success or failure of our course. Since this country was founded, each generation of Americans has been summoned to give testimony to its national loyalty. The graves of young Americans who answered the call to service surround the globe.

Now the trumpet summons us again—not as a call to bear arms, though arms we need—not as a call to battle, though embattled we are —but a call to bear the burden of a long twilight struggle, year in and year out, "rejoicing in hope, patient in tribulation"—a struggle against the common enemies of man: tyranny, poverty, disease and war itself.

Can we forge against these enemies a grand global alliance, North and South, East and West, that can assure a more fruitful life for all mankind? Will you join in that historic effort?

In the long history of the world, only a few generations have been granted the role of defending freedom in its hour of maximum danger. I do not shrink from this responsibility—I welcome it. I do not believe that any of us would exchange places with any other people or any other generation. The energy, the faith, the devotion which we bring to this endeavor will light our country and all who serve it—and the glow from that fire can truly light the world.

And so, my fellow Americans: ask not what your country can do for you—ask what you can do for your country.

My fellow citizens of the world: ask not what America will do for you, but what together we can do for the freedom of man.

Finally, whether you are citizens of America or citizens of the world, ask of us here the same high standards of strength and sacrifice which we ask of you. With a good conscience our only sure reward, with history the final judge of our deeds, let us go forth to lead the land we love, asking His blessing and His help, but knowing that here on earth God's work must truly be our own.

An Imperial President in Foreign Affairs?

DAVID BURNER

John Fitzgerald Kennedy was one of the most attractive men ever to be President of the United States. He was, Norman Mailer once wrote, "our leading man." His confidence that he could "get the nation moving again," his handsome and stylish wife, photogenic children, and appealing and able associates touched chords in American society that his predecessor Eisenhower, for all the love and respect the General generated, would not have tried to reach. Kennedy was the hero of the new men and women—in the professions, the universities, business and government—who were reaching positions of leadership, a new generation "born in this century."

The discussion here of Kennedy and his presidential term recognizes this elan and its vital—if intangible—effect on American foreign policy. The account that emerges stresses Kennedy's sophisticated and balanced approach to foreign policy crises.

John Kennedy was a foreign policy President. It has been common for the presidency in this century to receive much of its definition from the global events that impinge so dramatically upon it. Kennedy, even among recent Presidents, has been distinctive in the degree of his identification with those events.

That Kennedy, an occasional reader of Ian Fleming's James Bond novels, has been associated with them in the Kennedy image is appropriate to the cold war mentality of his times. Fleming's fiction is about more than an arrogant practitioner of secret war. The violence of his stories notwithstanding, they were early efforts in a spy genre that looked beyond the simplicities of a time when militant Westerners had resolved all the details of international politics into confrontations between a free world and a solid Communist bloc. The antagonists in a Fleming story play a game in which they act for larger forces, but these are shadowy and vary from one tale to the next. James Bond, moreover, is armed with light and dazzling mechanical devices that evoke the increasingly sophisticated technological world of the cold war itself. And this understanding of power and politics found a presidential spokesman in a war hero, the skipper of a small craft, who wanted a quicker, more mobile, more expert military capable of fighting in limited wars. Major General Chester Clifton has remembered: he "made me gather up all [the weapons] we had that might be used for guerrilla warfare. . . . There were about twenty weapons . . . the most recent of them was something that had been invented in 1944. This was 1961."

The "torch has been passed to a new generation of Americans, born in this century, tempered by war, disciplined by a hard and bitter peace"—so go the famous words of the inaugural at the transfer of power from the oldest elected President in the nation's history to the youngest.

The new generation, or much of it, had served under Eisenhower or MacArthur in a war. The claim is now familiar that the war had schooled the Kennedy people, made them quick to react to crisis, impatient with bureaucracy, swift to improvise. After victory in 1945 it must have seemed to the war generation that the world's ills would yield to the competent marshaling of power, and that the United States, the most powerful victor of the war, had the ability and the obligation to shape events. There was another side to the thought of this generation. Elvis Stahr, secretary of the army under Kennedy, reports that the President wished that every military officer would read *The Guns of August,* Barbara Tuchman's account of the world that stumbled into war in 1914. "It is a dangerous illusion," he said at Berkeley on March 23, 1962, "to believe that the policies of the United States, stretching as they do worldwide, under varying and different conditions, can be encompassed in one slogan or one adjective, hard or soft or otherwise." It was a "simple central theme of American foreign policy," Kennedy once said, "to support the independence of nations so that one bloc cannot gain sufficient power to finally overcome us." John Gaddis in *Strategies of Containment* calls this "the most precise public explanation by an American president of what all postwar chief executives had believed, but rarely stated: that the American interest was not to remake the world but to balance power within it." This belief has activist implications if the balancing is carried out in the Kennedy manner, by an incessant watchfulness, an infusing of military or economic aid to one region, an encouragement of progressive reform in another, a neutralization of a dangerous conflict, as in Laos, a development of a swift and versatile military, and the sending forth of a skilled force of Peace Corps volunteers. A world to be balanced and rebalanced, indeed, invites an activity more extensive and exact than a world to be remade once and for all.

"In general," writes the journalist Carey McWilliams, "the liberals Kennedy attracted to Washington were more aggressively anti-Communist than the bureaucrats they replaced." But their anticommunism sought more sophisticated expression than Washington had previously employed. In wanting to renovate the military so that it would be a defter instrument for use in a complex power politics, Kennedy was taking the same position that Generals Maxwell Taylor and Matthew Ridgway had earlier expounded in the Pentagon against the view that we should rely primarily on the nuclear deterrent. The United States, said Taylor, should be able to fight two wars and a half at once. Having retired in 1959, subsequently becoming president of the new Lincoln Center for the Performing Arts, Taylor returned in 1961 as an important adviser. Taylor was a liberal's general. A scholar who could speak several languages, he argues in *The Uncertain Trumpet* against founding national policy simplistically on the threat to use nuclear weapons. During the Berlin crisis of 1961 he was free enough of chauvinism to be able to say, in a note of July 7 to Secretary of State Dean Rusk, that it was not our rights in Berlin but our responsibilities to the West Berliners that mattered. A combination of the warrior, the seasoned critic of force, and the technician in Taylor favored tactical over strategic nuclear weapons, for the incorrect reason that they would produce virtually no fallout or danger to civilians. The Robert McNamaras of the administration, no spokesmen for the rhetoric that equated internal subversion with Soviet troops and negotiation with surrender, were given to the new militancy of surgical antiguerrilla tactics.

The counterforce strategy soon announced by the administration, the plan to prepare our missiles for strikes not at enemy cities but at missile bases, was equally expressive of the technocrat liberal mind. It trusted in the precision of which missile technology is capable, it was supposed to allow for greater flexibility of action, and McNamara apparently sincerely preferred it as more humane than a policy aiming weapons at civilians. In July 1962 Kennedy and McNamara finally equipped overseas nuclear missiles with electronic locks so that their crews could not fire them without information from the government. Advances in missile construction decreed the eventual use of the device, but it was fitting to an administration that looked to technology for power and for the restraint of power. . . .

As President Kennedy seemed to relish elitist competence and aristocratic gesture singly and in compound: his was the administration of experts, of the Special Forces or, as the service was popularly known, the Green Berets. An early plan for training the Green Berets, it seems, projected that troops parachuted into Hungary should be able to talk about the principal Hungarian poets and know the correct words for romance. (James Bond becomes an expert lepidopterist.) The President, who had our remaining PT boats routed to Vietnam, made suggestions for the equipping of the Green Berets, the substitution, for example, of sneakers for heavy combat boots. When the sneakers were found vulnerable to bamboo spikes, he recommended their reinforcement with flexible steel inner soles. He shared fully in the family regard for strength and courage, a regard that made Robert Kennedy respond longingly, on hearing his brother read from a citation for bravery Douglas MacArthur had received in World War I, "I would love to have that said about me." Like James Reston, John was aware of Hemingway's succinct definition of courage, "grace under pressure" (he remarked that it reminded him of a girl he had known). But to locate courage in an expert's or an aristocrat's conduct that is at once resolute and perfectly restrained makes for a precarious balance. The restraint could be the hard part. It has been observed that President Kennedy's fear of appearing weak could tempt him to overreact, as after his first confrontation with Khrushchev about Berlin.

The first days of Kennedy's presidency were a time not of militancy abroad but of domestic reconciliation. In a manner reminiscent of bringing Lyndon Johnson on the presidential ticket for balance, he met with Richard Nixon in Florida after the election. He later appointed Nixon's running mate and Kennedy's 1952 Senate race opponent, Henry Cabot Lodge, Jr., ambassador to South Vietnam. The inaugural address omitted a specific discussion of domestic issues for fear of divisiveness. Kennedy retained staple figures of government, such as Allen Dulles of the Central Intelligence Agency and J. Edgar Hoover of the Federal Bureau of Investigation, and appointed the conservative William McChesney Martin chairman of the Federal Reserve Board.

Robert McNamara, the cost-accounting president of the Ford Motor Company, became secretary of defense. "He really runs, rather than walks," even "running up and down the escalator steps"; so Kennedy's secretary of agriculture Orville Freeman has described McNamara. For secretary of state the President wanted William Fulbright of Arkansas, chairman of the Senate Foreign Relations Committee. He had worked with Fulbright in the Senate and found him capable. Robert Kennedy and others argued against the appointment on the ground that the southerner's civil rights record would make him undesirable to new African countries, while one source recalls that it was the opposition of supporters of Israel, thinking Fulbright too sympathetic to the Arab interest, that kept him from becoming secretary. President Kennedy also passed over Adlai Stevenson, who as early as the middle fifties had called for an end to nuclear testing; Stevenson instead became ambassador to the United Nations. Following the advice of the tough-minded foreign policy experts Robert Lovett and Dean Acheson, Kennedy chose imperturbable Dean Rusk secretary.

For undersecretary of state Kennedy picked a liberal of strong convictions, Chester Bowles. After less than a year, during which he was instrumental in selecting able ambassadors, Bowles was to be eased from his post into an ambassadorship himself. In the discussions preceding the administration's launching of the exiles' invasion of Cuba, Bowles was almost alone in opposition. Beyond that, he was the kind of liberal, in the Stevenson vein, with whom John Kennedy was uncomfortable. But that does not seem to have been the main trouble. A comment in the *Kiplinger Washington Letter* for December 2, 1961, in a discussion of inefficiency in the State Department, suggests a general incompatibility between the government and Bowles's administrative style: "*Bowles made the situation worse* with fireworks of bright *ideas*. . . . That's the real reason he was fired, then kicked upstairs." Kennedy himself confirmed that view in an interview with Robert Estabrook of the *Washington Post. . . .* Bowles was capable of serving as the conscience of the administration. In a letter to Kennedy dated September 30, 1961, he voiced his concern that the government's training of foreign military personnel was neglecting to inculcate "an understanding of the values and practices of a democratic society" and that "our aid programs have woefully underemphasized an integrated attack on poverty and despair." He later wrote Kennedy brilliant memoranda on the dangers of American involvement in Vietnam. Bowles's difficulties were one of few exceptions in remarkably warm relationships between a President and his advisers.

McNamara, a graduate and at one time a teacher at the Harvard Business School; Rusk, a Rhodes scholar and an academician who had published in *Foreign Affairs*; Elvis Stahr, another Rhodes scholar and after his services in Washington president of the University of Indiana; Walt Rostow of Yale University and MIT; McGeorge Bundy, dean of the faculty of arts and science at Harvard; the historian Arthur M. Schlesinger, Jr., a White House adviser; Bowles, an editor of the *Encyclopaedia Britannica*: these were among the people who constituted for the administration virtually a university faculty. . . . It was the right assemblage for a government that gave promise of quickening the scientific, technological, and intellectual instruments of national growth.

Dean Rusk's later connection with the Vietnam War has turned liberals against him, and during Kennedy's presidency his careful steadiness made him unpopular with the Kennedy White House advisers who prized their own bright, quick decisiveness. Rusk had a strong liberal background. Peace advocate before World War II (though also a member of his college ROTC), open opponent of McCarthyism, supporter of Stevenson even in 1960, he belonged to a now almost forgotten company of old-line southern liberals and, when such gestures meant something, once broke a color barrier by going with Ralph Bunche of the United Nations into the officers' mess at the Pentagon. As secretary of state he tried to reestablish the China experts purged in the Red-baiting days, but Robert Kennedy stopped him.

Rostow, Rusk's subordinate, was of a different character. At his worst he was capable of proposing in a note to the President during the Berlin crisis that we increase the risk of armed conflict by probing within Khrushchev's territory. That way both leaders would "share the burden of making sacrifice to avoid nuclear war." (Yet in a memorandum of August 14, 1961, to McGeorge Bundy, Rostow in proposing broad negotiations between the West and the Soviet Union on Germany and Berlin remarked, "This approach requires that the President reverse the bad Western postwar habit of regarding negotiation as a sign of weakness.") Later Kennedy apparently titled Rostow the Air Marshal for his inclination to advocate bombs as answers to our various troubles abroad. But he was a spokesman for peaceful competition with communism through aid for economic development. That idea, along with his notion that the military of the underdeveloped nations could be their hope—providing a leavening of educated and idealistic officers—represents the compound of toughness, progressivism, and trust in trained intelligence that the Kennedy circle expected to dictate foreign policy.

McNamara had a mind as severe and clean as a statistical table, so clean that because of Franklin D. Roosevelt, Jr.'s conduct in the West Virginia primary, McNamara would not countenance the President's making Roosevelt Secretary of the Navy. Once during his days at Ford, McNamara had upset a few of his corporate superiors with a passage in a commencement address at the University of Alabama that seemed to question whether money was a sufficient motive for going into business. "Today progressive taxation places limits on the earning power of the businessman, and hence upon his purely monetary motivation," said McNamara with an engaging innocence. "More and more he draws his incentive from a sense of public responsibility." McNamara would typify the liberal technocrat side of the administration in his pursuit of efficiency and his apparent belief, so his conduct during the Vietnam

War demonstrates, in information gathered by experts. His combination of militancy and respect for complexity represents what cold war liberalism was coming to.

Among the technocrats and new frontiersmen of the administration appeared a figure out of another time and style, New Dealer Adolf A. Berle. He now had a reputation for being a conservative, but it was not illogical for a New Dealer to be well content with American business civilization as the Roosevelt era had modified and confirmed it. But Berle could think like a post-war liberal, faithful to the spirit of New Deal progressivism. He was both a cold warrior and, toward the American continent, at any rate, a supporter of the Democratic left—a formula the New Frontier groped toward. Head of a task force for advising the President-elect on Latin America, Berle presented to Kennedy and Sorensen on January 6, so his diary entry for that day relates, a summary of the report that contains the injunctions: "Stabilization of social revolution at left-of-center. . . . U.S. cannot support dying dictatorships . . . or plutocracies—or any group including Communist parties." A portion of the summary attributed to Berle alone suggests this position on Cuba: "The '26th of July' revolution has the sympathy of U.S. It is incomplete, and should succeed. Castro aborted it; he is now dictatorial obstacle to be removed like Batista." Berle's entries for the years of the Kennedy administration reveal a grumbling hard-liner, complaining late in the fall of 1961 about the failure of the West to require the dismantling of the Berlin Wall—"The evidence coming in now suggests that a little nerve would have stopped the maneuver"—and noting just after the Cuba missile crisis that we had not completely expelled the effective Soviet presence from the island: "A half-done job."

Some of the new administration's mentality quickly revealed itself at the Bay of Pigs. In the Eisenhower years, the Central Intelligence Agency had prepared an invasion force that it believed would bring a Cuban uprising against Fidel Castro. Cuban refugee guerrillas awaited orders on a coffee plantation in a mountainous region of Guatemala. In the campaign debates, Kennedy had come out as the hard-liner on Cuba, implicitly holding the Eisenhower administration responsible for letting Cuba go Communist, while Nixon, the liberal Republican, observed that we were obliged to work within the Organization of American States. Conservative columnists praised Kennedy; liberal commentators lauded Nixon, somewhat inaccurately, for the Vice President knew of the plans for invasion. So Kennedy as President had to make a decision about a scheme that his opponent had needed to shroud with soft language. Several liberals dissented from the plan. Arthur Schlesinger and William Fulbright voiced their objections to the President. Others did not get to make their case: Chester Bowles, intelligence expert Roger Hilsman of the Department of State, and George Kennan, the intellectual architect of the policy of containment. Another set of advisers got through to Kennedy.

Notable among these were the Joint Chiefs of Staff, including Arleigh Burke, the legendary navy chief, whom Kennedy admired. As Kennedy would soon discover, all the chiefs had a habit of favoring belligerent operations. Allen Dulles told him that the probability of success for the act was higher than could have been predicted of the Eisenhower administration's successful intervention of 1954 in Guatemala. In April 1961 Kennedy gave the order for the assault on Cuba.

The landing spot, surrounded by swamps and allowing the rebels no opportunity to retreat to the mountains, was familiar in detail to Castro, for it was his favorite fishing spot. Maps studied for the invasion had little grasslike figures that one CIA participant could recognize as symbols for swamps. The other planners apparently did not possess the useful art of map reading and so could not see that the exiles would be pinched in. "I don't think we fully realized," writes Schlesinger, "that the Escambray Mountains lay *eighty miles* from the Bay of Pigs, across a hopeless tangle of swamps and jungles." He has also noted that one road believed to be important ended in a swamp. The force of 1,400 was challenging an army of 250,000 to 400,000, powerfully equipped by the Soviet Union. The invaders, using old freighters supplied by the United Fruit Company, carried radio equipment and much of their inadequate supply of munitions in a single boat, which was blown up; air cover by the exiles was inadequate. Coral reefs ripped the hulls of some craft. In its spirit the enterprise recalls some of Kennedy's moments in World War II. Yet the President had the restraint not to provide major United States air support. Or perhaps it was not self-restraint but, as Senator George Smathers of Florida has reported Kennedy's telling him, Adlai Stevenson's threat to resign from the ambassadorship to the United Nations. Another possible reason for Kennedy's forbearance was a message from Khrushchev that in the event of a more direct intervention the Soviet Union would take action—perhaps it would be in Berlin or Southeast Asia: "Cuba is not alone," Khrushchev announced. Kennedy's indefatigable champion Schlesinger was later to tell Robert Estabrook that while Eisenhower had contemplated American air and sea support and even American ground forces in a strike against the island, Kennedy had rejected that idea in March, before the invasion. Castro, in any event, destroyed the assault.

Just after the Bay of Pigs an analogy appeared several times in the press between the Russian invasion of Hungary in 1956, intended to protect the Soviet Union's sphere of influence, and the attempt on the part of the United States government to preserve its own international domain. As an exercise in *realpolitik*, the invasion was comparable. It would have been morally comparable only if the Soviets, instead of sending their own troops to kill thousands of Hungarians in order to crush a movement unpleasing to them, had sent in an army of Hungarian exiles, expecting them to rally the people in a coup against a repressive government. In 1961 the Cuban regime had more people in prison than the rightist former government had confined for an equal period, and the treatment of political prisoners was often brutal. Not only former supporters of Batista but anyone at whom the new order took political offense became victims of the mass trials and mass executions of the early days of the Castro regime. Kennedy was acting on one of the most generous, and most naïve, of American cold war beliefs.

He assumed, in effect, that every people in the world wishes to be free in the way that the Western democracies understand freedom: with elected parliaments, a diverse and argumentative press, competing political parties, and a citizenry that conducts itself not by neighborhood committees ruthlessly enforcing ideological orthodoxy but by private choices. It may be that Cuba under Castro is free in ways that it was not before: free from extremes of hunger, disease, illiteracy; free to participate in local forms of self-management. The freedom that Cubans do enjoy, if freedom is the right word, must be preferable to a life of malnutrition and sickness under governments that provide a measure of democratic debate for classes prosperous enough to relish or profit from it. Yet the beliefs that led legions of Americans to expect that nations would be content with nothing less than constitutional, parliamentary, civil libertarian freedom expressed the pride of the West in some of its finest political achievements of recent centuries. Kennedy would have had no patience with the species of radicalism that dismisses the liberties of the Western republics as merely bourgeois. . . .

Using the Bay of Pigs as a reason for acting, Kennedy pressed for an Alliance for Progress, a $10 billion decade-long program of economic aid to Latin America. At Punta del Este in Uruguay during 1962 the alliance committed itself to land and tax reform. Though the administration was never to carry its support for progressivism to the point of abandoning right-wing regimes that promised stability, the plan at its origins was assertively social reformist. Richard Goodwin, one of Kennedy's advisers, was instrumental in fashioning the alliance and worked to make it address political and social problems as well as economics. State Department officials had cooperated with rightist Latin American governments and were repelled when the President, in a speech of March 13, 1961, talked of "revolutionary ideas and efforts." The *alianza,* in Hilsman's words, "is saying a revolution is inevitable in Latin America. If you don't do it peacefully, you'll end up with blood." Juan Bosch, a progressive leader in the Dominican Republic whose politics Lyndon Johnson was to push aside with marines in 1965, has said of the Alliance, "That was the only time the U.S. ever followed a correct policy in Latin America."

Elsewhere as well the administration acted to the left of its defense spending. The Development Loan Fund in 1961 provided more than $1 billion in aid to underdeveloped nations. The administration united diverse foreign aid programs under the Agency for International Development. An objective of AID was counterinsurgency, but its plans for training local police in advanced technology were combined with progressive measures for emergency economic assistance to threatened areas and for technical aid for sanitation and transportation. Yet Congress in 1963, against Kennedy's wishes, sharply cut foreign aid in response to the recommendations of a conservative study group headed by General Lucius Clay that the President himself had appointed. Kennedy's hope had been that the committee would win conservatives to foreign aid, but the plan went askew. In the opinion of John Sherman Cooper, foreign aid benefited little under Kennedy, aside from some additional funds for Latin America. In Africa Kennedy did not seek out the kinds of rightist regimes that over the years have so beguiled us in Latin America. Washington showed no sympathy for the white supremacist government of South Africa and strongly supported the efforts of the United Nations to put down a secessionist movement in Katanga considered to be more friendly to Western neoimperialism than was the new government of the Congo.

It was not, however, these initiatives that preoccupied Kennedy's presidency. More sudden necessities of confrontation and conciliation determined the character of its foreign policy.

A major crisis began in June 1961, when the President went to Vienna—in "excruciating pain," O'Donnell reports, from dislocated muscles at the base of the spine—for a summit conference with Premier Khrushchev. The main object of the Soviet leader was to get a permanent separate status for Communist East Germany. That meant an abrogation of the original agreement among the Allies for a reunification of Germany under free elections. Khrushchev was particularly disturbed at the flow of East Germans through the passage from East to West Berlin, a migration that included much of the professional classes within the Russian satellite and threatened to collapse its economy.

Khrushchev's concern was understandable. Recent history had instructed the Russians to fear a strong Germany, which in this case would mean a strong West Germany with no Eastern European buffer. They feared also a Western thrust into the vulnerable Eastern European corridor that flanks the Soviet Union, a thrust that could come from Germany in alliance with the NATO powers or could follow economic and consequent political chaos in East Germany. The politics of the West German government and the speeches of its politicians had been so provocative that they would disturb any Kremlin government—czarist, Communist, or democratic. Soviet spies had even seen German pilots warming up planes that carried American nuclear weapons. Eisenhower as President, agreeing that Berlin was "abnormal," had proposed negotiating the size of the Western military presence in West Berlin and the uses of the city for West German propaganda and intelligence. Now the premier threatened to sign a separate peace treaty with the East German Communist state unless the Western powers gave him a satisfactory alternative. The American reaction was as understandable as the Soviet position. Years of cold war and Communist ruthlessness toward Eastern Europe had conditioned Americans to an inability to conceive of the Soviet Union as having any foreign policy interests that were defensive rather than aggressive. The Russians, moreover, were tearing up the original Allied plans. That may have been justifiable; conditions and needs change. Yet a generation of commentators excoriates the United States for going against the Geneva accords of 1954 on Vietnam, which Washington had not signed but was obliged not to disrupt, and it is not surprising that in 1961 Americans held Khrushchev to a similar accountability. Khrushchev's designs for a German settlement contemplated making West Berlin a free city under the supervision of the United Nations on condition that East Germans not be allowed egress through it. But the United States feared that a German Communist state would swallow up West Berlin, a possibility that the rights of Berliners and the honor of the Allies made unacceptable.

At Vienna Kennedy argued for the stabilization of the two blocs, while Khrushchev, who was working to insure that Eastern Europe would remain safely closed, insisted that the rest of the world be open to the spread of Communist revolution. The two leaders also discussed a developing confrontation in Laos, where the United States had been supporting a rightist, and the Soviet Union a Communist, faction. On that issue, at any rate, they managed to agree to some disengagement, actually effected later under a troika government composed of the right-wing, the Communist, and a neutral party. But on the overriding issue of Germany Khrushchev and Kennedy went home empty-handed. The meeting is remembered for an ideological argument between the two leaders, one of them by general account having little taste for abstraction, the other a spokesman for a society steeped in the language of ideology.

It was a prelude to some of the sharpest verbal and diplomatic clashes of the cold war. The Soviet Union had its reasons for arrogance. The Bay of Pigs had discredited the United States, and the Soviet space program, after years of spectacular success, had just launched the first of all manned satellites. But who, precisely, was confronting Kennedy? There was Khrushchev himself, possessing something of the belligerence, as well as the hearty good fellowship, of a peasant out of folklore. Yet it is a question how much of the truculence that he was to show throughout the crisis expressed his own personality and how much was for the sake of politics at home. Khrushchev, having presided over the ending of political terror in the Soviet Union and its replacement by a milder and more stable repression, was working to put the economy at the service of the population, while his more chauvinistic opponents, led by V. I. Kozlov, wanted the resources of the economy to flow into the military. Khrushchev's political situation bears a resemblance to that of Dean Acheson, Truman's secretary of state, who had been relentlessly firm toward the Soviet Union even while right-wingers accused him of appeasement. Khrushchev apparently needed to win enough from the West, and to be aggressive enough about winning it, in order to appease or outflank his domestic enemies, just as American politicians have to prove that they are not soft on communism. So Kennedy had to face a country confident in its recent achievements, resolved to settle the German danger, and speaking through a leader whose verbal manner and political troubles made him the image of bellicosity.

The first reactions to Khrushchev's demands were angry. Samuel Beer, head of the Americans for Democratic Action, said in the liberal manner of the time, "The crisis in our affairs is no less serious than that confronting the nation in 1933. Nothing less is at stake than the survival of freedom." Even before Vienna Dean Acheson, calling the Berlin question a "simple contest of wills," had recommended sending a division of American troops on the Autobahn through East Germany to Berlin and had urged Kennedy to declare a national emergency and make it clear that we would fight a nuclear war, if necessary. Since there was nothing to negotiate, a willingness to go to the conference table would be taken as a sign of weakness. After the meeting with Khrushchev, Kennedy seemed to be of like mind with such pugnacious advisers as Acheson. The President believed that Khrushchev was using the German question to probe Western resolve. He demanded a crash civil defense program that led to a popular stir about bomb shelters: the government, reported the *Kiplinger Washington Letter* for July 29, was testing NEAR (National Emergency Alarm Repeater) boxes, to be plugged into household wall outlets, that would receive from a central office warnings of impending attack. The President requested estimates on casualties in the event of nuclear war. Aided by the nation's reaction to the recent launching of a manned Soviet space satellite and possessed of a keen sense of historical event, he began a multibillion dollar effort that aimed at reaching the moon and, as a side effect, quickening the economy. It was in the atmosphere of Vienna and Berlin that he turned to heavy increases in defense spending. On July 25 he proposed a growth in military expenditures and an increase in the armed forces by 217,000 and announced doubled draft calls and a mobilization of 51,000 reserves. "We do not want to fight," he said, "but we have fought before." Berlin was "the great testing place of Western courage and will."

One incident that summer, though, was or seemed to be curiously at odds with the administration's announcements of its resoluteness. The large immediate issue was that of emigration from East Germany. Washington knew that the threat of the economic ruin of the Communist satellite could push the Soviet Union very far. On July 30 William Fulbright, chairman of the Senate Foreign Relations Committee, remarked on television that a Communist closing off of East Berlin might be acceptable. After widespread indignation in Germany, Fulbright retracted his statement. In answer to a question that referred to Fulbright's comments, the President in his press conference of August 10 was noticeably silent on the question of whether the East Germans had a right to free exit. Khrushchev was losing East Germany and could not allow that to happen, Walt Rostow recalls the President's remarking to him early in August. The Premier would have to halt the stream of refugees, perhaps by a wall, Kennedy observed, and he could not stop Khrushchev from doing it, though he could muster the Western alliance for defense of West Berlin. On August 28 an annoyed Kennedy, speaking to Robert Estabrook, was to deny the truth of a story in that day's paper that the closing of the border in Berlin had caught the United States by surprise.

Is it possible that the administration, having recognized how dangerous the situation had become, was giving signals that it would tolerate a sealing off of the passage into West Berlin, signals that could amount to encouragement to the Communists to do so? Then its policy would be a study in the dilemma of how to balance one evil against another. Should history, for example, be more understanding of those realistic antebellum statesmen who to preserve domestic peace would return fugitive slaves to the South? When in August East Germany, acting with the blessing of Khrushchev, began the construction of the Berlin Wall, thereby presenting itself as the sovereign force in an East Berlin in which the four-power arrangement no longer existed, Kennedy responded as though the act was uninvited and an outrage. McGeorge Bundy remembers the President as being surprised by the wall. Probably Fulbright's speculations and Kennedy's lack of response to them had not been meant after all as a message to the Soviet Union. Or perhaps the administration had contemplated something less harsh on the part of the Russians, possibly a negotiated slowing of the migration from the Eastern sector. Or was Kennedy attempting, through belligerent gestures, to reassure West Berliners that their allies would not also abandon them or to warn Khrushchev against trying his luck further?

Kenneth O'Donnell, summing up the remarks his cautious John Kennedy made in the course of the crisis, reports that the President, having read Barbara Tuchman's account of the beginning of World War I, commented, "All wars start from stupidity," and reasoned that it would be especially stupid to risk American lives over the question of access to an Autobahn or over the desire of Germans for unification. "Before I back Khrushchev against the wall, . . . the freedom of all of Western Europe will have to be at stake." Kennedy, according to O'Donnell, remarked "Why should Khrushchev put up a wall if he really intended to seize West Berlin? . . . This is his way out of his predicament. It's not a very nice solution, but a wall is a hell of a lot better than a war." In a memorandum to Bundy that summer the President observed, "I'm somewhat uneasy to have refusal to negotiate become a test of firmness." Kennedy chose a show of force. Aware of the possibility of a confrontation with the Communists, he sent 1,500 troops along the Autobahn from West Germany to West Berlin. Vice President Johnson went to the city to pledge American lives to its defense. To strengthen the confidence of the Berliners the President appointed as his representative to them General Lucius Clay, the determined organizer of the defiant and victorious airlift of 1948. The airlift, the rescue of West Berlin, had been Clay's idea, pressed upon Truman in the face of more conciliatory advice. With reason, the Berliners considered the general their special friend and champion. Yet the wall solved a big problem for the Soviet Union and perhaps a big problem for the United States. It also circumvented the wishes of Khrushchev's domestic enemies for some policy that would force all Berlin into Russian hands, and allowed him to compensate in part for having backed off from his six-month deadline for a separate treaty with East Germany.

But his decision not to press for a fully satisfactory solution must have remained a domestic political problem for him. Kennedy's stridency in his July 25 speech, Khrushchev later remarked to the banker John McCloy, put the premier under great duress from Kremlin militants to resume nuclear testing. His nation lagged behind the United States in nuclear weaponry. On August 30 the Soviet Union announced that it would begin tests. Thereupon a new issue compounded the crisis that Berlin had wrought. Kennedy and Britain's Tory prime minister, Harold Macmillan, appealed to Khrushchev not to set off further nuclear bombs in the air, adding that they would not insist on standard schemes for monitoring tests. The September 15 issue of *Life* carried an article by the President on fallout shelters, a subject that simply in being raised was an expression of militancy. The administration, meanwhile, had to decide on its own policy of nuclear tests. If the Russians really wanted a treaty on the issue, Rusk reasoned at a meeting of the National Security Council, we should not test. But Rusk guessed that they did not, and he argued that the hazards from fallout were minimal beside the hazards that misunderstandings about our nuclear strength might bring. Kennedy expressed concern that fallout might kill even a single person, but Rusk doggedly insisted, "Our security must be the primary consideration." In September Kennedy, angered at the intransigence of the Soviet Union on the issue, began a round of tests. Robert Kennedy's explanation is that his brother, though unenthusiastic about testing, feared that the Soviet Union would perfect an antimissile before we did. Our first explosions were underground. The next spring, after a presidential decision in February, atmospheric testing followed, most spectacularly with the Starfish, which turned the Hawaiian night into day, flashed the skies of Australia, and temporarily altered the Van Allen radiation belt.

Still, even as the tests were threatening to move the two superpowers toward confrontation, their leaders were seeking a formula to avert it. On September 5 the Soviet premier, telling C. L. Sulzberger of the *New York Times* that he would be happy to meet with Kennedy, suggested a resolution of the power struggle between Russia and the West in Laos in return for a settlement of the Berlin crisis. On September 25 before the United Nations, Kennedy made a conciliatory speech. And a letter on September 29 from Khrushchev to the President was part of a long correspondence between them that bypassed the usual institutions of negotiation and may in the end have considerably softened for a time the relations between the two powers. Then, in mid-October there was a tense moment in Berlin. On the border between the Western and the Eastern zones, American and Soviet tanks faced each other after a dispute over what rights the East German authorities had to restrict the movement of Western military between the sectors. The tanks pulled back and the Berlin crisis eased. Robert Estabrook, reflecting on an interview of November 11 with General Clay, recorded the conviction of the President, at odds with Clay, that insistence on the details of Western rights could be unnecessarily provocative.

Clay early in 1962 pleaded for greater authority to make decisions in any future clash; Clay told Dean Rusk that had he been there to take immediate, unilateral action on the ground, he could have stopped the wall. The general wired: "If we fail to exercise [our power] properly, we here are at fault. If we exercise it improperly, almost any error of judgment here can be corrected immediately by the prompt removal of the responsible official." Kennedy, after sending his brother to Berlin, pointedly praised Clay's "coolness" and assured him that his "convictions" were not being "lightly overridden." On another occasion the President told the General, "The clear impression of determination, calmness and unity which we have all sought to convey in recent actions is, I think, a major element in the success which we have had in sustaining our access and making Soviet tactics ineffective." Clay was home by May 1962.

Kennedy's words here come as close as anything to indicating how his handling of the Berlin crisis accorded with the style of a liberal cold warrior—a style presuming that both resolve and restraint, and more particularly a close balancing of the two, are the way of disciplined maturity. And either Kennedy's forbearance or his determination or both could claim at least one result: Khrushchev had withdrawn the deadline for Western assent to a separate East Germany as a condition for our continued access to West Berlin. Was there a victor? The Soviet Union, certainly, had not gotten all it wanted. But during the crisis furious voices had risen in the West, as they have from the beginning of the cold war no matter how strong our actions, complaining of the weakness of the Western posture. Bonn university students had sent Kennedy an umbrella symbolic of British Prime Minister Neville Chamberlain and his appeasement of Hitler at Munich. To such people, doubtless, the West was losing; to Khrushchev's Kremlin opponents, the Soviet Union was being sold out. At the end the superpowers had played out their tests of will, at no cost in blood to either, and with no harmful consequences at the time to anyone except, of course, the East Germans, who no longer could go West.

To a generation accustomed to the Vietnam War or to Reagan's war on Central American leftists, the Berlin crisis is a reminder that in the early years of the cold war the major objective had been to save a burned and broken Europe from Soviet domination. By the time of Kennedy's presidency Western Europe, having long since ceased to be a convalescent, was a powerful economic and military force. Kennedy encouraged Britain to enter into the European Common Market, and since a strengthened Common Market could become tariff-encased against the United States, he asked Congress for legislation, which late in 1962 he obtained, permitting him to bargain for tariff reductions. In 1962, going along with a plan conceived before his presidency, he worked without result for the formation of MLF, a multilateral European and American nuclear force that was supposed to operate within NATO.

The gravest incident of the cold war, however, was to come not in Europe but close to the United States. Earlier in 1962, several months after the United States had stopped altogether the importing of Cuban sugar, Castro had decided to allow the Russians to set up a great military installation on the island. The Soviet leaders secretly began preparing for forty-two medium-range (1,100-mile) ballistic missiles, twenty-four intermediate-range (2,200-mile) missiles—these, as it happened, would never arrive—forty-eight out-of-date bombers, and some 22,000 advisers. Access to the missiles was controlled by electronic locks much like those that Kennedy had installed on our missiles abroad. By October, none or few of the sites yet had the nuclear warheads intended for them. For the first time the Soviet Union was doing what the United States had done many years before. It was installing missiles outside its immediate sphere. Air surveillance revealed the sites as their construction neared completion. Thereupon the Kennedy administration, early in the autumn of 1962, was in the midst of a crisis of immeasurable magnitude.

The incident of the Bay of Pigs, it may be supposed, had given Khrushchev two somewhat contradictory impressions of the United States, both of them invitations to bellicose action: that this country was an adventurist nation against which the Soviet Union would have to fortify itself, and that we knew how to back off and therefore would not overreact to the emplacement of the missiles. It would once again have been to Khrushchev's advantage, moreover, to win a power play so great as to silence the Kremlin right. But why Cuba and the missiles?

One gain from the venture would be the strengthening of Soviet credibility with Cuba. In Moscow Raúl Castro, brother of the Cuban leader, had pleaded for more aid. The island had reason to want aid. By this time the Kennedy administration, obsessed with Cuba, was waging something close to undeclared war. Operation Mongoose it was called. Robert Kennedy championed it. In the course of the early sixties the CIA by one estimate launched hundreds of commando sabotage raids in Cuba involving 2,000 exiles working with 600 of the agency's people. Bombing of Cuban embassies in Latin America and Europe was plotted. Circumstantial evidence, moreover, indicates that both before and after the Bay of Pigs Kennedy, at the insistent nudging of elements in the CIA, had contemplated the assassination of Castro. If so, it is one of the seamiest stories of American foreign policy in recent years, and not because the plotting of an assassination is especially brutal—nations continually effect policies that bring widespread death and suffering—but because it would violate one of the implicit rules of good behavior that keep international relations from being even worse than they are.

Former Florida Senator George Smathers has recounted a conversation with Kennedy that took place after mid-March 1961, when the agency gave toxic pills to a Mafia chief in Miami, a second supply to be delivered in April. The President asked the senator how Latin America would respond to the killing of the Cuban premier. Smathers, answering that the United States would be held accountable, opposed the idea, and Kennedy replied that he was also opposed. The chief of the Cuba desk office of the CIA in 1961 has summed up the impression Richard Bissell passed on to him of a September meeting that year between Bissell and the Kennedy brothers: "They wanted the CIA to get rid of Castro, and they meant *get rid of Castro*." In a talk with a *New York Times* reporter in November, at a period when the CIA was again in touch with the Mafia on the matter, the President had a near repeat of his conversation with Smathers, asking for an opinion of Castro's assassination and then again, perhaps for the record, rejecting the idea. Whether or not the President was at odds with himself on the idea of assassination, in January 1962 he said of the removal of Castro, reports Thomas Powers, CIA officer at the time, "It's got to be done and will be done." McNamara once openly suggested Castro's assassination. Castro was a continuing preoccupation of the government. By the time of the missiles the CIA had been deeply involved in Operation Mongoose. Robert Kennedy, it seems, was angry at the CIA scheme for eliminating Castro, but what angered the purist and crime-fighting Bobby was the use of the Mafia. And whoever may have been behind them, in the middle seventies a select editorial committee chaired by Frank Church of Idaho was to document eight attempts on Castro.

In face even of the administration's overt sentiments about the island regime, the missiles could have appeared to Soviet and Cuban minds as defensive, rescuing Cuba from the threat of an invasion from the north. What Khrushchev actually did, it would turn out, was to rescue the United States, as Norman Mailer observes, from the moral disadvantage the Bay of Pigs had put us in.

The larger reason for installing missiles was that however much they might actually increase relative Soviet power at a time when additions to the destructive capability of nuclear weapons were becoming meaningless, they would at least add to the look of Soviet military might. Khrushchev's memoirs describe the venture as an attempt to establish a balance of power.

Kennedy, even after discovering that the missile gap so important to him during the campaign did not exist, had increased the nation's nuclear strength. The President and McNamara might have realized that the Cuba missiles were a response to that increase. Their failure to recognize that our build-up would bring a Soviet reaction belongs to the dreary history of a cold war in which each bloc has believed again and again that one more increase or show of force will right matters. It is known, too, that the Soviet military leaders had been alarmed to learn that the United States could measure Russia's nuclear strength. Kennedy's announcement of the counterforce strategy had been his way of informing Moscow that we knew where its missiles were and could take them out of action—possibly in a first strike—instead of making war on the whole population. Our intention was to tell the Soviet Union we were aware that there was no missile gap and thereby to restrain the Russians from any adventurism, especially toward Berlin, that they might be tempted to effect if they believed that the West thought itself too weak to resist. The placing of missiles so close to the United States could appear to compensate for the inferiority of Soviet long-range striking capacity to ours. Particularly provocative to the Soviets, too, were the American Jupiter missiles in Turkey, installed during the previous administration. Taking hours to fire, and so vulnerable that a sniper's bullet could disable them, they were virtually useless as a deterrent weapon, to be used in retaliation for a Soviet nuclear attack on the alliance. They were the ugliest of nuclear weapons, a missile having no effective purpose aside from beginning a nuclear war. President Kennedy, for once more cautious than his predecessor, had ordered a study of whether they should be removed.

That the Soviet Union was behind in the arms race undoubtedly constituted Khrushchev's biggest problem, bigger than the specifics of Berlin and Cuba, and could explain much of the urgency with which he pressed for advantages in both instances.

The format for the White House discussion preceding the Bay of Pigs had provided not a free and continuing conflict of ideas but orchestration by the CIA. Kennedy recognized that he now needed a broad exchange of ideas. For the mid-October strategy sessions to plan an American response to the missiles, Kennedy pulled together a group of advisers under a new heading, the Executive Committee of the National Security Council, or Ex-Comm as it was quickly and coldly termed. Sessions were informal and at times would break into groups, each having its own conversation, after which the participants would come back together for cross-examinations.

Ex-Comm spent much of its time on the issue of how much military force was necessary. On the one side was the alternative of air strikes against the missile bases or a larger military action. On the other was the policy the administration finally chose: a naval quarantine of Cuba for the interdiction of further weaponry, to be accompanied with the threat of bombardment or invasion if the bases were not dismantled. As the discussion proceeded, some participants switched from one plan to the other or back and forth.

All this sounds like a debate between belligerent advisers and those favoring relative restraint; between hawks and doves, to use terms that became popular in the sixties. Air raids were, of course, the more technically belligerent course, although the dovish Senator Fulbright argued in favor of air strikes that as a defensive measure they would be less provocative than attacking a Soviet ship in the open seas while it ran the quarantine. And in tone the debate sometimes divided as could be expected. Dean Acheson favored an attack on the missile sites to show that we were not to be cowed. The Joint Chiefs were set on air strikes, and the air force was urging the bombing not only of the missile sites but of other military installations. McNamara, proposing the quarantine as an alternative, suggested on October 16 a diplomatic way of presenting it to the world: we would declare a policy of open surveillance. Robert Kennedy argued that an air attack against a small nation unable to retaliate would be treason to the American ethos and compable to the Japanese attack on Pearl Harbor. He was McNamara's and the President's indispensable partner in facing down the military.

The debate, however, did not separate hawks from doves so neatly. There was, with the possible exception of Averell Harriman and Adlai Stevenson, no one who would have forsworn force or put off its use for long and risked giving the Soviet Union time to complete construction and to add the nuclear warheads. The goal was limited and technical: defining the proper economy of force that would insure the quick dismantling of the sites with the least likelihood of retaliation. That outcome, not the satisfaction of parading a triumphant American will, was what most of the President's advisers set themselves to achieving, not because they were above humiliating the Soviet Union but because the moment was too serious for self-indulgence. The President at first thought that we would have to take out the missiles, and he left open the question of whether to have a more general air attack. Walt Rostow, relishing the advanced and the unusual in military tactics and technology, contributed the suggestion, disordered but humane, that we drop nonexplosive pellets "of the kind we used to shoot out of BB guns." Thickly deposited, they would "quickly convert both the missiles and the installations into worthless junk." Toward the very end of the crisis, when it was uncertain whether Khrushchev would dismantle the missiles, the participants floated an idea that defied the categories of dove and hawk: we would unilaterally start dismantling the missiles in Turkey and let the Soviet Union know that we were doing it; then we would bomb the Cuba sites.

The Jupiter missiles in Turkey gave Ex-Comm virtually the only opportunity it could discern for diplomacy. If it could find some way of offering their removal that would not tempt Moscow to decide that its Cuba venture had been profitable and would be a model for future behavior, the crisis would have a peaceful resolution with no material loss to the United States, which was dissatisfied with the Jupiters anyway. They may have been a better touchstone than the air strikes for distinguishing hawkish from dovish sentiment, for while most advisers probably were prepared to accept whatever force was necessary for elimination of the Cuba bases, they could disagree over whether to present a plan of genuine or at least contrived reciprocity. Averell Harriman, once ambassador to the USSR and shrewd in his knowledge of that nation's leadership, had remarked to Schlesinger that we should not stop Soviet ships—that would injure Soviet pride—but instead ought to help strengthen the position of the more conciliatory Kremlin people. Now he suggested, on October 26, as a means of releasing Khrushchev from the confrontation without our backing down, that we proffer the dismantling of the Jupiters in Turkey not as a trade but as the beginning of a more general process of disarmament. But Thomas Finletter, American ambassador to NATO and a member of New York State's Liberal party, opposed the exchange, which is an object lesson in not confusing liberal with dove.

The discussions, as White House tapes and other records reveal them, catch the minds and temperaments of Kennedy's advisers in crisis. Dean Rusk, who today is measured by his stony defense of the war in Vietnam, showed on October 16 a careful sensitivity to diplomatic questions. He observed that an air strike would entangle our allies in the consequences, and he suggested approaching Castro and talking to the Organization of American States, from which the administration did obtain support for a blockade. McNamara on that day was insistent on close examination of what each action might bring and recommended writing down the possible result of every alternative the country might choose. Throughout the crisis the most pacific counselor was Adlai Stevenson, who wanted the United States to turn back to Cuba our naval base at Guantánamo and to negotiate the elimination of Soviet and American missile bases. His scheme would have the United Nations send inspection teams to all missile bases outside the homelands of the three major nuclear powers as insurance against secret attacks before the achievement of a broader agreement. Schlesinger remembers that as he was about to go to New York for the UN discussions of the crisis, Robert Kennedy told him, "We're counting on you to watch things in New York. That fellow [Stevenson] is ready to give everything away. We will have to make a deal at the end; but we must stand firm now." Yet Stevenson in United Nations debate that week pursued the Soviet delegation relentlessly. McGeorge Bundy has argued that reliance on the United Nations could have undermined our whole position at that desperate moment: "in public comment, especially in the United Kingdom, there was evidence of the difficulties we should have faced if we had been less clearly strong, restrained, and right."

Events, meanwhile, were unfolding before the public. Appearing on television on Monday, October 22, the President announced the presence of the missiles and informed the public of his response, the institution of a naval quarantine against Russian ships bringing additional missile equipment to Cuba. Kennedy set the barrier as close to the Caribbean as he dared, hoping that Khrushchev would decide not to risk an incident. He also placed McNamara in charge of supervising the details of the quarantine very closely, much to the distress of the chief of naval operations. The White House further provided that every ship enforcing the quarantine carry Russian-speaking personnel. Thereupon the events of the week made for a country at war but not at combat, a people at once participants and spectators. The United States permitted a harmless tanker to enter the quarantine area. After that the first ship carrying equipment applicable to the missile bases drew back. That was in radio and television reports by Wednesday evening, October 24. Still Americans waited, those in the big cities going about their work with resignation or affected nonchalance.

The navy, meanwhile, had been playing games. It had ignored instructions from the White House to pull the line still closer to Cuba. In contravention of the President's orders, its ships were on top of Soviet nuclear-bearing submarines in the Atlantic, keeping them from surfacing, which that generation of Russian submarines would have to do before it could launch missiles. An American U-2 plane accidentally strayed on Friday over Siberia, and our fighter-bombers sent to escort the plane met up with it over Soviet territory. Khrushchev's mild response was confined to complaining to Kennedy about American recklessness. On Saturday night, after an American spy plane had been shot down over Cuba, members of Ex-Comm argued again for an immediate assault on the missile bases. Kennedy rejected the idea.

Then, on Sunday, Americans awakened to hear of Khrushchev's announcement that he was removing the missiles, and they realized that for a time at least they could go back to a workaday universe in which nuclear weapons could seem remote and abstract. Khrushchev may have responded not so much to the quarantine itself as to an implicit warning by the President on Saturday night that the United States would not continue to refrain from military action against the Russian presence in Cuba. We were successful, according to Kennedy's later observation, because by then we had a conventional military capable of invading Cuba. In 1961 our forces would not have been equal to the task without reinforcement with troops sent home from Europe. The appraisal is consonant with the arguments put forth by liberals during Eisenhower's administration for a development of our conventional forces and with Kennedy's conviction in response to the Berlin trouble that we needed a larger military. But if the threat of a bombing or an invasion was the immediate reason for Khrushchev's backing off, it was the quarantine that made that threat credible.

What the American public had not known about during the crisis week was an intricate diplomacy between the United States and the Soviet Union. In one telegram received by President Kennedy the premier offered to take the missiles home in a return for a promise that we would not invade Cuba. Events, Khrushchev warned, would join the "knot of war" tighter and tighter. Another telegram asked for the removal of the American missiles from Turkey. Robert Kennedy championed this response: publicly this nation ignored the question of the Turkish bases but promised to stay out of Cuba; privately Bobby went to the Russians with the word that dismantling of the sites on the island would bring the withdrawal of the American missiles from Turkey. President Kennedy then told the world what he had indicated to Khrushchev: that the United States would not invade Cuba—though that December he was to tell the released prisoners from the Bay of Pigs that the battle flag of a free Cuba would be returned "in a free Havana."

To his countrymen Kennedy's performance appeared flawless. It made Americans feel good that their nation had stared down a major danger. It must have made Kennedy feel good that the humiliation of the Bay of Pigs was now behind him. That the outcome of the event did not make the Russians feel good, and that this might in time have dangerous consequences, were not at the moment considerations. Since the crisis occurred just before the midterm elections, it probably helped the Democrats gain seats in the Senate and hold their losses in the House to two, no small achievement for a first-term party in power. Khrushchev's position was left more precarious. This leader who had made life measurably better for the Soviet people by ending the worst terror of the Stalin era and by nourishing the consumer economy, and who toward the end of his career would make the world a little safer by following a policy of détente, had committed one inexcusably dangerous act from which his country was forced to retreat with embarrassment. Within a few years of the crisis he was out of power, replaced by a more militaristic leadership determined to increase Soviet arms so that the USSR would never have to back down again. Khrushchev's decline also slowed the course of de-Stalinization.

Some critics have called President Kennedy irresponsible for taking a military course, and if the horror that the quarantine could have brought is weighed against the probable benefits that it did bring, there can be no satisfactory answer to those critics. It is a partial vindication of Kennedy that among all the military actions available, his

was the most restrained—so much so that military people were mutter-
ing even after the resolution of the crisis that he had settled the affair
too mildly. At the President's suggestion Navy Chief of Staff Anderson,
who had disregarded instructions to pull in the quarantine boundary
and at the end of the crisis was complaining bitterly, resigned and was
named ambassador to Portugal. The President had determined during
the crisis to avoid anything that might invite from the Russians a
"spasm reaction." Still, the proper measure of Kennedy's actions is not
what other people would have done, but what the dangers were in his
own course of action. The recollections of John Sherman Cooper catch
the President at one moment saying that if the missiles were not removed, "they will be destroyed and Cuba will be destroyed."

Walter Lippmann on October 25 had made a more limited criticism of the President for bringing the issue to public light, which made
it more difficult for Khrushchev to get out of the crisis gracefully. But
then the public revelation and challenge may have been a way of sub-
jecting the Soviet Union to world opinion, an alternative to military
action. Lippmann also objected to the "suspension of diplomacy." Much
secret diplomacy, in fact, was going on, but Lippmann cannot be faulted
for ignorance of it. In failing to pursue a more formal diplomatic course,
Kennedy was acting consistently with his larger decision, which was to
treat the missiles as an intolerably dangerous adventure that must not
be allowed to become a precedent. That decision may have been wrong;
it was not separately wrong to avoid a public process of bargaining that
would have legitimized the missiles as objects to be bargained over.
During the time public negotiations would take, morever, the Soviet
Union might have completed the emplacement of the missiles. The
administration had needed to act quickly. The White House tapes for
October 16 have McNamara concluding that since photography revealed land still unfenced, the warheads were probably still not in place,
then remarking that he would strongly oppose an air strike against completed weaponry. Another accusation would fault Kennedy for refusing
during that dangerous week to make public his agreement to dismantle
the Turkish sites. That refusal, it can be claimed, increased the threat
that the Russians, seeking some other means of not looking as though
they were backing away, might draw out the crisis or do something
brash. To this the same response applies as to the claim that Kennedy
should have publicly negotiated: the proposition that the missiles were
unacceptable meant that nothing—in public, at any rate—could be traded
for them.

Khrushchev had been the aggressor in his attempt to overturn in
a stroke the status quo. That in itself, however, is not a sufficient answer to the critics of Kennedy. Scorched and flattened cities at the end
of a technically defensive American act would still be in cinders. The
same would hold for any attempt to defend Khrushchev for wishing
to place missiles not many miles nearer to United States soil than separated American warheads from the Soviet Union. A nuclear world has
too much to worry about to indulge the kind of reasoning that demands
technical parity of that sort. Khrushchev had violated the precarious

nuclear peace that obtained, and that, in a nuclear age, was an aggression that risked inviting a nation-killing response. Kennedy gave Khrushchev an ultimatum, and an ultimatum is so very humiliating for a nation to submit to that Kennedy was risking a nation-killing response. Khrushchev gambled, and Kennedy gambled, and not much more is to be said than that.

In a reply appearing in the *Christian Science Monitor* for November 25 to the question of what made our missiles in Turkey different from the Soviet missiles in Cuba, the administration explained that we had not deployed our missiles secretly and had put them there only after a Soviet threat of a nuclear attack on Europe. The response indicates much about our perceptions; it is less useful as an answer to the question. The West values openness, and the secrecy of the Russian maneuver, which reflects the character of Soviet officialdom, gave the undertaking all the more malevolent a look. But an overt emplacement of the missiles would not have made them acceptable to Washington either. The argument that our missiles in Turkey had been in reaction to a Soviet threat says only that the United States saw itself and its allies as peaceful and their weapons as defensive; that is, of course, the way nations see themselves. The administration could have pointed out that the Cuba missiles were much closer to Washington than our missiles were to Moscow. A sufficient accuracy in delivery would make this technically unimportant, but it does emphasize how politically provocative the Cuban weapons were.

One thing that the missile crisis and the events leading up to it did demonstrate is that short of actual firing of nuclear weapons, both the Soviet Union and the United States will as like as not respond to signs of strength or aggressiveness not by turning away from conflicts but by inviting them. The superiority of our nuclear force, along with the revelation of our ability to spot bases in the Soviet Union, should have frightened Moscow, and it did—into installing the missiles in Cuba. Khrushchev, in setting up the missiles, should have frightened the United States, and he did—into setting up the quarantine and finally into delivering an ultimatum. It is a continuing source of curiosity that some of our more hawkish political commentators expect American shows of force to produce Russian retreat, while they demand that Russian shows of force be met with American bellicosity. Out of the era of Khrushchev they have one incident to enforce their claim: when Khrushchev did not choose to push the confrontation farther to preserve his pride. And an eventual result of the crisis was a further increase in Soviet armaments, and a remote result of that has been an American arms policy designed to face down the Russians.

Yet if the missile crisis put the world at the edge of catastrophe, it is not because either side remotely considered or suspected the other of considering a nuclear strike under the circumstances. The danger rode on the momentum of the crisis itself. The event shaped the period of partial détente that followed because it revealed to the antagonists what they had probably been coming to know half-consciously: that they were in the end allies of a sort in the presence of a weapon that threatened to wrench itself loose from all control. The crisis gave Kennedy another occasion for that perception, which seems so inappropriate to what his presidency was supposed to mean: that the world will not go the way we wish it to go. Asked by a reporter in 1963 whether after the crisis he was more or less pessimistic about the future, he answered, more so: "I believe that sooner or later someone is going to make a mistake."

The two powers nevertheless started behaving as though they were not going to let that mistake happen. A hot line between the Kremlin and the White House insured instantaneous communication in emergencies; it was a fitting complement to a diplomacy of personal correspondence that Khrushchev and Kennedy had been carrying on. However angrily and however fearfully the Russians were to arm themselves in the years after the missile crisis, they also opposed the Maoist stridency. The administration had wanted to step up subversion within Cuba; then, in the midst of the crisis, it ordered a cessation. On June 10, 1963, Kennedy at American University in one of his most important speeches urged an era of cooperation between our country and the Soviet Union: "We all inhabit this small planet. We all breathe the same air. We all cherish our children's future. And we are all mortal." The address had the courtesy to refer to the sufferings of the Soviet Union in World War II, and the reference may have contributed to the good feeling that attended the test ban treaty that year. Then came a speech in the confrontational vein, in Berlin on June 26. Kennedy's famous announcement *"Ich bin ein Berliner"*—"I am a Berliner"—was warranted; the encircled people in the free part of the city were entitled to an assurance that the West would stand by them. Less called for was the declaration "There are some who say that communism is the wave of the future. Let them come to Berlin. And there are some"—Kennedy actually was now among them—"who say in Europe and elsewhere, 'We can work with the Communists.' Let them come to Berlin."

But two months before his death the President made a major speech against the proliferation of nuclear arms. Elsewhere he proposed that the Soviet Union and the United States make a joint flight to the moon. In October 1963 he initiated the first sale of surplus wheat to the Soviet Union. After the shaping of the wheat deal Khrushchev announced a reduction in Soviet defense funding. In his final days Kennedy, with the aid of Republican conservative Senator Everett Dirksen of Illinois, got ratification of the test ban treaty outlawing atmospheric testing of atomic weapons, and bringing to an end, so it seemed, the hopes of the right wing for a future of uncompromised hostility to all things Communist. The treaty was also a victory for Khrushchev over Soviet hardliners, whose political position had been weakened by the illness of Kozlov.

The Kennedy policy or style, the working toward a perfection of force and restraint, had achieved about as full a vindication as any politician could dare wish for. The Kennedy image, whether programmed or spontaneous, had its final polish, and technocratic liberals could argue confidently against both rightists, offended at the very thought of negotiating coexistence, and whoever to the left might reject the entire strategy of negotiation from a posture of military strength. Meanwhile, in a corner of Asia were unfolding events that would turn much of a whole generation of liberals against the memory of the Kennedy style.

Freedom Riders

HOWELL RAINES

On February 1, 1960, in downtown Greensboro, North Carolina, four
black students from North Carolina Agricultural and Technical College
walked into a Woolworth's store, purchased a few small items, and then
sat at the lunch counter to seek equal service with white patrons. Their
brave and dangerous action was a part of a long tradition of protest
in Greensboro. Parents like Ezell Blair, Sr., an NAACP activist, and
teachers like Nell Coley, who had inspired three of the four boys when
they attended Dudley High School, were not surprised by the sit-ins:
"We had been teaching those kids things all along." Yet, this action
threw a spark: within days the sit-in movement had spread to fifty-four
cities in nine states. Two months after the first sit-ins, the Student Non-
Violent Coordinating Committee (SNCC) was formed in Raleigh, North
Carolina. Within a year, more than 100 cities had at least partially desegregated public facilities in response to student-led demonstrations.

The sit-in tactic was simple and dramatic: human dignity was defined
by the right to be served in any restaurant, to register for a room in any
motel, or to take out a book at a public library. Yet the tactic had its
limits: the stress on the dramatic hid the long, slow, painful legal and
social revolution that lay behind these stunning moments. The tactic
was local, suggesting that an issue could be resolved by the community,
while the civil rights movement actually required the force of the nation and the weight of the federal government to end the system of
segregation. The following interviews were conducted by a white southern journalist, Howell Raines, for his superb oral history My Soul Is
Rested: Movement Days in the Deep South Remembered. Both the long
quiet history preceding the movement of the 1960's in the South and
the need for a strategy to promote intervention by the federal government are focused upon. The period of the sit-ins, the "freedom rides,"
the marches, and the demonstrations comprise one of the most dramatic stories in American history; a story we are now learning in detail
in the words and memories of the participants.

INTERVIEW WITH JAMES FARMER

JF: I was impressed by the fact that most of the activity thus far
had been of local people working on their local problems—Greensborans
sitting-in in Greensboro and Atlantans sitting-in in Atlanta—and the
pressure of the opposition against having outsiders come was very, very
great. If any outsider came in . . . , "Get that outside agitator." . . . I
thought that this was going to limit the growth of the Movement. . . .
We somehow had to cut across state lines and establish the position that
we were entitled to act any place in the country, no matter where we
hung our hat and called home, because it was our country.

We also felt that one of the weaknesses of the student sit-in movement of the South had been that as soon as arrested, the kids bailed out. . . . This was not quite Gandhian and not the best tactic. A better tactic would be to remain in jail and to make the maintenance of segregation so expensive for the state and the city that they would hopefully come to the conclusion that they could no longer afford it. Fill up the jails, as Gandhi did in India, fill them to bursting if we had to. In other words, stay in without bail.

So those were the two things: cutting across state lines, putting the movement on wheels, so to speak, and remaining in jail, not only for its publicity value but for the financial pressure it would put upon the segregators. We decided that a good approach here would be to move away from restaurant lunch counters. That had been the Southern student sit-in movement, and anything we would do on that would be anticlimactic now. We would have to move into another area and so we decided to move into the transportation, interstate transportation. . . .

It would be necessary, he decided, to violate custom and local law to focus attention on the federal laws barring discrimination in interstate transportation. He knew that in 1946 the Supreme Court had ruled against segregated seating on interstate buses, and in 1960, against segregated terminal facilities. The rulings were uniformly ignored throughout the South.

JF: So we, following the Gandhian technique, wrote to Washington. We wrote to the Justice Department, to the FBI, and to the President, and wrote to Greyhound Bus Company and Trailways Bus Company and told them that on May first or May fourth—whatever the date was, I forget now—we were going to have a Freedom Ride. Blacks and whites were going to leave Washington, D.C., on Greyhound and Trailways, deliberately violating the segregated seating requirements and at each rest stop would violate the segregated use of facilities. And we would be nonviolent, absolutely nonviolent, throughout the campaign, and we would accept the consequences of our actions. This was a deliberate act of civil disobedience. . . .

Did Justice try to head you off?

JF: No, we got no reply. We got no reply from Justice. Bobby Kennedy, no reply. We got no reply from the FBI. We got no reply from the White House, from President Kennedy. We got no reply from Greyhound or Trailways. *We got no replies.* [Laughs]

He recruited an interracial group of thirteen and brought them to Washington for a week's training.

JF: We had some of the group of thirteen sit at a simulated counter asking for coffee. Somebody else refused them service, and then we'd have others come in as white hoodlums to beat 'em up and knock them off the counter and club 'em around and kick 'em in the ribs and stomp 'em, and they were quite realistic, I must say. I thought they bent over backwards to be realistic. I was aching all over. [Laughs] And then we'd go into a discussion as to how the roles were played, whether there was something that the Freedom Riders did that they shouldn't have done, said that they shouldn't have said, something that they didn't say or do that they should have, and so on. Then we'd reverse roles and play it over and over again and have lengthy discussions of it.

I felt, by the way, that by the time that group left Washington, they were prepared for anything, even death, and this was a possibility, and we knew it, when we got to the Deep South.

Through Virginia we had no problem. In fact they had heard we were coming, Greyhound and Trailways, and they had taken down the For Colored and For Whites signs, and we rode right through. Yep. The same was true in North Carolina. Signs had come down just the previous day, blacks told us. And so the letters in advance did something.

In South Carolina it was a different story. . . . John Lewis started into a white waiting room in some town in South Carolina . . . and there were several young white hoodlums, leather jackets, ducktail haircuts, standing there smoking, and they blocked the door and said, "Nigger, you can't come in here." He said, "I have every right to enter this waiting room according to the Supreme Court of the United States in the Boynton case."

They said, "Shit on that." He tried to walk past, and they clubbed him, beat him, and knocked him down. One of the white Freedom Riders . . . Albert Bigelow, who had been a Navy captain during World War II, big, tall, strapping fellow, very impressive, from Connecticut—then stepped right between the hoodlums and John Lewis. Lewis had been absorbing more of the punishment. They then clubbed Bigelow and finally knocked him down, and that took some knocking because he was a pretty strapping fellow, and he didn't hit back at all. [They] knocked him down, and at this point police arrived and intervened. They didn't make any arrests. Intervened.

Well, we went through the rest of South Carolina without incident and then to Atlanta, Georgia, and there we met with Dr. King. We called him and told him we were coming, and he had dinner with us and wished us well. Went to Albany first and then Atlanta. And when we were in Atlanta—my father by the way, was in Freedman's Hospital here in Washington with cancer, and I got word just about two hours before the buses left Atlanta that my father had died, and I had to go back and bury him. My mother insisted until her death five years later that my father willed his death at that time, willed the timing of it because he had my schedule. I had talked with him here in Washington during our training session, when he was in the hospital before I left, and told him what we were going to do, and he said, "Well, that's an interesting idea and I hope you survive it." He said, "I think the most dangerous part of it will be through Bama," as he put it, "and Mississippi. There, somebody will probably take a potshot at you, and I just hope they miss." And my mother says that every morning he would take out my itinerary and look at it and say, "Well, now, let's see where Junior is today." And he was relaxed about it until I got to Atlanta, and he says, "Oh, tomorrow he goes through Bama."

He died, and she says that he willed the timing of it to bring me back. It's apocryphal I'm sure. At any rate I had to return then to bury him and informed the Freedom Riders that I would rejoin them as soon as I had gotten this family obligation out of the way. I must confess that while I felt guilty at leaving, there was also a sense of relief at missing this leg of the trip, because all of us were scared. There was one reporter who was one of the Freedom Riders at this stage, and that was Simeon Booker of Johnson publications, *Jet* and *Ebony*. Simeon had come to me just before I got the telegram telling me of my father's death, or the phone call, and he said, "Jim, you know, I've decided that you are the only Freedom Rider I can outrun. So what I'm going to do is to stick with you on this trip, and I figure it's the fellow bringing up the rear who's gonna get caught." [Laughs]

INTERVIEW WITH HANK THOMAS

HT: The Freedom Ride didn't really get rough until we got down in the Deep South. Needless to say, Anniston, Alabama, I'm never gonna forget that, when I was on the bus that they threw some kind of incendiary device on.

He was on the first of two buses to cross into "Bama." When it pulled into the depot at Anniston, a Klan hotbed about sixty miles from Birmingham, the bus was surrounded by white men brandishing iron bars. Anniston police held them back long enough for the bus to reach the highway again, but about six miles outside town the pursuing mob caught up.

HT: I got real scared then. You know, I was thinking—I'm looking out the window there, and people are out there yelling and screaming. They just about broke every window out of the bus. . . . I really thought that that was going to be the end of me.

How did the bus get stopped?

HT: They shot the tires out, and the bus driver was forced to stop. . . . He got off, and man, he took off like a rabbit, and might well have. I couldn't very well blame him there. And we were trapped on the bus. They tried to board. Well, we did have two FBI men aboard the bus. All they were there to do were to observe and gather facts, but the crowd apparently recognized them as FBI men, and they did not try to hurt them.

It wasn't until the thing was shot on the bus and the bus caught afire that everything got out of control, and . . . when the bus was burning, I figured . . . [pauses] . . . panic did get ahold of me. Needless to say, I couldn't survive that burning bus. There was a possibility I could have survived the mob, but I was just so afraid of the mob that I was gonna stay on that bus. I mean, I just got that much afraid. And when we got off the bus . . . first they closed the doors and wouldn't let us off. But then I'm pretty sure they realized, that somebody said, "Hey, the bus is gonna explode," because it had just gassed up, and so they started scattering then, and I guess that's the way we got off the bus.* Otherwise, we probably all would have been succumbed by the smoke, and not being able to get off, probably would have been burned alive or burned on there anyway. That's the only time I was really, really afraid. I got whacked over the head with a rock or I think some kind of a stick as I was coming off the bus.

What happened in Anniston after the bus was attacked?

HT: We were taken to the hospital. The bus started exploding, and a lot of people were cut by flying glass. We were taken to the hospital, most of us, for smoke inhalation.

By whom?

HT: I don't remember. I think I was half out of it, half dazed, as a result of the smoke, and, gosh, I can still smell that stuff down in me now. You got to the point where you started having the dry heaves. Took us to the hospital, and it was incredible. The people at the hospital would not do anything for us. They would not. And I was saying, "You're *doctors,* you're medical personnel." They wouldn't. Governor Patterson got on statewide radio and said, "Any rioters in this state will not receive police protection." And then the crowd started forming outside the hospital, and the hospital told us to leave. And we said, "No, we're not going out there," and there we were. A caravan from Birmingham, about a fifteen-car caravan led by the Reverend Fred Shuttlesworth, came up from Birmingham to get us out.

Without police escort, I take it?

---

* John Patterson, then governor of Alabama, maintains that he and his public safety director, Floyd Mann, were indirectly responsible for the Freedom Riders' getting off the burning bus: "Floyd recommended that we send a state plainclothes investigator to Atlanta to catch the bus and ride with the Freedom Riders, and we did. Now this has never been reported that I know of in any paper. . . . We sent a man named E. L. Cowling. . . . He went over to Atlanta and caught the bus, and he was on the bus when they came to Anniston. . . . So Cowling walked up to the door of the bus and drew his pistol and backed the crowd away from the bus and told them that if anybody touched anybody he'd kill them. And he got the Freedom Riders off the burning bus. That's true."

HT: Without police escort, but every one of those cars had a shot-gun in it. And Fred Shuttlesworth had got on the radio and said—you know Fred, he's very dramatic—"I'm going to get my people." [Laughs] He said, "I'm a nonviolent man, but I'm going to get my people." And apparently a hell of a lot of people believed in him. Man, they came there and they were a welcome sight. And each one of 'em got out with their guns and everything and the state police were there, but I think they all realized that this was not a time to say anything because, I'm pretty sure, there would have been a lot of people killed.

The black drivers were openly carrying guns?

HT: Oh, yeah. They had rifles and shotguns. And that's how we got back to Birmingham. . . . I think I was flown to New Orleans for medical treatment, because still they were afraid to let any of us go to the hospitals in Birmingham, and by that time—it was what, two days later—I was fairly all right. I had gotten most of the smoke out of my system.

No one received any attention in the hospital in Anniston?

HT: No, no. Oh, we did have one girl, Genevieve Hughes, a white girl, who had a busted lip. I remember a nurse applying something to that, but other than that, nothing. Now that I look back on it, man, we had some vicious people down there, wouldn't even so much as *treat* you. But that's the way it was. But strangely enough, even those bad things then don't stick in my mind that much. Not that I'm full of love and goodwill for everybody in my heart, but I chalk it off to part of the things that I'm going to be able to sit on my front porch in my rock-ing chair and tell my young'uns about, my grandchildren about.

Postscript: That same day, Mother's Day, May 14, 1961, the second bus escaped the mob in Anniston and made it to Birmingham. At the Trailways station there, white men armed with baseball bats and chains beat the Freedom Riders at will for about fifteen minutes before the first police arrived. In 1975 a former Birmingham Klansman, who was a paid informant of the FBI at the time, told the Senate Select Commit-tee on Intelligence that members of the Birmingham police force had promised the Klansmen that no policemen would show up to interfere with the beatings for at least fifteen minutes. In 1976 a Birmingham detective who refused to be interviewed on tape told me that account was correct—as far as it went. The detective said that word was passed in the police department that Public Safety Commissioner Eugene "Bull" Connor had watched from the window of his office in City Hall as the crowd of Klansmen, some brandishing weapons, gathered to await the Freedom Riders. Asked later about the absence of his policemen, Connor said most of them were visiting their mothers.

INTERVIEW WITH JOHN LEWIS

He had left the Freedom Ride in South Carolina to keep an appointment for a job interview. Returning to Nashville on May 14, he learned of the attacks in Anniston and Birmingham and that CORE, heeding Attorney General Robert Kennedy's request for a "cooling-off" period, had canceled the ride altogether. He and a group of sit-in veterans believed that if the Freedom Ride did not continue, segregationists would conclude that they could, indeed, defeat the Movement with violence and intimidation. Using money left over from the sit-in treasury and ignoring the advice of Nashville's SCLC affiliate, they bought tickets for Birmingham and announced that the Freedom Ride was on again.

At the Birmingham city limit, a policeman halted their bus and informed the driver that he was taking charge of the vehicle. When the bus pulled into the station, the "Birmingham police department put up newspapers all around the bus windows so you couldn't see out, and no one could see in." Shielded from inspection, they waited until "Bull" Connor arrived on the scene and ordered them taken into "protective custody." Thus began one of the most bizarre episodes of the Movement.

JL: So they took us all to the jail, the Birmingham city jail. Now this was on a Wednesday. We went to jail and stayed in jail Wednesday night. We didn't eat anything. We went on a hunger strike. . . .

What sort of treatment did you get from the police?

JL: They were very, very nice. They didn't rough us up or anything like that, just very nice, as I recall. They put us in jail, segregated us . . . and that Thursday we stayed in jail all day. That Thursday night around midnight, "Bull" Connor and two reporters . . . and maybe one or two detectives came up to the jail, and "Bull" Connor said they were going to take us back to Nashville, back to the college campus where we belonged. We said, "Well, we don't want to go back. We have a right to be on this Freedom Ride. We have a right to travel. We plan to go to Montgomery, and from Montgomery we're going to Jackson and to New Orleans." And he insisted. And people just sorta went limp, so they had people literally to pick us up and place us into these cars. . . .

Anyway, they drove us on the highway, and "Bull" Connor was really funny. I was in the car that he was in and this young lady, Katherine Burke. He was really funny, he was really joking with us, saying that he was gonna take us back to Nashville, and we told him we would invite him to the campus, and he could have breakfast with us and that type of thing. He said he would like that. It was that type of conversation that we had going with "Bull" Connor.

We got to the Tennessee-Alabama line . . . They dropped us off, saying . . . "You can take the bus back to Nashville." They literally left us there. We didn't know anybody, didn't know any place to go. This is true.

Did it cross your mind that you might be being set up?

JL: Oh, yeah, oh, yeah. We just didn't know what had happened, and it was still dark. It was early morning-like.

The Birmingham police, including the police commissioner, had physically loaded you up in a car and carried you to the state line, a matter of 150 miles.

JL: That's right. That's right. And *left* us, just left us. What we did, we started walking down a road, and we saw a railroad track, and we crossed this railroad track and went to an old house. There was an elderly couple there, must have been in their late sixties, early seventies. We knocked on the door, and they let us in, and they was just really frightened. They'd heard about the Freedom Riders.

This was a black couple?

JL: Black couple. They were just really, really frightened. They didn't know what to do. They didn't really want to let us in, but they did, and we called Nashville and told 'em what had happened. Called Diane Nash on the telephone. She was in the local student movement office there in Nashville, and she wanted to know whether we wanted to continue the ride or whether we wanted a car to pick us up to bring us back to Nashville. We told her to send a car to take us back to Birmingham. We wanted to continue the ride.

In the meantime, we hadn't had anything to eat, and we were very hungry. 'Cause this is now Friday morning, and we hadn't had anything to eat since, I guess, early Wednesday. This man, this elderly man, got in his pickup truck and went around during the early morning to two or three stores and bought something like bologna and bread and cornflakes. Anyway, we had a little meal there, and apparently some of the white people in the community came by, and he told 'em some of his relatives were visiting from Nashville. We waited around till the car from Nashville got there, and this was really something else. It was seven of us and the driver now, eight of us, got in that car on our way back to Birmingham, and we heard a reporter on the radio saying the students had been taken to the state line and apparently they were . . . back in Nashville on their college campuses. . . .

So we drove back to Birmingham, and Rev. Shuttlesworth and several other ministers from the Alabama Christian Movement for Human Rights met us there, and we went directly back to the Greyhound bus station. And we tried to get on the bus around, I recall, three o'clock, on the Greyhound bus from Birmingham to Montgomery, and apparently Greyhound canceled the bus taking off. We were going to try to get on one at five-something, and this bus driver said something that I'll never forget. He said, "I only have one life to give and I'm not going to give it to CORE or the NAACP."

He and his group, along with about twenty fresh volunteers from Nashville, spent the night on the wooden benches of the bus station. Departing from their previous practice, the police repelled a white mob which gathered during the night. Finally a reporter who was covering the story brought a message: "Apparently you all are going to get a chance to go. Attorney General Kennedy has been in contact with Greyhound."

JL: The same bus driver came out to the bus about eight-thirty on Saturday morning, and we got on a bus from Birmingham to Montgomery. And apparently the arrangement was that every so many miles there would be a state patrol car and there would be a plane. We did see—I don't know whether it was the arrangement or not—we did see a small plane flying up above the bus for so many miles and we did have the patrol car. . . .*

It was a nice ride between Birmingham and Montgomery. A few miles outside of Montgomery you just didn't see anything. You didn't see the plane, didn't see the state patrol car. It seemed like everything sort of disappeared, and the moment that we arrived in that station, it was the strangest feeling to me. It was something strange, that you knew something. It was really weird. It was an eerie feeling. There was a funny peace there, a quietness. You didn't see anything happening. Apparently, when you really look back, the mob there must have been so planned and was so out of sight . . . it just sorta appeared, just appeared on the scene.

You didn't see any sign of it as you went into the bus station?

JL: None. Just didn't see anything. When we drove up, we didn't see anything. . . . We got most of the young ladies in a cab. So they got in a cab and the black cab driver didn't want to drive, because at that time there was two white students, young ladies from Peabody or Scarritt, and in Alabama there was a law that you couldn't have an integrated cab. So the two young ladies got out, and at that very time, this mob started all over the place. So everybody, all the young ladies, got away, and the two young white girls were running down the street trying to get away. That's when John Siegenthaler got hit.** And at

---

* In fact, an airplane and sixteen highway patrol cars accompanied the bus, despite Governor Patterson's public statement that "we are not going to escort those agitators. We stand firm on that position."
** Robert Kennedy's administrative assistant, sent to Alabama as an observer.

that time, the rest of us, mostly fellas, just literally standing there because we couldn't run—no place to go really.***

This was out in the lot?

JL: Just out in the lot. And if you've been at the bus station, there's a rail there. . . . Down below is the entrance to the courthouse, the Post Office building. So when the mob kept coming, several of the people, several of the fellas jumped over and were able to get in the basement of the Post Office, and the postmaster there opened it and made it possible for people to come in and escape the mob. And I said—I remember saying that we shouldn't run, we should just stand there, 'cause the mob was beating people. And the last thing that I recall, I was hit with a crate, a wooden crate what you have soda in, and was left lying in the street. And I remember the Attorney General of Alabama, MacDonald Gallion, serving this injunction that Judge Walter B. Jones had issued saying that it was unlawful for interracial groups to travel. While I was lying there on the ground, he brought this injunction.

INTERVIEW WITH JAMES FARMER

After his father's funeral, he flew to Montgomery, where Dr. King and Reverend Abernathy had called a mass meeting at First Baptist Church as a show of support for the Freedom Riders.

JF: Fred Shuttlesworth met me at the airport with a couple of his guys. He said, "Well, gentlemen, it's going to be a touch-and-go as to whether we get to that church. Everybody's at the church; Martin has flown in . . . he's there and so we are under siege. A mob has it surrounded. . . ." And so he drove me back as close as he could, and mobs blocked the way, wouldn't let the car through, began trying to open the door. We backed up and tried another route. . . .

Approaching the church through a nearby graveyard, he and Shuttlesworth could get no closer than three blocks to the church before running into the white toughs again.

*** Freedom Rider William Harbour: "There was nobody there. I didn't see anybody standin' around the bus station. I saw some taxicabs there. That was about it. So the bus driver opened the bus door up and just walked away from the bus. I guess in less than fifteen minutes, we had a mob of people, five or six hundred people with ax handles, chains and everything else. . . . Soon as we walked off the bus, John Lewis said to me, 'Bill, it doesn't look right. . . .'

"Everything happened so quick. There was a standstill for the first two or three minutes . . . They were closin' in on us, and we were standin' still tryin' to decide what should we do in order to protect the whites we had with us. But then you had a middle-aged white female hollerin', 'Git them niggers, git them niggers . . . ,' and that urged the crowd on. From then on, they was constantly movin' in. I don't think she ever hit anybody or threw anything whatsoever. Just the idea she started, just kept pushin' and pushin' and pushin' . . . It started just like that."

JF: And so Fred Shuttlesworth walked into the mob. [Laughs] I must confess I was scared as hell, but Shuttlesworth—[He suddenly leaps from his chair and strides across the room, showing how the preacher shoved his way through the incredulous whites.] These goons were standing there, thousands of them with clubs. "Out of the way. Go on. Out of the way." He didn't have any trouble. They stopped and looked at him: *"That nigger's crazy."* [Laughs] And I was standing right behind him trying to be little. [Still laughing] And we got to the church and got in. . . .

Obviously, we were going to be there all night. . . . So we were singing, and King and I were consulting, sitting in the office of the church and talking and mapping alternative plans.

The mob kicked open the door of the church, and they just *poured* in. And people were screaming, backed up against the wall. I don't know where they came from or how they did it, but the marshalls materialized in that situation. It seemed almost fictional. *There they were* suddenly, the marshalls confronting the mob. They had arm bands on, U.S. marshalls. . . . They didn't draw their guns, but they used their clubs and forced them into a park and then dispersed those who had come to the church. Martial law was declared, and we were to stay in the church under heavy guard all night and not to attempt to leave.*

Then finally, when the mob was more or less permanently dispersed, we could leave the church. [We] went to homes, ministers' homes, and we had debates as to what to do, whether we should attempt the rest of the Freedom Ride, and the conclusion was that we would go on with it. We decided that we would go on. We had to, although I am sure that everybody was scared to death at this point. Dr. King declined to go on the grounds that he was on probation and it would be a violation of probation. The SNCC people wouldn't accept that though. They said, "Look, I'm on probation too." "So am I." "Me, too." "Me, too." "Me, too, and I'm going."

Did you try to prevail on King to go?

JF: No, no, no, no, no. I didn't feel that I should try to urge him to go, because I was debating whether I was going. [Laughs] I tried to fink out, I must confess. . . . The two buses were there, and they got on the buses, and I helped them put their luggage in and get on the bus, and I said, "Well, bye." [Laughs] And one of the CORE girls, Doris Castle, a girl from New Orleans, said, "Jim, you're going with us, aren't you?" I said, "Doris, I've been away from the office now for three weeks, and mail has piled up and somebody has to mind the store, so I think I've just got to get back to the office in New York to keep this thing

* Robert Kennedy sent in the U.S. marshalls because of Governor John Patterson's reluctance to promise protection for the Freedom Riders. Even so, the white mob, estimated at several thousand, would probably have overwhelmed the marshalls during the night had not Patterson finally relented. He declared martial law and sent eight hundred national guardsmen to the church. See John Patterson's account of his battle of wills with Kennedy.

going and raise the necessary money." She said, "Jim, *please*." I said, "Get my luggage out of the car and put it on the goddamn bus. I'm going." How was I going to face her afterwards if something happened, and I had finked out . . . ?"*

They rolled out of Montgomery under heavy guard, helicopters overhead, National Guard riflemen aboard the bus.

JF: I don't think any of us thought that we were going to get to Jackson, Mississippi, really. I know I didn't. I was scared and I am sure the kids were scared. . . . On the bus, I noticed that they were writing notes, many of them, and I walked across the aisle to see what they were writing, and they were writing names and addresses of next of kin. The girls were shoving them in their bosoms and the men putting them in pockets or wallets. . . .**

When the bus got to the state line, we saw this famous sign, Welcome to the Magnolia State. [Laughs] We had to chuckle at that in spite of the tenseness of the situation. The six Alabama national guardsmen left the bus, and the Mississippi national guardsmen took their place. The bus driver left the bus, and another bus driver came on. The state director of public safety came on the bus and whispered something to one of the reporters. This reporter's eyes bulged, and he passed this whispered message on to the other reporters on the bus. All except one of them left the bus and got in cars outside. So when the bus started, I asked this remaining reporter what the message had been, and he said, "The director of public safety tells us that they have it on excellent authority that this bus is going to be ambushed and destroyed inside the Mississippi border." And I said, "And you stayed on it?" He said, "What? Miss a story like that?" . . . [Laughs]

We had learned that Ross Barnett, who was governor at that time, had been on radio and TV several times a day for several days telling people to keep calm. He said, "Those Freedom Riders, so-called Freedom Riders, are coming into Mississippi. They're coming into Jackson, but don't come into town. Stay at home. Don't come into the city. Let us handle it according to our Mississippi laws. Anybody who breaks our laws is going to jail. But let us handle it. . . . Don't take the law into your own hands."

He was repeating that over and over and over again. And we passed one place where there were woods, heavy woods, on both sides of the road, and there was a cluster of Mississippi national guardsmen standing there on both sides of the road. I heard one of the officers of the Guard shout over a bullhorn, "Look behind every tree." So I guess

---

* John Lewis recalls: "That was one of the criticisms that many of the people in SNCC and CORE had of Dr. King. There's a fantastic picture of a young guy named Paul—I can't think of his last name—and the other guy was named Matthew Walker, waving out of a bus in Montgomery to Dr. King. . . . it was a big criticism that he came to the bus station and saw the people off and he refused to go."

** For another account of the tension on this trip, see Dave Dennis.

that's where the ambush was expected. They had their artillery pointed at the woods on both sides. A military operation, you know.

And when we got to Jackson, "Whew, well, the outskirts of Jackson now." We drove up to the Greyhound bus terminal. A crowd of people there. I said, "Well, this is it. This is where we get it." The door opened and I led the group off the bus. It turned out that the crowd of people were not hoodlums. They were plainclothesmen and reporters. [Laughs] *They* were the crowd. As soon as we walked out of the door, they parted, and they knew precisely where I was going, to the white waiting room and not to the colored waiting room. So they parted and made a path for me leading right to the white waiting room [laughing], and I thought maybe I could have pled entrapment when we got to court, because we couldn't go anyplace else.

He and a veteran of the Nashville sit-ins named Lucretia Collins joined arms and started walking toward the white restrooms. A Captain Ray of the Jackson police was waiting for them.

JF: He blocked the way. He said, "Move on." I said, "Where?" He said, "Move on out." I refused on the grounds of the Supreme Court decision in the Boynton case and gave the date of it. He said, "I said, 'Move on.' " I refused again on the same grounds.

He said, "Do you understand my order?"

I said, "Perfectly."

He said, "Well, I'm going to tell you one more time, move on."

I refused the third time on the same grounds.

He said, "What's your name?"

I said, "James Farmer."

He nodded. He said, "Follow that officer and get in the patrol wagon." So Lucretia and I and the people behind us climbed in the patrol, and we started singing "We Shall Overcome" and rocking that wagon with the song. And so it went. We made a symbol out of Captain Ray's pointed finger when he said, "Follow that patrol wagon." He was like the man who was sticking his finger in the hole in the dyke, trying to hold back the flood waters, but they would overwhelm him.

Jack Young, the only black attorney in Jackson, came to see him in the jailhouse.

JF: I sent word by him to call the CORE office and tell them to keep Freedom Riders coming into Jackson as fast as possible on every bus, every train . . . and recruit madly, and train. Didn't have to do much recruiting because by this time the volunteers were barraging us. CORE was jumping with telegrams coming in, phone calls: "Send me, I'll go." "Need more Freedom Riders? Take me. I'll go."

We had 325 or 326 jailed at one time. We filled up the jails.

We had trouble with some of the Freedom Riders because the training had to be hasty, and many of the people who rushed in, including some of the SNCC people, were not prepared for this sort of thing.

"We're gonna stay in 'til hell freezes over." But after two days, "You got money to bail me out?" [Laughs] "No, you're pledged to stay in for forty days." Forty days, it seems, was the maximum that you could stay in and still file an appeal. . . . We wanted to file appeals and get this thing adjudicated before the Supreme Court, if necessary. But we still wanted to stay in jail and make it expensive on Mississippi, and we made it expensive on them. One of the trustees in the jail brought in a newspaper that announced that there was a nuisance tax that they had in Jackson, auto-use tax, that they had planned to eliminate that year. Well, they announced they couldn't eliminate it, because the Freedom Riders were costing too much. . . .

And we were singing the songs, the freedom songs, which they hated. "You gotta stop that singing." You know, "O-o-h, freedom, o-o-o-o-h, free-*dom,* before I'd be a slave, I'd be buried in my grave and go home to my Lord and be free." . . . "Stop that singing!" The other prisoners upstairs began joining in on the singing. . . . They were in for murder, rape, theft, what have you. We developed a communications system by sending a message up a wire. They'd pull it up . . . an old electric wire that wasn't in use. "Stop that singing!" We refused to stop and kept on singing, and they then stopped bringing in the knickknacks. They'd bring in candy bars and chewing gum to sell, and they wouldn't bring that to us. The kids were looking forward to that coming in each day, so we found a way to get it. We would send the money upstairs and have them buy more than they wanted with our money.

One day a black trustee who had the run of the jail came to his cell with a whispered message: " 'They're gonna send you to the prison farm. That's where they're gonna try to break you. They're gonna try to whip your ass.' They transferred us there in the dead of night. . . ." The county prison farm proved to be but a way station on their passage to the legendary state prison at Parchman. There, black convicts in striped uniforms trailed mule-drawn plows across the endless vistas of the state's cotton fields, a tableau from another century. Yet "the singing went on, and there was still no brutality—physical brutality."

JF: They knew many of us were chain-smokers. They wouldn't allow any cigarettes in, and the guards would walk down the corridors blowing cigarette smoke into our cells. We were already climbing the walls for want of a cigarette. And they knew that most of these were college students. They wouldn't allow any books in, no books whatever. No newspapers . . .

And then psychological brutality—they passed out the clothing for us. We had to strip, and they then gave us shorts, just a pair of undershorts, that's all. The big guys got tiny little undershorts, and the little guys had huge undershorts. The big guys were trying to hold theirs shut, and the little guys were trying to stay in theirs and keep 'em from falling down. [Laughs] And they arranged to put two big guys in one cell and two little guys in one cell, so they couldn't swap.

The food was terrible. It was very, very bad. I went on a diet there and lost about thirty pounds. . . . We wanted to get out, because we were suffering in there. It was damp, and it was cold at night, too. And when they tried to get us to stop singing, we wouldn't stop singing, so they said, "If you don't stop singing, we'll take away your mattress." So they yanked those mattresses off those hard metal beds when we wouldn't stop singing. And we were sleeping on that cold, hard surface, and then they opened the window and turned on the exhaust fan, which brought cold air. I didn't know Mississippi could get that cold, but it felt cold at night. Almost everybody came down with a cold.

I finally—oh, by the way, Ross Barnett came by. Some of the other Freedom Riders recognized him from a picture. They said, "You know who that is that just walked in? That's Ross Barnett." Couldn't miss him. Not only his face, but he's a little man, small-boned man, with an enormous pot belly. [Laughs] So Ross came in, and he just walked around the cell block, just looking in, saying nothing. He stopped at my cell and says, "What's your name?" I said, "James Farmer." He said, "They treatin' you all right here?" I said, "Well, no violence, no physical brutality." He said, "So they treatin' you all right. No complaints, huh?" [Laughs] I said, "I didn't say that. We have lots of complaints. The biggest complaint is that we're in here, and we shouldn't be in here." So he nodded and walked off.

I then demanded to see the director of prisons. . . . Two guards came to escort me. Here I was with my tiny little shorts, trying to keep 'em up, couldn't fasten 'em, other than that, naked, walking along and going to meet the director of prisons. And he was seated there, smoking a big cigar, and there was only one chair. That was his. So I could not sit down. I had to stand. It was really quite a humiliating situation. Here he was, well-dressed, Palm Beach suit, smoking his big cigar; me standing, barefoot, too, no shoes or anything else. And I told him that we respectfully requested—the other Freedom Riders had authorized me to request that we be allowed to go outside and work, work on the farm, work in the field. "Naw, we cain't do that, 'cause the other prisoners'll kill you, and we're responsible for keeping you alive." I said, "We'll take our chances on that." He said, "No, ain't gonna do it. And furthermore," he says, "we want you to stay in there and rot. That's what we want you to do. We got to feed you, because the law says we gotta feed you, and the government will see to it we feed you. But we can make that food so damn unpalatable that you can't eat it. We can put so much salt in it that it'll turn your stomach if you swallow it, and that's just what we may do." Then he signaled that the interview was over.

At the end of forty days, CORE posted a $500 appeal bond for each of the Freedom Riders. Only after they had left the state did Mississippi spring its last surprise. Each of the three-hundred odd cases would have to be tried in the state appeals courts. The matter would not be settled through the arguing of a few selected "test cases."

JF: They agreed to that, yet one week before the arraignment, the state of Mississippi said, "Oh, no, every last one of them Freedom Riders gotta be back here in Jackson, Mississippi, for the arraignment, and anyone who doesn't show will have to forfeit that $500 bond that CORE has put up." And the prosecuting attorney told our lawyer very frankly. "We're gonna bankrupt CORE." . . . They almost did it, too.

In an ironic final act to the spring's high drama, CORE found itself chartering buses to haul the Freedom Riders back to Mississippi. But this time the riders were under strict orders to stay out of jail, for CORE was now saddled with legal fees, bail bond, and transportation costs of over $300,000.

JF: I called Roy Wilkins and told him of the problem, and Roy said, "Well, Jim, the NAACP will send you a check for a thousand dollars."

I said, "Fine, but a thousand dollars won't help."

Well, it helped a little bit, I guess. We put down the deposit on the buses that we were chartering. . . .

Thurgood Marshall saved us. I don't know, now that he's a Supreme Court justice, if he would want that known, but he saved us. I was at a cocktail party and Thurgood was there during this period, and he said, "Jim, how you coming along on that Freedom Ride now?"

I said, "Thurgood, Mississippi is gon' knock us out of the box. They're trying to bankrupt us and they don't know it, but they're just about succeeding 'cause we are *really* hard up now."

He said, "What's the problem, bail bond?"

I said, "Yeah. . . ."

He said, "The Inc. Fund* has got a bail bond fund. I don't know just what is in it, maybe $200,000, $250,000. It's not doing nothin'. It's just sitting there, salted away, drawing interest. You might as well use it as long as it lasts."

When he said that, I hugged him. [Laughs]

Postscript: CORE finally won in the Supreme Court and Mississippi had to refund the bond money. At the insistence of Robert Kennedy the Interstate Commerce Commission issued a directive which really did end bus segregation in parts of the South.

But the first phase of the Movement was over. So was James Farmer's moment as its leader, and so was CORE's day as the pacesetter of the Southern Movement. Now the torch would pass to SCLC and its preachers and to SNCC and its students, to these two organizations born in the South and tempered by Southern resistance for the long battle ahead in Alabama and Mississippi. And on the roadside at Anniston, at the terminal in Montgomery, in the drafty corridors of Parchman, the white folks who counted in those states had served notice that it would be a battle.

* The Inc. Fund, the NAACP Legal Defense and Education Fund, Inc., was administered by Marshall independently of the NAACP proper, the parent organization run by Wilkins.

Letter from Birmingham Jail

MARTIN LUTHER KING, JR.

Martin Luther King began writing his Letter from Birmingham Jail on the margins of the Birmingham News *issue that contained a letter from eight Christian and Jewish clergymen condemning the black demonstrations in Alabama. He continued writing on scraps of toilet paper, and completed the letter on a legal pad provided by his lawyers, who had also smuggled in the pen with which he composed this great document of the civil rights movement.*

Birmingham was King's thirteenth experience of jail. Only months before, he had been imprisoned in Albany, Georgia. At that time he had worried about his children's reaction to seeing him in jail. The children's mother had explained to their daughter Yolanda that, "Daddy was in jail so that all people could go where they liked." This had satisfied the child, who commented, "Good, tell him to stay in jail until I can go to Funtown [a local amusement park]." This reply was so important to King that he alluded to it in this famous letter. This reference was significant because King's most controversial tactic in Birmingham, barely mentioned in the letter, was the inclusion of children, even small grade-school children, among his marchers. Shortly after writing the letter and leaving jail, King had watched a confrontation between an angry policeman and an eight-year-old girl walking with her mother: "What do you want?" asked the policeman; "Freedom," replied the child, looking straight at him. During this scene, King remembered an old woman who had said about her involvement in the Montgomery bus boycott: "I'm doing it for my children and for my grandchildren." In 1963, seven years later, King commented, "The children and grandchildren are doing it for themselves."

The vision of policemen clubbing men, women, and children, of police dogs attacking crowds, of women and children bruised, bloodied, and smashed against walls and pavement by high pressure fire hoses shocked the world and transformed American public opinion. In February 1963 a weak administration's civil rights bill had died for lack of interest: "Nobody paid any attention," said Robert Kennedy. After the Birmingham demonstration of 1963 and its glorious symbolic coda, the March on Washington of August 1963, everyone paid attention. The eight Christian and Jewish clergymen from Alabama never answered King's letter, which was, in fact, unanswerable, but the churches of the nation did quickly move into the forefront of the coalition of concern that produced the great civil rights legislation of the mid-1960's. These enactments remain the great legacy of the movement and a substantial, although partial, realization of the dream King presented in the letter from Birmingham Jail and the "I Have a Dream" speech at the Lincoln Memorial later that same year.

My Dear Fellow Clergymen:

While confined here in the Birmingham city jail, I came across your recent statement calling my present activities "unwise and untimely." Seldom do I pause to answer criticism of my work and ideas. If I sought to answer all the criticisms that cross my desk, my secretaries would have little time for anything other than such correspondence in the course of the day, and I would have no time for constructive work. But since I feel that you are men of genuine good will and that your criticisms are sincerely set forth, I want to try to answer your statement in what I hope will be patient and reasonable terms.

I think I should indicate why I am here in Birmingham, since you have been influenced by the view which argues against "outsiders coming in." I have the honor of serving as president of the Southern Christian Leadership Conference, an organization operating in every southern state, with headquarters in Atlanta, Georgia. We have some eighty-five affiliated organizations across the South, and one of them is the Alabama Christian Movement for Human Rights. Frequently we share staff, educational and financial resources with our affiliates. Several months ago the affiliate here in Birmingham asked us to be on call to engage in a nonviolent direct-action program if such were deemed necessary. We readily consented, and when the hour came we lived up to our promise. So I, along with several members of my staff, am here because I was invited here. I am here because I have organizational ties here.

But more basically, I am in Birmingham because injustice is here. Just as the prophets of the eighth century B.C. left their villages and carried their "thus saith the Lord" far beyond the boundaries of their home towns, and just as the Apostle Paul left his village of Tarsus and carried the gospel of Jesus Christ to the far corners of the Greco-Roman world, so am I compelled to carry the gospel of freedom beyond my own home town. Like Paul, I must constantly respond to the Macedonian call for aid.

Moreover, I am cognizant of the interrelatedness of all communities and states. I cannot sit idly by in Atlanta and not be concerned about what happens in Birmingham. Injustice anywhere is a threat to justice everywhere. We are caught in an inescapable network of mutuality, tied in a single garment of destiny. Whatever affects one directly, affects all indirectly. Never again can we afford to live with the narrow, provincial "outside agitator" idea. Anyone who lives inside the United States can never be considered an outsider anywhere within its bounds.

You deplore the demonstrations taking place in Birmingham. But your statement, I am sorry to say, fails to express a similar concern for the conditions that brought about the demonstrations. I am sure that none of you would want to rest content with the superficial kind of social analysis that deals merely with effects and does not grapple with underlying causes. It is unfortunate that demonstrations are taking place in Birmingham, but it is even more unfortunate that the city's white power structure left the Negro community with no alternative.

In any nonviolent campaign there are four basic steps: collection of the facts to determine whether injustices exist; negotiation; self-purification; and direct action. We have gone through all these steps in Birmingham. There can be no gainsaying the fact that racial injustice engulfs this community. Birmingham is probably the most thoroughly segregated city in the United States. Its ugly record of brutality is widely known. Negroes have experienced grossly unjust treatment in the courts. There have been more unsolved bombings of Negro homes and churches in Birmingham than in any other city in the nation. These are the hard, brutal facts of the case. On the basis of these conditions, Negro leaders sought to negotiate with the city fathers. But the latter consistently refused to engage in good-faith negotiation.

Then, last September, came the opportunity to talk with leaders of Birmingham's economic community. In the course of the negotiations, certain promises were made by the merchants—for example, to remove the stores' humiliating racial signs. On the basis of these promises, the Reverend Fred Shuttlesworth and the leaders of the Alabama Christian Movement for Human Rights agreed to a moratorium on all demonstrations. As the weeks and months went by, we realized that we were the victims of a broken promise. A few signs, briefly removed, returned; the others remained.

As in so many past experiences, our hopes had been blasted, and the shadow of deep disappointment settled upon us. We had no alternative except to prepare for direct action, whereby we would present our very bodies as a means of laying our case before the conscience of the local and the national community. Mindful of the difficulties involved, we decided to undertake a process of self-purification. We began a series of workshops on nonviolence, and we repeatedly asked ourselves: "Are you able to accept blows without retaliating?" "Are you able to endure the ordeal of jail?" We decided to schedule our direct-action program for the Easter season, realizing that except for Christmas, this is the main shopping period of the year. Knowing that a strong economic-withdrawal program would be the by-product of direct action, we felt that this would be the best time to bring pressure to bear on the merchants for the needed change.

Then it occurred to us that Birmingham's mayoralty election was coming up in March, and we speedily decided to postpone action until after election day. When we discovered that the Commissioner of Public Safety, Eugene "Bull" Connor, had piled up enough votes to be in the run-off, we decided again to postpone action until the day after the run-off so that the demonstrations could not be used to cloud the issues. Like many others, we waited to see Mr. Connor defeated, and to this end we endured postponement after postponement. Having aided in this community need, we felt that our direct-action program could be delayed no longer.

You may well ask: "Why direct action? Why sit-ins, marches and so forth? Isn't negotiation a better path?" You are quite right in calling for negotiation. Indeed, this is the very purpose of direct action. Nonviolent direct action seeks to create such a crisis and foster such a tension that a community which has constantly refused to negotiate is forced to confront the issue. It seeks so to dramatize the issue that it can no longer be ignored. My citing the creation of tension as part of the work of the nonviolent-resister may sound rather shocking. But I must confess that I am not afraid of the word "tension." I have earnestly opposed violent tension, but there is a type of constructive, nonviolent tension which is necessary for growth. Just as Socrates felt that it was necessary to create a tension in the mind so that individuals could rise from the bondage of myths and half-truths to the unfettered realm of creative analysis and objective appraisal, so must we see the need for nonviolent gadflies to create the kind of tension in society that will help men rise from the dark depths of prejudice and racism to the majestic heights of understanding and brotherhood.

The purpose of our direct-action program is to create a situation so crisis-packed that it will inevitably open the door to negotiation. I therefore concur with you in your call for negotiation. Too long has our beloved Southland been bogged down in a tragic effort to live in monologue rather than dialogue.

One of the basic points in your statement is that the action that I and my associates have taken in Birmingham is untimely. Some have asked: "Why didn't you give the new city administration time to act?" The only answer that I can give to this query is that the new Birmingham administration must be prodded about as much as the outgoing one, before it will act. We are sadly mistaken if we feel that the election of Albert Boutwell as mayor will bring the millennium to Birmingham. While Mr. Boutwell is a much more gentle person than Mr. Connor, they are both segregationists, dedicated to maintenance of the status quo. I have hope that Mr. Boutwell will be reasonable enough to see the futility of massive resistance to desegregation. But he will not see this without pressure from devotees of civil rights. My friends, I must say to you that we have not made a single gain in civil rights without determined legal and nonviolent pressure. Lamentably, it is an historical fact that privileged groups seldom give up their privileges voluntarily. Individuals may see the moral light and voluntarily give up their unjust posture; but, as Reinhold Niebuhr has reminded us, groups tend to be more immoral than individuals.

We know through painful experience that freedom is never voluntarily given by the oppressor; it must be demanded by the oppressed. Frankly, I have yet to engage in a direct-action campaign that was "well timed" in the view of those who have not suffered unduly from the disease of segregation. For years now I have heard the word "Wait!" It rings in the ear of every Negro with piercing familiarity. This "Wait" has almost always meant "Never." We must come to see, with one of our distinguished jurists, that "justice too long delayed is justice denied."

We have waited for more than 340 years for our constitutional and God-given rights. The nations of Asia and Africa are moving with jet-like speed toward gaining political independence, but we still creep at horse-and-buggy pace toward gaining a cup of coffee at a lunch counter. Perhaps it is easy for those who have never felt the stinging darts of segregation to say, "Wait." But when you have seen vicious mobs lynch your mothers and fathers at will and drown your sisters and brothers at whim; when you have seen hate-filled policemen curse, kick and even kill your black brothers and sisters; when you see the vast majority of your twenty million Negro brothers smothering in an airtight cage of poverty in the midst of an affluent society; when you suddenly find your tongue twisted and your speech stammering as you seek to explain to your six-year-old daughter why she can't go to the public amusement park that has just been advertised on television, and see tears welling up in her eyes when she is told that Funtown is closed to colored children, and see ominous clouds of inferiority beginning to form in her little mental sky, and see her beginning to distort her personality by developing an unconscious bitterness toward white people; when you have to concoct an answer for a five-year-old son who is asking: "Daddy, why do white people treat colored people so mean?"; when you take a cross-country drive and find it necessary to sleep night after night in the uncomfortable corners of your automobile because no motel will accept you; when you are humiliated day in and day out by nagging signs reading "white" and "colored"; when your first name becomes "nigger," your middle name becomes "boy" (however old you are) and your last name becomes "John," and your wife and mother are never given the respected title "Mrs."; when you are harried by day and haunted by night by the fact that you are a Negro, living constantly at tiptoe stance, never quite knowing what to expect next, and are plagued with inner fears and outer resentments; when you are forever fighting a degenerating sense of "nobodiness"—then you will understand why we find it difficult to wait. There comes a time when the cup of endurance runs over, and men are no longer willing to be plunged into the abyss of despair. I hope, sirs, you can understand our legitimate and unavoidable impatience.

You express a great deal of anxiety over our willingness to break laws. This is certainly a legitimate concern. Since we so deligently urge people to obey the Supreme Court's decision of 1954 outlawing segregation in the public schools, at first glance it may seem rather paradoxical for us consciously to break laws. One may well ask: "How can you advocate breaking some laws and obeying others?" The answer lies in the fact that there are two types of laws: just and unjust. I would be the first to advocate obeying just laws. One has not only a legal but a moral responsibility to obey just laws. Conversely, one has a moral responsibility to disobey unjust laws. I would agree with St. Augustine that "an unjust law is no law at all."

Now, what is the difference between the two? How does one determine whether a law is just or unjust? A just law is a man-made code that squares with the moral law or the law of God. An unjust law is a code that is out of harmony with the moral law. To put it in the terms of St. Thomas Aquinas: An unjust law is a human law that is not rooted in eternal law and natural law. Any law that uplifts human personality is just. Any law that degrades human personality is unjust. All segregation statutes are unjust because segregation distorts the soul and damages the personality. It gives the segregator a false sense of superiority and the segregated a false sense of inferiority. Segregation, to use the terminology of the Jewish philosopher Martin Buber, substitutes an

"I—it" relationship for an "I—thou" relationship and ends up relegating persons to the status of things. Hence segregation is not only politically, economically and sociologically unsound, it is morally wrong and sinful. Paul Tillich has said that sin is separation. Is not segregation an existential expression of man's tragic separation, his awful estrangement, his terrible sinfulness? Thus it is that I can urge men to obey the 1954 decision of the Supreme Court, for it is morally right; and I can urge them to disobey segregation ordinances, for they are morally wrong.

Let us consider a more concrete example of just and unjust laws. An unjust law is a code that a numerical or power majority group compels a minority group to obey but does not make binding on itself. This is *difference* made legal. By the same token, a just law is a code that a majority compels a minority to follow and that it is willing to follow itself. This is *sameness* made legal.

Let me give another explanation. A law is unjust if it is inflicted on a minority that, as a result of being denied the right to vote, had no part in enacting or devising the law. Who can say that the legislature of Alabama which set up that state's segregation laws was democratically elected? Throughout Alabama all sorts of devious methods are used to prevent Negroes from becoming registered voters, and there are some counties in which, even though Negroes constitute a majority of the population, not a single Negro is registered. Can any law enacted under such circumstances be considered democratically structured?

Sometimes a law is just on its face and unjust in its application. For instance, I have been arrested on a charge of parading without a permit. Now, there is nothing wrong in having an ordinance which requires a permit for a parade. But such an ordinance becomes unjust when it is used to maintain segregation and to deny citizens the First-Amendment privilege of peaceful assembly and protest.

I hope you are able to see the distinction I am trying to point out. In no sense do I advocate evading or defying the law, as would the rabid segregationist. That would lead to anarchy. One who breaks an unjust law must do so openly, lovingly, and with a willingness to accept the penalty. I submit that an individual who breaks a law that conscience tells him is unjust, and who willingly accepts the penalty of imprisonment in order to arouse the conscience of the community over its injustice, is in reality expressing the highest respect for law.

Of course, there is nothing new about this kind of civil disobedience. It was evidenced sublimely in the refusal of Shadrach, Meshach and Abednego to obey the laws of Nebuchadnezzar, on the ground that a higher moral law was at stake. It was practiced superbly by the early Christians, who were willing to face hungry lions and the excruciating pain of chopping blocks rather than submit to certain unjust laws of the Roman Empire. To a degree, academic freedom is a reality today because Socrates practiced civil disobedience. In our own nation, the Boston Tea Party represented a massive act of civil disobedience.

We should never forget that everything Adolf Hitler did in Germany was "legal" and everything the Hungarian freedom fighters did in

Hungary was "illegal." It was "illegal" to aid and comfort a Jew in Hitler's Germany. Even so, I am sure that, had I lived Germany at the time, I would have aided and comforted my Jewish brothers. If today I lived in a Communist country where certain principles dear to the Christian faith are suppressed, I would openly advocate disobeying that country's antireligious laws.

I must make two honest confessions to you, my Christian and Jewish brothers. First, I must confess that over the past few years I have been gravely disappointed with the white moderate. I have almost reached the regrettable conclusion that the Negro's great stumbling block in his stride toward freedom is not the White Citizen's Counciler or the Ku Klux Klanner, but the white moderate, who is more devoted to "order" than to justice; who prefers a negative peace which is the absence of tension to a positive peace which is the presence of justice; who constantly says: "I agree with you in the goal you seek, but I cannot agree with your methods of direct action"; who paternalistically believes he can set the timetable for another man's freedom; who lives by a mythical concept of time and who constantly advises the Negro to wait for a "more convenient season." Shallow understanding from people of good will is more frustrating than absolute misunderstanding from people of ill will. Lukewarm acceptance is much more bewildering than outright rejection.

I had hoped that the white moderate would understand that law and order exist for the purpose of establishing justice and that when they fail in this purpose they become the dangerously structured dams that block the flow of social progress. I had hoped that the white moderate would understand that the present tension in the South is a necessary phase of the transition from an obnoxious negative peace, in which the Negro passively accepted his unjust plight, to a substantive and positive peace, in which all men will respect the dignity and worth of human personality. Actually, we who engage in nonviolent direct action are not the creators of tension. We merely bring to the surface the hidden tension that is already alive. We bring it out in the open, where it can be seen and dealt with. Like a boil that can never be cured so long as it is covered up but must be opened with all its ugliness to the natural medicines of air and light, injustice must be exposed, with all the tension its exposure creates, to the light of human conscience and the air of national opinion before it can be cured.

In your statement you assert that our actions, even though peaceful, must be condemned because they precipitate violence. But is this a logical assertion? Isn't this like condemning a robbed man because his possession of money precipitated the evil act of robbery? Isn't this like condemning Socrates because his unswerving commitment to truth and his philosophical inquiries precipitated the act by the misguided populace in which they made him drink hemlock? Isn't this like condemning Jesus because his unique God-consciousness and never-ceasing devotion to God's will precipitated the evil act of crucifixion? We must come to see that, as the federal courts have consistently affirmed, it is wrong to urge an individual to cease his efforts to gain his basic constitutional rights because the quest may precipitate violence. Society must protect the robbed and punish the robber.

I had also hoped that the white moderate would reject the myth concerning time in relation to the struggle for freedom. I have just received a letter from a white brother in Texas. He writes: "All Christians know that the colored people will receive equal rights eventually, but it is possible that you are in too great a religious hurry. It has taken Christianity almost two thousand years to accomplish what it has. The teachings of Christ take time to come to earth." Such an attitude stems from a tragic misconception of time, from the strangely irrational notion that there is something in the very flow of time that will inevitably cure all ills. Actually, time itself is neutral; it can be used either destructively or constructively. More and more I feel that the people of ill will have used time much more effectively than have the people of good will. We will have to repent in this generation not merely for the hateful words and actions of the bad people but for the appalling silence of the good people. Human progress never rolls in on wheels of inevitability; it comes through the tireless efforts of men willing to be co-workers with God, and without this hard work, time itself becomes an ally of the forces of social stagnation. We must use time creatively, in the knowledge that the time is always ripe to do right. Now is the time to make real the promise of democracy and transform our pending national elegy into a creative psalm of brotherhood. Now is the time to lift our national policy from the quicksand of racial injustice to the solid rock of human dignity.

You speak of our activity in Birmingham as extreme. At first I was rather disappointed that fellow clergymen would see my nonviolent efforts as those of an extremist. I began thinking about the fact that I stand in the middle of two opposing forces in the Negro community. One is a force of complacency, made up in part of Negroes who, as a result of long years of oppression, are so drained of self-respect and a sense of "somebodiness" that they have adjusted to segregation; and in part of a few middle-class Negroes who, because of a degree of academic and economic security and because in some ways they profit by segregation, have become insensitive to the problems of the masses. The other force is one of bitterness and hatred, and it comes perilously close to advocating violence. It is expressed in the various black nationalist groups that are springing up across the nation, the largest and best-known being Elijah Muhammad's Muslim movement. Nourished by the Negro's frustration over the continued existence of racial discrimination, this movement is made up of people who have lost faith in America, who have absolutely repudiated Christianity, and who have concluded that the white man is an incorrigible "devil."

I have tried to stand between these two forces, saying that we need emulate neither the "do-nothingism" of the complacent nor the hatred and despair of the black nationalist. For there is the more excellent way of love and nonviolent protest. I am grateful to God that, through the influence of the Negro church, the way of nonviolence became an integral part of our struggle.

If this philosophy had not emerged, by now many streets of the South would, I am convinced, be flowing with blood. And I am further convinced that if our white brothers dismiss as "rabble-rousers" and "outside agitators" those of us who employ nonviolent direct action, and if they refuse to support our nonviolent efforts, millions of Negroes will, out of frustration and despair, seek solace and security in black-nationalist ideologies—a development that would inevitably lead to a frightening racial nightmare.

Oppressed people cannot remain oppressed forever. The yearning for freedom eventually manifests itself, and that is what has happened to the American Negro. Something within has reminded him of his birthright of freedom, and something without has reminded him that it can be gained. Consciously or unconsciously, he has been caught up by the *Zeitgeist,* and with his black brothers of Africa and his brown and yellow brothers of Asia, South America and the Caribbean, the United States Negro is moving with a sense of great urgency toward the promised land of racial justice. If one recognizes this vital urge that has engulfed the Negro community, one should readily understand why public demonstrations are taking place. The Negro has many pent-up resentments and latent frustrations, and he must release them. So let him march; let him make prayer pilgrimages to the city hall; let him go on freedom rides—and try to understand why he must do so. If his repressed emotions are not released in nonviolent ways, they will seek expression through violence; this is not a threat but a fact of history. So I have not said to my people: "Get rid of your discontent." Rather, I have tried to say that this normal and healthy discontent can be channeled into the creative outlet of nonviolent direct action. And now this approach is being termed extremist.

But though I was initially disappointed at being categorized as an extremist, as I continued to think about the matter I gradually gained a measure of satisfaction from the label. Was not Jesus an extremist for love: "Love your enemies, bless them that curse you, do good to them that hate you, and pray for them which despitefully use you, and persecute you." Was not Amos an extremist for justice: "Let justice roll down like waters and righteousness like an ever-flowing stream." Was not Paul an extremist for the Christian gospel: "I bear in my body the marks of the Lord Jesus." Was not Martin Luther an extremist: "Here I stand; I cannot do otherwise, so help me God." And John Bunyan: "I will stay in jail to the end of my days before I make a butchery of my conscience." And Abraham Lincoln: "This nation cannot survive half slave and half free." And Thomas Jefferson: "We hold these truths to be self-evident, that all men are created equal . . ." So the question is not whether we will be extremists, but what kind of extremists we will be. Will we be extremists for hate or for love? Will we be extremists for the preservation of injustice or for the extension of justice? In that dramatic scene on Calvary's hill three men were crucified. We must never forget that all three were crucified for the same crime—the crime of extremism. Two were extremists for immorality, and thus fell below their environment. The other, Jesus Christ, was an extremist for love, truth and goodness, and thereby rose above his environment. Perhaps the South, the nation and the world are in dire need of creative extremists.

I had hoped that the white moderate would see this need. Perhaps I was too optimistic; perhaps I expected too much. I suppose I should have realized that few members of the oppressor race can understand the deep groans and passionate yearnings of the oppressed race, and still fewer have the vision to see that injustice must be rooted out by strong, persistent and determined action. I am thankful, however, that some of our white brothers in the South have grasped the meaning of this social revolution and committed themselves to it. They are still all too few in quantity, but they are big in quality. Some—such as Ralph McGill, Lillian Smith, Harry Golden, James McBride Dabbs, Ann Braden and Sarah Patton Boyle—have written about our struggle in eloquent and prophetic terms. Others have marched with us down nameless streets of the South. They have languished in filthy, roach-infested jails, suffering the abuse and brutality of policemen who view them as "dirty nigger-lovers." Unlike so many of their moderate brothers and sisters, they have recognized the urgency of the moment and sensed the need for powerful "action" antidotes to combat the disease of segregation.

Let me take note of my other major disappointment. I have been so greatly disappointed with the white church and its leadership. Of course, there are some notable exceptions. I am not unmindful of the fact that each of you has taken some significant stands on this issue. I commend you, Reverend Stallings, for your Christian stand on this past Sunday, in welcoming Negroes to your worship service on a non-segregated basis. I commend the Catholic leaders of this state for integrating Spring Hill College several years ago.

But despite these notable exceptions, I must honestly reiterate that I have been disappointed with the church. I do not say this as one of those negative critics who can always find something wrong with the church. I say this as a minister of the gospel, who loves the church; who was nurtured in its bosom; who has been sustained by its spiritual blessings and who will remain true to it as long as the cord of life shall lengthen.

When I was suddenly catapulted into the leadership of the bus protest in Montgomery, Alabama, a few years ago, I felt we would be supported by the white church. I felt that the white ministers, priests and rabbis of the South would be among our strongest allies. Instead, some have been outright opponents, refusing to understand the freedom movement and misrepresenting its leaders; all too many others have been more cautious than courageous and have remained silent behind the anesthetizing security of stained-glass windows.

In spite of my shattered dreams, I came to Birmingham with the hope that the white religious leadership of this community would see the justice of our cause and, with deep moral concern, would serve as the channel through which our just grievances could reach the power structure. I had hoped that each of you would understand. But again I have been disappointed.

I have heard numerous southern religious leaders admonish their worshipers to comply with a desegregation decision because it is the law, but I have longed to hear white ministers declare: "Follow this decree because integration is morally right and because the Negro is your brother." In the midst of blatant injustices inflicted upon the Negro, I have watched white churchmen stand on the sideline and mouth pious irrelevancies and sanctimonious trivialities. In the midst of a mighty struggle to rid our nation of racial and economic injustice, I have heard many ministers say: "Those are social issues, with which the gospel has no real concern." And I have watched many churches commit themselves to a completely other-worldly religion which make a strange, un-Biblical distinction between body and soul, between the sacred and the secular.

I have traveled the length and breadth of Alabama, Mississippi and all the other southern states. On sweltering summer days and crisp autumn mornings I have looked at the South's beautiful churches with their lofty spires pointing heavenward. I have beheld the impressive outlines of her massive religious-education buildings. Over and over I have found myself asking: "What kind of people worship here? Who is their God? Where were their voices when the lips of Governor Barnett dripped with words of interposition and nullification? Where were they when Governor Wallace gave a clarion call for defiance and hatred? Where were their voices of support when bruised and weary Negro men and women decided to rise from the dark dungeons of complacency to the bright hills of creative protest?"

Yes, these questions are still in my mind. In deep disappointment I have wept over the laxity of the church. But be assured that my tears have been tears of love. There can be no deep disappointment where there is not deep love. Yes, I love the church. How could I do otherwise? I am in the rather unique position of being the son, the grandson and the great-grandson of preachers. Yes, I see the church as the body of Christ. But, oh! How we have blemished and scarred that body through social neglect and through fear of being nonconformists.

There was a time when the church was very powerful—in the time when the early Christians rejoiced at being deemed worthy to suffer for what they believed. In those days the church was not merely a thermometer that recorded the ideas and principles of popular opinion; it was a thermostat that transformed the mores of society. Whenever the early Christians entered a town, the people in power became disturbed and immediately sought to convict the Christians for being "disturbers of the peace" and "outside agitators." But the Christians pressed on, in the conviction that they were "a colony of heaven," called to obey God rather than man. Small in number, they were big in commitment. They were too God-intoxicated to be "astronomically intimidated." By their effort and example they brought an end to such ancient evils as infanticide and gladiatorial contests.

Things are different now. So often the contemporary church is a weak, ineffectual voice with an uncertain sound. So often it is an arch-defender of the status quo. Far from being disturbed by the presence of the church, the power structure of the average community is consoled by the church's silent—and often even vocal—sanction of things as they are.

But the judgment of God is upon the church as never before. If today's church does not recapture the sacrificial spirit of the early church, it will lose its authenticity, forfeit the loyalty of millions, and be dismissed as an irrelevant social club with no meaning for the twentieth century. Every day I meet young people whose disappointment with the church has turned into outright disgust.

Perhaps I have once again been too optimistic. Is organized religion too inextricably bound to the status quo to save our nation and the world? Perhaps I must turn my faith to the inner spiritual church, the church within the church, as the true *ekklesia* and the hope of the world. But again I am thankful to God that some noble souls from the ranks of organized religion have broken loose from the paralyzing chains of conformity and joined us as active partners in the struggle for freedom. They have left their secure congregations and walked the streets of Albany, Georgia, with us. They have gone down the highways of the South on tortuous rides for freedom. Yes, they have gone to jail with us. Some have been dismissed from their churches, have lost the support of their bishops and fellow ministers. But they have acted in the faith that right defeated is stronger than evil triumphant. Their witness has been the spiritual salt that has preserved the true meaning of the gospel in these troubled times. They have carved a tunnel of hope through the dark mountain of disappointment.

I hope the church as a whole will meet the challenge of this decisive hour. But even if the church does not come to the aid of justice, I have no despair about the future. I have no fear about the outcome of our struggle in Birmingham, even if our motives are at present misunderstood. We will reach the goal of freedom in Birmingham and all over the nation, because the goal of America is freedom. Abused and scorned though we may be, our destiny is tied up with America's destiny. Before the pilgrims landed at Plymouth, we were here. Before the pen of Jefferson etched the majestic words of the Declaration of Independence across the pages of history, we were here. For more than two centuries our forebears labored in this country without wages; they made cotton king; they built the homes of their masters while suffering gross injustice and shameful humiliation—and yet out of a bottomless vitality they continued to thrive and develop. If the inexpressible cruelties of slavery could not stop us, the opposition we now face will surely fail. We will win our freedom because the sacred heritage of our nation and the eternal will of God are embodied in our echoing demands.

Before closing I feel impelled to mention one other point in your statement that has troubled me profoundly. You warmly commended the Birmingham police force for keeping "order" and "preventing violence." I doubt that you would have so warmly commended the police force if you had seen its dogs sinking their teeth into unarmed, nonviolent Negroes. I doubt that you would so quickly commend the policemen if you were to observe their ugly and inhumane treatment of Negroes here in the city jail; if you were to watch them push and curse old Negro women and young Negro girls; if you were to see them slap and kick old Negro men and young boys; if you were to observe them, as they did on two occasions, refuse to give us food because we wanted to sing our grace together. I cannot join you in your praise of the Birmingham police department.

It is true that the police have exercised a degree of discipline in handling the demonstrators. In this sense they have conducted themselves rather "nonviolently" in public. But for what purpose? To preserve the evil system of segregation. Over the past few years I have consistently preached that nonviolence demands that the means we use must be as pure as the ends we seek. I have tried to make clear that it is wrong to use immoral means to attain moral ends. But now I must affirm that it is just as wrong, or perhaps even more so, to use moral means to preserve immoral ends. Perhaps Mr. Connor and his policemen have been rather nonviolent in public, as was Chief Pritchett in Albany, Georgia, but they have used the moral means of nonviolence to maintain the immoral end of racial injustice. As T. S. Eliot has said: "The last temptation is the greatest treason: To do the right deed for the wrong reason."

I wish you had commended the Negro sit-inners and demonstrators of Birmingham for their sublime courage, their willingness to suffer and their amazing discipline in the midst of great provocation. One day the South will recognize its real heroes. They will be the James Merediths, with the noble sense of purpose that enables them to face jeering and hostile mobs, and with the agonizing loneliness that characterizes the life of the pioneer. They will be old, oppressed, battered Negro women, symbolized in a seventy-two-year-old woman in Montgomery, Alabama, who rose up with a sense of dignity and with her people decided not to ride segregated buses, and who responded with ungrammatical profundity to one who inquired about her weariness: "My feets is tired, but my soul is at rest." They will be the young high school and college students, the young ministers of the gospel and a host of their elders, courageously and nonviolently sitting in at lunch counters and willingly going to jail for conscience' sake. One day the South will know that when these disinherited children of God sat down at lunch counters, they were in reality standing up for what is best in the American dream and for the most sacred values in our Judaeo-Christian heritage, thereby bringing our nation back to those great wells of democracy which were dug deep by the founding fathers in their formulation of the Constitution and the Declaration of Independence.

Never before have I written so long a letter. I'm afraid it is much too long to take your precious time. I can assure you that it would have been much shorter if I had been writing from a comfortable desk, but what else can one do when he is alone in a narrow jail cell, other than write long letters, think long thoughts and pray long prayers?

If I have said anything in this letter that overstates the truth and indicates an unreasonable impatience, I beg you to forgive me. If I have said anything that understates the truth and indicates my having a patience that allows me to settle for anything less than brotherhood, I beg God to forgive me.

I hope this letter finds you strong in the faith. I also hope that circumstances will soon make it possible for me to meet each of you, not as an integrationist or a civil-rights leader but as a fellow clergyman and a Christian brother. Let us all hope that the dark clouds of racial prejudice will soon pass away and the deep fog of misunderstanding will be lifted from our fear-drenched communities, and in some not too distant tomorrow the radiant stars of love and brotherhood will shine over our great nation with all their scintillating beauty.

Yours for the cause of Peace and Brotherhood,

Martin Luther King, Jr.

On Revolution

MALCOLM X

*Malcolm X emerged as one of the first to attack the civil rights move-
ment from the left. As a member of the Black Muslims (Nation of
Islam), a black nationalist group, Malcolm X rejected the Christian
millennialism of Martin Luther King, Jr., the belief in nonviolence,
and the notion that whites could be converted to racial integration.
This speech delivered in November 1963, three months after King's "I
Have a Dream" speech, strikes the themes that dominated black power
movements in the ensuing years: solidarity with African nationalism,
emphasis on revolution with the attendant threat of violence, and insistence on black separatism rather than integration with whites.*

*During the years after Malcolm X left the Muslims, he moderated
some of his rhetoric. But overall he remains important as one of the
first major black voices in the 1960's to speak from the city streets rather
than from the rural southern base that King represented. Of course, the
principal successes in the drive against segregation and discrimination
did come in the South; the issues Malcolm X raised—what future lies
beyond civil rights for black Americans—remain to be resolved.*

．　．　．

Of all our studies, history is best qualified to reward our research.
And when you see that you've got problems, all you have to do is
examine the historic method used all over the world by others who have
problems similar to yours. Once you see how they got theirs straight,
then you know how you can get yours straight. There's been a revolution, a black revolution, going on in Africa. In Kenya, the Mau Mau
were revolutionary; they were the ones who brought the word "Uhuru"
to the fore. The Mau Mau, they were revolutionary, they believed in
scorched earth, they knocked everything aside that got in their way, and
their revolution also was based on land, a desire for land. In Algeria,
the northern part of Africa, a revolution took place. The Algerians were
revolutionists, they wanted land. France offered to let them be integrated into France. They told France, to hell with France, they wanted
some land, not some France. And they engaged in a bloody battle.

So I cite these various revolutions, brothers and sisters, to show you
that you don't have a peaceful revolution. You don't have a turn-the-
other-cheek revolution. There's no such thing as a nonviolent revolution. The only kind of revolution that is nonviolent is the Negro
revolution. The only revolution in which the goal is loving your enemy
is the Negro revolution. It's the only revolution in which the goal is
a desegregated lunch counter, a desegregated theater, a desegregated
park, and a desegregated public toilet; you can sit down next to white
folks—on the toilet. That's no revolution. Revolution is based on land.

Land is the basis for all independence. Land is the basis for freedom, justice, and equality.

The white man knows what a revolution is. He knows that the black revolution is world-wide in scope and in nature. The black revolution is sweeping Asia, is sweeping Africa, is rearing its head in Latin America. The Cuban Revolution—that's a revolution. They overturned the system. Revolution is in Asia, revolution is in Africa, and the white man is screaming because he sees revolution in Latin America. How do you think he'll react to you when you learn what a real revolution is? You don't know what a revolution is. If you did, you wouldn't use that word.

Revolution is bloody, revolution is hostile, revolution knows no compromise, revolution overturns and destroys everything that gets in its way. And you, sitting around here like a knot on the wall, saying, "I'm going to love these folks no matter how much they hate me." No, you need a revolution. Whoever heard of a revolution where they lock arms . . . singing "We Shall Overcome?" You don't do that in a revolution. You don't do any singing, you're too busy swinging. It's based on land. A revolutionary wants land so he can set up his own nation, an independent nation. These Negroes aren't asking for any nation—they're trying to crawl back on the plantation.

When you want a nation, that's called nationalism. When the white man became involved in a revolution in this country against England, what was it for? He wanted this land so he could set up another white nation. That's white nationalism. The American Revolution was white nationalism. The French Revolution was white nationalism. The Russian Revolution too—yes, it was—white nationalism. You don't think so? Why do you think Khrushchev and Mao can't get their heads together? White nationalism. All the revolutions that are going on in Asia and Africa today are based on what?—black nationalism. A revolutionary is a black nationalist. He wants a nation. . . . If you're afraid of black nationalism, you're afraid of revolution. And if you love revolution, you love black nationalism.

To understand this, you have to go back to what the young brother here referred to as the house Negro and the field Negro back during slavery. There were two kinds of slaves, the house Negro and the field Negro. The house Negroes—they lived in the house with the master, they dressed pretty good, they ate good because they ate his food—what he left. They lived in the attic or the basement, but still they lived near the master; and they loved the master more than the master loved himself. They would give their life to save the master's house—quicker than the master would. If the master said, "We got a good house here," the house Negro would say, "Yeah, we got a good house here." Whenever the master said "we," he said "we." That's how you tell a house Negro.

If the master's house caught on fire, the house Negro would fight harder to put the blaze out than the master would. If the master got sick, the house Negro would say "What's the matter, boss, *we* sick?" *We* sick! He identified himself with his master, more than his master identified with himself. And if you came to the house Negro and said, "Let's run away, let's escape, let's separate," the house Negro would look at you and say, "Man, you crazy. What you mean, separate? Where is there a better house than this? Where can I wear better clothes than this? Where can I eat better food than this?" That was that house Negro. In those days he was called a "house nigger." And that's what we call them today, because we've still got some house niggers running around here.

This modern house Negro loves his master. He wants to live near him. He'll pay three times as much as the house is worth just to live near his master, and then brag about "I'm the only Negro out here." "I'm the only one on my job." "I'm the only one in this school." You're nothing but a house Negro. And if someone comes to you right now and says, "Let's separate," you say the same thing that the house Negro said on the plantation. "What you mean, separate? From America, this good white man? Where you going to get a better job than you get here?" I mean, this is what you say. "I ain't left nothing in Africa," that's what you say. Why, you left your mind in Africa.

On that same plantation, there was the field Negro. The field Negroes—those were the masses. There were always more Negroes in the field than there were Negroes in the house. The Negro in the field caught hell. He ate leftovers. In the house they ate high on the hog. The Negro in the field didn't get anything but what was left of the insides of the hog. They call it "chitt'lings" nowadays. In those days they called them what they were—guts. That's what you were—gut-eaters. And some of you are still gut-eaters.

The field Negro was beaten from morning to night; he lived in a shack, in a hut; he wore old, castoff clothes. He hated his master. I say he hated his master. He was intelligent. That house Negro loved his master, but that field Negro—remember, they were in the majority, and they hated the master. When the house caught on fire, he didn't try to put it out; that field Negro prayed for a wind, for a breeze. When the master got sick, the field Negro prayed that he'd die. If someone came to the field Negro and said, "Let's separate, let's run," he didn't say "Where we going?" He'd say, "Any place is better than here." You've got field Negroes in America today. I'm a field Negro. The masses are the field Negroes. When they see this man's house on fire, you don't hear the little Negroes talking about "*our* government is in trouble." They say, "*The* government is in trouble." Imagine a Negro: "*Our* government!" I even heard one say "*our* astronauts." They won't even let him near the plant—and "*our* astronauts!" "*Our* Navy"—that's a Negro that is out of his mind, a Negro that is out of his mind.

Just as the slavemaster of that day used Tom, the house Negro, to keep the field Negroes in check, the same old slavemaster today has Negroes who are nothing but modern Uncle Toms, twentieth-century Uncle Toms, to keep you and me in check, to keep us under control, keep us passive and peaceful and nonviolent. That's Tom making you nonviolent. It's like when you go to the dentist, and the man's going to take your tooth. You're going to fight him when he starts pulling.

So he squirts some stuff in your jaw called novocaine, to make you think they're not going to do anything to you. So you sit there and because you've got all of that novocaine in your jaw, you suffer—peacefully. Blood running all down your jaw, and you don't know what's happening. Because someone has taught you to suffer—peacefully.

The white man does the same thing to you in the street, when he wants to put knots on your head and take advantage of you and not have to be afraid of your fighting back. To keep you from fighting back, he gets these old religious Uncle Toms to teach you and me, just like novocaine, to suffer peacefully. Don't stop suffering—just suffer peacefully. As Rev. Cleage pointed out, they say you should let your blood flow in the streets. This is a shame. You know he's a Christian preacher. If it's a shame to him, you know what it is to me.

There is nothing in our book, the Koran, that teaches us to suffer peacefully. Our religion teaches us to be intelligent. Be peaceful, be courteous, obey the law, respect everyone; but if someone puts his hand on you, send him to the cemetery. That's a good religion. In fact, that's that old-time religion. That's the one that Ma and Pa used to talk about: an eye for an eye, and a tooth for a tooth, and a head for a head, and a life for a life. That's a good religion. And nobody resents that kind of religion being taught but a wolf, who intends to make you his meal.

This is the way it is with the white man in America. He's a wolf—and you're sheep. Any time a shepherd, a pastor, teaches you and me not to run from the white man and, at the same time, teaches us not to fight the white man, he's a traitor to you and me. Don't lay down a life all by itself. No, preserve your life, it's the best thing you've got. And if you've got to give it up, let it be even-steven.

. . .

The Port Huron Statement

STUDENTS FOR A DEMOCRATIC SOCIETY

The radical tradition in America is a series of episodes, not a continuous story. Where conservatives and liberals never cease reaching back for real or imaginary forbears, radicals have generally insisted on forgetting the history of radicalism as the first act in any new beginning. In the early 1960's, when the Students for a Democratic Society spread from campus to campus, drawing together activists in the civil rights and peace movements, the group received compliments for precisely this tendency to forget the radical past. It was "pragmatic," "non-ideological," and "non-programmatic." The movement worried little about its intellectual underpinnings; its main concern was action. The Port Huron Statement, *drawn up at the first SDS convention in 1962, achieved wide circulation on the campuses as an "agenda for a generation."*

The document, written principally by Tom Hayden, is impressive in surprising ways. Its tentative assertions, social science language, and generally nationalistic and cooperative stance contrast sharply with the image of campus militancy of the later 1960's. In its quiet way, however, it states the main themes of the youth political movement: rejection of bureaucracy, anti-communism, alienation, and the lack of community. It is clearly the beginning of a quest, not a set of final answers. Where that quest led was one of the fascinating subjects of the decade. It raises the inevitable question—to what extent did the young radicals relive the experience of earlier radicals because they began by rejecting its lessons?

INTRODUCTION: AGENDA FOR A GENERATION

We are people of this generation, bred in at least modest comfort, housed now in universities, looking uncomfortably to the world we inherit.

When we were kids the United States was the wealthiest and strongest country in the world; the only one with the atom bomb, the least scarred by modern war, an initiator of the United Nations that we thought would distribute Western influence throughout the world. Freedom and equality for each individual, government of, by, and for the people—these American values we found good, principles by which we could live as men. Many of us began maturing in complacency.

As we grew, however, our comfort was penetrated by events too troubling to dismiss. First, the permeating and victimizing fact of human degradation, symbolized by the Southern struggle against racial bigotry, compelled most of us from silence to activism. Second, the enclosing fact of the Cold War, symbolized by the presence of the Bomb, brought awareness that we ourselves, and our friends, and millions of abstract "others" we knew more directly because of our common peril, might die at any time. We might deliberately ignore, or avoid, or fail to feel all other human problems, but not these two, for these were too immediate and crushing in their impact, too challenging in the demand that we as individuals take the responsibility for encounter and resolution.

While these and other problems either directly oppressed us or rankled our consciences and became our own subjective concerns, we began to see complicated and disturbing paradoxes in our surrounding America. The declaration "all men are created equal . . ." rang hollow before the facts of Negro life in the South and the big cities of the North. The proclaimed peaceful intentions of the United States contradicted its economic and military investments in the Cold War status quo.

We witnessed, and continue to witness, other paradoxes. With nuclear energy whole cities can easily be powered, yet the dominant nation-states seem more likely to unleash destruction greater than that incurred in all wars of human history. Although our own technology is destroying old and creating new forms of social organization, men still tolerate meaningless work and idleness. While two-thirds of mankind suffers undernourishment, our own upper classes revel amidst superfluous abundance. Although world population is expected to double in forty years, the nations still tolerate anarchy as a major principle of international conduct and uncontrolled exploitation governs the sapping of the earth's physical resources. Although mankind desperately needs revolutionary leadership, America rests in national stalemate, its goals ambiguous and tradition-bound instead of informed and clear, its democratic system apathetic and manipulated rather than "of, by, and for the people."

Not only did tarnish appear on our image of American virtue, not only did disillusion occur when the hypocrisy of American ideals was discovered, but we began to sense that what we had originally seen as the American Golden Age was actually the decline of an era. The worldwide outbreak of revolution against colonialism and imperialism, the entrenchment of totalitarian states, the menace of war, overpopulation, international disorder, supertechnology—these trends were testing the tenacity of our own commitment to democracy and freedom and our abilities to visualize their application to a world in upheaval.

Our work is guided by the sense that we may be the last generation in the experiment with living. But we are a minority—the vast majority of our people regard the temporary equilibriums of our society and world as eternally-functional parts. In this is perhaps the outstanding paradox: we ourselves are imbued with urgency, yet the message of our society is that there is no viable alternative to the present. Beneath the reassuring tones of the politicians, beneath the common opinion that America will "muddle through," beneath the stagnation of those who have closed their minds to the future, is the pervading feeling that there simply are no alternatives, that our times have witnessed the exhaustion not only of Utopias, but of any new departures as well.

Feeling the press of complexity upon the emptiness of life, people are fearful of the thought that at any moment things might be thrust out of control. They fear change itself, since change might smash whatever invisible framework seems to hold back chaos for them now. For most Americans, all crusades are suspect, threatening. The fact that each individual sees apathy in his fellows perpetuates the common reluctance to organize for change. The dominant institutions are complex enough to blunt the minds of their potential critics, and entrenched enough to swiftly dissipate or entirely repel the energies of protest and reform, thus limiting human expectancies. Then, too, we are a materially improved society, and by our own improvements we seem to have weakened the case for further change.

Some would have us believe that Americans feel contentment amidst prosperity—but might it not be better be called a glaze above deeply-felt anxieties about their role in the new world? And if these anxieties produce a developed indifference to human affairs, do they not as well produce a yearning to believe there *is* an alternative to the present, that something *can* be done to change circumstances in the school, the workplaces, the bureaucracies, the government? It is to this latter yearning, at once the spark and engine of change, that we direct our present appeal. The search for truly democratic alternatives to the present, and a commitment to social experimentation with them, is a worthy and fulfilling human enterprise, one which moves us and, we hope, others today. On such a basis do we offer this document of our convictions and analysis: as an effort in understanding and changing the conditions of humanity in the late twentieth century, an effort rooted in the ancient, still unfulfilled conception of man attaining determining influence over his circumstances of life. . . .

THE STUDENTS

In the last few years, thousands of American students demonstrated that they at least felt the urgency of the times. They moved actively and directly against racial injustices, the threat of war, violations of individual rights of conscience and, less frequently, against economic manipulation. They suceeded in restoring a small measure of controversy to the campuses after the stillness of the McCarthy period. They succeeded, too, in gaining some concessions from the people and institutions they opposed, especially in the fight against racial bigotry.

The significance of these scattered movements lies not in their success or failure in gaining objectives—at least not yet. Nor does the significance lie in the intellectual "competence" or "maturity" of the students involved—as some pedantic elders allege. The significance is in the fact the students are breaking the crust of apathy and overcoming the inner alienation that remain the defining characteristics of American college life.

If student movements for change are still rareties on the campus scene, what is commonplace there? The real campus, the familiar campus, is a place of private people, engaged in their notorious "inner emigration." It is a place of commitment to business-as-usual, getting ahead, playing it cool. It is a place of mass affirmation of the Twist, but mass reluctance toward the controversial public stance. Rules are accepted as "inevitable," bureaucracy as "just circumstances," irrelevance as "scholarship," selflessness as "martyrdom," politics as "just another way to make people, and an unprofitable one, too."

Almost no students value activity as citizens. Passive in public, they are hardly more idealistic in arranging their private lives: Gallup concludes they will settle for "low success, and won't risk high failure." There is not much willingness to take risks (not even in business), no settling of dangerous goals, no real conception of personal identity except one manufactured in the image of others, no real urge for personal fulfillment except to be almost as successful as the very successful people. Attention is being paid to social status (the quality of shirt collars, meeting people, getting wives or husbands, making solid contacts for later on); much, too, is paid to academic status (grades, honors, the med school rat race). But neglected generally is real intellectual status, the personal cultivation of the mind.

"Students don't even give a damn about the apathy," one has said. Apathy toward apathy begets a privately-constructed universe, a place of systematic study schedules, two nights each week for beer, a girl or two, and early marriage; a framework infused with personality, warmth, and under control, no matter how unsatisfying otherwise.

Under these conditions university life loses all relevance to some. Four hundred thousand of our classmates leave college every year.

But apathy is not simply an attitude; it is a product of social institutions, and of the structure and organization of higher education itself. The extracurricular life is ordered according to *in loco parentis* theory, which ratifies the Administration as the moral guardian of the young.

The accompanying "let's pretend" theory of student extracurricular affairs validates student government as a training center for those who want to spend their lives in political pretense, and discourages initiative from the more articulate, honest, and sensitive students. The bounds and style of controversy are delimited before controversy begins. The university "prepares" the student for "citizenship" through perpetual rehearsals and, usually, through emasculation of what creative spirit there is in the individual.

The academic life contains reinforcing counterparts to the way in which extracurricular life is organized. The academic world is founded on a teacher-student relation analogous to the parent-child relation which characterizes *in loco parentis*. Further, academia includes a radical separation of the student from the material of study. That which is studied, the social reality, is "objectified" to sterility, dividing the student from life—just as he is restrained in active involvement by the deans controlling student government. The specialization of function and knowledge, admittedly necessary to our complex technological and social structure, has produced an exaggerated compartmentalization of study and understanding. This has contributed to an overly parochial view, by faculty, of the role of its research and scholarship, to a discontinuous and truncated understanding, by students, of the surrounding social order; and to a loss of personal attachment, by nearly all, to the worth of study as a humanistic enterprise.

There is, finally, the cumbersome academic bureaucracy extending throughout the academic as well as the extracurricular structures, contributing to the sense of outer complexity and inner powerlessness that transforms the honest searching of many students to a ratification of convention and, worse, to a numbness to present and future catastrophes. The size and financing systems of the university enhance the permanent trusteeship of the administrative bureaucracy, their power leading to a shift within the university toward the value standards of business and the administrative mentality. Huge foundations and other private financial interests shape the under-financed colleges and universities, not only making them more commercial, but less disposed to diagnose society critically, less open to dissent. Many social and physical scientists, neglecting the liberating heritage of higher learning, develop "human relations" or "morale-producing" techniques for the corporate economy, while others exercise their intellectual skills to accelerate the arms race.

Tragically, the university could serve as a significant source of social criticism and an initiator of new modes and molders of attitudes. But the actual intellectual effect of the college experience is hardly distinguishable from that of any other communications channel—say, a television set—passing on the stock truths of the day. Students leave college somewhat more "tolerant" than when they arrived, but basically unchallenged in their values and political orientations. With administrators ordering the institution, and faculty the curriculum, the student learns by his isolation to accept elite rule within the university, which prepares him to accept later forms of minority control. The real function of the educational system—as opposed to its more rhetorical function of "searching for truth"—is to impart the key information and styles that will help the student get by, modestly but comfortably, in the big society beyond.

THE SOCIETY BEYOND

Look beyond the campus, to America itself. That student life is more intellectual, and perhaps more comfortable, does not obscure the fact that the fundamental qualities of life on the campus reflect the habits of society at large. The fraternity president is seen at the junior manager levels; the sorority queen has gone to Grosse Pointe; the serious poet burns for a place, any place, to work; the once-serious and never-serious poets work at the advertising agencies. The desperation of people threatened by forces about which they know little and of which they can say less; the cheerful emptiness of people "giving up" all hope of changing things; the faceless ones polled by Gallup who listed "international affairs" fourteenth on their list of "problems" but who also expected thermonuclear war in the next few years; in these and other forms, Americans are in withdrawal from public life, from any collective effort at directing their own affairs.

Some regard these national doldrums as a sign of healthy approval of the established order—but is it approval by consent or manipulated acquiescence? Others declare that the people are withdrawn because compelling issues are fast disappearing—perhaps there are fewer bread-lines in America, but is Jim Crow gone, is there enough work and work more fulfilling, is world war a diminishing threat, and what of the revolutionary new peoples? Still others think the national quietude is a necessary consequence of the need for elites to resolve complex and specialized problems of modern industrial society—but, then, why should *business* elites help decide foreign policy, and who controls the elites anyway, and are they solving mankind's problems? Others, finally, shrug knowingly and announce that full democracy never worked anywhere in the past—but why lump qualitatively different civilizations together, and how can a social order work well if its best thinkers are skeptics, and is man really doomed forever to the domination of today?

There are no convincing apologies for the contemporary malaise. While the world tumbles toward final war, while men in other nations are trying desperately to alter events, while the very future qua future is uncertain—America is without community, impulse, without the inner momentum necessary for an age when societies cannot successfully perpetuate themselves by their military weapons, when democracy must be viable because of the quality of life, not its quantity of rockets.

The apathy here is, first *subjective*—the felt powerlessness of ordinary people, the resignation before the enormity of events. But subjective apathy is encouraged by the *objective* American situation—the actual structural separation of people from power, from relevant knowledge, from pinnacles of decision-making. Just as the university influences the student way of life, so do major social institutions create the circumstances in which the isolated citizen will try hopelessly to understand his world and himself.

The very isolation of the individual—from power and community and ability to aspire—means the rise of a democracy without publics. With the great mass of people structurally remote and psychologically hesitant with respect to democratic institutions, those institutions themselves attenuate and become, in the fashion of the vicious circle, progressively less accessible to those few who aspire to serious participation in social affairs. The vital democratic connection between community and leadership, between the mass and the several elites, has been so wrenched and perverted that disastrous policies go unchallenged time and again.

POLITICS WITHOUT PUBLICS

The American political system is not the democratic model of which its glorifiers speak. In actuality it frustrates democracy by confusing the individual citizen, paralyzing policy discussion, and consolidating the irresponsible power of military and business interests.

A crucial feature of the political apparatus in America is that greater differences are harbored within each major party than the differences existing between them. Instead of two parties presenting distinctive and significant differences of approach, what dominates the system is a natural interlocking of Democrats from Southern states with the more conservative elements of the Republican party. This arrangement of forces is blessed by the seniority system of Congress which guarantees congressional committee domination by conservatives—ten of 17 committees in the Senate and 13 of 21 in the House of Representatives are chaired currently by Dixiecrats.

The party overlap, however, is not the only structural antagonist of democracy in politics. First, the localized nature of the party system does not encourage discussion of national and international issues: thus problems are not raised by and for people, and political representatives usually are unfettered from any responsibilities to the general public except those regarding parochial matters. Second, whole constituencies are divested of the full political power they might have: many Negroes in the South are prevented from voting, migrant workers are disenfranchised by various residence requirements, some urban and suburban dwellers are victimized by gerrymandering, and poor people are too often without the power to obtain political representation. Third, the focus of political attention is significantly distorted by the enormous lobby force, composed predominantly of business interests, spending hundreds of millions each year in an attempt to conform facts about productivity, agriculture, defense, and social services, to the wants of private economic groupings.

What emerges from the party contradiction and insulation of privately-held power is the organized political stalemate: calcification dominates flexibility as the principle of parliamentary organization, frustration is the expectancy of legislators intending liberal reform, and Congress becomes less and less central to national decision-making especially in the area of foreign policy. In this context, confusion and blurring is built into the formulation of issues, long-range priorities are not discussed in the rational manner needed for policy-making, the politics of personality and "image" become a more important mechanism than the construction of issues in a way that affords each voter a challenging and real option. The American voter is buffeted from all directions by pseudo-problems, by the structurally-initiated sense that nothing political is subject to human mastery. Worried by his mundane problems which never get solved, but constrained by the common belief that politics is an agonizingly slow accommodation of views, he quits all pretense of bothering.

A most alarming fact is that few, if any, politicians are calling for changes in these conditions. Only a handful even are calling on the President to "live up to" platform pledges; no one is demanding structural changes, such as the shuttling of Southern Democrats out of the Democratic Party. Rather than protesting the state of politics, most politicians are reinforcing and aggravating that state. While in practice they rig public opinion to suit their own interests, in word and ritual they enshrine "the sovereign public" and call for more and more letters. Their speeches and campaign actions are banal, based on a degrading conception of what people want to hear. They respond not to dialogue, but to pressure: and knowing this, the ordinary citizen sees even greater inclination to shun the political sphere. The politician is usually a trumpeter to "citizenship" and "service to the nation," but since he is unwilling to seriously rearrange power relationships, his trumpetings only increase apathy by creating no outlets. Much of the time the call to "service" is justified not in idealistic terms, but in the crasser terms of "defending the free world from communism"—thus making future idealistic impulses harder to justify in anything but Cold War terms.

In such a setting of status quo politics, where most if not all government activity is rationalized in Cold War anti-communist terms, it is somewhat natural that discontented, super-patriotic groups would emerge through political channels and explain their ultra-conservatism as the best means of Victory over Communism. They have become a politically influential force within the Republican Party, at a national level through Senator Goldwater, and at a local level through their important social and economic roles. Their political views are defined generally as the opposite of the supposed views of communists: complete individual freedom in the economic sphere, non-participation by the government in the machinery of production. But actually "anti-communism" becomes an umbrella by which to protest liberalism, internationalism, welfareism, the active civil rights and labor movements. It is to the disgrace of the United States that such a movement should become a prominent kind of public participation in the modern world—but, ironically, it is somewhat to the interests of the United States that such a movement should be a public constituency pointed toward realignment of the political parties, demanding a conservative Republican Party in the South and an exclusion of the "leftist" elements of the national GOP.

THE ECONOMY

American capitalism today advertises itself as the Welfare State. Many of us comfortably expect pensions, medical care, unemployment compensation, and other social services in our lifetimes. Even with one-fourth of our productive capacity unused, the majority of Americans are living in relative comfort—although their nagging incentive to "keep up" makes them continually dissatisfied with their possessions. In many places, unrestrained bosses, uncontrolled machines, and sweat-shop conditions have been reformed or abolished and suffering tremendously relieved. But in spite of the benign yet obscuring effects of the New Deal reforms and the reassuring phrases of government economists and politicians, the paradoxes and myths of the economy are sufficient to irritate our complacency and reveal to us some essential causes of the American malaise.

We live amidst a national celebration of economic prosperity while poverty and deprivation remain an unbreakable way of life for millions in the "affluent society," including many of our own generation. We hear glib references to the "welfare state," "free enterprise," and "shareholder's democracy" while military defense is the main item of "public" spending and obvious oligopoly and other forms of minority rule defy real individual initiative or popular control. Work, too, is often unfulfilling and victimizing, accepted as a channel to status or plenty, if not a way to pay the bills, rarely as a means of understanding and controlling self and events. In work and leisure the individual is regulated as part of the system, a consuming unit, bombarded by hard-sell, soft-sell, lies and semi-true appeals to his basest drives. He is always told that he is a "free" man because of "free enterprise." . . .

THE MILITARY-INDUSTRIAL COMPLEX

The most spectacular and important creation of the authoritarian and oligopolistic structure of economic decision-making in America is the institution called "the military-industrial complex" by former President Eisenhower—the powerful congruence of interest and structure among military and business elites which affects so much of our development and destiny. Not only is ours the first generation to live with the possibility of world-wide cataclysm—it is the first to experience the actual social preparation for cataclysm, the general militarization of American society. In 1948 Congress established Universal Military Training, the first peacetime conscription. The military became a permanent institution. Four years earlier, General Motors' Charles E. Wilson had heralded the creation of what he called the "permanent war economy," the continuous use of military spending as a solution to economic problems unsolved before the post-war boom, most notably the problem of the seventeen million jobless after eight years of the New Deal. This has left a "hidden crisis" in the allocation of resources by the American economy.

Since our childhood these two trends—the rise of the military and the installation of a defense-based economy—have grown fantastically. The Department of Defense, ironically the world's largest single organization, is worth $160 billion, owns 32 million acres of America and employs half the 7.5 million persons directly dependent on the military for subsistence, has an $11 billion payroll which is larger than the net annual income of all American corporations. Defense spending in the Eisenhower era totaled $350 billions and President Kennedy entered office pledged to go even beyond the present defense allocation of 60 cents from every public dollar spent. Except for a war-induced boom immediately after "our side" bombed Hiroshima, American economic prosperity has coincided with a growing dependence on military outlay—from 1941 to 1959 America's Gross National Product of $5.25 trillion included $700 billion in goods and services purchased for the defense effort, about one-seventh of the accumulated GNP. This pattern has included the steady concentration of military spending among a few corporations. In 1961, 86 percent of Defense Department contracts were awarded without competition. The ordnance industry of 100,000 people is completely engaged in military work; in the aircraft industry, 94 percent of 750,000 workers are linked to the war economy; shipbuilding, radio and communications equipment industries commit 40 percent of their work to defense; iron and steel, petroleum, metal-stamping and machine shop products, motors and generators, tools and hardware, copper, aluminum and machine tools industries all devote at least 10 percent of their work to the same cause.

The intermingling of Big Military and Big Industry is evidenced in the 1,400 former officers working for the 100 corporations who received nearly all the $21 billion spent in procurement by the Defense Department in 1961. The overlap is most poignantly clear in the case of General Dynamics, the company which received the best 1961 contracts, employed the most retired officers (187), and is directed by a former Secretary of the Army. A *Fortune* magazine profile of General Dynamics said: "The unique group of men who run Dynamics are only incidentally in rivalry with other U.S. manufacturers, with many of whom they actually act in concert. Their chief competitor is the USSR. The core of General Dynamics' corporate philosophy is the conviction that national defense is a more or less permanent business." Little has changed since Wilson's proud declaration of the Permanent War Economy back in the 1944 days when the top 200 corporations possessed 80 percent of all active prime war-supply contracts.

MILITARY-INDUSTRIAL POLITICS

The military and its supporting business foundation have found numerous forms of political expression, and we have heard their din endlessly. There has not been a major Congressional split on the issue of continued defense spending spirals in our lifetime. The triangular relations of the business, military, and political arenas cannot be better expressed than in Dixiecrat Carl Vinson's remarks as his House Armed Services Committee reported out a military construction bill of $808 million throughout the 50 states, for 1960-61: "There is something in this bill for everyone," he announced. President Kennedy had earlier acknowledged the valuable anti-recession features of the bill.

Imagine, on the other hand, $808 million suggested as an anti-recession measure, but being poured into programs of social welfare: the impossibility of receiving support for such a measure identifies a crucial feature of defense spending—it is beneficial to private enterprise, while welfare spending is not. Defense spending does not "compete" with the private sector; it contains a natural obsolescence; its "confidential" nature permits easier boondoggling; the tax burdens to which it leads can be shunted from corporation to consumer as a "cost of production." Welfare spending, however, involves the government in competition with private corporations and contractors; it conflicts with immediate interests of private pressure groups; it leads to taxes on business. Think of the opposition of private power companies to current proposals for river and valley development, or the hostility of the real estate lobby to urban renewal; or the attitude of the American Medical

Association to a paltry medical care bill; or of all business lobbyists to
foreign aid; these are the pressures leading to the schizophrenic public-
military, private-civilian economy of our epoch. The politicians, of
course, take the line of least resistance and thickest support: warfare,
instead of welfare, is easiest to stand up for: after all, the Free World
is at stake (and our constituency's investments, too). . . .

THE STANCE OF LABOR

Amidst all this, what of organized labor, the historic institutional
representative of the exploited, the presumed "countervailing power"
against the excesses of Big Business? The contemporary social assault on
the labor movement is of crisis proportions. To the average American,
"big labor" is a growing cancer equal in impact to Big Business—nothing
could be more distorted, even granting a sizeable union bureaucracy.
But in addition to public exaggerations, the labor crisis can be measured
in several ways. First, the high expectations of the newborn AFL-CIO
of 30 million members by 1965 are suffering a reverse unimaginable
five years ago. The demise of the dream of "organizing the unorganized"
is dramatically reflected in the AFL-CIO decision, just two years after
its creation, to slash its organizing staff in half. From 15 million members when the AFL and CIO merged, the total has slipped to 13.5 million. During the post-war generation, union membership nationally has
increased by four million—but the total number of workers has jumped
by 13 million. Today only 40 percent of all non-agricultural workers are
protected by any form of organization. Second, organizing conditions
are going to worsen. Where labor now is strongest—in industries—automation is leading to an attrition of available work. As the number of
jobs dwindles, so does labor's power of bargaining, since management
can handle a strike in an automated plant more easily than the older
mass-operated ones.

More important, perhaps, the American economy has changed
radically in the last decade, as suddenly the number of workers producing goods became fewer than the number in "nonproductive" areas—
government, trade, finance, services, utilities, transportation. Since
World War II "white collar" and "service" jobs have grown twice as
fast as have "blue collar" production jobs. Labor has almost no organization in the expanding occupational areas of the new economy, but
almost all of its entrenched strength in contracting areas. As big government hires more, as business seeks more office workers and skilled technicians, and as growing commercial America demands new hotels, service
stations and the like, the conditions will become graver still. Further,
there is continuing hostility to labor by the Southern states and their
industrial interests—meaning "runaway" plants, cheap labor threatening
the organized trade union movement, and opposition from Dixiecrats to
favorable labor legislation in Congress. Finally, there is indication that
Big Business, for the sake of public relations if nothing more, has acknowledged labor's "right" to exist, but has deliberately tried to contain
labor at its present strength, preventing strong unions from helping

weaker ones or from spreading to unorganized sectors of the economy. Business is aided in its efforts by proliferation of "right-to-work" laws at state levels (especially in areas where labor is without organizing strength to begin with), and anti-labor legislation in Congress.

In the midst of these besetting crises, labor itself faces its own problems of vision and program. Historically, there can be no doubt as to its worth in American politics—what progress there has been in meeting human needs in this century rests greatly with the labor movement. And to a considerable extent the social democracy for which labor has fought externally is reflected in its own essentially democratic character: representing millions of people, not millions of dollars; demanding their welfare, not eternal profit.

Today labor remains the most liberal "mainstream" institution—but often its liberalism represents vestigial commitments, self-interestedness, unradicalism. In some measure labor has succumbed to institutionalization, its social idealism waning under the tendencies of bureaucracy, materialism, business ethics. The successes of the last generation perhaps have braked, rather than accelerated labor's zeal for change. Even the House of Labor has bay windows: not only is this true of the labor elites, but as well of some of the rank-and-file. Many of the latter are indifferent unionists, uninterested in meetings, alienated from the complexities of the labor-management negotiating apparatus, lulled to comfort by the accessibility of luxury and the opportunity of long-term contracts. "Union democracy" is not simply inhibited by labor-leader elitism, but by the related problem of rank-and-file apathy to the tradition of unionism. The crisis of labor is reflected in the co-existence within the unions of militant Negro discontents and discriminatory locals, sweeping critics of the obscuring "public interest" marginal tinkering of government and willing handmaidens of conservative political leadership, austere sacrificers and business-like operators, visionaries and anachronisms—tensions between extremes that keep alive the possibilities for a more militant unionism. Too there are seeds of rebirth in the "organizational crisis" itself: the technologically unemployed, the unorganized white collar men and women, the migrants and farm workers, the unprotected Negroes, the poor, all of whom are isolated now from the power structure of the economy, but who are the potential base for a broader and more forceful unionism.

HORIZON

In summary: a more reformed, more human capitalism, functioning at three-fourths capacity while one-third of America and two-thirds of the world goes needy, domination of politics and the economy by fantastically rich elites, accommodation and limited effectiveness by the labor movement, hard-core poverty and unemployment, automation confirming the dark ascension of machine over man instead of shared abundance, technological change being introduced into the economy by the criteria of profitability—this has been our inheritance. However inadequate, it has instilled quiescence in liberal hearts—partly reflecting the extent to which misery has been overcome, but also the eclipse of social ideals. Though many of us are "affluent," poverty, waste, elitism, manipulation are too manifest to go unnoticed, too clearly unnecessary to go accepted. To change the Cold War status quo and other social evils, concern with the challenges to the American economic machine must expand. Now, as a truly better social state becomes visible, a new poverty impends: a poverty of vision, and a poverty of political action to make that vision reality. Without new vision, the failure to achieve our potentialities will spell the inability of our society to endure in a world of obvious, crying needs and rapid change. . . .

TOWARDS AMERICAN DEMOCRACY

Every effort to end the Cold War and expand the process of world industrialization is an effort hostile to people and institutions whose interests lie in perpetuation of the East-West military threat and the postponement of change in the "have not" nations of the world. Every such effort, too, is bound to establish greater democracy in America. The major goals of a domestic effort would be:

1 *America must abolish its political party stalemate.*

Two genuine parties, centered around issues and essential values, demanding allegiance to party principles shall supplant the current system of organized stalemate which is seriously inadequate to a world in flux. . . . What is desirable is sufficient party disagreement to dramatize major issues, yet sufficient party overlap to guarantee stable transitions from administration to administration.

Every time the President criticizes a recalcitrant Congress, we must ask that he no longer tolerate the Southern conservatives in the Democratic Party. Every time a liberal representative complains that "we can't expect everything at once" we must ask if we received much of anything from Congress in the last generation. Every time he refers to "circumstances beyond control" we must ask why he fraternizes with racist scoundrels. Every time he speaks of the "unpleasantness of personal and party fighting" we should insist that pleasantry with Dixiecrats is inexcusable when the dark peoples of the world call for American support.

2 *Mechanisms of voluntary association must be created through which political information can be imparted and political participation encouraged.*

Political parties, even if realigned, would not provide adequate outlets for popular involvement. Institutions should be created that engage people with issues and express political preference, not as now with huge business lobbies which exercise undemocratic *power* but which carry political *influence* (appropriate to private, rather than public, groupings) in national decision-making enterprise. Private in nature, these should be organized around single issues (medical care, transportation systems reform, etc.), concrete interest (labor and minority group organizations); multiple issues or general issues. These do not exist in America in quantity today. If they did exist, they would be a significant politicizing and educative force bringing people into touch with public life and affording them means of expression and action. Today, giant lobby representatives of business interests are dominant, but not educative. The Federal government itself should counter the latter forces whose intent is often public deceit for private gain, by subsidizing the preparation and decentralized distribution of objective materials on all public issues facing government.

3 *Institutions and practices which stifle dissent should be abolished, and the promotion of peaceful dissent should be actively promoted.*

The First Amendment freedoms of speech, assembly, thought, religion and press should be seen as guarantees, not threats, to national security. While society has the right to prevent active subversion of its laws and institutions, it has the duty as well to promote open discussion of all issues—otherwise it will be in fact promoting real subversion as the only means of implementing ideas. To eliminate the fears and apathy from national life it is necessary that the institutions bred by fear and apathy be rooted out: the House Un-American Activities Committee, the Senate Internal Security Committee, the loyalty oaths on Federal loans, the Attorney General's list of subversive organizations, the Smith and McCarran Acts. The process of eliminating the blighting institutions is the process of restoring democratic participation. Their existence is a sign of the decomposition and atrophy of participation.

4 *Corporations must be made publicly responsible.*

It is not possible to believe that true democracy can exist where a minority utterly controls enormous wealth and power. The influence of corporate elites on foreign policy is neither reliable nor democratic; a way must be found to subordinate private American foreign investment to a democratically-constructed foreign policy. . . .

Labor and government as presently constituted are not sufficient to "regulate" corporations. A new re-ordering, a new calling of responsibility is necessary: more than changing "work rules" we must consider changes in the rules of society by challenging the unchallenged politics of American corporations. Before the government can really begin to control business in a "public interest," the public must gain more substantial control of government: this demands a movement for political as well as economic realignments. We are aware that simple government "regulation," if achieved, would be inadequate without increased worker participation in management decision-making, strengthened and independent regulatory power, balances of partial and/or complete public ownership, various means of humanizing the conditions and types of work itself, sweeping welfare programs and regional *public* development authorities. These are examples of measures to re-balance the economy toward public—and individual—control.

5 *The allocation of resources must be based on social needs. A truly "public sector" must be established, and its nature debated and planned.*

At present the majority of America's "public sector," the largest part of our public spending, is for the military. When great social needs are so pressing, our concept of "government spending" is wrapped up in the "permanent war economy." . . .

The main *private* forces of economic expansion cannot guarantee a steady rate of growth, nor acceptable recovery from recession—especially in a demilitarizing world. Government participation will inevitably expand enormously, because the stable growth of the economy demands increasing "public" investments yearly. Our present outpour of more than $500 billion might double in a generation, irreversibly involving government solutions. And in future recessions, the compensatory fiscal action by the government will be the only means of avoiding the twin disasters of greater unemployment and a slackening rate of growth. Furthermore, a close relationship with the European Common Market will involve competition with numerous planned economies and may aggravate American unemployment unless the economy here is expanding swiftly enough to create new jobs.

All these tendencies suggest that not only solutions to our present social needs but our future expansion rests upon our willingness to enlarge the "public sector" greatly. Unless we choose war as an economic solvent, future public spending will be of non-military nature—a major intervention into civilian production by the government. . . .

6 *America should concentrate on its genuine social priorities: abolish squalor, terminate neglect, and establish an environment for people to live in with dignity and creativeness.*

A. A program against *poverty* must be just as sweeping as the nature of poverty itself. It must not be just palliative, but directed to the abolition of the structural circumstances of poverty. At a bare minimum it should include a *housing* act far larger than the one supported by the Kennedy Administration, but one that is geared more to low- and middle-income needs than to the windfall aspirations of small and large private entrepreneurs, one that is more sympathetic to the quality of communal life than to the efficiency of city-split highways. Second, *medical care* must become recognized as a lifetime human right just as vital as food, shelter and clothing—the Federal government should guarantee health insurance as a basic social service turning medical treatment into a social habit, not just an occasion of crisis, fighting sickness among the aged, not just by making medical care financially feasible but by reducing sickness among children and younger people. Third, existing institutions should be expanded so the Welfare State cares for *everyone's* welfare according to need. *Social Security* payments should be extended to everyone and should be proportionately greater for the poorest. A *minimum wage* of at least $1.50 should be extended to all workers (including the 16 million currently not covered at all). Programs for equal *educational opportunity* are as important a part of the battle against poverty.

B. A full-scale public initiative for civil rights should be undertaken despite the clamor among conservatives (and liberals) about gradualism, property rights, and law and order. The executive and legislative branches of the Federal government should work by enforcement *and* enactment against any form of exploitation of minority groups. No Federal cooperation with racism is tolerable—from financing of schools, to the development of Federally-supported industry, to the social gatherings of the President. Laws hastening school desegregation, voting rights, and economic protection for Negroes are needed right now. The moral force of the Executive Office should be exerted against the Dixiecrats specifically, and the national complacency about the race question generally. Especially in the North, where one-half of the country's Negro people now live, civil rights is not a problem to be solved in isolation from other problems. The fight against poverty, against slums, against the stalemated Congress, against McCarthyism, are all fights against the discrimination that is nearly endemic to all areas of American life.

C. The promise and problems of long-range *Federal economic development* should be studied more constructively. It is an embarrassing paradox that the Tennessee Valley Authority is a wonder to most foreign visitors but a "radical" and barely influential project to most Americans. The Kennedy decision to permit private facilities to transmit power from the $1 billion Colorado River Storage Project is a disastrous one, interposing privately-owned transmitters between publicly-owned generators and their publicly (and cooperatively) owned distributors. The contrary trend, to public ownership of power, should be generated in an experimental way.

The Area Redevelopment Act of 1961 is a first step in recognizing the underdeveloped areas of the United States. It is only a drop in the bucket financially and is not keyed to public planning and public works on a broad scale. It consists only of a few loan programs to lure industries and some grants to improve public facilities to lure these industries. The current public works bill in Congress is needed—and a more sweeping, higher-priced program of regional development with a proliferation of "TVAs" in such areas as the Appalachian region are needed desperately. However, it has been rejected already by Mississippi because the improvement it bodes for the unskilled Negro worker. This program should be enlarged, given teeth, and pursued rigorously by Federal authorities.

D. We must meet the growing complex of "city" problems; over 90 percent of Americans will live in urban areas within two decades. Juvenile delinquency, untended mental illness, crime increase, slums, urban tenantry and non-rent controlled housing, the isolation of the individual in the city—all are problems of the city and are major symptoms of the present system of economic priorities and lack of public planning. Private property control (the real estate lobby and a few selfish landowners and businesses) is as devastating in the cities as corporations are on the national level. But there is no comprehensive way to deal with these problems now amidst competing units of government, dwindling tax resources, suburban escapism (saprophitic to the sick central cities), high infrastructure costs and no one to pay them.

The only solutions are national and regional. "Federalism" has thus far failed here because states are rural-dominated; the Federal government has had to operate by bootlegging and trickle-down measures dominated by private interests, with their appendages through annexation or federation. A new external challenge is needed, not just a Department of Urban Affairs but a thorough national *program* to help the cities. The *model* city must be projected—more community decision-making and participation, true integration of classes, races, vocations—provision for beauty, access to nature and the benefits of the central city as well, privacy without privatism, decentralized "units" spread horizontally with central, regional democratic control—provision for the basic facility-needs, for everyone, with units of planned *regions* and thus public, democratic control over the growth of the civic community and the allocation of resources.

E. *Mental health institutions* are in dire need; there were fewer mental hospital beds in relation to the numbers of mentally-ill in 1959 than there were in 1948. Public hospitals, too, are seriously wanting; existing structures alone need an estimated $1 billion for rehabilitation. Tremendous staff and faculty needs exist as well, and there are not enough medical students enrolled today to meet the anticipated needs of the future.

F. Our *prisons* are too often the enforcers of misery. They must be either re-oriented to rehabilitative work through public supervision or be abolished for their dehumanizing social effects. Funds are needed, too, to make possible a decent prison environment.

G. *Education* is too vital a public problem to be completely entrusted to the province of the various states and local units. In fact, there is no good reason why America should not progress now toward internationalizing rather than localizing, its education system—children and young adults studying everywhere in the world, through a United Nations program, would go far to create mutual understanding. In the meantime, the need for teachers and classrooms in America is fantastic. This is an area where "minimal" requirements should hardly be considered as a goal—there always are improvements to be made in the education system, e.g., smaller classes and many more teachers for them, programs to subsidize the education for the poor but bright, etc.

H. America should eliminate *agricultural policies* based on scarcity and pent-up surplus. In America and foreign countries there exist tremendous needs for more food and balanced diets. The Federal government should finance small farmers' cooperatives, strengthen programs of rural electrification, and expand policies for the distribution of agricultural surpluses throughout the world (by Food-for-Peace and related

UN programming). Marginal farmers must be helped to either become productive enough to survive "industrialized agriculture" or given help in making the transition out of agriculture—the current Rural Area Development program must be better coordinated with a massive national "area redevelopment" program.

I. *Science* should be employed to constructively transform the conditions of life throughout the United States and the world. Yet at the present time the Department of Health, Education, and Welfare and the National Science Foundation together spend only $300 million annually for scientific purposes in contrast to the $6 billion spent by the Defense Department and the Atomic Energy Commission. One-half of all research and development in America is directly devoted to military purposes. Two imbalances must be corrected—that of military over non-military investigation, and that of biological-natural-physical science over the sciences of human behavior. Our political system must then include planning for the human use of science: by anticipating the political consequences of scientific innovation, by directing the discovery and exploration of space, by adapting science to improved production of food, to international communications systems, to technical problems of disarmament, and so on. For the newly-developing nations, American science should focus on the study of cheap sources of power, housing and building materials, mass educational techniques, etc. Further, science and scholarship should be seen less as an apparatus of conflicting power blocs, but as a bridge toward supra-national community: the International Geophysical Year is a model for continuous further cooperation between the science communities of all nations.

The Great Society

LYNDON B. JOHNSON

Lyndon Johnson announced his Great Society program in a speech delivered at the University of Michigan in 1964. This, in effect, was his "I Have a Dream" speech, and Johnson was indeed a man of large dreams and grandiose vision. He promised to tackle the full range of social problems that American society faced in the mid-1960's: racial injustice, poverty, a decaying environment, as well as the need to improve the quality of life by applying American economic advances in the twentieth century to the resolution of these problems.

In this speech Johnson spoke of leading the nation's intelligentsia toward formulation of social polices to solve the problems he identified. This dream was the source of the Great Society legislation of the mid- and late 1960's. The implementation of this far-reaching social program became sadly tangled with the parallel pursuit of elusive victory in the Vietnam War. The outcome of these noble dreams has had a mixed reception. To some extent, a fair assessment of Johnson's programs is still premature. The Great Society was clearly a major effort in the history of American reform. Much of our opinion of the reform tradition in American politics will be colored by the eventual assessment that American historians reach of the programs that Lyndon Johnson created in a few frenetic years.

I have come today from the turmoil of your capital to the tranquility of your campus to speak about the future of your country.

The purpose of protecting the life of our nation and preserving the liberty of our citizens is to pursue the happiness of our people. Our success in that pursuit is the test of our success as a nation.

For a century we labored to settle and to subdue a continent. For half a century we called upon unbounded invention and untiring industry to create an order of plenty for all of our people.

The challenge of the next half century is whether we have the wisdom to use that wealth to enrich and elevate our national life, and to advance the quality of our American civilization.

Your imagination, your initiative, and your indignation will determine whether we build a society where progress is the servant of our needs, or a society where old values and new visions are buried under unbridled growth. For in your time we have the opportunity to move

Speech at Ann Arbor, Mich., May 22, 1964. *Public Papers of the Presidents of the United States: Lyndon B. Johnson,* Government Printing Office (Washington, D.C., 1965), I (1963-1964), 704-707.

not only toward the rich society and the powerful society, but upward to the Great Society.

The Great Society rests on abundance and liberty for all. It demands an end to poverty and racial injustice, to which we are totally committed in our time. But that is just the beginning.

The Great Society is a place where every child can find knowledge to enrich his mind and to enlarge his talents. It is a place where leisure is a welcome chance to build and reflect, not a feared cause of boredom and restlessness. It is a place where the city of man serves not only the needs of the body and the demands of commerce but the desire for beauty and the hunger for community.

It is a place where man can renew contact with nature. It is a place which honors creation for its own sake and for what it adds to the understanding of the race. It is a place where men are more concerned with the quality of their goals than the quantity of their goods.

But most of all, the Great Society is not a safe harbor, a resting place, a final objective, a finished work. It is a challenge constantly renewed, beckoning us toward a destiny where the meaning of our lives matches the marvelous products of our labor.

So I want to talk to you today about three places where we begin to build the Great Society—in our cities, in our countryside, and in our classrooms.

Many of you will live to see the day perhaps fifty years from now, when there will be 400 million Americans—four-fifths of them in urban areas. In the remainder of this century urban population will double, city land will double, and we will have to build homes, highways, and facilities equal to all those built since this country was first settled. So in the next forty years we must rebuild the entire urban United States.

Aristotle said: "Men come together in cities in order to live, but they remain together in order to live the good life." It is harder and harder to live the good life in American cities today.

The catalogue of ills is long: there is the decay of the centers and the despoiling of the suburbs. There is not enough housing for our people or transportation for our traffic. Open land is vanishing and old landmarks are violated.

Worst of all expansion is eroding the precious and time-honored values of community with neighbors and communion with nature. The loss of these values breeds loneliness and boredom and indifference.

Our society will never be great until our cities are great. Today the frontier of imagination and innovation is inside those cities and not beyond their borders. . . .

A second place where we begin to build the Great Society is in our countryside. We have always prided ourselves on being not only America the strong and America the free, but America the beautiful. Today that beauty is in danger. The water we drink, the food we eat, the very air that we breathe, are threatened with pollution. Our parks are overcrowded, our seashores overburdened. Green fields and dense forests are disappearing.

A few years ago we were greatly concerned about the "Ugly American." Today we must act to prevent an ugly America.

For once the battle is lost, once our natural splendor is destroyed, it can never be recaptured. And once man can no longer walk with beauty or wonder at nature his spirit will wither and his sustenance be wasted.

A third place to build the Great Society is in the classrooms of America. There your children's lives will be shaped. Our society will not be great until every young mind is set free to scan the farthest reaches of thought and imagination. We are still far from that goal. . . .

Each year more than 100,000 high school graduates, with proved ability, do not enter college because they cannot afford it. And if we cannot educate today's youth, what will we do in 1970 when elementary school enrollment will be 5 million greater than 1960? And high school enrollment will rise by 5 million. College enrollment will increase by more than 3 million.

In many places, classrooms are overcrowded and curricula are outdated. Most of our qualified teachers are underpaid, and many of our paid teachers are unqualified. So we must give every child a place to sit and a teacher to learn from. Poverty must not be a bar to learning, and learning must offer an escape from poverty.

But more classrooms and more teachers are not enough. We must seek an educational system which grows in excellence as it grows in size. This means better training for our teachers. It means preparing youth to enjoy their hours of leisure as well as their hours of labor. It means exploring new techniques of teaching, to find new ways to stimulate the love of learning and the capacity for creation.

These are three of the central issues of the Great Society. While our government has many programs directed at those issues, I do not pretend that we have the full answer to those problems. . . .

But I do promise this: We are going to assemble the best thought and the broadest knowledge from all over the world to find those answers for America. I intend to establish working groups to prepare a series of White House conferences and meetings—on the cities, on natural beauty, on the quality of education, and on other emerging challenges. And from these meetings and from this inspiration and from these studies we will begin to set our course toward the Great Society.

The solution to these problems does not rest on a massive program in Washington, nor can it rely solely on the strained resources of local authority. They require us to create new concepts of cooperation, a creative federalism, between the national capital and the leaders of local communities.

Within your lifetime powerful forces, already loosed, will take us toward a way of life beyond the realm of our experience, almost beyond the bounds of our imagination.

For better or for worse, your generation has been appointed by history to deal with those problems and to lead America toward a new age. You have the chance never before afforded to any people in any age. You can help build a society where the demands of morality, and the needs of the spirit, can be realized in the life of the nation.

So, will you join in the battle to give every citizen the full equality which God enjoins and the law requires, whatever his belief, or race, or the color of his skin?

Will you join in the battle to give every citizen an escape from the crushing weight of poverty?

Will you join in the battle to make it possible for all nations to live in enduring peace—as neighbors and not as mortal enemies?

Will you join in the battle to build the Great Society, to prove that our material progress is only the foundation on which we will build a richer life of mind and spirit?

There are those timid souls who say this battle cannot be won; that we are condemned to a soulless wealth. I do not agree. We have the power to shape the civilization that we want. But we need your will, your labor, your hearts, if we are to build that kind of society.

Those who came to this land sought to build more than just a new country. They sought a new world. So I have come here today to your campus to say that you can make their vision our reality. So let us from this moment begin our work so that in the future men will look back and say: It was then, after a long and weary way, that man turned the exploits of his genius to the full enrichment of his life.

Keynesian Economics
in the 1960s

ALLEN MATUSOW

*Classical economic theory viewed government intervention as a threat
to economic progress. Early in the twentieth century, however, the great
British economist John Maynard Keynes proposed, to the contrary, that
an interventionist government can rejuvenate a declining economy. Its
spending policies can send wealth churning through society by demand
for goods and services, or a well-planned tax cut can suddenly release
funds that the taxpayer had counted on losing, thereby awakening a
psychology of spending and investment. The Kennedy tax cut, which
spurred the economy, actually increased the first tax collection after his
death. This program, unlike the recent Reagan tax cut, was generous
to Americans of low income and seemed to prove the accuracy of
Keynesian economic theory. Social engineering had come of age. It
appeared that government in the hands of experts could improve the
economy.*

*The apparent success of Keynesian economics reinforced America's
confidence in hard-edged economics. The people of this era exalted
social and natural scientists. Television adventure shows had dashing
heroes addressed as "doctor" or "professor." This mood of the 1960's
accompanied the burgeoning of higher education, in which enrollments
had more than doubled. But by the end of the 1960's Keynesian economics no longer produced miracles, and economists had to reevaluate
theories.*

. . . The Great Inflation damaged not only the economy but the reputation of the economists who presumed to manage it. They had come to
Washington in 1961, seeking converts to Keynes. They had seen their
labors of persuasion crowned by passage of the 1964 tax cut, which
wrote the Keynesian multiplier into national policy. And they had con-
quered most unbelief by mid-decade when the prosperity they prophe-
sied actually materialized. But, as it says in Proverbs, "Pride goeth before destruction, and an haughty spirit before a fall."

The turning point for the economy, as for so much else in the
decade, occurred during the fiscal year coinciding with Year One of
Johnson's ground war—July 1, 1965 to June 30, 1966. As this year approached, most Americans were bullish. Unemployment stood at 4.5
percent, prices were rising at the politically acceptable rate of 1.6 percent annually, and private investment was advancing briskly. When,
in May 1965, J. K. Galbraith described the Keynesian Revolution as
one of the "great modern accomplishments in social design," he was
merely retailing the latest conventional wisdom. But privately Gardner
Ackley, the chief Keynesian in the White House, was not rejoicing. A

University of Michigan economist noted for unflappable calm and professional caution. Ackley had joined the Council of Economic Advisers in 1962 and become its chairman when Walter Heller resigned after the 1964 election. Though he lacked Heller's ingratiating public personality, Ackley, too, possessed qualities esteemed by presidents—brains, loyalty, conciseness, and political savvy. And he, no less than Heller, regarded full employment as the ultimate end of policy, which was why his mood was somber in the spring of 1965. The true state of things was being obscured "by an artificial glow," Ackley told the president in May. The effects of the 1964 tax cut were wearing off, the economy was going to stall out short of full employment, and the unemployment rate might climb back to 5.5 percent within a year. The time had come, he urged, to begin considering a new round of tax cuts in 1966.

Pessimism remained Ackley's mood until July 28, 1965, when Johnson announced his decision to dispatch ground troops to Vietnam. The president offered no estimates of the costs of escalation on this occasion, and he skillfully dodged a question about whether "down the road a piece the American people may have to face the problem of guns or butter." Evasion suited Johnson's political purpose, but he could not have knowledgeably answered the question even if he had wanted to. Concerned as always with secrecy, he had proceeded into the Vietnam quagmire without taking his economic advisers into his confidence. Ackley immediately sought his own sources of information and within two days of Johnson's announcement submitted his unsolicited view of the new situation.

"The current thinking in DOD [Department of Defense], as relayed to me by Bob McNamara on a super-confidential basis," Ackley wrote Johnson on July 30, 1965, "points to a gradual and modest build-up of expenditures and manpower." Ackley could scarcely contain his pleasure at this intelligence. He had wanted a dose of fiscal stimulus, and thanks to the war, he was going to get it. "We are certainly not saying that a Vietnam crisis is just what the doctor ordered for the American economy in the next 12 months. But on a coldly objective analysis, the over-all effects are most likely to be favorable to our prosperity." The upward creep of prices might accelerate a bit during the next year, Ackley admitted, but the Council's wage-price guideposts could help contain inflationary pressures. No tax increase to finance the war would be needed unless costs got "into the $10 billion range"—a possibility that he termed "remote." In view of the economy's rapid growth in productive capacity, Ackley foresaw ample room "for both more butter, and if needed, more guns."

Ackley's buoyant forecast derived from McNamara's assurances that the costs of the war over the next year would be modest. In a way, they were. The United States had a large standing army in 1965 and a vast store of military supplies. The cost of shifting part of this existing force to Vietnam, which principally occupied the military in the war's early stages, was relatively small. Indeed, actual federal expenditures for Vietnam in Year One of the war totaled only $6 billion, approximately the fiscal stimulus deemed appropriate by the Council to resume the march to full employment.

The great imponderable, as the buildup got underway, was prices. In view of prevailing economic doctrine, Ackley had to take the problem seriously. In 1958 an economist named A. W. Phillips had demonstrated a statistical relationship between unemployment and wages. When unemployment fell, wages—hence prices—rose. This relationship, enshrined in the textbooks as the Phillips Curve, described only too well the nation's last inflationary episode. In the mid-1950s when unemployment had fallen to almost 4 percent, prices increased 3 percent annually, enough to send shivers of fear through the body politic. The task of policy, as the Council saw it in the early sixties, was to achieve a more favorable trade-off between unemployment and prices—namely, 4 percent unemployment with a 2 percent inflation rate.

Gearing up in the fall of 1965 to reshape the Phillips Curve, the Council located the probable source of inflationary danger not in excess demand fueled by the war, but in monopoly. When markets tightened, big unions and corporations could exploit their discretionary power over wages and prices by raising them. This was "cost-push" inflation, which most economists blamed for the upward trend of prices in the mid-fifties. In 1962, anticipating future cost-push outbreaks, the Council had devised a handy standard for measuring the social responsibility of wage and price decisions. According to the Council's famed guideposts, if wages rose no faster than output per worker, labor costs per unit would remain constant, and corporations would ordinarily have no excuse to raise prices. Since long-run output had been rising by 3.2 percent a year, the Council implicitly argued that wages too should rise no more than 3.2 percent. Even before the war's escalation, the administration had begun rigorously applying "moral suasion" to obtain guidepost compliance from business and labor. Immediately after the war's escalation in mid-1965, the guideposts became the main weapon in Ackley's battle with the Phillips Curve.

The big test for the guideposts that year, as in 1962, was steel. Ackley wrote Johnson in June that even though the deadline for current wage bargaining in the industry was not until September 1, the administration should begin developing a strategy. "If the steel settlement is close to guideposts, and the companies hold the price line, then industrial prices generally can't move up very much," he said. When steel talks broke down on August 29, 1965, the Council met the crisis by deploying its ultimate weapon—the president himself. In a virtuoso display of the "Johnson treatment," Johnson summoned both sides to Washington, virtually held them prisoner in the White House, appealed in person for a noninflationary settlement on behalf of our boys in Vietnam, sent in his own proposal for a settlement, and paced the alley outside the Executive Office Building, waiting for the final word. At 6:30 P.M. on September 3, an exultant president appeared on TV to announce a wage increase for steel workers estimated by the Council to be exactly 3.2 percent. After following up this success with equally dramatic tactics against an aluminum price rise in Novermber, the Council pursued the policy of moral suasion far into 1966.

"As long as total demand in the economy remains clearly within our overall production potential, guideposts can make a useful contribution to price stability," Ackley told Johnson on November 13, 1965. The qualification was crucial. Moral suasion might restrain the greed of unions and corporations; it could not repeal the law of supply and demand. If aggregate demand outstripped supply, prices would rise, in which case workers would inevitably smash the guideposts. For to accept a wage increase of, say, 3 percent when the inflation rate was 3 percent, would be to receive no wage increase at all. The guideposts were obviously only as good as the Council's belief that demand still had a way to go to catch up with supply—Vietnam spending notwithstanding.

Throughout the fall of 1965 the Council clung to its optimistic assessment. When Federal Reserve chairman William McChesney Martin argued for higher interest rates to slow expansion, Ackley wrote the president, "We see no need for sedatives." In late November Ackley thought that price rises in the next twelve months "could well be smaller" than in the past twelve. It would be "premature," he said, "to conclude that even our interim goal of 4 percent unemployment is just around the corner." On December 2 Ackley dismissed fears of a runaway boom by telling the president, "We remain determined to make policy on the basis of facts not nightmares."

One day later, December 3, 1965, when the Council got an advance look at the government's survey of business investment, nightmare became fact. Businessmen had substantially revised upward their investment plans, throwing the administration's expectations into disarray. On December 4 Johnson's advisers finally told him, "We are in danger of too much steam." Indeed, a tremendous boom had been gathering force for months—as the economic statistics for December were to establish beyond any doubt. Unemployment that month fell to 4.1 percent, virtually the Council's goal; consumer prices rose 0.4 percent, the highest December increase since the Korean War; and GNP was galloping out of control. The genie of inflation had escaped the bottle.

Once it caught the economy's true drift, the Council attempted to switch course. Johnson was already at work on the budget for the next fiscal year, beginning July 1, 1966. In mid-December 1965, he asked his economists a question. Given that spending this fiscal year, as measured by the conventional administrative budget, would be $100 billion, what would happen if next year's expenditures reached $110 billion or $115 billion? Ackley replied, "If the budget is $115 billion, there is little question in my mind that a significant tax increase will be needed to prevent an intolerable degree of inflationary pressure." Even if the budget was $110 billion, he still thought "a tax increase would probably be necessary." That same day, another of Johnson's Keynesian advisers, Budget Director Charles Schultze, urged a tax increase of $5 billion. Less spending by taxpayers would mean less overall demand

and a reduction in inflationary pressure. If fiscal policy could revive an economy in the doldrums, it could just as successfully restore calm in an episode of hyperactivity. Or so Johnson's Keynesian advisers reasoned.

Johnson now confronted one of the most difficult decisions of his presidency. To squeeze an unpopular tax increase from a reluctant Congress, he would have to wrap himself in the flag and frankly ask for a war tax. But, if he did so, conservatives would enforce austerity on his Great Society programs, and liberals would have additional evidence that the war was hurting America. In his notorious guns and butter budget submitted to Congress on January 24, 1966, Johnson resolved the dilemma by a combination of wish projection and deceit. Johnson estimated total expenditures for the coming fiscal year at $112.8 billion, with $10.3 billion earmarked for Vietnam. Except for a temporary reinstatement of some excise taxes, he refrained from requesting a tax increase. And he unblushingly described his budget as consistent with "an environment of strong but noninflationary economic growth." Johnson did not say that his own economists disagreed with him. And he left to Secretary McNamara the disagreeable task of informing Congress that official estimates of Vietnam costs assumed the war's end by June 30, 1967. No one expected that, least of all McNamara. In fact, in the fiscal year beginning July 1, 1966, budgetary expenditures would be not $112.8 but in excess of $126 billion, with Vietnam costing not $10 billion but almost $20 billion. In the Keynesian version of history, this budget, with its refusal to raise taxes, opened the floodgates to the Great Inflation.

Throughout the winter of 1966 the tremendous boom, first detected in December, kept accelerating. Real growth, termed "phenomenal" by the Council, exceeded an annual rate of 7 percent, and unemployment dropped to 3.8 percent, the lowest rate since Korea. By March Johnson was besieged by Keynesians, columnists, and some congressmen demanding that he raise taxes. It was a topic that could be counted on to turn him surly. In the 1950s he said, you couldn't walk in any hostess's home without them saying, " 'What do you think about McCarthy?' . . . Now it is, 'What do you think about inflation?' "

But once again the economy fooled the economists. In the spring of 1966 growth in GNP slowed down, unemployment stopped falling, and industrial production no longer increased faster than capacity. Thanks to unexpected restraint in consumer spending, the temperature of the economy had cooled. The reason: taxes had increased substantially after all. A previously scheduled rise in social security taxes had taken place in January; and in March Congress passed the "bits and pieces" tax program that Johnson had submitted earlier in the year—higher excise taxes, improved withholding on personal income tax, and accelerated collection of corporate taxes. Though the investment boom proceeded, the saner pace of activity elsewhere eased the worst fears of Johnson's economists. Their pleas for higher taxes continued, but not their sense of urgency. Nevertheless, as the new fiscal year began in July 1966—Year Two of Johnson's ground war—one statistic dominated all the others. The consumer price index had risen 2.5 percent in the past twelve months. Low by later standards, this rate signaled to the public the end of several years of price stability and awakened widespread anxieties.

It had been a hard year for the president's economists. Their forecasts had been off the mark, their advice had been ignored, and prices had risen more than they had gambled on. Still, after the fact, they could plausibly account for events. Year One of Johnson's war had generated too much demand in relation to supply, and prices had gone up. The $6 billion direct cost of Vietnam did not, by itself, trigger inflation. In fact, according to the national income accounts budget, which gave a better picture of the government's fiscal impact on the economy than did the conventional administrative budget, government revenue had risen just as fast as defense expenditures. The national income accounts budget showed not a deficit but a $1 billion surplus for the fiscal year, compared to $2 billion the previous year. It was the indirect effects of war spending, the Council argued, that propelled the economy out of control. Businessmen, interpreting escalation to mean that good times would roll on, had gone on an investment binge. If Johnson had raised taxes in time, the inflationary effects of war spending and booming investment would have been offset, aborting the Great Inflation. This was the Keynesian story, which, though consistent with events, was not the only story possible.

In the late 1960s Milton Friedman emerged as one of the most influential intellectuals in the United States. Diminutive, combative, and brilliant enough to win a Nobel Prize for economics, Friedman spent most of his academic life dueling with liberals and Keynesians. In a sense Friedman's economics were incidental to his philosophy. Valuing individual liberty as the highest good, he cherished the free market as its best defense. Accordingly, Friedman was bound to dispute two of Keynes's central doctrines—that economic instability originated in the private sector and that government should manage aggregate demand to cure the problem. To refute the Keynesians, Friedman not only attacked the logic of their system; he championed a rival explanation of reality. Rehabilitating and revising the ancient quantity theory of money, he used it to argue that economic instability originated in the public sector and that government could best serve the economy by remaining neutral. Friedman's remarkable success in popularizing the quantity theory in the Johnson years had three causes: his skills as an advocate, the simplicity of his theory, and the stumbling performance of his Keynesian adversaries.

Friedman's position was often misstated as "only money matters." In the long run, he said, the only factors that really mattered in determining output were real ones, like technological change, the rate of savings, and relations among nations. But in the short run, money possessed a unique power to throw smoothly running economies out of gear. In the United States the Federal Reserve, familiarly known as the Fed, regulated the money supply. When the Fed decided to increase the rate of growth of money, output and then prices rose. When the

Fed decided to put on the monetary brakes, recession inevitably followed. It took anywhere from six to eighteen months for a change in money to affect the business cycle; but despite the long and variable lags Friedman never doubted the causal short-run relationship between money and output.

Why was money so potent? Friedman's answer to this question hinged on his empirical claim that "people seem to be extraordinarily stubborn about the real amount of money that they want to hold." For example, say the public wishes to hold money (narrowly defined here as currency plus checking accounts) equivalent to seven months' income. For any one of a number of reasons, the Fed decides to expand the money supply by purchasing bonds from dealers with checks drawn on itself and subsequently deposited in the banking system. As the banks spend or lend these additions to their reserves, the public comes to hold more money—equivalent, say, to eight months' income. To restore their money holdings to the desired level, individuals begin spending their excess balances—on consumer goods or equities or by paying off debts. Some of the increased spending will translate initially into increased output; but if monetary growth is prolonged and significant, all of it will eventually translate into higher prices. For no matter how hard individuals try to reduce their money balances, collectively they cannot possibly succeed, since one person's expenditures are another's receipts. But, as prices rise, the real value of money falls—until finally the public finds itself once again holding money balances whose purchasing power is equivalent to seven months' income. In the end, then, the only lasting consequence of an increased rate of monetary growth is price inflation. Friedman believed that if only the Fed would permit the money supply to grow at about the same rate as output, without starts and stops, the main source of economic instability would be eliminated and so would the main excuse for government intervention.

Keynesian giants including James Tobin, Paul Samuelson, and Walter Heller entered the lists to joust with Friedman. They did not believe, as he did, that the demand for money was stable. They denied that the money supply was determined solely by the monetary authorities, stressed the failure of quantity theorists (also called monetarists) to agree on which of the various definitions of money was the important one, and scoffed at a model that could not account for wide variations in lags between money and output. As scientists, they were particularly offended that Friedman's theorizing was so "casual." Indeed, even his disciples referred to his "black box." Money went in, and income and prices came out, but what happened inside remained a mystery.

In truth, both the Keynesians and the quantity theorists were less like scientists than they were akin to religious prophets. The competing models of reality they advanced in the 1960s relied mainly on unproved premises and lacked satisfactory validation. Despite the passionate loyalty each side felt for its own system of belief, events would, in time, damage the credibility of both. Only as critics of one another did they prove entirely sound. But in the Johnson years Friedman had the advantage. Because Keynesians controlled policy, he could act as gadfly, pointing out the logical errors of his opponents and winning converts as their policies failed. In addition, his model proved more successful, at least for a while, in accounting for events. Not the least telling of his points was that the quantity of money mattered a whole lot more than Johnson's economists, for example, had once believed.

Predictably, Friedman's account of the Great Inflation differed from that of the Council. "Inflation is always and everywhere a monetary phenomenon, resulting from and accompanied by a rise in the quantity of money relative to output," he said. Friedman traced the origins of inflation not to Johnson's 1965 escalation or to the accompanying investment boom, but to the decisions of the Fed some years before to step up monetary growth. In his famous letter of October 1965 to the Federal Reserve Board Friedman surveyed recent monetary history and predicted its consequences. From August 1962 through August 1965, he said, money growth had increased significantly faster than the historic average. Printing money faster had so far translated into higher output because people had been expecting stable prices and because excess capacity in the economy existed. But, he warned, "past experience suggests that a continuation of the present rate of [monetary growth] . . . is not indefinitely sustainable without a price rise."

The villain in Friedman's story, then, was the Fed. This was ironic. No man in public life had spoken more frequently and emotionally against inflation than the Fed's chairman, William McChesney Martin, Jr. Past president of the New York Stock Exchange, Martin was a Democrat appointed by Harry Truman in 1951. He liked to play his daily game of tennis, keep in personal touch with financial markets, and make policy according to his intuitive feel of conditions. In Friedman's view Martin was the classic example of the misguided money manager who regarded interest rates, not the quantity of money, as the proper measure of whether money was easy or tight. Interest rates were inching up in 1965, so Martin concluded that money was tightening. Actually, rising rates stemmed from the brisk demand by business borrowers for investment loans, a demand that the Fed's metaphorical printing presses all too willingly accommodated.

On December 5, 1965, two days after the government's survey of current business investment had confirmed his premonitions of inflation, Martin took what seemed to him to be the logical step. To discourage borrowing he announced a rise in the discount rate (the interest rate the Fed charges on loans to member banks) from 4 percent to $4\frac{1}{2}$ percent. Martin's action infuriated both Lyndon Johnson, who opposed high interest rates on populist principle, and Gardner Ackley, who resented the Fed's failure to consult the administration beforehand. In fact, all that Martin did was ratify the upward movement of interest rates originating in the market. While skirmishing with the Fed over interest rates, the White House ignored the recent ominous trend in the money supply. From June 1965 to May 1966, money would grow at the exuberant annual rate of more than 6 percent—compared to a

2.8 percent historic average. In Friedman's view, the Fed was the true engine of inflation and did not even know it.

If Friedman was right about inflation, then not only Martin but the president's economists were wrong. Friedman thought the Keynesians were wrong, for example, to take seriously the threat of cost-push inflation. No such phenomenon could logically exist, he declared. Suppose the steel workers exact a wage increase that forces steel companies to raise prices. Two outcomes are possible. Demand for steel declines at the higher prices, leading to unemployment in the industry; or steel consumers pay the higher prices, leaving them less to spend for other goods. Either way, the inflationary effects of higher steel prices are offset by increased unemployment or perhaps by lower prices in competitive sectors. A rise in steel prices could nudge up the price indexes only temporarily—unless, said Friedman, the Fed stepped in to restore the former level of output and employment by printing more money. Then, as always, the true cause of inflation would be an increase in money relative to output.

Whether or not Friedman was right about cost-push inflation, all economists agreed that it was not the cause of the initial inflationary spurt of 1965–1966. Price increases began in raw materials, services, and non-unionized industries, not in sectors characterized by concentrated economic power. "Market pressures—not monopoly power—made the difference between the good price record of the early sixties and its deterioration in 1966," wrote Council member Arthur Okun later.

And if Friedman was right about inflation, then the president's economists were also wrong in believing that fiscal policy could counter it. As good Keynesians, they had advocated a tax increase in December 1965, theorizing that reduced spending by taxpayers would reduce pressure on prices. More bad logic, said Friedman. If taxes rose, taxpayers would, indeed, have less to spend. But increased federal revenue would also reduce the need of government to borrow from the public. Funds that would otherwise have been lent to the Treasury would now be available for more lending or spending in the private economy, offsetting the deflationary effect of higher taxes. Friedman conceded one possible deflationary consequence of a tax increase. Reduced borrowing by the government would lower interest rates; and lower rates in turn might induce people to lend less and hold more of their income in the form of idle cash. To the extent this happened, aggregate demand in fact would fall. But, believing as he did that people's desire to hold money was stable, Friedman expected the impact of lower interest rates on lending to be slight. There was only one way to reduce inflation, Friedman said, and that was to slow down the rate of growth of the money supply.

The curious thing was how little attention the quantity theory attracted during the initial phase of the Great Inflation. The financial press virtually ignored money growth. The Fed conducted policy with blithe unconcern for its rate of increase. And the Council of Economic Advisers, though theoretically committed to the view that monetary policy could affect aggregate demand through interest rates, treated money as a distinctly secondary topic. Friedman noted that in the chapter on prices in its 1966 *Annual Report,* the Council referred only twice to monetary policy and managed to avoid using the word "money" at all. This, he said is "strictly comparable to the way a rigid Puritan writing a book about love might have handled 'sex.' "

The quantity theory came into its own in the fiscal year beginning July 1, 1966, and ending June 30, 1967—Year Two of Johnson's ground war. As the year began, Keynesians were once again gloomy about prices. Though the economy was straining against capacity, fiscal policy would be expansionary, showing a $7 billion deficit in the national income accounts budget, the largest in years. Given their premises, Johnson's economists produced an inevitable forecast, namely, excess demand and 4 percent inflation by mid-1967. The Council took no note that over at the Fed Chairman Martin had turned off the money spigot.

Deeply worried by deficit spending and feverish business investment, Martin switched course in the spring of 1966 and decided to kill the boom himself. Specifically, he curbed credit by drastically reducing the supply of new reserves to the commercial banks. For quantity theorists the chief consequence of Martin's tough new line was this: the money supply, which had been growing at a 6 percent annual rate for almost a year, grew not at all from May through December 1966. If money was as important as Friedman said, the economy faced dangers quite different from those anticipated by the budget-conscious Keynesians. As it turned out, danger took the form of the famous Credit Crunch of 1966, the first in a series of crunches that periodically racked the economy over the next decade.

The shortage of credit, created by the Fed, sent ever-widening shock waves through the financial world in the summer of 1966, nearly causing its ruin. First hit were the thrift institutions (savings and loan associations and mutual savings banks), which provided the major source of money for the home-building industry. In April 1966, for the first time in the post–World War II era, commercial banks began paying higher interest rates (5½ percent) on savings deposits than did the thrifts. Because their funds were tied up in long-term, low-interest-rate mortgages, the thrifts were not earning enough to pay their own depositors competitive rates. Net deposits in thrift institutions stopped growing, and for a while it appeared that a large segment of the industry would go under. When the thrifts get squeezed, the home-building industry feels the pain. Mortgage money dried up, private nonfarm housing starts in the last half of 1966 fell to approximately 60 percent of what they had been in the similar period of 1965, and depression gripped the home-building industry.

By August 1966 the shortage of money was driving interest rates to levels unknown since the 1920s. The stock market went into a severe slump, and insurance companies were besieged by customers taking advantage of their legal right to borrow against their policies at interest rates now below the market. The commercial banks, desperate for money to lend their favorite customers and unable to replenish their reserves at the Fed, began selling off their large holdings of state and municipal bonds. As the price of municipals plummeted, state and local governments found it nearly impossible to find buyers for their long-term securities. By mid-August the commercial banks themselves had reached a crisis. Market rates edged above $5\frac{1}{2}$ percent—the legal limit they could pay their depositors—and corporations began threatening to withdraw their large certificates of deposit. The banks had no choice except to curtail their loans. Now it was the turn of business to scream. For a few days it appeared that credit to finance American business might not be available at any rate of interest. The head of the New York Federal Reserve Bank reported that at the end of August "the financial community was experiencing growing and genuine fear of a financial panic."

The resolution of the crisis came on September 1, 1966, in the form of an unprecedented letter from the Fed to its member banks. The Fed called on the banks to moderate their business loans and to stop selling municipals. In return the Fed would reopen its discount window to cooperating banks. In other words, if banks would voluntarily ration credit, the Fed would ease up. Tension in financial markets diminished immediately.

In the fall of 1966, the volume of bank loans fell, interest rates eased, the market for municipals firmed, and thrift institutions foresaw brighter days. The pace of GNP growth slowed down, and the inflation rate did not speed up. Heaving a sigh of relief, Johnson's economists privately admitted in November 1966, "Monetary policy has done more than some of us expected it would or could." The Council estimated that tight money had had about the same effect on the economy as the tax increase it had unsuccessfully urged on the president earlier in the year. Reducing the quantity of money had, after a fashion, worked.

Among those critical of the Fed's performance was Milton Friedman. He had always said that too little was known about how monetary policy actually worked to use it for purposes of short-run stabilization. The Credit Crunch only confirmed his view. Though the Fed had jammed on the brakes to curb business investment, businessmen proved ingenious in finding new sources of credit outside the banks. Investment did slow down, but only because of bottlenecks in industrial construction and the producers' goods industry. While the bludgeon of tight money missed business investment, it landed a nearly lethal blow on housing, whose depressed state had chiefly caused economic activity to moderate in the last half of 1966. This consequence of tight money the Fed had neither expected nor desired.

Once they were past the Credit Crunch, economists debated the effects of tight money in 1966 on output in 1967. In September 1966 Gardner Ackley, who was more impressed by the growing budget deficit than by the Fed's stringency, predicted resumption of excess demand and accelerating inflation. Friedman, disregarding the budget and looking only at money, predicted a recession. As money grew scarce, Friedman believed, individuals would hoard it to maintain their desired cash balances, thereby spending less and reducing output. The economy now became not merely a source of goods and services but a grand experiment to test the rival models of Keynesian and quantity theorists.

Friedman almost got his recession (defined as declining output in two successive quarters), but not quite. In the first quarter of calendar 1967, real GNP did not grow at all, and in the second quarter it rose slightly. For the full six months, output increased by only 1 percent. Friedman found consolation in the decline of industrial production over both quarters. The "mini-recession" of 1967, as the press called it, embarrassed the Keynesians more than Friedman. Back in September 1966 they had been so worried about inflation that they had persuaded Congress to repeal the investment tax credit. In April 1967, fearful of a slump, they sheepishly asked for its immediate restoration. In the midst of war, a big deficit, and 4 percent unemployment, the economy trod water for half a year. Prices, meanwhile, rose in Year Two of Johnson's ground war not by 4 percent, as Johnson's economists had predicted, but by 2.7 percent, approximately the same rate as the year before. Wholesale prices did not rise at all. The quantity of money suddenly emerged as the hottest topic in the economics profession. . . .

It was among the public's most firmly held beliefs that inflation was a bad thing. When Gallup asked Americans in the fall of 1967 to name "the most urgent problem facing you and your family," an astounding 60 percent answered the "high cost of living." At that time the inflation rate was still around 3 percent. Some economists shared the public's anxieties, arguing that inflation was a cruel tax that arbitrarily and unfairly robbed some and enriched others. Other economists, especially of the Keynesian variety, failed to understand why so many were so afraid.

Who had been helped by the inflation in the Johnson years and who hurt? Old people living on private pensions were clear losers. So were small savers, less because of inflation than because of the government's refusal to let banks pay competitive interest rates. And so, too, were steadily employed factory workers, whose real wages had stagnated. But there were winners also, most notably poor Americans for whom the war in Vietnam was an inefficient but highly successful antipoverty program, the only one in the Johnson years that actually worked.

The war helped the poor, at least temporarily, mainly by increasing the demand for labor. The defense budget was $30 billion higher in 1968 than when the war began, an increase almost entirely attributable to Vietnam. These extra billions directly paid for 767,000 more soldiers, 185,000 civilian government employees, and 1,472,000 jobs in defense production. War spending, financed by the Fed, also unleashed excess demand for the products of the private sector and so indirectly generated further demand for labor. Tight labor markets meant more rapid promotion for the working poor, new jobs for the unemployed poor, and more wage earners in the families of the poor. As employers scraped the bottom of the labor barrel, they bid up the wages of marginal workers—bid them up faster than the wages of skilled workers. Blacks made exceptionally large relative gains in these years. Median family income for blacks was 52 percent that of whites in 1959, 54 percent in 1965, and 60 percent in 1968. The war not only shoved millions above Johnson's fixed poverty line, it even temporarily reduced income inequality.

Among the war's losers might be counted the nation's businessmen. The war brought an end to the spectacular profits of the decade's first half, as rising costs, especially labor costs, cut into profit margins. Labor's share of aftertax national income grew from 72.2 percent in 1966 to 77.5 percent in 1970; the share going to corporate profits fell from 10.6 percent to 7.2 percent. Louis B. Lundborg, chairman of the board of the Bank of America, the largest bank in the world, said in 1970, "protestations of the new left to the contrary, the fact is that an end to the war would be good, not bad, for American business." Lundborg was right.

"What's so bad about inflation?" a reviewer in the *New Republic* asked, after reading an essay on the subject by Arthur Okun. "Prices go up, but so do incomes. The nickel candy bar is no longer, but neither is the $1.25-an-hour hospital orderly or the $5000 per year teacher." No less an authority than James Tobin was of similar mind. The Phillips Curve taught that the cost of reducing unemployment would be some degree of inflation. Because he, along with most liberals, had no policy objective higher than full employment, this was a cost Tobin was willing to pay. Once, the Council of Economic Advisers had hoped to achieve 4 percent unemployment with a 2 percent inflation rate. Toward the end of the Vietnam era Tobin admitted that the price of "full employment" might be a 4 or 5 percent annual inflation rate. But any attempt to reduce inflation would only wring out the economy and hurt the poor. "So," he concluded, "let us aim at the 4 percent unemployment rate . . . and accept the 4 percent inflation that comes with it."

Friedman rejected this logic because he rejected the Phillips Curve. Phillips and Tobin believed that the trade-off between unemployment and inflation was permanent, that if unemployment fell to 4 percent and stayed there, prices would rise at a constant rate, say 4 percent annually. In his 1967 presidential address before the American Economic Association, Friedman introduced the concept of the "natural rate of unemployment," which he defined as the rate of unemployment that would exist if supply and demand were in balance at stable prices. Governments could attempt to peg the unemployment rate below the natural rate by pumping up aggregate demand, Friedman said. He conceded that for a while the policy would succeed: Prices would rise, and because workers did not anticipate inflation, wages would lag behind. As real wages fell, employers would have an incentive to hire more workers, lowering unemployment. Temporarily, the Phillips Curve described reality: prices rose, unemployment fell. But eventually workers would wise up to the higher price level and demand compensating wage increases. As real wages rose to their original level, unemployment would fall back to the natural rate. Everything would be the same as before, except that the price level would be higher. To reduce unemployment again, the government would have to inflate still more, which would work only until employees anticipated the new inflation rate. Contrary to the Phillips Curve—argued Friedman—the cost of pegging unemployment below the natural rate was not a constant, but an accelerating rate of inflation.

Laymen had intuited from the beginning that a little inflation would lead to more, and that the higher the price level, the worse off they would be. Time proved them right. Inflation made winners of some, but society was one of the losers. By the late 1970s accelerating inflation discouraged savings, added to the risks of long-term investment, cut real transfer payments to the poor, destabilized financial markets, automatically siphoned off a growing proportion of national income to the federal government, and eroded social stability. By then, even Keynesians began to concede that inflation might be a bad thing after all.

In the 1960s Keynesian economists went back to school. Testing their theories in the laboratory of the nation's economy, they obtained results that were something less than vindication. When the period ended, they had to rewrite their textbooks, taking account of recent experience and Friedman's critique. Calling themselves post-Keynesians, mainstream economists developed models so sophisticated that Heller's 1961 version of orthodoxy came to seem both archaic and naïve. Even a partial list of revisions conveys some sense of the intellectual distance traveled.

On unemployment: Friedman's concept of "the natural unemployment rate" became widely accepted, replacing the older notion of "full employment." Retrospective calculations estimated the natural rate in the 1960s above 5 percent. Pegging unemployment at 4 percent, therefore, was bound to generate inflation.

On the Phillips Curve: Friedman was right in denying any permanent trade-offs between prices and unemployment. The cost of pegging unemployment below the natural rate would be accelerating inflation. For an illustrative case, the 1960s would do.

On the Keynesian multiplier: In its 1963 Annual Report the Council of Economic Advisers explained how one dollar of a tax cut (with no cut in federal spending) would generate two dollars of GNP. Friedman countered that, unless the Fed financed the defict by printing money faster, the Treasury would have to borrow from the public, driving up interest rates. Higher interest rates were prominent among the reasons why Friedman believed that the stimulating effects of a pure fiscal policy would be "crowded out." Post-Keynesians, repudiating the Council's simple version of the multiplier, conceded that some crowding out would occur. It would be partial, however, and fiscal policy still contained some kick.

On the business cycle: In the sixties Keynesians on the Council had paid scant attention to the quantity of money as a determinant of output. Though denying money the potency ascribed to it by Friedman, post-Keynesians developed a healthy respect for its short-run influence on the business cycle. The quantity of money mattered after all.

On inflation: Post-Keynesians regarded Friedman's simple explanation of inflation as extreme. Inflations were *not* always and everywhere a monetary phenomenon. Supply shocks—for example, an oil embargo or bad harvests—could cause cost-push inflations and drive up the price indexes for considerable periods. But the textbooks now taught that eventually cost-push inflations would have deflationary side effects and could not be sustained without printing up more money. Friedman's simple definition was not refuted but amended. No one was likely ever again to write about inflation, as the Council did in 1966, without mentioning the word "money."

On the role of government in economic stabilization: Post-Keynesians continued to believe that the private economy was inherently unstable and that government policy could steady it. But they knew now that fiscal policy was a less effective and more erratic tool than they had once supposed and that monetary policy performed in mysterious ways. They also conceded that government was the prime source of recent instability. While not abandoning Walter Heller's old faith, post-Keynesians advanced their claims with considerably more humility.

The fate of Keynesian ideas had relevance for politics. In the 1960s liberals and Keynesians, sharing abhorrence of unemployment and trust in government, struck up a natural alliance. Keynesian professors supplied the brains, and liberal politicians supplied the power, their fates intertwining as the decade proceeded. When the Keynesians were riding high, as they were midway through, the liberals rode with them. When they hit the skids in the war years, the liberals did too. If 4 percent unemployment was the wrong goal, if fiscal policy was the wrong tool, if inflation was underrated and the forces governing the economy misunderstood, the liberals paid the political price for Keynesian error. Keynesian ideas played no small role in the unraveling of both liberalism and the economy—and no small role, therefore, in the unraveling of America.

Vietnam: Lessons of the Past

ERNEST MAY

The American philosopher George Santayana made the famous comment that those who do not remember the past are condemned to repeat it. Ernest May's book The Lessons of the Past *modifies Santayana's statement, saying, in effect, that those who know some history draw false conclusions due to incomplete information and false assumptions. French and English statesmen determined to avoid another Munich met humiliation and disaster in Suez in 1956. However, statesmen are not alone in misreading "the lessons" of the past. The French military, in learning so thoroughly the lessons of World War I, turned themselves into "sitting ducks" before the German* blitzkrieg *in World War II.*

One of the most distinguished American diplomatic historians, May examines how Vietnam policy makers misread the past. Men who would not for a moment have thought to analyze economic policy without the help of trained economists, who would have called on small armies of military thinkers to devise a strategy, and who employed batteries of lawyers to make recommendations on legal matters, casually interpreted "the lessons" of history in deciding major policy directions in Vietnam. May's fascinating analysis of the way these statesmen uncritically selected their historical parallels illustrates the need for a more discriminating use of history and historians in the policy-making process. The philosopher Hegel argued that we only learn from history that we cannot learn from history, but May argues that analysis of an extensive array of precedents, instead of merely seizing upon an apparently apt parallel, can provide an imaginative reconstruction of the options. This broader view of history opens the possibility for well informed decisions. May's analysis poses a challenge not only to policy makers but also to historians who would have to develop their art in a way that could have such utility.

. . . . When Kennedy became President in 1961, he faced problems in many areas abroad. Vietnam did not lead the list. After the French defeat there in 1954, a conference at Geneva had partitioned the country, with Ho Chi Minh setting up a communist-controlled state north of the seventeenth parallel, and non-communists putting together a government for the territory south of that line. At the time almost everyone assumed that the communists would soon take over all of the country. Surprisingly, this did not occur. Under President Ngo Dinh Diem, South Vietnam retained its independence. Supplied with large amounts of American aid, his regime even began to seem stable and hardy. Despite increasing guerrilla activity by the communist-led National Liberation Front, Diem was judged by Americans in Saigon to need only marginally greater American assistance in order to retain power. Kennedy there-

fore saw the need to decide how much the United States should contribute to South Vietnam and for what, but his choices chiefly concerned
his budget, and he had to deal with many such issues.

Of far greater concern to the new President was Vietnam's neighbor
Laos. There, the North Vietnamese had long supported a Pathet Lao
group which from time to time had seemed on the verge of triumph.
Clandestinely, American agencies had aided anti-communist factions.
Just before Kennedy's inauguration, the Soviet government openly
joined the North Vietnamese in supplying the Pathet Lao. Fleets of
Soviet planes delivered weapons and equipment to landing fields in the
sparsely settled Laotian highlands. Like Berlin, Laos became a place
where the two super-powers stood fist to fist.

During the new administration's settling-in period, Laos temporarily took second place to Cuba. In that country, guerrillas had won
power in 1959. Their leader, Fidel Castro, had then proclaimed himself a communist and established an alliance with the Soviet Union.
Anti-communist Cuban refugees secured backing from the C.I.A. for
plots against the Cuban regime, and Kennedy gave approval to a C.I.A.
plan for landing refugee military units on the island. The operation,
taking place at the Bay of Pigs, proved a fiasco. Kennedy publicly took
the blame. Privately, he vowed in future to place less trust in advice and
recommendations from the bureaucracy.

Returning to the Laotian problem, he pressed questions about the
possible consequences of alternative courses of action. Some in his entourage advocated sending in American troops. Remembering vexedly
that the Joint Chiefs of Staff had failed to warn him of what might
happen at the Bay of Pigs, the President insisted that the chiefs spell
out the possible consequences. He found them unwilling to give any
assurance of success unless authorized to deploy large ground forces
and, if necessary, use nuclear weapons.

This counsel caused Kennedy to turn much more decidedly toward
a course of action for which he had shown some inclination even during
a pre-inauguration interview with Eisenhower. While leaving open the
possibility of ordering troops into Laos, he bent his efforts toward
negotiating a compromise. If the Laotian leaders could be brought into
a coalition and if the United States and the Soviet Union both undertook to keep hands off, Laos would cease to be a battlefield of the Cold
War and become instead a testing ground for a global armistice. So
reasoning, Kennedy came to regard successful neutralization of Laos as
an objective transcending most others.

It was with negotiations over Laos in the background that the
Kennedy administration studied Vietnam. Reports from that country
told of marked increases in guerrilla activity, and Americans on the
scene expressed certainty not only that the North Vietnamese supplied
and directed the guerrillas but that the new level of warfare reflected
a conscious decision in Hanoi to bring down Diem and install a communist or communist-controlled government in Saigon. Warned that
the North Vietnamese might well succeed, Kennedy faced the question

of whether or not to commit the United States to preventing Diem's fall.

The President and his advisers appreciated the gravity of the issue. Although an American military advisory group functioned in Saigon and almost four billion dollars in economic and military aid had been contributed to South Vietnam since 1954, the fate of the country still depended in large part on the South Vietnamese themselves. If the communists won, Washington could say that the United States had done as much as a distant friendly power could, but that Diem had proved incapable of enlisting the loyalty of his people. If, on the other hand, Americans assumed a direct role in combating the guerrillas, a victory for the communists would seem more a defeat for the United States.

In the early autumn of 1961, Kennedy sent to Vietnam two members of the White House staff, General Maxwell Taylor and former M.I.T. professor Walt Rostow. Taylor, once chief of staff of the army, had been added to Kennedy's entourage after the Bay of Pigs as an independent adviser on military questions. Upon return, Taylor and Rostow recommended:

1. A quick U.S. response to the present crisis which would demonstrate by deeds—not merely words—the American commitment seriously to help save Vietnam rather than to disengage in the most convenient manner possible. To be persuasive this commitment must include the sending to Vietnam of some U.S. military forces.
2. A shift in the American relation to the Vietnamese effort from advice to limited partnership.

Cables to diplomatic and military missions in Asia, memoranda exchanged in Washington, and a number of face-to-face meetings in the Pentagon, State Department, C.I.A., and White House assessed the pros and cons of these recommendations. Secretary of Defense McNamara, an energetic, self-confident, and analytically brilliant former president of the Ford Motor Company, reported to the President that, if the Taylor-Rostow recommendations were followed and if the North Vietnamese and even possibly the Chinese were to respond in kind, the United States might have to deploy as many as 205,000 troops. "To accept the stated objective," observed McNamara, "is . . . a most serious decision."

Kennedy's Secretary of State was Dean Rusk. Having spent some of his World War II army service in the China-Burma-India theater and having been Assistant Secretary of State for Far Eastern Affairs during the final years of the Truman administration, he had kept up with news from Asia. More than most of his colleagues, or for that matter most Foreign Service officers, he recognized the apparent solidity of the Diem regime as a possible illusion. Absent on an official trip at the time when Taylor and Rostow delivered their report, he cabled the President, "While attaching greatest possible importance to security in SEA [Southeast Asia], I would be reluctant to see U.S. make major additional commitment American prestige to a losing horse."

Viewed simply in the circumstances of 1961, the arguments against the Taylor-Rostow recommendations were mostly summed up in Rusk's comment and in an appraisal prepared in Honolulu by the staff of the Commander-in-Chief, Pacific. The Diem government might prove to have no staying power. American troops might be seen by the Vietnamese as agents of a new colonial power, threatening their independence. If so, the insurgents could gain strength. In any case, the North Vietnamese and perhaps the Chinese would have a valid pretext for stepping up support of the communists or perhaps intervening themselves. Americans would inevitably become involved in counter-guerrilla operations for which they were ill-prepared, and large numbers might be so engaged for a long period of time.

In terms of factors immediately in play, the arguments for adopting the Taylor-Rostow recommendations were more complex. If the North Vietnamese were to win control over South Vietnam, the likelihood of their accepting any compromise in Laos would probably disappear, no matter what might be the disposition of the Soviet Union. Laos could not then serve as a test of possibilities for a broader American-Soviet détente. Many people in the American government thought a Laotian settlement unlikely in any case, and communist takeover of Laos probable. On these assumptions, it could be contended that the United States ought to make a stand in Vietnam in order to prove that willingness to negotiate about Laos did not signify willingness to abandon all of Southeast Asia.

It could further be argued that, if Laos and South Vietnam both came under communist domination, Cambodia, Thailand, Burma, Malaya, and Indonesia would quickly follow suit. Speaking of the countries of Southeast Asia, Eisenhower had once used the simile of a row of standing dominoes. At the time, Democrats criticized his figure of speech. When asked about the so-called "domino theory," Kennedy responded, however, "I believe it. I believe it."

Were communists or their sympathizers to take over all or most of Southeast Asia, it was held, China and the Soviet Union would achieve a major gain in the Cold War. When avowing his faith in the domino theory, Kennedy had explained, "China is so large, looms so high just beyond the frontiers, that if South Viet-Nam went, it would not only give them an improved geographic position . . . but would also give the impression that the wave of the future in Southeast Asia was China and the Communists." Always militant in rhetoric, the Chinese leaders had recently deployed troops to install a protégé in Tibet, conducted skirmishes on the Indian frontier, and offered military "volunteers" to help President Sukarno suppress a revolt in Indonesia. With a large army, the world's third-ranking air force, and a crash program under way for development of nuclear weapons, China seemed likely soon to have strength for even more adventurous moves. And most observers could not yet credit evidence of Chinese-Soviet antagonism. In any case, Kennedy was to remark in a 1963 speech that "hope must be tempered with caution. For the Soviet-Chinese disagreement is over means, not ends."

Analyzing the scene as of 1961, men around the President could argue for putting troops in Vietnam to conserve hope of an American-Soviet agreement on Laos, to have an advanced position in Southeast Asia in case such an agreement did not materialize, to demonstrate to Thai leaders and others that, in spite of seeking to neutralize Laos, the United States would support non-communist governments in the region, and above all, to hold a line against the aggressive advance of the Chinese. These were, in fact, the contentions at the core of memoranda advising a military commitment in Vietnam.

In the end every member of Kennedy's inner circle supported such a commitment. Despite his earlier words of caution, Rusk joined McNamara in recommending to the President that "We now take the decision to commit ourselves to the objective of preventing the fall of South Viet-Nam to Communism and that, in doing so, we recognize that the introduction of United States . . . forces may be necessary to achieve this objective." The formula which the secretaries proposed and the President accepted involved dispatch of several thousand soldiers, but with instructions at the outset to serve only as advisers to Diem's commanders and administrators. Although their engaging in combat against the guerrillas seemed almost inevitable, Kennedy could forbear giving orders to such effect and thus leave open some limited opportunity for later reconsideration. At the time, however, he and the men around him clearly saw the arguments for fighting in Vietnam as much more compelling than those against.

Although the principal items in this balance sheet concerned current conditions and future prospects, beliefs about the past entered into the weighings and the tallies.

With varying degrees of precision, every participant in the debate remembered France's experiences in Indo-China. In the spring of 1961 when the new administration first examined Diem's pleas for more help, a State Department memorandum commented that the French commitment had run to 200,000 men. Probably this reminder traced to Deputy Under Secretary George Ball, who had represented the French government as a lawyer during the last year of its humiliating effort to hold the colony. After the Taylor-Rostow report became the focus of discussion, Deputy Assistant Secretary of Defense William P. Bundy was a principal adviser to McNamara. Earlier, Bundy had spent ten years in the C.I.A., working chiefly on broad estimates of current and future trends. He offered an opinion, "based on very close touch with Indochina in the 1954 war and civil war afterwards till Diem took hold," which said that "an early and hard-hitting operation has a good chance (70% would be my guess) of *arresting* things and giving Diem a chance to do better and clean up. . . . The 30% chance is that we would wind up like the French in 1954; white men can't win this kind of fight."

Harvard economics professor John Kenneth Galbraith, whom Kennedy had appointed ambassador to India, sent the President the only emphatic recommendation against committing American troops to Vietnam. Warning of the administration's "bright promise being sunk under the rice fields," Galbraith urged Kennedy to remember that Eisenhower and Secretary of State John Foster Dulles had decided not to risk an effort to rescue the French after their calamitous defeat at Dienbienphu. "Dulles in 1954," he remarked, "saw the dangers in this area."

Kennedy himself had taken a special interest in Indo-China as a member of the House and Senate in the early 1950's. He had even had his French-speaking wife, Jacqueline, translate reading matter for him. As with Ball and William Bundy, recollection of what had befallen the French probably entered his thoughts as an important count against committing American soldiers.

To some extent, memories of the Korean War produced a similar effect. Although almost no one questioned the correctness and courageousness of Truman's decision to fight that war, everyone in the government recalled that early United Nations victories, including a march deep into North Korea, had been followed by Chinese intervention. Hard fighting had dragged on for two years, taken over 54,000 American lives, and left more than 100,000 others wounded or in captivity. Moreover, the war had divided the public. On the one hand, millions had clamored for bombing or blockading of China in spite of the Truman administration's estimate that such actions could lead to an all-out war with the Soviet Union. On the other hand, quieter millions had evidenced impatience with continuing casualty reports and economic controls and appeared willing to see the war ended on almost any terms. Public approval of Truman, as measured by Gallup polls, fell as low as 23 per cent. Promises by Eisenhower that he would bring peace played a part in his 6.6 million-vote margin, and the actual armistice in 1953, even though involving some concessions to the communists, was greeted with relieved approval throughout the country.

These experiences were thought to convey two lessons. First, they confirmed that the United States should never fight a land war in Asia. Second, they demonstrated that the American people had little stomach for a prolonged, limited war.

Available documents on the Vietnam debate of 1961 contain few references to the Korean War and its alleged lessons. Since documents of 1964 and later contain many, this fact is surprising. The probable explanation is that the debate over Laos had made men sensitive about mentioning Korea. Roger Hilsman's retrospective account of that debate suggests why. Then head of the State Department's Bureau of Intelligence and Research, Hilsman was a former Columbia University political science professor and one of the cluster of intellectuals and academics close to the throne. He believed the Joint Chiefs to have exaggerated when they estimated requirements for intervention in Laos. He writes,

it was a shibboleth among the Joint Chiefs of Staff that the United States ought never again to fight a limited war on the ground in Asia. . . . Some who held this view—among the staff of the JCS and even among the JCS themselves—seemed suspicious that even a show of force in Asia might be a White House or State Department plot to trap them into a situation where a limited war could not be avoided. . . . Not all of the Joint Chiefs fully subscribed to the "Never Again" view, but it seemed to the White House that they were at least determined to build a record that would protect their position and put the blame entirely on the President no matter what happened.

Feeling that the "lessons" of Korea might be exaggerated by the military, civilians in the administration refrained from touching on them. Doubtless aware that they were suspected of timidity, the careerists did likewise. Further, as Hilsman relates, some "never again" sentiment appeared in the press and in Congress.

On occasion, advisers to the President alluded to widespread fears of a ground war in Asia. When urging firm support of Diem, Vice President Lyndon Johnson mentioned as one problem "the extent that fear of ground troop involvement dominates our political responses to Asia in Congress or elsewhere." When Taylor recommended the dispatch of military advisers, he took pains to say, "The risks of backing into a major Asian war . . . are present but not impressive." Describing North Vietnam as "extremely vulnerable to conventional bombing," Taylor forecast that both the North Vietnamese and the Chinese "would face severe logistical difficulties in trying to maintain strong forces in the field. . . . There is no case for fearing a mass onslaught of Communist manpower." Probably, the President and most of his advisers refrained from invoking the alleged lessons of Korea because, in the first place, they regarded them as too well understood to require mention and in the second place, because they suspected that any such reference would concede a point to the military. Even so, the Korean example undoubtedly remained at the back of their minds, warning against a war in Vietnam.

On the other hand, analogies from experience elsewhere in Asia seemed to argue in favor of military action by the United States. A few years after World War II, communist-led insurgents had developed strength in both the Philippine Islands and Malaya. By deploying small, specially trained military units, policing secured areas, confining captured rebels in isolated reconcentration camps, curbing corruption, and improving public services, Ramon Magsaysay and his associates regained almost complete control of the Philippines. In Malaya, British and native forces cut off supplies, rounded up rebels, and resettled them in controlled areas. Both cases were taken by American officials as demonstrating that relatively specialized small-scale military operations, coupled with positive measures of other types, could overcome guerrillas. These cases suggested that an effort different from and below that of the Korean War could yield success in Vietnam.

In 1961 President Kennedy and his intimates tended to see Vietnam much more in the image of the Philippines and Malaya than in that of Korea. According to Arthur Schlesinger, Jr., Kennedy's own judgment was that Magsaysay's campaign in the Philippines provided a model for Vietnam—"tough counter-guerrilla action, generous provisions for amnesty, real and sweeping reforms." The President and his younger brother, Attorney General Robert F. Kennedy, superintended creation by the army of elite Special Forces trained for counter-guerrilla operations. They even selected headgear and shoes for these units. And White House representatives criticized the army high command for thinking in Korean War terms and through its advisory mission preparing South Vietnam to fight a war like that of 1950–53. Instead, the chief of staff was told, the army should be thinking of a Malayan-style campaign.

While denying that army planning was as charged, the chief of staff paused to tick off five reasons why the Vietnamese and Malayan situations were not comparable:

a. Malayan borders were far more controllable. . . .
b. The racial characteristics of the Chinese insurgents in Malaya made identification and segregation a relatively simple matter as compared with the situation in Vietnam. . . .
c. The scarcity of food in Malaya versus the relative plenty in South Vietnam made the denial of food to the guerrillas a far more important and readily usable weapon in Malaya.
d. Most importantly, in Malaya the British were in actual command. . . .
e. Finally, it took the British nearly 12 years to defeat an insurgency that was less strong than the one in South Vietnam.

It does not appear, however, that such analysis had any impact in the White House or for that matter among civilians in the Defense Department or the State Department. As late as 1964 McNamara was to cite Malaya as a precedent for Vietnam, and Rusk in the same year was to recommend Magsaysay as the example to be copied by South Vietnam's president.

If leaders of the Kennedy administration viewed Vietnam itself as analogous to Malaya and the Philippines, they saw it as symbolically akin to China. They remembered Republican charges that the Democrats had "lost" China as having harmed their party for a decade. That they believed the wellsprings of public emotion to remain unchanged had been indicated by Kennedy's efforts in the 1960 campaign to pin the blame for "losing" Cuba on the Republicans. When advising the President to accept the Taylor-Rostow recommendations, Rusk and McNamara stressed that "loss of South Vietnam would stimulate bitter domestic controversies in the United States and would be seized upon by extreme elements to divide the country and harass the Administration." Explaining publicly in 1963 all his efforts to shore up the South Vietnamese, Kennedy said, "Strongly in our mind is what happened in the case of China at the end of World War II, where China was lost. . . . We don't want that." Although members of the administration seldom made such explicit admissions, it seems almost beyond doubt that recollection of congressional and public outcries about the "loss" of China cast a shadow whenever the possibility of abandoning the South Vietnamese flickered through their thoughts.

Finally, a commitment to defend South Vietnam was made to seem necessary and almost inevitable by the historical framework of the issue, as it was conventionally portrayed. Careerists repeatedly told the newly arrived political appointees that the communists had a plan for the conquest of the world and that their action in Vietnam was a calculated strategic move. The Joint Chiefs asserted to the Secretary of Defense and the President:

It is recognized that the military and political effort of Communist China in South Vietnam . . . is part of a major campaign to extend communist control beyond the periphery of the Sino-Soviet bloc and overseas to both island and continental areas in the Free World. . . . It is, in fact, a planned phase in the communist timetable for world domination.

In the State Department, the premier careerist and expert on Southeast Asia was Deputy Under Secretary U. Alexis Johnson. With twenty-five years in the Foreign Service, he had been in Japan with Grew and, after the war, with MacArthur he was Rusk's deputy in the Far Eastern bureau during the Korean War; and most recently he had been ambassador to Thailand. Alexis Johnson believed that the communist design for taking over Southeast Asia dated back before World War II, and he had a hand in drafting the earliest analysis of the Vietnam problem submitted to the President. This document warned that "turmoil . . . throughout the area . . . provides an ideal environment for the Communist 'master plan' to take over all of Southeast Asia." The long Taylor-Rostow report, partially drafted by careerists acting as staff assistants, said, "the Communists are pursuing a clear and systematic strategy in Southeast Asia."

This representation of the historical background probably had some effect on the calculations of Kennedy and his advisers. To be sure, they were predisposed to view communism as an expanding and aggressive force. They also regarded all countries not allied with either the Soviet Union or the United States as battlegrounds in a global struggle between the two. These conceptions were widely shared. They permeated most American commentary on international politics, including that by scholars. During 1960 and 1961, the government and much of the press displayed concern lest communists gain the upper hand in the former Belgian Congo. It would not have been easy for members of the Kennedy administration to see Southeast Asia as anything but a battlefront in the Cold War.

In any case, the President's decision was to prevent the "loss" of Vietnam. Soon American military advisers were interlaced into the South Vietnamese command, down even to the platoon level, and American helicopter crews ferried Vietnamese soldiers and spotted targets for their artillery.

Despite increasing American aid and involvement, the likelihood of South Vietnam's falling to the communists seemed to grow. The guerrillas became more numerous and more bold, and North Vietnamese reinforcement of them at least matched American reinforcement of Saigon. By late 1964 actual North Vietnamese combat units had entered the south.

Increasingly, American observers saw reason to fear the Saigon regime's dissolution. Diem's administration reportedly became both more arbitrary and more corrupt. Non-communist groups demonstrated against it. American officials felt obliged to utter public reproach. Army leaders then effected a coup, overthrowing Diem and arranging for him to be murdered. Subsequently, one group of generals or politicians succeeded another, with no individual emerging as anything more than a factional leader.

Lyndon Johnson, who had become President after Kennedy's assassination, inherited the question of what to do about the worsening situation in Vietnam. To some extent, he faced the same choice as his predecessor. It remained open to him to wash his hands of Vietnam or, alternatively, to commit the United States to preventing communist victory. For Johnson, however, the former choice appeared much less attractive because of the extent to which Kennedy had already engaged American prestige. At the same time, it was more obvious that the second choice would involve heavy costs, for Johnson's advisers told him almost from the beginning that success might require bombing North Vietnam and ordering substantial American forces into combat in South Vietnam. In effect, Johnson had to decide whether or not to go to war.

Considerations on one side or the other were much like those of 1961. Recent events in Saigon argued for disengagement, for they made it seem more questionable than ever that South Vietnam deserved to be termed "free." Also, they increased significantly the chances of failure. Further, the possibility that the American public might not support a war in Vietnam had become far more apparent. Although polls, editorial commentary, and congressional votes all gave emphatic support to each militant step which the President actually took, disinclination to see American lives expended in Southeast Asia manifested itself when questioners at press conferences and congressional hearings asked sharply whether American advisers participated in combat. It also found expression in the election campaign of 1964, when Johnson defeated his bellicose opponent, Barry Goldwater, by a margin of sixteen million votes. And in early 1965, when the President approached decisions for war, significant numbers of Congressmen and editorial writers voiced opposition.

Domestically, the arguments against war rose not only from the possibility of its being unpopular but also from the near certainty that its costs would make more difficult the funding of various social welfare programs to which Johnson had a deep commitment. The 1964 elections also brought increases in the Democratic majorities in Congress. Using the persuasive skills which he had perfected as majority leader in the Senate, Johnson planned to press enactment of a number of major reforms. Many would entail new spending, and the President could see that, while the two houses might pass his bills, they would be more resistant to putting up the necessary money if at the same time they had to appropriate billions for a war in Southeast Asia.

The analytical arguments in favor of war had much more to do with what might happen outside the United States if the war were not fought. As compared with 1961, the reasoning remained practically unchanged. It was summarized succinctly in a National Security Action Memorandum endorsed by Johnson in March 1964:

We seek an independent non-Communist South Vietnam. . . .
    Unless we can achieve this objective . . . almost all of Southeast Asia will probably fall under Communist dominance (all of Vietnam, Laos, and Cambodia), accommodate to Communism so as to remove effective U.S. and anti-Communist influence (Burma), or fall under the domination of forces not now explicitly Communist but likely then to become so (Indonesia taking over Malaysia). Thailand might hold for a period without help, but would be under grave pressure. Even the Philippines would become shaky, and the threat to India on the West, Australia and New Zealand to the South, and Taiwan, Korea, and Japan to the North and East would be greatly increased.

Beyond the immediate region, it was feared, Vietnam might be taken as a test of American resoluteness and of the integrity of other American commitments. To withdraw, said Secretary Rusk, "would mean not only grievous losses to the free world in Southeast and southern Asia but a drastic loss of confidence in the will and capacity of the free world to oppose aggression." Specifically, Rusk and others were concerned lest the NATO states and other American allies find reason for questioning whether the United States would actually come to their defense.

    Were the communists to succeed in Vietnam, members of the administration believed, the Soviet Union and China would be inspired to stir up new insurgencies. In January 1961 Khrushchev had applauded "wars of national liberation." Many read this statement as proclaiming a new communist strategy and declaring Vietnam its first serious trial. Rusk said, "If Hanoi and Peiping prevail in Viet-nam in this key test of the new communist tactics of 'wars of national liberation,' then the Communists will use this technique with growing frequency elsewhere in Asia, Africa, and Latin America."

    As in 1961, so in 1964–65 debate involved not only calculations concerning present and future but also inferences from historical experience. The possible parallel with pre–1954 France continued to provoke doubts. It was very much in the mind of George Ball, now Under Secretary of State, who stood as the one convinced and consistent opponent of further military action. It also entered the thoughts of William Bundy, now the Assistant Secretary of State for Far Eastern Affairs, and John T. McNaughton, a Harvard law professor recruited by McNamara to replace Bundy as Assistant Secretary of Defense for International Security Affairs. The two men guided intensive staff work on Vietnam from the autumn of 1964 to the summer of 1965, and McNaughton once spoke of a "French-defeat syndrome" as an obstacle to detached consideration of large-scale troop deployments.

    The parallel had enough persuasiveness so that those who favored war felt some compulsion to argue its invalidity. McNamara offered public assurances that the two situations were not comparable, and a spokesman for the Joint Chiefs protested to William Bundy in November 1964:

French errors . . . included major political delays and indecisions, which amongst other things tolerated if not enforced a military fiasco. Rather than now lamely resurrecting the story of how the French couldn't do the job, it seems to me we should instead make sure we don't repeat their mistakes. (The French also tried to build the Panama Canal.)

More powerful still was the possible parallel with the Korean War. In specific ways, it had some effect on almost everyone. The thought that some action by the United States might provoke massive Chinese intervention, as had the United Nations invasion of North Korea, entered almost every discussion of possible action against North Vietnam. As it happened, the new chief of State's Bureau of Intelligence and Research was Allen S. Whiting. In private life, he had written a book on China's intervention in Korea. By calling the attention of his colleagues to every signal even faintly resembling ones heard in the autumn of 1950, he contributed to keeping that particular experience alive in men's minds. Even the Joint Chiefs hedged their recommendation for bombing North Vietnam by noting that "there is a fair chance that Peiping would introduce limited numbers of Chinese ground forces as 'volunteers.' " Similarly, some who yearned for a negotiated solution somehow freeing the United States from its dilemma expressed the view that the government should not get entrapped, as it had in the Korean War, into talking while the enemy continued to fight.

In broad outline as well as in detail, the Korean parallel preoccupied planners in the State Department. In a draft paper for the National Security Council, Assistant Secretary Bundy wrote,

we cannot guarantee to maintain a non-Communist South Viet-Nam short of committing ourselves to whatever degree of military action would be required to defeat North Viet-Nam and probably Communist China militarily. Such a commitment . . . could not be confined to air and naval action but would almost inevitably involve a Korean-scale ground action and possibly even the use of nuclear weapons at some point.

Uncomfortable with all the options they could discern, the officials thinking about Vietnam gravitated toward the idea of going to war by escalating stages. The United States would do some bombing in North Vietnam. This would demonstrate American determination to persevere. If the communists did not desist, the bombing would intensify and spread to new targets. The question of introducing ground troops could be faced somewhat later. The planners came to refer to this scheme as "the slow squeeze." Although William Bundy saw merits in it, he observed that:

This course of action is inherently likely to stretch out and to be subject to major pressures both within the U.S. and internationally. As we saw in Korea, an "inbetween" course of action will always arouse a school of thought that believes things should be tackled quickly and conclusively. On the other side, the continuation of military action and a reasonably firm posture will arouse sharp criticism in other political quarters.

In a memorandum to Rusk, McNamara, and other presidential advisers, Bundy addressed the question of whether "the slow squeeze" could be "carried out in practice under the klieg lights of a democracy." He commented, "This is a key point. . . . The parallel to Korea in 1951–53 is forbidding."

Rusk, whose memories of that period were full and vivid, felt similar concern. At one point, he said to one of South Vietnam's transitory heads of government that the United States "would never again get involved in a land war in Asia limited to conventional forces." Down to the last moment, he expressed qualms about "the slow squeeze," saying "that the consequences of both escalation and withdrawal are so bad that we simply must find a way of making our present policy work."

McNaughton referred to the "Korea syndrome" as another obstacle to stepped-up warfare, and the Joint Chiefs felt impelled to argue explicitly that the parallel was invalid. If they had earlier been gripped by fear of reliving that war, they were not any longer. American troops had gone into action, albeit as advisers. Officers in Washington, Honolulu, and Saigon had worked out detailed plans for winning in Vietnam, and the chiefs were now intent only on obtaining from their political superiors a signal to proceed at full speed. Their expressed reservations had to do not with going to war but with going to war in stages. They advocated a "fast squeeze." In response to William Bundy's prediction of Korean-scale ground action, their representative commented,

Our first objective is to cause the DRV [North Vietnam] to terminate support of the SEA [Southeast Asian] insurgencies. . . . To achieve this objective does not necessarily require that we "defeat North Viet-Nam," and it almost certainly does not require that we defeat Communist China. Hence our commitment to SVN [South Vietnam] does not involve a high probability . . . of a major conflict in Southeast Asia. . . . Certainly, no responsible person proposes to go about such a war, if it should occur, on a basis remotely resembling Korea. "Possibly even the use of nuclear weapons at some point" is of course why we spend billions to have them.

The chiefs did not address the possibility that domestic reactions might parallel those of the Korean War. One of their representatives came closest to doing so when noting, chiefly in reference to probable foreign criticism, that "We recognize quite clearly that any effective military action taken by the United States will generate a hue and cry in various quarters. The influence that this kind of 'pressure' may have upon the United States will be no more than what we choose to permit it to be."

While recollections of the Korean War fuelled doubt, they also, paradoxically, encouraged boldness. Every participant in the governmental debate looked back with admiration at Truman's 1950 decision. Together with his decisions to defend Greece and Berlin and to create NATO, they believed, the intervention in Korea had demonstrated America's willingness to risk war in order to protect the integrity of other nations. They wanted to act in Vietnam in keeping with Truman's example.

This theme ran through all the debates of 1964 and 1965. Adlai Stevenson, then ambassador to the United Nations, said publicly in the summer of 1964, "The point is the same in Vietnam today as it was in Greece in 1947 and in Korea in 1950." President Johnson himself declared during the same summer, "The challenge that we face in Southeast Asia today is the same challenge that we have faced with courage and that we have met with strength in Greece and Turkey, in Berlin and Korea."

In a ruminative draft memorandum, McNaughton wrote:

It is essential—however badly SEA [Southeast Asia] may go over the next 2–4 years—that U.S. emerge as a "good doctor." We must have kept promises, been tough, taken risks, gotten bloodied, and hurt the enemy very badly. We must avoid appearances which will affect judgments by, and provide pretexts to, other nations regarding U.S. power, resolve and competence. . . . The questions will be:

a. Has U.S. policy of containment against overt and covert aggression changed, at least as to SEA? How will we behave in new confrontations à la South Vietnam, Korea (1950), Berlin? . . .
b. Is U.S. *power* to contain insufficient, at least at the fringes?
c. Is the U.S. *hobbled by restraints* which might be relevant in future cases (fear of illegality, of U.N. or neutral reaction, of domestic pressures, of U.S. losses, of deploying U.S. ground forces in Asia, of war with China or Russia, of use of nuclear weapons, etc.)?

When intensively studying the problem during the autumn, McNaughton and William Bundy explored alternatives to war. In doing so, they groped for ways of distinguishing a decision on Vietnam from the 1950 decision on Korea. A document jointly composed described the following as part of a fallback position: "To make clear to the world, and to nations in Asia particularly, that failure in South Vietnam, if it comes, was due to special local factors—such as a bad colonial heritage and a lack of will to defend itself—that do not apply to other nations." Amplifying the point, Bundy wrote,

The honest fact is that South Viet-Nam and Laos have not really been typical cases from the beginning, which accounts in part for our inability to enlist the kind of international support we had in Korea and for our having to carry the load so largely alone. Most of the world had written off both countries in 1954, and our ability to keep them going—while an extraordinary and praiseworthy effort—has never given them quite the standing of such long-established national entities as Greece, Turkey, and Iran, or the special ward-of-the-U.N. status that South Korea had in 1950.

Taking the lead in opposition to war, George Ball attacked the Korean analogy very much as the chairman of the Joint Chiefs had earlier attacked comparisons between South Vietnam and Malaya. Writing to Rusk, McNamara, and McGeorge Bundy, he ticked off points of dissimilarity between the situation facing Johnson and that which had faced Truman in 1950. "South Viet-Nam is not Korea," he declared, "and in making fundamental decisions it would be a mistake for us to rely too heavily on the Korean analogy."

First, Ball noted, intervention in Korea had express sanction from the United Nations. Second, the United States had, as a result, active support from other countries, including fifty-three that contributed troops. "In Viet-Nam," he observed, "we are going it alone." Third, South Korea had a stable government. South Vietnam by contrast exemplified "governmental chaos." Fourth, the South Koreans were newly independent and willing to fight for their nation. Having been at war for twenty years, the South Vietnamese had no such energy or sense of commitment. Ball concluded,

Finally, the *Korean War* started with a massive land invasion by 100,000 troops. This was a classical type of invasion across an established border. . . . It gave us an unassailable political and legal base for counteraction.

In South Viet-Nam there has been no invasion—only a slow infiltration. . . . The . . . insurgency does have substantial indigenous support. Americans know that the insurgency is actively directed and supported by Hanoi, but the rest of the world is not so sure. . . . And, as the weakness of the Saigon government becomes more and more evident, an increasing number of governments will be inclined to believe that the . . . insurgency is, in fact, an internal rebellion.

Neither the Joint Chiefs nor Ball succeeded, however, in stripping the Korean example of its force. It was subsequently to be cited time and again both in internal memoranda and in public statements.

While Korea figured much more in the debate of 1964–65 than in that of 1961, the Philippine and Malayan analogies no longer did. McNaughton once mused that perhaps some Vietnamese leader might achieve an unexpected turn-around in public opinion such as Magsaysay had effected in the Philippines. In general, however, officials tended simply to make passing mention of these earlier Southeast Asian cases as evidence that communist guerrillas could be defeated.

Officials now cited as seemingly stronger evidence the instance of Greece after American aid commenced in 1947. Perhaps Greece drew such notice because the Greek insurgents had had support from outside. Perhaps it was because the insurgency there had died down in two years instead of ten or twelve. In any case, many people mentioned it or thought of it. Henry Cabot Lodge, the ambassador in Saigon, did so. So did William Bundy, who had worked for the Greek government as a lawyer during the very period of its success against the guerrillas. Walt Rostow, now head of the State Department's Policy Planning Council, contributed the observation that if the United States used its military power with determination, "The odds are pretty good . . . that . . . we will see the same kind of fragmentation of the Communist movement in South Viet Nam that we saw in Greece."

Arguing for ground force deployments as well as bombing, Rostow even offered what purported to be a systematic analysis of past guerrilla wars. Citing not only Greece, the Philippines, and Malaya but also Ireland after World War I, China, North Vietnam in the 1950's and Laos, he argued that such wars nearly always ended in clear-cut victory or defeat. At some point, he alleged, the guerrillas usually commanded most of the countryside. Often they menaced the capital. When they won, it was by all-out conventional war (China), a political take-over (North Vietnam), a coalition settlement which permitted eventual take-over (Eastern Europe, rather than any of the cases supposedly under the microscope), or a partition arrangement (North Vietnam again, Laos, and Ireland). All the United States had to do, Rostow proffered, was to ensure that all these routes to communist victory remained closed. As of 1964, however, Rostow had only a fugitive role in the debate. Everyone knew that he had been urging war against North Vietnam for years. Neither his enthusiasm for such a course, his optimism about its prospects, nor his opinion of the special relevance of previous guerrilla wars was widely shared.

How significant memories of public reaction to the fall of China remained is hard to estimate. In available documents, one finds only faint allusions. The last comprehensive analysis of policy options prior to the President's first critical decision was made by William Bundy's younger brother, McGeorge Bundy, a former Harvard dean who had come to Washington with Kennedy and remained to work for Johnson, occupying throughout the crucial post of Special Assistant to the President for National Security Affairs. Often the last man to review an issue for the President, he had influence at least equal to that of McNamara and Rusk. Johnson had sent Bundy and McNamara in person for a last look around in South Vietnam, and Bundy reported that he and the Secretary of Defense both favored bombing North Vietnam. He continued,

We . . . cannot estimate the odds of success with any accuracy—they may be somewhere between 25% and 75%. What we can say is that even if it fails, the policy will be worth it. At a minimum it will damp down the charge that we did not do all that we could have done, and this charge will be important in many countries, including our own.

In retrospect, we can see that when ranking the arguments for war in Vietnam President Johnson placed this consideration high on his list, second only to the danger that the rest of Southeast Asia would fall. "A divisive debate about 'who lost Vietnam' would be," he was to write, ". . . even more destructive to our national life than the argument over China had been."

Deliberations about what the United States should do in Vietnam were probably also influenced by the alleged lessons of the 1930's. After examining all the options, the President decided to proceed with "the slow squeeze." He ordered limited bombing of North Vietnam and dispatch to South Vietnam of some ground combat units. In July, after a further exhaustive canvass of the pros and cons, he authorized sending 125,000 ground troops on the understanding that more would follow if necessary.

Defending these decisions publicly, administration spokesmen invoked over and over experience prior to World War II. Rusk was to cite it incessantly. Loyally defending a course of action which he continued to oppose, George Ball employed much the same brief. He said, for example:

We have . . . come to realize from the experience of the past years that aggression must be dealt with wherever it occurs and no matter what mask it may wear. . . . In the 1930's Manchuria seemed a long way away. . . . Ethiopia seemed a long way away. The rearmament of the Rhineland was regarded as regrettable but not worth a shooting war. Yet after that came Austria, and after Austria, Czechoslovakia. Then Poland. Then the Second World War.

The central issue we face in South Viet-Nam . . . is whether a small state on the periphery of Communist power should be permitted to maintain its freedom. And that is an issue of vital importance to small states everywhere.

Intra-governmental memoranda may have failed to refer to events of the 1930's because their authors so took for granted the consensus about its lessons that they thought it unnecessary to mention them. Or it may be that these events lacked saliency for many. The Bundy brothers, McNamara, and McNaughton had all been in college or graduate school until at least the outbreak of the Second World War. Rusk, though several years older, had been a professor and dean on the West Coast prior to going on active service with the army in 1940. While all of them had been interested observers (and partisans of American intervention), none had been in public life. It is perhaps not surprising that events after World War II should have been more vivid in most of their minds, and it is worth noting that McNamara, who had been preoccupied with his business career prior to 1961, seldom referred to any event of earlier date.

The "lessons" of the 1930's may nevertheless have weighed heavily with the President's advisers. Certainly they had a place in Johnson's own thought. Fifty-seven in 1965, he had worked in Washington throughout the New Deal years, been elected to Congress in 1936, and served continuously thereafter in either the House or Senate. In his memoirs, he says that he continually bore in mind the failures of the American government prior to World War II. As a supporter of Greek-Turkish aid, NATO, and the intervention in Korea, he had cited the teachings of pre-war experience. And his speeches justifying the decisions of 1965 were filled with similar rhetoric. For example, he was to say at a press conference that defeat in South Vietnam "would encourage and spur on those who seek to conquer all free nations within their reach. . . . This is the clearest lesson of our time. From Munich until today we have learned that to yield to aggression brings only greater threats." Lacking any other record of his private thoughts during 1964–65, we cannot estimate whether certainty about the lessons of the 1930's had as powerful an influence on Johnson as on Truman in 1950. His memoir account of the critical Vietnam decisions refers primarily to the Korean precedent.

In any case, it is quite clear that beliefs about at least the very recent past penetrated the thinking of men who determined America's course of action in Vietnam. In 1961 the examples of France's defeat and of American public controversy over the Korean War prompted doubts. Perceiving South Vietnam as more analogous to the Philippines and Malaya than to Korea, officials saw reason, however, to expect that the country could be saved without wholesale engagement of American forces. Recollection of the bitter public debate over the fall of China deterred them from considering seriously the abandonment of South Vietnam. And the presumed experts on long-term trends encouraged a commitment to South Vietnam by portraying the conflict there as a planned phase in a communist timetable for world conquest.

When the Johnson administration faced the choice of whether or not to go to war in 1964–65, the French parallel and the Korean War experience still figured in the arguments against military action. On the other hand, officials saw in the intervention in Korea and other events of 1947–50 compelling precedents for a determined resort to force. Memories of the aftermath of communist victory in China continued to urge them in the same direction. So perhaps did shared assumptions about lessons taught by the experience of the 1930's.

As with decisions by Roosevelt and Truman, so with those of Kennedy and Johnson one can plausibly argue that the outcome would have been the same even if inferences from history had played no part in the reasoning. The Presidents of the 1960's and their advisers saw Southeast Asia as important in itself. Both McNamara and the Joint Chiefs insisted that a position there was indispensable to retention of any defense line in the western Pacific. Kennedy, Johnson, and their associates judged that as Vietnam went so would go the entire region, and they believed that in the Cold War communist success in Southeast Asia would represent an enormous gain to the enemy. On these assumptions, they might have decided to fight for South Vietnam even if nothing in previous experience seemed either relevant or comparable. The only element in the debate that would almost certainly have been different would have been the argument about the domestic consequences of the "loss" of Vietnam, for without recollections of the controversy over China, officials would surely have seen an adverse public reaction as at least no more likely than an adverse reaction to war.

Since arguments from history did play a part in the debate, it is nevertheless apropos to examine here their character and quality. One cannot say, as of the possibly unique case of intervention in Korea in 1950, that they were allowed to preclude other analyses of the issues. Nor, in fact, can Kennedy and Johnson be accused, like Truman in 1950, of over-hasty decision-making. On the contrary, both Presidents permitted months of careful staff work and assigned to it some of the ablest minds around them. But it can be said that the historical reasoning entering into decisions about Vietnam was at best superficial.

As a rule, examples were cited as if there could be no dispute about the facts or their meaning, and they were employed indiscriminately in two quite different ways. Sometimes, the surrounding grammar suggested that the logic ran, "X happened before and therefore X is likely to happen again." At other times, the implicit logic ran, "Such and such is a regular pattern in human affairs; X serves as an illustration." Most references to the French were of the first variety. That is, the official asserted that the French had been defeated and therefore the Americans were also likely to be defeated. On occasion, however, such references took the second form. A cautionary cable from Maxwell

Taylor in February 1965 said, for example, "White-faced soldier armed, equipped and trained as he is not suitable guerrilla fighter for Asian forests and jungles. French tried to adapt their forces to this mission and failed; I doubt that U.S. forces could do much better." References to the Philippines and Malaya in 1961 implied that, since the insurgents had been defeated there, they would be defeated in Vietnam. By 1964–65, these examples along with that of Greece had become mere illustrations of the proposition that guerrillas could be defeated. On the other hand, statements about Korea and about aid to Greece and the defense of Berlin seemed almost always to assert simply that the past pattern would or should reproduce itself. The same was true of allusions to the domestic debate over China.

Few of the surviving documents evidence any effort to assess the actual comparability of apparent precedents or to extend the search for possibly comparable cases. The only contrary examples are the Joint Chiefs' comments on the Malayan parallel and George Ball's evaluation of the Korean analogy. The chiefs' remark that the French failed to build the Panama Canal, while effective in debate, hardly ranked as analysis. Nor did Rostow's memorandum on victory in guerrilla wars. Even though Rostow had once been a professor of economic history and had written prolifically on the recent past, his memorandum was transparently a brief for a particular course of action and not in any sense an essay of relevant data.

In fact, the historical evidence actually or potentially entering into the deliberation about Vietnam could have received much closer analysis. Where the underlying proposition was that X had occurred and would occur again, the peculiar characteristics of X could certainly have been put under scrutiny. The chiefs' notes on Malaya, and Ball's on Korea, suggest what might have been tried. The chiefs themselves might usefully have been pressed to develop their Panama Canal remark, for it implied that the failure of the French resulted from shortcomings in equipment and technical skill. This contention was at least open to debate.

Where a proposition was of the second type, a systematic review of possible precedents surely should have seemed in order. Thus, for instance, Taylor's assertion about white soldiers in Asian forests and jungles could have been examined in light not only of French experience in the 1950's but also of British and French experience in Asia from the nineteenth century onward and American experience in the so-called Philippine insurrection. In fact, various broad assertions made about guerrilla wars could well have been refined by reflection additionally on some Latin American wars for independence, the short-lived French-supported empire in Mexico, and more recent conflicts in Palestine and during World War II, in Southeastern Europe. Had the war in Vietnam been perceived as in some respects a civil war, attention could conceivably have gone also to sixteenth-century France, seventeenth-century England, the United States in 1861–65, and Spain in the 1930's.

To the extent that the Korean War experience served merely as an illustration of difficulties likely to beset a democratic country waging a limited war, the nature and causes of those difficulties could surely have been better understood not only by a careful review of the actualities of 1951–53 but also by some scrutiny of public reactions to the Indian wars, the Spanish-American War, and the prolonged low-level military operations in Cuba, Nicaragua, the Dominican Republic, and Haiti between 1906 and 1934. Consideration of, say, British domestic reactions to the Egyptian campaigns, the Boer War, and the Palestine conflict and French domestic reactions to the Mexican adventure and the Tonkin expedition could also have been illuminating.

Like the strategic and diplomatic arguments, the historical arguments in favor of war concerned for the most part probable effects outside the United States and indeed outside Vietnam. The logic in references to Greece, Berlin, and Korea ran roughly as follows. Other governments saw in these precedents evidence that the United States would not hesitate to use its military power if an ally or ward were threatened or if an independent state were the victim of aggression. If the American government failed to act unhesitatingly in Vietnam, these governments would infer that the United States had changed its resolve. Non-communist states would doubt American determination to protect them. The communist powers would be inclined to take greater risks in order to gain new territory.

Underpinning such reasoning was a set of unspoken assumptions. In his brilliant book, *Essence of Decision,* Graham T. Allison has pointed out that when thinking of international relations, most of us visualize nations as rational unitary actors, defining objectives, laying plans, and following sequences of coherent actions in pursuit of their ends. In doing so, we ignore important ways in which complex organizations do not behave like individual men and women. We also slight the parochialism, internal conflict, and rivalry which are characteristics of all governments. The authors of memoranda about Vietnam plainly thought of other nations as rational unitary actors. To some extent, they conceived of the United States in the same way, for it was certainly a rational unitary actor that would show determination, keep its commitments, etc. In certain respects, however, they envisioned rational calculation in other governments as different from that in the United States.

Officials assumed that other nations would revise their estimates of the United States as soon as in any one instance the American government showed itself unwilling to wage war. They themselves, however, were quite hesitant to make comparable recalculations even on the basis of repeated actions by other states. They believed, for example, that the United States had faced down the Soviet Union in successive crises over Berlin and over the emplacement of offensive missiles in Cuba. When considering the possibility of mining or blockading North Vietnamese harbors, they recognized that the result could be a crisis with Moscow, for many of the ships carrying supplies to North Vietnam were Russian. Yet they did not read recent experience as indicating that the Soviets would be weak or accommodating. On the contrary, they assumed throughout that the Soviet government had a greater interest in North Vietnam than it had had in either Berlin or Cuba and that mine-laying or the imposition of a blockade would be likely to provoke a war. Similarly, they recalled the crises of the 1950's over Quemoy and Matsu and the Chinese-Indian border war of 1962 as instances in which China had buckled before the menace of American air and nuclear power. Yet memoranda on Vietnam expressed just as much concern about China's initiating hostilities in Vietnam as if these episodes had never occurred. In other words, American officials visualized their principal adversaries as nations whose behavior could not be predicted by individual past actions but which would instead be a function of interests and capabilities.

Had American officials analyzed their own reasoning and, insofar as historical evidence permitted, that of men in other governments, they might have qualified their forecasts of what would happen if the United States deserted South Vietnam. Their memoranda might have conceded that men in Moscow, Peking, Tokyo, Bonn, London, and even Bangkok were no more likely to revise their expectations of future American behavior than to assume that the action was not indicative of how the United States might act in other situations where its interests were clear or the odds of success were better.

Finally, to make the most obvious point of all, members of the Kennedy and Johnson administrations could profitably have sought some understanding of the history of Vietnam itself. To be sure, most works on Vietnam were by men who did not know Vietnamese, wrote from French sources, and focused heavily on the colonialists rather than the colonials. Even so, there were books and articles outlining the peculiar evolution of the country. By reading them, men making decisions about Vietnam might have discovered at the outset some truths later painfully learned. Presidents, cabinet officers, ambassadors, and bureaucrats were to speak, for example, of alliance or a partnership with South Vietnam. Any study of the history of Vietnam or, indeed, of the Chinese culture area would have brought awareness that the concept of co-operation between governments was alien to Vietnamese thought. In their tradition, there were only patrons and clients, each exploiting the other. Such study might also have suggested that the separateness of the two Vietnams was largely a Western juridical fiction, not a notion internalized by Vietnamese on either side of the artificial boundary. As indicated earlier, it might also have led to recognition that the conflict in Vietnam was in many if not most respects a civil war, the determining forces of which were outgrowths of the Vietnamese past and likely to be affected only marginally by foreigners.

Given the assumptions generally shared by Americans in the 1960's, it seems probable that any collection of men or women would have decided as did members of the Kennedy and Johnson administrations. Nevertheless, at the moment I write, almost everyone regards those decisions as mistaken. Many find them incredible. It may well be that the fashion will change and that some future generations will see these decisions as not only understandable but also as, in the circumstances, right. I doubt it. My expectation is that, like the decisions of Napoleon III concerning Mexico, they will have a sustained reputation as misbegotten blunders.

Because of this reputation, an autopsy of these decisions provides especially convincing evidence of how history can be misused in efforts to determine the national interest and what to do in its behalf. Here one can see men who would have been scandalized by an inelegant economic model or a poorly prepared legal brief making significant use of historical parallels, analogies, and trends with utter disregard for expertise or even the inherent logic of their assertions. No example illustrates better both the importance of history for men in government and the carelessness and lack of system with which they characteristically use it.

Report from Vietnam

MICHAEL HERR

The United States war in Vietnam, as Jean-Paul Sartre described it in his remarkable essay "On Genocide," was a "war of example." It was primarily an assertion of American willingness to resist "wars of national liberation" sponsored by major communist powers. Sartre pointed out that such a war could have no specific outcome. The limitlessness of the goal of demonstrating the great price a country would have to pay if it pursued a war of national liberation made genocide a part of strategy. The United States would bomb the smaller nation "back to the Stone Age," "defoliate" its forests and farmlands, "zippo" its villages, "pattern bomb" its towns and countrysides. With mindless destruction raised to a strategic objective, a certain type of rogue warrior would be the only possible hero; the rest were "grunts" mired in the slaughter, having to kill, hoping to survive, breathing in and breathing out, as Michael Herr says, but doomed to live with a horror of purposelessness that they could never share with the everyday world to which they prayed to return. This was not the John Wayne kind of war the generation after World War II grew up with, where purpose and heroism weighed in against the horrors. This was the world of Apocalypse Now, *of an anger without focus that is the only legacy of Vietnam.*

Michael Herr's book Dispatches *has been widely acclaimed as the most successful depiction of the American war in Vietnam. It was a media war: reporters at least represented a bit of the gratuitous heroism, the choosing to live dangerously that we Americans have been pleased to identify with war since the days of Richard Harding Davis and Ernest Hemingway. It was a battle of technology against the silent black-pajama-clad Viet Cong. (And of the modern globalism of the United States set so incongruously against obscurely understood struggles that drifted back through three thousand years of history and may continue for three thousand more.) It was also a defense of Saigon, where, for a scant century or so, the West had comfortably exploited the East. Michael Herr's stacatto prose captures the images the war holds at a point in our experience when its larger meanings for the United States remain still beyond the grasp of our imaginations, which are still glutted by the years of televised horrors witnessed in our living rooms.*

I   THE REPORTER

Going out at night the medics gave you pills, Dexedrine breath like dead snakes kept too long in a jar. I never saw the need for them myself, a little contact or anything that even sounded like contact would give me more speed than I could bear. Whenever I heard something outside of our clenched little circle I'd practically flip, hoping to God that I wasn't the only one who'd noticed it. A couple of rounds fired off in the dark a kilometer away and the Elephant would be there kneeling on my chest, sending me down into my boots for a breath. Once I thought I saw a light moving in the jungle and I caught myself just under a whisper saying, "I'm not ready for this, I'm not ready for this." That's when I decided to drop it and do something else with my nights. And I wasn't going out like the night ambushers did, or the Lurps, long-range recon patrollers who did it night after night for weeks and months, creeping up on VC base camps or around moving columns of North Vietnamese. I was living too close to my bones as it was, all I had to do was accept it. Anyway, I'd save the pills for later, for Saigon and the awful depressions I always had there.

I knew one 4th Division Lurp who took his pills by the fistful, downs from the left pocket of his tiger suit and ups from the right, one to cut the trail for him and the other to send him down it. He told me that they cooled things out just right for him, that he could see that old jungle at night like he was looking at it through a star-light scope. "They sure give you the range," he said.

This was his third tour. In 1965 he'd been the only survivor in a platoon of the Cav wiped out going into the Ia Drang Valley. In '66 he'd come back with the Special Forces and one morning after an ambush he'd hidden under the bodies of his team while the VC walked all around them with knives, making sure. They stripped the bodies of their gear, the berets too, and finally went away, laughing. After that, there was nothing left for him in the war except the Lurps.

"I just can't hack it back in the World," he said. He told me that after he'd come back home the last time he would sit in his room all day, and sometimes he'd stick a hunting rifle out the window, leading people and cars as they passed his house until the only feeling he was aware of was all up in the tip of that one finger. "It used to put my folks real uptight," he said. But he put people uptight here too, even here.

"No man, I'm sorry, he's just too crazy for me," one of the men in his team said. "All's you got to do is look in his eyes, that's the whole fucking story right there."

"Yeah, but you better do it quick," someone else said. "I mean, you don't want to let him catch you at it."

But he always seemed to be watching for it, I think he slept with his eyes open, and I was afraid of him anyway. All I ever managed was one quick look in, and that was like looking at the floor of an ocean. He wore a gold earring and a headband torn from a piece of camouflage parachute material, and since nobody was about to tell him to get his hair cut it fell below his shoulders, covering a thick purple scar. Even at division he never went anywhere without at least a .45 and a knife, and he thought I was a freak because I wouldn't carry a weapon.

"Didn't you ever meet a reporter before?" I asked him.

"Tits on a bull," he said. "Nothing personal."

But what a story he told me, as one-pointed and resonant as any war story I ever heard, it took me a year to understand it:

"Patrol went up the mountain. One man came back. He died before he could tell us what happened."

I waited for the rest, but it seemed not to be that kind of story; when I asked him what had happened he just looked like he felt sorry for me, fucked if he'd waste time telling stories to anyone dumb as I was.

His face was all painted up for night walking now like a bad hallucination, not like the painted faces I'd seen in San Francisco only a few weeks before, the other extreme of the same theater. In the coming hours he'd stand as faceless and quiet in the jungle as a fallen tree, and God help his opposite numbers unless they had at least half a squad along, he was a good killer, one of our best. The rest of his team were gathered outside the tent, set a little apart from the other division units, with its own Lurp-designated latrine and its own exclusive freeze-dry rations, three-star war food, the same chop they sold at Abercrombie & Fitch. The regular division troops would almost shy off the path when they passed the area on their way to and from the mess tent. No matter how toughened up they became in the war, they still looked innocent compared to the Lurps. When the team had grouped they walked in a file down the hill to the lz across the strip to the perimeter and into the treeline.

I never spoke to him again, but I saw him. When they came back in the next morning he had a prisoner with him, blindfolded and with his elbows bound sharply behind him. The Lurp area would definitely be off limits during the interrogation, and anyway, I was already down at the strip waiting for a helicopter to come and take me out of there. . . .

II AIRMOBILITY

In the months after I got back the hundreds of helicopters I'd flown in began to draw together until they'd formed a collective metachopper, and in my mind it was the sexiest thing going; saver-destroyer, provider-waster, right hand—left hand, nimble, fluent, canny and human; hot steel, grease, jungle-saturated canvas webbing, sweat cooling and warming up again, cassette rock and roll in one ear and door-gun fire in the other, fuel, heat, vitality and death, death itself, hardly an intruder. Men on the crews would say that once you'd carried a dead person he would always be there, riding with you. Like all combat people they were incredibly superstitious and invariably self-dramatic, but it was (I knew) unbearably true that close exposure to the dead sensitized you to the force of their presence and made for long reverberations; long. Some people were so delicate that one look was enough to wipe them away, but even bone-dumb grunts seemed to feel that something weird and extra was happening to them.

Helicopters and people jumping out of helicopters, people so in love they'd run to get on even when there wasn't any pressure. Choppers rising straight out of small cleared jungle spaces, wobbling down onto city rooftops, cartons of rations and ammunition thrown off, dead and wounded loaded on. Sometimes they were so plentiful and loose that you could touch down at five or six places in a day, look around, hear the talk, catch the next one out. There were installations as big as cities with 30,000 citizens, once we dropped in to feed supply to one man. God knows what kind of Lord Jim phoenix numbers he was doing in there, all he said to me was, "You didn't see a thing, right Chief? You weren't even here." There were posh fat air-conditioned camps like comfortable middle-class scenes with the violence tacit, "far away"; camps named for commanders' wives, LZ Thelma, LZ Betty Lou; number-named hilltops in trouble where I didn't want to stay; trail, paddy, swamp, deep hairy bush, scrub, swale, village, even city, where the ground couldn't drink up what the action spilled, it made you careful where you walked.

Sometimes the chopper you were riding in would top a hill and all the ground in front of you as far as the next hill would be charred and pitted and still smoking, and something between your chest and your stomach would turn over. Frail gray smoke where they'd burned off the rice fields around a free-strike zone, brilliant white smoke from phosphorus ("Willy Peter/Make you a buh liever"), deep black smoke from 'palm, they said that if you stood at the base of a column of napalm smoke it would suck the air right out of your lungs. Once we fanned over a little ville that had just been airstruck and the words of a song by Wingy Manone that I'd heard when I was a few years old snapped into my head, "Stop the War, These Cats Is Killing Themselves." Then we dropped, hovered, settled down into purple lz smoke, dozens of children broke from their hootches to run in toward the focus of our landing, the pilot laughing and saying, "Vietnam, man. Bomb 'em and feed 'em, bomb 'em and feed 'em."

Flying over jungle was almost pure pleasure, doing it on foot was nearly all pain. I never belonged in there. Maybe it really was what its people had always called it, Beyond; at the very least it was serious, I gave up things to it I probably never got back. ("Aw, jungle's okay. If you know her you can live in her real good, if you don't she'll take you down in an hour. Under.") Once in some thick jungle corner with some grunts standing around, a correspondent said, "Gee, you must really see some beautiful sunsets in here," and they almost pissed themselves laughing. But you could fly up and into hot tropic sunsets that would change the way you thought about light forever. You could also fly out of places that were so grim they turned to black and white in your head five minutes after you'd gone.

That could be the coldest one in the world, standing at the edge of a clearing watching the chopper you'd just come in on taking off again, leaving you there to think about what it was going to be for you now: if this was a bad place, the wrong place, maybe even the last place, and whether you'd made a terrible mistake this time.

There was a camp at Soc Trang where a man at the lz said, "If you come looking for a story this is your lucky day, we got Condition Red here," and before the sound of the chopper had faded out, I knew I had it too. . . .

Airmobility, dig it, you weren't going anywhere. It made you feel safe, it made you feel Omni, but it was only a stunt, technology. Mobility was just mobility, it saved lives or took them all the time (saved mine I don't know how many times, maybe dozens, maybe none), what you really needed was a flexibility far greater than anything the technology could provide, some generous, spontaneous gift for accepting surprises, and I didn't have it. I got to hate surprises, control freak at the crossroads, if you were one of those people who always thought they had to know what was coming next, the war could cream you. It was the same with your ongoing attempts at getting used to the jungle or the blow-you-out climate or the saturating strangeness of the place which didn't lessen with exposure so often as it fattened and darkened in accumulating alienation. It was great if you could adapt, you had to try, but it wasn't the same as making a discipline, going into your own reserves and developing a real war metabolism, slow yourself down when your heart tried to punch its way through your chest, get swift when everything went to stop and all you could feel of your whole life was the entropy whipping through it. Unlovable terms.

The ground was always in play, always being swept. Under the ground was his, above it was ours. We had the air, we could get up in it but not disappear in *to* it, we could run but we couldn't hide, and he could do each so well that sometimes it looked like he was doing them both at once, while our finder just went limp. All the same, one place or another it was always going on, rock around the clock, we had the days and he had the nights. You could be in the most protected space in Vietnam and still know that your safety was provisional, that early death, blindness, loss of legs, arms or balls, major and lasting disfigurement— the whole rotten deal—could come in on the freakyfluky as easily as in the so-called expected ways, you heard so many of those stories it was a wonder anyone was left alive to die in firefights and mortar-rocket attacks. After a few weeks, when the nickel had jarred loose and dropped and I saw that everyone around me was carrying a gun, I also saw that any one of them could go off at any time, putting you where it wouldn't matter whether it had been an accident or not. The roads were mined, the trails booby-trapped, satchel charges and grenades blew up jeeps and movie theaters, the VC got work inside all the camps as shoeshine boys and laundresses and honey-dippers, they'd starch your fatigues and burn your shit and then go home and mortar your area. Saigon and Cholon and Danang held such hostile vibes that you felt you were being dry-sniped every time someone looked at you, and choppers fell out of the sky like fat poisoned birds a hundred times a day. After a while I couldn't get on one without thinking that I must be out of my fucking mind. . . .

"Boy, you sure get offered some shitty choices," a Marine once said to me, and I couldn't help but feel that what he really meant was that you didn't get offered any at all. Specifically, he was just talking about a couple of C-ration cans, "dinner," but considering his young life you couldn't blame him for thinking that if he knew one thing for sure, it was that there was no one anywhere who cared less about what *he* wanted. There wasn't anybody he wanted to thank for his food, but he was grateful that he was still alive to eat it, that the mother-fucker hadn't scarfed him up first. He hadn't been anything but tired and scared for six months and he'd lost a lot, mostly people, and seen far too much, but he was breathing in and breathing out, some kind of choice all by itself.

He had one of those faces, I saw that face at least a thousand times at a hundred bases and camps, all the youth sucked out of the eyes, the color drawn from the skin, cold white lips, you knew he wouldn't wait for any of it to come back. Life had made him old, he'd live it out old. All those faces, sometimes it was like looking into faces at a rock concert, locked in, the event had them; or like students who were very heavily advanced, serious beyond what you'd call their years if you didn't know for yourself what the minutes and hours of those years were made up of. Not just like all the ones you saw who looked like they couldn't drag their asses through another day of it. (How do you feel when a nineteen-year-old kid tells you from the bottom of his heart that he's gotten too old for this kind of shit?) Not like the faces of the dead or wounded either, they could look more released than over-taken. These were the faces of boys whose whole lives seemed to have backed up on them, they'd be a few feet away but they'd be looking back at you over a distance you knew you'd never really cross. We'd talk, sometimes fly together, guys going out on R&R, guys escorting bodies, guys who'd flipped over into extremes of peace or violence. Once I flew with a kid who was going home, he looked back down once at the ground where he'd spent the year and spilled his whole load of tears. Sometimes you even flew with the dead.

Once I jumped on a chopper that was full of them. The kid in the op shack had said that there would be a body on board, but he'd been given some wrong information. "How bad do you want to get to Danang?" he'd asked me, and I'd said, "Bad."

When I saw what was happening I didn't want to get on, but they'd made a divert and a special landing for me, I had to go with the chopper I'd drawn, I was afraid of looking squeamish. (I remember, too, thinking that a chopper full of dead men was far less likely to get shot down than one full of living.) They weren't even in bags. They'd been on a truck near one of the firebases in the DMZ that was firing support for Khe Sanh, and the truck had hit a Command-detonated mine, then they'd been rocketed. The Marines were always running out of things, even food, ammo and medicine, it wasn't so strange that they'd run out of bags too. The men had been wrapped around in ponchos, some of them carelessly fastened with plastic straps, and loaded on board. There was a small space cleared for me between one of them and the door gunner, who looked pale and so tremendously furious that I thought he was angry with me and I couldn't look at him for a while. When we went up the wind blew through the ship and made the ponchos shake and tremble until the one next to me blew back in a fast brutal flap, uncovering the face. They hadn't even closed his eyes for him.

The gunner started hollering as loud as he could, "Fix it! Fix it!," maybe he thought the eyes were looking at him, but there wasn't anything I could do. My hand went there a couple of times and I couldn't, and then I did. I pulled the poncho tight, lifted his head carefully and tucked the poncho under it, and then I couldn't believe that I'd done it. All during the ride the gunner kept trying to smile, and when we landed at Dong Ha he thanked me and ran off to get a detail. The pilots jumped down and walked away without looking back once, like they'd never seen that chopper before in their lives. . . .

III SAIGON

In Saigon I always went to sleep stoned so I almost always lost my dreams, probably just as well, sock in deep and dim under that information and get whatever rest you could, wake up tapped of all images but the ones remembered from the day or the week before, with only the taste of a bad dream in your mouth like you'd been chewing on a roll of dirty old pennies in your sleep. I'd watched grunts asleep putting out the REM's like a firefight in the dark, I'm sure it was the same with me. They'd say (I'd ask) that they didn't remember their dreams either when they were in the zone, but on R&R or in the hospital their dreaming would be constant, open, violent and clear, like a man in the Pleiku hospital on the night I was there. It was three in the morning, scary and upsetting like hearing a language for the first time and somehow understanding every word, the voice loud and small at the same time, insistent, calling, "*Who? Who?* Who's in the next room?" There was a single shaded light over the desk at the end of the ward where I sat with the orderly. I could only see the first few beds, it felt like there were a thousand of them running out into the darkness, but actually there were only twenty in each row. After the man had repeated it a few times there was a change like the break in a fever, he sounded like a pleading little boy. I could see cigarettes being lighted at the far end of the ward, mumbles and groans, wounded men returning to consciousness, pain, but the man who'd been dreaming slept through it. . . . As for my own dreams, the ones I lost there would make it through later, I should have known, some things will just naturally follow until they take. The night would come when they'd be vivid and unremitting, that night the beginning of a long string, I'd remember then and wake up half believing that I'd never really been in any of those places.

Saigon *cafarde*, a bitch, nothing for it but some smoke and a little lie-down, waking in the late afternoon on damp pillows, feeling the emptiness of the bed behind you as you walked to the windows looking down at Tu Do. Or just lying there tracking the rotations of the ceiling fan, reaching for the fat roach that sat on my Zippo in a yellow disk of grass tar. There were mornings when I'd do it before my feet even hit the floor. Dear Mom, stoned again.

In the Highlands, where the Montagnards would trade you a pound of legendary grass for a carton of Salems, I got stoned with some infantry from the 4th. One of them had worked for months on his pipe, beautifully carved and painted with flowers and peace symbols. There was a reedy little man in the circle who grinned all the time but hardly spoke. He pulled a thick plastic bag out of his pack and handed it over to me. It was full of what looked like large pieces of dried fruit. I was stoned and hungry, I almost put my hand in there, but it had a bad weight to it. The other men were giving each other looks, some amused, some embarrassed and even angry. Someone had told me once, there were a lot more ears than heads in Vietnam; just information. When I handed it back he was still grinning, but he looked sadder than a monkey.

In Saigon and Danang we'd get stoned together and keep the common pool stocked and tended. It was bottomless and alive with Lurps, seals, recondos, Green-Beret bushmasters, redundant mutilators, heavy rapers, eye-shooters, widow-makers, nametakers, classic essential American types; point men, *isolatos* and outriders like they were programmed in their genes to do it, the first taste made them crazy for it, just like they knew it would. You thought you were separate and protected, you could travel the war for a hundred years, a swim in that pool could still be worth a piece of your balance.

We'd all heard about the man in the Highlands who was "building his own gook," parts were the least of his troubles. In Chu Lai some Marines pointed a man out to me and swore to God they'd seen him bayonet a wounded NVA and then lick the bayonet clean. There was a famous story, some reporters asked a door gunner, "How can you shoot women and children?" and he'd answered, "It's easy, you just don't lead 'em so much." Well, they said you needed a sense of humor, there you go, even the VC had one. Once after an ambush that killed a lot of Americans, they covered the field with copies of a photograph that showed one more young, dead American, with the punch line mimeographed on the back, "Your X-rays have just come back from the lab and we think we know what your problem is."

Beautiful for once and only once, just past dawn flying toward the center of the city in a Loach, view from a bubble floating at 800 feet. In that space, at that hour, you could see what people had seen forty years before, Paris of the East, Pearl of the Orient, long open avenues lined and bowered over by trees running into spacious parks, precisioned scale, all under the soft shell from a million breakfast fires, camphor smoke rising and diffusing, covering Saigon and the shining veins of the river with a warmth like the return of better times. Just a projection, that was the thing about choppers, you had to come down sometimes, down to the moment, the street, if you found a pearl down there you got to keep it.

By 7:30 it was beyond berserk with bikes, the air was like L.A. on short plumbing, the subtle city war inside the war had renewed itself for another day, relatively light on actual violence but intense with bad feeling: despair, impacted rage, impotent gnawing resentment; thousands of Vietnamese in the service of a pyramid that wouldn't stand for five years, plugging the feed tube into their own hearts, grasping and gorging; young Americans in from the boonies on TDY, charged with hatred and grounded in fear of the Vietnamese; thousands of Americans sitting in their offices crying in bored chorus, "You can't get these people to do a fucking thing, you can't get these people to do a fucking thing." And all the others, theirs and ours, who just didn't want to play, it sickened them. That December the GVN Department of Labor had announced that the refugee problem had been solved, that "all refugees [had] been assimilated into the economy," but mostly they seemed to have assimilated themselves into the city's roughest corners, alleyways, mud slides, under parked cars. Cardboard boxes that had carried air-conditioners and refrigerators housed up to ten children, most Americans and plenty of Vietnamese would cross the street to avoid trash heaps that fed whole families. And this was still months before Tet, "refugees up the gazops," a flood. I'd heard that the GVN Department of Labor had nine American advisors for every Vietnamese.

In Broddards and La Pagode and the pizzeria around the corner, the Cowboys and Vietnamese "students" would hang out all day, screaming obscure arguments at each other, cadging off Americans, stealing tips from the tables, reading Pléiade editions of Proust, Malraux, Camus. One of them talked to me a few times but we couldn't really communicate, all I understood was his obsessive comparison between Rome and Washington, and that he seemed to believe that Poe had been a French writer. In the late afternoon the Cowboys would leave the cafés and milk bars and ride down hard on Lam Son Square to pick the Allies. They could snap a Rolex off your wrist like a hawk hitting a field mouse; wallets, pens, cameras, eyeglasses, anything; if the war had gone on any longer they'd have found a way to whip the boots off your feet. They'd hardly leave their saddles and they never looked back. There was a soldier down from the 1st Division who was taking snapshots of his friends with some bar girls in front of the Vietnamese National Assembly. He'd gotten his shot focused and centered but before he pushed the button his camera was a block away, leaving him in the bike's backwash with a fresh pink welt on his throat where the cord had been torn and helpless amazement on his face, "Well I'll be dipped in shit!"; as a little boy raced across the square, zipped a piece of cardboard up the soldier's shirtfront and took off around the corner with his Paper Mate. The White Mice stood around giggling, but there were a lot of us watching from the Continental terrace, a kind of gasp went up from the tables, and later when he came up for a beer he said, "I'm goin' back to the war, man, this fucking Saigon is too much for me." There was a large group of civilian engineers there, the same men you'd see in the restaurants throwing food at each other, and one of them, a fat old boy, said, "You ever catch one of them li'l nigs just pinch 'em. Pinch 'em hard. Boy, they hate that."

Five to seven were bleary low hours in Saigon, the city's energy ebbing at dusk, until it got dark and movement was replaced with apprehension. Saigon at night was still Vietnam at night, night was the war's truest medium, night was when it got really interesting in the villages, the TV crews couldn't film at night, the Phoenix was a night bird, it flew in and out of Saigon all the time.

Maybe you had to be pathological to find glamour in Saigon, maybe you just had to settle for very little, but Saigon had it for me, and danger activated it. The days of big, persistent terror in Saigon were over, but everyone felt that they could come back again any time, heavy like 1963–5, when they hit the old Brinks BOQ on Christmas Eve, when they blew up the My Canh floating restaurant, waited for it to be rebuilt and moved to another spot on the river, and then blew it up again, when they bombed the first U.S. embassy and changed the war forever from the intimate inside out. There were four known VC sapper battalions in the Saigon-Cholon area, dread sappers, guerrilla superstars, they didn't even have to do anything to put the fear out. Empty ambulances sat parked at all hours in front of the new embassy. Guards ran mirrors and "devices" under all vehicles entering all installations, BOQ's were fronted with sandbags, checkpoints and wire, high-gauge grilles filled our windows, but they still got through once in a while, random terror but real, even the supposedly terror-free safe spots worked out between the Corsican mob and the VC offered plenty of anxiety. Saigon just before Tet; guess, guess again.

Those nights there was a serious tiger lady going around on a Honda shooting American officers on the street with a .45. I think she'd killed over a dozen in three months; the Saigon papers described her as "beautiful," but I don't know how anybody knew that. The commander of one of the Saigon MP battalions said he thought it was a man dressed in an *ao dai* because a .45 was "an awful lot of gun for a itty bitty Vietnamese woman."

Saigon, the center, where every action in the bushes hundreds of miles away fed back into town on a karmic wire strung so tight that if you touched it in the early morning it would sing all day and all night. Nothing so horrible ever happened upcountry that it was beyond language fix and press relations, a squeeze fit into the computers would make the heaviest numbers jump up and dance. You'd either meet an optimism that no violence could unconvince or a cynicism that would eat itself empty every day and then turn, hungry and malignant, on whatever it could for a bite, friendly or hostile, it didn't matter. Those men called dead Vietnamese "believers," a lost American platoon was "a black eye," they talked as though killing a man was nothing more than depriving him of his vigor.

It seemed the least of the war's contradictions that to lose your worst sense of American shame you had to leave the Dial Soapers in Saigon and a hundred headquarters who spoke goodworks and killed nobody themselves, and go out to the grungy men in the jungle who talked bloody murder and killed people all the time. It was true that the grunts stripped belts and packs and weapons from their enemies; Saigon wasn't a flat market, these goods filtered down and in with the other spoils: Rolexes, cameras, snakeskin shoes from Taiwan, air-brush portraits of nudc Vietnamese women with breasts like varnished beach balls, huge wooden carvings that they set on their desks to give you the finger when you walked into their offices. In Saigon it never mattered what they told you, even less when they actually seemed to believe it. Maps, charts, figures, projections, fly fantasies, names of places, of operations, of commanders, of weapons; memories, guesses, second guesses, experiences (new, old, real, imagined, stolen); histories, attitudes—you could let it go, let it all go. If you wanted some war news in Saigon you had to hear it in stories brought from the field by friends, see it in the lost watchful eyes of the Saigonese, or do it like Trashman, reading the cracks in the sidewalk.

Sitting in Saigon was like sitting inside the folded petals of a poisonous flower, the poison history, fucked in its root no matter how far back you wanted to run your trace. Saigon was the only place left with a continuity that someone as far outside as I was could recognize. Hue and Danang were like remote closed societies, mute and intractable. Villages, even large ones, were fragile, a village could disappear in an afternoon, and the countryside was either blasted over cold and dead or already back in Charles' hands. Saigon remained, the repository and the arena, it breathed history, expelled it like toxin, Shit Piss and Corruption. Paved swamp, hot mushy winds that never cleaned anything away, heavy thermal seal over diesel fuel, mildew, garbage, excrement, atmosphere. A five-block walk in that could take it out of you, you'd get back to the hotel with your head feeling like one of those chocolate apples, tap it sharply in the right spot and it falls apart in sections. Saigon, November 1967: "The animals are sick with love." Not much chance anymore for history to go on unselfconsciously.

You'd stand nailed there in your tracks sometimes, no bearings and none in sight, thinking, *Where the fuck am I?*, fallen into some unnatural East-West interface, a California corridor cut and bought and burned deep into Asia, and once we'd done it we couldn't remember what for. It was axiomatic that it was about ideological space, we were there to bring them the choice, bringing it to them like Sherman bringing the Jubilee through Georgia, clean through it, wall to wall with pacified indigenous and scorched earth. (In the Vietnamese sawmills they had to change the blades every five minutes, some of our lumber had gotten into some of theirs.)

There was such a dense concentration of American energy there, American and essentially adolescent, if that energy could have been channeled into anything more than noise, waste and pain it would have lighted up Indochina for a thousand years. . . .

Cambodia and Kent State:
Two Memoirs

RICHARD NIXON and HENRY KISSINGER

The war question that ripped domestic politics in the Vietnam years was without a successful resolution. Several administrators supported a war effort that piled up bodies of Vietnamese and Americans with what we now know was no chance of military success. Yet the conduct of the communist governments that have since seized Indochina have given little cause for satisfaction at the outcome.

The American and South Vietnamese incursion into Cambodia in 1970 raised anger among various segments of the political opposition—those who opposed the entire American cause and those who believed the invasion would interfere with the achievement of an orderly negotiated peace. In any event, Vietnam was a war beyond solutions.

President Richard Nixon and Secretary of State Henry Kissinger, the individuals most responsible for the invasion, were not simplistic right-wingers who tried to reduce international politics to a confrontation between communism and anticommunism; they had respect for the subtle compositions and shifts of international power. Still, the war and the situation in Cambodia eluded their logic of power and revealed a perhaps questionable morality that each in his way labors to justify.

I RICHARD NIXON

The whole situation over Cambodia and Vietnam was becoming so tense that I felt I had to make a very painful personal decision. Although I knew how much Pat and Julie were counting on it, I canceled our plans to attend David's graduation from Amherst and Julie's graduation from Smith later in the spring. Pat had never known the joy of having a parent attend any of her graduations, and I knew that she had been looking forward to Julie's. Julie was also terribly disappointed. She tried to hold back her tears, and she pointed out that only a few small radical groups were involved, and that everyone she knew—including students who opposed the war and my administration—felt that I should be able to attend the ceremony.

Ted Agnew felt particularly strongly about this. "Don't let them intimidate you, Mr. President," he said, barely restraining his indignation. "You may be President, but you're her father, and a father should be able to attend his daughter's graduation." The Secret Service, however, had received reports of several protest demonstrations that were already being planned against me, and the possibility of an ugly incident that would mar the graduation, not just for us but for all the other students and parents, was too great a risk.

Despite the impasse in the secret talks and the worsening military situation in Cambodia, I decided to go ahead with the troop withdrawal scheduled for April 20 [1970]. I discussed the issue at length with Kissinger, and we agreed that the time had come to drop a bombshell on the gathering spring storm of antiwar protest.

Vietnamization had progressed to the point that, for the first time, we felt we could project our troop withdrawals over the next year. We decided, therefore, that instead of announcing a smaller number over a shorter period, I would announce the withdrawal of 150,000 men over the next year.

The withdrawal figure came as a dramatic surprise when I revealed it in a speech on April 20. The only Communist reaction was an escalation of the fighting.

By the end of April, the Communists had a quarter of Cambodia under control and were closing in on Phnom Penh. It was clear that Lon Nol needed help to survive. If the Communists succeded in overthrowing him, South Vietnam would be threatened from the west as well as the north. This situation would jeopardize our troop withdrawal program and would also virtually assure a Communist invasion of South Vietnam as soon as the last American had left. . . .

The Communist sanctuaries in Cambodia were in two main areas. The Parrot's Beak is a sliver of land that pushes into South Vietnam and reaches within thirty-three miles of Saigon. A particularly strong ARVN [South Vietnamese Army] force was stationed on the border in this area. Our intelligence reports indicated that the heaviest Communist concentration was in another border area, the Fishhook, a thin, curving piece of Cambodian territory jutting right into the heart of South Vietnam, about fifty miles northwest of Saigon. This was the primary area of operation for what intelligence referred to as COSVN— the Central Office of South Vietnam. COSVN was the Communists' floating command post of military headquarters, supplies, food, and medical facilities. The Fishhook was thus the nerve center of the Communist forces in the sanctuaries, and it would be strongly defended. The initial intelligence estimates projected that the heavy fortifications and the concentration of Communist troops in the area might result in very high casualties in the first week of operation.

I began to consider letting the ARVN go into the Parrot's Beak and sending a mixed force of American and South Vietnamese troops into the Fishhook. Giving the South Vietnamese an operation of their own would be a major boost to their morale as well as provide a practical demonstration of the success of Vietnamization. It would also be a good diversionary cover for the more important and more difficult Fishhook operation.

I never had any illusions about the shattering effect a decision to go into Cambodia would have on public opinion at home. I knew that opinions among my major foreign policy advisers were deeply divided over the issue of widening the war, and I recognized that it could mean personal and political catastrophe for me and my administration.

On Sunday night, April 26, I reached my decision. We would go for broke. The ARVN would go into the Parrot's Beak and a joint ARVN—U.S. force would go into the Fishhook.

On Monday morning I met with Rogers, Laird, and Kissinger. It was a tense meeting, because even though Rogers and Laird had by now given up hope of dissuading me from taking some action in Cambodia, they still thought they could convince me not to involve American troops. Rogers said, "It will cost us great casualties with very little gain. And I just don't believe it will be a crippling blow to the enemy." Laird said, "I'm not really opposed to going after the COSVN, but I'm not happy with the way this is being implemented." He was more upset, it seemed, with an apparent snub of the Pentagon in our decision-making process. He also suggested that General Abrams might not approve of the COSVN operation, but backed away when Kissinger contradicted him. Nevertheless, immediately after our meeting I sent a back-channel cable to Abrams, ordering him to send me the "unvarnished truth" about the way he felt.

A joint response from Abrams and U.S. Ambassador Ellsworth Bunker indicated full support on their part. Speaking specifically of the attack on the Fishhook, they wrote: "We both agree that attack on this area should have maximum unsettling effect on the enemy, who has considered until now his sanctuaries immune to ground attack." Abrams added his personal views in a separate paragraph: "It is my independent view that these attacks into the enemy's sanctuaries in Cambodia are the military move to make at this time in support of our mission in South Vietnam both in terms of security of our own forces and for advancement of the Vietnamization program."

That night I sat alone going over the decision one last time. It was still not too late to call the operation off: the Parrot's Beak action would not begin until the next morning, and the Fishhook not until two days after that. I took a pad and began to make a list of the pluses and minuses of both operations. The risk and danger involved were undeniably great; there was no assurance of success on the battlefield and there was the certainty of an uproar at home. But there was also no question that the continued existence of the Cambodian sanctuaries would threaten the safety of the remaining American troops in South Vietnam and almost guarantee a Communist invasion as soon as we had pulled out.

Early the next morning I showed Kissinger my notes. He blinked his eyes as he took a piece of paper from the folder he was carrying and handed it to me. It was a list almost identical to mine. "I did the same thing, Mr. President," he said, "and it looks like we're both able to make a good case both ways on it."

I said that as far as I was concerned, the simple fact of showing the Communists that we intended to protect ourselves and our allies put all the weight on one side. "Now that we have made the decision there must be no recriminations among us," I said. "Not even if the whole thing goes wrong. In fact, *especially* if the whole thing goes wrong."

South Vietnam's announcement of the Parrot's Beak operation came over the wires on Wednesday, April 29. Within minutes the leading Senate doves were in front of the TV cameras, demanding that I disavow Thieu's offensive and not send any American troops into Cambodia. All during the day I continued to work on the speech I would deliver the next night announcing the operation. I asked Rose to call Julie for me. "I don't want to get her upset, but it's possible that the campuses are really going to blow up after this speech," I said, "so could you just say I asked if she and David could come down from school to be with us."

That night I found it difficult to get to sleep. After tossing fitfully for an hour or so, I got up and sat in the Lincoln Sitting Room until 5:30. At nine o'clock I walked over to my EOB office to go over the first pages of the typed speech. That afternoon I had Haldeman and Kissinger come over so I could read the announcement to them. I asked Kissinger to brief George Meany, because I knew that labor support would be vital. A little later he reported that Meany supported my decision wholeheartedly. Kissinger had less success with his own NSC staff. Three of his top assistants decided to resign in protest over my decision.

Shortly before delivering the speech from the Oval Office, I went to the White House Theatre to brief the bipartisan congressional leadership. I said I understood that many of them would oppose the decision I had made. I knew how they felt about it, and I respected their feelings. "I just want you to know that whether you think it's right or wrong, the reason I have decided to do this is that I have decided it's the best way to end the war and save the lives of our soldiers," I told them.

I looked around the room. The faces were intent and strained. Some of the strongest doves were there: Fulbright, Mansfield, Aiken, Kennedy. The sincerity of my words must have reached them, even though they remained opposed to the decision I had made. As I left the room, everyone stood and applauded.

I began the speech by describing how the Communists had responded to my recently announced troop withdrawal by stepping up their attacks throughout Indochina. "To protect our men who are in Vietnam and to guarantee the continued success of our withdrawal and Vietnamization programs," I said, "I have concluded that the time has come for action."

I used a map to explain the geographic and strategic importance of the Cambodian sanctuaries and to describe the South Vietnamese operation in the Parrot's Beak. Then I announced that a joint U.S.–Vietnamese force would go into the Fishhook.

I stressed that this was not an invasion of Cambodia. The sanctuaries were completely occupied and controlled by North Vietnamese forces. We would withdraw once they had been driven out and once their military supplies were destroyed. The purpose, I said, was not to expand the war into Cambodia, but to end the war in Vietnam by making peace possible.

Setting my decision in its widest context, I continued, "If, when the chips are down, the world's most powerful nation, the United States of America, acts like a pitiful, helpless giant, the forces of totalitarianism and anarchy will threaten free nations and free institutions throughout the world."

For an hour after the speech I sat with my family in the Solarium while they discussed the speech and tried to gauge the reactions to it. Then I went to the Lincoln Sitting Room and began returning calls that had come in after the speech.

Just after 10:30 I was informed that Chief Justice Warren Burger was at the gate with a letter for me. I instructed the Secret Service agent on duty to have him shown up immediately.

"I didn't want to disturb you, Mr. President," Burger said, "but I wanted you to know that I think your speech tonight had a sense of history and destiny about it."

I said that the critics had already begun denouncing the speech and the decision, but he said that he was sure it would be supported by the people. "I think anyone who really listened to what you said will appreciate the guts it took to make the decision," he added. He also pointed out that anyone who thought about it would realize that, as a shrewd politician, I would obviously not do anything that might damage Republican chances in the November elections unless I felt that it was absolutely necessary for national security.

"Speaking in the greatest confidence, Mr. Chief Justice," I said, using his formal title as I always did when addressing him, "I am realist enough to know that if this operation doesn't succeed—or if anything else happens that forces my public support below a point where I feel I can't be re-elected—I would like you to be ready to be in the running for the nomination in 1972." . . .

Despite very little sleep, I was up early on the morning after the speech. I went to the Pentagon for a firsthand briefing on the Cambodian operation from the Joint Chiefs and their top advisers. As I walked through the halls to the briefing room, I was mobbed by people cheering and trying to shake my hand. "God bless you!" "Right on!" "We should have done this years ago!" they shouted.

The atmosphere in the briefing room was generally positive if somewhat more restrained. A huge map of the battle area almost covered one wall. Different colored pins indicated the positions and movements of the various forces. As the briefers described the initial success of the operation, I found myself studying the map more and more intently. I noted that in addition to the Parrot's Beak and the Fishhook, four other areas were marked as occupied by Communist forces.

Suddenly I asked, "Between the ARVN and ourselves, would we be able to mount offensives in all of those other areas? Could we take out *all* the sanctuaries?"

The reply to my question emphasized the very negative reaction any such action would receive in the media and Congress.

"Let me be the judge as far as the political reactions are concerned," I said. "The fact is that we have already taken the political heat for this particular operation. If we can substantially reduce the threat to our forces by wiping out the rest of the sanctuaries, now is the time to do it."

Everyone seemed to be waiting for someone else to speak. Usually I like to mull things over, but I made a very uncharacteristic on-the-spot decision. I said, "I want to take out all of those sanctuaries. Make whatever plans are necessary, and then just do it. Knock them all out so that they can't be used against us again. Ever."

As I left the Pentagon after the briefing, once again employees rushed into the halls. By the time I reached the lobby, I was surrounded by a friendly, cheering crowd. One woman was particularly emotional as she thanked me on behalf of her husband, who was serving in Vietnam. As I thought of these men and women with loved ones fighting in Vietnam, I could not help thinking about those students who took advantage of their draft deferments and their privileged status in our society to bomb campuses, set fires, and tyrannize their institutions.

"I have seen them," I said about our soldiers in Vietnam. "They're the greatest. You see these bums, you know, blowing up the campuses. Listen, the boys that are on the college campuses today are the luckiest people in the world, going to the greatest universities, and here they are burning up the books, storming around about this issue. . . . Then out there, we have kids who are just doing their duty. And I have seen them. They stand tall, and they are proud."

That afternoon, while the tempest of reaction over Cambodia continued to build, I decided to get my family away from the White House for at least a few hours of relaxation after the great tension we had all experienced. It was a warm, clear day, so I suggested that we sail down the Potomac to Mount Vernon on the *Sequoia*.

It is the custom for all naval vessels passing Mount Vernon to honor George Washington, who is buried there. When we neared the spot, I had everyone move onto the deck and face the shore. Pat was next to me, then David, Julie, and Bebe Rebozo. As we passed by the first President's tomb, over the *Sequoia*'s loudspeaker came "The Star-Spangled Banner." We all stood at attention until the last note died away.

By the time the *Sequoia* had returned to Washington, the indignant reaction to my "bums" statement that morning at the Pentagon had almost overwhelmed the response to the Cambodia speech itself.

All through the spring of 1970 the country had faced wave after wave of violent campus unrest. As with the disturbances at the beginning of 1969, the issues were largely campus-oriented, dealing with disciplinary regulations, campus administration, and minority admissions.

What distinguished many of the 1970 campus disturbances from all earlier ones was the increase in bombings and violence connected with them. Radical groups openly encouraged the bombing of institutions of which they disapproved.

In the academic year 1969–70 there were 1,800 demonstrations, 7,500 arrests, 462 injuries—two-thirds of them were to police—and 247 arsons and 8 deaths.

April 1970 had been a particularly violent month. For the second time, a bank near the University of California at Santa Barbara was set on fire. A fire was set at the University of Kansas that destroyed buildings worth $2 million. At Ohio State University protesters demanding the admission of more black students and the abolition of ROTC on campus engaged in a six-hour battle with police. There were 600 arrests and 20 wounded. Governor James Rhodes finally had to call in 1,200 national guardsmen and impose a curfew to quiet the campus.

It was criminal and barbarous to burn banks as a protest against capitalism or to burn ROTC buildings as a protest against militarism. But to me the most shocking incidents were those that I considered to be directed at the very quality of intellectual life that should characterize a university community. In March, an arsonist caused $320,000 damage to the University of California library at Berkeley. At the end of April, as part of a demonstration in support of Black Panthers charged with murder in New Haven, $2,500 worth of books were set on fire in the basement of the Yale Law School.

The most shameful incident occurred at Stanford University. On April 24 an anti-ROTC group set a fire at the university's center for behavioral studies. One of the offices that was completely gutted belonged to a visiting Indian anthropologist, Professor M. N. Srinivas. His personal notes, files, and manuscripts went up in flames.

When Pat Moynihan told me about this tragedy, I wrote to Professor Srinivas:

As did countless other Americans, I responded with disbelief at the news that your study at the Center for Advanced Studies in the Behavioral Sciences had been firebombed, and that much of the work of a lifetime had been destroyed.

It can be small consolation for you to know that the overwhelming proportion of the American people, and of the American academic community, utterly reject the tactics of the person or persons who did this. To say that they are deranged, does not excuse them. To say, what is more probably the case, that they are simply evil, does not make them go away.

I hope that the great insights of social anthropology that you have brought to your studies might serve in this moment to help you understand this tragedy. Please at all events know that you are an honored and welcome guest, whose work is appreciated and valued in this nation as indeed throughout the world.

I do not think that anyone who heard my comments at the Pentagon or who heard the tape recording of it had any doubt that when I talked about "bums" burning up the books and blowing up the campuses, I was referring to the arsonists at Berkeley and Yale and the Stanford firebombers and others like them. The Washington *Post* headline the next morning accurately reflected my meaning: *Nixon Denounces Campus "Bums" Who Burn Books, Set Off Bombs.*

But the front-page headline in the New York *Times* conveyed a slightly different meaning: *Nixon Puts "Bums" Label on Some College Radicals*; and the inside continuation of the story was headlined: *Nixon Denounces "Bums" on Campus.*

Within a few days, it was the widespread impression that I had referred to all student protesters as "bums."

The media coverage and interpretation of the "bums" statement added fuel to the fires of dissent that were already getting out of control on many campuses. The National Student Association called for my impeachment, and editors of eleven Eastern colleges, including most of the Ivy League schools, ran a common editorial in their campus newspapers calling for a nationwide academic strike.

At the University of Maryland, just outside Washington, fifty people were injured when students ransacked the ROTC building and skirmished with police. In Kent, Ohio, a crowd of hundreds of demonstrators watched as two young men threw lighted flares into the Army ROTC building on the campus of Kent State University, and burned it to the ground. Governor Rhodes called in the National Guard. He said that 99 percent of the Kent State students wanted the school to remain open, and that the rest were "worse than the brownshirts."

On Monday, May 4, I asked Haldeman to come to the EOB office to go over trip schedules with me. He looked agitated. "Something just came over the wires about a demonstration at Kent State," he said. "The National Guard opened fire, and some students were shot."

I was stunned. "Are they dead?" I asked.

"I'm afraid so. No one knows why it happened."

It appeared that an uneasy confrontation had begun brewing around noon. Finally, a large crowd of students began throwing rocks and chunks of concrete at the guardsmen, forcing them up a small hill. At the top the soldiers turned, and someone started shooting.

In the newspaper the next day I saw the pictures of the four young people who had been killed. Two had been bystanders; the other two had been protesting a decision they felt was wrong. Now all four were dead, and a call was going out for nationwide demonstrations and student strikes. Would this tragedy become the cause of scores of others? I could not get the photographs out of my mind. I could not help thinking about the families, suddenly receiving the news that their children were dead because they had been shot in a campus demonstration. I wrote personal letters to each of the parents, even though I knew that words could not help.

Those few days after Kent State were among the darkest of my presidency. I felt utterly dejected when I read that the father of one of the dead girls had told a reporter, "My child was not a bum."

Kent State also took a heavy toll on Henry Kissinger's morale.

Members of his staff had resigned because of Cambodia, and former Harvard colleagues whom he had considered among his most loyal friends wrote bitter letters to him demanding that he make his professed moral position credible by resigning.

On a day several of these letters arrived, he came into my office and sat staring disconsolately out the window. Finally he said, "I still think you made the right decision as far as foreign policy considerations were involved. But in view of what has happened I fear I may have failed to advise you adequately of the domestic dangers."

I told him that I had been fully aware of both the military and the political risks. I had made the decision myself, and I assumed full responsibility for it. Finally I said, "Henry, remember Lot's wife. Never turn back. Don't waste time rehashing things we can't do anything about."

I was shocked and disappointed when an apparently intentional leak to the press revealed that Bill Rogers and Mel Laird had been opposed to my Cambodian decision. The operation was still in a critical stage, and I called Rogers and told him that I felt the Cabinet should get behind a decision once it had been made by the President.

Walter Hickel, the Secretary of the Interior, chose a more public way to express his conviction that I should listen to the students and spend more time with the Cabinet. In what he later explained as a mishap, a copy of a letter he had written to me raising these points was already going out over the AP wire before it had been delivered to the White House. Several other Cabinet and administration members also took public positions of less than full support.

In the midst of all the furor, it meant a great deal to me when one of the two living Americans who could really know what I was going through wrote to me.

I received a note from Johnson City: "Dear Mr. President," it read, "I hope you have a chance to read this. My best always. LBJ." Attached to it was a recent column by one of Johnson's former assistants, John P. Roche, entitled "The President Makes the Decisions." It began: "What distinguishes the Republican regime from that of Lyndon Johnson is that Mr. Nixon announced an 'open administration,' with the consequence that everyone above the rank of GS-15 feels free to comment on the wisdom of the President's actions." After noting examples of Cabinet members dissociating themselves from my Cambodian decision, Roche concluded by making the point that "Nixon was elected to make a choice and he made it. One can attack it on the merits if he so chooses, that is, say it was mistaken. Or one can support his actions (as I do). But under the Constitution no one has the right to impeach his decision because he did not consult Senator Fulbright, Secretary Finch, Pat Moynihan or the International Security Affairs section of the Pentagon."

Kent State triggered a nationwide wave of campus protests. The daily news reports conveyed a sense of turmoil bordering on insurrection. Hundreds of college campuses went through a paroxysm of rage, riot, and arson. By the end of the first week after the killings, 450 colleges and universities were closed by student or faculty protest strikes. Before the month was over, the National Guard had been called out twenty-four times at twenty-one campuses in sixteen states.

A national day of protest was hastily called to take place in Washington on Saturday, May 9. I felt that we should do everything possible to make sure that this event was nonviolent and that we did not appear insensitive to it. Ehrlichman urged that we make whatever gestures of communication were possible. Kissinger, however, took a particularly hard line on the demonstrators. He was appalled at the violence they provoked and at the ignorance of the real issues they displayed. He felt strongly that I should not appear more flexible until after the Cambodian operation was successfully completed. As he put it, we had to make it clear that our foreign policy was not made by street protests.

I decided to try to defuse the tension by holding a press conference. The risks were high, and my staff was deeply divided about the wisdom of having one at this time. Most of the reporters and commentators were bound to be bitterly critical, and it was highly possible that an acrimonious session would only make things worse. Nonetheless I decided to go ahead, and the conference was announced for prime time on Friday evening, May 8.

I could feel the emotions seething beneath the hot TV lights as I entered the East Room at ten o'clock Friday night. Almost all the questions were about the Cambodian operation and Kent State.

The first question was whether I had been surprised by the intensity of the protests and whether they would affect my policy in any way. I replied that I had not been surprised by the intensity of the protests. I knew that those who protested did so because they felt that my decision would expand the war, our involvement in it, and our casualties. "I made the decision, however, for the very reasons that they are protesting," I said. "I am concerned because I know how deeply they feel. But I know that what I have done will accomplish the goals that they want. It will shorten this war. It will reduce American casualties. It will allow us to go forward with our withdrawal program. The 150,000 Americans that I announced for withdrawal in the next year will come home on schedule. It will, in my opinion, serve the cause of a just peace in Vietnam."

One reporter asked what I thought the students were trying to say in the demonstration that was about to take place in Washington. I wanted my answer to this question to be compassionate but not weak. I said, "They are trying to say that they want peace. They are trying to say that they want to stop the killing. They are trying to say that they want to end the draft. They are trying to say that we ought to get out of Vietnam. I agree with everything that they are trying to accomplish. I believe, however, that the decisions that I have made, and particularly this last terribly difficult decision of going into the Cambodian sanctuaries which were completely occupied by the enemy—I believe that that decision will serve that purpose, because you can be sure that everything that I stand for is what they want."

Immediately after the press conference I began returning some of the dozens of phone calls that had come in and placing calls to others. I was agitated and uneasy as the events of the last few weeks raced through my mind.

I slept for a few hours and then went to the Lincoln Sitting Room. I put on a record of Rachmaninoff's Second Piano Concerto and sat listening to the music. Manolo heard that I was up and came in to see if I would like some tea or coffee. Looking out the windows I could see small groups of young people beginning to gather on the Ellipse between the White House and the Washington Monument. I mentioned that I considered the Lincoln Memorial at night to be the most beautiful sight in Washington, and Manolo said that he had never seen it. Impulsively I said, "Let's go look at it now."

This event was spontaneous on my part and I purposely did not take any staff members along or alert any reporters to accompany me. Thus it was especially frustrating when the newspapers reported that I had been unable to communicate with the young people I met, and that I had shown my insensitivity to their concerns by talking about inconsequential subjects like sports and surfing. Some of this mistaken impression apparently came from the students themselves. One of them told a reporter, "He wasn't really concerned with why we were here." Another said that I had been tired and dull and rambled aimlessly from subject to subject. . . .

II HENRY KISSINGER

Historians rarely do justice to the psychological stress on a policymaker. What they have available are documents written for a variety of purposes—under contemporary rules of disclosure, increasingly to dress up the record—and not always relevant to the moment of decision. What no document can reveal is the accumulated impact of accident, intangibles, fears, and hesitation.

March and April of 1970 were months of great tension. My talks with Le Duc Tho were maddeningly ambiguous. We faced what looked like a significant offensive in Laos; there was the coup in Cambodia soon to be followed by North Vietnamese attacks all over the country; Soviet combat personnel appeared in Egypt—the first time that the Soviet Union had risked combat outside the satellite orbit. Amid all these events, the President was getting testy. Nixon blamed his frustrations on the bureaucracy's slow and erratic response to his wishes, which he ascribed to the legacy of thirty years of Democratic rule. Haldeman joked that the President was in a "charming mood"; in the course of covering one subject on the telephone Nixon had hung up on him several times.

On April 13, just as Cambodia was approaching the decisive turn, an extraneous event occurred that took a heavy toll of Nixon's nervous energy: the mishap of *Apollo 13*. Soon after its launch on April 11 it became apparent that there was a severe malfunction and that the astronauts might have to circumnavigate the moon in the cramped and fragile vehicle designed for the brief lunar landing. I learned of the accident around 11:00 P.M. I sought to inform the President but ran into one of the mindless edicts by which Haldeman established his authority: The President could not be awakened without his specific authorization. This he refused to give for what he considered a technical problem involving no foreign policy considerations. I warned Haldeman that keeping the President ignorant would be hard to explain; he insisted that public relations was his province. The next morning Ron Ziegler had to go through verbal contortions to imply, without lying outright, that the President had been in command all night. . . .

Revisionist history has painted a picture of a peaceful, neutral Cambodia wantonly assaulted by American forces and plunged into a civil war that could have been avoided but for the American obsession with military solutions. The facts are different. Sihanouk declared war on the new Cambodian government as early as March 20, two days after his overthrow, throwing in his lot with the Communists he had held at bay and locating himself in Peking, then still considered the most revolutionary capital in the world and with which, moreover, we had no means of communication whatever. April saw a wave of Communist attacks to overthrow the existing governmental structure in Cambodia. Le Duc Tho on March 16 had rejected all suggestions of de-escalation of military activities and on April 4 had rejected all suggestions of neutralization. He had asserted that the Cambodian, Laotian, and Vietnamese peoples were one and would fight shoulder to shoulder to win the whole of Indochina. By the second half of April, the North Vietnamese were systematically expanding their sanctuaries and merging them into a "liberated zone." They were surrounding Phnom Penh and cutting it off from all access—using the very tactics that five years later led to its collapse.

If these steps were unopposed, the Communist sanctuaries, hitherto limited to narrow unpopulated areas close to the Vietnamese border, would be organized into a single large base area of a depth and with a logistics system which would enable rapid transfer of units and supplies. We would have preferred the old Sihanouk government, I told a group of Republican Senators on April 21. But Sihanouk's pronouncements left little doubt that this option was no longer open to us. If Lon Nol fell, the Sihanouk who returned would no longer balance contending forces in neutrality but lead a Communist government. His necessities (as well as his outraged vanity) would force him to purge the moderate groups on which his freedom of maneuver between contending factions had previously depended; he would be reduced to a figurehead. Sihanoukville would reopen to Communist supplies. Security throughout the southern half of South Vietnam would deteriorate drastically.

By April 21 the basic issue had been laid bare by Hanoi's aggressiveness; it was whether Vietnamization was to be merely an alibi for an American collapse or a serious strategy designed to achieve an honorable peace. If the former, neither the rate of withdrawal nor events in neighboring countries were important; in fact, anything that hastened the collapse of South Vietnam was a blessing in disguise. Some of the opposition, like Senator George McGovern, took this position. Though I considered it against the national interest, it was rational and honest. My intellectual difficulties arose with those who pretended that there was a middle course of action that would avoid collapse in Vietnam and yet ignore the impending Communist takeover in Cambodia.

There was no serious doubt that Hanoi's unopposed conquest of Cambodia would have been the last straw for South Vietnam. In the midst of a war, its chief ally was withdrawing forces at an accelerating rate and reducing its air support. Saigon was being asked to take the strain at the very moment Hanoi was increasing reinforcements greatly over the level of the preceding year. If Cambodia were to become a single armed camp at this point, catastrophe was inevitable. Saigon needed time to consolidate and improve its forces; the United States had to pose a credible threat for as long as possible; and Hanoi's offensive potential had to be weakened by slowing down its infiltration and destroying its supplies. It was a race between Vietnamization, American withdrawal, and Hanoi's offensives.

Strategically, Cambodia could not be considered a country separate from Vietnam. The indigenous Cambodian Communist forces—the murderous Khmer Rouge—were small in 1970 and entirely dependent on Hanoi for supplies. The forces threatening the South Vietnamese and Americans from Cambodia were *all* North Vietnamese; the base areas were part of the war in Vietnam. North Vietnamese forces that were busy cutting communications had already seized a quarter of the country. The danger of being "bogged down in a new war in Cambodia" was a mirage; the enemy in Cambodia and Vietnam was the same one. Whatever forces we fought in Cambodia we would not have to fight in Vietnam and vice versa. The war by then was a single war, as Le Duc Tho had proclaimed; there was turmoil in Cambodia precisely because Hanoi was determined to use it as a base for its invasion of South Vietnam and to establish its hegemony over Indochina.

By April 21 we had a stark choice. We could permit North Vietnam to overrun the whole of Cambodia so that it was an indisputable part of the battlefield and then attack it by air and sea—even Rogers told me on April 21 that if the Communists took over Cambodia, he believed all bombing restrictions should be ended. Or we could resist Cambodia's absorption, supporting the independence of a government recognized by the United Nations and most other nations, including the Soviet Union.

Momentous decisions are rarely produced by profound discussions. By the time an issue reaches the NSC [National Security Council], it has been analyzed by so many lower-level committees that the Cabinet members perform like actors in a well-rehearsed play; they repeat essentially what their subordinates have already announced in other forums. In the Nixon NSC there was the additional factor that every participant suspected that there was almost certainly more going on than he knew. As usual, there was also an ambivalence between taking positions compatible with their complicated chief's designs and fear of the domestic consequences. There was a sinking feeling about anything that could be presented as escalation in Vietnam. No one around the table questioned the consequences of a Communist takeover of Cambodia. But we all knew that whatever the decision another round of domestic acrimony, protest, and perhaps even violence was probable. If Cambodia collapsed we would be even harder pressed to pull out unilaterally; if we accepted any of the other options we would be charged with "expanding the war." There was no middle ground.

The initial decision to attack the sanctuaries was thus taken at a subdued and rather random NSC meeting. Rogers opposed substantial cross-border operations even by South Vietnamese, but he took it for granted that unrestricted bombing of Cambodia would follow the overthrow of the government in Phnom Penh. Laird had been the strongest advocate of shallow cross-border operations, but he opposed General Abrams's recommendation of destroying the sanctuaries altogether. Helms was in favor of any action to neutralize the sanctuaries. Nixon normally announced his decisions after, not during, an NSC meeting; he would deliberate and then issue instructions in writing or through intermediaries. He did this to emphasize that the NSC was an advisory, not a decision-making, body and to avoid a challenge to his orders. On this occasion Nixon altered his usual procedure. He told his colleagues that he approved attacks on the base areas by South Vietnamese forces with US support. Since the South Vietnamese could handle only one offensive, Wheeler recommended that they go after Parrot's Beak. This led to a debate about American participation; Laird and Rogers sought to confine it to an absolute minimum, opposing even American advisers or tactical air support.

At this point Vice President Spiro Agnew spoke up. He thought the whole debate irrelevant. Either the sanctuaries were a danger or they were not. If it was worth cleaning them out, he did not understand all the pussyfooting about the American role or what we accomplished by attacking only one. Our task was to make Vietnamization succeed. He favored an attack on *both* Fishhook and Parrot's Beak, including American forces. Agnew was right. If Nixon hated anything more than being presented with a plan he had not considered, it was to be shown up in a group as being less tough than his advisers. Though chafing at the bit, he adroitly placed himself between the Vice President and the Cabinet. He authorized American air support for the Parrot's Beak operation but only "on the basis of demonstrated necessity." He avoided committing himself to Fishhook. These decisions were later sent out in writing. After the meeting, Nixon complained bitterly to me that I had not forewarned him of Agnew's views, of which I had in fact been unaware. I have no doubt that Agnew's intervention accelerated Nixon's ultimate decision to order an attack on all the sanctuaries and use American forces. . . .

I was becoming increasingly restless with the decision at the NSC meeting that was in effect my recommendation: to limit the attack on the sanctuaries to South Vietnamese forces. Agnew was right; we should either neutralize all of the sanctuaries or abandon the project. It was hard to imagine how a limited operation into just one sanctuary, in which South Vietnamese forces had at best strictly limited American air support, could make a decisive difference. We were in danger of combining the disadvantages of every course of action. We would be castigated for intervention in Cambodia without accomplishing any strategic purpose.

Before I could present these views to Nixon, there occurred another of those seemingly trivial events that accelerate the process of history. Journalist William Beecher in the *New York Times* reported the contents of a highly classified cable informing our chargé in Phnom Penh that we had decided to provide captured Communist rifles to the Cambodian government. Nixon exploded. Leaks infuriated him in the best of circumstances; this one seemed to him a clear attempt by the bureaucracy to generate Congressional and public pressures against any assistance to Cambodia. To make matters worse, at about the same moment Nixon found out that the signal equipment and CIA representative that he had ordered into Phnom Penh on April 1 and again on April 16 had still not been sent.

He flew into a monumental rage. On the night of April 23 he must have called me at least ten times—three times at the house of Senator Fulbright, where I was meeting informally with members of the Senate Foreign Relations Committee. As was his habit when extremely agitated he would bark an order and immediately hang up the phone. He wanted our chargé, Rives, relieved immediately; he ordered Marshall Green fired; on second thought his deputy Bill Sullivan was to be transferred as well; an Air Force plane with CIA personnel aboard should be dispatched to Phnom Penh immediately; everybody with access to the cable should be given a lie-detector test; a general was to be appointed immediately to take charge of Cambodia.

In these circumstances it was usually prudent not to argue and to wait twenty-four hours to see on which of these orders Nixon would insist after he calmed down. As it turned out, he came back to none of them. (I did get the CIA communications sent into Phnom Penh by military plane.) But his April 23 outburst did finally propel him to accept Agnew's advice: to proceed against Fishhook and Parrot's Beak simultaneously, using American forces against Fishhook. He called a meeting on the morning of April 24 with Admiral Moorer, Acting Chairman of the Joint Chiefs, and Helms and Cushman of the CIA. Nixon wanted to discuss the feasibility of a combined US–South Vietnamese operation against Fishhook, in parallel with the Parrot's Beak operation. It was a reflection of his extreme irritation at bureaucratic foot-dragging that he excluded both Rogers and Laird, on the pretext that he merely wanted a military and intelligence briefing. Helms and Moorer were both strongly in favor of an attack on the Fishhook sanctuary. They felt it would force the North Vietnamese to abandon their effort to encircle and terrorize Phnom Penh. The destruction of supplies would gain valuable time for Vietnamization. But Nixon was not prepared to announce a decision yet. Instead, he helicoptered to Camp David to reflect further and to figure out a way to bring along his Cabinet on a course toward which he was increasingly tending. In the meantime he left me to manage the bureaucracy.

The situation had its bizarre aspects. The departments were still dragging their feet on American air support of a South Vietnamese operation against *one* sanctuary when the President was beginning to lean more and more toward *combined* South Vietnamese–American operations against *all* sanctuaries. I did not think it right to keep the Secretary of Defense ignorant of a meeting between the Acting Chairman of the Joint Chiefs and the President; I therefore called Laird, describing it as a military briefing of options. including an American attack on Fishhook. Laird stressed that it would be highly desirable to avoid authorizing any American operation before Rogers's testimony to the Senate Foreign Relations Committee on April 27; this would enable Rogers to state truthfully that no Americans were involved in Cambodia. Laird reported that even the usually hawkish Armed Services Committees were restive about American involvement in Cambodia. Laird also argued—as he was to do on several occasions over the next few days—that Abrams and Wheeler were really opposed to the Fishhook operation. I checked with Admiral Moorer, who claimed (in a rough translation from his more colorful naval jargon) that his Secretary was under a misapprehension.

Once he was launched on a course, Nixon's determination was equal to his tactical resourcefulness. He decided to adopt Rogers's suggestion of scaring the Congress with the prospect of monumental aid requests from Cambodia but to use it to justify *American* operations in the sanctuaries, which Rogers never intended. . . .

The final decision to proceed was thus not a maniacal eruption of irrationality as the uproar afterward sought to imply. It was taken carefully, with much hesitation, by a man who had to discipline his nerves almost daily to face his associates and to overcome the partially subconscious, partially deliberate procrastination of his executive departments. It was a demonstration of a certain nobility when he assumed full responsibility. The decision was not made behind the backs of his senior advisers, as has been alleged—though later on others were. Nixon overruled his Cabinet members; he did not keep them in the dark. This is the essence of the Presidency, the inescapable loneliness of the office, compounded in Nixon's case by the tendency of his senior Cabinet colleagues to leave him with the burden and to distance themselves publicly from him. His secretive and devious methods of decision-making undoubtedly reinforced their proclivity toward selfwill. But his views were well known; the agencies had had many opportunities to argue their case. The fact remains that on the substance of Cambodia, Nixon was right. And he was President. There is no doubt that the procrastination in carrying out direct Presidential directives, the exegesis of clear Presidential wishes in order to thwart them, helped confirm Nixon's already strong predilection for secretive and isolated decision-making from then on.

A confrontation with people who disagreed with him took a lot out of Nixon. After the meeting in the Oval Office he withdrew to his hideaway in the Executive Office Building, not to emerge until he delivered his speech of April 30 announcing the Cambodian incursion. I spent hours with him every day, bringing him up to date on the planning. Pat Buchanan drafted the basic speech from a rough outline supplied by my staff. But its major thrust was Nixon's. He supplied the rhetoric and the tone; he worked for hours each day on successive drafts. . . .

On the fateful day of April 30 the President delivered his speech at 9:00 P.M., explaining to an anxious public that "the actions of the enemy in the last ten days clearly endanger the lives of Americans who are in Vietnam now and would constitute an unacceptable risk to those who will be there after withdrawal of another 150,000." He opened by explaining, with a map, that the North Vietnamese had begun to threaten Phnom Penh and expand their previously separated base areas into "a vast enemy staging area and a springboard for attacks on South Vietnam along 600 miles of frontier." We had three options: to do nothing; to "provide massive military assistance to Cambodia itself"; to clean out the sanctuaries. The decision he now announced was a combined US–South Vietnamese assault on "the headquarters for the entire Communist military operation in South Vietnam." The action was limited, temporary, not directed against any outside country, indispensable for Vietnamization and for keeping casualties to a minimum.

Adding rhetoric out of proportion to the subject though not to the stresses of the weeks preceding it, the President emphasized that America would not be "humiliated"; we would not succumb to "anarchy"; we would not act like a "pitiful, helpless giant." Nor would he take "the easy political path" of blaming it all on the previous administrations. It was vintage Nixon. He had "rejected all political considerations":

Whether my party gains in November is nothing compared to the lives of 400,000 brave Americans fighting for our country and for the cause of peace and freedom in Vietnam. Whether I may be a one-term President is insignificant compared to whether by our failure to act in this crisis the United States proves itself to be unworthy to lead the forces of freedom in this critical period in world history. I would rather be a one-term President and do what I believe is right than to be a two-term President at the cost of seeing America become a second-rate power and to see this Nation accept the first defeat in its proud 190-year history. . . .

None of these successes had any effect on the eruptions of the spring of 1970, thereby turning the period of the Cambodian incursion into a time of extraordinary stress. I had entered government with the hope that I could help heal the schisms in my adopted country by working to end the war. I sympathized with the anguish of the students eager to live the American dream of a world where ideas prevailed by their purity without the ambiguities of recourse to power. The war in Vietnam was the first conflict shown on television and reported by a largely hostile press. The squalor and suffering and confusion inseparable from any war became part of the living experience of Americans; too many ascribed its agony to the defects of their own leaders.

Repellent as I found the self-righteousness and brutality of some protesters, I had a special feeling for the students. They had been brought up by skeptics, relativists, and psychiatrists; now they were rudderless in a world from which they demanded certainty without sacrifice. My generation had failed them by encouraging self-indulgence and neglecting to provide roots. I spent a disproportionate amount of time in the next months with student groups—ten in May alone. I met with protesters at private homes. I listened, explained, argued. But my sympathy for their anguish could not obscure my obligation to my country as I saw it. They were, in my view, as wrong as they were passionate. Their pressures delayed the end of the war, not accelerated it; their simplifications did not bring closer the peace, of the yearning for which they had no monopoly. Emotion was not a policy. We had to end the war, but in conditions that did not undermine America's power to help build the new international order upon which the future of even the most enraged depended.

Nor is it fair to blame the upheaval primarily on Nixon's inflated rhetoric or even on the events at Kent State. The dialogue in our democracy had broken down previously. The antiwar movement had been dormant since November, awaiting a new opportunity. In mid-April there were protests in some two hundred cities and towns, and the temper was such that the April 28 news of the purely South Vietnamese operation in the Parrot's Beak evoked condemnation as a major escalation of the war. This was two days before the involvement of American soldiers or Nixon's speech. North Vietnamese forces had been romping through Cambodia for well over a month, without a word of criticism of Hanoi. Yet the South Vietnamese response was denounced in the *New York Times* ("a virtual renunciation of the President's promise of disengagement from South East Asia"), the *Wall Street Journal* ("Americans want an acceptable exit from Indochina, not a deeper entrapment") and the *St. Louis Post-Dispatch* ("a shocking escalation"). The South Vietnamese thrust was intended to assist our orderly retreat. But in Congress barriers were being erected almost immediately against helping Cambodia, itself suffering a savage invasion by the same enemies and indeed the identical units that were fighting us in Vietnam. Senator J. William Fulbright, Chairman of the Senate Foreign Relations Committee, told NBC news on April 27 after the briefing that had given Rogers so much anticipatory anguish that the Committee was virtually unanimous in the view that assisting Cambodia in its resistance to North Vietnamese conquest "would be an additional extension of the war."

All the critical themes of the later explosion were present before the President's speech: We were escalating the war. No military action could possibly succeed; hence, claims to the contrary by the government were false. We were alleged to be so little in control of our decisions that the smallest step was seen as leading to an open-ended commitment of hundreds of thousands of American troops. A credibility gap had been created over any effort to achieve an honorable exit from the war. Thus, the press greeted the arguments in Nixon's speech on April 30 with a simple counterassertion: They did not believe him. It was "Military Hallucination—Again" according to the *New York Times:* "Time and bitter experience have exhausted the credulity of the American people and Congress." To the *Washington Post* it was a "self-renewing war" supported by "suspect evidence, specious argument and excessive rhetoric." To the *Miami Herald* "the script in Cambodia shockingly is the same as the story in Vietnam in the days of Kennedy and Johnson. We have heard it all before—endless times." Debate was engulfed in mass passion.

Just as it was burgeoning before April 30, the new increase in tempo had begun with calls for strikes and marches by the student leaders, who had proved their skill in producing confrontation in previous seasons of protest. The President's statements, oscillating between the maudlin and the strident, did not help in a volatile situation where everything was capable of misinterpretation. His May 1 off-the-cuff reference to "bums . . . blowing up campuses," a gibe overheard by reporters during a visit to the Pentagon, was a needless challenge, although it was intended to refer only to a tiny group of students who had firebombed a building and burned the life's research of a Stanford professor. When on May 4, four students at Kent State University were killed by rifle fire from National Guardsmen dispatched by Ohio Governor James Rhodes to keep order during several days of violence, there was a shock wave that brought the nation and its leadership close to psychological exhaustion.

The Administration responded with a statement of extraordinary insensitivity. Ron Ziegler was told to say that the killings "should remind us all once again that when dissent turns to violence it invites tragedy."

The momentum of student strikes and protests accelerated immediately. Campus unrest and violence overtook the Cambodian operation itself as the major issue before the public. Washington took on the character of a besieged city. A pinnacle of mass public protest was reached by May 9 when a crowd estimated at between 75,000 and 100,000 demonstrated on a hot Saturday afternoon on the Ellipse, the park to the south of the White House. Police surrounded the White House; a ring of sixty buses was used to shield the grounds of the President's home.

After May 9 thousands more students, often led by their faculty, descended on the capital to denounce "escalation" and the "folly" of their government. A thousand lawyers lobbied Congress to end the war, followed by thirty-three heads of universities, architects, doctors, health officers, nurses, and one hundred corporate executives from New York. The press fed the mood. Editorials expressed doubts about the claims of success in Cambodia emanating from the Pentagon. Beyond these peaceful demonstrations antiwar students proved adept at imaginative tactics of disruption merging with outright violence. Some two thousand Columbia University students sat down in the road in the rush hour. Fires were set on several college campuses as bonfires for peace. At Syracuse University fire destroyed a new building as twenty-five hundred students demonstrated nearby. Students demonstrated in the financial district of New York City on May 7 and 8. In retaliation, construction workers building the World Trade Center descended on Wall Street and beat the protesters with clubs and other makeshift weapons. The incident shocked some into the realization that a breakdown of civil order could backfire dangerously against the demonstrators. But it did not slow down the pace of protest; it only encouraged Nixon in the belief that the masses of the American public were on his side.

Indeed, the Gallup Poll showed considerable support for the President's action. When people were asked, "Do you think the US should send arms and material to help Cambodia or not?" 48 percent of those questioned responded yes, 35 percent no, 11 percent expressed no opinion, while 6 percent gave a qualified answer. When they were asked, "Do you approve or disapprove of the way President Nixon is handling the Cambodian situation?" 50 percent expressed approval; 35 percent expressed disapproval; 15 percent expressed no opinion. And 53 percent of those questioned expressed approval of the way President Nixon was handling the situation in Vietnam; 37 percent expressed disapproval; 10 percent had no opinion.

The tidal wave of media and student criticism powerfully affected the Congress. From not unreasonable criticism of the President's inadequate consultation it escalated to attempts to legislate a withdrawal from Cambodia and to prohibit the reentry of American troops. On May 13 debate began in the Senate on the Foreign Military Sales Bill, to which Senators Frank Church and John Sherman Cooper proposed an amendment prohibiting the extension of US military aid to, and US military activities in, Cambodia after June 30. On the other hand, an amendment offered by Senator Robert Byrd would have granted the President authority to take whatever action he deemed necessary to protect US troops in South Vietnam. This amendment was narrowly defeated, 52–47, on June 11, in what was seen as a trial heat. Senate debate and parliamentary skirmishing lasted seven weeks, until on June 30 the Senate approved the Cooper-Church amendment in a 58–37 roll-call vote. The Senate had voted to give the Communists a free hand in Cambodia even though in the judgment of the Executive Branch this doomed South Vietnam. The bill then went to a House-Senate Conference. The entire Foreign Military Sales Bill remained in conference for the remainder of 1970, deadlocked over the House's refusal to agree to the Senate-passed amendment. By then the damage was substantially done; in the middle of a blatant North Vietnamese invasion, the enemy was being told by the Senate that Cambodia was on its own.

Whereas the Cooper-Church amendment focused on Cambodia, the McGovern-Hatfield amendment to the Defense Procurement Bill aimed at ending the Indochina war by the simple expedient of cutting off all funds by the end of 1970, later extended to December 31, 1971. The move was finally defeated by the Senate on September 1 by a 55–39 margin. But the pattern was clear. Senate opponents of the war would introduce one amendment after another, forcing the Administration into unending rearguard actions to preserve a minimum of flexibility for negotiations. Hanoi could only be encouraged to stall, waiting to harvest the results of our domestic dissent.

All this accelerated the processes of disenchantment. Conservatives were demoralized by a war that had turned into a retreat and liberals were paralyzed by what they themselves had wrought—for they could not completely repress the knowledge that it was a liberal Administration that had sent half a million Americans to Indochina. They were equally reluctant to face the implications of their past actions or to exert any serious effort to maintain calm. There was a headlong retreat from responsibility. Extraordinarily enough, all groups, dissenters and others, passed the buck to the Presidency. It was a great joke for undergraduates when one senior professor proclaimed "the way to get out of Vietnam is by ship." The practical consequence was that in the absence of any serious alternative the government was left with only its own policy or capitulation.

PART THREE

1973-Present

The story that set the political tone for the early 1970's was hardly front page news when it first appeared. The report on June 18, 1972, that five men had been arrested in the headquarters of the Democratic National Committee in the Watergate complex only appeared on page 30 of *The New York Times*. Readers on that day, unaware of the future significance of this apparently trivial item, would have had reason for optimism in most of national life. The Vietnam War seemed to be winding down, relations with the Soviet Union were improving, and the Nixon administration seemed headed for another four years, promising economic and diplomatic progress and a further healing of the political wounds of the 1960's.

Yet by August 1974, only two years later, Nixon had resigned in disgrace, the nation's economy was threatened by foreign events out of its control, and Vietnam was on the verge of falling to the Communists. The nation was also about to see the dark side of its technological prowess: ecological time bombs existed in our chemical dumps and nuclear plants as well as in our streams, lakes, and oceans. Many of the hopes of the 1960's appeared to have died.

In the late seventies the new Democratic administration led by Jimmy Carter seemed as if it would lead the nation into a post-Watergate era. Carter was a Southerner, a former governor of Georgia, a successful businessman, an outsider to the Washington establishment, and a born-again Christian. He combined themes from the perennial New Deal sensibility with an innate conservatism that seemed to reflect the mood of the 1970's. But his promise was never fulfilled. Foreign dilemmas and domestic economic problems ultimately doomed the Carter administration. In 1980 the American people overwhelmingly rejected Carter and replaced him with Ronald Reagan, a conservative who harkened back to old virtues and old hopes.

The themes of the Reagan administration were as clear as their meanings were elusive. It sought to build up American military power, adopted a bellicose stance against the Soviet Union, continued the Carter administration's movement toward deregulation of the economy, and cut taxes, social services, and investment in education and research while attempting to stimulate the private sector of the economy. Ronald Reagan emerged as perhaps the most ideological president in American history, but the administration's ideology was delivered in terms that the American public has found comfortable and even reassuring. Ralph Waldo Emerson long ago spoke of the opposition of the "party of hope" and the "party of memory" as the primary dialogue of American politics; Reagan intertwined hopes and memories in a way that none of his critics had succeeded in disentangling. For the past quarter century, every presidential election has differed markedly from the previous one, a pattern unusual in American political history, where stable coalitions enduring for a full generation had been the norm. The Reagan administration may be the last effort at saving a vanished ideology, or it may represent the temporary solidification of a new political coalition.

Watergate

JONATHAN SCHELL

*The Watergate crisis with its bizarre, abrupt rhythm of mysterious
events following one upon another, each out of beat with the one before—trivial burglaries, odd dealings with reclusive billionaires, Saturday night massacres during which no blood was shed, statements that
the President of the United States is not a "crook," unseemly hassles
with reporters, the impeachment and resignation of a president—was
perhaps the greatest piece of political theatrics in American history.
The story dominated not just the news but the national imagination
for many months. Since its dramatic conclusion, theories about its
meaning, even about its cause, flourish like weeds in a horticulturist's
nightmare. Impeachment is such a drastic measure that a president
must experience almost every kind of failure to fall under its threat.
He must find his political support hopelessly collapsed, his morality
highly suspect, his associates seriously tainted, his policies in disarray. But
even then he must be unlucky as well. It is almost impossible for a president to be forced to resign. But this happened to Richard M. Nixon.*

*Jonathan Schell offers one of the more persuasive and even-tem-
pered views of the spectacle. Schell emphasizes the problems of con-
ducting foreign policy in secret as well as Nixon's personality as
contributing influences leading to the Watergate scandals. Other
writers, however, have with equal plausibility emphasized entirely other
explanations. The journalists J. Anthony Lucas and Norman Mailer
have viewed Nixon's involvements with the eccentric billionaire Howard
Hughes as a key element in the coverup. Other arguments emphasize
different issues: new Nixon men undermining old party arrangements,
new Texas and California money threatening the East. In many ways,
we must understand the whole history of the Cold War, the intelligence
apparatus it spawned, and the domestic political and economic arrangements that it influenced before a full assessment of this catastrophe will
become apparent.*

In mid-1972, as President Nixon returned to the United States from
his trip to Russia—where he had signed the first Soviet-American agreements on the limitation of nuclear arms—and as his reëlection campaign
got under way, the systemic crisis that had been threatening the survival of Constitutional government in the United States ever since he
took office was deepening. The crisis had apparently had its beginnings
in the war in Vietnam. Certainly the lines connecting the crisis to the
war were numerous and direct. The war had been the principal issue
in the struggle between the President and his political opposition—a
struggle that had provoked what he called the Presidential Offensive,
which was aimed at destroying independent centers of authority in the

nation. In more specific ways, too, the evolution of the Administration's usurpations of authority had been bound up with the war. Almost as soon as the President took office, he had ordered a secret bombing campaign against Cambodia (theretofore neutral). When details of the campaign leaked out, he had placed warrantless wiretaps on the phones of newsmen and White House aides. And when J. Edgar Hoover, the Director of the Federal Bureau of Investigation, seemed to be on the verge of getting hold of summaries of those tapped conversations, the President, in his efforts to prevent this, had entered into a venomous hidden struggle with the Director, and the Nixon White House had tried to damage the Director's reputation in the press. In another incident growing out of the war, the White House had hired undercover operatives to "nail" Daniel Ellsberg (as their employers expressed it) after Ellsberg gave the Pentagon Papers to the press; and then some of these operatives had been transferred to the Committee for the Re-Election of the President, where they went on to plan and execute criminal acts against the Democrats.

The evolution of the warrantless-wiretap incident and of the Pentagon Papers incident illustrated one of the ways in which the crisis of the Constitutional system was deepening. Large quantities of secret information were building up in the White House, first in connection with the war policy and then in connection with the President's plans to insure his reëlection. Every day, as the White House operatives went on committing their crimes, the reservoir of secrets grew. And the very presence of so many secrets compelled still more improper maneuverings, and thus the creation of still more secrets, for to prevent any hint of all that information from reaching the public was an arduous business. There had to be ever-spreading programs of surveillance and incrasing efforts to control government agencies. Only agencies that unquestioningly obeyed White House orders could be relied upon to protect the White House secrets, and since in normal times it was the specific obligation of some of the agencies to uncover wrongdoing, wherever it might occur, and bring the wrongdoers to justice, some agencies had to be disabled completely. In effect, investigative agencies such as the F.B.I. and the Central Intelligence Agency had to be enlisted in the obstruction of justice.

At some point back at the beginning of the Vietnam war, long before Richard Nixon became President, American history had split into two streams. One flowed aboveground, the other underground. At first, the underground stream was only a trickle of events. But during the nineteen-sixties—the period mainly described in the Pentagon Papers—the trickle grew to a torrent, and a significant part of the record of foreign affairs disappeared from public view. In the Nixon years, the torrent flowing underground began to include events in the domestic sphere, and soon a large part of the domestic record, too, had plunged out of sight. By 1972, an elaborate preëlection strategy—the Administration strategy of dividing the Democrats—was unfolding in deep secrecy. And this strategy of dividing the Democrats governed not only a program of secret sabotage and espionage but the formation of

Administration policy on the most important issues facing the nation. Indeed, hidden strategies for consolidating Presidential authority had been governing expanding areas of Administration policy since 1969, when it first occurred to the President to frame policy not to solve what one aide called "real problems" but to satisfy the needs of public relations. As more and more events occurred out of sight, the aboveground, public record of the period became impoverished and misleading. It became a carefully smoothed surface beneath which many of the most significant events of the period were being concealed. In fact, the split between the Administration's real actions and policies was largely responsible for the new form of government that had arisen in the Nixon White House—a form in which images consistently took precedence over substance, and affairs of state were ruled by what the occupants of the White House called scenarios. The methods of secrecy and the techniques of public relations were necessary to one another, for the people, lacking access to the truth, had to be told something, and it was the public-relations experts who decided what that something would be.

When the President made his trip to Russia, some students of government who had been worried about the crisis of the American Constitutional system allowed themselves to hope that the relaxation of tensions in the international sphere would spread to the domestic sphere. Since the tensions at home had grown out of events in the international sphere in the first place, it seemed reasonable to assume that an improvement in the mood abroad would give some relief in the United States, too. These hopes were soon disappointed. In fact, the President's drive to expand his authority at home was accelerated; although the nation didn't know it, this was the period in which White House operatives advanced from crimes whose purpose was the discovery of national-security leaks to crimes against the domestic political opposition. The Presidential Offensive had not been called off; it had merely been routed underground. The President spoke incessantly of peace, and had arranged for his public-relations men to portray him as a man of peace, but there was to be no peace—not in Indo-China, and not with a constantly growing list of people he saw as his domestic "enemies." Détente, far from relaxing tensions at home, was seen in the White House as one more justification for its campaign to crush the opposition and seize absolute power.

On Sunday, June 18, 1972, readers of the front page of the *Times* learned, among other things, that heavy American air strikes were continuing over North Vietnam, that the chairman of President Nixon's Council of Economic Advisers, Herbert Stein, had attacked the economic proposals of Senator George McGovern, who in less than a month was to become the Presidential nominee of the Democratic Party, and that the musical "Fiddler on the Roof" had just had its three-thousand-two-hundred-and-twenty-fifth performance on Broadway. Readers of page 30 learned, in a story not listed in the "News Summary and Index," that five men had been arrested in the headquarters of the Democratic National Committee, in the Watergate office building, with burglary tools, cameras, and equipment for electronic surveillance in their possession. In rooms that the men had rented, under aliases, in the adjacent Watergate Hotel, thirty-two hundred-dollar bills were found, along with a notebook containing the notation "E. Hunt" (for E. Howard Hunt, as it turned out) and, next to that, the notation "W. H." (for the White House). The men were members of the Gemstone team, a White House undercover group, which had been attempting to install bugging devices in the telephones of Democrats.

Most of the high command of the Nixon Administration and the Nixon reëlection committee were out of town when the arrests were made. The President and his chief of staff, H. R. Halderman, were on the President's estate in Key Biscayne, Florida. The President's counsel, John Dean, was in Manila, giving a lecture on drug abuse. John Mitchell, the former Attorney General, who was then director of the Comimttee for the Re-Election of the President, and Jeb Magruder, a former White House aide, who had become the committee's assistant director, were in California. In the hours and days immediately following the arrests, there was a flurry of activity at the headquarters of the committee, in a Washington office building; in California; and at the White House. Magruder called his assistant in Washington and had him remove certain papers—what later came to be publicly known as Gemstone materials—from his files. Gordon Liddy, by then the chief counsel of the Finance Committee to Re-Elect the President, went into the headquarters himself, removed from his files other materials having to do with the break-in, including other hundred-dollar bills, and shredded them. At the White House, Gordon Strachan, an aide to Haldeman, shredded a number of papers having to do with the setting up of the reëlection committee's undercover operation, of which the break-in at the headquarters of the Democratic National Committee was an important part. Liddy, having destroyed all the evidence in his possession, offered up another piece of potential evidence for destruction: himself. He informed Dean that if the White House wished to have him assassinated he would stand at a given street corner at an appointed time to make things easy. E. Howard Hunt went to his office in the Executive Office Building, took from a safe ten thousand dollars in cash he had there for emergencies, and used it to hire an attorney for the burglars. In the days following, Hunt's name was expunged from the White House telephone directory. On orders from John Ehrlichman, the President's chief domestic-affairs adviser, his safe was opened and his papers were removed. At one point, Dean—also said to have been acting under instructions from Ehrlichman—gave an order for Hunt to leave the country, but then the order was rescinded. Hunt's payment to an attorney for the burglars was the first of many. The President's personal attorney, Herbert Kalmbach, was instructed by Dean and, later, by Ehrlichman, Haldeman, and Mitchell to keep on making payments, and he, in turn, delegated the task to Anthony Ulasewicz, a retired New York City policeman who had been hired to conduct covert political investigations for the White House. Theirs was a hastily improvised operation. Kalmbach and Ulasewicz spoke to each other from phone booths. (Phone booths apparently had a strong attraction for Ulasewicz. He attached a change-maker to his belt to be sure to have enough coins for his calls, and he chose to make several of his "drops" of the payoff money in them.) He and Kalmbach used aliases and code language in their conversations. Kalmbach became Mr. Novak and Ulasewicz became Mr. Rivers—names that seem to have been chosen for no specific reason. Hunt, who had some forty mystery stories published, was referred to as "the writer," and Haldeman, who wore a crewcut, as "the brush." The payoff money became "the laundry," because when Ulasewicz arrived at Kalmbach's hotel room to pick up the first installment he put it in a laundry bag. The burglars were "the players," and the payoff scheme was "the script." Apparently, the reason the White House conspirators spoke to one another from phone booths was that they thought the Democrats might be wiretapping them, just as they had wiretapped the Democrats. In late June, the President himself said to Haldeman, of the Democrats, "When they start bugging us, which they have, our little boys will not know how to handle it. I hope they will, though." Considerations like these led Kalmbach, Ulasewicz, and others working for the White House to spend many unnecessary hours in phone booths that summer.

All these actions were of the sort that any powerful group of conspirators might take upon the arrest of some of their number. Soon, however, the White House was taking actions that were possible only because the conspirator occupied high positions in the government, including the highest position of all—the Presidency. For almost four years, the President had been "reorganizing" the executive branch of the government with a view to getting the Cabinet departments and the agencies under his personal control, and now he undertook to use several of these agencies to cover up crimes committed by his subordinates. In the early stages of the coverup, his efforts were directed toward removing a single evidentiary link: the fact that the Watergate burglars had been paid with funds from his campaign committee. There was a vast amount of other information that needed to be concealed—information concerning not just the Watergate break-in but the whole four-year record of the improper and illegal activities of the White House undercover operators, which stretched from mid-1969, when the warrantless wiretaps were placed, to the months in 1972 when the secret program for dividing the Democrats was being carried out—but if this one fact could somehow be suppressed, then the chain of evidence would be broken, and the rest of it might go undetected. On June 23rd, the President met with Haldeman and ordered him to have the C.I.A. request that the F.B.I. halt its investigation into the origin of the Watergate burglars' funds, on the pretext that C.I.A. secrets might come to light if the investigation went forward The problem, Haldeman told the President, was that "the F.B.I. is not under control, because Gray doesn't exactly know how to control it." Patrick Gray was Acting Director of the F.B.I. "The way to handle this now," he went on, "is for us to have Walters call Pat Gray and just say, 'Stay to hell out of this.' " The reference was to Vernon Walters, Deputy

Director of the C.I.A. A moment later, Haldeman asked the President, concerning the F.B.I., "And you seem to think the thing to do is get them to stop?" "Right, fine," the President answered. But he wanted Haldeman to issue the instructions. "I'm not going to get that involved," he said. About two hours later, Haldeman and Ehrlichman met with C.I.A. Director Richard Helms and Deputy Director Walters, and issued the order.

The maneuver gave the White House only a temporary advantage. Six days later, on June 29th, Gray did cancel interviews with two people who could shed light on the origin of the burglars' funds. (On the twenty-eighth, Ehrlichman and Dean had handed him all the materials taken from Hunt's safe, and Dean had told him that they were never to "see the light of day." Gray had taken them home, and later he burned them.) But soon a small rebellion broke out among officials of the F.B.I. and the C.I.A. Meetings were held, and at one point Gray and Walters told each other they would rather resign than submit to the White House pressure and compromise their agencies. Several weeks after the request was made, the F.B.I. held the interviews after all. The rebellion in the ranks of the federal bureaucracy was not the first to break out against the Nixon White House. As early as 1969, some members of the Justice Department had fought Administration attempts to thwart the civil-rights laws. In 1970, members of the State Department and members of the Office of Education, in the Department of Health, Education, and Welfare, had protested the invasion of Cambodia. In 1970, too, J. Edgar Hoover had refused to go along with a White House scheme devised by a young lawyer named Tom Huston for illegal intelligence-gathering. The executive bureaucracy was one source of the President's great power, but it was also acting as a check on his power. In some ways, it served this function more effectively than the checks provided by the Constitution, for, unlike the other institutions of government, it at least had some idea of what was going on. But ultimately it was no replacement for the Constitutional checks. A President who hired and fired enough people could in time bring the bureaucracy to heel. And although a Gray, a Walters, or a Helms might offer some resistance to becoming deeply involved in White House crimes, they would do nothing to expose the crimes. Moreover, the bureaucracy had no public voice, and was therefore powerless to sway public opinion. Politicians of all persuasions could—and did—heap abuse on "faceless," "briefcase-toting" bureaucrats and their "red tape," and the bureaucracy had no way to reply to this abuse. It had only its silent rebellions, waged with the passive weapons of obfuscation, concealment, and general foot-dragging. Decisive opposition, if there was to be any, had to come from without.

With respect to the prosecutorial arm of the Justice Department, the White House had aims that were less ambitious than its aims with respect to the F.B.I. and the C.I.A., but it was more successful in achieving them. Here, on the whole, the White House men wished merely to keep abreast of developments in the grand-jury room of the U.S. District Court, where officials of the Committee for the Re-Election of the President were testifying on Watergate, and this they accomplished through the obliging coöperation of Henry Petersen, the chief of the Criminal Division, who reported regularly to John Dean and later to the President himself. Dean subsequently described the coöperation to the President by saying, "Petersen is a soldier. He played —he kept me informed. He told me when we had problems, where we had problems, and the like. Uh, he believes in, in, in you. He believes in this Administration. This Administration had made him." What happened in the grand-jury room was further controlled by the coördinating of perjured testimony from White House aides and men working for the campaign committee. As for the prosecutors, a sort of dim-wittedness—a failure to draw obvious conclusions, a failure to follow up leads, a seeming willingness to construe the Watergate case narrowly—appeared to be enough to keep them from running afoul of the White House.

While all these moves were being made, the public was treated to a steady stream of categorical denials that the White House or the President's campaign committee had had anything to do with the break-in or with efforts to cover up the origins of the crime. The day after the break-in, Mitchell, in California, described James McCord, one of the burlars, as "the proprietor of a private security agency who was employed by our Committee months ago to assist with the installation of our security system." Actually, McCord was the committee's chief of security at the moment when he was arrested. Mitchell added, "We want to emphasize that this man and the other people involved were not operating either in our behalf or with our consent. . . . There is no place in our campaign or in the electoral process for this type of activity, and we will not permit nor condone it." On June 19th, two days after the break-in, Ronald Ziegler, the President's press secretary, contemptuously dismissed press reports of White House involvement. "I'm not going to comment from the White House on a third-rate burglary attempt," he said. On June 20th, when Lawrence O'Brien, the chairman of the Democratic Party, revealed that the Party had brought a one-million-dollar civil-damages suit against the Committee for the Re-Election of the President and the five burglary suspects, charging invasion of privacy and violation of the civil rights of the Democrats, Mitchell stated that the action represented "another example of sheer demagoguery on the part of Mr. O'Brien." Mitchell said, "I reiterate that this committee did not authorize and does not condone the alleged actions of the five men apprehended there."

Among the nation's major newspapers, only one, the Washington *Post,* consistently gave the Watergate story prominent headlines on the front page. Most papers, when they dealt with the story at all, tended to treat it as something of a joke. All in all, the tone of the coverage was not unlike the coverage of the Clifford Irving affair the previous winter, and the volume of the coverage was, if anything, less. "Caper" was the word that most of the press settled upon to describe the incident. A week after the break-in, for instance, the *Times* headlined its Watergate story "WATERGATE CAPER." When another week had passed, and Howard Hunt's connection with the break-in had been made known, *Time* stated that the story was "fast stretching into the most provocative caper of 1972, an extraordinary bit of bungling of great potential advantage to the Democrats and damage to the Republicans in this election year." In early August, the *Times* was still running headlines like "THE PLOT THICKENS IN WATERGATE WHODUNIT" over accounts of the repercussions of the burglary. "Above all, the purpose of the break-in seemed obscure," the *Times* said. "But these details are never explained until the last chapter." The President held a news conference six weeks after the break-in, and by then the story was of such small interest to newsmen that not one question was asked concerning it.

Disavowals such as those made by Mitchell and Ziegler carried great weight in the absence of incontrovertible evidence refuting them. The public had grown accustomed to deception and evasion in high places, but not yet to repeated, consistent, barefaced lying at all levels. The very boldness of the lies raised the cost of contradicting them, for to do so would be to call high officials outright liars. Another effective White House technique was to induce semi-informed or wholly uninformed spokesmen to deny charges. One of these spokesmen was Clark MacGregor, a former member of Congress from Minnesota, who became reëlection-campaign director early in July, when John Mitchell resigned, pleading family difficulties. A few weeks later, when Senator McGovern described the break-ins as "the kind of thing you expect under a person like Hitler," MacGregor called McGovern's remark "character assassination." The practice of using as spokesmen officials who were more or less innocent of the facts was one more refinement of the technique of dissociating "what we say" from "what we do." In this manner, honest men could be made to lend the weight of their integrity to untruths. They spoke words without knowing whether the words were true or false. Such spokesmen lent their vocal cords to the campaign but left their brains behind, and confused the public with words spoken by nobody.

On Septembter 15th, the five men who had been caught in the Democratic National Committee headquarters were indicted—together with E. Howard Hunt and G. Gordon Liddy, who were elsewhere in the Watergate complex at the time of the break-in—for the felonies of burglary, conspiracy, and wiretapping. A few days later, the seven defendants pleaded not guilty. As the case stood at that moment, their crimes were officially motiveless. The prosecutors had not been able to suggest who might have asked employees of the Committee for the Re-Election of the President to wiretap the Democratic headquarters, or why a check belonging to that committee should have found its way into the bank account of Bernard Barker. That afternoon, the President met with Haldeman and Dean, and congratulated Dean on his work, "Well," he said, "the whole thing is a can of worms. . . . But the, but the way you, you've handled it, it seems to me, has been very skillful, because you— putting your fingers in the dikes every time that leaks have sprung here and sprung there." Representative Wright Patman, the chairman of the House Banking and Currency Committee, was planning to hold hearings on the Watergate break-in, and the President, Dean, and Haldeman went on to discuss ways of "turning that off," as Dean put it. Dean reported to the two others that he was studying the possibility of blackmailing members of the Patman committee with damaging information about their own campaigns, and then the President suggested that Gerald Ford, the minority leader of the House, would be the man to pressure Patman into dropping the hearings. Ford should be told that "he's got to get at this and screw this thing up while he can," the President said. Two and a half weeks later, a majority of the members of the committee voted to deny Patman the power to subpoena witnesses. But Patman made the gesture of carrying on anyway for a while, and asked questions of an empty chair.

At the end of September—more than a month before the election —the Washington *Post* reported that John Mitchell had had control of a secret fund for spying on the Democrats. Throughout October, denials continued to pour out from the Administration. As before, some were outright lies by men who knew the facts, and others were untruths spoken by men who were simply repeating what they had been told. On October 2nd, Acting Director Gray of the F.B.I. said that it was unreasonable to believe that the President had deceived the nation about Watergate. "Even if some of us [in federal law enforcement agencies] are crooked, there aren't that many that are. I don't believe everyone is a Sir Galahad, but there's not been one single bit of pressure put on me or any of my special agents." In reality, of course, Gray had once considered resigning because the pressure from the White House to help with the coverup had been so intense, and even as he spoke he was keeping the contents of E. Howard Hunt's safe in a drawer of a dresser at his home in Connecticut. Gray went on to say, "It strains the credulity that the President of the United States—if he had a mind to —could have done a con job on the whole American people." Gray added, "He would have to control the United States."

In the months since the election, the issue of Watergate had faded, and the papers had devoted their front pages to other news. Shortly after the trial began, however, the front-page news was that all the defendants but two had pleaded guilty. In the courtroom, Judge John Sirica, who presided, found himself dissatisfied with the questioning of witnesses by the government prosecutors. The prosecutors now had a suggestion as to the burglars' motive. They suggested that it might be blackmail. They did not say of whom or over what. At the trial, the key prosecution witness, the former F.B.I. agent Alfred Baldwin, related that on one occasion he had taken the logs of the Watergate wiretaps to the headquarters of the Committee for the Re-Election of the President. But this suggested nothing to the Justice Department, one of whose spokesmen had maintained when the indictment was handed up in September that there was "no evidence" showing that anyone except the defendants was involved. Sirica demurred. "I want to know where the money comes from," he said to the defendant Bernard Barker.

"There were hundred-dollar bills floating around like coupons." When Barker replied that he had simply received the money in the mail in a blank envelope and had no idea who might have sent it, Sirica commented, "I'm sorry, but I don't believe you." When the defense lawyers protested Sirica's questioning, he said, "I don't think we should sit up here like nincompoops. The function of a trial is to search for the truth."

All the Watergate defendants but one were following the White House scenario to the letter. The exception was James McCord. He was seething with scenarios of his own. He hoped to have the charges against him dismissed, and, besides, he had been angered by what he understood as a suggestion from one of his lawyers that the blame for the Watergate break-in be assigned to the C.I.A., his old outfit, to which he retained an intense loyalty. There was some irony in the fact that McCord's anger had been aroused by an Administration plan to involve the C.I.A. in its crimes. McCord believed that Nixon's removal of C.I.A. director Richard Helms, in December of 1972—at the very time that McCord himself was being urged to lay the blame for Watergate at the door of the C.I.A.—was designed to pave the way for an attempt by the Administration itself to blame the break-in on the agency and for a takeover of the agency by the White House. He had worked for the White House, but he did not see the reorganizational wars from the White House point of view. He saw them from the bureaucrats' point of view; in his opinion, President Nixon was attempting to take over the C.I.A. in a manner reminiscent of attempts by Hitler to take control of German intelligence agencies before the Second World War. The White House, that is, belatedly discovered that it had a disgruntled "holdover" on its hands. And this particular holdover really was prepared to perform sabotage; he was prepared, indeed, to sabotage not just the President's policies but the President himself, and, what was more, he had the means to do it. McCord was putting together a scenario that could destroy the Nixon Administration. In a letter delivered to his White House contact, the undercover operative John Caulfield, McCord pronounced a dread warning: If the White House continued to try to have the C.I.A. take responsibility for the Watergate burglary, "every tree in the forest will fall," and "it will be a scorched desert." Piling on yet another metaphor of catastrophe, he wrote, "Pass the message that if they want it to blow, they are on exactly the right course. I am sorry that you will get hurt in the fallout." McCord was the first person in the Watergate conspiracy to put in writing exactly what the magnitude of the Watergate scandal was. Many observers had been amazed at the extreme hard line that the President had taken since his landslide reëlection—the firings in the bureaucracies, the incomprehensible continuation of the attacks' on Senator McGovern, the renewed attacks on the press, the attacks on Congress's power of the purse, the bombing of Hanoi. They could not know that at the exact moment when President Nixon was wreaking devastation on North Vietnam, James McCord was threatening to wreak devastation on him.

On February 7th, the Senate, by a vote of seventy-seven to none, established a Select Committee on Presidential Campaign Activities, to look into abuses in the Presidential campaign of 1972, including the Watergate break-in; and the Democratic leadership appointed Senator Sam Ervin, of North Carolina, the author of the resolution to establish the Select Committee, to be its chairman. Three days later, the Administration secretly convened a Watergate committee of its own, in California—at the La Costa Resort Hotel and Spa, not far from the President's estate in San Clemente, with John Dean, H. R. Haldeman, John Ehrlichman, and Richard Moore, a White House aide, in attendance. The meeting lasted for two days. Its work was to devise ways of hampering, discrediting, and ultimately blocking the Ervin committee's investigation.

The President's drive to take over the federal government was going well. By the end of March those legislators who were worried about the possibility of a collapse of the Constitutional system were in a state of near-hopelessness. It seemed that the President would have his will, and Congress could not stop him; as for the public, it was uninterested in Constitutional matters. Senator Muskie had now joined Senator McGovern in warning against the dangers of "one-man rule," and he said that the Administration's proposal for preventing the release of "classified" information, no matter how arbitrarily the "classified" designation had been applied, could impose "the silence of democracy's graveyard." Senator William Fulbright, of Arkansas, had expressed fear that the United States might "pass on, as most of the world has passed on, to a totalitarian system." In the press, a new feeling seemed to be crystallizing that Congress had had its day as an institution of American life. Commentators of all political persuasions were talking about Congress as though it were moribund. Kevin Phillips, a political writer who had played an important role in formulating "the Southern strategy," and who had once worked in John Mitchell's Justice Department, wrote, in an article in *Newsweek* called "Our Obsolete System," that "Congress's separate power is an obstacle to modern policy-making." He proposed a "fusion of powers" to replace the Constitution's separation of powers. "In sum," he wrote, "we may have reached a point where separation of powers is doing more harm than good by distorting the logical evolution of technology-era government." In *The New Republic,* the columnist TRB, who, like Senator McGovern and Senator Muskie, was worried that "one-man rule" was in prospect, wrote, "President Nixon treats Congress with contempt which, it has to be admitted, is richly deserved. We have a lot of problems—the economy, inflation, the unfinished war, Watergate —but in the long run the biggest problem is whether Congress can be salvaged, because if it can't, our peculiar 18th-century form of government, with separation of powers, can't be salvaged," And he wrote, "A vacuum has to be filled. The authority of Congress has decayed till it is overripe and rotten. Mr. Nixon has merely proclaimed it." At the Justice Department, Donald Santarelli, who was shortly to become head of the Law Enforcement Assistance Administration, told a reporter, "Today, the whole Constitution is up for grabs." These observers took the undeniable fact that the Congress was impotent as a sign that the Congress was obsolete. And the executive branch, having helped reduce the Congress to helplessness, could now point to that helplessness as proof that the Congress was of no value.

The coverup and the takeover had merged into a single project. For four years, the President's anger at his "enemies" had been growing. As his anger had grown, so had that clandestine repressive apparatus in the White House whose purpose was to punish and destroy his enemies. And as this apparatus had grown, so had the need to control the Cabinet departments and the agencies; and the other branches of government, because they might find out about it—until, finally, the coverup had come to exceed in importance every other matter facing the Administration. For almost a year now, the coverup had been the motor of American politics. It had safeguarded the President's reëlection, and it had determined the substance and the mood of the Administration's second term so far. In 1969, when President Nixon launched his Presidential Offensive, he had probably not foreseen that the tools he was developing then would one day serve him in a mortal struggle between his Administration and the other powers of the Republic; but now his assault on the press, the television networks, the Congress, the federal bureaucracy, and the courts had coalesced into a single, coordinated assault on the American Constitutional democracy. Either the Nixon Administration would survive in power and the democracy would die or the Administration would be driven from power and the democracy would have another chance to live. If the newly reëlected President should be able to thwart investigations by the news media, the agencies of federal law enforcement, the courts, and Congress, he would be clear of all accountabiilty, and would be above the law; on the other hand, if the rival institutions of the Republic should succeed in laying bare the crimes of his Administration and in bringing the criminals to justice, the Administration would be destroyed.

In the latter part of March, the pace of events in this area of the coverup quickened. Under the pressure of the pending sentences, two of the conspirators were breaking ranks: James McCord and Howard Hunt. McCord, who had been threatening the White House with exposure since December, now wrote a letter to Judge Sirica telling what he knew of the coverup. Hunt, for his part, was angry because he and the other defendants and their lawyers had not been paid as much money as they wanted in return for their silence. In November, 1972, he called Charles Colson to remind him that the continuation of the coverup was a "two-way street," and shortly after the middle of March he told Paul O'Brien, an attorney for the reëlection committee, that if more funds weren't forthcoming immediately he might reveal some of the "many things" he had done for John Haldeman—an apparent reference to the break-in at the office of Daniel Ellsberg's psychiatrist. Shortly thereafter, O'Brien informed Dean of Hunt's demand. These events on one edge of the coverup had an immediate influence on the chemistry of the whole enterprise. On March 21st, John Dean, convinced now that the coverup could not be maintained, met with the President and told him the story of it as he knew it from beginning to end. The President's response was to recommend that the blackmail money be paid to Hunt. "I think you should handle that one pretty fast," he said. And later he said, "But at the moment don't you agree that you'd better get the Hunt thing? I mean, that's worth it, at the moment." And he said, "That's why, John, for your immediate thing you've got no choice with Hunt but the hundred and twenty or whatever it is. Right?" The President was willing to consider plans for limited disclosure, and the meeting ended with a suggestion from Haldeman, who had joined the two other men: "We've got to figure out where to turn it off at the lowest cost we can, but at whatever cost it takes."

The defection of Hunt and McCord had upset the delicate balance of roles demanded by the coverup. Information that had to be kept secret began to flow in a wide loop through the coverup's various departments. Not only Hunt and McCord but Dean and Magruder began to tell their stories to the prosecutors. The prosecutors, in turn, relayed the information to Attorney General Kleindienst and Assistant Attorney General Petersen, who then relayed it to the President, who then relayed it to Haldeman and Ehrlichman, who in this period were desperately attempting to avoid prosecution, and were therefore eager to know what was happening in the Grand Jury room. Any defections placed the remaining conspirators in an awkward position. In order to get clear of the collapsing coverup, they had to become public inquisitors of their former subordinates and collaborators. Such a transformation, however, was not likely to sit well with the defectors, who were far from eager to shoulder the blame for the crimes of others, and who, furthermore, were in possession of damaging information with which to retaliate.

Notwithstanding these new tensions, the President sought to continue the coverup. In the weeks following his meeting with Dean on March 21st, his consistent strategy was what might be called the hors d'oeuvre strategy. The President described the strategy to Haldeman and Ehrlichman after a conversation with Dean on April 14th by saying, "Give 'em an hors d'oeuvre and maybe they won't come back for the main course." His hope was that by making certain public revelations and by offering a certain number of victims to the prosecutors he could satisfy the public's appetite, so that it would seek no more revelations and no more victims. (This technique, which Ehrlichman, on another occasion, called a "modified limited hang-out," was also what Haldeman had had in mind when he suggested that they should "turn it off at the lowest cost" they could.) Hors d'oeuvres of many kinds came under consideration. Some were in the form of scapegoats to be turned over to the prosecutors, and others were in the form of incomplete or false reports to be issued to the public. By now, the country's appetite for revelations was well developed, and in the White House it was decided that no less a man than Mitchell was needed to satisfy it.

As Ehrlichman explained the new plan to the President, Mitchell would be induced to make a statement saying, "I am both morally and legally responsible."

"How does it redound to our advantage?" the President asked.

"That you have a report from me based on three weeks' work," Ehrlichman replied, "that when you got it, you immediately acted to call Mitchell in as the provable wrongdoer, and you say, 'My God, I've got a report here. And it's clear from this report that you are guilty as hell. Now John . . . go on in there and do what you should.' "

That way, the President could pose as the man who had cracked the conspiracy.

Shortly thereafter, Mitchell was called down to the White House, and Ehrlichman proposed the plan. Mitchell did not care for it. He not only maintained his innocence but suggested that the guilt lay elsewhere; namely, in the White House. Ehrlichman told the President when Mitchell had left that Mitchell had "lobbed, uh, mud balls at the White House at every opportunity." Faced with Mitchell's refusal to play the scapegoat, the President, Haldeman, and Ehrlichman next invited Dean to step into the role. Soon after Ehrlichman's unsatisfactory experience with Mitchell, the President met with Dean and attempted to induce him to sign a letter of resignation because of his implication in the scandal.

The President approached the subject in an offhand manner. "You know, I was thinking we ought to get the odds and ends, uh . . . we talked, and, uh, it was confirmed that—you remember we talked about resignations and so forth," he said.

"Uh huh," Dean replied.

"But I should have in hand something, or otherwise they'll say, 'What the hell did you—after Mr. Dean told you all of this, what did you do?' " the President went on.

Again Dean answered "Uh huh."

The President then related that even Henry Petersen had been concerned about "this situation on Dean," and Dean once more answered with an "uh huh."

"See what I mean?" the President asked the uncommunicative Dean.

"Are we talking Dean, or are we talking Dean, Ehrlichman, and Haldeman?" Dean finally asked.

"Well, I'm talking Dean," the President answered.

But Dean, like Mitchell before him, was talking Ehrlichman and Haldeman, too, and would not resign unless they also resigned. He did not want to be an hors d'oeuvre any more than Mitchell did. And since Dean was in possession of highly detailed information that implicated not only Haldeman and Ehrlichman but the President as well, the President was unable to "bite the Dean bullet," as he put it, until he also was willing to let Haldeman and Ehrlichman go. Their turn came quickly. By now the President was under intense pressure to act soon. If he did not, he could hardly pose as the man who had cracked the case. On April 17th, the day after the unproductive conversation with Dean, the President said to Haldeman and Ehrlichman, "Let me say this. . . . It's a hell of a lot different [from] John Dean. I know that as far as you're concerned, you'll go out and throw yourselves on a damned sword. I'm aware of that. . . . The problem we got here is this. I do not want to be in a position where the damned public clamor makes, as it did with Eisenhower, with Adams, makes it necessary or calls—to have Bob come in one day and say, 'Well, Mr. President, the public—blah, blah, blah—I'm going to leave.' " But Ehrlichman was not willing to throw himself on a sword. The person he was willing to throw on a sword was Dean. "Let me make a suggestion," he responded. It was that the President give Dean a leave of absence and then defer any decision on Ehrlichman and Haldeman until the case had developed further. However, the President pursued the point, seeming at times to favor Haldeman's and Ehrlichman's resignation, and finally Ehrlichman did what McCord, Hunt, Mitchell, and Dean had done before him. He lobbed mud balls at the White House—which in this case meant the President.

If he and Haldeman should resign, Ehrlichman observed, "we are put in a position of defending ourselves." And he went on, "The things that I am going to have to say about Dean are: basically that Dean was the sole proprietor of this project, that he reported to the President, he reported to me only incidentally."

" 'Reported to the President'?" the President inquired.

A moment later, speaking in his own defense, the President said, "You see the problem you've got there is that Dean does have a point there which you've got to realize. He didn't see me when he came out to California. He didn't see me until the day you said, 'I think you ought to talk to John Dean.' "

At this point, Ehrlichman retreated into ambiguity, and said, "But you see I get into a very funny defensive position then vis-à-vis you and vis-à-vis him, and it's very damned awkward. And I haven't thought it clear through. I don't know where we come out."

On April 17th, the President made a short statement saying simply that there had been "major developments in the case concerning which it would be improper to be more specific now." He was unable to offer any diversionary reports or propitiatory victims to deflect the public's wrath at the forthcoming disclosures. He and his aides had talked over countless schemes, but all of them had foundered on the unwillingness of any of the aides to sacrifice themselves for him—or for "the Presidency," as he had asked them to do. The coverup was all one piece, and it cohered in exposure just as it had cohered in concealment.

The President had become adept at recollecting whatever was needed at a particular moment. By April of 1973, he and his aides were spending most of their time making up history out of whole cloth to suit the needs of each moment. Unfortunately for them, the history they were making up was self-serving history, and by April their individual interests had grown apart. Each of them had begun to "re-collect" things to his own advantage and to the detriment of the others. As their community of interests dissolved under the pressure of the investigation, each of them was retreating into his own private, self-interested reality. The capacity for deception which had once divided them from the country but united them with one another now divided them from one another as well.

In the White House, the fabric of reality had disintegrated altogether. What had got the President into trouble from the start had been his remarkable capacity for fantasy. He had begun by imagining a host of domestic foes. In retaliating against them, he had broken the law. Then he had compounded his lawbreaking by concealing it. And, finally, in the same way that he had broken the law although breaking it was against his best interests, he was bringing himself to justice even as he thought he was evading justice. For, as though in anticipation of the deterioration of his memory, he had installed another memory in the Oval Office, which was more nearly perfect than his own, or anyone else's merely human equipment: he had installed the taping system. The Watergate coverup had cast him in the double role of conspirator and investigator. Though the conspirator in him worked hard to escape the law, it was the investigator in him that gained the upper hand in the end. While he was attempting to evade the truth, his machines were preserving it forever.

At the moment when the President announced "major developments" in the Watergate case, the national process that was the investigation overwhelmed the national process that was the coverup. The events that followed were all the more astounding to the nation because, at just the moment when the coverup began to explode, the President, in the view of many observers, had been on the point of strangling the "obsolete" Constitutional system and replacing it with a Presidential dictatorship. One moment, he was triumphant and his power was apparently irresistible; the next moment, he was at bay. For in the instant the President made his announcement, the coverup cracked—not just the Watergate coverup but the broader coverup, which concealed the underground history of the last five years—and the nation suffered an inundation of news. The newspaper headlines now came faster and thicker than ever before in American history. The stories ran backward in time, and each day's newspaper told of some event a little further in the past as reporters traced the underground history to the early days of the Administration, and even into the terms of former Administrations. With the history of half a decade pouring out all at once, the papers were stuffed with more news than even the most diligent reader could absorb. Moreover, along with the facts, nonfacts proliferated as the desperate men in the White House put out one false or distorted statement after another, so that each true fragment of the story was all but lost in a maze of deceptions, and each event, true or false, came up dozens of times, in dozens of versions, until the reader's mind was swamped. And, as if what was in the newspapers were not already too much, television soon started up, and, in coverage that was itself a full-time job to watch, presented first the proceedings of the Ervin committee and then the proceedings of the House Judiciary Committee, when it began to weigh the impeachment of the President. And, finally, in a burst of disclosure without anything close to a precedent in history, the tapes were revealed—and not just once but twice. The first set of transcripts was released by the White House and was doctored, and only the second set, which was released by the Judiciary Committee, gave an accurate account of the President's conversations.

As the flood of information flowed into the public realm, overturning the accepted history of recent years, the present scene was also transformed. The Vice-President was swept from office when his bribe-taking became known, but so rapid was the pace of events that his departure was hardly noticed. Each of the institutions of the democracy that had been menaced by the President—and all had been menaced—was galvanized into action in its turn: the press, the television networks, the Senate, the House of Representatives, and, finally, in a dispute over release of the tapes, the Supreme Court. The public, too, was at last awakened, when the President fired the Special Proscutor whom he had appointed to look into the White House crimes. In an outpouring of public sentiment that, like so much else that happened at the time, had no precedent in the nation's history, millions of letters and telegrams poured in to Congress protesting the President's action. The time of letters sent by the President to himself was over, and the time of real letters from real people had come. No one of the democracy's institutions was powerful enough by itself to remove the President; the efforts of all were required—and only when those efforts were combined was he forced from office.

The Environmental Decline

BARRY COMMONER

*The 1970's may well become known to historians as the age of environ-
mentalism. Important initiatives in conserving the natural environment
date back nearly one hundred years, but mass public awareness of environmental problems and the development of an elaborate legal structure to deal with them have been phenomena of recent times. After a
moment in the late 1960's and early 1970's, when everyone was "for"
the environment, the issues to which Barry Commoner speaks became
major sources of controversy in a society worried as much about economic stagnation as about the quality of the environment.*

*Commoner, one of the nation's most distinguished environmental
scientists (and the Citizens Party presidential candidate in 1980), analyzes
the connection between the nature of economic growth and its impact
on the environment. He shows that environmental pollution is the result not of economic growth alone, but rather of alterations in the kinds
of products the economy produces. The substitution of plastics and
aluminum for wood and steel, synthetic fibers for cotton and wool, and
fertilizer for the use of additional acreage needlessly consumes resources
and degrades the environment. While much political debate pits environmental quality against economic needs, Commoner's analysis points
to a convergence between these issues. More dependence on renewable
energy, Commoner argues, will both solve the energy problem and improve the environment while maintaining the nation's standard of
living. Clearly, the issues he addresses in the selection that follows will
be lively concerns during the decades ahead.*

We have now arrived at the following position in the search for the
causes of the environmental crisis in the United States. We know that
something went wrong in the country after World War II, for most of
our serious pollution problems either began in the postwar years or have
greatly worsened since then. While two factors frequently blamed for the
environmental crisis, population and affluence, have intensified in that
time, these increases are much too small to account for the 200 to 2,000
per cent rise in pollution levels since 1946. The product of these two
factors, which represents the total output of goods (total production
equals population times production per capita), is also insufficient to
account for the intensification of pollution. Total production—as measured by GNP—has increased by 126 per cent since 1944 while most pollution levels have risen by at least several times that rate. Something else
besides growth in population and affluence must be deeply involved in
the environmental crisis. . . .

The growth of the United States economy is recorded in elaborate
detail in a variety of government statistics—huge volumes tabulating the

amounts of various goods produced annually; the expenditures involved, the value of the goods sold, and so forth. Although these endless columns of figures are rather intimidating, there are some useful ways to extract meaningful facts from them. In particular, it is helpful to compute the rate of growth of each productive activity, a procedure that nowadays can be accomplished by committing the tables of numbers to an appropriate programmed computer. In order to compare one kind of economic activity with another, it is useful to arrange the computer to yield a figure for the percentage increase, or decrease, in production or consumption.

Not long ago, two of my colleagues and I went through the statistical tables and selected from them the data for several hundred items, which together represent a major and representative part of overall United States agricultural and industrial production. For each item, the average annual percentage change in production or consumption was computed for the years since 1946, or since the earliest date for which the statistics were available. Then we computed the overall change for the entire twenty-five year period—a twenty-five-year growth rate. When this list is rearranged in decreasing order of growth rate, a picture of *how* the United States economy has grown since World War II begins to emerge.

The winner of this economic sweepstakes, with the highest postwar growth rate, is the production of nonreturnable soda bottles, which has increased about 53,000 per cent in that time. The loser, ironically, is the horse; work animal horsepower has declined by 87 per cent of its original postwar value. The runners-up are an interesting but seemingly mixed bag. In second place is production of synthetic fibers, up 5,980 per cent; third is mercury used for chlorine production, up 3,920 per cent; succeeding places are held as follows: mercury used in mildew-resistant paint, up 3,120 per cent; air conditioner compressor units, up 2,850 per cent; plastics, up 1,960 per cent; fertilizer nitrogen, up 1,050 per cent; electric housewares (such as can-openers and corn-poppers), up 1,040 per cent; synthetic organic chemicals, up 950 per cent; aluminum, up 680 per cent; chlorine gas, up 600 per cent; electric power, up 530 per cent; pesticides, up 390 per cent; wood pulp, up 313 per cent; truck freight, up 222 per cent; consumer electronics (TV sets, tape recorders), up 217 per cent; motor fuel consumption, up 190 per cent; cement, up 150 per cent.

Then there is a group of productive activities that, as indicated earlier, have grown at about the pace of the population (i.e., up about 42 per cent): food production and consumption, total production of textiles and clothes, household utilities, and steel, copper, and other basic metals.

Finally there are the losers, which increase more slowly than the population or actually shrink in total production: railroad freight, up 17 per cent; lumber, down 1 per cent; cotton fiber, down 7 per cent; returnable beer bottles, down 36 per cent; wool, down 42 per cent; soap, down 76 per cent; and, at the end of the line, work animal horsepower, down 87 per cent.

What emerges from all these data is striking evidence that while production for most basic needs—food, clothing, housing—has just about kept up with the 40 to 50 per cent or so increase in population (that is, production *per capita* has been essentially constant), the *kinds* of goods produced to meet these needs have changed drastically. New production technologies have displaced old ones. Soap powder has been displaced by synthetic detergents; natural fibers (cotton and wool) have been displaced by synthetic ones; steel and lumber have been displaced by aluminum, plastics, and concrete; railroad freight has been displaced by truck freight; returnable bottles have been displaced by nonreturnable ones. On the road, the low-powered automobile engines of the 1920's and 1930's have been displaced by high-powered ones. On the farm, while per capita production has remained about constant, the amount of harvested acreage has decreased; in effect, fertilizer has displaced land. Older methods of insect control have been displaced by synthetic insecticides, such as DDT, and for controlling weeds the cultivator has been displaced by the herbicide spray. Range-feeding of livestock has been displaced by feedlots.

In each of these cases, what has changed drastically is the technology of production rather than overall output of the economic good. Of course, part of the economic growth in the United States since 1946 has been based on some newly introduced goods: air conditioners, television sets, tape recorders, and snowmobiles, all of which have increased absolutely without displacing an older product.

Distilled in this way, the mass of production statistics begins to form a meaningful pattern. In general, the growth of the United States economy since 1946 has had a surprisingly small effect on the degree to which individual needs for basic economic goods have been met. That statistical fiction, the "average American," now consumes, each year, about as many calories, protein, and other foods (although somewhat less of vitamins); uses about the same amount of clothes and cleaners; occupies about the same amount of newly constructed housing; requires about as much freight; and drinks about the same amount of beer (twenty-six gallons per capita!) as he did in 1946. However, his food is now grown on less land with much more fertilizer and pesticides than before; his clothes are more likely to be made of synthetic fibers than of cotton or wool; he launders with synthetic detergents rather than soap; he lives and works in buildings that depend more heavily on aluminum, concrete, and plastic than on steel and lumber; the goods he uses are increasingly shipped by truck rather than rail; he drinks beer out of nonreturnable bottles or cans rather than out of returnable bottles or at the tavern bar. He is more likely to live and work in air-conditioned surroundings than before. He also drives about twice as far as he did in 1946, in a heavier car, on synthetic rather than natural rubber tires, using more gasoline per miles, containing more tetraethyl lead, fed into an engine of increased horsepower and compression ratio.

These primary changes have led to others. To provide the raw materials needed for the new synthetic fibers, pesticides, detergents, plastics, and rubber, the production of synthetic organic chemicals has also grown very rapidly. The synthesis of organic chemicals uses a good deal of chlorine. Result: chlorine production has increased sharply. To make chlorine, an electric current is passed through a salt solution by way of a mercury electrode. Consequently, mercury consumption for this purpose has increased—by 3,930 per cent in the twenty-five-year postwar period. Chemical products, along with cement for concrete and aluminum (also winners in the growth race), use rather large amounts of electric power. Not surprisingly, then, that item, too, has increased considerably since 1946.

All this reminds us of what we have already been told by advertising—which incidentally has *also* grown; for example, the use of newsprint for advertising has grown faster than its use for news—that we are blessed with an economy based on very modern technologies. What the advertisements do not tell us—as we are urged to buy synthetic shirts and detergents, aluminum furniture, beer in no-return bottles, and Detroit's latest creation—is that *all this "progress" has greatly increased the impact on the environment.*

This pattern of economic growth is the major reason for the environmental crisis. A good deal of the mystery and confusion about the sudden emergence of the environmental crisis can be removed by pinpointing, pollutant by pollutant, how the postwar technological transformation of the United States economy has produced not only the much-heralded 126 per cent rise in GNP, but also, at a rate about ten times faster than the growth of GNP, the rising levels of environmental pollution.

Agriculture is a good place to start. . . . Between 1949 and 1968 total United States agricultural production increased by about 45 per cent. Since the United States population grew by 34 per cent in that time, the overall increase in production was just about enough to keep up with population; crop production *per capita* increased 6 per cent. In that period, the annual use of fertilizer nitrogen increased by 648 per cent, surprisingly larger than the increase in crop production. One reason for this disparity also turns up in the agricultural statistics: between 1949 and 1968 harvested acreage *declined* by 16 per cent. Clearly, more crop was being produced on less land (the yield per acre increased by 77 per cent). Intensive use of fertilizer nitrogen is the most important means of achieving this improvement in yield per acre. Thus, the intensive use of fertilizer nitrogen allowed "agribusiness" to just about meet the population's need for food—and at the same time to reduce the acreage used for that purpose.

These same statistics also explain the resulting water pollution problem. In 1949, an average of about 11,000 tons of fertilizer nitrogen were used *per USDA unit of crop production*, while in 1968 about 57,000 tons of nitrogen were used for the *same* crop yield. This means that the efficiency with which nitrogen contributes to the growth of the crop declined fivefold. Obviously, a good deal of the fertilizer nitrogen did not enter the crop and must have ended up elsewhere in the ecosystem. . . .

What the new fertilizer technology has accomplished for the farmer is clear: more crop can be produced on less acreage than before. Since the cost of fertilizer, relative to the resultant gain in crop sales, is lower than that of any other economic input, and since the Land Bank pays the farmer for acreage not in crops, the new technology pays him well. The cost—in environmental degradation—is borne by his neighbors in town who find their water polluted. The new technology is an economic success—but only because it is an ecological failure. . . .

In marketing terms, detergents are probably one of the most successful of modern technological innovations. In a scant twenty-five years this new invention has captured more than two-thirds of the laundry market from one of man's oldest, best-established, and most useful inventions—soap. This technological displacement is typical of many that have occurred since World War II: the replacement of a natural organic product by an unnatural synthetic one. In each case the new technology has worsened the environmental impact of the economic good.

Soap is produced by reacting a natural product, fat, with alkali. A typical fat used in soap making is palm oil. This is produced by the palm tree, using water and carbon dioxide as raw materials, and sunlight to provide the necessary energy. These are all freely available, renewable resources. No environmental impact results from the synthesis of the palm oil molecule. Of course, with inadequate husbandry a palm plantation can deplete the soil, and when the oil is extracted from the coconut, fuel is used and the resultant burning contributes to air pollution. The manufacture of soap from oil and alkali also consumes fuel and produces wastes.

Once used and sent down the drain, soap is broken down by the bacteria of decay—for the natural fat is readily attacked by the bacterial enzymes. In most places, this bacterial action takes place within the confines of a sewage treatment plant. What is then emitted to surface waters is only carbon dioxide and water, since fat contains only carbon, hydrogen, and oxygen atoms. Hence there is little or no impact on the aquatic ecosystem due to biological oxygen demand (which accompanies bacterial degradation of organic wastes) arising from soap wastes. Nor is the product of soap degradation, carbon dioxide, usually an important ecological intrusion since it is already in plentiful supply from other environmental sources. In its production and use, soap has a relatively light impact on the environment.

In comparison with soap, the production of detergents is likely to exert a more intense environmental impact. Detergents are synthesized from organic raw materials originally present in petroleum along with a number of other substances. To obtain the raw materials, the petroleum is subjected to distillation and other energy-consuming processes—and the burned fuel pollutes the air. Then the purified raw materials are used in a series of chemical reactions, involving chlorine and high temperatures, finally yielding the active cleaning agent. This is then mixed with a variety of additives, designed to soften hard water, bleach stains, "brighten" wash (this additive strongly reflects light and dazzles the eye to achieve a simulated whiteness), and otherwise gladden the heart of the advertising copywriter. Suitably boxed, this is the detergent. The total energy used to produce the active agent alone—and therefore the resultant air pollution—is probably three times that needed to produce oil for soap manufacture. And to produce the needed chlorine, mercury is used—and released to the environment as a pollutant. In substituting man-made chemical processes for natural ones, detergent manufacture inevitably produces a greater environmental stress than does the manufacture of soap. . . .

Another pollution problem arises from the phosphate content of detergents, whether degradable or not, for phosphate can stimulate algal overgrowths, which on their death overburden the aquatic ecosystem with organic matter. Phosphate is added to detergents for two purposes: to combat hard water (because it helps to tie up materials, such as calcium, which cause water hardness) and to help suspend dirt particles so that they can be readily rinsed away. Soap itself accomplishes the second of these functions, but not the first. In hard water, soap is rather ineffective, but can be improved by adding a water-softening agent such as phosphate. Thus, phosphate is needed only to solve the hard-water problem. But where water is hard, it can be treated by a household water-softener, a device which could also be built into washing machines. In other words, successful washing can be accomplished without resorting to phosphate, which when added to detergents, worsens their already serious environmental effects. Thus the actual need to replace soap is slight. As a recent chemical engineering textbook states: "There is absolutely no reason why old-fashioned soap cannot be used for most household and commercial cleaning." . . .

Electric power is one of the fast-growing features of the postwar United States economy. This industry is also the source of major pollution problems: sulfur dioxide, nitrogen oxides, and dust emitted by fossil-fuel burning plants; radioactive emissions and the small but enormously catastrophic potential of an accident from the operation of nuclear power plants; and the emission of waste heat to the air and nearby surface waters by both types of plants. This growth in the use of electric power is, justifiably, associated with the modernity of our economy and—with much less cause—to our supposed "affluence." The statistics appear to be straightforward enough. In the United States, annual power consumption is about 20,540 kilowatt hours per capita (the United States consumes 34 per cent of the world's electric power output), as opposed to about 2,900 kw-h per capita for Chile, 260 kw-h per capita for India, and 230 kw-h per capita for Thailand. However, electric power, unconverted, is not in itself capable of satisfying any known human need, and its contribution to human welfare needs to be measured in terms of the economic goods that power can produce. Here we discover another serious failing—when measured in terms of human welfare—of postwar technology: the new productive technologies are more costly than the technologies they have displaced, in consumption of electric power and other forms of fuel-generated energy *per unit economic good*. For example, aluminum, which has increasingly displaced steel and lumber as a construction material, requires for its production about 15 times more fuel energy than steel and about 150 times more fuel energy than lumber. Even taking into account that less aluminum, by weight, is needed for a given purpose than steel, the power discrepancy remains. For example, the energy required to produce metal for an aluminum beer can is 6.3 times that needed for a steel beer can.

The displacement of natural products by synthetic organic chemicals and of lumber and steel by concrete has a similar effect, for both chemical manufacturing and the production of cement for concrete are intense consumers of electric power. Aluminum and chemical production alone account for about 28 per cent of total industrial use of electric power in the United States. Thus the expansion of power production in the United States is not an accurate measure of increased economic good, being badly inflated by the growing tendency to displace power-thrifty goods with power-consumptive ones. The cost of this inefficiency is heavily borne by the environment.

Another technological displacement is readily visible to the modern householder in the daily acquisition of rubbish, most of it from packaging. It is a useful exercise to examine the statistics relevant to some economic good—beer, let us say—and determine from them the origin of the resultant impact on the environment. We can begin the exercise by recalling that the relevant economic good is chiefly the beer, not the bottle or can in which it is delivered. The relevant pollutant is the non-returnable bottle or can, for these, when "disposed of" in rubbish, cannot be assimilated in any natural ecological cycle. Therefore, they either accumulate or must be reprocessed at some expenditure of energy and cost in power-produced pollutants. The exercise consists in determining the relative effects of the three factors that might lead to an increased output of pollution, in this case, in the period from 1950 to 1967. In that time, the total consumption of nonreturnable beer bottles increased by 595 per cent and the consumption of beer increased by 37 per cent. Since the population increased by 30 per cent, the "affluence" factor, or the amount of beer consumed per capita, remained essentially constant (actually a 5 per cent increase). The remainder of the increased output of pollutant—beer bottles—is due to the technological factor—that is, the number of nonreturnable bottles produced per gallon of beer, which increased by 408 per cent. The relative importance of the three factors is evident.

It will be argued, of course, that the use of a nonreturnable beer bottle is more desirable than a returnable one to the individual beer drinker. After all, some human effort must be expended to return the bottle to the point of purchase. We can modify the earlier evaluation, then, by asserting that for the sake of whatever improvement in well-being is involved in avoiding the effort of returning the bottle, the production of beer in nonreturnable bottles incurs a 408 per cent intensification of environmental impact. No such subtlety is involved in comparing the environmental impacts of two alternative nonreturnable beer containers: steel beer cans and aluminum ones. The energy involved in producing the aluminum can—and therefore the amount of combustion and the resultant output of pollutants—is 6.3 times that required for a steel can.

Similar computations can be made for the added environmental impact incurred when extra layers of packaging are added to foods and other goods or when plastic wrappers (nondegradable) are substituted for degradable cellulosic ones. In general, modern industrial technology has encased economic goods of no significantly increased human value in increasingly larger amounts of environmentally harmful wrappings. Result: the mounting heaps of rubbish that symbolize the advent of the technological age.

It should be recognized that such computations of environmental impact are still in a primitive, only partially developed stage. What is needed, and what—it is to be hoped—will be worked out before long, is an ecological analysis of every major aspect of the production, use, and disposition of goods. What is needed is a kind of "ecological impact inventory" for each productive activity, which will enable us to attach a sort of pollution price tag to each product. We would then know, for example, for each pound of detergent: how much air pollution is generated by the electric power and fuel burned to manufacture its chemical ingredients; how much water pollution is due to the mercury "loss" by the factory in the course of manufacturing the chlorine needed to produce it; the water pollution due to the detergent and phosphate entering sewage systems; the ecological effect of fluoride and arsenic (which may contaminate the phosphate), and of mercury, which might contaminate any alkali used to compound the detergent. Such pollution price tags are needed for all major products if we are to judge their relative *social* value. The foregoing account shows how far we are from this goal, and once again reminds us how blind we are about the environmental effects of modern technology.

More Work for Mother

RUTH SCHWARTZ COWAN

The word housework *is, as Ruth Schwartz Cowan points out in* More Work for Mother, *a fairly recent coinage. The Oxford English Dictionary notes its earliest appearance in 1841 in England and not until 1871 in the United States. Before that time, Cowan states, "the word* housework *would probably have been nonsensical since—with the exception of seamen, miners, soldiers, and peddlers—almost all people worked in or on the grounds of a house, their own, or someone else's." Prior to industrialization, the work of maintaining a house was not distinguished from other forms of labor. Men had their chores: butchering meat, hauling wood, and weaving cloth, among others; and women had theirs: cooking, sewing, and cleaning, in addition to others. Men's work and women's work were both necessary to the household, both onerous, and both unpaid. And the paid labor of an agricultural world was largely shared as well: for example, men plowed and attended to crops and herds, and women maintained vegetable patches and churned butter.*

Industrialism and the development of a new household technology radically changed this picture. The house became a "home": woman's "place" and man's "refuge." After about 1840 housework was distinguished from men's paid work, and a technology external to the home, developed largely by men, magically eliminated most of their role in the home and freed them to work in a cash economy. The production of food, the preparing of meats, the provision of heat and light to houses, all became part of this external technology. Meanwhile, the new demands of housework multiplied as washable cottons replaced wool and created the need for an army of launderers; as standards of cleanliness rose sharply; as new cookbooks exploited the versatility of stoves and increased expectations for the variety and quality of the family diet; and as the demands of childrearing were thrown back on mothers who lacked relatives within the house or services from outside to share the burden. By the middle of the twentieth century, this pattern—women supported by a new household technology and having a defined place within the home, and men as "breadwinners" and recipients of women's services—had become a cultural norm.

This selection from Ruth Schwartz Cowan's book traces this complicated social revolution up to the mid-twentieth century. Women's actual role, as the author makes clear, changed more rapidly than did the ideal of domesticity presented not only in magazines, sermons, novels, and the speeches of politicians, but also in the very structure of technology which had, in a peculiar way, industrialized the home without reducing the amount of labor that it exacted from women. This role change is more difficult to recognize than the transformation in American life created by the new technologies of telecommunication and medicine. More Work for Mother *offers a subtle picture of the interdependence of men, women, and machines and how this last partner to every American marriage has silently molded our innermost thoughts about who and what we are.*

After World War II some women found that they were working harder inside their homes than their mothers had worked, because they employed fewer servant-hours than their mothers had employed; other women found that they were working just as hard as their mothers, but were achieving greater results. As time wore on, their daughters, members of the second postwar generation, discovered that they were working even longer hours than *their* mothers had worked, because of the double burden of housework and outside employment. Either way, the end result of the long historical process that began when the shooting stopped in 1945, has been more work for mother.

Today . . . weary women know that, whether what they have been doing all day is called "consumption" or "purchasing" or "maintaining our social status," it still takes time and energy. Infants still want to be fed when they are hungry, toddlers still want to be comforted in the middle of the night, and schoolchildren still want someone to be at home when the school day has ended. School nurses expect someone to be at home when a child becomes ill during the day, and plumbers expect someone to be there to open the door when a sewer has backed up or a radiator is leaking. Men still marry—and, if divorced, marry soon again—as if they knew (leaving aside considerations of companionship, sexuality, and affection, on the one hand, and of modern technologies, on the other) that the skills women possess are difficult to live without. The work processes of housework may have changed substantially since 1940, but the work itself has not gone away.

To say that the postwar decades have been decades of affluence is to say not that poverty has disappeared, but, rather, that its face has changed, as have the numbers of people afflicted by it. By 1960, the American who could afford to live at a "decent" and "healthful" level had become the average American; decency, cleanliness, rudimentary nutrition, and rudimentary healthfulness were no longer the privileges of an élite. The minimum subsistence budget that was used to determine welfare payments in New York City in 1960 specified a set of material conditions for family life that would have been regarded as fairly luxurious in 1910 and even, for that matter, in 1930. A four-person family was permitted to rent a five-room flat, so that each member of the family who wanted to could be "alone in a room"—a luxury inconceivable to most poor families earlier in the century. The flat was to be outfitted with a complete bathroom (hot and cold running water, toilet, bath or shower, and a sink), a complete kitchen (sink with a drain, hot and cold water, refrigerator, and a gas or electric range), and central heat. Plain but adequate furnishings were allowed (each person was to have a bed and a complete set of eating utensils) as well as annual replacement clothing for the children (shoes that fit, dresses that were new and not made over from hand-me-downs). The diet for such a family was not to contain luxurious foods such as steak, but did allow meat, milk, fresh fruits, and vegetables to be served at least once a day. The family was also allowed an iron and a vacuum cleaner (although not a washing machine or a dryer) and linoleum (although not carpeting) to cover all the floors. That set of material conditions is doubly significant: first, because it was regarded as deprivation in terms of the general standard applying throughout the country in 1960: and, second, because it was luxurious in comparison to how people had lived in earlier decades.

As the standard of "minimum health and decency" has risen profoundly in the past forty years, so the portion of the population that has been unable to attain that standard has fallen. The horrors of poverty have not disappeared, but they are not nearly as horrible as they used to be, and not nearly as many people are beset by them. When computed in terms not of a specific rate of wages, but of standards of minimum decency and health established in each decade, the proportion of the population living at or below the poverty level has fallen from 33 percent (44 million people) in 1940 to 27 percent (41 million) in 1950, to 21 percent (39 million) in 1960, and to 11 percent (23 million) in 1970. Although those who remain poor are justifiably angry that the so-called affluent society cannot provide more for them than it does, "those who remain poor" are a much smaller part of our population than ever before in history. Thus, when viewed in terms of the entire contemporary world and our own immediate past, the vast majority of Americans are staggeringly well-off. As we struggle to make ends meet from one paycheck to the next, we forget how really luxurious is the life to which we have become accustomed. Even if our minds forget, however, our behavior remembers, for the memory of poverty is enshrined in the habits of our housework.

For many people the diffusion of affluence meant the diffusion of toilets, refrigerators, and washing machines, not Cadillacs, stereos, and vacation homes. In 1940, just as the Depression was drawing to a close and the economy was shifting to wartime production, one out of every three Americans was still carrying water in buckets, and two out of three Americans did not enjoy the comforts of central heating. Forty years later, there were roughly eighty-seven million "year-round housing units" in the country: only one million of these did not have running water (1 out of 87). In 1940, only 53 percent of all households had any sort of built-in bathing equipment; thus forty years ago, taking a bath for just under half of all Americans involved a lot more work than just turning on a faucet. In 1980, only three million housing units did not have a complete bathroom. Similarly, in 1941—roughly thirty years after they had first come on the market, and twenty years after the prices had fallen to more or less reasonable levels as the result of mass production—only 52 percent of the families in the United States owned or had "interior access" to a washing machine. Thus, just under half the families in the land were either still hand rubbing or hand cranking their laundry or using commercial services. About the same percentage of families had mechanical refrigerators as had washing machines in 1941 (52 percent); but ten years later, this proportion had increased to 80 percent; and by 1980, access to mechanical refrigeration was virtually universal. Before the United States entered the Second World War, one third of the households in the country were still cooking with wood and coal, so that there was both back-breaking labor on someone's part to provide fuel and equally intense labor to provide cleanliness. By 1980, gas and electric cooking was common everywhere. Conversely, only one third of all the dwellings in the country had central heating in 1940. In 1980, however—even after the energy crises of the 1970s had sent millions of people out to buy coal stoves and kerosene heaters—only sixteen million of the eighty-seven million dwellings lacked central heating, and the vast majority of those were in parts of the country where such comforts were not necessary. In the forty years since the end of the Second World War, the amenities that were once reserved for just part of the population have become the basic standard for the lives of almost everyone.

Over, under, around, and through those statistics about the technological systems with which we live, lies a daily reality about the work processes of housework that we often forget. If the basic material conditions of life have become homogenized for all Americans (the fact that the less-than-basic material conditions have not is another matter, relevant to another book), so have the work processes of housework. In times past, housewives of the "uncomfortable" classes were manual laborers in their own homes, but housewives of the "comfortable" classes were both managers and laborers. Nowadays, the general expansion of both the economy and the welfare system has led fewer people than ever before into the market for paid domestic labor; and the diffusion of appliances into households, and of households into suburbs, has encouraged the disappearance of various commercial services. The end result is that housewives, even of the most comfortable classes (in our generally now comfortable population) are doing their housework themselves. Similarly, the extension of schooling for those who are young, the proliferation of school-related activities, and the availability of jobs for those who have finished their schooling has led to the disappearance of even those helpers upon whom the poverty-stricken housewife had once been able to depend. Hence, in almost all economic sectors of the population (except the very, very rich), housework has become manual labor: the wife of the lawyer is just as likely to be down on her knees cleaning her kitchen floor as is the wife of the bricklayer or the garbageman. In 1914, the wife of a college professor had two different kinds of household assistant (a laundress, who washed and did heavy cleaning; a student who cleared after meals, did light cleaning, and supervised the children when their mother was away) and did much of her marketing over the telephone. Forty years later, the wife of another college professor described her typical day this way:

I get up at 6 A.M. and put up coffee and cereal for breakfast and go down to the basement to put clothes into the washing machine. When I come up I dress Teddy (1–½) and put him in his chair. Then I dress Jim (3–½) and serve breakfast to him and to my husband and feed Teddy.

While my husband looks after the children I go down to get the clothes out of the machine and hang them on the line. Then I come up and have my own breakfast after my husband leaves. From then on the day is as follows: Breakfast dishes, clean up kitchen. Make beds, clean the apartment. Wipe up bathroom and kitchen floor. Get lunch vegetable ready and put potatoes on to bake for lunch. Dress both children in outdoor clothes. Do my food shopping and stay out with children until 12. Return and undress children, wash them up for lunch, prepare lunch, feed Teddy and put him to nap. Make own lunch, wash dishes, straighten up kitchen. Put Jim to rest. Between 1 and 2:30, depending on the day of the week, ironing (I do my husband's shirts home and, of course, all the children's and my own clothes), thorough cleaning of one room, weekend cooking and baking, etc.; 3 P.M., give children juice or milk, put outdoor clothes on. Out to park; 4:30 back. Give children their baths. Prepare their supper. Husband usually home to play with them a little after supper and help put them to bed. Make dinner for husband and myself. After dinner, dishes and cleaning up.

After 8 P.M. often more ironing, especially on the days when I cleaned in the afternoon. There is mending to be done; 9 P.M., fall asleep in the living room over a newspaper or listening to the sound of the radio; 10 P.M., have a snack of something with my husband and go to bed.

And just as striking were the comments of another housewife in the same decade—a twenty-four-year-old woman living in the then newly built Levittown, Pennsylvania; she was described by those who interviewed her as a member of the "working class." This housewife, whose grandmother might well have been grateful to have bread and soup on the table at night, described her day in terms virtually identical to those of the college professor's wife:

Well, naturally, I get up first, make breakfast for my husband and put a load of clothes in my washer while breakfast cooks. Then I wake him up, give him his breakfast and he's off to work. Then I make breakfast for the children. After the children eat I dress them and they go out to play. Then I hang the clothes up and clean lightly through the house. In between times I do the dishes—that's understood of course. Then I make lunch for the children and myself and I bring them in, clean them up, and they eat. I send them out to play when they're done and I do the dishes, bring the clothes in and iron them. When I'm done ironing it's usually time to make supper, or at least start preparing it. Sometimes I have time to watch a TV story for half an hour or so. Then my husband comes home and we have our meals. Then I do the dishes again. Then he goes out to work again—he has a part time job—at his uncle's beverage company. Well, he does that two or three nights a week. If he stays home he watches TV and in the meantime I get the kids ready for bed. He and I have a light snack, watch TV a while and then go to bed.

In the 1950s (and the 1980s) the housewife of the "professional classes" and the housewife of the "working classes" were assisted only by machines. Few such women had paid household help, and fewer still had food or milk or clean laundry delivered to their doors. The differences between these women were no doubt profound—differences in levels of education, in families of origin, in annual household income; but those profound differences did not produce, as they would have done in the past, equally profound variations in the ways in which the women did their work.

Apparently, also, there were no significant variations in the time that women spent at that work. One sophisticated statistical analysis of time-use data collected from a large national sample of households in 1965 found that the average American woman spent about four hours a day doing housework (or twenty-eight hours a week) and about three and one-half hours a day (or twenty-six and a half hours per week) caring for children (a fifty-four-hour week). These figures were startling in two respects. First, they were not strikingly different from what Leeds had found for affluent housewives in 1912 or from what other researchers had reported for rural and urban housewives in 1935. Second, these averages were not markedly affected either by the income level of the household or by the educational attainment of the housewife: women who managed on less than four thousand dollars a year in household income spent 245 minutes per day at housework and 207 at child care; while, at the other end of the income scale, housewives who could dispose of over fifteen thousand dollars put in 260 and 196 minutes at housework and child care, respectively. Housewives with college educations were logging in 474 minutes a day of housework and child care (a little under eight hours); and housewives who had not completed grade school put in almost equally tiring days of 453 minutes (or seven and one-half hours).

Neither the working-class wife nor her middle-class contemporary could have expected her husband to help much with this work. For a while, in the 1950s, there was a hullabaloo in the popular press about "new husbands" in suburbia who were diapering babies and drying dishes and cooking barbecues and otherwise becoming "feminized." Again, in the late 1970s, a spate of books and national magazine articles appeared touting the virtues of "househusbandry," most of these articles written, it turned out, by free-lance writers and journalists who had decided to stay home for a while with their children when their wives went back to work. If the results of sociological studies are to be trusted, not much lay behind either one of those journalistic episodes. Men do very little housework; and the few "househusbands" there have ever been seem not to have stuck to it for long. Whether men are asked to estimate the time that they spend at housework, or wives are asked to estimate their husbands' time, or outside observers actually clock the amount of time that men spend at it, no one has ever estimated men's share of housework at anything higher than one and a half hours per day. Housewives who are not employed in the labor market spend, roughly speaking, fifty hours a week doing housework; housewives who are employed outside their homes spend, again roughly speaking, thirty-five hours on their work in and for their homes. Men whose wives are employed spend about ten minutes more a day on housework than men whose wives "stay home," and men who have small children add yet another ten—a grand total, for these particularly helpful husbands, of just under eleven hours of housework a week. Men who do housework tend not to do the same work that their wives are doing: they take out the garbage, they mow the lawns, they play with children, they occasionally go to the supermarket or shop for household durables, they paint the attic or fix the faucet; but by and large, they do not launder, clean, or cook, nor do they feed, clothe, bathe, or transport children. These latter—the most time-consuming activities around the home—are exclusively the domain of women. In households that are particularly well equipped with appliances, men do even less housework, partly because they believe that the work simply cannot be onerous, but also because some of the "extra" appliances actually relieve them of sex-related, or sex-acceptable chores. In homes where there are garbage disposals, men give up removing the small quantities of garbage that still need to be carried to the curb; and in households where there are dishwashers, men cease providing whatever help with the dishes they had formerly proffered.

Thus, there is more work for a mother to do in a modern home because there is no one left to help her with it. Almost all of the work that once stereotypically fell to men has been mechanized. Families tend to live a considerable distance from the place where the male head of the household is employed; hence, men leave home early in the morning and return, frequently exhausted, late at night. Children spend long hours in school and, when school is over, have "after-school activities," which someone must supervise and from which they must be transported. Older children move away from home as soon as they reasonably can, going off to college or to work. No one delivers anything (except bills and advertisements) to the door any longer, or at least not at prices that most people can afford; and domestic workers now earn salaries that have priced them out of the reach of all but the most affluent households. The advent of washing machines and dishwashers has eliminated the chores that men and children used to do as well as the accessory workers who once were willing and able to assist with the work. The end result is that, although the work is more productive (more services are performed, and more goods are produced, for every hour of work) and less laborious than it used to be, for most housewives it is just as time consuming and just as demanding.

The modern technological systems on which our households and our standard of living depend were constructed on the assumption that women would remain at home, that they would continue to function as pre-industrial workers (without paychecks, time clocks, or supervisors), and that, as a corollary, they would not be tempted to enter the labor market except under unusual (and usually temporary) circumstances. Ironically, the last of these assumptions proved erroneous. In the postwar years, more and more married women, and more and more mothers, entered the labor force, the comforts of full-time wifehood and motherhood and the existence of washing machines and dishwashers notwithstanding.

In the decades after the Second World War, the national economy shifted its focus from production to service, from manufacturing to communication; and, in the process, jobs were opened up for which women were considered to be appropriate candidates: jobs as typists, clerks, and receptionists; as waitresses, store clerks, and stenographers; as teachers, social workers, nurses, administrative assistants; and, later, as computer programmers. To various women, at various times, those jobs and the salaries they provided, proved to be attractions too great to resist. In different households, the decision that wife and/or mother would "go back to work" or "continue working" was made at different times, determined either by what was going on in the world outside the family or by a particular family's development. Some women "continued to work" in the postwar years because they were reluctant to give up the life and the income to which they had become accustomed during the war; some women went home and had babies and did not re-enter the labor force until their children were grown and out of the house; other women never went back to work. As the years passed, some younger women decided not to interrupt their careers when their babies arrived, because the high level of education that they had attained, and the high salaries that they could consequently hope to command, seemed to compensate for the double burden of motherhood and career which they had to shoulder. Other women found that, whether or not they were graced with higher education and higher incomes, the growing pressure of inflation was so seriously eroding the purchasing power of their husbands' income that, small children or no, they had to go back to work. Furthermore, as a result of divorce, desertion, or the decision to remain single, other women, in increasing numbers, had no husband's income to fall back upon. The end result was that, by 1980, just over 40 percent of the total workforce was female (up from 25 percent in 1940), women with children at home constituted almost 20 percent of the labor force, and more than half of the nation's children under the age of six had mothers who were working full time. Even though different women achieved the status of being "homemakers with jobs" at different times, very large numbers of them did achieve it; and if present trends continue unabated, even more of them will do so in the future.

It is hardly surprising that, in the immediate postwar years, many women struggled mightily with the decision to take a job, since cultural pressures of the most extraordinary kind were being brought to bear against the employment of wives and mothers. If many husbands and children opposed that decision even before they had had a chance to discover its consequences, they, too, can barely be blamed, since the public debates on the subject gave them not the slightest reason to believe that the venture would end successfully. In the 1950s and the 1960s, psychiatrists, psychologists, and popular writers inveighed against women who wished to pursue a career, and even against women who wished to have a job, and referred to such "unlovely women" as "lost," "suffering from penis envy," "ridden with guilt complexes," or just plain "man-hating." Mass-circulation magazines almost never depicted a working wife, unless to paint her in derogatory terms: working mothers were blamed for the rise in juvenile delinquency in the 1950s, for the soaring divorce rate of the 1960s, and for the rise in male impotence in the 1970s. Women's magazine fiction of the day was populated by "glowing" pregnant women and "barren" working women, whose "hungers were not yet appeased, whose destinies were not yet fulfilled"; by children who felt abandoned when their mothers were not there to greet them on the day the teacher had finally given them an "A"; and by husbands who, while tempted by the career women in their offices, always returned to their less glamorous, but more feminine wives with a warm smile and a rose behind their backs. Betty Friedan, who worked for and wrote for some of those magazines in the postwar years, recalls:

When you wrote about an actress for a woman's magazine you wrote about her as a housewife. You never showed her doing or enjoying her work as an actress, unless she eventually paid for it by losing her husband or her child, or otherwise admitting failure as a woman.

Friedan might well have added that newspaper and magazine profits depended upon the sale of advertising space to manufacturers and retailers of consumer goods; and that in the postwar years, many advertising specialists and market researchers, who advised the manufacturers and the retailers, viewed the working woman as someone who was either too poor or too preoccupied to spend time and money in the stores. Hence, profit-conscious editors, and the writers who desired their custom, were not inclined to enhance the image of the working wife, even if they happened to be one themselves.

Sociologists and other academic social scientists, rather than be left on the sidelines, joined in the debate about women's proper place by adopting what has come to be called the "functionalist" interpretation of the recent history of the family and then by broadcasting that interpretation in countless textbooks and lectures. This argument suggested that since industrialization began, households have been deprived of their essential productive roles in the economy and, consequently, housewives have been deprived of their essential productive functions. Modern women are in trouble, the analysis continued, because modern technology has either eliminated or eased most of their earlier burdens, but modern ideologies have not kept pace with the change. One solution to the problem, the social scientists noted, would be for women to take their place in the market economy; but this solution, many of the experts argued, would be contrary to female instincts and biological needs and would interfere with the few remaining functions that housewives still perform at home—namely, socialization of young children and tension management. A better solution would be to create a new ideology, one that would rationalize the woman's situation and diminish the likelihood that she would suffer "role anxiety."

Ironically, the ideology that became popular in the years when functionalism dominated sociology constituted a symbolic (but only a symbolic) reflection of the very set of conditions that had made it possible for many Americans to have the comfort both of indulging in ideological pursuits and of attending lectures in sociology. One perceptive observer referred to this ideology as the "backward search for femininity." If women who lived before the Industrial Revolution had led happy, fruitful, and productive lives (as the sociologists were suggesting), then it seemed reasonable to assume that modern discontents could be wiped away if women would return at least to some of the conditions that had pertained in Martha Washington's day. In communities across the land (especially in those that were particularly affluent and, therefore, farthest removed from the horrors of pre-industrial conditions), people were acting out the sociologists' prescriptions by bearing numerous children (the baby boom appears to have been a result of a deliberate decision on the part of affluent couples to have more children than their parents had), by breastfeeding those numerous children, raising vegetables in their backyards, crocheting afghans, knitting argyle socks, entertaining at barbecues, hiding appliances behind artificial wood paneling, giving homemade breads for Christmas presents, and decorating their living rooms with spinning wheels. "I interviewed a woman," Betty Friedan reported,

in the huge kitchen of a house that she had helped build herself. She was busily kneading the dough for her famous homemade bread; a dress she was making for a daughter was half-finished on the sewing machine; a handloom stood in one corner. Children's art materials and toys were strewn all over the floor of the house, from front door to stove: in this expensive modern house, like many of the open plan houses in this era, there was no door at all between kitchen and living room. Nor did this mother have any dream or wish or thought or frustration of her own to separate her from her children. She was pregnant now with her seventh; her happiness was complete, she said, spending her days with her children.

The wiles of the "backward search for femininity" apparently enticed men as well as women—as is nowhere more strikingly illustrated than in the writings of Kurt Vonnegut, whose novels ruthlessly dissect postwar mentality. In *Player Piano* (1952), Vonnegut created Paul Proteus, an archetypically unhappy "organization man" (an engineer working for a big electrical manufacturing company), who lives with his wife, Anita, in an archetypically "backward looking" home, replete with a huge fieldstone fireplace with candle molds over the mantel:

Paul narrowed his eyes, excluding everything from his field of vision but the colonial tableau, and imagined that he and Anita had pushed this far into the upstate wilderness, with the nearest neighbor twenty-eight miles away. She was making soap, candles, and thick wool clothes for a hard winter ahead, and he, if they weren't to starve, had to mold bullets and go shoot a bear. Concentrating hard on the illusion, Paul was able to muster a feeling of positive gratitude for Anita's presence, to thank God for a woman at his side to help with the petrifying amount of work involved in merely surviving. As, in his imagination, he brought home a bear to Anita, and she cleaned it and salted it away, he felt a tremendous lift—the two of them winning by sinew and guts a mountain of strong, red meat from an inhospitable world. And he would mold more bullets, and she would make more candles and soap from the bear fat, until late at night, when Paul and Anita would tumble down together on a bundle of straw in the corner, dog-tired and sweaty, make love, and sleep hard until the brittle-cold dawn.

Such erotic and historical fantasies were (and still are) potent cultural forces; they help us to understand not only why some people have difficulty coming to terms with the reality of their lives, but also why some people (most notably affluent housewives) are still spending so very much time at their work. People who believe that family solidarity can be bolstered by hand-dipped chocolates and hand-grown string beans are bound to spend a lot of time dipping chocolates and growing string beans.

In any event, even if these ideological props for full-time house-wifery had not existed, historical experience itself would have militated against widespread enthusiasm for the entry of married women into the labor force. The adults who were worrying about these matters in 1950 (and even in 1960) had been children of the Depression; hence, they had good reason to remember that in their youth a "working mother" had been a person to be pitied, and her family had quite possibly been a family to be shunned. If "mother worked" during the 1920s and the 1930s, her family was more than likely to be poor, the father more than likely to be unemployed, the children more than likely to be dirty, the house more than likely to be in disrepair; when "mother worked," there were children who had no one to nurse them through illnesses, meals that were hastily thrown together from whatever could be found ready-made in the markets, poor teeth, clothing that did not fit, dirty floors, skin rashes, and bad breath. It hardly mattered that only a few of these symptoms of poverty were likely to have been directly attributable to the mother's employment, because the fact of her employment served as symbol for all of them. Similarly, at the other end of the economic scale, the presence of a full-time housewife served as symbol not just for the status of the family, but also for its degree of good health and for its decent living standards. Whether she actually did the work or whether she directed the work that was to be done, the presence of a full-time wife and mother meant careful supervision of the family's health, a well-appointed living room, white stockings, ironed hair ribbons, regular church attendance, Sunday dinner, birthday parties. All those small (and large) comforts both helped to demonstrate the family's status and to ensure that it did not fall. The postwar working-class husband who complained that he would be embarrassed in front of his friends if his wife went out to work, was as much a product of this historical experience as his middle-class contemporary who claimed that two well-organized dinner parties a month would do more for his family's annual income than the salary his wife would be able to earn at a job.

In the end, whatever the complaints of husbands may have been (and there were many of them), and however ambivalent wives and mothers may have felt (as many of them did), by the time the children of the baby boom had come to maturity, the "working mother" had become the "normal American housewife"; and many people believed that the widespread diffusion of modern technology was, in and of itself, responsible for this transformation. On common-sense grounds alone, a causal connection between the washing machine and the working wife seems justified: if it takes less time to do the wash with a Bendix than it did with a washtub, and to cook a meal since the advent of Birdseye, then housework must take less time (and certainly less energy) than it used to, and women must thus be tempted to fill their free time with paid employment.

The only trouble with this argument is that one empirical investigation after another has failed to find evidence for it; common sense, in this case as in many others, is not a reliable guide to the truth. As we have seen, even with washing machines and frozen vegetables, housewives do not have much free time; 50 hours per week is ten hours more than what is now considered the standard industrial week. Housewives began to enter the labor market many years before modern household technologies were widely diffused; and the housewives then entering the workforce were precisely those who could not afford to take advantage of the amenities that then existed. Even in the postwar labor market the sociological variable that correlates most strongly with a married woman's participation in the labor force is her husband's income. And the correlation is strongly negative: the housewives who are most likely to enter the labor market are the ones who are least likely to have many labor-saving devices and household amenities. Indeed, in the early postwar years, some married women were entering the labor force precisely in order to acquire those attributes of affluence.

Where the sociologists and economists have failed to find a causal connection, the historians may be able to suggest a substitute. The washing machine, the dishwasher, and the frozen meal have not been *causes* of married women's participation in the workforce, but they have been *catalysts* of this participation: they have acted, in the same way that chemical catalysts do, to break certain bonds that might otherwise have impeded the process. Most American housewives did not enter the job market because they had an enormous amount of free time on their hands (although this may have been true in a few cases). Rather, American housewives discovered that, for one reason or another, they needed full-time employment; and subsequently, they discovered that, with the help of a dishwasher, a washing machine, and an occasional frozen dinner, they could undertake that employment without endangering their family's living standards. The symbolic connection between "working wife" and "threatened family" was thus severed, not by ideologues but by housewives with machines. Working mothers discovered that, although they were weary when they left the office or factory, they could still manage to get a decent dinner on the table that night and clean clothes on everyone's back the next morning. Husbands discovered that they had been deprived of few, if any, of the comforts to which they had become accustomed, and that additional comforts (namely, ones connected with having more cash on hand) had appeared. Children discovered that they could, if need be, make their lunches and their breakfasts themselves.

Viewed from a national perspective, American housewives entered the labor market without destroying either the level of health or the level of comfort to which they and their parents had become accustomed. If the movement of married women into the labor force proceeded with what some social critics regarded as unseemly speed, it did so because many members of the generation that had been raised in the affluent society (those who were children of the baby boom, not of the Depression, and who came to maturity and began forming their households in the 1960s and the 1970s) saw little reason to worry about the various social ills that might result from cold cereal for breakfast, from an occasional meal in a restaurant, from slightly dirty bathroom sinks and unironed sheets. Modern household technology facilitated married women's workforce participation not by freeing women from household labor but by making it possible for women to maintain decent standards in their homes without assistants and without a full-time commitment to housework.

The work that women do when they are being paid to do it is easy to recognize, because there are so many standard indicators that allow us to account for it—personnel records, time clocks, pay sheets, and the like. On the other hand, the productive labor that is still being done in American homes is difficult to recognize, because the reigning theory of family history tells us that it should not be there, because the reigning methodology of the social sciences cannot be applied to it, because ordinary language has a penchant for masking it, and because advertisers have had a vested interest in convincing us that it has evaporated. Economists and sociologists do not consider housework to be "productive work," at least in part because they cannot measure it. They can easily quantify what people are consuming (how many cans of peas? how many dollars' worth of stockings?), but they cannot place a dollar value (to choose a particularly simple example) on a nutritious meal—and they cannot begin to estimate how many such meals are prepared in households throughout the year (in part, because the workers who prepare them are not paid nor are their hours timed). People who write advertising copy for microwave ovens, toilet bowl cleaners, and paper toweling seem to believe that they will lose their jobs if they confess that it still takes time to prepare food for the oven, scrub the brown stains out of the toilet, and wipe down counters after dinner has been consumed. Virtually every lecture on the history of the family, and every textbook on the sociology of the family, and every new inquiry into the state of the family begins with the sentiment that "households do not produce anything valuable any more." And, in our everyday conversations, we cannot even refer to housewives as "laboring" or as "working" or even as being "employed," without confusing our listeners, even though we all know that housework is work.

The technological systems that presently dominate our households were built on the assumption that a full-time housewife would be operating them, since very few people in the last one hundred years (when the foundations for these systems were being laid) wanted adult women to leave their homes in order to work in the labor market, or believed that adult women themselves would ever want to go out to work. In the earliest stages of industrialization, in the early decades of the nineteenth century, as some of men's work in the home was eliminated (fuel gathering, leather working, grain processing), some men were thereby freed to work (at least part of the year) in factories and offices. Some of women's housework was eliminated at that time also (principally spinning and weaving), but no one then expected or desired women to leave their homes to work for wages elsewhere (unless the women were single or exceedingly poor) because so much of what had always been considered women's work still remained to be done at home: cooking, sewing, laundering, cleaning, child care. In the next stages of industrialization, even more of men's household work was eliminated, as was much of children's work; but, again, no one expected or desired women to leave their homes in order to go out to work because, whether rich or poor, a family's sustenance and status still depended on the presence of a full-time homemaker. In this stage of industrialization (roughly from 1880 to 1920), the foundations for the modern household technologies were laid: municipalities began to supply households with clean water and ample sewers; gas and electric companies figured out how to bring in modern fuels; merchandisers and retailers developed new techniques for selling durable goods to households. Almost no one who participated in this process—whether rich or poor, whether female or male, whether producer or consumer— seems to have doubted that the individual household would be the ultimate consumption unit, and that most of the work of that household would be done by housewives who would continue to work, as they had in the past, without pay and without timeclocks. If the utility companies had had any reason to believe that households would stop functioning after five or six o'clock—as offices, stores, and many factories do —they would have had precious little motivation for trying to supply them with electricity, water, and gas. Similarly, if householders had believed that they would have to pay every adult woman for every hour that she labored in their homes, they would have had precious little economic incentive for preferring washing machines to commercial laundry services and automobiles to deliverymen. Whether for good or ill, women were the only workers whose "place" was still at home in the years when homes were becoming mechanized, and the vast majority of these women were housewives who were not paid hourly, weekly, or even annual wages. When, in the decades after the Second World War, our economy finally became capable of realizing the potential benefits of these technological systems, the individual household, the individual ownership of tools, and the allocation of housework to women had, almost literally, been cast in the stainless steel, the copper, and the aluminum out of which those systems were composed.

The implications of this arrangement and the ironies implicit in it became particularly clear to those millions upon millions of families who moved out of urban areas and into suburban ones in the postwar decades. The move to the suburbs carried with it the assumption that someone (surely mother) would be at home to do the requisite work that made it possible for someone else (surely father) to leave early in the morning and return late at night, without worrying either about the welfare of his family or the maintenance of his domicile. Having made the move and purchased the house and invested in the cars and the appliances without which the suburban way of life simply was not possible, people discovered that the technological systems in which they had invested (not only so much money, but also so much emotion) simply would not function unless someone stayed home to operate them.

When this "someone" had, however, decided that, for whatever reason, staying at home was no longer her cup of tea, neither the house nor the cars nor the appliances nor the way of life that they all implied could simply be thrown into the dustbin, nor did anyone wish to throw them there. All of these were long-term investments (consumer *durables*); and the technological systems of which they were a part (houses, roads, telephone lines, gas mains) were built to last for more than one lifetime. The transition to the two-income family (or to the female-headed household) did not occur without taking a toll—a toll measured in the hours that employed housewives had to work in order to perform adequately first as employees and then as housewives. A thirty-five-hour week (housework) added to a forty-hour week (paid employment) adds up to a working week that even sweatshops cannot match. With all her appliances and amenities, the status of being a "working mother" in the United States today is, as three eminent experts have suggested, virtually a guarantee of being overworked and perpetually exhausted.

The technological and social systems for doing housework had been constructed with the expectation that the people engaged in them would be full-time housewives. When the full-time housewives began to disappear, those systems could not adjust quickly. Not even the most efficient working wife in the world can prepare, serve, and clean up from a meal in four minutes flat; and even the best organized working mother still cannot feed breakfast to a toddler in thirty seconds. Homes cannot automatically be moved close to a job or even close to public transportation, so someone still has to be available to drive the man of the family to the train or a child to the soccer field or to a party; and day-care centers cannot quickly be built where they have not existed before, so someone still has to leave a career behind for a while when babies are born—or find a helpful grandmother.

Indeed, given the sacred feelings that most Americans seem to attach to meals, infants, private homes, and clean laundry—and given the vast investment individuals, corporations, and municipalities have made in the technological systems that already exist—our household technologies may never evolve so as to make life easier for the working wife and mother. In the generations to come, housework is not likely to disappear. Barring a catastrophic economic or nuclear disaster, the vast majority of today's children will form families when they grow up, will buy houses, and will outfit those houses with tools for doing housework. Home computers may be added to the repertoire, but there will still be at least functional equivalents of cooking stoves and refrigerators, telephones and automobiles, washing machines and dishwashers. However much trouble these technologies may be, however much they may cost to obtain and then to maintain, and however much they may induce us to engage in amounts or forms of work that are often irritating and sometimes infuriating, the standard of living and the way of living that they make possible is one to which many Americans aspired in the past and that many are unlikely to forsake in the future. The washing machine may not save as much time as its advertisers might like us to believe, and electricity may not bring as many good things to living as the manufacturers of generating equipment would like us to think, but the daily lives that are shaped by washing machines and electricity are so much more comfortable and healthy than the ones that were shaped by washtubs and coal (or, before that, dirty clothes and open hearths) that we will probably not give them up.

Still, while enjoying the benefits that these technological systems provide, we need not succumb entirely to the work processes that they seem to have ordained for us. If we regard these processes as unsatisfactory, we can begin to extricate ourselves from them not by destroying the technological systems with which they are associated but by revising the unwritten rules that govern the systems. Some of these rules —to change our sheets once a week and keep our sinks spotless and greaseless, to wipe the table after every meal, to flush the toilet, brush our teeth, change our clothes and wash our hair, to give music lessons to our children and keep our dirty linen literally and figuratively to ourselves—generate more housework than may really be necessary. These rules were passed down to us by members of an earlier generation (our parents) and sprang from fear of the deprivations that poverty engenders and from a desire either to rise above those deprivations or to stave them off. Now that profound poverty has ceased to be an imminent threat for most of us, the time has surely come to re-evaluate the amount of time that we spend maintaining the symbols of our status.

Others of these rules—that, for example, men who dry dishes or change diapers are insufficiently masculine, that only women can properly nurture infants, that young girls should help their mothers in the kitchen and young boys assist their fathers in the garage, that husbands can undertake long commutes but wives cannot—ensure that the work processes of housework will be confined to members of only one sex, not only in this generation but in generations to come. These latter rules, connected as they are to aspects of our sexuality and our self-conception, are not easy to revise. Even those brave members of the postwar generations who learned to sever the bond between "working mother" and "social disaster" could not erase more than one social stereotype at a time; and when they chose spouses and formed households, they adopted virtually the same sexual division of household labor with washing machines and microwave ovens as had their ancestors with washtubs and open hearths: the men responsible for fuel and for lawns (those symbolic remnants of fields of waving grain) and the women responsible for cooking, cleaning, laundering, and child care. If centuries upon centuries of social conditioning have led us to prefer the private household and the individual ownership of tools, then centuries upon centuries of social conditioning also prepared these young women to be housewives and these young men to believe that the work of cooking, cleaning, and caring for infants would threaten their masculinity. Indeed, when the children of the baby boom were still children, when they were forming their sense of "what it means to be a woman" or "what it means to be a man," all the adults upon whom these adolescents might have been modeling themselves—their parents, the people down the block, celebrities, creators of plots for movies, authors of magazine articles and textbooks—were still engaged in the backward search for femininity and still suggesting (in the strongest affective terms) that dishwashers and diapers were objects to be manipulated by females, and that wrenches and lawnmowers were objects to be manipulated by males, and that the manipulation of inappropriate objects was, to put it anthropologically, sexually polluting.

The rules that stem from a fear of poverty, and the rules that stem from fear of sexual pollution, were the product of specific historical periods, with social and technological constraints of their own. The widespread diffusion of modern household technology and the widespread entrance of married women into the labor force have markedly loosened those constraints; and thus the time has come to begin changing the rules. We can best solve the problems that beset many working wives and their families not by returning to the way things used to be (since that is probably impossible and, in view of the ways things really used to be, hardly attractive), not by destroying the technological systems that have provided many benefits (and that much of the rest of the world is trying, for fairly good reasons, to emulate), and not by calling for the death of the family as a social institution (a call that the vast majority of people are unlikely to heed)—but by helping the next generation (and ourselves) to neutralize both the sexual connotation of washing machines and vacuum cleaners and the senseless tyranny of spotless shirts and immaculate floors.

The Elvis Presley Phenomenon

GREIL MARCUS

Rock and roll developed primarily from two long-established strains of American music: "race" and "hillbilly," politely renamed "rhythm and blues" and "country and western" by the record industry. These musical styles existed before the Second World War on the fringes of American popular music. During the late 1940's changes in both the music and its availability brought these styles into increasing prominence. First, the record industry came into its own, producing cheap records in vast quantities so that recorded songs became the standard form of radio music. Second, rhythm and blues, along with country and western, sounded harder, louder, and more urbanized as blacks and Southerners moved from country to city. Blues were now played in crowded bars, and electric guitars pounded a beat that could penetrate urban noise. Popular music had already developed the cult of the singer; Frank Sinatra made girls swoon or scream in the forties much as Pat Boone and Elvis Presley did in the fifties.

In 1951 a disc jockey named Alan Freed, alerted by a record store owner to the rising popularity of rhythm-and-blues records outside the black ghetto, organized "Moondog's Rock-and-Roll Party" on station WJW, in Cleveland. Rock and roll did not develop a life of its own, however, until 1954, when Freed joined a medium-sized New York station and drove both the new music and its new name to the top of radio ratings. A white band, Bill Haley and the Comets, was the first to label itself as a rock-and-roll group; their song "Shake Rattle and Roll" reached the "Top Ten" late in 1954. A new era began in May 1955 when Haley's hit "Rock Around the Clock" opened the highly successful movie, The Blackboard Jungle, *thus linking rock and roll with wild and rebellious teenagers. Adolescents made such films an instant success. In 1956 Bill Haley and the Comets produced a low-budget movie called* Rock Around The Clock, *which grossed a million dollars in that year alone. In England minor riots occurred as theaters showing the film turned into dance halls. The* Encyclopaedia Britannica *yearbook described the new music as "insistent savagery."*

Elvis Presley, the greatest of the rock-and-roll singers, came out of the country music tradition but, through records and radio, was a close student of the black rhythm-and-blues music. Before his sudden leap to a national audience in 1956, he was an acclaimed country music performer who had worked in the Grand Ole Opry in Nashville. In that year he appeared on the Ed Sullivan Show, his gyrations photographed only from the waist up, and recorded "Heartbreak Hotel," which topped country, popular, and rhythm-and-blues charts. All the elements of past tradition of music had been drawn together into a new form by this amazing urban hillbilly, and the beat of American life would never again be quite the same.

They called Elvis the Hillbilly Cat in the beginning; he came out of a stepchild culture (in the South, white trash; to the rest of America, a caricature of Bilbo and moonshine) that for all it shared with the rest of America had its own shape and integrity. As a poor white Southern boy, Elvis created a personal culture out of the hillbilly world that was his as a given. Ultimately, he made that personal culture public in such an explosive way that he transformed not only his own culture, but America's.

It was, as Southern chambers of commerce have never tired of saying, A Land of Contrasts. The fundamental contrast, of course, could not have been more obvious: black and white. Always at the root of Southern fantasy, Southern music, and Southern politics, black Americans were poised in the early fifties for an overdue invasion of American life, in fantasy, music, and politics. As the North scurried to deal with the problem, the South would be pushed farther and farther into the weirdness and madness its best artists had been trying to exorcise from the time of Poe on down. Its politics would dissolve into night-riding and hysteria; its fantasies would be dull for all their gaudy paranoia. Only the music got away clean.

The North, powered by the Protestant ethic, had set men free by making them strangers; the poor man's South that Elvis knew took strength from community.

The community was based on a marginal economy that demanded cooperation, loyalty, and obedience for the achievement of anything resembling a good life; it was organized by religion, morals, and music. Music helped hold the community together, and carried the traditions and shared values that dramatized a sense of place. Music gave pleasure, wisdom, and shelter.

"It's the only place in the country I've ever been where you can actually drive down the highway at night, and if you listen, you hear music," Robbie Robertson once said. "I don't know if it's coming from the people or if it's coming from the air. It lives, and it's rooted there." Elegant enough, but I prefer another comment Robbie made. "The South," he said, "is the only place we play where everybody can clap on the off-beat."

Music was also an escape from the community, and music revealed its underside. There were always people who could not join, no matter how they might want to: tramps, whores, rounders, idiots, criminals. The most vital were singers: not the neighbors who brought out their fiddles and guitars for country picnics, as Elvis used to do, or those who sang in church, as he did also, but the professionals. They were men who bridged the gap between the community's sentimentalized idea of itself, and the outside world and the forbidden; artists who could take the community beyond itself because they had the talent and the nerve to transcend it. Often doomed, traveling throughout the South enjoying sins and freedoms the community had surrendered out of necessity or never known at all, they were too ambitious, ornery, or simply different to fit in.

The Carter Family, in the twenties, was the first to record the old songs everyone knew, to make the shared musical culture concrete, and their music drew a circle around the community. They celebrated the landscape (especially the Clinch Mountains that ringed their home), found strength in a feel for death because it was the only certainty, laughed a bit, and promised to leave the hillbilly home they helped build only on a gospel ship. Jimmie Rodgers, their contemporary, simply hopped a train. He was every boy who ever ran away from home, hanging out in the railroad yards, bumming around with black minstrels, pushing out the limits of his life. *He* celebrated long tall mamas that rubbed his back and licked his neck just to cure the cough that killed him; he bragged about gunplay on Beale Street; he sang real blues, played jazz with Louis Armstrong, and though there was a melancholy in his soul, his smile was a good one. He sounded like a man who could make a home for himself anywhere. There's so much *room* in this country, he seemed to be saying, so many things to do—how could an honest man be satisfied to live within the frontiers he was born to?

Outside of the community because of the way they lived, the singers were tied to it as symbols of its secret hopes, of its fantasies of escape and union with the black man, of its fears of transgressing the moral and social limits that promised peace of mind. Singers could present the extremes of emotion, risk, pleasure, sex, and violence that the community was meant to control; they were often alcoholic or worse, lacking a real family, drifters in a world where roots were life. Sometimes the singer tantalized the community with his outlaw liberty; dying young, he finally justified the community by his inability to survive outside of it. More often than not, the singer's resistance dissolved into sentiment. Reconversion is the central country music comeback strategy, and many have returned to the fold after a brief fling with the devil, singing songs of virtue, fidelity, and God, as if to prove that sin only hid a deeper piety—or that there was no way out.

By the late forties and early fifties, Hank Williams had inherited Jimmie Rodgers' role as the central figure in the music, but he added an enormous reservation: that margin of loneliness in Rodgers' America had grown into a world of utter tragedy. Williams sang for a community to which he could not belong; he sang to a God in whom he could not quite believe; even his many songs of good times and good lovin' seemed to lose their reality. There were plenty of jokes in his repertoire, novelties like "Kaw-Liga" (the tale of unrequited love between two cigar store Indians); he traveled Rodgers' road, but for Williams, that road was a lost highway. Beneath the surface of his forced smiles and his light, easy sound, Hank Williams was kin to Robert Johnson in a way that the new black singers of his day were not. Their music, coming out of New Orleans, out of Sam Phillips' Memphis studio and washing down from Chicago, was loud, fiercely electric, raucous, bleeding with lust and menace and loss. The rhythmic force that was the practical legacy of Robert Johnson had evolved into a music that overwhelmed *his* reservations; the rough spirit of the new blues, city R&B, rolled right over his nihilism. Its message was clear: What life doesn't give me, I'll take.

Hank Williams was a poet of limits, fear, and failure; he went as deeply into one dimension of the country world as anyone could, gave it beauty, gave it dignity. What was missing was that part of the hillbilly soul Rodgers had celebrated, something Williams' music obscured, but which his realism could not express and the community's moralism could not contain: excitement, rage, fantasy, delight—the feeling, summed up in a sentence by W. J. Cash from *The Mind of the South*, that "even the Southern physical world was a kind of cosmic conspiracy against reality in favor of romance"; that even if Elvis's South was filled with Puritans, it was also filled with natural-born hedonists, and the same people were both.

To lie on his back for days and weeks [Cash wrote of the hillbilly], storing power as the air he breathed stores power under the hot sun of August, and then to explode, as that air explodes in a thunderstorm, in a violent outburst of emotion—in such a fashion would he make life not only tolerable, but infinitely sweet.

In the fifties we can hardly find that moment in white music, before Elvis. Hank Williams was not all there was to fifties country, but his style was so pervasive, so effective, carrying so much weight, that it closed off the possibilities of breaking loose just as the new black music helped open them up. Not his gayest tunes, not "Move It on Over," "Honky Tonkin'," or "Hey Good Lookin'," can match this blazing passage from Cash, even if those songs share its subject:

To go into the town on Saturday afternoon and night, to stroll with the throng, to gape at the well-dressed and the big automobiles, to bathe in the holiday cacaphony . . . maybe to have a drink, maybe to get drunk, to laugh with the passing girls, to pick them up if you had a car, or to go swaggering or hesitating into the hotels with the corridors saturated with the smell of bicloride of mercury, or the secret, steamy bawdy houses; maybe to have a fight, maybe against the cops, maybe to end, whooping and god-damning, in the jailhouse. . . .

The momentum is missing; that will to throw yourself all the way after something better with no real worry about how you are going to make it home. And it was this spirit, full-blown and bragging, that was to find its voice in Elvis's new blues and the rockabilly fever he kicked off all over the young white South. Once Elvis broke down the door, dozens more would be fighting their way through. Out of nowhere there would be Carl Perkins, looking modest enough and sounding for all the world as if he was having fun for the first time in his life, chopping his guitar with a new kind of urgency and yelling: "Now Dan got happy and he started ravin'—He jerked out his razor but he wasn't shavin' "—

He hollered R-R-RAVE ON *chillen, I'm with ya!*
RAVE ON CATS *he cried*
It's almost dawn and the cops're gone
Let's allllllll get dixie fried!

Country music (like the blues, which was more damned and more honestly hedonistic than country had ever been) was music for a whole community, cutting across lines of age, if not class. This could have meant an openly expressed sense of diversity for each child, man, and woman, as it did with the blues. But country spoke to a community fearful of anything of the sort, withdrawing into itself, using music as a bond that linked all together for better or for worse, with a sense that what was shared was less important than the crucial fact of sharing. How could parents hope to keep their children if their kids' whole sense of what it meant to live—which is what we get from music when we are closest to it—held promises the parents could never keep?

The songs of country music, and most deeply, its even, narrow sound, had to subject the children to the heartbreak of their parents: the father who couldn't feed his family, the wife who lost her husband to a honky-tonk angel or a bottle, the family that lost everything to a suicide or a farm spinning off into one more bad year, the horror of loneliness in a world that was meant to banish that if nothing else. Behind that uneasy grin, this is Hank Williams' America; the romance is only a night call.

Such a musical community is beautiful, but it is not hard to see how it could be intolerable. All that hedonism was dragged down in country music; a deep sense of fear and resignation confined it, as perhaps it almost had to, in a land overshadowed by fundamentalist religion, where original sin was just another name for the facts of life.

Now, that Saturday night caught by Cash and Perkins would get you through a lot of weekdays. Cash might close it off—"Emptied of their irritations and repressions, left to return to their daily tasks, stolid, unlonely, and tame again"—and he's right, up to a point. This wasn't any revolution, no matter how many cops got hurt keeping the peace on Saturday night. Regardless of what a passport to that Southern energy (detached from the economics and religion that churned it up) might do for generations of restless Northern and British kids, there is no way that energy can be organized. But the fact that Elvis and the rest could trap its spirit and send it out over a thousand radio transmitters is a central fact of more lives than mine; the beginning of most of the stories in this book, if nothing near the end of them.

For we are treading on the key dividing line that made Elvis "King of Western Bop" (they went through a lot of trouble finding a name for this music) instead of just another country crooner or a footnote in someone's history of the blues: the idea (and it was just barely an "idea") that Saturday night could be the whole show. You had to be young and a bit insulated to pull it off, but why not? Why not trade pain and boredom for kicks and style? Why not make an escape from a way of life—the question trails off the last page of *Huckleberry Finn*—into a way of life?

You might not get revered for all time by everyone from baby to grandma, like the Carter Family, but you'd have more fun. Reality would catch up sooner or later—a pregnant girlfriend and a fast marriage, the farm you had to take over when your daddy died, a dull and pointless job that drained your desires until you could barely remember them—but why deal with reality before you had to? And what if there was a chance, just a chance, that you *didn't* have to deal with it? "When I was a boy," said Elvis not so long ago, "I was the hero in comic books and movies. I grew up believing in a dream. Now I've lived it out. That's all a man can ask for."

Elvis is telling us something quite specific: how special he was; how completely he captured and understood what for most of us is only a tired phrase glossing the surfaces of our own failed hopes. It is one thing, after all, to dream of a new job, and quite another to dream of a new world. The risks are greater. Elvis took chances dreaming his dreams; he gambled against the likelihood that their failure would betray him, and make him wish he had never dreamed at all. There are a hundred songs to tell that story, but perhaps Mott the Hoople, chasing the rock 'n' roll fantasy Elvis made of the American dream, said it best: "I wish I'd never wanted then/What I want now twice as much."

Always, Elvis felt he was different, if not better, than those around him. He grew his sideburns long, acting out that sense of differentness, and was treated differently: in this case, he got himself kicked off the football team. Hear him recall those days in the midst of a near-hysterical autobiography, delivered at the height of his comeback from the stage at the International Hotel in Las Vegas: ". . . Had pretty long hair for that time and I tell you it got pretty weird. They used to see me comin down the street and they'd say, 'Hot dang, let's get him, he's a squirrel, he's a squirrel, get him, he just come down outta the trees.' "

High school classmates remember his determination to break through as a country singer; with a little luck, they figured, he might even make it.

Out on the road for the first time with small-change country package tours, though, Elvis would plot for something much bigger—for everything Hollywood had ever shown him in its movies.

On North Main in Memphis, as Harmonica Frank recalls Elvis, this was nothing to put into words. Talking trash and flicking ash, marking time and trying to hold it off, what did Elvis really have to look forward to? A year or so of Saturday nights, a little local notoriety, then a family he didn't quite decide to have and couldn't support? It would be all over.

Elvis fancied himself a trucker (if there weren't any Memphis boys in the movies, there were plenty on the road), pushing tons of machinery through the endless American night; just his version of the train whistle that called out to Johnny B. Goode and kept Richard Nixon awake as a boy. If it is more than a little odd that what to Elvis served as a symbol of escape and mastery now works—as part of his legend—as a symbol of everything grimy and poor he left behind when he did escape, maybe that only tells us how much his success shuffled the facts of his life—or how much he raised the stakes.

You don't make it in America—Emerson's mousetrap to the contrary—waiting for someone to come along and sign you up. You might be sitting on the corner like a Philly rock 'n' roller and get snatched up for your good looks, but you'll be back a year later and you'll never know what happened. Worst of all, you may not even care. What links the greatest rock 'n' roll careers is a volcanic ambition, a lust for more than anyone has a right to expect; in some cases, a refusal to know when to quit or even rest. It is that bit of Ahab burning beneath the Huck Finn rags of "Freewheelin'" Bob Dylan, the arrogance of a country boy like Elvis sailing into Hollywood, ready for whatever kind of success America had to offer.

So if we treat Elvis's words with as much respect as we can muster —which is how he meant them to be taken—we can see the first point at which his story begins to be his own. He took his dreams far more seriously than most ever dare, and he had the nerve to chase them down.

Cash's wonderful line—"a cosmic conspiracy against reality in favor of romance"—now might have more resonance. Still, if the kind of spirit that romance could produce seems ephemeral within the context of daily life, you would not expect the music it produced to last very long either. Not even Elvis, as a successful young rocker, could have expected his new music to last; he told interviewers rock 'n' roll was here to stay, but he was taking out plenty of insurance, making movies and singing schmaltz. You couldn't blame him; anyway, he liked schmaltz.

Within the realm of country music, the new spirit dried up just like Saturday fades into Monday, but since rock 'n' roll found its own audience and created its own world, that hardly mattered. Rock 'n' roll caught that romantic conspiracy on records and gave it a form. Instead of a possibility within a music, it became the essence; it became, of all things, a tradition. And when that form itself had to deal with reality— which is to say, when its young audience began to grow up—when the compromise between fantasy and reality that fills most of this book was necessary to preserve the possibility of fantasy, the fantasy had become part of the reality that had to be dealt with; the rules of the game had changed a bit, and it was a better game. "Blue Suede Shoes" had grown directly into something as serious and complex, and yet still off-hand, still take-it-or-leave-it-and-pass-the-wine, as the Rolling Stones' "You Can't Always Get What You Want," which asks the musical question, "Why *are you* stepping on my blue suede shoes?"

Echoing through all of rock 'n' roll is the simple demand for peace of mind and a good time. While the demand is easy to make, nothing is more complex than to try to make it real and live it out. It all sounds plain, obvious; but that one young man like Elvis could break through a world as hard as Hank Williams', and invent a new one to replace it, seems obvious only because we have inherited Elvis's world, and live in it.

Satisfaction is not all there is to it, but it is where it all begins. Finally, the music must provoke as well as delight, disturb as well as comfort, create as well as sustain. If it doesn't, it lies, and there is only so much comfort you can take in a lie before it all falls apart.

The central facts of life in Elvis's South pulled as strongly against the impulses of hedonism and romance as the facts of our own lives do against the fast pleasures of rock 'n' roll. When the poor white was thrown back on himself, as he was in the daytime, when he worked his plot or looked for a job in the city, or at night, when he brooded and Hank Williams' whippoorwill told the truth all too plainly, those facts stood out clearly: powerlessness and vulnerability on all fronts. The humiliation of a class system that gave him his identity and then trivialized it; a community that for all its tradition and warmth was in some indefinable way not enough; economic chaos; the violence of the weather; bad food and maybe not enough of that; diseases that attached themselves to the body like new organs—they all mastered him. And that vulnerability produced—along with that urge to cut loose, along with that lively Southern romance—uncertainty, fatalism, resentment, acceptance, and nostalgia: limits that cut deep as the oldest cotton patch in Dixie.

Vernon Presley was a failed Mississippi sharecropper who moved his family out of the country with the idea of making a go in the city; it's not so far from Tupelo to Memphis, but in some ways, the journey must have been a long one—scores of country songs about boys and girls who lost their souls to the big town attest to that. Listen to Dolly Parton's downtown hooker yearning for her Blue Ridge mountain boy; listen to the loss of an America you may never have known.

They don't make country music better than that anymore, but it's unsatisfying, finally; too classical. This country myth is just one more echo of Jefferson pronouncing that, in America, virtue must be found in the land. I like myths, but this one is too facile, either for the people who still live on the land or for those of us who are merely looking for a way out of our own world, for an Annie Green Springs utopia. The myth is unsatisfying because the truth is richer than the myth.

"King Harvest (Has Surely Come)," the Band's song of blasted country hopes, gives us the South in all of its earthly delight and then snuffs it out. All at once, the song catches the grace and the limbo of the life that must be left behind.

The tune evokes a man's intimacy with the land and the refusal of the land to respond in kind. The music makes real, for the coolest city listener, a sense of place that is not quite a sense of being at home; the land is too full of violence for that. One hears the farmer's fear of separating from the land (and from his own history, which adhering to the land, is not wholly his own); one hears the cold economic necessities that have forced him out. The melody—too beautiful and out of reach for any words I have—spins the chorus into the pastoral with a feel for nature that is *really* hedonistic—

Corn in the field
Listen to the rice as the wind blows cross the water
KING HARVEST HAS SURELY COME*

—and a desperate, ominous rhythm slams the verses back to the slum streets that harbor the refugees of the pastoral disaster: "Just don't judge me by my shoes!" Garth Hudson's organ traces the circle of the song, over and over again.

The earliest picture of Elvis shows a farmer, his wife, and their baby; the faces of the parents are vacant, they are set, as if they cannot afford an unearned smile. Somehow, their faces say, they will be made to pay even for that.

You don't hear this in Elvis's music; but what he left out of his story is as vital to an understanding of his art as what he kept, and made over. If we have no idea of what he left behind, of how much he escaped, we will have no idea what his success was worth, or how intensely he must have wanted it.

Elvis was thirteen when the family left Tupelo for Memphis in 1948, a pampered only child; ordinary in all respects, they say, except that he liked to sing. True to Chuck Berry's legend of the Southern rocker, Elvis's mother bought him his first guitar, and for the same reason Johnny B. Goode's mama had in mind: keep the boy out of trouble. Elvis sang tearful country ballads, spirituals, community music. On the radio, he listened with his family to the old music of the Carter Family and Jimmie Rodgers, to current stars like Roy Acuff, Ernest Tubb, Bob Wills, Hank Williams, and to white gospel groups like the Blackwood Brothers. Elvis touched the soft center of American music when he heard and imitated Dean Martin and the operatics of Mario Lanza; he picked up Mississippi blues singers like Big Bill Broonzy, Big Boy Crudup, Lonnie Johnson, and the new Memphis music of Rufus Thomas and Johnny Ace, mostly when no one else was around, because that music was naturally frowned upon. His parents called it "sinful music," and they had a point—it was dirty, and there were plenty of blacks who would have agreed with Mr. and Mrs. Presley —but Elvis was really too young to worry. In this he was no different from hundreds of other white country kids who wanted more excitement in their lives than they could get from twangs and laments—wanted a beat, sex, celebration, the stunning nuances of the blues and the roar of horns and electric guitars. Still, Elvis's interest was far more casual than that of Jerry Lee Lewis, a bad boy who was sneaking off to black dives in his spare time, or Carl Perkins, a musician who was consciously working out a synthesis of blues and country.

The Presleys stumbled onto welfare, into public housing. Vernon Presley found a job. It almost led to the family's eviction, because if they still didn't have enough to live on, they were judged to have too much to burden the county with their troubles. Elvis was a loner, but he had an eye for flash. He sold his blood for money, ushered at the movies, drove his famous truck, and divided the proceeds between his mother and his outrageous wardrobe. Looking for space, for a way to set himself apart.

Like many parents with no earthly future, the Presleys, especially Gladys Presley, lived for their son. Her ambition must have been that Elvis would take all that was good in the family and free himself from the life she and her husband endured; she was, Memphian Stanley Booth wrote a few years ago, "the one, perhaps the only one, who had told him throughout his life that even though he came from poor country people, he was just as good as anybody."

On Sundays (Wednesdays too, sometimes) the Presleys went to their Assembly of God to hear the Pentecostal ministers hand down a similar message: the last shall be first. This was democratic religion with a vengeance, lower class and gritty. For all those who have traced Elvis's music and his hipshake to his religion (accurately enough—Elvis was the first to say so), it has escaped his chroniclers that hillbilly Calvinism was also at the root of his self-respect and his pride: the anchor of his ambition.

His church (and the dozens of other Pentecostal sects scattered throughout the South and small-town America) was one part of what was left of the old American religion after the Great Awakening. Calvinism had been a religion of authority in the beginning; in the middle-class North, filtered through the popular culture of Ben Franklin, it became a system of tight money, tight-mindedness, and gentility; in the hillbilly South, powered by traveling preachers and their endless revivals, the old holiness cult produced a faith of grace, apocalypse, and emotion, where people heaved their deepest feelings into a circle and danced around them. Momentum scattered that old authority; all were sinners, all were saints. Self-consciously outcast, the true faith in a land of Philistines and Pharisees, it was shoved into storefronts and tents and even open fields, and no less sure of itself for that.

Church music caught moments of unearthly peace and desire, and the strength of the religion was in its intensity. The preacher rolled fire down the pulpit and chased it into the aisle, signifying; men and women rocked in their seats, sometimes onto the floor, bloodying their fingernails scratching and clawing in a lust for absolute sanctification. No battle against oppression, this was a leap right through it, with tongues babbling toward real visions, negating stale red earth, warped privvies, men and women staring from their sway-backed porches into nothingness. It was a faith meant to transcend the grimy world that called it up. Like Saturday night, the impulse to dream, the need to escape, the romance and the contradictions of the land, this was a source of energy, tension, and power.

Elvis inherited these tensions, but more than that, gave them his own shape. It is often said that if Elvis had not come along to set off the changes in American music and American life that followed his triumph, someone very much like him would have done the job as well. But there is no reason to think this is true, either in strictly musical terms, or in any broader cultural sense. It is vital to remember that Elvis was the first young Southern white to sing rock 'n' roll, something he copied from no one but made up on the spot; and to know that even though other singers would have come up with a white version of the new black music acceptable to teenage America, of all that did emerge in Elvis's wake, none sang as powerfully, or with more than a touch of his magic.

Even more important is the fact that no singer emerged with anything like Elvis's combination of great talent and conscious ambition, and there is no way a new American hero could have gotten out of the South and to the top—creating a whole new sense of how big the top was, as Elvis did—without that combination. The others—Perkins, Lewis, Charlie Rich—were bewildered by even a taste of fame and unable to handle a success much more limited than Presley's.

If Elvis had the imagination to come up with the dreams that kept him going, he had the music to bring them to life and make them real to huge numbers of other people. It was the genius of his singing, an ease and an intensity that has no parallel in American music, that along with his dreams separated him from his context.

Jimmy Carter: A Crisis of Confidence

PETER CARROLL

With the exception of Dwight Eisenhower, no president has served two full terms since the 1930's. Jimmy Carter, sharply aware of the public's lack of confidence in its political institutions, was elected president by running against politics, against Washington, and against "insiders." Once selected, he found himself the victim of all that he had campaigned against: the Washington establishment, the media, the exaggerated and unrealistic expectations of the American people, and the demand for a political smoothness that the public mistrusts in candidates but admires in presidents. Being fuzzy on the issues as a candidate proved profitable, but as president his shifts were harmful. However, on some issues in which he expressed a clear policy, such as energy, he was opposed.

Carter never succeeded in overcoming the crisis of legitimacy that gripped American institutions throughout the 1970's. In 1975 a national poll indicated that 69 percent of the country thought that "over the last ten years, this country's leaders have consistently lied to the people." In 1976 another poll indicated that public confidence had dropped in the past decade from 73 to 42 percent for the medical profession and from 55 to 16 percent for major companies. Similar declines were reported for other institutions. A nation that was adjusting from the abundance and sense of control of the 60's to the scarcities and sense of closing frontiers of the 70's was extraordinarily critical of its leaders. Historians, more knowledgeable of the problems, may have been less harsh with the leaders of the 1970's than the public, and more willing to see the era as a period of painful transition which neither policy nor rhetoric could greatly soften or legitimize. The hard, strident years of Kennedy, Johnson, and Nixon had thrust the nation toward moral catastrophe; future generations may put a surprisingly high value on the simple decency of men like Ford, Carter, and Reagan.

"Our people were sick at heart," said Jimmy Carter, explaining his election victory, "and wanted new leadership that could heal us, and give us once again a government of which we could feel proud." Carter's inauguration symbolized this affirmation of traditional values. Instead of formal attire, the two chief executives, Carter and Ford, wore ordinary business suits, and the new President took the oath of office with the nickname "Jimmy." Then, he stirred the Washington crowds by leading the parade from Capitol Hill to the White House on foot. ("He's walking!" people shrieked. "He's walking!") "I have no new dream to set forth today," he admitted, "but rather urge a fresh faith in the old dream. . . . We must once again have full faith in our country—and in one another." Evoking "a new spirit"—the phrase appeared five times in his inaugural speech—Carter called for the restoration of political morality, a government "at the same time . . . competent and compassionate."

Carter's appeal for moral leadership, effective as campaign oratory, raised new problems once the mantle of authority passed to his own shoulders. "This is not the time to tax Mr. Carter again for his fuzziness on the issues," acknowledged *The New York Times* on his first day in office. "But he should recognize that he lacks the eloquence to hide it." With a paper-thin electoral victory and a rising proportion of citizens who refused to vote, the new administration took power in an atmosphere of persistent distrust. "One result was certain," observed veteran reporter Haynes Johnson. "The [new] president would be watched more critically than ever before."

Recognizing these suspicions, Carter attempted to demystify the operations of government and create an impression of rule by ordinary people. He reduced the size of the White House staff by one-third, ordered cabinet officers to drive their own cars, and required that government regulations be written "in plain English for a change." His administration instituted new ethical guidelines for executive employees, mandating public disclosure of financial holdings, divestiture of potential conflicts of interest, and closing what Carter called "the revolving door" between government service and corporate appointment. "Government officials can't be sensitive to your problems," the President remarked in a televised "fireside chat" two weeks after taking office, "if we are living like royalty here in Washington."

Carter's disavowal of professional politicians, partly a function of his own inexperience, partly the result of a self-conscious style, determined the structure of power within the White House. As his closest advisers, he retained the people who had shaped his campaign strategy —all Washington outsiders from Georgia: Hamilton Jordan, Jody Powell, and Charles Kirbo. More problematic was his nomination to head the Office of Management and Budget, Georgia banker Bert Lance, state highway commissioner under Carter and an early, generous contributor to the presidential campaign. "What has been Mr. Lance's experience in the federal government?" asked Senator William Proxmire scornfully. "He has none—zero, zip, zilch, not one year, not one week, not one day." Even more controversial was the choice for attorney general, former federal judge Griffin Bell, also from Georgia. Bell's political views—membership in clubs that excluded Jews and blacks, enthusiastic support for Nixon's nomination of Judge Carswell, and a legal ruling that upheld the removal from office of Georgia legislator Julian Bond for opposing the Vietnam war—aroused liberal suspicions about the administration's political sympathies. But despite unexpected angry rhetoric, the Democratic Senate indulged the President's preferences.

While public attention focused on questions of inexperience and cronyism, however, the bulk of Carter's high-level nominations revealed the administration's close ties to another, even more powerful interlocking establishment, the corporate elite that supported the Trilateral Commission. "If after the inauguration you find a Cy Vance as secretary of state and Zbigniew Brzezinski as head of national security," Hamilton Jordan told an interviewer during the recent campaign, "then I would say we failed." Yet Carter appointed Vance and Brzezinski to those very posts! And besides these two administrators and Vice President Mondale, Carter also turned to the Trilateral Commission for Secretary of the Treasury W. Michael Blumenthal, Secretary of Defense Harold Brown, United Nations ambassador Andrew Young, and a dozen other slightly lower appointees. "Conservatives with high integrity," consumer advocate Ralph Nader described them, who would "follow the wrong policies straight instead of crooked."

It was perhaps no coincidence, then, that the only Carter selection rejected by the Senate was an apparent insider who inadvertently had become associated with genuine outsiders, Theodore Sorensen, a former Kennedy adviser, nominated by Carter to head the CIA. Six years earlier, Sorensen had filed an affidavit in the *Pentagon Papers* case, in which he acknowledged leaving government service in 1964 with sixty-seven boxes of documents, including papers marked "classified." Such confessions confirmed Senate fears about Sorensen's antipathy to extralegal activities by the intelligence organization. "It is now clear," maintained Sorensen in withdrawing his name, "that a substantial portion of the United States Senate and the intelligence community is not yet ready to accept . . . an outsider who believes as I believe."

The orthodoxy of Carter's appointments, however, could not compensate for their lack of political experience. Within one month of the inauguration, the administration needlessly aroused the fury of the Democratic leadership of Congress, surely its most valuable political ally, by announcing the cancellation of nineteen water projects in the interests of fiscal austerity. Challenged by this attack on traditional "pork-barrel" legislation—the division of public spoils among the politicians in power—congressional leaders roared defiance, threatened to crush the remainder of the President's programs, and authorized the disputed appropriations anyway. In the face of such opposition, Carter prudently retreated, neither vetoing nor even denouncing the unwanted measure. He had lost not only the immediate issue, but considerable goodwill on Capitol Hill as well. Yet after one hundred days in office, Carter enjoyed rising popularity, garnering a 75 percent approval rating in the Harris poll. There was, observed the venerable presidential adviser Clark Clifford, "a return of the confidence of the people in our government."

Carter's ability to revitalize public spirit nevertheless depended on the cooperation of Congress. Since the fall of Richard Nixon, congressional leaders had become especially jealous of legislative power, reluctant to compromise with any administration and, often, even with each other. Moreover, the elections of 1974, 1976, and 1978 brought to office a spate of new politicians—half the House Democrats had not served under Nixon—who remained uncommitted to the traditional committee system and hostile to the control of party leaders. A survey conducted at the University of Pittsburgh showed party loyalty and party voting within Congress at the lowest level in thirty-six years. "If this were France," grieved Speaker Thomas "Tip" O'Neill, "the Democratic Party would be five parties."

The administration's attempt to restore public confidence in the federal government also collided with a more sinister dimension of congressional independence: the penchant of numerous representatives for graft. On the eve of Carter's election, *The Washington Post,* chief sleuth in the Watergate scandals, accused over one hundred congressmen of taking bribes from South Korea lobbyist Tongsun Park in exchange for enacting favorable legislation. The resulting "Koreagate" investigation, headed by former Watergate prosecutor Leon Jaworski, found "substantial" support for the charges. But because of intelligence restraints on the evidence, only three sitting congressmen were reprimanded for their conduct, and one former representative, Richard Hanna of California, went to prison. In a separate case, thirteen-term Michigan Democrat Charles Diggs was convicted of taking illegal kickbacks from staff employees, but managed to win reelection in 1978. The next year, he became the first congressman since 1921 to be censured by the House of Representatives for padding his payroll and taking public funds for personal use.

The discovery of widespread congressional corruption also smeared the White House. When United States attorney David Marston, a former aide of Republican Senator Schweiker, probed too closely into a kickback scheme involving two Pennsylvania Democrats, one of the suspects, Representative Joshua Eilberg, telephoned the President to recommend cashiering Marston, a proposal Carter endorsed. "This was a routine matter for me," said the President in self-defense, "and I did not consider my taking the telephone call . . . nor relaying his request to the attorney general to be ill advised at all." But the Marston affair evoked memories of Watergate and kept the case alive. Indicted on conflict-of-interest charges and defeated at the polls, Eilberg pleaded guilty in 1979. Representative Daniel Flood, charged with similar violations, won a mistrial, then pleaded ill-health to avoid a retrial; he retired in 1980. Meanwhile, FBI investigators were gathering some remarkable evidence, including videotaped motion pictures of congressmen taking bribes from mysterious Arab millionaires. The cases, coded Abscam, broke the headlines in 1980.

For two prestigious senators—liberal Republican Edward Brooke of Massachusetts, the only black in the upper house, and Herman Talmadge, scion of southern conservatism—messy divorce trials led to revelations of the illegal accumulation of funds. The charges contributed to Brooke's electoral defeat in 1978. Talmadge, having recovered from alcoholism, staged a strong personal defense. But in 1979, the Senate denounced his "reprehensible" conduct for bringing "dishonor and disrepute" on that body, and he lost a bid for reelection in 1980.

The reluctance of Congress to discipline its members intensified public distrust of the political process. "For some citizens," warned Carter in his first state of the union message, "the government has almost become like a foreign country." Responding to the decline of voter participation, the President proposed a liberalization of voter registration, urging the removal of "antiquated and unnecessary obstacles." But a Congress content with its own rule felt no need for reform. In the 1978 elections, voter participation dropped under 38 percent, the lowest turnout since 1942. Though most congressional incumbents won reelection, party loyalty virtually disappeared. In the state elections, voters readily split tickets in response to single issues and candidate personality, and while Republicans made only modest gains in Congress, they captured 298 new seats in the state legislatures. "This is the most profound change for us," said a gloating Republican National Chairman Bill Brock. The mood of the citizenry emerged clearly in the low television ratings obtained by election-night news shows, which in New York City ran third behind a rerun of Peter Sellers's *The Pink Panther.* It was no surprise, then, that by the summer of 1979, a Gallup poll found public approval of Congress at an abysmal 19 percent.

The intractability of Congress severely diminished the political power of Jimmy Carter, leaving the nominal head of the Democratic party with a shrinking constituency in the country which, in turn, further weakened his influence on Capitol Hill. "Nixon had his enemies list," quipped Senator James Abourezk. "Carter has his friends list." As White House proposals vanished in Congress, the President's popularity steadily declined, raising what *Newsweek* magazine called "the Eptitude Question—the suspicion abroad in Washington's power factories that Carter and his Georgia irregulars have not yet fully mastered their jobs." After one year in office, Carter's approval rating slid below 50 percent. "He is a soothing flatterer and a sensible president," noted *The New York Times,* "but not yet a leader, or teacher, even for a quiet time." This disenchantment fed upon itself, the erosion of support causing presidential failure, which eroded still more support until the ominous summer weekend in 1979 when Carter's popularity statistics dropped even below those of Richard Nixon on the eve of resignation.

Carter's declining fortunes surely reflected his political incompetence. But he suffered as much for his personal style as he did for the policies he pursued. The very traits that had made the Georgian such an attractive candidate in 1976—images of compassion, homeyness, innocence—contradicted popular expectations of presidential authority, the decisive manipulation of power. Where Nixon personified a callous imperiousness and Ford simple bumbling, Carter, by contrast, epitomized neither boldness nor dullness, instead communicated images of hesitancy, obfuscation, ultimately of impotence. Carter's attempt to exercise compassionate power, almost by definition, could satisfy no one.

The difficulty of balancing moral justice with raw power emerged during Carter's first full day in office when, to fulfill one of his most controversial campaign pledges, the President offered "full, complete, and unconditional pardon" to the draft resisters of the Vietnam war, provided only that they had not engaged in violent crimes. (With considerably less fanfare, Carter later commuted the prison sentence of the unrepentant Watergate burglar G. Gordon Liddy.) Such gestures attempted to separate the administration from the troubles of the past. But Carter underestimated the force of memory. "It's the saddest day in American history," complained the director of the Veterans of Foreign Wars upon learning of the presidential pardon, "sadder than Watergate and Vietnam itself." "The most disgraceful thing a President has every done," protested Barry Goldwater. "If I had known this would happen," snapped one bitter veteran, "I would have gone to Canada, too, and hung out." A Harris survey found that public opinion opposed the reprieve, and the Senate nearly passed a resolution criticizing the President's action. "I don't intend to pardon any more people from the Vietnam era," Carter soon assured a radio audience.

Nor did the Vietnam pardon win the gratitude of the peace movement. By excluding military offenders—deserters and veterans with less-than-honorable discharges—the President ignored a far larger group of war resisters which was also, according to the American Civil Liberties Union, "more likely to be poor, from minority groups and less educated." Though Carter instructed the Defense Department to re-examine the status of antiwar veterans, the Pentagon established strict criteria for upgrading discharges, and Congress specifically prohibited the expediture of funds to advertise the project. When the program terminated in October 1977, only 9 percent of the eligible veterans had applied for review. By then, the President had also signed the Cranston-Thurmond bill which denied veterans' benefits to participants in the upgrading program. Carter's much publicized moralism, in perpetuating the distinction between civilian and military opposition to the Vietnam war, thus surrendered to political expediency.

The President demonstrated considerably greater compassion for intimate associates accused of crimes—but also bore unfortunate consequences for this loyalty. In 1977, budget director Lance drew congressional criticism for his loose financial practices—taking large personal overdrafts from his bank—prior to assuming federal office. Carter remained staunchly supportive of his friend, dodging reporters' questions and denying any improprieties. But public pressure forced Lance's resignation anyway and the President suffered for his unswerving faith. Lance did not win acquittal until 1980. The President showed similar tolerance for the harmful commentary of his brother, Billy, who insulted Jews and blacks with impunity. But Billy Carter's financial transactions as a lobbyist for Libya smacked of corruption and the "Billygate" scandal tarnished the administration. Carter also defended his close adviser, Hamilton Jordan, against charges of personal misconduct, snorting cocaine at New York's Club 54. Such allegations called into question the President's own standards.

The blurring of morality and power politics also affected Carter's foreign policy—and returned to plague the administration when it encountered moral values different from its own. "Our commitment to human rights must be absolute," said Carter in his inaugural speech, "but let no one confuse our idealism with weakness." While pursuing détente with the Soviet Union and negotiating SALT II, the President determined to promote "human rights" within Soviet borders. Such a program contradicted the assumptions of recent diplomacy, the acceptance of big-power spheres of influence in which other powers exerted no leverage. "We must replace balance-of-power politics with world order politics," the Trilateralist had suggested in the recent campaign. Soon after taking office, Carter personally wrote to Soviet dissident Andrei Sakharov, assuring that "the American people . . . will continue our firm commitment to promote respect for human rights not only in our country but also abroad." By unexpectedly altering American policy, the administration challenged the Soviet leadership, which responded by hardening its position on SALT. "Washington's claims to teach others how to live cannot be accepted by any sovereign state," retorted President Brezhnev.

Besides delaying SALT, the human rights issue exposed obvious contradictions in United States policy. The State Department used Carter's stand to justify the cessation of military aid to repressive regimes such as Argentina and Uruguay, but for reasons of national security rationalized continuing aid to South Korea. Even worse, administration policy raised an ugly specter of revenge. Challenged by Carter's attack, the Soviet Union could not afford to retreat from its traditional suppression of dissent. "Carter painted himself into a corner," observed Harvard's Adam Ulam. Nor would the White House halt SALT negotiations in protest. "It's not worth going into another cold war," explained a Carter aide. To protest Soviet domestic conduct, the President ordered minor retaliations—the cancellation of a computer sale to Tass for use at the 1980 Olympics, the delay of a shipment of drill bits—and allowed such symbols to serve as a substitute for policy. Utterly ineffective in influencing the Soviet leadership, Carter's denunciations also made the idea of rapprochement unpalatable to the American public.

The defense of human rights soon embroiled the United States in a new type of diplomacy, the manipulation of individual lives as a way of rendering impotent the most powerful government on earth. Seeking to demonstrate his consistency of policy, Carter referred in his second press conference to atrocities committed by Uganda's Idi Amin which, said the President, "disgusted the entire civilized world." The African dictator promptly clamped travel restrictions on the two hundred Americans living in Uganda and ordered them to attend a personal meeting. Fearing reprisals, the White House briefly considered landing troops to defend American citizens. But the futility of such action persuaded the President to settle for a protest letter that denounced the taking of hostages. Scorning American hypocrisy, Amin kept the world in suspense over a long weekend, before conceding he had no evil intent.

Two weeks later, the seizure of hostages came closer to home when a small group of Hanafi Muslims occupied three buildings in Washington, D.C., holding 134 people at gunpoint to protest their persecution by Black Muslims. Sensitive to what *Newsweek* magazine called "the ghosts of Attica," the administration ordered negotiations with the invaders, finally ending the siege peacefully after three days. The result, said the President, "was a vivid proof that a slow and careful approach was the effective way."

Such takeovers, spawned in terrorist politics, reached epidemic proportions in the late seventies. In New York, an American Nazi held an entire factory at bay; in Indianapolis, an angry debtor wired a shotgun to the head of his mortgage holder for sixty-two hours. One gunman in Cleveland refused to surrender until he had talked to President Carter. "Taking hostages is a very creative act," explained an experienced police psychiatrist. "It gives you real power." In such situations, federal authorities recommended continued negotiations. "Society should aim to outwit the terrorist," advised a government manual, "rather than to outfight him." But indulging terrorism lent credibility to the tactic. Commenting on Carter's "dealing *viva voce* with hostage-holders," the recently paroled Watergate conspirator E. Howard Hunt expressed an ominous thought: "I'll bet he hasn't answered the telephone for the last time."

Carter's confidence in the power of moral persuasion miscalculated the strength of entrenched interests to resist presidential appeals, an error that soon devastated the administration's attempt to settle what it considered the most pressing domestic issue of the age: the energy crisis. The terrible winter of 1977 underscored the problem. As record snowfalls and subzero temperatures forced the closing of schools and factories, causing layoffs for an estimated 1.6 million workers, a grim President told the nation to "face the fact that the energy shortage is permanent." "Live thriftily," he advised, "and remember the importance of helping our neighbors."

These moral homilies served as the centerpiece of the President's much-awaited energy program, unveiled in a series of televised speeches in April 1977. Comparing the crisis to moral warfare, Carter reiterated the importance of old-fashioned frugality: energy conservation. "It is the cheapest, most practical way to meet our energy needs," he told a joint session of Congress, "and to reduce our dependence on foreign oil." To stimulate conservation, the President proposed a tax package to penalize energy waste and to encourage greater efficiency. The program offered few alternatives to the continued reliance on imported oil (which by 1977 amounted to half the nation's energy supply), suggesting small tax credits for the installation of solar devices and describing nuclear power "as a last resort." Opposing the development of breeder reactors, Carter insisted that "effective conservation efforts can minimize the shift toward nuclear power."

The President's emphasis on reduced energy consumption immediately challenged entrenched corporate interests. "This country did not conserve its way to greatness," protested a defender of the Texas gas industry. "It produced itself to greatness." Carter's plan to raise consumer prices through taxation rather than deregulation threatened corporate profits; "a windfall loss," complained an economist at Standard Oil. "Our problem isn't a shortage of oil," stated Ronald Reagan, "it's a surplus of government." The wrath of the business community descended quickly on Congress, which rallied to protect its diverse constituents. "It's like it was the day after Pearl Harbor," suggested Representative Morris Udall, "and you interviewed the Congressman from Detroit and he said, 'The Japanese attack was outrageous, but before we rush into war, let's see how it would affect the [auto] industry,' and then somebody else said, 'It was dastardly, but consider the effect on oil,' and another Congressman said, 'War could be very serious for recreation and tourism.'" Such pressures rapidly transformed Carter's clarion call for the "moral equivalent of war" into its acronym, MEOW, a pussycat proposal that could not slide through the legislature.

Though the President obtained approval for a Department of Energy to coordinate government policy, the remainder of his program collapsed in shambles. Unable to rally public opinion ("I don't feel much like talking about energy and foreign policy," an unemployed steelworker told him at an "Energy Round Table." "I am concerned about how I am going to live."), the President watched helplessly while the Senate dismantled the energy tax program and even overcame a two-week filibuster to endorse the deregulation of natural gas. "The moral equivalent of the Vietnam war," exclaimed a White House aide. When the President took his crusade for conservation to yet another television audience, *The Boston Globe* extended that metaphor further, calling the speech "the moral equivalent of Sominex."

Having failed in 1977, the President renewed his battle for an energy program the next year. "Further delay will only lead to more harsh and painful solutions," he warned. But the absence of fuel shortages—indeed, the existence of surpluses on the West Coast—encouraged consumers to burn ever larger quantities of imported oil. "I don't see the inevitability of a crunch," assured a petroleum industry spokesman. "The possibility is there but it's not a crisis." On the anniversary of his first energy speech, Carter conceded the importance of stimulating new oil production and recommended the decontrol of prices paired with a windfall profits tax to allow rebates for the poor. But Congress rebuffed the proposal. Nor did alternative technologies attract political support. "To think of alternative energy sources," observed economist Lester Thurow, "is to think of vigorous well-organized opponents." On May 3, 1978, advocates of solar power sponsored a Sun Day, reminiscent of the environmentalists' Earth Day of 1970, but won no inroads in government policy. Nuclear power remained economically suspect. "It's time for it to compete," said a Carter official in rejecting additional government subsidies. "It's been too much a pampered child of the federal government."

The National Energy Act, finally passed in November 1978, bore scant resemblance to Carter's initial program, leaving the nation ill-prepared for an impending crisis of resources. "I have not given up on my original proposal that there should be some constraint on consumption," said Carter in signing the bill, "and thus on oil imports." Within two months, news from the Middle East reinforced that advice. The eruption of civil war in Iran against the rule of the Shah sharply curtailed oil production, and the OPEC nations took the opportunity to announce a 14.5 percent increase in oil prices. "Market conditions do not warrant a price increase of this magnitude," protested the White House. But the administration did little more than plead for reconsideration. To the American people, the President urged that they "honor the 55-m.p.h. speed limit, set thermostats no higher than 65 degrees and limit discretionary driving."

While the public calmly accommodated these inconveniences, the problem of energy resources suddenly escalated beyond the bounds of ordinary imagination. "The world has never known a day quite like today," announced Walter Cronkite on March 30, 1979. "It faced the considerable uncertainties and dangers of the worst nuclear power plant accident of the atomic age. And the horror tonight is that it could get much worse." Two days earlier, a stuck valve at the nuclear power facility at Three Mile Island, Pennsylvania, had overheated the reactor core, threatening to wash the countryside in a shower of deadly radiation. While technicians worked feverishly to avert a cataclysmic meltdown, one hundred thousand civilians fled their homes for safety. It took nearly two weeks to bring the errant reactor under control. "We were damn lucky," admitted a member of a special presidential commission established to investigate the calamity. "No one understood what was going on at the time, and it scares the hell out of me." The then popular film, *China Syndrome,* the story of a similar reactor failure, dramatized a growing public suspicion about nuclear power—an anxiety not just about the dangers of radioactivity, but about the failure of the industry and the regulatory agencies to tell the truth about the omnipresent risk.

Such fears sent a chill through the troubled industry. Even before the Three Mile Island calamity, the rising cost of nuclear reactors had caused cancellation of twenty planned projects. Soon afterward, eleven more were dropped and no new orders were made in 1979. The seventy-one plants remaining in operation provided about 11 percent of the nation's electrical energy, far below earlier estimates. But despite sharp criticism of the nuclear industry as well as condemnation of the safety procedures established by the Nuclear Regulatory Commission, the President's advisers recommended the continuation of nuclear power. "We cannot simply shut down our nuclear power plants," insisted Carter; they "must play an important role in our energy future."

The near disaster at Three Mile Island, by exposing the limitations of technological performance, shocked the nation into a reconsideration of the energy crisis. Taking advantage of the unsettled mood, Carter again appealed for support of his energy program. "The fundamental cause of our nation's energy crisis," he told a prime-time television audience in April 1979, "is petroleum," and he warned about overdependence on "a thin line of oil tankers stretching halfway around the earth . . . [to] one of the most unstable regions in the world." To encourage domestic production, Carter announced the gradual decontrol of oil prices beginning immediately and pleaded with Congress for a windfall profits tax to equalize the sacrifice. He also requested "standby authority" to impose a national rationing plan. At a time when gasoline cost seventy cents a gallon, pessimistic observers predicted that the President's scheme would produce an increase of twenty cents per gallon.

Despite the recent peril, however, Congress remained unimpressed. While praising the decontrol decision, most congressional leaders criticized the tax proposal. In May, the legislature handed the President a major defeat by rejecting the plan for standby rationing. "The members don't pay any attention to him," said Speaker O'Neill. "They put their heads in the sand," Carter complained. "The average motorist is going to be faced with more shortages of gasoline in the future. We ought to be ready for it, and we're not."

The crisis came sooner than expected. By May, gasoline lines in California ran as long as five hundred cars, and prices at the pump already touched one dollar per gallon. "It's sort of like sex," assured an official of Gulf Oil. "Everybody's going to get all the gasoline they need, but they're damn sure not going to get all they want." Then, in June, OPEC announced a gigantic 50 percent hike in oil prices. The news created panic conditions. Despite odd-even rationing schemes, tempers steamed easily, causing fistfights, stabbings, and shootings, and in Levittown, Pennsylvania, the cradle of suburbia, gasoline shortages provoked a full-scale riot. To make matters worse, the nation's independent truckers staged a wildcat strike to protest rising diesel costs, idling 60 percent of the long-haul interstate traffic. "When the President and all them senators can't get no steak," said a striker, "then they'll do something."

"The future of the Democratic Party is tied to energy," Carter had recently advised congressional leaders. "It could cost us control of the Senate and White House. It could be the issue that puts the Democrats out of power for a very long time." Cutting short a vacation, the President retreated to his Camp David hideaway to prepare another address on the energy crisis. But the speech never came. As his popularity ratings cascaded to all-time lows, Carter recognized the futility of moral appeal. "If I give this speech," he told an aide, "they'll kill me." Canceling the broadcast, the President summoned teams of consultants to Camp David to discuss the sorry state of the nation. Mayors, governors, congressmen, academics, and private citizens—135 in all—spoke candidly, while the President and his wife Rosalynn took notes. After a week of suspense, Carter returned from the mountain.

"All the legislation in the world can't fix what's wrong with America," a solemn President addressed the nation. "It is a crisis of confidence. It is a crisis that strikes at the very heart and soul and spirit of our nation . . . and [it] is threatening to destroy the social and political fabric of America." Stressing the decline of traditional values—"hard work, strong families, close-knit communities and our faith in God"— Carter lamented the growing loss of assurance about the American future. "Looking for a way out of this crisis, our people have turned to the federal government and found it isolated from the mainstream of our nation's life; Washington, D.C., has become an island. . . . This is not a message of happiness or reassurance," he concluded. "But it is the truth. And it is a warning."

The struggle for renewal, Carter suggested, should begin "on the battlefield of energy." For the third time in his administration, the President revealed a major energy package, promising to "win for our nation a new confidence—and . . . seize control of our common destiny." First, he ordered a freeze on the amount of oil imported from abroad and recommended additional cutbacks during the next decade. Second, he proposed the formation of an $88 billion government-funded corporation to produce synthetic fuel from coal and shale. Third, he suggested the creation of an "energy mobilization" committee to cut through bureaucratic red tape. "We will protect our environment," he pledged. "But when this nation critically needs a refinery or pipeline, we will build it."

Carter's dramatic appeal struck close to the national conscience, rapidly improving his political prospects. But just as quickly, the President destroyed his advantage. Two days after promising to restore a sense of national unity, the White House announced that the entire cabinet had offered to resign and that Carter had accepted the departure of five top administrators, producing a major reorganization of the executive branch. The upheaval shocked public opinion and renewed fears that the government had drifted out of control. By the end of July, surveys showed Carter's approval ratings at a dismal 25 percent—exactly the nadir on the eve of the Camp David meetings.

Emboldened by the administration's self-defeating maneuvers, Congress delayed enactment of the President's plan, carefully cultivating exemptions to the windfall profits tax. Not until the spring of 1980, after nearly a year of oil decontrol, did the legislature approve a modified profits tax, which brought substantially lower funds for the government. Congress also authorized stricter safety rules for nuclear power, ordering reactors kept away from population centers and establishing stringent penalties for violations. To encourage production, Congress established the U.S. Synthetic Fuels Corporation, provided a solar-energy bank, and authorized funding for an alcohol fuel program and for a Strategic Petroleum Reserve. "If OPEC tries to blackmail us," explained Majority Leader Wright, "we'll have a spare tire."

By the time Congress enacted an energy program, however, the issue of resources had been subsumed by its larger consequences—an economy on the brink of collapse. The deterioration of the American economy under Carter reflected as much the failures of presidential policy as it did persistent and fundamental structural problems that no administration could meet. Basic to these difficulties was the question of faith— the impact of future expectations as a driving force for inflation and as a drag on corporate investment. Having inherited an inflation rate below 5 percent, Carter saw the figure increase to 6 percent in 1977, 9 percent in 1978, and 13.3 percent in 1979, while official unemployment statistics fell slightly from 7.4 percent to about 6 percent. Worse, the rate of productivity of United States business steadily declined, running at −.9 percent in 1979.

Upon taking office, Carter expected to speed recovery from the recession of 1974–75 by cutting taxes and increasing government spending. But his refusal to fund public works projects antagonized organized labor, and conservatives criticized the growing deficit. "The increase in the federal budget is stirring up new fears," warned Arthur Burns, "new expectations of inflation that to some degree may be a self-fulfilling prophecy." As unemployment continued to drop, however, and the severe cold boosted prices, the administration decided to scrap a promised tax rebate. Opting for fiscal restraint, Lance predicted "no new programs if we are going to . . . get a balanced budget by 1981." Retorted Senator Hubert Humphrey, "There is *no* way to balance the budget by 1981."

Even if Carter had managed, as he promised in April 1977, "to discipline the growth of government spending," the rate of inflation would have continued to increase. Cost-of-living escalators, built into labor and business contracts as a hedge against inflation, had developed a self-generating momentum, one increase automatically stimulating the next. A lag of investment in the modernization of facilities—partly because of preferred opportunities abroad and partly because of fear of inflation—contributed to a decline of productivity. "We already have so much capacity," explained Stanford economist Ezra Solomon, "it's much easier to buy a company ready-made than to add capacity." Such trends weakened American competition with foreign manufacturers, causing a decline of such basic industries as steel and automobiles. These losses, combined with a growing reliance on imported oil, produced unprecedented deficits in the balance of trade, reaching $28 billion in 1979. The result was a rapid depreciation of the dollar overseas, which returned in the form of further inflated prices for imported goods such as OPEC oil. Finally, the rising cost of energy added across-the-board increases throughout the economy.

By the late seventies, these economic trends were threatening the survival of the nation's tenth largest business, the Chrysler Corporation. After losing $205 million in 1978 and over $700 million in the first three quarters of 1979, the third largest automobile manufacturer appealed to the federal government for a billion-dollar tax credit to remain solvent. The misfortunes of Chrysler closely mirrored the general predicament of American capitalism. Slow to convert to small-car manufacturing, Chrysler chose not to build its own factory and instead contracted with Volkswagen to import four-cylinder engines. These arrangements severely limited Chrysler's productivity, especially when the small-car Dodge Omni and Plymouth Horizon became the corporation's best-sellers. Yet even these vehicles suffered from basic deficiencies—the only American cars ever rated "Not Acceptable" by Consumers Union. With a shrinking share of the automobile market, Chrysler sold its European holdings to foreign manufacturers and reduced its facilities at home.

Chrysler's appeal for public assistance ignited an angry debate about the limits of government responsibility for the economy. "You just can't have a free-enterprise system without failures," asserted Senator Proxmire. "Are we going to guarantee businessmen against their own incompetence by eliminating any incentive for avoiding the specter of bankruptcy?" But the collapse of Chrysler, warned its president Lee Iacocca, "would have a falling-dominoes effect" in the economy. "The people who made the bad decisions at Chrysler are no longer there," argued Michigan Representative James Blanchard. "No one should hold half a million workers responsible for the decisions of a few officials long since gone." After forcing Chrysler to make significant economic concessions, including renegotiation of its contract with the United Auto Workers, Congress finally approved a $1.5 billion loan guarantee in 1979.

The structural problems of the American economy were intensified by new government legislation—agricultural price supports, increases in the minimum wages, benefits for the steel industry, and higher social security payroll taxes. Together with rising food and fuel costs and a depreciated dollar, such expenditures sparked a new inflationary spiral in 1978. "You can't figure your real return, so you postpone investments," Treasury Secretary Blumenthal explained. "Your costs rise, your real profits shrink, your stock values go down; it costs more to borrow. It goes on and on." A May 1978 Gallup poll showed that a majority of Americans saw inflation as the nation's most serious problem. Yet the administration hesitated to act, pleading simply for voluntary restraint.

The relentless inflation, however, together with the trade deficit, imperiled the stability of the dollar in international markets, moving the economy closer to a crisis situation. At an economic summit conference in Bonn and in a subsequent meeting of the World Bank in Washington, the President pledged "my own word of honor" to fight inflation. "I do not have all the answers," Carter told a television audience in October. "Nobody does." But he proposed a program of voluntary guidelines, calling for 7 percent limits on wage gains and 6.5 percent rises in prices. "We must face a time of national austerity," he urged. "Hard choices are necessary if we want to avoid consequences that are even worse." But, commented *The Wall Street Journal,* "few believed that the Carter plan would win the battle."

The lack of confidence in the Carter remedy precipitated another run on the dollar, further toppling its value. To halt this erosion, the administration intervened boldly, raising the discount rate a full percentage point, tightening credit, purchasing dollars abroad, and accelerating the sale of gold. But the policy aroused new fears of a recession. "Using high interest rates to psychologically support the dollar and try to fight inflation is part of the old-time conservative religion," protested consumer advocate Roger Hickey. "Millions of Americans will be sacrificial lambs in the anti-inflation war."

The sudden announcement of a major boost in OPEC prices—they would soar sixty percent in 1979—quickly undermined the credibility of Carter's economic program. "Sometimes a party must sail against the wind," declared Senator Kennedy in protesting the administration's commitment to balance the budget. "The party that tore itself apart over Vietnam in the 1960s cannot afford to tear itself apart today over budget cuts in basic social programs." As the inflation rate soared to 13 percent in January 1979, labor leader George Meany called for "equality of sacrifice, not the sacrifice of equality." Ignoring the President's plea for wage restraints, the Teamsters and United Airlines workers went on strike while an AFL-CIO local in Washington won a lawsuit that denied the legality of the administration's voluntary guidelines. Lacking effective controls, the White House encouraged the Federal Reserve system to raise interest rates to a record-breaking 15 percent in 1979, virtually assuring a recession in the coming election year. "There are no economic miracles waiting to be performed," conceded Carter in his 1980 economic report to Congress.

The weaknesses of the American economy and mounting concern about the nation's energy resources provided the framework for the implementation of a foreign policy. Like his Republican predecessors, Trilateralist Carter placed preeminence on stabilizing American trade with other nations, particularly the "lesser developed countries" that constituted the third world. After the failure in Vietnam, however, the traditional commitment to the Open Door was now tempered by a recognition, if not a fear, of the limits of American power. Not only had the United States suffered ignominious military defeat in trying to enforce a capitalist regime in a small country, but the rejuvenated economies of Western Europe and Japan also competed more aggressively for American markets and sources of raw materials.

By the time Carter took office, the United States could no longer expect easy accommodation even in its own backyard, Latin America. Recognizing the changes in international power, the nations in this traditional American sphere of influence had charted a more independent course by seeking trade with other economic blocs, including the Soviet Union. One obstacle to better relations in the Western Hemisphere was Latin American opposition to United States interventionism. To eliminate the most obvious symbol of American aggression—United States control of the Panama Canal—Presidents Nixon and Ford had discussed a new treaty relationship with the Torrijos regime of Panama.

Carter resolved to complete these unfinished negotiations. By the summer of 1977, he announced the signing of two related treaties which provided for the gradual transfer of the canal to Panama by the year 2000. "Fairness, not force," said the President, "should lie at the heart of our dealings with the nations of the world." Yet the administration carefully protected the right of the United States to intervene to preserve the neutrality of the canal beyond 2000 and retained certain privileges in times of emergency. To avoid misunderstandings, the two nations also signed a subsequent statement distinguishing between acceptable intervention in the name of neutrality and unwanted interference "in the internal affairs of Panama."

Revelation of the treaties provoked angry debate around the nation, which showed that public opinion generally disapproved the arrangements. "The fatal flaw," warned Ronald Reagan, "is the risk they contain for our national security and for hemisphere defense. We're turning one of the world's most important waterways over to a country no one can believe." Antitreaty groups promptly launched a massive advertising campaign to block ratification. "There is *no* Panama Canal," asserted the American Conservative Union. "There is an *American* Canal in Panama. Don't let President Carter give it away." To overcome this opposition, the administration developed an elaborate public relations strategy, flooding the nation with prominent supporters, including Kissinger and Ford. "If the treaties are rejected," lobbied Carter, "Communist radicals from Cuba and other places would have rich hunting ground in Panama." Such pressure slowly shifted the balance of public opinion. "After receiving thousands of letters opposing the treaties, we were so happy to receive protreaty letters," quipped one senator, "that we framed both of them." But by the spring of 1978, the administration had persuaded the requisite two-thirds of the Senate to approve the pacts.

The ratification of the Panama treaties represented a fundamental shift in American power, heralding what Carter called "a new era" in relations with small countries. "The Panama Canal," remarked a United States diplomat, "was to our Latin policy what Vietnam was to our global policy—blood poisoning. Now that's over." When Sandinista guerrillas attacked Nicaragua dictator Anastasio Somoza in 1979, the Carter administration refused to support the doomed regime beyond offering the fallen president exile in Miami. "We're trying to carve out a moderate solution in Nicaragua," explained one government official, "that would inspire moderate opposition in El Salvador." The age of Big Stick diplomacy seemed at an end. TODAY THE PANAMA CANAL, warned a picket at Capitol Hill, TOMORROW TAIWAN.

The prophecy came sooner than expected. In a major departure from past foreign policy, Carter told a surprised nation that effective January 1, 1979, the United States extended formal diplomatic recognition to the People's Republic of China and terminated its mutual defense treaty with the regime on Taiwan. "Normalization," explained the President, "—and the expanded commercial and cultural relations that it will bring—will contribute to the well-being of our own Nation . . . , and it will also enhance the stability of Asia." Though the President promised the temporary preservation of the Taiwan government, conservatives deplored what former ambassador to Peking George Bush called "a major blow to our already declining credibility." Reagan immediately cabled regrets to Taiwan's president, while Goldwater filed suit to block "an outright abuse of presidential power." Carter could find solace, however, not only in the courts, which upheld his decision, but also in the quadrupling of American exports to China in 1978.

The importance of advancing American trade also shaped the administration's policy toward the nations of Africa. In 1978, Carter became the first President to visit black Africa, making assurances to Nigeria, the second largest supplier of crude oil to the United States, of a "departure from past aloofness." Fearful of offending this crucial ally, the White House rebuffed congressional pressure to lift economic sanctions imposed against Rhodesia for its policies of white supremacy. Carter also placed priority on economic interests by joining France and Belgium in ousting Zairian rebels from the mineral-rich province of Shaba in 1978. But the administration carefully limited United States involvement to air transportation and criticism of alleged "external intervention."

Underlying these alterations of American foreign policy, one basic assumption remained unchanged: the Soviet Union constituted a menace to world peace. Like Nixon and Ford, Carter had no illusions about the possibility of ending Soviet-American rivalry. But he did hope to stabilize the arms race and reduce the likelihood of nuclear war. As the administration reopened SALT talks in 1977, therefore, Carter made several significant gestures of good faith. To the dismay of traditional cold warriors, he canceled production of the B-1 bomber, withheld approval of the deadly neutron radiation bomb, and announced opposition to the reinstitution of the draft. (Unknown to the public and to the Soviets, Carter did approve the "Stealth" bomber as an alternative to the B-1.) "Peace will not be assured," he told the United Nations General Assembly, "until the weapons of war are finally put away."

These conciliatory postures, however, brought few Soviet concessions. Evidence of Soviet intervention in Ethiopia and Zaire infuriated the President. In a series of public addresses in the spring of 1978, Carter rekindled the cold war. "We, like our forebears," he declared in a Kennedy-like call to arms, "live in a time when those who would destroy liberty are restrained less by their respect for freedom itself than by the knowledge that those of us who cherish freedom are strong." But despite this rhetorical militance, Carter opposed suspension of SALT negotiations. "If we spend all our time jawboning against the Soviet Union," observed a White House aide, "we're going to have a real problem convincing the American people that the Russians can be trusted."

The new SALT treaty, signed by Carter in Vienna in June 1979, satisfied neither dove nor hawk. The agreement established ceilings on strategic weapons, limited qualitative improvements, and assured a basic parity of numbers between the two powers, while permitting a doubling of the number of nuclear warheads. "SALT II will not end the arms competition," the President admitted to Congress, "but it does make that competition safer and more predictable, with clear rules and verifiable limits." Protesting the continuation of the arms race, liberal senators led by McGovern vowed to vote against the treaty. But the loudest objections came from conservative quarters. "The danger is real," advised Senator Jackson, "that seven years of détente are becoming a decade of appeasement."

The domestic attack on SALT produced a remarkable change in administration policy. With the likelihood of expanded trade in China, the United States no longer needed economic détente with the Soviet Union. Carter could afford more easily to clash with the Soviets. To silence his domestic critics, therefore, and at the same time demonstrate

United States resolve to its allies, the President adopted the contradictory goals of arms limitations and greater military expenditures. He endorsed construction of advanced Trident submarines, pleaded for the mobile MX missile system, and supported the return of compulsory "national service" for men and women. The administration also resurrected the dormant Civil Defense system, calling for doubled appropriations to facilitate the evacuation of major cities. But even these proposals failed to persuade opponents of SALT. Seeking a reevaluation of "deterrence"—the idea that fear of retribution would prevent either power from launching a first attack—conservatives urged the implementation of a strategy capable of destroying Soviet missiles. Paired with a civil defense program that could protect American citizens from counterattack, such a scheme challenged the very essence of SALT, threatened to restore only a balance of terror.

The taut era before détente, symbolized by the Cuban Missile Crisis of 1962, assumed special relevance in 1979 when, in a curious replay of events seventeen years earlier, American intelligence reported the presence of a Soviet combat brigade in Cuba. Carter quickly called the situation "unacceptable" and pleaded with the Soviet Union to make some token retreat. But when the Soviets refused, the President merely assured a television audience "that the brigade issue is certainly no reason for a return to the cold war." For conservatives, the President's willingness to tolerate the presence of Soviet forces in the Western Hemisphere dramatized the decline of United States world leadership. "We stood toe-to-toe with the Soviet Union," objected Senate Minority Leader Howard Baker, "and, unlike 1962, we blinked instead of the Russians."

Carter's determination to assert American hegemony by peaceful means produced the most extraordinary diplomatic triumph of his administration—a peace treaty ending thirty years of warfare between Egypt and Israel. Taking advantage of Egyptian leader Anwar Sadat's willingness to confer directly with Israeli Prime Minister Menachem Begin, Carter invited the two leaders to a summit conference in September 1978 at Camp David. After thirteen days of intensive conversations, the three heads of state presented the world with "A Framework for Peace," heralded as the first step toward stabilizing power in the Middle East. Overnight Carter's rating in public opinion polls soared, the only significant interruption in what otherwise appeared as an endless decline.

Despite great fanfare, however, the arrangements left considerable unfinished business, not the least of which concerned the status of the Palestinian refugees and the legitimacy of the Palestine Liberation Organization. Even the staunch American ally, Saudi Arabia, the main supplier of oil to the United States, was outraged by the exclusion of Palestinian negotiators. To mollify the Saudis, Carter sent substantial military aid to North Yemen, a buffer state between Soviet-supported South Yemen and the Saudi border. Sensitive to the power of the pro-Israel lobby, however, the President refused to press for Israel's withdrawal from occupied territory. In an embarrassing showdown in the

United Nations Security Council, the United States voted to condemn Israel, but the next day apologized for the "error" and reversed its stand. Supporters of both sides were indignant.

"We have no illusions," said Carter after signing a second accord with Sadat and Begin in March 1979, "—we have hopes, dreams, prayers, yes—but no illusions." In an attempt to bridge the stalemate, UN Ambassador Young initiated secret talks with a PLO representative. But revelation of the meeting, followed by Young's disingenuous denial, raised a storm of protest, which forced the ambassador to resign; "a scapegoat for the entire muddled mess in the Middle East," protested Shirley Chisholm. Though Carter had managed to forge a solid alliance with Egypt and Israel, obtaining added leverage in that tempestuous part of the world, a general peace eluded his grasp. Having failed by mid-1979 to persuade either Egypt or Israel to meet with the PLO, a government official admitted that "the credibility of the United States is eroding."

The frustrations of American policy in the Middle East reflected an inability to understand, much less encourage, the forces of revolutionary nationalism outside the context of the cold war, a myopia that soon undermined United States interests in the Persian Gulf. Despite the rhetoric of human rights, the Carter administration preferred to overlook State Department reports of violations committed by the government of the Shah against so-called "terrorists." "Because of the great leadership of the Shah," the President toasted his ally on New Year's Eve 1977, Iran was "an island of stability in one of the more troubled areas of the world." Following the policies of Nixon and Ford, Carter allowed Iran to receive the largest quantities of American arms with sales amounting to $15 billion between 1974 and 1978. So supportive was Carter of the Shah that the administration forbade American intelligence agents to establish contact with Iranian dissidents, lest their presence imply a weakening of the regime.

The eruption of revolutionary violence in Iran in 1978 caused no shift in Carter's policies. In public statements, he reiterated support for the Shah and authorized the continuation of the sale of arms and crowd-control equipment. As a show of strength, the President ordered a task force to sail in the Persian Gulf. But three days later, he countermanded the order. "We've learned our lessons the hard way," he said, "in Vietnam." Meanwhile, the State Department tried to instigate a military coup to ensure emergence of a friendly regime, but seriously underestimated the strength of the revolution. Nor could the United States protect American citizens from the harassment of crowds. Bell Helicopter employees in Teheran began wearing T-shirts emblazoned with bullet holes; KEEP A LOW PROFILE, they read. Not until January 1979 did the administration accept the inevitability of change, persuading the Shah to surrender his peacock throne.

Carter's prolonged support of the Shah undermined the possibility of accommodation with the new regime. Quickly the United States lost access to Iranian oil and saw the cancellation of $7 billion of uncompleted arms contracts, a serious blow to the balance of payments. The

United States also surrendered sensitive listening posts used to monitor Soviet missiles, raising questions about the ability to verify the new SALT treaty. Within Iran, anti-American tempers continued to erupt. On Valentine's Day 1979, revolutionary forces in Teheran overran the United States embassy, seizing seventy employees. But other soldiers, loyal to the Ayatollah Khomeini, ended the siege after two hours. "There is no way we could get those people out by using force," admitted a White House official. "We just have to wheedle them out the best we can." Unable to protect American lives, the State Department prepared to evacuate the seven thousand Americans remaining in Iran. "This is a volatile world," concluded Senator Church, chairman of the Foreign Relations Committee. "The thing we must learn is that the U.S. can live with a great deal of change and upheaval. But the one thing we can't do is stabilize it. There's no way to put a lid on it."

While relations between the United States and Iran deteriorated, the Shah basked in exile in the Bahamas, visited frequently by associates of David Rockefeller and Henry Kissinger, who urged the administration to give the former ally refuge. "The 10,000 Iranian students in the U.S. make this a rather less safe place than other countries," explained one government official. "How would you like it," replied another in May 1979, "if the U.S. mission in Teheran were taken hostage and held in return for the Shah? It might make good copy, but it would also make for a hell of a tough decision."

Five months later, the fantasy turned to nightmare. When the President, responding to Rockefeller pressure, finally agreed to allow the Shah to enter the United States for a gall bladder operation, militants in Iran seized the American embassy, captured sixty hostages, and demanded the repatriation of the Shah and his fortune. Showing contempt for international laws that had protected diplomats even in major conflagrations, the militants threatened their captives with death, paraded them blindfolded in scenes that would reappear on American television screens for a year. "Death to Carter," chanted the angry crowds.

"My initial reaction," said Carter, "is to do something." But "none of us would want to do anything that would worsen the danger in which our fellow Americans have been placed." Frustrated by the impotence of government, citizens vented their rage by attacking Iranian students, burning Iranian flags, and boycotting Iranian products. NO MORE IRANIAN STUDENTS WILL BE PERMITTED ON THESE PREMISES, read a sign posted on the Mustang Ranch, a bordello near Reno, UNTIL THE HOSTAGES ARE RELEASED. The crisis instilled a new sense of patriotism as Americans closed ranks behind the President. According to a Gallup poll, Carter's approval ratings jumped from 30 percent to 61 percent in the four weeks after the capture of the embassy.

While the nation poised for action, the administration worked to soothe public passion. "It is a time not for rhetoric," advised Secretary Vance, "but for quiet, careful and firm diplomacy." But appeals to the United Nations, to the World Court, to American allies throughout the world, brought no relief. To eliminate economic pressure, the ad-

ministration clamped an embargo on imported Iranian oil and to prevent the removal of Iranian assets from Rockefeller's Chase Manhattan
Bank, it froze Iranian deposits. There the matter rested. "It would not
be possible, or even advisable," Carter told a press conference one week
before he announced his candidacy for reelection, "for me to set a deadline about when, or if, I would take certain action in the future."

Carter's credibility now hinged on the patience of the American
people, their willingness to accept the limits of American power. "If
one works for years at becoming a pitiful, helpless giant," observed
former Energy Secretary James Schlesinger in a paraphrase of Nixon's
plea on the eve of the Cambodia invasion, "one might just succeed.
It all goes back to the retreat and rout of American foreign policy in
recent years. Wild as he is, the Ayatollah Khomeini would not have
touched the Soviet Embassy." Harkening to Carter's cold war metaphors,
Americans recoiled from this vision of global impotence—and wondered,
too, how it all had happened.

Nicaragua: The System Overthrown

WALTER LA FEBER

Interpretations of Central America quickly become outmoded: historians' accounts must be placed against today's and tomorrow's headlines. Walter LaFeber, a leading historian of American foreign policy, poses disquieting questions about American diplomacy in Inevitable Revolutions. *United States' interests in Central America date back to the 1840's during the administration of James K. Polk. Desiring an isthmian canal and a balance in the power of Great Britain and Mexico in the region, Polk established an American presence in the area that grew enormously in the twentieth century as the power of Great Britain waned.*

The five countries of Central America have in common a scarcity of natural resources and a sharply uneven distribution of wealth, which is derived primarily from the raising of export crops such as bananas and coffee. Widespread poverty and tightly knit elites dependent on foreign investors for their wealth, LaFeber asserts, make revolution inevitable. But revolution against the status quo in Central America implies revolution against the United States, for the economic elites of those countries are closely connected to American investments and markets. Therefore, in LaFeber's analysis, the United States emerged as the great anti-revolutionary power in Central America supporting oligarchies against revolutions, both home-grown and imported.

This is not a position with which American policymakers have felt comfortable. They have sought a middle ground between dictatorship and revolution. LaFeber argues that the middle ground has not existed, except perhaps in Costa Rica, and American policy has inevitably come, in effect, to support dictators against the forces of change. In the 1970's and 1980's inflation, worldwide recession and revolutionary movements threw Central America into turmoil. In the following selection LaFeber concentrates on the problems in Nicaragua.

Revolution triumphed first in Nicaragua. With the exception of Costa Rica, no Central American nation in 1970 had seemed more safe from upheaval. Anastasio Somoza and his National Guard controlled the country. In 1969 the Guard trapped and killed five leaders of the Sandinist revolutionaries. Somoza pronounced the Sandinist Front (the FSLN) dead. The dictator, moreover, enjoyed total support from Washington. His relations with President Nixon were so close that he paid a state visit to the White House during Nixon's first term and allegedly dispatched his mother to Washington with $1,000,000 in her handbag for Nixon's reelection campaign. Nicaragua, Somoza proclaimed in

1974, did not belong to any third-world nonaligned group, but was "totally aligned with the United States and the Western world."

During the new cold war, as nationalist, third-world leaders chipped away at U.S. power, Somoza was a welcome relief: he did as he was told. He consequently did well. In 1972, Nixon performed a much appreciated symbolic act by terminating the 1916 Bryan-Chamorro treaty that had given the United States monopoly rights to build an isthmian canal in Nicaragua. More concretely, North American aid and private investment flooded into Nicaragua. Much of this money directly enriched the Somoza family and the Guard officers. Nicaragua was blessed with a highly favorable person-to-land ratio, but after the Guard officers and Somozas took what they wanted, 200,000 peasants had no land at all. (The officers and the family also monopolized the high profit industries: prostitution, gambling, construction kickbacks, taxation.) Nicaragua enjoyed the highest annual increase in agricultural production (5 percent) between 1950 and 1977 of any Central American nation. By the end of that era, however, the landless rural labor force in some areas was more than 1,000 percent larger than during the fifties.

As late as 1976 the country boasted a $46 million trade surplus, inflation dropped to 3 percent, and the gross national product grew 8 percent. But such aggregate figures had little meaning for most Nicaraguans. Within three years, Somoza and the Guard had to flee the country. One reason for their disappearance after decades of extraordinary economic growth was offered by a leading Nicaraguan banker after the revolution had triumphed: "It was an ingenious thing. For 45 years the Somoza family ran this country like their own private enterprise. The country was only a mechanism to invest abroad."

Without exception, U.S. Presidents did not care. Nixon's administration never flagged in its support. It sent bilateral aid and urged large contributions to Nicaragua from international lending agencies. A Nixon friend, Turner B. Shelton, arrived in Managua as ambassador. Shelton had been only a run-of-the-mill foreign service officer, but in his travels had come to know Bebe Rebozo, a Florida wheeler-dealer who was perhaps Nixon's closest friend, and multibillionaire Howard Hughes, who contributed to Nixon's campaign. For a brief time Hughes even found refuge in Managua when Shelton was ambassador. The new appointee did not know Spanish, but, as *Time* correspondent Bernard Diederich phrased it, he "had a special way of bowing when he clasped [Somoza's] outstretched hand." Knowing his man, the dictator soon made decisions after consulting no one in Managua but Shelton.

But the end was near. When an earthquake destroyed much of the capital and leveled many villages in 1972, Nixon sprang to the rescue, sending $32 million for reconstruction. Even so, the National Guard proved to be incapable of keeping order in the devastated areas; Shelton therefore ordered 600 U.S. troops to fly in from the Panama Canal Zone so Somoza could maintain control.

The earthquake had started a chain of events that climaxed in the success of the Sandinists. They and others watched with surprise as the National Guard, even Somoza's personal elite guard, faded into the chaos. Discipline collapsed as soldiers deserted to find their families or join in the looting. Those officers who did not loot publicly did so privately when they and the Somozas handled all the U.S. funds and medical supplies. Of the $32 million sent by Nixon, the Nicaraguan Treasury finally accounted for about $16 million. The Guard sold relief supplies for its own profit. When reconstruction began, Somoza and his fellow officers drove out other businessmen to control construction funds. Managua was never totally rebuilt, but a new city rose on the outskirts of town where Somoza's friends made a fortune in land speculation and building. The business class never forgave the dictator. As a leading U.S. businessman in Nicaragua recalled in 1979: "He robbed us blind. He was not at all interested in us, except for what we could give, and we gave him plenty. . . . Right now it is showing up in a backfire."

Somoza then made another mistake. With Shelton's help, he had swung a political deal that guaranteed him no opposition and a lifetime in power. As the 1974 election approached, his greed outpaced itself. He filed criminal charges against those who urged a boycott of the voting, then declared nine parties illegal. The Roman Catholic bishops issued a pastoral letter that denounced attempts to force people to vote, and indeed denounced the entire campaign. (Later the bishops refused to attend the inauguration.) The small liberal press, led by Pedro Joaquín Chamorro's *La Prensa,* published stories about the post-earthquake corruption and urged a boycott of the election. Chamorro was among those whom Somoza arrested and tried in the courts. Somoza won by a margin of twenty to one, leaving nothing to chance: his henchmen bribed voters with money, food, and rum. He had, however, stirred powerful enemies.

The election results meant little. They impressed only those who believed that statistics generated by voting in an authoritarian Central American country were somehow blows struck on behalf of the free world. The Church and Chamorro were actually signalling that Somoza was becoming vulnerable. Just how vulnerable became clear in late 1974 when a faction of the FSLN seized a number of Nicaraguan and foreign officials at a dinner party (Shelton had left only minutes earlier), and held them until Somoza promised to release political prisoners, pay $5 million—which he obtained without delay in New York City—and allow the thirteen guerrillas to fly out of the country. As the guerrillas traveled to the airport, crowds cheered them. Somoza retaliated by launching terrorist campaigns against areas suspected of harboring the Sandinists.

For a time, Somoza's forces scored significant victories in the field. They killed several FSLN leaders, and the movement broke into three sections: the Proletarian Tendency, which urged urban warfare; the Prolonged Popular War (PPW), which argued for mobilizing campesinos to fight a long-term conflict; and the Third-World Tendency *(Terceristas),* which was the most open and pluralistic (although it did oppose the Communist party), and advocated war in both the cities and villages. But the factionalism did not entirely benefit Somoza. The

Tercerista's pluralism and moderate rhetoric won over conservative businessmen who had given up on the regime. The *Terceristas* built a broad ideological umbrella under which all anti-Somoza forces could organize. The revolution thus gained momentum despite the Guard's victories. Anti-Somoza feeling also spread in the United States during 1975 and 1976 when priests testified before Congress about Guard atrocities. The torture included not only the usual rape and electric shocks, but more imaginative devices, such as forcing a prisoner to swallow a button on a string while a Somoza official kept tugging it up.

When Jimmy Carter became president and dedicated himself to upholding human rights, Nicaraguan Archbishop Obando y Bravo issued a pastoral letter condemning the National Guard's atrocities. The White House made no significant response. But a group on Capitol Hill led by Representative Ed Koch (Dem.-N.Y.) and Senator Edward Kennedy (Dem.-Mass.) moved to stop all military aid to Nicaragua. After a bitter fight, the so-called "Somoza lobby" defeated the move. Congressman John Murphy (Dem.-N.Y.) led the pro-Somoza forces; he had been a classmate of the dictator at LaSalle Academy and remained a close friend. Murphy received help from high-powered lobbyists, including the former legal counsel of the Republican party, William Cramer, who received at least $50,000 from Somoza. Koch and Kennedy, however, forced the Carter administration to take a stand. Human rights had to be improved or, according to congressional legislation and the president's campaign rhetoric, aid would be severed. Neither side, the State Department or Somoza, wanted a cutoff to occur.

As every president after Hoover knew, Somozas did as they were told. The National Guard eased up on its victims. Freedom of the press reappeared. From the dictator's point of view, however, requests by Carter ("that Baptist," as Somoza disgustedly called him) to deal more gently with his enemies turned out to be useless advice. The rebellion spread. A group of professional people, later known as "the twelve," publicly condemned Somoza and demanded that he resign. The growing chaos was partly due to his absence during the summer of 1977. (He had suffered a heart attack while at the villa of his mistress, Dinorah Sampson, and his doctors rushed him to Miami for treatment. Hospitals in Nicaragua were apparently little better than when his father had suddenly needed a good one in 1956.) The disorder also resulted from growing concern over a sudden decline in the economy, a decline forced by ever-higher military spending, the fleeing of capital to New York and Switzerland, and guerrilla attacks on large farms and power plants.

But the crisis soon testified to the contradictions of Carter's human rights policy. As long as the United States stressed opening up the political process and limiting Guard violence, while at the same time doing nothing to redistribute wealth or opportunity, Carter's policy was a recipe for disaster. His administration moved from the assumption that by changing political methods Somoza could weaken the revolution. The assumption had no basis in reality. Modifying the political process did little to ameliorate the economic maldistribution and built-in corruption that initially gave the revolution its life.

North American conservatives later condemned Carter's policy as a primary reason for Somoza's fall. Their condemnation had little basis in fact. The problem was that Carter and his predecessors never pushed Somoza far enough, early enough, so that either he or another Nicaraguan leader could begin to remove the socioeconomic causes of the revolution. Neither Carter nor his critics can escape that judgment by answering that the United States should have interfered only so far, or not at all, in Nicaraguan affairs: the Somoza dynasty had been a subsidiary of the United States since 1936.

Another contradiction also plagued Carter's policy. He valued human rights, but he preferred Somoza to the FSLN. Consequently when the dictator eased his repression, the United States sent in $2.5 million in arms in late 1977 (while continuing to hold back economic aid). The military supplies arrived just as the rebels launched a major offensive during "Sandinista October," as it came to be known. After months of silence, the revolutionaries demonstrated their considerable military power. On 10 January 1978, Joaquín Chamorro of *La Prensa* was murdered by pro-Somoza gunmen. The killing launched the first mass uprising against the regime, and for the first time people from the urban slums joined the rebellion. The National Guard met the uprising with renewed repression.

Carter was trapped. He wanted both to send aid and to force Somoza toward reform. The president, moreover, came under much pressure from the Somoza lobby on Capitol Hill. One member, Representative Charles Wilson (Dem.-Tex.), threatened to hold up all foreign aid appropriations until Nicaragua received its millions. Somoza bragged that he had more friends in the U.S. Congress than did Carter. State Department officials argued at length whether to send arms secretly, but finally decided to do it publicly because secrecy was impossible in Nicaraguan affairs, and any revelation could only further embarrass the Carter administration. Somoza complained loudly that Carter's human rights policy interfered in Nicaragua's internal affairs, but the dictator played the game: he gave amnesty to some political prisoners and allowed an OAS team to investigate human rights violations. The situation had grown too serious for either Carter or Somoza to stand on principle. As the *Washington Post* editorialized in early August, the central question no longer revolved around human rights violations, because the United States "is really dealing with . . . a revolution. . . . A 'second Cuba' in Central America? It is not out of the question."

As Somoza's regime tottered, a major debate broke out within the Carter inner circle. Zbigniew Brzezinski and the National Security Council began to play a more active role. An initial result of the debate was a secret letter in which Carter congratulated Somoza for improving his human rights record. The State Department's original evaluation proved true: little remained secret in U.S.-Nicaraguan relations. News of the letter leaked, probably through a State Department official. The media interpreted it as indicating Carter's strong support for the dictator's regime. But the message was not that simple. The State Department, which had fought against sending the letter, had finally succeeded in adding language that politely ordered Somoza to open up his political system.

Within a month, the importance of the human-rights debate all but disappeared. Led by Edén Pastora ("Commandante Zero" as he became known), thirteen FSLN guerrillas dramatically seized the National Legislative Palace, kidnapping nearly all of Somoza's congress and several of his relatives. Pastora extracted a string of concessions from the humiliated ruler before leaving via the Nicaraguan airport. Again, crowds lined the streets to cheer, and they were particularly enthusiastic along the airport road that passed through some of Managua's worst slums. Another general strike and urban uprising followed the incident. The FSLN army multiplied ten times to 7,000 members.

Somoza retaliated by turning the Guard loose in September 1978. It levelled parts of towns and massacred thousands of people. One survivor later testified, "I could see what they did to my Mother after they killed her—they slit her stomach open with a bayonet. They cut off the genitals of my brother-in-law and stuffed them in his mouth." Amnesty International declared that in some areas all males over fourteen years of age were murdered systematically. At this moment, the OAS human rights investigating team arrived and recorded the atrocities.

Anti-Somoza uprisings occurred spontaneously and without FSLN direction. Venezuela, Mexico, Costa Rica, and Panama sensed the kill. They moved supplies to the revolutionaries while the Costa Ricans—José Figueres and his countrymen had long memories—allowed the FSLN to establish its government-in-exile in San José. The Costa Ricans did not care for the radicalism of some FSLN leaders and programs, but understanding that the revolution had moved into its final phase, they worked to make its results as acceptable as possible. The Costa Ricans received help in this task during February 1979: the three FSLN factions merged under *Tercerista* leadership into the Government for National Reconstruction (GRN). More moderate, less doctrinaire revolutionaries gained considerable political control, but all the groups agreed on the primary objective of totally removing Somoza and the Guard.

Only the United States refused to accept the inevitable. As they have done almost automatically since Woodrow Wilson's dealings with Mexican, Chinese, and Russian revolutionaries, U.S. officials began the search once again for an acceptable (and now nonexistent) middle. For eleven months (September 1978 to July 1979), Washington teams tried to split moderates away from the FSLN coalition, and to keep Somoza—or at least the Guard—in business until the scheduled 1981 elections.

But nothing worked. No middle could be found. The United States turned to other tactics. These were described by Alfonso Robelo, probably the most important moderate and pro-North American figure in the FSLN movement:

First, the U.S. came and told everyone they would put pressure on Somoza to go. They created false expectations. When Somoza's reaction was to say, "Come and [remove me] physically," they backed down. They actually downplayed the process and at the end put little pressure on Somoza and gave him valuable time to build up his National Guard.

In early 1979 Carter tried to pressure Somoza by cutting off military and economic aid, while sharply reducing U.S. diplomatic personnel in Nicaragua. That move also turned out to be unproductive. It publicly announced that Somoza no longer enjoyed the unwavering support of the White House, but it did not reduce his military effectiveness. The United States had already trained his Guard. As North American supply lines dried up, the Israelis and Argentines sold Somoza arms and ammunition during his last months. The purchases drained more money out of Nicaragua. Facing huge debts, Somoza asked the International Monetary Fund for emergency help. As late as May 1979, two months before Somoza fled, the United States supported his request for a $66 million loan from the IMF. U.S. officials somehow hoped to prop up the Somoza regime, but not prop up Somoza.

On 29 May 1979, the FSLN troops moved out of their Costa Rican bases to launch a "final offensive." For its part Mexico conducted a diplomatic offensive by breaking relations with Somoza and then, to Washington's anger, sent missions urging other nations to follow suit. Suffering a series of military defeats, the National Guard retaliated by rocket-bombing the slums that supplied increasing numbers of FSLN fighters and killing thousands of women and children. Most of the men had already departed to fight.

U.S. officials understood this was their last opportunity. Policymaking was concentrated in the White House where Carter, Brzezinski, and CIA and Pentagon officials could overbalance the State Department's growing reluctance to support the Guard. A White House spokesman even declared the Guard had to be kept to "preserve order"; at that moment Somoza's troops were dive-bombing slums, murdering unarmed people in the streets, and looting the cities. Carter and Brzezinski reverted to tactics that had worked before: they called an emergency OAS meeting to urge an inter-American force that could move into Nicaragua, stop the fighting, and establish an acceptable regime. A propaganda campaign was launched emphasizing Cuba's role. The FSLN soon seemed to many North Americans little more than a puppet controlled by Castro and the Kremlin.

Nothing worked. The U.S. proposal for an OAS "peacekeeping force" ran into united opposition from the other states in the hemisphere. The Mexican delegation led the fight against Washington's idea. Carter suffered a humiliating defeat. For the first time since its origins in 1948, the OAS had rejected a U.S. proposal to intervene in an American state.

In seeking to replay Johnson's exercise of 1965 in the Dominican Republic, Carter discovered that the two situations were not similar. The Dominican episode had involved not a mass revolution but two army-supported factions opposing each other in a small strip of territory. Nor was U.S. influence the same as in 1965. The ghosts of past U.S. interventions could not be laid to rest; if North Americans had poor memories the Latin Americans did not. Assistant Secretary of State Viron P. Vaky accurately observed that the OAS rejection "reflected how deeply the American states were sensitized by the Dominican intervention of 1965, and how deeply they fear physical intervention."

Carter had no more luck convincing other governments that Castro pulled the strings controlling the FSLN. Cuba had supported the revolutionaries since 1961, although the extent of the support varied greatly over the years. During the final climactic months, however, at least four other Latin American nations provided more support and political guidance than did Cuba. As one revolutionary leader, Father Ernest Cardenál, observed, his colleagues did not want "any help from Cuba" because "we don't want to give the pretext" for intervention to the United States government. During the final offensive of April through June, however, Castro did send in as much as one hundred and fifty tons of munitions on planes flown by Costa Rican and Panamanian pilots. One shipment arrived the day Somoza left Nicaragua forever. Castro helped lead the cheers, but by no means called the plays.

U.S. officials did not publicly distinguish between the two functions. But then their purpose was not to be discriminating; it was to mobilize U.S. opinion with the anti-Communist rhetoric used so successfully by Truman in 1947, Dulles in 1954, and Johnson in 1965. This time Carter mobilized few except already convinced conservatives who neatly used the administration's own assessments of Castro's influence among the revolutionaries to embarrass the president politically in 1980. (If, they could claim with some logic, Cuban involvement was as deep as Carter claimed, he should have stopped at nothing to prevent a total FSLN victory.)

On 20 June 1979 most other North Americans witnessed a horror that pushed Castro out of their minds. National Guard soldiers took an ABC-TV newsman, Bill Stewart, out of his car, made him kneel in the middle of a street, and shot him through the head. Unknown to the killers, Stewart's camera crew caught every moment of the murder on film. Within hours after Stewart's death, North American television viewers saw for themselves the senseless brutality that Nicaraguans had suffered at Somoza's hands for years.

Confronted with total failure, U.S. officials scrambled to make the best possible deal with the revolutionary Government of National Reconstruction (GRN). Since late 1978, State Department official William Bowdler had led the mediation attempts. Carter now dispatched Lawrence Pezzullo to join Bowdler. Pezzullo had a decade of experience in Latin American affairs. Carter ordered him to demand Somoza's resignation then use it as bait to obtain FSLN agreement for a moderate post-Somoza regime. (At their first meeting, Pezzullo found Congressman John Murphy sitting next to the dictator as an adviser.) After some dallying, Somoza gave his resignation to the ambassador. Pezzullo and Bowdler then asked the GRN to enlarge its five-person governing junta (Sergio Ramírez, Alfonso Robelo, Violeta Barrios de Chamorro, Moises Hassan, and Daniel Ortega) to at least seven members by adding two or more "moderates." A New York Times correspondent watched the bargaining and reported from Managua that "the United States seems to be assuming its traditional role as final arbiter of Nicaragua's political destiny."

Traditions, however, were changing in Central America. The junta rejected key parts of Carter's proposal. The first U.S. demand—that no mass executions be held after the FSLN victory—caused no problems. The revolutionaries had long promised to allow no mass killings, even of the hated Guard officers, and the junta made good that promise. (Some *Somacistas* were even allowed to leave for neighboring Honduras or the United States, where they began scheming to overthrow the new government.) Nor was the U.S. Embassay or any North Americans ever threatened by revolutionary mobs. A second demand—that the junta be enlarged—was rejected. The junta argued that it already represented a broad-based group. Carter turned to Venezuela and Mexico for help. Wanting to ensure post-victory moderation, these two nations leaned on the junta to be more flexible. The revolutionaries complied by appointing an eighteen-member "Cabinet" with only one Sandinist representative; the remainder were businessmen and professionals. But the five-member junta was not enlarged.

On the third U.S. demand, that elements of a "purged" National Guard be preserved and brought into the government, no compromise was possible. Nicaraguans hated the Guard. They were appalled that Carter tried to maintain some of its power. In his Sunday message issued during the negotiations, Archbishop Obando y Bravo declared, "We lament the ambiguity of those governments who have thought or continue to think of their own political interests before the common good of the Nicaraguan people." The Guard was an empty, rotted shell. It delighted in its reputation of toughness, but its officers had grown fat and lazy from corruption. The Guard's toughness, moreover, had been proved by the murder and brutalizing of women, children, and unarmed men. That has turned out to be insufficient preparation for fighting armed, dedicated revolutionaries. Since 1979 U.S. conservatives have tried to rewrite the history of the Nicaraguan revolution's last days to make it appear that the Guard never lost—or lost because of the U.S. arms cutoff. Somoza's troops, however, had been given all the arms they should have needed; between 1975 and 1978 the United States alone provided $14 million of arms for the 8000-man Guard. As for the actual result, a foreign mercenary fighting for Somoza disgustedly described the Guard towards the end: "There was nothing gutsy about those guys. . . . They ran like rats."

As the Guard disintegrated, so did U.S. policy. Somoza finally fled on 17 July 1979. After several intermediate steps, he and his mistress (his U.S.-born wife had long since moved to London) settled in a fortress in Paraguay, a gray, stifling dictatorship that Somoza had once described as "the last place on earth for the worst people in the world." In 1980, bazooka shells shredded Somoza, his armor-plated Mercedes, and a U.S. businessman riding with him. Several suspects were arrested, but the killers were not found.

Debate meanwhile erupted in the United States, just as the 1980 presidential campaign began, over whether Carter "lost" Nicaragua. Henry Kissinger accused the president of "actively working to overthrow Somoza without having any idea [of] what to replace him [with]. . . . I think we should have been prepared simultaneously to put in in his place a moderate alternative." Kissinger's view became a common criticism. It was also an irony. Carter had worked to replace Somoza with the most "moderate alternative" possible: Somoza's National Guard. But the president could not have maintained the Guard's authority, it turned out, unless he had been willing to land U.S. troops unilaterally —no other OAS nation would join the operation—then use those troops not only to fight revolutionaries that were supported by all the major regional powers, but to put down spontaneous uprisings in Nicaraguan towns and villages. No other alternative appeared. And no knowledgeable observer, including Kissinger, suggested sending in marines in July 1979.

The United States now had to live with a revolutionary government whose authority it had fought to the end. Both sides clearly wanted to avoid repeating the disaster during the years 1959 through 1961 when U.S.-Cuban differences pushed Castro into the Soviet camp. Long before their victory, the Sandinists repeatedly declared their intention to become economically dependent on no one and to follow a "nonaligned" foreign policy. The Sandinists, however, had the misfortune to gain power just as the Soviets invaded Afghanistan, the U.S. Congress rejected the SALT–II agreements to limit the arms race with Russia, and North American conservatives gathered strength for the 1980 elections.

In this charged atmosphere few acts could be nonaligned. Within a week after taking Managua the top Sandinist leaders flew to Havana where Castro celebrated them as heroes. Nicaragua next joined the "Movement of Non-Aligned Countries" and openly criticized U.S. assistance to El Salvador's military regime. Most notably, the Sandinists supported self-determination in Afghanistan, but joined major nonaligned countries (such as India) in refusing to vote for a U.S.-sponsored UN resolution that condemned the Soviet invasion. The Nicaraguans publicly defended all of these policies. They feared the UN resolution could lead to increased U.S. involvement in Southwest Asia and perhaps create a major East-West conflict. Neither the new regime nor most other emerging nations wanted to be trapped in that kind of struggle between the giants.

Discussing the touchy issue of Salvador, the Nicaraguan Ambassador to the United Nations worried that U.S. intervention "could turn all of Central America into Vietnam" and spread "counterrevolutionary intervention" into his own country. He also argued that Cuban-Sandinist relations had always been close, and that Castro's help—especially in the health and educational areas—was critical as well as without strings. (Or at least without visible strings. Castro must have realized that by involving thousands of Cubans in the most fundamental grass-roots organizations, he had considerable influence in a new Nicaragua. He also must have wondered why North Americans did not have the same insight.) The Cuban leader had warned the Sandinists not to copy his model, but to maintain a large private business sector and retain as many ties as possible to United States funds. The Sandinists intended to follow that advice. They had excellent reasons for their foreign policy strategy: self-preservation and maintenance of maximum freedom of action. This kind of behavior, however, was not what North Americans had experienced historically with Central Americans—especially Nicaraguans.

For all their searching, the Sandinists needed immediate U.S. help on an emergency basis. The country had lost 40,000 to 50,000 people in the war (the equivalent of 4 million U.S. deaths). One-fifth of the population was homeless, 40,000 children were orphaned. Somoza and the Guard officers had plundered the economy. They left behind only a $1.5 billion debt. (Somoza personally made off with a fortune estimated at upwards of $100 million.) At the end, the dictator's Guard had turned industrial plants into rubble. The country was little more than a ruin.

The United States responded in mid–1979 by sending in nearly $20 million in aid. North American businessmen reentered the country to be welcomed by the revolutionaries. When radical union organizers tried to foment a strike against Coca-Cola and other U.S. companies, Commander Daniel Ortega, emerging as the junta's strongman, expelled the organizers from the country. United Brands and Standard Fruit resumed operations. As it had promised, the junta did create a huge public sector simply by nationalizing Somoza's former properties. The banks (looted by the dictator) were also nationalized and turned over to respected bankers to operate. Nationalization went no farther. One experienced U.S. businessman in Nicaragua told a congressional committee that the Sandinist "economic team" was of high quality: "Communists are not in control, and unless we democratic and private types concede the issue by default, the chances are against Communism in Nicaragua."

Ambassador Pezzullo had no illusions after bargaining with the junta. He told Congress much the same:

It is very much a Nicaraguan phenomenon. There is no question about that. Sandinismo, whatever its opportunities ought to be, is a Nicaraguan, home-grown movement. Sandino predates Castro. He was a man, he lived. So there is no reason to believe they are going out and borrow from elsewhere when they really have something at home. The nature of this thing is such that you have to see it take its own form, rather than make prejudgments about it.

The autumn of 1979 was the high-water mark of U.S.-Sandinist relations. Decline quickly set in. The Sandinists gave the relationship a severe jolt when they delayed long-promised national elections. From Washington's point of view, the delay meant that the revolutionaries intended to impose a Communist-style regime. From the Nicaraguan perspective, however, the announcement meant that the Sandinists were splitting into factions; any election campaign could turn into a struggle that would fragment and even destroy the revolution. That possibility could not be risked. In mid–1980, Defense Minister Humberto Ortega formally announced that elections would not be held until 1985. Another such jolt and good relations could be impossible.

Important U.S. congressional leaders had already reached that conclusion. In September 1979 Carter asked Congress for an $80 million aid package for Central America, $75 million of which was to go to Nicaragua. Nearly one-third of the amount was for the U.S. training of Sandinist soldiers. The State Department declared that prompt approval would be an "important symbol" to show that the United States could respond positively to revolutionary change in Latin America. But Carter had lost most of his influence over Congress. The legislature itself was burdened by too little discipline and too many old-style Somoza lobbyists. Congress did not debate the request until January 1980. The House then added sixteen conditions, including one that required 60 percent of the aid to go to the private business sector, another insisting that no funds could go to projects using Cuban personnel (that provision effectively cut out aid to health and educational facilities), and yet another making aid conditional on the Sandinists following high human rights standards and holding elections in a "reasonable period of time." The Nicaraguans bridled at these conditions (20,000 marched in one anti-Yankee protest), but the junta realized that more was at stake than $75 million: unless the measure passed to indicate Washington's confidence in the regime, international banks would be reluctant to make loans. The Nicaraguans consequently continued to ask for the money, even after the House added another clause requiring some of the money to be used for propaganda that told the recipients how much the United States was helping them. By March, the House and Senate had still not reached agreement. The Sandinists were desperate. Their Treasury was virtually empty, and the spiraling oil prices created a new economic crisis.

Then Nicaragua opened expanded diplomatic relations with the Soviet Union. A series of trade agreements with the Soviet bloc followed. Amounting to $100 million in value, they provided help in agriculture, power generating, transportation, and communications. This shock was not the last. The Sandinist government (and others, including Mexico), channeled aid to revolutionaries who stepped up campaigns in El Salvador. The Nicaraguans meanwhile began building their own army and tightening internal controls. They feared, justifiably, that Somoza's forces were preparing a counterrevolution. Finally, the two leading moderates, Violeta Chamorro and Alfonso Robelo, resigned from the junta in May 1980. For them, the government had moved too far to the left. At the same time they also urged U.S. non-interference, and Robelo particularly defended his country's nonaligned foreign policy. The two wanted the arguments kept within the revolutionary regime. Two of the most respected members of the Managua establishment —Rafael Cordova Rivas of the Supreme Court, and Arturo Cruz, head of the Central Bank—joined the junta.

Lines hardened while Congress dawdled, but it finally passed the aid measure in June 1980, eight months after Carter had submitted it.

The reasons for the final passage after the traumas of the spring are varied: a desire to maintain leverage on the Sandinists, an attempt to counter the Soviet-bloc aid, the fear that without such help the Sandinists—as had Castro in 1960 and 1961—would move sharply to the left.

But another critical reason was the desire by 120 of the largest North American, European, and Japanese banks to avoid a Nicaraguan default on the country's $1.5 billion debt. After long, tough negotiations (at one point the largest creditor, Citibank of New York City, tried to push for debt-service payments that would hand over to the bankers nearly one-third of the country's entire export revenue in 1980), a deal was struck in September 1980. The junta agreed to reschedule nearly $600 million of debt—piled up by Somoza, not the revolutionaries—for payment over the next twelve years. Assuming the debt meant assuming also an austerity program to pay it off, the traditional year-end bonuses for workers, for example, had to be sharply cut in 1980. But the Nicaraguans had few alternatives. If they were to stay out of the Soviet bloc they had little choice but to tie themselves to the international bankers and lending agencies. Nicaraguan bankers wanted the United States government involved. They lobbied hard in Congress for the $75 million aid package during the spring. Once these steps were taken, a third would follow: the Nicaraguans could obtain over $200 million in long-term loans from the IADB, World Bank, and other lending agencies. The importance of this series of deals, all interrelated, could not be overestimated. As former Assistant Secretary of State Viron Vaky observed, the debt arrangements with the banks "locked Nicaragua into the private money market, and Nicaragua's willingness to do so was a significant move toward a pragmatic, pluralistic course."

Yet no sooner were these deals completed than the United States and Nicaraguan governments resumed their collision course. Mistrust increased. Nicaragua's economy deteriorated despite the agreement with the bankers. Disillusion spread within the country. After Reagan's victory in November, the Sandinists tightened their control. They prohibited opposition political rallies and increased censorship. The junta arrested members of the private sector for allegedly plotting to overthrow the government, and one private sector leader was killed by Sandinist troops who claimed they caught him running guns.

Both sides, Nicaraguan and North American, had vowed to learn from history, not be trapped by it. But half a century of U.S. intimacy with Somoza held sway; neither could avoid the path taken by U.S.-Cuban relations between 1959 and 1961. The North American system was unable to tolerate revolutionaries. And vice versa. . . .

The rewriting of history was of special importance. After the experiences of Vietnam, many North Americans were reluctant to become involved in another indigenous revolution. The new administration and its supporters tried to circumvent that problem by declaring, in the president's words, that the Vietnam conflict was "a noble cause," and—more important—the problems in Central America were not indigenous but caused by Castro and the Soviet Union.

Within a month after taking office, Secretary of State Alexander

Haig warned NATO delegates that "a well-orchestrated Communist campaign designed to transform the Salvadoran crisis from the internal conflict to an increasingly internationalized confrontation is underway." In mid-March, a "senior official"—obviously Haig—declared the revolutions were part of "a global problem," so "we have to talk to the Russians about them." The mistakes in Vietnam would not be repeated; instead of trying to resolve the problem within only Central America, the administration intended to "go to the source" of the problem. The phrase meant a possible attack on Cuba, since Castro's regime, in the words of Assistant Secretary of State for Inter-American Affairs Thomas Enders, "is a Soviet surrogate."

Reagan then raised tensions with Cuba to the highest pitch since the 1962 missile crisis. Some officials demurred. The top U.S. official in Havana, Wayne Smith, told the State Department that Castro's aid to the revolutionaries had been greatly overestimated, and that the Cuban leader wanted to negotiate with—not confront—the United States. Enders nevertheless repeatedly accused Castro of uniting revolutionary factions together so, as they had in Nicaragua, the rebels could establish "more Marxist-Leninist regimes in this hemisphere." At best this was a partial truth. Not Castro, but the Church and professional groups had been most critical in creating a united front against Somoza in 1978 and 1979. But that interpretation threatened the administration's simpler views about Central American revolutionaries. Enders was correct in claiming that Cuban arms helped the Sandinists. He neglected to add, however, that they received more weapons from other sources, including Venezuela and the U.S. Mafia. . . .

The Reagan administration moved quickly to weaken the Sandinists' hold on power. The 1980 election results in the United States made little difference in this regard; a high Nicaraguan official declared privately that if Carter had remained in office, "we would still be at loggerheads." The problem was historical and ideological, not personal or partisan. Reagan only turned the screws more rapidly and tightly. By late February 1981 economic aid was turned off. In the summer Washington officials accused the Sandinists of moving close to the Soviet bloc. By the end of the year the president endorsed a CIA plan that aimed at destabilizing the Nicaraguan government. He also accepted a Pentagon program for rapidly building up Honduran forces. Those troops, aided by more than 100 U.S. military advisers and as many as 5,000 ex-Somoza supporters, were poised to wage war against the Sandinists.

Two particular issues pushed Reagan's policy so far so fast. One was Sandinist military aid to the Salvadoran revolutionaries. The other was the Nicaraguan regime's tightening of internal controls that drove out private business and threatened to turn the country into a consolidated socialist state. In 1981 the two issues were closely related. Broken by the Somozas' forty-year-long robbery, tied by terms negotiated with the international bankers in 1979 and 1980, and saddled with an economy devastated by the civil war, the Nicaraguans needed U.S. economic help above all else. Only the United States could provide the three million dollars a day that one top Nicaraguan official estimated his country needed to survive. Only U.S. approval could open doors to international lending agencies or encourage other nations to help. "We need 10 years to regain the 1977 gross national product," the Nicaraguan official declared. Without Washington's aid the Sandinists would not accomplish even that goal.

Holding the high cards, U.S. officials demanded in late January 1981 that Nicaragua stop helping their "revolutionary brothers" in El Salvador and pull back from a growing relationship with Cuba and the Soviet bloc. Haig announced he was stopping $15 million of economic aid headed for Managua, as well as nearly $10 million of wheat, for thirty days to test whether the Sandinists would stop helping the Salvadoran rebels. Bread lines appeared in Nicaraguan cities. One of Reagan's National Security Council officials warned a Nicaraguan, "The question is not whether U.S.-Nicaraguan relations are good or bad, but whether there will be any relations at all."

In early April the State Department announced good news: the Nicaraguan "response has been positive. We have no hard evidence of arms movements through Nicaragua during the past few weeks, and propaganda and some other support activities have been curtailed." But then came the non sequitur: because "some arms traffic may [sic] be continuing and other support very probably continues," aid would be cancelled anyway. The announcement was illogical. Politically, however, it made sense because it appeased the extreme right-wing of the Republican party led by powerful Senator Jesse Helms of North Carolina. Helms, who chaired the Foreign Relations Subcommittee on Latin America, had demanded an end to the assistance. Diplomatically, moreover, it demonstrated to the administration's satisfaction a toughness that failed to appear in the confusion and failure that marked Reagan's foreign policy elsewhere, including El Salvador.

With its economic leverage gone, the United States could no longer use it to discipline the Sandinists as they reopened the arms flow to El Salvador and employed Communist-bloc equipment and advisers to build a 25,000–man army (the largest in Central America) and a 30,000–strong militia. The Sandinists wanted to develop a 50,000–man force if they could find the resources. They did find help behind the iron curtain, and obtained tanks, helicopters, heavy artillery, and surface-to-air missiles. They also sent seventy men to Bulgaria for jet training. ("Yes, they are there," a high Nicaraguan official admitted privately, "but don't worry. They are flunking the course." His North American listeners were not amused.)

But if the United States had lost some leverage, the Sandinists had lost most of their alternatives for development. As a member of their three-man governing junta, Sergio Ramírez Mercado, noted in early 1982, "We know that we cannot produce the profound social gains we want if we are in confrontation with the United States." To accomplish such gains, the Sandinists believed they had to dismantle the system inherited from Somoza. They intended to develop light industry and agriculture for internal consumption as well as export. Sandinists planned to rebuild by controlling capital movement, and by combining state controls with a private sector that accounted for over 60 percent of the economy. Political pluralism had to be limited. National efforts could not be spent on political struggles. North Americans, however, viewed such one-party states with alarm.

By mid–1981 all U.S. aid had stopped. The revolution moved sharply to the Left. Businessmen who criticized the government were arrested or exiled. (The regime carefully tried to maintain the appearance of balance by simultaneously jailing several Communist party members.) Cut off from U.S. money, Sandinists found help not only in Western Europe and Mexico, but in the Soviet bloc and General Qaddafi's Libya. But the aid was insufficient. The Russian promise of $166 million over five years, with perhaps more to come, hardly touched Nicaraguan needs. The Sandinists tightened up at home. Aid to the private sector dropped. Incentives for foreign investors disappeared. State controls and nationalization spread. But without U.S. aid, little seemed to help. Inflation and unemployment rose. "We have failed so far economically," a high Nicaraguan official admitted in late 1981.

Political repercussions quickly followed. The three-man junta and the nine-person directorate (which theoretically held ultimate power) divided between pragmatists who wanted to slow down use of state controls and self-styled Marxist-Leninists who pushed for rapid centralization. Officials who tried to restrain the Marxist-Leninists began to quit or were expelled from the regime. Many who left, however, continued to plead for U.S. help. Robelo, for example, warned that U.S. hostility played into the hardliners' hands. Arturo Cruz, a respected banker, revolutionary, and ambassador to Washington before he quit the Nicaraguan government, remarked as he left his home country that although he disagreed with the Sandinists, he would do all in his power to support them rather than have the regime fall because of U.S. pressure or internal opposition.

The moderates were trapped. As the Roman Catholic leaders cooled towards the revolution, unsympathetic clergy were picked out for political attack and humiliation by the Sandinists. Church leaders became more hostile and the Sandinists responded in kind. The regime cracked down on 50,000 Miskito Indians in distant provinces along the Atlantic Ocean and the Honduran border. Never hispanized, the Miskitos had historically opposed attempts by Managua to control them. They had become fertile ground for ex-Somoza supporters. Some 10,000 of the Indians moved into Honduras for refuge. As they did so, their village priests also turned against the government. A large, rebellious force had developed, and in turn the radical Sandinists urged further centralization of power and aid from the Soviet bloc to deal with that force.

Reagan's hope of slowly strangling the Managua regime appeared to be working. Caught in what one Sandinist leader called "a vicious circle," the more the government extended its control to protect itself, the more it alienated key segments of the population. Ex-Somoza henchmen and disaffected Sandinists found support among the Indians and from Salvadoran military. They also found friends in Florida and California, where the United States government allowed anti-Sandinists troops to drill, although most former Sandinists would have nothing to do with these remnants of the hated National Guard. Reagan did little to stop the old Somoza supporters. "Under the Carter and Nixon administration, what we were doing was a crime," said the leader of one private army. "With the Reagan administration no one has bothered us for ten months."

In November 1981 Reagan approved a $19 million CIA plan to undercut the Sandinist regime. In December, Haig refused to rule out a U.S. blockade of Nicaragua or the mining of harbors. Enders told the Senate that plans had been drawn up, but not yet approved, for military action against both Cuba and Nicaragua.

Reagan's advisers planned to use Honduras as a staging area for the attacks. The choice was not surprising. If Somoza's Nicaragua had been the most cooperative of all Latin American countries in supporting U.S. policies, Honduras had run a close second. The Hondurans had long been more fully controlled by North American capital than even Nicaragua. Their new professional army had been produced by U.S. advisers and training schools. As many as five thousand Somoza followers made Honduras home base. Honduras once again became what it had frequently been since its independence 150 years earlier: a launching area for attacks on neighboring regimes. Eisenhower had used Honduras for this purpose when he overthrew the Guatemalan government in 1954.

Once again, U.S. policy began to turn during the final months of the Carter administration. It nearly doubled military aid for Honduras to $5 million in 1980. Reagan again doubled military assistance, then raised it to $15 million for 1982. He also dispatched a team of Green Berets to operate along the Salvadoran border. In mid–1982 and again in early 1983 U.S. troops went through maneuvers with the Honduran army (merely to test "communications procedures," said one U.S. officer), and built a large base camp located just forty-five miles from a major Nicaraguan military station. Honduras possessed a 20,000–man army and the largest, best-equipped air force in Central America. The United States sent in even more transport planes and large helicopters to increase the army's mobility. In mid–1982 skirmishes broke out in which Nicaragua claimed forty soldiers died.

A war between Honduras and Nicaragua could involve El Salvador and Guatemala. The latter two countries could not pass up the opportunity to attack their rebels who found sanctuary in Honduran jungles or obtained help from Nicaragua. The entire region could ignite. . . .

Ronald Reagan: Cold War Certainties

ROBERT DALLEK

The administration of Ronald Reagan is unusual in American history for its ideological clarity. Other recent administrations have projected confusion and uncertainty about America's role within the world; the Reagan administration has had a distinct rationale, which Robert Dallek calls "anti-Sovietism." Other politicians and thinkers have struggled over the past generation to analyze changes in the world diplomatic order; Ronald Reagan believes that the patterns of the world have changed little since the years after World War II. The Soviet Union remains an "evil empire" seeking world domination. Following the logic of this position, the administration has pressed for a substantial buildup of the American military and an aggressive foreign policy almost everywhere in the world. The Carter administration was confused and vascillating and the Nixon administration unpredictable and capable of sharp shifts. President Reagan has maintained the consistency we identify with geniuses and madmen, and this distinction is the central question of American politics in the mid–1980's as Professor Dallek formulates it.

The organizing principle of Ronald Reagan's defense and foreign policies is anti-Sovietism—the need to confront and overcome the Soviet Communist danger in every part of the globe. Reagan shares the legitimate concern, expressed by all American presidents since 1945, with the threat to America and its allies from a totalitarian Soviet Union hostile to their way of life. Unlike those predecessors, however, Reagan sees almost no room for reasonable compromise with the Soviets and looks forward to the day when the West "will transcend Communism. We will not bother to denounce it," he said in a 1981 speech, "we'll dismiss it as a sad, bizarre chapter in human history whose last pages are even now being written."

What explains this anti-Soviet evangelism? Reagan's rhetoric and actions suggest that in some fundamental way it is a symbolic protest against the state of his own nation. His anti-Soviet attitude arises as much from inner conservative tensions about government authority and social change as from any realistic understanding of Soviet aims and capabilities. For Ronald Reagan, the world outside the United States is little more than an extension of the world within: the struggle to defend freedom and morality abroad is a more intense version of the battle to preserve these virtues at home. In the eyes of Reagan and other conservatives, the communism of the Soviet Union represents the end point, the logical culmination of dangerous currents—big government, atheism, and relaxed moral standards—that they see running so powerfully in America. More broadly, as former *Harper's* editor Lewis H. Lapham has written, America sees in the Soviet Union "what it most fears in itself . . . Americans portray [it] as a monolithic prison, a dull and confined place where nobody is safe and nobody is free." It is a land of stereotyped commissars and peasants, of "cruel ideologues bent on world domination" and hapless victims of a repressive government. Through these caricatures, Lapham concluded, "Americans aim at the targets of their own despotism."

Reagan's portrait of Soviet communism, unchanged since the 1950s, is of a ruthless, power-mad movement bent on the creation of a "one-world Communist state" in which individuals and the traditional Western concepts of freedom and morality count for nothing. Children growing up under Russian communism, Reagan said during his 1980 presidential campaign, are taught that a human being's "only importance is its contribution to the state—that they are wards of the state—that they exist only for that purpose, and that there is no God, they are just an accident of nature . . . This is why they have no respect for human life, for the dignity of an individual." At his first press conference in January 1981, the president made similar observations when asked if détente with the Kremlin was possible. Soviet Communist leaders had repeatedly affirmed their desire for "world revolution and a one-world Socialist or Communist state . . . Now, as long as they do that and as long as they, at the same time, have openly and publicly declared that the only morality they recognize is what will further their cause, meaning they reserve unto themselves the right to commit any crime, to lie, to cheat, in order to attain that, and that is moral, not immoral, and we operate on a different set of standards, I think when you do business with them, even at a détente, you keep that in mind."

In speeches during 1981 and 1982 he struck similar themes when discussing world affairs. Quoting Pope John Paul II, in a commencement address at Notre Dame in May 1981, Reagan denounced "economic theories that use the rhetoric of class struggle to justify injustice, that in the name of an alleged justice the neighbor is sometimes destroyed, killed, deprived of liberty or stripped of fundamental human rights." Ten days later at West Point he told the cadets that after World War II the United States had "prevented what could have been a retreat into the Dark Ages. Unfortunately, another great power in the world was marching to a different drum beat, creating a society in which everything that isn't compulsory is prohibited. The citizens of that society have little more to say about their government than a prison inmate has to say about the prison administration."

The danger to free peoples everywhere, he also emphasized, was that the Soviets aimed to export their totalitarian system to all points on the globe. He told the United Nations Special Session on Disarmament in June 1982 that the history of Soviet foreign policy since World War II was a "record of tyranny" that "included violation of the Yalta

Agreements, leading to domination of Eastern Europe, symbolized by the Berlin wall, a grim gray monument to repression . . . It includes the takeovers of Czechoslovakia, Hungary, and Afghanistan and the ruthless repression of the proud people of Poland. Soviet-sponsored guerrillas and terrorists," he added, "are at work in Central and South America, in Africa, the Middle East, in the Caribbean and in Europe, violating human rights and unnerving the world with violence. Communist atrocities in Southeast Asia, Afghanistan, and elsewhere continue to shock the free world as refugees escape to tell their horror."

Reagan's description of Soviet communism is plausible. It has been a repressive, totalitarian regime at home and has exhibited an evangelistic fervor for influence abroad, especially when its national security is involved, as in Eastern Europe, where it has established a kind of imperial empire. Other American presidents and foreign policy makers have used language similar to Reagan's to describe the Soviets, but unlike him they have recognized that Moscow is also a self-interested nation-state that is open to a certain amount of give-and-take in world affairs. Reagan has been much less willing to accept this as a fact of international politics because his depiction of the Soviet Union is less a balanced realistic view of its internal conditions and external aims than an amalgam of conservative complaints about conditions in the United States. When Reagan speaks of Soviet statism, of Communist indifference to personal freedom and the dignity of the individual, he is referring as much to conservative perceptions of recent trends in America as to the state of Russian affairs. After World War II, Reagan told an interviewer in 1980, "when the Soviet Union—when it looked as if the world might go into a thousand years of darkness—Pope Pius XII said, 'The American people have a great genius and capacity for performing great and generous deeds. Into the hands of America, God has placed an afflicted mankind.' I want to see," Reagan said, "I want to help get us back to those fiercely independent Americans, those people that can do those great deeds, and I've seen them robbed of their independence, I've seen them become more and more dependent on government because of these great social reforms." To Reagan and a certain group of middle-class, educated, suburban conservatives, there are striking similarities between a Communist Russia and a welfare-state America that they see as abandoning its traditional spirit of rugged individualism. The mission for a conservative president, Reagan believes, is to oppose both forces at the same time—to limit the size and power of government at home while repelling and, if possible, destroying, Communist power abroad.

Although the United States had faltered for a while in its response to these dangers, he described this as only "a temporary aberration. There is a spiritual revival going on in this country, a hunger on the part of the people to once again be proud of America, all that it is and all that it can be . . . The era of self-doubt is over," he announced at West Point. "We've stopped looking at our warts and rediscovered how much there is to love in this blessed land . . . Let friend and foe alike be made aware of the spirit that is sweeping across our land, because it means we will meet our responsibilities to the free world. Very much a part of this new spirit is patriotism, and with that goes a heartfelt appreciation for the sacrifices of those in uniform . . . Today, you are . . . [a] chain," he told the cadets, "holding back an evil force that would extinguish the light we've been tending for 6,000 years."

For Reagan and some lower-middle-class Christian fundamentalists, anticommunism is also a crusade to restore traditional assumptions about God, family, and country to a central place in American life. These people, Richard Hofstadter has written, "are less concerned with the battle against communism in the world theater than they are with the alleged damage it does to politics and morals at home. The cold war serves as a constant source of recriminations about our moral and material failure, but as an objective struggle in the arena of world politics it is less challenging to them than it is as a kind of spiritual wrestling match with the minions of absolute evil." The visceral, evangelistic anticommunism of these Americans is another way of demanding recognition for their values and their importance as a social group. It is a way of reasserting the conventional American verities they identify with so strongly and of boosting their self-esteem.

Those upwardly mobile, middle-class Americans who make anticommunism an extension of their fight for greater personal freedom at home also derive a sense of status from their militancy against the Soviets abroad. Indeed, both groups use the crusade against communism as a demonstration of their Americanism and their importance in preserving the nation. Superpatriotism, pride in country, pride in the flag, pride in America's men and women in uniform are central elements of this "cold war fundamentalism." An emotional patriotism has been a stock ingredient of Reagan's speeches for years. His inaugural address celebrated America's heroes and gave recognition to a fallen American soldier in World War I who cheerfully made the supreme sacrifice for his country. This nationalism is also meant to compel a revival of respect for America overseas, a renewed deference to the United States by friends and foes. For its staunchest advocates, the aim of this resurgent nationalism is to assure that other nations will no longer defy or ignore America or, perhaps more to the point, ignore them. The deference these superpatriots demand from other countries differs little from what they ask of their fellow citizens at home.

Reagan's national security and foreign policy advisers all share these attitudes toward Soviet communism in one degree or another. Secretary of Defense Caspar Weinberger, a conservative corporate attorney with a Harvard law degree and strong credentials as a budget cutter of domestic spending, and an advocate of less government, came to the Defense Department after serving as Reagan's finance director in Sacramento and as President Nixon's director of the Office of Management and Budget and as secretary of health, education, and welfare. His efforts in these two positions to limit federal spending on social programs, even using the legally questionable method of impounding of federal funds, won him the nickname "Cap the Knife." Yet as secretary of defense, Weinberger has turned one hundred eighty degrees on spending and has been an unbending supporter of a huge arms buildup to combat Soviet power. Ronald Brownstein and Nina Easton, the authors of *Reagan's Ruling Class,* point out that despite massive budget deficits, Weinberger has "defended nearly every tank, missile, and machine gun, every . . . weapon system that has come across his desk. On arms control, on Poland, on trade with the Soviets, Weinberger has taken a harder line than even the most . . . [extreme] hawks in the Administration." In the view of one former admiral, he is "one of the few genuine anti-communist cold warriors in Washington." His anti-Soviet rhetoric, *Time* magazine has pointed out, is at least as bellicose as that of other leading hawks in the administration. "He strongly believes détente has worked to the strategic advantage of the USSR. As he told the NATO ministers: 'If the movement from the cold war to détente is progress, . . . we cannot afford much more progress.' " He comes across like "a Roman proconsul," a West German newspaper complained.

Others in the Reagan defense establishment echo Weinberger's anti-Soviet views. Deputy Secretary of Defense Frank Carlucci, an ex-foreign service officer and former deputy director of the Central Intelligence Agency, is said to have been involved in coups d'état and assassination plots in Third World countries. Though none of these charges has ever been "irrefutably proven," Carlucci prides himself on his anticommunism and freely tells of being accused of plotting "the assassination of Patrice Lumumba in the Congo, the overthrow of Allende in Chile and Abeid Karume in Zanzibar and of Goulart in Brazil." He shares Weinberger's belief, which is disputed by many, that the United States has fallen behind the Soviet Union in "nuclear-war-fighting capability" and must now develop the same capacity to fight and win a nuclear war. Similarly, Fred Ikle, under secretary of defense for policy, depicts the United States as militarily inferior to the Soviet Union, which is as determined as ever "to expand the Communist empire." Ikle is an outspoken exponent of an arms buildup which will close America's military "window of vulnerability" and prevent the ultimate subjugation of the West by Soviet power. However, he opposes the proliferation of nuclear weapons and the deterrence theory known as Mutual Assured Destruction (MAD); according to this theory the U.S. nuclear arsenal should be able to absorb a first strike and answer with a massive assault on the enemy's population. Other leading figures in the Defense Department, like Secretary of the Navy John Lehman and Assistant Secretary for International Security Policy Richard Perle, share an apocalyptic vision of the Soviet danger, which they consider little different from the threat posed by Nazi Germany. Like the Nazis, the Soviets have built up their military power and are ready to use it. They are prepared to fight, survive, and win an all-out nuclear war.

Reagan's State Department does not trail far behind his defense officials in taking a hard anticommunist line. Although considered moderates in the Reagan administration, former Secretary of State Alexander Haig and his successor George Shultz are vigorous advocates of standing up to the Soviets. As a prominent member of Henry Kissinger's National Security Council and as Nixon's White House chief of staff, Haig was identified with détente and was attacked by the radical Right as a compromiser who was willing to reach agreements with the USSR. But any rational estimate of Haig's record suggests that he was an appropriate head of the State Department in the conservative Reagan administration. A former general and commander of NATO, a veteran of the Pentagon bureaucracy and Washington's political wars, a hawk on Vietnam—Kissinger described him as a deciding voice in the Christmas bombings of 1972—an alleged architect of United States efforts to overturn the Allende regime in Chile, Haig had impeccable credentials as an anti-Soviet cold warrior.

On foreign policy in general and the Soviet Union in particular, *Time* magazine said in March 1981, Haig's "ideas dovetail so neatly with Reagan's that the President hardly considered anyone else as his No. 1 foreign policymaker . . . The essence of their combined view: the prime threat to peace and stability in the world is Soviet expansionism, and the U.S. must restore the confidence of its allies and the entire free world that it can and will contain such aggression." While Haig considered the United States as being opposed to "anything military" since the Vietnam war, he described the Soviets as transforming "a continental and largely defensive land army into a global offensive army, navy, and air force fully capable of supporting an imperial foreign policy." Although the Soviet military buildup is unquestionable, Haig was too quick to view it as principally serving an aggressive and expansionist foreign policy. Yet, like Reagan, "for all his somber view of Soviet power, he believes that the historical tide is running against Marxism, and that with a prompt buildup of American military might and a consistent policy of checking Soviet adventurism, including strong support for all anticommunist governments around the world, the United States will come out on top." Stated another way, Reagan and Haig see the United States as holding the fate of the world in its own hands; the struggle to eclipse the USSR depends less on what happens overseas than on what we commit ourselves to in the United States.

When Haig resigned in June 1982, Reagan replaced him with another conservative Republican, George Shultz, a professional economist who had served as Nixon's director of the Office of Management and Budget, secretary of labor, and secretary of the treasury. Shultz, a fiscal conservative and an advocate of free trade, helped shape Reagan's initial economic program. He is widely viewed as a pragmatist with a flair for reconciling conflicting positions. His appointment aroused the ire of archconservatives, who see him as part of the Nixon-Ford-Kissinger establishment backing détente, and as even more of a "détentist" than Haig. "We had only two seconds to enjoy Haig's firing," one radical Right leader complained. Shultz's selection as secretary of state moved another New Right critic to observe: "Now we've got what we helped to prevent." As an Ivy League graduate and former dean of the University of Chicago Business School, Shultz is much too understated for the evangelistic conservatives who are moved by rhetorical bombast about Communist evils. Unlike Reagan, who speaks that sort of language to the Moral Majority, Shultz is a reserved, quiet man who prefers compromise to confrontation.

He is less moderate than he has been given credit for, however, and his credentials as a stern anticommunist are unassailable. Disturbed by the strategic arms limitation (SALT) agreements with the Soviet Union, Shultz was a founding member in 1976 of the Committee on the Present Danger, a group of prominent American foreign policy experts who considered Reagan's predecessors' approach to the Russians as much too soft. At the time of Shultz's appointment, Washington insiders predicted that he would "focus more sharply on exerting economic and political pressure against the Soviet Union." He "would probably take a harder line [than Haig] toward dealing with the Soviets," one senior White House official believed. Emphasizing that Shultz had been Reagan's original choice for secretary of state, the White House encouraged the belief that the new secretary would be more attuned ideologically to other Reagan advisers on the issues that had separated Haig from the president. Although these assertions may be seen as part of the administration's efforts to disarm New Right hostility to someone it considered too moderate, Shultz does genuinely share Reagan's concern with advancing the cause of freedom against Communist totalitarianism, as his tenure in the State Department has demonstrated.

Other national security and diplomatic assignments have given the New Right less reason to complain. Reagan's selection of Richard Allen as national security adviser softened conservative complaints about having first Haig and then Shultz as secretary of state. Initially "the Right's principal spokesman in internal Reagan administration debates on national security matters," Allen is an evangelistic anticommunist who was a member of conservative think tanks at Georgetown and Stanford universities. In the 1970s he served on Nixon's National Security Council, from which he resigned after personal and political clashes with Henry Kissinger. During his year in the Reagan administration he fought repeatedly with Haig over policy and power. In March 1981, two months after becoming national security adviser, Allen told the Conservative Political Action Conference, in a speech not cleared by the State Department, that America's West European allies should be upbraided for their "pacifist sentiments" toward the Soviet Union. Richard Pipes, a professor of Russian history at Harvard and a member of Allen's National Security staff, reinforced the picture of a new cold war militancy in Washington when he declared that détente was at an end and that the Soviets would have to choose between evolving along Western lines or going to war. A hallmark of Allen's career, a news magazine pointed out, has been controversy over his "unyielding hostility to the Soviet Union."

In January 1982 Allen's fights with Haig and the impropriety of his acceptance of gifts from Japanese journalists embarrassed the administration and forced him to resign. He was succeeded by William Clark, a former California attorney, Reagan's chief of staff in Sacramento, and a state supreme court justice. Clark came to the National Security Office with only limited experience in foreign affairs, having been appointed deputy secretary of state under Haig in 1981. As his Senate confirmation hearings demonstrated, Clark's only credentials for the job were his long-standing relationship with the president, a flair for administration and for resolving conflicts between strong-minded officials, and a devotion to conservative principles and patriotic sentiments. His inability to identify the leaders of South Africa or Zimbabwe or the names of the NATO countries opposed to long-range nuclear missiles on their soil and his open acknowledgment that he could speak only in the most general terms about major foreign policy questions exposed the administration to ridicule in the world press. Yet he has been effective as national security adviser to the president by being a "conciliatory presence" rather than an abrasive self-promoter, and he has staunchly supported Reagan's tough approach to the Russians and his military buildup to meet the Soviet challenge, attitudes that have endeared him to the Right.

No one in the field of foreign affairs in the administration has done more to satisfy the Right than Ambassador to the United Nations Jeane Kirkpatrick. A former political science professor and member of the Center for Strategic and International Studies at Georgetown University, as well as a resident scholar at the conservative American Enterprise Institute, Kirkpatrick caught the president's attention in 1979 with a *Commentary* article entitled "Dictatorships and Double Standards." An attack on Jimmy Carter's human rights policy, the essay distinguished between right-wing authoritarian governments that were friendly to the United States and left-wing totalitarian regimes that were linked to the Soviet Union and threatened American security. Kirkpatrick criticized Carter's "posture of continuous self-abasement and apology" toward leftist "autocrats" and his antagonism to rightist rulers like Nicaragua's Somoza and the shah of Iran as destructive to the United States. Where the left-wing governments were clients of the Soviets, the right-wing ones were "not only anticommunist, they were positively friendly to the U.S." As ambassador to the UN, she has been an outspoken advocate of American support for South Africa's government and the anticommunist military regimes in Chile and Argentina. She has explained Third World revolutions as the product of Soviet expansionism and has urged American intervention in Third World countries like El Salvador to defend ourselves against the Soviet threat.

Kirkpatrick's view of the world, like Reagan's and that of his other principal foreign policy advisers, rests upon an exaggerated fear of Soviet power and control. This is not to imply that the Soviet Union is a benign, reasonable state with which the United States can easily achieve an accommodation. The Soviets' suspicions, illusions, and aggressive determination to serve their own interests make the USSR a difficult and dangerous adversary which will take advantage of any sign of idealized hopes and timidity in international exchange. But the Reagan picture of a power-hungry, evangelistic nation inspired by an unyielding determination to fasten totalitarian communism on all parts of the globe reveals more about Reagan's conservative inner tensions over issues of authority, dependence, and control than about Soviet capabilities and aims. Most conservatives, having had a rigid, stern, authoritarian upbringing, are both submissive to and rebellious against authority. Advocates of traditional values and the moral life, to which they insist all Americans must conform, conservatives oppose an oppressive government seeking to stymie initiative and personal freedom. And yet the paradox is that they themselves are authoritarian. They are ready to exclude many freedoms nonconservatives consider important—the right to have an abortion, to breathe clean air, and not to have a religion are but a few examples. It is not surprising that they are tolerant of right-wing regimes abroad that they see sharing their values of family, church, and country. Jeane Kirkpatrick, for example, describes rightists in Latin America as "traditional rulers in semi-traditional societies." In contrast, they see leftist regimes as defying the conventional wisdoms American conservatives live by and as extensions of liberal impulses in the United States which subject the individual to excessive government restraints on economic choices and social actions. Going well beyond the genuine fears of the Soviet Union's imperialistic and totalitarian drives, the Reagan administration's foreign policy is less a realistic response to actual conditions abroad than a kind of symbolic objection to conditions in the United States.

Reagan's defense buildup is a good case in point. Throughout his campaign for the presidency and from his first day in office, Reagan stressed the need to expand America's military might to meet the Soviet threat. "Let us not delude ourselves," he said in 1980. "The Soviet Union underlies all the unrest that is going on. If they weren't engaged in this game of dominoes, there wouldn't be any hot spots in the world." More important, according to this view, Soviet adventurism is supported by a massive growth of military power. The administration argues that although the United States still holds a nine-to-seven advantage over the Soviets in the number of nuclear warheads, Moscow has nearly a two-to-one edge in the megatonnage, or destructive power, of its nuclear weapons. Moreover, the Soviets have achieved a clear superiority in land-based ballistic missiles, and administration defense specialists describe this as part of a plan to achieve "military superiority in all fields."

Where Moscow depicts its reach for nuclear parity as essential to its security, the administration interprets it as a drive for an offensive advantage. "It is neither reasonable nor prudent to view the Soviet military buildup as defensive," Secretary Weinberger told the Senate Armed Services Committee in March 1981. The administration's answer to this danger was to propose the largest and most expensive peacetime expansion of military might in American history. In the five years between 1981 and 1986 the annual defense budget was to more than double, from $171 billion to $367.5 billion, with the total expenditure amounting to $1.8 trillion. The program in part called for expanding the navy from 456 to 600 ships to counter the recent expansion of Soviet naval power. "Control of the seas is as essential to our security as control of their land borders is to the Soviet Union," Weinberger said.

Development of nuclear weapons was considered an equally pressing priority. Warning that the United States faced "the prospect of Soviet strategic superiority" unless it built up its land-based missiles and bomber forces, Weinberger advocated yet again, even though it had been declared unneeded by earlier Congresses, a new manned bomber capable of penetrating Soviet air defenses. He also pushed harder for the MX intercontinental ballistic missile system, to be based in Nevada and Utah. As for the SALT agreement that the Carter administration had negotiated with the Soviets, Weinberger, despite the contrary view of many reputable arms control experts, dismissed the treaty as permitting "an enormous further increase in Soviet offensive capability while presenting the danger of lulling us into a false sense of security." Though Weinberger also avowed that the administration was "not abandoning hopes for arms control," it still had not identified an arms control strategy after six months in office. At his confirmation hearings in June 1981, Eugene V. Rostow, Reagan's proposed director of the Arms Control and Disarmament Agency, admitted that the administration had not yet settled on a policy. "It may be that a brilliant light will strike our officials," Rostow said. "But I don't know anyone who knows what it is yet that we want to negotiate about." Moreover, Rostow estimated that it would be at least another nine months before the administration was ready for any serious new SALT talks.

The administration's plans immediately produced a barrage of criticism. Former government officials and defense experts contended that the Reagan-Weinberger rearmament plan rested on an exaggerated view of the nation's present and future strategic vulnerability. They argued that the manned bombers and land-based missiles the administration wished to construct would be useful in fighting the kind of war the United States was least likely to confront: a nuclear conflict with the Soviets. Critics also pointed out that such weapons would do little to deter limited Soviet aggression in such places as Poland or Central America. To meet this challenge the United States would have to strengthen its conventional forces, and while the administration had indicated its intention to do so, it had offered no persuasive blueprint for how this would be done. Indeed, critics complained that Reagan and Weinberger wanted to spend billions of dollars on defense without a close assessment of what the money would buy. The experts wanted to know: "What kind of global strategic doctrine will govern the deployment of U.S. forces? What kind of weapons are needed to carry out that doctrine? What is the proper mix of spending between strategic nuclear forces and conventional forces? . . . Can U.S. industry, for which military production is essentially a sideline, turn out weapons in the quantity required by the buildup Ronald Reagan contemplates?" As *Time* magazine observed, critics worried that the administration was "preparing to spend indiscriminately for everything the Pentagon can think of—missiles, ships, planes, tanks, guns, ammunition, spare parts, training, military pay—in the hope that money alone will solve all problems, which it emphatically will not." Had the Democrats been the sponsors of this defense plan, Reaganites would surely have described them as simply "throwing money at a problem."

Liberal economists like Lester Thurow also expressed fears that the Reagan defense program could "wreck the economy" by gobbling up scarce resources and causing runaway inflation. "The military build-up that is currently being contemplated," Thurow wrote in May 1981, "is three times as large as the one that took place during the Vietnam War." Johnson's failure to raise taxes to pay for that war and the Great Society, which he refused to spend less on, "wrecked the economy." Thurow saw Reagan's determination to cut taxes and have an even larger military buildup as a recipe for long-term economic catastrophe. He foresaw "tremendous strains . . . on the domestic economy, unless measures are taken to restrain private consumption. Without tax increases the military can only get the necessary capital capacity, skilled manpower, and raw materials by paying more than the civilian economy is willing to pay. This drives up prices and creates civilian shortages."

Cuts in domestic programs would come nowhere near making up the difference. "President Reagan talks as if his cuts in civilian government consumption are going to pay for the extra military spending. But he also talks as if those civilian budget cuts are going to pay for the loss in revenue from business tax cuts and from the 30 percent cut in personal income taxes . . . But the sums that will be spent and saved do not match. A $138 billion cut . . . in civilian expenditures . . . simply does not counterbalance a $196 billion tax cut and $181 billion increase in military spending." Nevertheless, the administration saw the burden of total government spending shrinking "not because of a decrease in that spending, but because there will be an explosion of economic output" of some 23 percent in the next five years. But Thurow considered this supply-side wisdom as unconvincing and damaging. With the growth in American economic productivity slowing down since 1965 and running at a negative rate for the three years before 1981, Thurow challenged the assumption that productivity would "return to a 3 percent rate of growth almost instantly . . . Such an increase in productivity has never happened before in our history," he said, "and there are good technical reasons for believing that it will not happen now." What made the whole thing particularly dangerous, Thurow concluded, was that Reagan's mistakes would not become obvious until long after they had been made, and by then it would be too late to correct them.

Why is the administration so much on the wrong track in its arms buildup? If the threat from Moscow is less than what the administration sees, why does the White House exaggerate the Soviet danger? Again, it is because the Soviets are a convenient whipping boy for conservative concerns. Moscow does represent a genuine danger to the United States, so conservatives have not had to invent the peril, only to make more of it than actually exists. It is not simply the actual Soviet threat with which conservatives are engaged but also the Soviet Union as the symbol of those unpleasant developments at home they are striving to combat.

Principally for this reason, none of the criticisms of the Reagan defense plans had any perceptible impact on the administration's military buildup. In the summer of 1981 Weinberger gave Reagan a proposal for regaining nuclear superiority over the Soviet Union within this decade. According to the *New York Times,* the plan went "well beyond previous plans to strengthen those forces" and would "encompass intercontinental ballistic missiles, long-range bombers, Trident submarines armed with more accurate missiles and, especially, a vast rebuilding of the extensive communications apparatus through which the strategic forces are controlled." It aimed to create "a capacity to fight nuclear wars that range from a limited strike through a protracted conflict to an all-out exchange."

At the same time the administration announced that it would build the neutron bomb, a weapon "designed to kill as many people as a regular hydrogen bomb ten times its size, and yet cause less damage to nearby buildings." American military chiefs described the weapon as the best way to deter or counter a massive Soviet tank assault across Central Europe. Opponents of the bomb warned that its restricted effects might encourage NATO generals to use it hastily against a Soviet attack, making it "the catalyst for escalating a conventional war into a nuclear confrontation." When the Soviets attacked the action as a "further spiraling of the arms race," the president replied: "They are squealing like they're sitting on a sharp nail simply because we are now showing the will that we are not going to let them get to the point of dominance where they can someday issue to the free world an ultimatum of 'Surrender or die.'" Reagan added that some of those opposing the decision "are really carrying the propaganda ball for the Soviet Union."

In the view of Reagan and his defense advisers, the principal point is that the Soviets had undertaken a huge buildup of ICBMs and were ready to use them, should a crisis require it. "The Soviets have sufficient forces to attack and destroy our ICBMs," Lieutenant General Edward Rowny, Reagan's chief arms control negotiator said in August 1981. "I have no doubt that we could still launch a second strike with our other missiles and wreak untold damage on the Soviet Union, causing more than 100 million casualties. But the fundamental problem is that the Soviets don't believe that. They believe nuclear weapons are there to be used . . . So we must think about nuclear exchanges not because they will ever occur necessarily but because as long as the Soviets believe they're possible, they will have the power of blackmail over us." It is difficult to follow Rowny's logic. Does he see the Soviets as doubting our second-strike capability or the will to use it? Is he saying that only the Soviets think of using nuclear weapons and that this opens us to blackmail? If this is his argument, then he himself refutes it by planning for a possible nuclear exchange. His assertion is also countered by the fact that the president also thinks in terms of a possible nuclear war. In October 1981 Reagan made clear that he was determined to prevent the United States from being blackmailed by announcing that this country would begin producing MX missiles and B-1 bombers and by indicating, in a conversation with newspaper editors, that he could imagine a limited nuclear war in Europe. The Soviets were now to understand that the United States was as ready as Moscow to use its nuclear arsenal.

Revelations by Thomas K. Jones, deputy under-secretary of defense for strategic and nuclear forces, about the administration's civil defense plans gave further indications of the president's determination to face down the Soviets by preparing to fight and survive a nuclear war. In an interview with Robert Scheer, a national reporter for the *Los Angeles Times,* Jones predicted that the United States would be able to fully recover in two to four years from an all-out nuclear exchange with the Soviet Union. Jones's optimism rested on the assumption that people could be evacuated from cities to the countryside, where they would dig holes and cover them with a couple of doors and three feet of dirt. Jones believed that in this way the American people could survive a nuclear war. "It's the dirt that does it," he told Scheer. "What is truly astounding about my conversation with T.K.," Scheer wrote, "is not simply that one highly placed official in the Reagan administration is so horribly innocent of the effects of nuclear war. More frightening is that T. K. Jones' views are all too typical of the thinking of those at the core of the Reagan administration, as I have discovered through hundred of hours of interviews with the men who are now running our government. The only difference is that T.K. was more outspoken than the others."

Jones's ideas were dismissed by informed people as preposterous. The *New York Times* ridiculed his views in an editorial entitled "The Dirt on T.K. Jones": "Is the Thomas K. Jones who is saying those funny things about civil defense . . . only a character in 'Doonesbury'? . . . Or is T.K. . . . the peace movement's mole inside the Reagan Administration?" Yet, as Scheer points out, "Jones's notions of civil defense, odd as they may have seemed, are crucial to the entire Reagan strategic policy." Central to the administration's thinking about nuclear war is the conviction that the Soviets have developed an effective civil defense plan, including fallout shelters and city evacuation plans, and that this program has allowed the Russians to assume that they could reasonably survive and win a nuclear conflict. As long as the United States fails to imitate the Soviet civil defense program, the administration's defense planners believe, we are vulnerable to a Soviet first strike. The prime objective, Jones told Scheer, is to convince the American people that they can survive a nuclear war if they learn how to build and supply a proper shelter. "In the business of nuclear war," Jones declared, "what you don't know can kill you." But surely it is Jones's fantasy of millions of evacuees from cities sheltering themselves in shallow holes covered with "a couple of doors and three feet of dirt" that is more likely to kill us. The belief that any such civil defense program could allow the country to survive a nuclear conflict encourages the administration to contemplate fighting such a war. Jones' presence in the Defense Department is enough to make any sensible person lose all trust in the administration's ability to lay rational plans for the security and survival of the United States.

The administration's optimistic plans for delivering the mail after a nuclear attack also testified to its determination to prepare the country for such a conflict. "Those that are left will get their mail," the Postal Service Civil Defense Coordinator told a House subcommittee. First-class mail "would be delivered even if the survivors ran out of stamps." One subcommittee member could not believe his ears: "There will be no addresses, no streets, no blocks, no houses," he exclaimed. Denouncing the postal plan as "idiotic" and "deceitful," subcommittee members said "there would also be no trucks, trains or airplanes for delivering the mail." One defense policy expert reinforced the committee's skepticism: "I can assure you that while neither snow nor rain nor heat nor gloom of night will stay the postal couriers from the swift completion of their appointed rounds, nuclear war will."

The administration now came under a barrage of criticism for its so-called defense plans. The diplomat and historian George Kennan pointed to "the futility of any war fought with these weapons." He reminded the country that every president from Eisenhower to Carter had emphasized that "there could be no such thing as victory in a war fought with such weapons." He warned against the continued multiplication of these devices, saying that we and the Russians together had achieved "levels of redundancy" in destructiveness "of such grotesque dimensions as to defy rational understanding." To those who would invoke the need for deterrence, Kennan replied: "If the same relative proportions were to be preserved, something well less than 20 percent of these stocks would surely suffice for the most sanguine concepts of deterrence . . . Whatever their suspicions of each other, there can be no excuse on the part of these two governments for holding, poised in a sense against each other and poised in a sense against the whole Northern Hemisphere, quantities of these weapons so vastly in excess of any demonstrable requirements."

While asserting that Moscow had contributed its share to getting us into "this dangerous mess," Kennan urged against "blaming it all on our Soviet adversaries . . . It has been we Americans," he said, "who, at almost every step of the road, have taken the lead in the development of this sort of weaponry. It was we who first produced and tested such a device; we who were the first to raise its destructiveness to a new level with the hydrogen bomb; we who introduced the multiple warhead; we who have declined every proposal for the renunciation of the principle of 'first use.'" Whatever then might be blamed on the Russians, and "they too have made their mistakes," Kennan allowed, ". . . let us not, in the face of this record, so lose ourselves in self-righteousness and hypocrisy as to forget the measure of our own complicity in creating the situation we face today."

Men more knowledgeable about nuclear weapons than Kennan echoed and expanded upon his point of view. Hans Bethe, a Nobel Prize-winning physicist, a prominent figure in the development of the atomic bomb, and a leading adviser to the U.S. government on issues relating to strategic nuclear weapons, spoke for numerous other American scientists when he publicly took issue with the administration's assertions about the need for a nuclear buildup to eliminate Soviet superiority to the United States in ICBMs. In testimony before the Senate Foreign Relations Committee in May 1982, Bethe disputed the idea of American inferiority: "We have more nuclear warheads than the Russians, and I consider this to be the most important measure of relative strength." Our so-called vulnerability, Bethe said, rests on the belief that the Russians will soon be able to use their ICBMs to destroy our land-based ICBMs. Even if this were technically feasible, which it may not be, Bethe claimed "that such a first strike would give no significant military advantage to the Russians." Since ICBMs make up only one-fourth of the U.S. strategic nuclear forces, "invulnerable nuclear-powered submarines" and bombers carrying cruise missiles could effectively retaliate. Dismissing the argument that our submarine-based missiles do not have "sufficient accuracy," he described numerous targets for which these "missiles would have plenty of accuracy." Moreover, he outlined the United States' significant progress in the development of sophisticated submarine warheads, which "permits our submarines to operate over most of the North Atlantic, and to still hit Russia."

But the most important addition he saw to America's arsenal was the cruise missile. It "can penetrate into the Soviet Union. No defense system against it exists. The elaborate and costly Russian air defense system has been made obsolete by the cruise missile, 3,000 of which are to be installed on our B-52 bombers . . . Because the cruise missile can penetrate the Soviet Union as no bomber can, and because it has extreme accuracy, we do not need a new bomber, the B-1, and even less its follow-up, the STEALTH." The need for these new bombers would be made superfluous by the cruise missile, which would be able to do the job "much more effectively and cheaply." Given the substantial invulnerability of our submarine and bomber forces, Bethe thought it "a futile expenditure of money" to deploy additional land-based ICBMs, which had become increasingly vulnerable to attack. Indeed, because the Soviets rely mostly on land-based strategic weapons, and the United States has more nuclear warheads overall, it is in fact this country that has superiority. "If anyone has a window of vulnerability, it is the Soviet Union." The greatest threat to our national security, then, is not from our inferiority to the Russians in strategic armaments, but from "the grotesque size and continuing growth of both nuclear arsenals."

Other strategy experts and scientists supported Bethe's conclusions. Herbert Scoville, Jr., a former deputy director of the CIA, denied President Reagan's claim that the "Soviets now have a definite margin of superiority over the United States . . . The president doesn't seem to realize," Scoville said, "that even if all our . . . [ICBMs] are destroyed, we would still have 3,000 warheads at sea placed on invulnerable submarines and another 2,000 on bombers on alert status. Each of these warheads has an explosive force many times that of the bomb

that destroyed Hiroshima. These can destroy military as well as industrial targets. They could contaminate hundreds of thousands of square
miles with deadly radioactivity." George Kistiakowsky, a Harvard professor of chemistry, who had been science adviser to President Eisenhower, and George Rathjens, a political scientist at Massachusetts
Institute of Technology and a former official in the State and Defense
departments, joined Scoville in complaining, that "on arms control,
Reagan hasn't earned our trust." "The president has asserted that our
strategic forces are inferior to those of the Soviet Union, that we could
not deter a Soviet attack on this country, and that we must postpone
arms control and procure new weapons to deal with what he calls a
'window of vulnerability.' But he ignores three-quarters of our strategic
forces, our invulnerable submarine missiles and alert bombers, which
provide us with a much more survivable overall deterrent than that of
the Soviet Union. This poor-mouthing of U.S. strength does great dis-
service to our security and undercuts our influence on friend and foe."

In response to what many people now perceived as the administration's "negative and hopeless . . . cold war policies," promising "increasing political tension and nuclear danger," an antinuclear war
movement spontaneously began to spread across the United States and
Western Europe. At the heart of this movement, George Kennan said,
are "some very fundamental and reasonable and powerful motivations:
among them a growing appreciation by many people of the true horrors
of a nuclear war; a determination not to see their children deprived
of life, or their civilization destroyed, by a holocaust of this nature;
and finally . . . a very real exasperation with their governments for the
rigidity and traditionalism that . . . prevents them from finding, or
even seriously seeking, ways of escape from the fearful trap into which
the cultivation of nuclear weapons is leading us." Echoing Kennan's
ideas, Admiral Hyman G. Rickover, the developer of nuclear-powered
ships, called for an international conference to outlaw nuclear weapons
and nuclear reactors. Pointing to the Washington Arms Conference of
1921–22, Rickover said that "it would be the finest thing in the world
for the President of the United States to initiate immediately another
disarmament conference" to halt and reverse the arms race.

A solid majority of Americans agreed. Fourteen months into the
Reagan term, 57 percent of those asked in a nationwide poll favored
"an immediate freeze on the testing, production and deployment of
nuclear weapons by the United States and the Soviet Union." In spite
of the president's insistence on the need for a nuclear buildup to assure
national security, a majority of Americans regardless of age, sex, or
political allegiance, said that increased production of these bombs
would not make them feel more secure. At the same time 140 congressmen publicly offered backing for nuclear freeze petitions, and local
and state governments across the nation did likewise. Calling the president's military buildup "voodoo arms control, which says you must
have more in order to have less," Senator Edward Kennedy joined Republican Senator Mark Hatfield of Oregon in supporting a bipartisan
resolution urging a bilateral freeze by the United States and the Soviet

Union in the production and deployment of all nuclear weapons, as a prelude to arms reduction talks. The resolution was simply a recommendation; it did not compel the United States to halt its nuclear buildup, and any freeze would occur only in conjunction with the Soviets. In June 1982 more than half a million people jammed Central Park in New York in support of an end to the arms race. Described as possibly the largest protest meeting in American history, it included many people who had never been to a demonstration in their lives, seeming to confirm George Kennan's belief that the movement was achieving dimensions which would make it impossible "for the respective governments to ignore it. It will continue to grow until something is done to meet it," Kennan said. . . .

Suggested Further Readings

I. 1945–1960

A good survey of postwar American foreign policy is Seyom Brown, *The Faces of Power,* rev. ed. (New York: Columbia University Press, 1983). An important revisionist work critical of administration cold war policy is Gabriel and Joyce Kolko, *The Limits of Power* (New York: Harper & Row, 1972). A more moderate, yet still revisionist, account is Walter LaFeber, *America, Russia, and the Cold War, 1945–1966,* rev. ed. (New York: Wiley, 1972). A more recent study of the cold war is John Gaddis, *Strategies of Containment* (New York: Oxford University Press, 1982). Dean Acheson offers a memoir in *Present at the Creation* (New York: Norton, 1969). A most suggestive book is Richard Aliano, *American Defense Policy from Eisenhower to Kennedy* (Athens, Ohio: Ohio University Press, 1975). Alonzo Hamby has written the standard book on the Truman administration: *Beyond the New Deal* (New York: Columbia University Press, 1973). Robert Ferrell has published an up-to-date biography: *Harry Truman* (Boston: Little, Brown, 1983). See also the more critical anthology edited by Barton J. Bernstein and Allen J. Matusow, *The Truman Administration: A Documentary History* (New York: Harper & Row, 1966), as well as Bernstein's *Toward a New Past* (New York: Random House, 1967), and his *Political Policies of the Truman Administration* (Chicago: Quadrangle, 1970). For a defense of Joseph McCarthy, at variance with the Michael Paul Rogin book excerpted here, see William F. Buckley, Jr., and L. Brent Bozell, *McCarthy and His Enemies* (Chicago: Henry Regnery, 1954).

In addition to the recent Fred I. Greenstein book excerpted here, see Herbert S. Parmet, *Eisenhower and the American Crusades* (New York: Macmillan, 1972); Emmet John Hughes, *The Ordeal of Power* (New York: Atheneum, 1963); and Arther Larson, *Eisenhower: The President Nobody Knew* (New York: Scribner's, 1968). See also John Bartlow Martin, *Adlai E. Stevenson and the World* (Garden City, N.Y.: Doubleday, 1976). The Alger Hiss–Whittaker Chambers controversy is the subject of Allen Weinstein's *Perjury* (New York: Alfred A. Knopf, 1978). Some outstanding works of social criticism from this period are David Reisman et al., *The Lonely Crowd* (New Haven: Yale University Press, 1950); Daniel Bell, *The End of Ideology,* rev. ed. (New York: Free Press, 1965); C. Wright Mills, *The Power Elite* (New York: Oxford University Press, 1956); and John Kenneth Galbraith, *American Capitalism* (Boston: Houghton Mifflin, 1956).

II. 1960–1973

A Thousand Days by Arthur Schlesinger, Jr. (Boston: Houghton Mifflin, 1965) is still the best book on the Kennedy administration, and Herbert Parmet's *Jack: The Struggles of John F. Kennedy* (New York:

Dial, 1980) and *JFK: The Presidency of John F. Kennedy* (New York: Dial, 1983) constitute the standard biographies. Most recent books have been critical, even hypercritical, of Kennedy. See, for example, Garry Wills, *The Kennedy Imprisonment* (Boston: Little, Brown, 1983); Henry Fairlie, *The Kennedy Promise* (Garden City, N.Y.: Doubleday, 1973); Louise Fitzsimons, *The Kennedy Doctrine* (New York: Random House, 1972); and Nancy Gager Clinch, *The Kennedy Neurosis* (New York: Grosset and Dunlap, 1973). David Burner and Thomas R. West have recently published *The Torch is Passed: The Kennedy Brothers and American Liberalism* (New York: Atheneum, 1984). Good books on Martin Luther King, Jr., are John A. Williams, *The King God Didn't Save* (New York: Coward McCann, 1970) and Stephen Oates, *Let the Trumpet Sound: The Life of Martin Luther King, Jr.* (New York: Harper, 1982). See also David J. Garrow, *The FBI and Martin Luther King, Jr.* (New York: Penguin Books, 1983). A statement by a more radical figure is Eldridge Cleaver, *Soul on Ice* (New York: McGraw Hill, 1967). A book both critical of and sympathetic to President Johnson is *Lyndon Johnson and the American Dream* by Doris Kearns (New York: Harper & Row, 1976); Robert Caro is critical in *The Path to Power* (New York: Alfred A. Knopf, 1982). A good historical account of the Vietnam War is Stanley Karnow, *Vietnam: A History* (New York: Viking, 1983). A good account of the election of 1968—and of the events of that startling year itself—is Lewis Chester et al., *An American Melodrama* (New York: Viking, 1969). The best book on Richard Nixon is the revised *Nixon Agonistes* by Garry Wills (Boston: Houghton Mifflin, 1979). On the economy from the liberal viewpoint see Robert Lekachman, *Inflation: The Permanent Problem of Boom and Bust* (New York: Vintage, 1973).

III. 1973–PRESENT

Books on Watergate include Jonathan Schell, *The Time of Illusion* (New York: Alfred A. Knopf, 1975); John Dean, *Blind Ambition* (New York: Simon & Schuster, 1976); Philip B. Kurland, *Watergate and the Constitution* (Chicago: University of Chicago Press, 1978); and John A. Labovitz, *Presidential Impeachment* (New Haven: Yale University Press, 1977). On Kissinger there is Roger Morris's *Uncertain Greatness: Henry Kissinger and American Foreign Policy* (New York: Harper & Row, 1977). Betty Glad has written *Jimmy Carter: From Plains to the White House* (New York: Norton, 1980). Books on Reagan, besides the Dallek book excerpted here, include Ronnie Dugger, *On Reagan: The Man and His Presidency* (New York: McGraw-Hill, 1984); and Laurence L. Barrett, *Gambling with History: Ronald Reagan in the White House* (Garden City, N.Y.: Doubleday, 1983). Reagan's troubles with Latin America are detailed in Walter LaFeber's up-to-date study, excerpted here. On politics generally, see Kirkpatrick Sale, *Power Shift: The Rise of the Southern Rim and Its Challenge to the Eastern Establishment* (New York: Random House, 1975); and Sidney Verba, *Political*

Participation in America (Ann Arbor: Inter-University Consortium for Political Research, 1975). On society, there is Robert Heilbroner's *An Inquiry into the Human Prospect* (New York: Norton, 1980). A stimulating anthology on popular music is Jonathan Eisen, *The Age of Rock* (New York: Vintage, 1969). The classic on the women's liberation movement is Betty Friedan's *The Feminine Mystique,* excerpted here. One of the many recent books on the movement is Sara Evans, *Personal Politics* (New York: Knopf, 1979). A classic on the environmental movement is Barry Commoner, *The Closing Circle* (New York: Knopf, 1969). On American liberalism see Theodore J. Lowi, *The End of Liberalism* (New York: Norton, 1969); on conservatism, George Will, *Statecraft as Soulcraft* (New York: Simon & Schuster, 1983).

"On Revolution" by Malcolm X. From "Message to the Grass Roots" in *Malcolm X Speaks* by Malcolm X. Copyright © by Merit Publishers and Mrs. Betty Shabazz. Reprinted by permission of Pathfinder Press.

"Keynesian Economics in the 1960s" by Allen Matusow. From *The Unraveling of America: A History of Liberalism in the 1960s* by Allen J. Matusow. Copyright © 1984 by Allen J. Matusow. Reprinted by permission of Harper & Row, Publishers, Inc.

"Vietnam: The Bed of Procrustes" by Ernest May. From *'Lessons' of the Past: The Use and Misuse of History in American Foreign Policy*. Copyright © 1973 by Ernest R. May. Reprinted by permission of Oxford University Press, Inc.

"Report from Vietnam" by Michael Herr. From *Dispatches* by Michael Herr. Copyright © 1977 by Michael Herr. Reprinted by permission of Alfred A. Knopf, Inc.

"Cambodia and Kent State: Two Memoirs" by Richard Nixon and Henry Kissinger. 1. Reprinted by permission of Warner Books/New York. From *RN: The Memoirs of Richard Nixon*. Copyright © 1978 by Richard Nixon. 2. From *White House Years* by Henry Kissinger. Copyright © 1979 by Henry A. Kissinger. By permission of Little, Brown and Company.

PART THREE 1974–PRESENT

"Watergate" by Jonathan Schell. Condensed by permission of Alfred A. Knopf, Inc. from *The Time of Illusion*, by Jonathan Schell. Copyright © 1975 by Jonathan Schell. Most of the book originally appeared in *The New Yorker*.

"The Environmental Decline" by Barry Commoner. From *The Closing Circle: Nature, Man, and Technology*, by Barry Commoner. Reprinted by permission of Alfred A. Knopf, Inc. Portions of this book originally appeared in *The New Yorker*.

"More Work for Mother" by Ruth Schwartz Cowan. From *More Work for Mother* by Ruth Schwartz Cowan. Copyright © 1983 by Basic Books, Inc., Publishers. Reprinted by permission of the Publisher.

"The Elvis Presley Phenomenon" by Greil Marcus. From *Mystery Train*. Copyright © 1975 by Greil Marcus. Reprinted by permission of the publisher, E. P. Dutton, Inc.

"A Crisis of Confidence" by Peter Carroll. From *It Seemed Like Something Happened* by Peter Carroll. Copyright © 1982 by Peter Carroll. Reprinted by permission of Holt, Rinehart and Winston, Publishers.

"Nicaragua: The System Overthrown" by Walter LaFeber. Reprinted from *Inevitable Revolutions: The United States in Central America*, by Walter LaFeber, by permission of W. W. Norton & Company, Inc. Copyright © 1983 by Suzanne Margaret LaFeber.

"Ronald Reagan: Cold War Certainties" by Robert Dallek. Reprinted by permission of the publishers from *Ronald Reagan: The Politics of Symbolism* by Robert Dallek, Cambridge, Mass.: Harvard University Press, Copyright © 1984 by Robert Dallek.